Christmas 2015

To, Harry   Lots of Love xxx
From, Emily.

The GPO Garrison
Easter Week 1916

A Biographical Dictionary

JIMMY WREN

 GEOGRAPHY PUBLICATIONS

This book has been published with generous financial suppport from Dublin County Board GAA and Dublin City Council Central Area Committee.

Published in Ireland by Geography Publications,
24, Kennington Road, Templeogue, Dublin 6w.
Copyright © 2015 Jimmy Wren
All rights reserved
ISBN 978-0906602-744
Illustrations and cover illustration by Jimmy Wren
Cover design by Niall O'Sullivan
Design & Typesetting by Keystrokes Digital, Dublin 2.
Printed by Grehan Printers, Dublin 2

Contents

Introduction

A personal quest

A visit to the 1916 Room in the National Museum of Ireland in the mid 1950s with a teenage neighbourhood friend engendered in me an interest in the 1916 Rising and the fight for Irish independence. Charlie Murtagh discovered that Paddy Murtagh, his father, had signed the Roll of Honour for the Four Courts Garrison and I found that James Wren, my father, had signed the Roll of Honour for the GPO Garrison. Through the years I met many of the participants of the Rising and the subsequent struggle. Rarely, did they speak of their experiences.

Mary Chadwick, nee Kelly, the founder of the Clann na Gael Girl Scouts and her husband Mick, who was vice-commandant of the 6th Battalion Dublin Brigade, were friends of my parents. My sister and I always looked forward to their visits to our home, because they always brought treats for us. Thomas Reilly, who was in Jacob's Garrison, lived in Elm Road, Donnycarney, near where I was born. His grandfather, Charles Reilly, was a founding member of the Land League in north County Dublin and an associate of Charles Stewart Parnell. Thomas was employed as a driver in Dublin Corporation prior to the Rising. In that capacity he was often engaged to drive Rory O'Connor, an engineer with the Corporation, in the course of his work. Thomas Reilly gave me detailed information on the War of Independence in north Dublin but rarely spoke about his own role either in the Easter Rising.

I knew Donal O'Reilly, who worked as a plasterer with the Housing Maintenance Department of Dublin Corporation and was a member of the Dublin Trades Council. As a fourteen year old he followed his father and four brothers to the GPO on Easter Monday. He made his way home on Monday night, but returned to the GPO on Tuesday and sold the *War News* in the streets. On Thursday he got away and hid in derelict buildings in Berkeley Road until Sunday. He took the Republican side in the Civil War and was a member of the Four Courts Garrison in that conflict.

Jimmy Carrigan was another family friend, who served as a Fianna member in the GPO. He later became a member of the Active Service Unit in the War of Independence and was the driver with the IRA party when Kevin Barry was captured in Church Street in August 1920. Paddy and Tommy Mahon were first cousins of my father and they were the sons of Councillor Paddy Mahon, the printer of *An t-Óglach*. His printing works in Yarnhall Street was frequently raided and the machinery destroyed. Paddy Mahon Senior was imprisoned on many occasions. Tom Crimmins, who was beside The O'Rahilly when he was fatally wounded in Moore Street and was probably the last person to speak to him, spent many years in the United States. He was a member of Saint Laurence O'Toole's GAA Club and on his return to Ireland he often met with old club members, including myself.

Sources

Diarmuid Lynch, who served in the GPO Garrison, conducted research on behalf of the Easter Week Memorial Committee to prepare the 1916 Roll of Honour and it was presented to Éamon de Valera on 21 April 1935, the nineteenth anniversary of the Rising. There were 328 names on the list for the GPO. Lynch subsequently extended his research by sending a questionnaire to surviving members of the various garrisons asking them to list their posts, superior officers and 'duties performed, incidents of special interest recalled' (NLI, Eph D82a, 1937).[1] A list of the members of all the Dublin garrisons in 1916 was drawn up and signed by the survivors or, in the case of deceased members, by the senior surviving officers. There were 1,104 names of those still alive and 254 names of those executed, killed in action or deceased since 1916. Three hundred and fifty-seven signed the Roll of Honour for the GPO but Lynch added a further 47 that he believed were in the Garrison but hadn't signed. This adjustment gave Lynch a total of 404.

Subsequent research by John M. Heuston included estimates from four other sources, all of which give different numbers.[2] Desmond Ryan is quoted by Heuston as stating that 'no more than 200 marched into Moore Street for the surrender'. Sean McLoughlin, who marshalled the surrender, estimated the number as 'three hundred and twenty odd' but this excluded the wounded, who were left behind on the pavement in Moore Street. Heuston calculated that between the wounded, those killed in action and the executed leaders a further 54 could be added to McLoughlin's figures bringing the total to between 375 and 380. The index of the Headquarters Company Association estimated the number at 423 but Heuston, on the basis of his own research, adjusted this to a total 'as high as four hundred and sixty or four hundred and seventy'. The British military authorities gave a figure of 376 for the GPO Garrison assembled after their arrests at the Rotunda.

The release of state records relating to military service during the period from 1913 to 1923 has been invaluable in researching this book and qualifying Lynch and Heuston's numbers. The Military Service (1916-1923) Pensions Collection (MSPC) originated in legislation in June 1923 and has details of applications for pensions for military service in the revolutionary period. According to this source, 459 persons received pensions for service in the GPO Garrison during Easter Week. This number includes 33 whose files have not yet been released. The Bureau of Military History 1913-1921 was established in January 1947 by Oscar Traynor, TD, Minister for Defence and a surviving member of the GPO Garrison. It consists of 1,773 witness statements, 334 sets of contemporary documents and associated material including photographs.

In addition to the 459 participants on the pension list, further numbers have been ascertained from the 1916 Roll of Honour and newspaper obituaries in all the Dublin newspapers from 1916 onwards. From all these sources a figure of 572 emerges as the credible total number of insurgents that served at various times throughout Easter Week in the GPO area. It has to be noted that the earlier estimates did not include the women members of the Garrison who had escorted the wounded to Jervis Street Hospital on Friday before the general evacuation occurred.

In some instances discrepancies can be found between pension records, newspaper obituaries and other sources. In the case of Joseph Trimble, for example, his pension application stated that he ceased activity after his release from Frongoch, in December 1916, while newspaper obituaries refer to him having taken part in the War of Independence and of being a member of the Four Courts Garrison, during the Civil War. Similarly, other deceased persons are credited with participating in the Rising in newspaper obituaries but these cases are difficult to substantiate when you consult the Roll of Honour, the Witness Statements, or the Pension Records (see appendix 13).

Easter Week Dublin 1916

In the glorious sunshine of Easter Monday morning 1916, many of Dublin's citizens headed to the mountains, the seaside, or the Fairyhouse races. In Liberty Hall, beside the Custom House, there was a different type of gathering taking place as the first army of the Irish Republic prepared to take possession of the General Post Office building in Sackville (O'Connell) Street and other strong points throughout the city. A rising, which had been planned by the Irish Republican Brotherhood led Irish Volunteers under the cover of manoeuvres for the previous day, had been cancelled by Eoin MacNeill, President of the Irish Volunteers. Despite the MacNeill countermanding order, it was decided to strike on Monday, but with a much depleted force due to the confusion.

The first column to leave Liberty Hall at 11.50am was led by Captain Richard McCormack of the Irish Citizen Army to the St Stephen's Green area and it numbered about 36 men and boys. They were later followed to the Green by Commandant Michael Mallin and Countess Markievicz, his second-in-command, and about 32 men and some women. This force increased in number to about 137 all through the week. Captain Sean Connolly led 45 men and women to the City Hall area and Captain Seán Heuston, initially led 12 men to the Mendicity Institute, at Usher's Quay. Across the River Liffey, Commandant Edward Daly had a combined force of 320 men and women in the Four Courts area that included Church Street and North King Street. Commandant Thomas MacDonagh occupied Jacob's Biscuit Factory on Bishop Street, with about 170 men that included Major John McBride. Commandant Éamon de Valera was in charge of a further 170 men that took control of Boland's Mills & Bakery, on Grand Canal Place, with outposts at Mount Street Bridge. The South Dublin Union area, under the command of Commandant Eamon Ceannt and

Cathal Brugha, included Marrowbone Lane Distillery, Watkin's Brewery, Ardee Street, Roe's Distillery and Mount Brown, had a combined force of about 200 men.

In North County Dublin, Commandant Thomas Ashe and Lieutenant Richard Mulcahy, his second-in-command, led about 65 men and women, who would later be involved in the Battle of Ashbourne. The last party of about 150 men and one woman left Liberty Hall before noon and marched to the GPO, led by Commandant General P.H. Pearse and Commandant General James Connolly. The column included 54 members of the Kimmage Garrison (mainly Irish exiles from England and Scotland), who had arrived in the city centre on a tram from Kimmage shortly beforehand. As the column stopped outside the Post Office Headquarters, James Connolly gave the order, 'GPO....charge!' and as the rebels took possession of the building the public were ordered out.

Shortly after the occupation, P.H. Pearse came outside in front of the GPO and read the Proclamation of the Irish Republic to a curious but unenthusiastic crowd. At 1.20 pm as a troop of British lancers galloped down Sackville Street, some 40 Volunteers from the Rathfarnham Company approached the building, but failed to gain entry. As they broke through a side window a volley of shots rang out, causing casualties among the lancers and causing the remainder to retreat in the direction of the Parnell Monument.

The first rebel casualty of the Rising was Rathfarnham Volunteer, Jack Kealy, who was shot as he tried to enter the GPO from Prince's Street. He was taken to Jervis Street Hospital and died shortly afterwards. Before the arrival of the lancers a number of outposts were secured, including Reis's Chambers at the corner of Abbey Street and Sackville Street. Here, a wireless apparatus was erected with the intention of transmitting a radio message, stating that an Irish Republic had been declared. Kelly's Gunpowder Shop, known as 'Kelly's Fort', at the corner of Bachelor's Walk, was occupied, because of its commanding view of the O'Connell Bridge approach, and Hopkin's & Hopkin's Jewellery Shop, at the corner of Eden Quay, was commandeered for the same reason. Several houses in Henry Street were also occupied.

At 3.00 pm on Monday, as a party of 120 Volunteers from the 2nd Battalion, under the command of Captain Tom Weafer, was advancing to the GPO they came under machine-gun fire from the railway line at Ballybough Road. Captain Weafer sent 30 men under Captain Leo Henderson to engage the enemy and another party under Frank Henderson to take up a defensive position at Ballybough Bridge. He then proceeded to the GPO with about 64 men. Other late-comers who arrived at the GPO on Monday, included 45 men from Liberty Hall, about 50 Cumann na mBan members, 25 Volunteers from Parnell Square and 20 members of the Hibernian Rifles, who arrived at midnight from North Frederick Street. On Monday afternoon several groups were sent to reinforce the defenders of Ballybough Bridge and the Vitriol

Works at Annesley Bridge. Also on Monday, Captain Brennan-Whitmore led a party that was sent across the street to occupy Tyler's Boot Shop and Noblett's Sweet Shop at North Earl Street and erect a barricade there.

Tom Byrne, a veteran of the Irish Brigade, who fought with the Boers against the British in South Africa, led a party of 13 Volunteers from Maynooth that arrived at the GPO at 7.00 am on Tuesday morning. They were sent across the Liffey to reinforce the defenders of City Hall. When they reached Parliament Street they came under heavy fire and took up positions in several buildings and inflicted a number of losses on the enemy. With the fall of the City Hall and with little ammunition left they came back to the GPO. Another party under the command of Captain Frank Thornton returned to the GPO on Tuesday. They had also been sent to reinforce the City Hall Garrison, but had failed to get through the British military cordon. This group of about 20 men was then sent across the street to occupy the Imperial Hotel and Clery's Store. Before noon on Tuesday the Hibernian Bank at the corner of Abbey Street and Sackville Street was occupied by Captain Tom Weafer and about 15 Volunteers, and women from Cumann na mBan set up a field hospital in the adjacent building.

Captain Richard Coleman arrived in the GPO with 20 Volunteers from North County Dublin and 5 of this group were sent to reinforce 'Reilly's Fort' at the junction of Church Street and North King Street, while the remainder were sent to the Mendicity Institute, at Usher's Quay. By 5.30 pm the wireless apparatus in Reis's was in working order and the news that an Irish Republic was declared and that Dublin City was in the possession of the Insurgents was transmitted. The transmission was picked up by ships at sea and subsequently reached the outside world. Later in the evening at about 7.00 pm a further 70 Volunteers were recalled to the GPO from the Fairview and Ballybough positions, and Lieutenant Oscar Traynor occupied the Metropole Hotel next-door with about 40 of this contingent and broke through the walls to Mansfield's, at the corner of Abbey Street. Widespread looting also broke out in the city on Tuesday and Volunteers dealing with these incidents fired shots over the heads of the looters to disperse them. By Tuesday evening the British forces in the city were greatly increased with reinforcements arriving from Athlone, Belfast, Templemore, the Curragh and a brigade from England.

By early Wednesday morning vantage positions were taken up by the British at Tara Street Fire Station, Amiens Street Railway Station, the Gresham Hotel, and Trinity College and at many other city centre locations. The British gunboat, the Helga, shelled Liberty Hall at about 8.00am and left the building in ruins. In the afternoon 'Kelly's Fort' came under artillery fire from D'Olier Street and College Street junction and the Volunteers there were forced to retreat to the Metropole Hotel. Later in the afternoon a misinterpreted order caused the Reis's position to be evacuated and the Volunteer party to return to the GPO. However, a few hours later they returned across Sackville Street under heavy machine-gun and rifle fire and re-occupied the building.

On Thursday afternoon several positions were occupied in the Henry Street, Liffey Street, and Abbey Street areas, including the Henry Street Warehouse, O'Neill's Public House, Lucas Bicycle Shop and the Independent Newspaper Offices. James Connolly received a flesh wound to his arm, while inspecting barricades in the vicinity of the GPO. Later he received a serious leg wound when he stepped out into Abbey Street to see the progress of the group of Volunteers, under the command of Sean McLoughlin, as they gained entry to the Independent Newspaper Offices. He was discovered dragging himself along William's Lane and into Prince's Street and was carried into the GPO. His shattered ankle was treated by Captain John Mahoney, a captured British Army doctor, and by medical students, James Ryan and Dan McLoughlin. The shelling in the vicinity increased on Thursday and the Metropole –Mansfield block was hit and another shell landed on the roof of the GPO. On the opposite side of Sackville Street incendiary shells fell on the roof of the Imperial Hotel and by nightfall the entire block, as far as Noblett's, was in flames. The garrison on this side of the street were compelled to evacuate their posts at midnight. With the exception of a few, who successfully retreated to the GPO, the majority of the insurgents retreated to the north inner-city, where most were eventually captured.

Early on Friday morning those manning the outposts in Abbey Street and Liffey Street were recalled to the GPO. During the morning the GPO came under an intense artillery bombardment with incendiary shells setting the roof on fire and desperate attempts were made to fight the flames. At noon, Commandant General Pearse ordered all women, except nursing staff, to leave the building under a Red Cross flag and make their way to their homes. They were arrested and interrogated at the North Dublin Union, before they were released. The garrison was now confined to the ground floor of the GPO as fire took hold of the upper-floors. At 6.00 pm a party of about 20 women and the wounded, led by Father John Flanagan and Captain Mahoney, the captured British Army doctor, left the GPO under the protection of a Red Cross flag. A Volunteer escort accompanied them to Jervis Street Hospital, where they were refused entry and ordered back to the GPO.

At 8.00 pm on Friday evening an advanced party of Volunteers, under the command of The O'Rahilly left the GPO by the Henry Street entrance and moved into Moore Street. As they advanced in columns on each side of Moore Street they came under intense machine-gun and rifle fire from British troops at the barricade on the Parnell Street end. The O'Rahilly was mortally wounded and Volunteers Charles Carrigan, Harry Coyle, Francis Macken, Michael Mulvihill and Patrick Shortis, also died, while many more were wounded. The other members of this party took cover in the adjacent laneways, warehouses and stables in the area. The main body of men left the GPO and retreated through Henry Place, carrying James Connolly on a stretcher. They were stopped in Henry Place and Moore Lane by the machine-gun fire, before eventually reaching the Moore Street end of Henry Place. The corner house was entered and the walls were then bored from house to house along Moore Street. This work of boring through the walls continued through the night until they reached the end of the block and the GHQ was set up at Plunkett's Butcher Shop, 16 Moore Street.

At noon on Saturday a party of Volunteers stood in Sackville Lane in readiness to charge the British army barricade around the corner at Parnell Street, less than 30 yards away. They were led by 20 year old Sean McLoughlin, who had earlier been given the rank of Commandant by James Connolly. It was intended that when this action took place, the garrison would break through towards the Four Courts. The charge was called off when P.H. Pearse decided to surrender 'in order to prevent the further slaughter of Dublin citizens'. On Saturday evening the men of the GPO Garrison laid down their arms outside the Gresham Hotel in Sackville Street and spent the night as prisoners on the lawn of the Rotunda Hospital. Commandant General James Connolly was carried by his men on a stretcher along with other badly wounded men to the emergency hospital that was set up at Dublin Castle.

REFERENCES

1. The best account of Liam Lynch's research is in Eileen McGough, *Diarmuid Lynch. A forgotten patriot* (Cork, 2013), pp 182-3, 218-19. See also Diarmuid Lynch, *The IRB and the 1916 Insurrection* edited by Florence O'Donoghue (Cork, 1957)

2. J.M. Heuston, a brother of the executed 1916 leader, Seán Heuston, published his findings in *Headquarters Battalion, Army of the Irish Republic, Easter Week 1916* (Carlow, 1966), pp 5-10.

Réamhrá / Foreword

Má shamhlaítear aon fhoirgneamh amháin le hÉirí Amach 1916, is é an GPO é – ba í Ard-Oifig an Phoist ar Shráid Uí Chonaill, nó Sráid Sackville mar a tugadh uirthi san am sin, ceanncheathrú agus lárionad an Éirí Amach i mBaile Átha Cliath agus, go deimhin, an tír ar fad. Sheas Pádraig Mac Piarais taobh amuigh de chun Forógra na Poblachta a léamh ag meán lae ar 24 Aibreán 1916 agus bhí an chathair ina cíor thuathail ina dhiaidh sin ag troid a mhair ar feadh sé lá. Bhí príomhshráid na tíre agus an GPO féin slogtha ag dóiteáin i ndeireadh na dála, rud a chiallaigh gur dheacair Sráid mhór mhaorga Sackville a aithint a thuilleadh.

Cérbh iad na fir agus mná a ghabh seilbh ar an GPO in éineacht leis an bPiarsach agus Ó Conghaile ar Luan na Cásca 1916? Anois, a bhuíochas ar Jimmy Wren, tá eolas cinnte againn fúthu go léir, faoina n-ainmneacha agus a sonraí, a gcúlraí agus an méid a tharla dóibh tar éis an Éirí Amach fiú. Is taisce é an saothar is déanaí le Jimmy: tá sé mar thoradh ar a thaighde géarchúiseach ar feadh blianta fada go bhfuil liosta cuimsitheach beathaisnéiseach againn de gach fear agus bean a bhí páirteach sa troid i ngarastún an GPO. Nuair a chuirtear a líníochtaí pinn agus dúigh de na reibiliúnaigh san áireamh, tá imleabhar ar leith againn agus is breá an saothar é a chuirfidh go mór le staireolaíocht 1916.

Tá a fhios againn anois go raibh 498 fear agus 74 bean sa GPO i rith Sheachtain na Cásca in 1916. A bhuíochas ar an anailís ar throdaithe an GPO, tá eolas againn faoina ngairmeacha, a n-oideachas, cá háit a raibh cónaí orthu agus an méid a bhí ar siúl acu in Éirinn tar éis don tír neamhspleáchas a bhaint amach. Tá a fhios againn go raibh an chuid is mó acu óg – ní raibh an duine ab óige acu, Charlie McMahon, ach dhá bhliain déag d'aois; tá a fhios againn gur bhain an chuid is mó acu le lár thuaidh na cathrach agus go raibh gné mhuinteartha ag baint leis an troid a bhí ar siúl ag cuid mhaith acu; bhí iomlán 106 teaghlach ag troid san Éirí Amach. Bhí post ag seacht nduine is fiche acu i mBardas Bhaile Átha Cliath tar éis an Éirí Amach agus bhí cúig dhuine is fiche acu ina dTeachtaí Dála ina dhiaidh.

Tá an-áthas ar Chomhairle Cathrach Bhaile Átha Cliath tacú leis an leabhar seo mar chuid de Chlár Comórtha 1916. Tá Jimmy Wren, iarfhostaí de Bhardas Bhaile Átha Cliath, ina thaighdeoir agus scríbhneoir ar stair na Cathrach le fada an lá. Bhí tábhacht leis na chéad leabhair a scríobh Jimmy, *The Villages of Dublin* (1982) agus *Crinan, Dublin: a history of 13 north inner-city streets* (1993) agus bhí ráchairt orthu mar startha áitiúla, agus baintear úsáid astu mar thagairtí go minic go fóill i leabharlanna poiblí na Cathrach seo. Tréaslaím leis as an saothar luachmhar gan chúiteamh seo a chur i gcrích agus tá súil agam go léifear agus go n-úsáidfear é mar thagairt go forleathan ar feadh blianta fada amach anseo.

If any one building is synonymous with the 1916 Rising it is the GPO – the General Post Office on O'Connell Street, or Sackville Street as it was then, was the headquarters and the epicentre of the Rising in Dublin and indeed the entire country. Patrick Pearse stood outside the GPO to read the Proclamation at noon on 24th April 1916, and thereafter the city was convulsed by fighting for six days with the country's principal street and the GPO itself eventually engulfed by fire, leaving the once great Sackville Street almost unrecognisable.

Who were the men and women who took over the GPO with Pearse and Connolly on Easter Monday 1916? Now, thanks to Jimmy Wren, we definitively know them all, their names and details, their backgrounds and even what happened to them after the Rising. Jimmy's latest work is a treasure: his meticulous research over many years has led to a comprehensive biographical listing of every man and woman involved in the fighting in the GPO garrison. Add to this his pen and ink drawings of the rebels and we have a truly unique volume and one that is a very welcome addition to the historiography of 1916.

We now know that 498 men and 74 women were present in the GPO during Easter Week 1916. Thanks to the analysis of the GPO fighters we have information on their professions, education, where they lived and what they worked at in post-Independent Ireland. We know that the majority of them were young - the youngest, Charlie McMahon was only twelve years of age; we know the majority were from Dublin's north inner city and we know that for many the fighting was a family affair, with a total of 106 families fighting in the Rising. After the Rising, twenty-seven of them held positions in Dublin Corporation and twenty-five went on to serve in Dáil Eireann.

Dublin City Council is delighted to support this book as part of our 1916 Commemorations Programme. Jimmy Wren, a former employee of Dublin Corporation, is a long-time researcher and writer on the history of the City. Jimmy's earlier books, *The Villages of Dublin* (1982) and *Crinan, Dublin: a history of 13 north inner-city streets* (1993) were important and popular local histories, still consulted regularly today in our City's public libraries. I congratulate him on bringing to fruition this valuable labour-of-love and hope it will be widely read and referenced for years to come.

Críona Ní Dhálaigh
Ardmhéara Bhaile Átha Cliath
Lord Mayor of Dublin

Foreword

Coisde Co. Áth Cliath CLG, The Dublin County Board GAA, is honoured to be able to assist with the publication of The GPO Garrison Easter Week 1916: a biographical dictionary by Jim Wren. The author of this monumental work is a proud member of St. Laurence O'Tooles, one of the oldest GAA clubs in the county, and he has represented club and county in senior hurling. Previously, Jim has contributed to the three-volume history of the GAA in the county, a work which was commissioned by the Dublin County Board in 2005, and is without doubt one of the greatest living authorities on the interconnections between sport and politics in his native city.

The GAA was a non-political organisation but its agenda of reviving what were believed to be Ireland's ancient games brought its members into contact with those engaged in building up a national identity and seeking separation from Britain through physical force if necessary. Jim Wren has identified 302 members of the GAA who participated in the Rising and 69 of these were in the GPO Garrison. Harry Boland, as chairman of Dublin County Board, was the most senior GAA official in the GPO. He was also a well-known hurler having represented Rathmines and then Faughs at club level and was a regular on the Dublin Senior Hurling team from 1911 to 1916. When Dublin won the All-Ireland Senior Hurling Championship in 1917, the County Board had a special All-Ireland medal presented to him in recognition of his services. Harry Boland's father, Jim, had been chairman of the County Board in 1892 and Edmund, his brother, also in the GPO garrison, won a Dublin Senior Football Championship with Parnells on 20 August 1916. Seán T. O'Kelly, the future President of Ireland, was a playing member of the Confederates Hurling Club.

Both Tom Clarke and Seán MacDiarmada were associated with O'Toole's GAA Club through its Piper's Band and Gaelic League Branch, respectively. P.H. Pearse had helped establish the Leinster Colleges GAA Board and his team from Scoil Éanna participated in its hurling competitions. Two former Scoil Éanna pupils, Frank Burke and Brian Seoige, who were in the GPO Garrison, represented Dublin at inter-county level. Burke, from Carbury, Co. Kildare, won two All-Ireland Senior Hurling medals and three All-Ireland Senior Football medals with Dublin. He played on the Dublin team which met Tipperary in that fatal encounter on Bloody Sunday 21 November 1920; his direct opponent in that game was Michael Hogan the Tipperary player shot dead by British forces.

Charlie McMahon was the youngest member of the GPO Garrison; he was subsequently wounded in the attack on the Custom House in 1921. Though he had a metal plate inserted in his skull he went on to represent Kevins and then Young

Ireland HC. He played senior hurling for Dublin from the late 1920s to the early 1940s and was a member of the last Dublin team to win an All-Ireland Senior Hurling Championship in 1938. Jim Wren has documented the lives of other GAA players in this extraordinary book, including Tom Ennis (O'Tooles), Harry Coyle (Thomas Davis H.C.), Stephen Mulvey (Bray Emmets), who walked from Bray to join the GPO Garrison on Easter Monday, Paddy English (St. Margarets and Erin's Isle) and many more.

One is struck by how normal things appeared to be for those GAA members who were in the GPO Garrison in the weeks prior to the Rising. The Dublin County Board at its annual convention held on 11 April devoted much time to discussing how it should oppose the proposed imposition of an entertainment duty on the GAA. It decided to canvass the Irish MPs at Westminster for their support and the minutes were signed by Harry Boland. Boland was present in his capacity as chairman of Dublin County Board at the GAA Annual Congress on Easter Sunday. The following day he took up arms in support of the newly proclaimed Provisional Government.

Jim Wren will be always in our debt for his sterling research. His work will be invaluable for all the Dublin GAA clubs and the County Board in their commemorative programmes to mark the centenary of the 1916 Rising. Cómhgháirdeachas le Jim Wren agus le gach duine a raibh baint aige leis an bhfoilseachán tábhachtach seo. Tá Coisde Co. Áth Cliath CLG an-bhródúil cúnamh a thabhairt don obair údarásach seo a chur faoi bhráid an pobal.

John Costello,
Dublin County Board GAA Chief Executive.

Foreword

Brendan Behan was fond of quipping that the British wouldn't have felt it necessary to shell the GPO during the Easter Rising if all those who later claimed to have been inside the building on that fateful week had actually been there. With tongue in cheek, he suggested that the walls of Francis Johnston's masterpiece would have literally collapsed due to internal pressure caused by the presence of so many self-elected 'patriots'. However, if Brendan was still with us today he would be forced to drop that particular joke from his repertoire because we now know not only how many volunteers were in the building in 1916 but, more importantly, who they were. This is thanks to the diligent research conducted by Jimmy Wren and his resultant book, beautifully illustrated by the author, which, without question will prove indispensable to all those who are interested in that seminal period of Irish history.

Robert Ballagh

Acknowledgements

When I first began this research a number of years ago I was privileged to have met a number of the participants in the Easter Rising 1916, all of whom are now deceased. These were Nicholas Burke, Jimmy Carrigan, May Chadwick nee Kelly, Tom Crimmins, Tommy Mahon and Donal O'Reilly (G.P.O.); Paddy Murtagh and Mark Wilson (Four Courts); Johnny McDonald and Frank Robbins (Stephen's Green); Paddy McDonnell and Tom Reilly (Jacobs).

The relatives of participants in the 1916 Rising have been particularly helpful in furnishing details from family archives and memories. I am therefore grateful to Arthur Agnew, Charles Billings, Paul Callery, Patrick and Oscar Canny, Jim Corr, Ciaran Coyle, Billy Drea, Terry Fagan, Eamon Flynn, Ciaran Forde, Michael Giffney, Des Goulding, Eamon, Dan and Liam Heery, Niall Henderson, James Hendrick, Danny Hughes, Johnny Joyce, Patricia Kelly, David Kilmartin, Frank McAllister, Charles McDermott, Pádraig McGrane, Hugo McGuinness, Andy McKenna, Siobhán Mulligan, Charley Murtagh, Peadar Nolan, Robert Norgrove, Peter O'Brien, Mary O'Halloran, Kevin O'Rorke, Niall Ring, Brian Roche, Mary Anne Sanderson née Hughes, Val Scott, Mick Smyth, Donie Stritch, Elizabeth Turner, Noel Wearan, Frank Whearity, John Wren, Marian Wren and Margaret Kennedy née Wren.

I am indebted to Jim Corr, Seamus Cullen, Brian Hanley, Gerard MacAtasney, Padraig McGrane, Hugo McGuiness, Charlie McGuire, Rory Quinn, Noel Stapleton and Robin Stocks who provided information and photographs. Des O'Brien, chairman of the 1916 Committee, O'Toole's GAA Club, encouraged me in every way as did all the members of this historic club. The members of the 1916 Relatives Association helped me greatly in researching this book.

Much of the research work on newspapers was completed in the congenial surroundings of the National Library of Ireland and I am particularly grateful to the staff there for their unfailing courtesy and kindness. Ms Bernie Metcalfe of the National Library staff was most helpful with sourcing illustrations; apart from typing the manuscript, Gerard Kavanagh, National Library of Ireland, assisted with the research and his knowledge of Dublin City was invaluable. I acknowledge the help of Lar Joye, National Museum of Ireland, in sourcing information. David Gorry read early drafts of the work and made many valuable suggestions; he also contributed to the epilogue. I am grateful to Dr. Máire Kennedy, Dublin City Public Libraries and Archive, Pearse Street,who helped shape this work in the early stages. All students of this period in Irish history are indebted to the staffs of the Military History Bureau, and I am especially indebted to the late Commandant Peter Young. The information contained in the witness statements and the Military Pensions Collection (1916-1923) is essential for compiling a book of this kind. I wish to thank the National Archives of Ireland for the great work they have collectively done in making so much source material available online. I wish to thank Niamh O'Sullivan and Mícheál Ó Doibhilín and the staff of Kilmainham Gaol for their kind help.

The production of this book was completed in its entirety within Ireland. It was most appropriate that the book was printed by Grehan Printers of Brunswick Place close to the birthplace of P.H. and Willie Pearse, two of the executed leaders of the Easter Rising. Frank Kearney, whose relative Dick Gogan was in the GPO Garrison, typeset the book and Duffy Binders, North Wall, did an expert job on the binding. I am most grateful to Eamonn Murphy and Trevor Grehan for their advice at the typesetting and printing stages.

Coisde Baile Áth Cliath, CLG, made a subvention towards the cost of production and John Costello, its chief executive, was always supportive of the project. I wish to acknowledge the financial support given to this publication by Dublin City Council Central Area Committee and the assistance of Brendan Teeling, Deputy City Librarian, and Tara Doyle, Senior Librarian, Dublin City Public Libraries and Archive, in securing the grant. The 1916-1921 Club also gave financial assistance for which I am grateful. I am also indebted to the personnel of An Post for securing the use of the GPO for the launch of the book

Finally I wish to acknowledge the important role played by Willie and Teresa Nolan of Geography Publications in bringing this project to a successful conclusion.

Abbreviations

app: an appreciation
Batt.: Battalion
BMH (WS): Bureau of Military History, Witness Statement
CLG/GAA: Cumann Lúthchleas Gael / Gaelic Athletic Association
Coy.: Company
DHR: *Dublin Historical Record*
DIB: *Dictionary of Irish Biography*
dn: death notice
fr: funeral report
GHQ: General Headquarters
HI: *History Ireland*
ICA: Irish Citizen Army
IMA: Irish Military Archive
inq: inquest
MSPC: Military Service Pensions Collection
na: newspaper article
NLI: National Library of Ireland
obit: obituary
O/C: Officer Commanding
RH: Roll of Honour

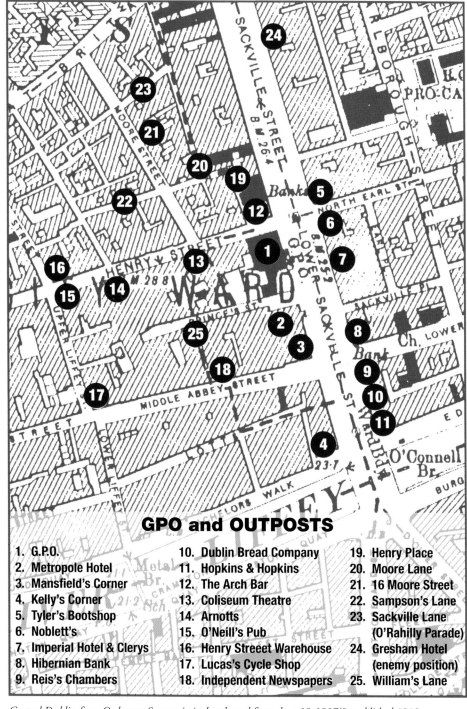

GPO and OUTPOSTS

1. G.P.O.
2. Metropole Hotel
3. Mansfield's Corner
4. Kelly's Corner
5. Tyler's Bootshop
6. Noblett's
7. Imperial Hotel & Clerys
8. Hibernian Bank
9. Reis's Chambers
10. Dublin Bread Company
11. Hopkins & Hopkins
12. The Arch Bar
13. Coliseum Theatre
14. Arnotts
15. O'Neill's Pub
16. Henry Streeet Warehouse
17. Lucas's Cycle Shop
18. Independent Newspapers
19. Henry Place
20. Moore Lane
21. 16 Moore Street
22. Sampson's Lane
23. Sackville Lane
    (O'Rahilly Parade)
24. Gresham Hotel
    (enemy position)
25. William's Lane

Central Dublin from Ordnance Survey six inch enlarged from sheet 18-1907/8, published 1912.
Reproduced with permission of the Board of Trinity College Dublin.

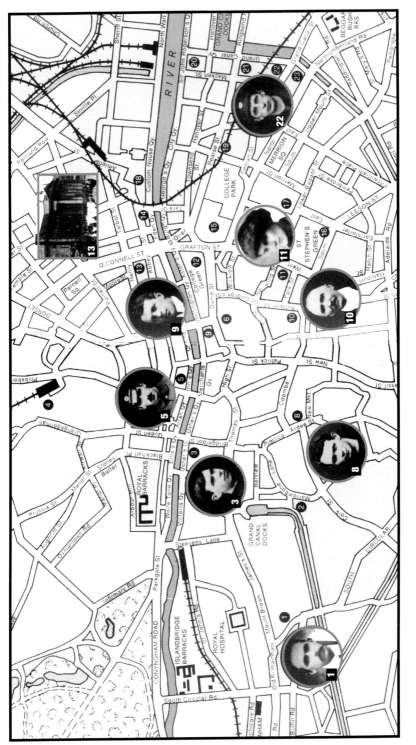

Republican positions Dublin, Easter Week, 1916: **1.** South Dublin Union (Eamonn Ceannt); **3.** Mendicity Institute (Seán Heuston); **5.** Four Courts (Edward Daly); **8.** Watkin's Distillery (Con Colbert); **9.** Dublin City Hall (Seán Connolly); **10.** Jacob's Factory (Seán McBride/Thomas McDonagh); **11.** College of Surgeons (Countess Markievicz); **13.** Post Office (Headquarters of Provisional Government); **22.** Boland's Mills (Eamon deValera). [CBS Records, *The Irish Uprising 1916-1922*, (New York, 1966), pp 34-5].

*In Memory of my father, James Wren
and my grandfather, John Wren*

Mary (Molly) Adrien: (1875 - 1949)

Cumann na mBan. Roll of Honour

Molly Adrien was born in 1875, daughter of Dr Adrien, of Oldtown, Co. Dublin. Her great-grandfather, also Dr Adrien, attended Lord Edward Fitzgerald in 1798. Educated in the Loreto Convent, Balbriggan and in Surbiton, England, she joined the Árd Croabh Branch of Cumann na mBan in November 1915, and shortly after founded a local branch at Lusk, County Dublin.

Throughout Easter Week she acted as a scout for Commandant Thomas Ashe of the Fingal Brigade. On Tuesday she cycled from the Volunteer Camp at Finglas to the GPO with despatches and as she returned, she scouted the coastline area. She returned to the GPO on Wednesday and spent time working with the Cumann na mBan women there, before returning with further despatches for the Fingal Brigade from P.H. Pearse. On Thursday she witnessed the wounded James Connolly being carried back into the GPO and she left the building for the final time shortly after noon on Friday.

She travelled to Ashbourne and was described as "a heroine ranking with the bravest" for assisting Doctor Richard Hayes in attending the wounded, both Volunteers and RIC, during and after the Battle of Ashbourne.

After the Rising, she was prominent in the service of Cumann na mBan and was a despatch rider during the War of Independence before taking the Republican side during the Civil War.

Throughout a distinguished career in the public service in north county Dublin, she was the local representative of the National Aid Organisation, chairperson of the Balrothery Board of Guardians and secretary to the Balrothery Old Age Pensions Committee.

Mary Adrien died on July 17th 1949 and was buried at the family burial ground in Crickstown, County Meath.

References:

RH; IMA, MSPC; 1911 Census; NLI, *Lynch Papers*, (Ms 11,131); Seán O'Luing, *I Die in a Good Cause*, (1970); *Drogheda Independent*, 23rd July 1949, (obit); *Evening Herald* & *Irish Press*, 20th July 1949, (obit); *Skerries News*, 6th October 2006, (na, *Frank Whearity*).

Arthur P. Agnew: (1892 – 1973)

Liverpool Company, (Kimmage Garrison). Roll of Honour

Arthur Agnew was born in Liverpool to Irish parents in 1892, and was employed as a shoemaker. He joined the Bootle Branch of the IRB in 1910, and became a member of the Liverpool Volunteers in 1914. He travelled with a group of Liverpool Volunteers to Dublin in March 1916, after receiving his conscription notice, and joined the Volunteer Camp in Kimmage. For several hours on Easter Monday, he was placed on duty across O'Connell Bridge with Joe Good of the London Volunteers and Paddy Morrin of the Glasgow Volunteers. They later joined the outpost at Kelly's Gun Shop. On Thursday he was transferred to the Metropole Hotel, and on Friday he was involved in the removal of explosives from the basement of the GPO. After the evacuation of the GPO on Friday evening, he spent the night in the Moore Street houses. He was deported to Stafford Jail on May 1st, and later interned in Frongoch until Christmas, 1916.

After his release from prison, he worked in Belfast where he became quartermaster of the Antrim and East Down Brigade, until the formation of the 3rd Northern Division of the IRA. He continued to serve during the War of Independence and in 1921 he took a position with the Belfast Division's Intelligence Dept., until March 1922. His Belfast born wife, Kathleen, was a member of Fianna Éireann in that city. He took no part in the Civil War.

He moved to Swords, County Dublin in 1932 and worked in the civil service until his retirement in 1967.

Arthur Agnew died on March 21st 1973 and was buried in Swords.

References:
RH; IMA, MSPC; NLI, *Lynch Papers*, (Ms. 11,131); Ann Matthews, *The Kimmage Garrison 1916*, (2010); *Irish Independent* & *Irish Press*, 22nd March 1973, (dn).

Kathleen Barber (nee O'Kelly)

Cumann na mBan. Roll of Honour

Kathleen O'Kelly was a member of Cumann na mBan and served in the GPO throughout Easter Week. After the Rising she was detained in custody until May 22nd. Cumann na mBan, Secretary, L. O'Reilly stated that she served with the GPO garrison and this was vouched for by Mary O'Hanrahan, 149 North Strand Road. However she never received her pension.

Kathleen Barber's last known residence was 26 Carleton Road, Marino, in 1939.

References:
RH; IMA, MSPC.

Leslie Bean de Barra (nee Price): (1893-1984)

Cumann na mBan. Roll of Honour

Leslie Price was born in Dublin in 1893. She qualified as a national schoolteacher at St Mary's Dominican College, Belfast and became active in the Gaelic League. In 1915 she joined Cumann na mBan in Dublin and acted as a courier, carrying messages to and from Tom Clarke's shop in Parnell Street.

She reported to Blessington Street as requested on Easter Monday morning, and after some time she went to the GPO with her friend, Bríd Dixon. She was sent by Tom Clarke to the Hibernian Bank on the corner of Abbey Street, and was beside Captain Tom Weafer when he was shot and fatally wounded on Wednesday, saying an Act of Contrition in his ear before he passed away.

After returning to the GPO she carried ammunition and despatches between there and the Fr Mathew Hall in Church Street, with Bríd Dixon. Tom Clarke asked her to go and get a priest from the Pro-Cathedral, Marlborough Street on Thursday afternoon and she returned with Father John Flanagan. On Friday she was among a group of Cumann na mBan women asked to leave the GPO and accompanied the wounded Volunteers to Jervis Street Hospital. She was later arrested in the Capel Street area and taken to Broadstone Station, where she was questioned and released after a few hours. She made her way to Eccles Street Convent and later back to north county Dublin and remained with the Fingal Brigade until the surrender. Two of her brothers also fought in the rising, Seán in the GPO and Eamon in the Jacobs Garrison. Another brother, Michael, later fought in the War of Independence.

In 1917 she was elected to the Executive of Cumann na mBan and became director, travelling the country, recruiting and establishing branches. She married General Tom Barry, Commander of the West Cork Flying Column in 1921, and continued on active service, as Director of Cumann na mBan until 1923. During the Civil War she served on the Republican side in Barry's Hotel, the Tara Hall, Seán McDermott Street and The Hamman Hotel in O'Connell Street until its evacuation.

A member of the Irish Red Cross Society from its inception in 1939, she was chairperson from 1950 to 1973 and was decorated by the Irish, German, Italian and Dutch governments for her service to the Society, receiving the International Committee's highest award, the Henri Dunant Award, in 1978. She was also chairperson of the Irish National Committee for Refugees, from 1955 to 1960 and national president of Gorta, from 1960 to 1965. She was awarded an honorary L.L.D. Degree by the National University of Ireland.

Leslie Bean de Barra died at St Finbarr's Hospital, Cork, on April 9th 1984 and was buried in St Finbarr's Cemetery.

References:

RH; IMA, MSPC; NLI, *Lynch Papers*, (Ms 11,131); *DIB*, John McGuire, (James Quinn, Ed, 2009); Ruth Taillon, *Women in 1916*, (1996); Liz Gillis, *Women of the Irish Revolution*, (2014); *Irish Press*, 18th December 1959, (na); *Irish Independent*, 7th February 1964, (na); *Irish Press*, 30th April 1966 & 7th April 1980, (na); *Irish Independent, Irish Press & Irish Press*, 11th April 1984, (obit).

David (Dave) Begley: (1897 -   )

London Company, (Kimmage Garrison)

Dave Begley was born in London in 1897 to Irish parents. He joined Volunteers in London in 1915 and came to Dublin in January 1916. During Easter Week he was ordered to occupy and protect a room, containing a water tank, in the GPO with Volunteer Patrick Caldwell. He was engaged as a sniper and on Friday he helped remove explosions from the basement, when the fire took hold in the GPO. After the evacuation, he was one the Volunteers who broke into the grocery shop at the corner of Moore Street and Henry Place. He was deported to Stafford Jail on May 1st and then interned in Frongoch until July 27th 1916.

His cousin, Dan Begley, fought with the Four Courts Garrison in the Rising and the pair, along with Dave's brother Patrick and his cousin Denis, were active in E. Company, 2nd Battalion during the War of Independence. He was a member of the St Laurence O'Toole's GAA Club and worked as a bricklayer with MGR Railway Co. He returned to England in 1921 and in later years his health declined.

Dave Begley's last known address in 1939 was 68 Brondesbury Villas, High Road, Kilburn, London.

References:
IMA, MSPC; NLI, *Lynch Papers*, (Ms 11,131); John Heuston OP, *Headquarters Battalion, Easter Week 1916*, (1966); Ann Matthews, *The Kimmage Garrison 1916*, (2010).

James Behan: (1898 - 1954)

B. Coy, 2nd Batt, Dublin Brigade

James Behan was born in 1898 and resided at 257 Richmond Road, Drumcondra. An apprentice printer, he was walking with companions along Summerhill on Easter Monday, when a group of Volunteers, led by Captain Tom Weafer, passed by and asked them to join them. He accompanied the Volunteers to the GPO although he was not attached to any unit. On entering the building, he was handed a shotgun and posted at a barricaded window on the ground floor at the Princes Street side. He fought there beside another youth, Peter Byrne, until the evacuation on Friday. His older brother, Michael, a member of F. Company, 2nd Battalion, was also a member of the GPO garrison. James spent Friday night in Moore Street and after the surrender he was detained in Richmond Barracks. He was released after nine days because of his young age. He became a member of B. Company, 2nd Battalion, Dublin Brigade and served from September 1916 until he was arrested in December 1920. Detained in Ballykinlar Camp, he and was released on December 22nd 1921.

He later lived at 24 Botanic Avenue, Glasnevin, and was employed by Monsor, Robinson & Co. Printers.

James Behan died on February 8th 1954 and was buried two days later in Glasnevin Cemetery.

References:
IMA, MSPC; 1911 Census; *Irish Independent* & *Irish Press*, 9th February 1954, (dn).

Michael Behan: (1893 - 1963)
F. Coy, 2nd Batt. Dublin Brigade. Roll of Honour

Michael Behan was born in 1893 and resided at 257 Richmond Road. A member of F. Company, 2nd Battalion, Dublin Brigade he was in a group under the command of Captain Frank Henderson, that occupied the Gilbeys premises in Ballybough. On Tuesday evening they were ordered into the GPO and he fought there and in the Sackville Street area for the rest of the week. He rejoined his unit and continued on active service during the War of Independence. His younger brother, James, was also in the GPO in Easter Week.

A printer by trade, he worked for Alex Thom & Co., Abbey Street . Michael Behan passed away on May 12th 1963 and was buried in St Fintan's Cemetery, Sutton.

References:
RH; 1911 Census; *Evening Herald*, 13th May 1963, (dn).

Andrew J. Bermingham: (- 1956)
C. Coy, 1st Batt, Dublin Brigade. Roll of Honour

Andrew Bermingham resided at 24 St Ignatius Road, Drumcondra and was educated with his brother Seán, at O'Connell Schools, North Richmond Street. He joined C. Company, 1st Battalion, Dublin Brigade in 1914 and fought in the GPO throughout Easter Week. Deported to Knutsford Barracks on May 1st, he was interned in Frongoch until July 27th 1916.

He rejoined C. Company's Cyclist Section and was on active service, acting as a scout, during the War of Independence. He was one of the firing-party at the funeral of Thomas Ashe in 1917. Bermingham took part in the operation when Robert Barton escaped by rope ladder over the walls of Mountjoy Jail and was involved in the unsuccessful attempt to rescue Kevin Barry from the prison in October 1920. Having taken the Republican side in the Civil War he fought in Hughes Hotel, Lower Gardiner Street in July 1922.

During the emergency years he was a member of 26th Infantry Battalion (War of Independence Veterans).

Andrew Bermingham, of 66 Brian Road, Marino, died on June 3rd 1956 and was buried at Glasnevin Cemetery.

References:
RH; IMA, MSPC; *Irish Press*, 4th June 1956, (dn).

John J. (Seán) Bermingham: (1895 - 1973)

C. Coy, 1st Batt, Dublin Brigade. Roll of Honour

Seán Bermingham, was born in 1895 and resided at 24 St Ignatius Road, Drumcondra. Educated at O'Connell Schools, North Richmond Street, he was a coachmaker by trade. In November 1913 he joined the Volunteers at the Rotunda Rink, and took part in the Howth gun running in 1914 and attended the funeral of O'Donovan Rossa in 1915. With his brother, Andrew, he was a member of C. Company, 1st Battalion, Dublin Brigade and they reported to the GPO together on Easter Monday. He was stationed at the top-floor windows, and on Tuesday he was sent with a party across the street to Reis's Chambers, at the corner of Abbey Street. On Wednesday he was employed as a sniper on the tower of the Dublin Bread Company. From early on Thursday he posted on the roof of the GPO until forced down by the fire. He helped bore through the walls of the houses in Moore Street after the GPO was evacuated. He was deported to Knutsford Barracks on May 1st and later interned in Frongoch until July 27th 1916.

After his release from internment, he rejoined C. Company, 1st Battalion and served in the War of Independence, until March 1920, when he resigned on health grounds.

Seán Bermingham, of 124 Leix Road, Cabra, died on March 27th 1973 and was buried in Glasnevin Cemetery.

References:
RH; IMA, MSPC; NLI, *Lynch Papers*, (Ms 11,131); *Evening Herald*, 27th March 1973, (dn).

Joseph Billings: (1895 - 1975)

B. Coy, 2nd Batt, Dublin Brigade. Roll of Honour

Joseph Billings was born in 1895 and resided at 24 Bayview Avenue, North Strand. He was educated at O'Connell Schools, North Richmond Street and was an upholsterer by trade. He was related on his mother's side, to Joe Brady, one of the Invincibles executed in 1882. A member of B. Company, 2nd Battalion, Dublin Brigade, on Easter Monday 1916 he was among a group of Volunteers who held positions in the Fairview area. On the Tuesday evening they were ordered back to the GPO and he fought there and in the Sackville Street area, throughout Easter Week. After the surrender, he was deported to Knutsford Barracks on May 1st, and interned in Frongoch until July 26th 1916.

He rejoined B. Company, 2nd Battalion, Dublin Brigade and served until March 1918, when he transferred to the 3rd Northern Division, A. Company, Belfast Brigade. He was involved in armed operations, during the Belfast pogroms and was appointed Captain in October 1920. In April 1921 he transferred to the Active Service Unit, Belfast Brigade and he returned to Dublin in August 1921 and served with K. Company, 2nd Battalion. During the Civil War, he took the Republican side and fought in Barry's Hotel and in the Dublin area.

Joseph Billings died on the December 16th 1975 and was buried at Cruagh Cemetery, Rathfarnham.

References:
RH; IMA, MSPC; *Irish Independent*, 17th December 1975, (dn).

Patrick Bird: (1890 - 1938)
D. Coy, 2nd Batt, Dublin Brigade. Roll of Honour

Patrick Bird was born in 1890 and was employed as a baker in Kennedy's Bakery, Parnell Street in 1916. A member of D. Company, 2nd Battalion, Dublin Brigade, he was not mobilised on Easter Monday, but reported to Father Mathew Park and was posted to the Vitriol Works, at Ballybough Bridge. At 3.00 p.m. he went with a body of Volunteers under the command of Captain Weafer to the GPO. He was then sent across the street to the Hibernian Bank. When Captain Weafer was shot, he was sent with a Cumann na mBan nurse to bring an ambulance to the back of the Hibernian Bank, but the driver refused to return with them. He spent Wednesday night and Thursday at the rear of Clerys, before making his way to a house in Gloucester Street with three other volunteers. On Friday he got to Kennedy's Bakery and evaded capture.

In 1917 he was living at 1 Ben Edar Road, Arbour Hill and he rejoined his old unit on the re-organisation of the Volunteers and fought in the War of Independence.

He later resided at 88 West Street, Drogheda.

Patrick Bird died on December 29th 1938 and was laid to rest two days later in Glasnevin Cemetery.

References:
RH; IMA, MSPC; 1911 Census; *Irish Independent*, 31st December 1938, (dn).

Edmund (Ned) Boland: (1893 - 1928)

F. Coy, 2nd Batt, Dublin Brigade

Ned Boland was born in Dalymount Terrace, Phibsboro, the younger brother of Gerry and Harry. His father, James, was the Chairman of the Dublin County Board of the GAA in 1892 and all brothers became members of the GAA from a very young age. Having played initially with O'Donovan Rossas, he later won a Dublin senior championship medal with Parnells in 1916.

He joined the Volunteers in 1913, and on Easter Monday reported to the F. Company, 2nd Battalion Dublin Brigade's headquarters at Fr Mathew Park in Fairview with his brother Harry. Gerry, who lived in Crooksling on the Blessington Road, cycled into Jacob's biscuit factory to join a section of the 2nd Battalion that was stationed there, while Ned stayed with the remainder of the battalion that held positions in the Fairview area until they moved into the GPO late on Tuesday night. He was sent with a group across the street to occupy the Imperial Hotel. The following day he and Joseph Whelan of the Irish Citizen Army ran out and carried Noel Lemass, who had been wounded in the leg while crossing O'Connell Street, to safety while under heavy sniper fire. At the time of surrender he managed to evade capture and returned to the family home at Marino Crescent.

He continued to play an active part in the War of Independence and fought on the anti-Treaty side during the Civil War. Ned and his brothers, Harry and Gerry, joined the Republican forces at Blessington after the fall of the Four Courts and later returned to the city with Oscar Traynor.

After the Civil War, Ned Boland emigrated to the United States, where he passed away in 1928.

References:
David Fitzpatrick, *Harry Boland's Irish Revolution*, (2003); Jim Maher: *Harry Boland*, (1998); Andrew Brasier, *Harry Boland, a man divided*, (2000).

Henry (Harry) Boland: (1887 – 1922)

F. Coy, 2nd Batt, Dublin Brigade. Roll of Honour

Harry Boland was born at Dalymount Terrace, Phibsboro, in 1887. His father, James, was a Manchester born Fenian and pioneer of the GAA who died as a result of head injuries received during a fracas between Parnellites and Healyites in 1895. He was educated at Synge St CBS and later at the De La Salle College in Castletown, County Laois. After serving his time as a tailor with Todd Burns in Henry Street, he set up his own business in Abbey Street. He became a member of the Keating Branch of the Gaelic League and he joined the IRB in 1904 with his brother Gerry. With his two brothers, Ned and Gerry, he became a member of the O'Donovan Rossa Gaelic Football Club and the Rathmines Hurling Club. As well as being a first class hurler, he was also involved in administration and was Chairman of the Dublin County Board from 1911 to 1916. He won a Leinster Junior Championship with Dublin in 1909 and later won Dublin Senior Championship and League medals with Faughs in 1914 and 1915. From 1911 to 1916, he was a regular on the Dublin Senior Hurling team.

He joined the Irish Volunteers at the inaugural meeting at the Rotunda in 1913. On Easter Monday 1916 he was one of a detachment from F. Company, 2nd Battalion, Dublin Brigade, under Captain Frank Henderson, that occupied Gilbey's at Ballybough Bridge. Called to the GPO late on Tuesday night, he was sent to the Metropole Hotel and later Mansfield's Corner, where he was an effective marksman in halting the advancing military. Following the surrender, he was sentenced to 10 years penal servitude with 5 years remission and was sent to Dartmoor Prison. In December, 1916 he was transferred to Lewes Prison and remained there, until the June 16th 1917.

In 1918 he was elected to the First Dáil for Sinn Féin, in South Roscommon. During DeValera's American fund raising campaign Boland acted as his secretary. Although he was a close friend of Michael Collins, he voted against the Treaty. When the Provisional Government forces attacked the Four Courts on June 28th 1922, he volunteered for service with the Republican forces, under Oscar Traynor, O/C Dublin Brigade. He fought with the Republican forces at Blessington in July and when a large force of Provisional Government troops moved on the Blessington Garrison, he evaded capture and went on the run in Dublin. In the early hours of August 1st 1922, Provisional Government forces burst into his room at the Grand Hotel in Skerries, where he was sleeping and in the struggle that ensued he was shot in the abdomen and died hours later in St Vincent's Hospital. Harry Boland was laid to rest in the Republican Plot in Glasnevin Cemetery on August 4th 1922.

References:

RH; *DIB*, David Fitzpatrick, (James Quinn, Ed, 2009); Piaras Béaslaí, *Michael Collins and the Making of a New Ireland,* (1926); Seán Cronin, *The McGarrity Papers,* (1972); Marcus de Burca, *The GAA, a History,* (1980); Diarmuid Lynch, *The IRB and the 1916 Insurrection,* (1987); Jim Maher, *Harry Boland,* (1998); Michael Hopkinson, *Green against Green:the Irish Civil War,* (1992); David Fitzpatrick, *Harry Boland's Irish Revolution,* (2003): Andrew Brasier & John Kelly, *Harry Boland, a man divided,* (2000); *The Gaelic Athletic Association in Dublin, 1884-2000,* (William Nolan, Ed, 2005); Charlie McGuire, *Seán McLoughlin: Ireland's Forgotten Revolutionary,* (2011).

Michael Boland: (1876 - 1942)

O/C, E. Coy, 4th Batt, Dublin Brigade. Roll of Honour

Michael Boland was born in 1876 and worked as a carter. He was a lieutenant in E. Company, 4th Battalion, Dublin Brigade, and was O/C of the Volunteers that left Rathfarnham village for the GPO on Easter Monday. While in charge of the defence unit on the roof of the GPO, he was wounded while under heavy fire. His command was taken by Lieutenant Eamon Bulfin, until the position was abandoned because of the fire engulfing the roof. He was later among the wounded taken to Jervis Street Hospital and was transferred to the military hospital in Dublin Castle. A former soldier in the British Army, he had fought in the Boer War and believed the Volunteers should have taken to the hills during the Rising, just as the Boers had done.

He was deported to Wakefield Prison on May 6th, and then interned in Frongoch until Christmas 1916. On his release from internment, he took an active part in the re-organisation of the Volunteers and fought in the War of Independence. In the civil war he took the Republican side and assisted in medical duties.

Michael Boland died on November 8th 1942 at his home at Grange Avenue, Rathfarnham and was buried in Templeogue Cemetery.

References:
RH; IMA, MSPC; NLI, *Lynch Papers*, (Ms 11,131); Thomas Coffey, *Agony at Easter*, (1969); Max Caulfield, *The Easter Rebellion*, (1963); Desmond Ryan, *The Rising: the complete story of Easter Week*, (1949); *Irish Independent*, 10th November 1942, (obit).

John Bolger

Liverpool Company, (Kimmage Garrison). Roll of Honour

John Bolger, a native of Blackwater, Co. Wexford, went to Liverpool as a teenager in 1912 and worked as a barman. While there he joined the Volunteers. He returned to Dublin in January, 1916 and was employed as a motor driver. He joined the Kimmage Camp and assisted in making bombs and buckshot. On Easter Sunday, he was one of four men from the Kimmage Garrison who took part in the raid for gelignite at the De Selby quarries, Jobstown, Co. Dublin. After the occupation of the GPO he took part in the attempt to blow up the railway bridge at the North Circular Road. He returned to the GPO on Tuesday and fought there throughout Easter Week. After the surrender, he was deported to Stafford Jail on May 1st and then interned in Frongoch until Christmas, 1916. He returned to Wexford after his release from Frongoch and served with the 4th Battalion, Wexford Brigade in the War of Independence. He enlisted in the Free State Army in February 1923 and served as a Marine Coastal Service Inspector. He was demobilised in March 1924 and was employed as a temporary civil servant. He emigrated to the United States and married in Chicago, in 1927.

John Bolger died in Barrington, Illinois, USA on November 17th 1974.

References:
RH; IMA, MSPC.

David Bourke: (1890 - 1978)
Tipperary Brigade

David Bourke was born in 1890 and joined the Volunteers at Emly, County Tipperary, in 1913. On the Tuesday preceding Easter Week, he was summoned to Dublin and on Good Friday he and Con Keating were sent to Kerry to seize the Government's wireless apparatus. When their car drove off the pier at Ballykissane, Keating was drowned but Bourke survived. He returned to the GPO on Easter Monday and was sent with Fergus Kelly, a former British Army Signals Corps operator, across the street to the Dublin Wireless School of Telegraphy in Reis's Chambers, situated between Abbey Street and Eden Quay. They worked through the night and on Tuesday morning, after some difficulty re-connecting the dismantled wireless apparatus; they transmitted a message that was picked up by ships at sea stating that a Rising had taken place. After both Reis's Chambers and the Dublin Bread Company building on the same block were evacuated on Wednesday night, he and several others made their way into the north inner city area. With Volunteer James Conroy (Junior), he got through the military cordon to Conroy's home at Richmond Parade, Summerhill on Saturday. The following morning the house was surrounded by troops and they were taken Arbour Hill for interrogation. He was deported to Knutsford Jail and was released after three months.

He returned to his native Emly and joined Dinny Lacy's 1st Flying Column, 3rd Tipperary Brigade. He was appointed a captain and served in the Tipperary region until March 1919, when he was ordered to transfer to the Cork 7th Brigade because of a warrant for his arrest. He took the Republican side in the Civil War and was part of a flying column that engaged with Free State troops in the Knockmealdown Mountains. He was arrested in September 1923 and detained at Limerick Jail until June 1924. He was later employed by the Irish Land Commission and lived at 64 Gracepark Road, Drumcondra.

David Bourke passed away on July 28th 1978 and was buried in Glasnevin Cemetery.

References:
IMA, MSPC; Max Caulfield, *The Easter Rebellion*, (1963); *Irish Press*, 29th July 1978, (dn).

John Boylan: (1878 – 1941)
Irish Citizen Army, (High St Section)

John Boylan was born in 1878 and resided at 23 St Michael's Terrace, Blackpitts. A member of the Irish Citizen Army, High Street Section, he reported to Liberty Hall on Easter Saturday 1916. He remained on duty there until Easter Monday, when he brought supplies to the GPO. He then went to the Fairview area with a group of Irish Citizen Army men under the command of Captain Vincent Poole, where they occupied the Vitriol Works, Ballybough. He also fought at Annesley Bridge and was cut off from the main body of insurgents when they retreated to the GPO on Tuesday evening.

He suffered ill health for a long period and was hospitalised with chronic bronchitis.

John Boylan died on March 9th 1941 and was buried at Mount Jerome Cemetery, Harold's Cross.

References:
IMA, MSPC.

Joseph Bracken: (1882 - 1968)

B. Coy, 2nd Batt, Dublin Brigade. Roll of Honour

Joseph Bracken, the son of a civil servant, was born at 106 St Lawrence Road, Clontarf, in 1882. He was educated at St Joseph's CBS, Fairview and on leaving school joined the civil service. In 1913 he joined the Irish Volunteers and became a member of B. Company, 2nd Battalion, Dublin Brigade. On entering the GPO on Easter Monday, he was sent out as a scout reporting on troop movements. When he returned later he was handed a rifle and fought there until the evacuation of the building on Friday evening. Deported to Wandsworth Prison on May 9th , he was then interned in Wormwood Scrubbs, Woking and Frongoch. He was released from Frongoch on August 29th 1916 and returned to Dublin, but took no further part in the struggle.

He was reinstated in the Congested District Board and was later employed for many years as a clerical officer in the Dept. of Defence until he retired in 1951.

Joseph Bracken died in 1968.

References:
RH; IMA, MSPC; *Scoil Iósaif, Marino, 1916-1966: (a 1916 Jubilee Publication)*, (1966).

Peadar Bracken: (1887 - 1961)

Commandant. Offaly Company, Athlone Brigade, (Kimmage Garrison).
Roll of Honour

Peadar Bracken was born in Tullamore, in 1887. He joined the IRB at the age of eighteen and became Commandant of the Offaly Company, Athlone Brigade. On March 20th 1916, Volunteers had assembled for revolver practice in the Sinn Féin Rooms in William Street, Tullamore, when a hostile crowd gathered outside. It appears the crowd's anger towards the Volunteers was a reaction to the large number of casualties in WWI in the preceding weeks. Peadar Bracken fired a revolver in the air to disperse the crowd and this alerted the police. In the subsequent struggle to escape, he fired at Inspector Crane and seriously wounded Sergeant Ahern. He remained on the run in the Westmeath area in the following weeks and returned to Tullamore on Good Friday to mobilise the Volunteers for the Rising which was to take place on Easter Sunday. He received the countermanding orders, issued by Eoin MacNeill, from Liam O'Brien. He and Seamus Brennan accompanied O'Brien on his return car journey to Dublin on Sunday, where they joined the Kimmage Garrison.

He reported to Liberty Hall on Easter Monday and was commissioned captain by James Connolly. On entering the GPO he took charge of a group of Kimmage Garrison men, who occupied Kelly's Gunpowder Shop, at the corner of Bachelor's Walk, overlooking Westmoreland Street. They held out until Thursday, when they came under intense artillery fire and sniper fire from Trinity College and were ordered to return to the GPO. After the

Rising he was detained and court-martialled in Richmond Barracks on charges relating to the Tullamore incident, and after his release from Kilmainham Jail in June 1916 he reorganised the Athlone Brigade. During the War of Independent he was involved in an ambush of British forces at Raheen, Geashill, County Offaly. He was imprisoned in March 1921 and escaped from Rath Camp in the Curragh in October 1921. Following his escape, he helped organise Republican Courts in Westmeath, Offaly, Meath and Kildare. He took the Republican side in the Civil War and took part in an unsuccessful attempt to secure arms in County Offaly.

He was the Tullamore District Court Clerk for many years.

Peadar Bracken, of the Lawn, Tullamore, died on January 19th 1961 and was buried at St Mary's Cemetery, Clonminch, Tullamore, County Offaly.

References:

RH; IMA, MSPC; Michael Foy & Brian Barton, *The Easter Rising*, (1999); *Sunday Independent*, 26th March 1954, (na); *Irish Independent*, 20th January 1961, (obit); *Midland Tribune*, April 1966, (*1916 Jubilee Supplement*).

Michael Brady: (1868 – 1954)

Lieutenant. E. Coy, 2nd Batt, Dublin Brigade. Roll of Honour

Michael Brady was born in Cavan in 1868. He later came to Dublin to work as a draper's assistant and in the years prior to the Rising, he owned a tobacconist shop at 63a Talbot Street. A member of the local St Laurence O'Toole's GAA Club, he joined E. Company, 2nd Battalion, Dublin Brigade in 1914. In 1915 he was promoted Company Staff Lieutenant and his shop was used for concealing arms.

On Easter Monday he reported to the GPO and was engaged in manning the ground floor windows there throughout the week. On Friday evening he was leading the advance party, under the command of The O'Rahilly, into Moore Street and when O'Rahilly was shot, he led a small group of Volunteers into Samson's Lane. They spent the night at the rear of William's Stores in Henry Street until the surrender the following afternoon. He was court-martialled and sentenced to death, which was commuted to three years penal servitude. He was imprisoned in Dartmoor Prison for six months, in Lewes Jail for seven months and Parkhurst Prison for two weeks, before being released on June 16th 1917.

On his release from prison he fought in the War of Independence. He served as an intelligence officer under Captain Dick McKee and his shop in Talbot Street was raided by the Black and Tans on many occasions. With the outbreak of the Civil War he went to the anti-Treaty forces at Barry's Hotel, but was refused entry because of his age. He then joined the Fingal Brigade as an intelligence officer and served until 1923.

Michael Brady, who suffered ill health for many years, died at St Patrick's Nursing Home, Kilmainham, on May 22nd 1954 and was buried at Deansgrange Cemetery.

References:

RH; IMA, MSPC; *Irish Press*, 27th May 1954, (obit).

William (Liam) Breen: (1886 – 1919)

Captain. O/C Engineering, 2nd Batt, Dublin Brigade. Roll of Honour

Liam Breen was born in 1886 and resided at 76 Fairview Strand. He was employed by Dockrell's Builder's Providers and was one the Dublin Brigade's engineering officer's attached to the 2nd Battalion, in 1916. He was a member of the GPO Garrison and fought in the Abbey Street area early in Easter Week. He was in the group that left the burning building on Friday evening with The O'Rahilly, intending to establish a new headquarters at William & Woods, in Great Britain Street. He was the only one of five from that group who came through unscathed, after The O'Rahilly fell mortally wounded in Moore Street. He led the Volunteers from Moore Street to Sackville Street, carrying a white flag at the surrender. He was then deported to Stafford Jail and later interned in Frongoch until July 26th 1916.

Liam Breen died at his home at Fairview Strand on July 28th 1919 and was buried at Glasnevin Cemetery. His son, the Rev. W. Breen, was a curate in Bray in 1966, the year of the 50th anniversary of the Rising.

References:
RH; Desmond Ryan, *The Rising: the complete story of Easter Week,* (1949); Seán MacEntee, *Episode at Easter,* (1966); *Evening Herald,* 29th July 1919, (obit); *Evening Herald,* 13th April 1966, (na).

Daniel (Dan) Brophy: (1892 - 1961)

Lieutenant, Lusk Coy, Fingal Brigade. Roll of Honour

Dan Brophy, a native of Lusk, County Dublin, was born in 1892 and sworn into the IRB by Thomas Ashe in 1908. He was played hurling for his local club, Lusk and was also lieutenant in the Lusk Company, Fingal Brigade. On Easter Monday, he and his company of Lusk Volunteers reported to Commandant Ashe at Finglas. The following day he was one of twenty Volunteers from the Fingal Brigade, who were sent to the GPO. He fought at Kelly's Gunshop, Bachelor's Walk and then at the GPO for the remainder of the week. After the surrender, he was sent to Knutsford on May 1st and then interned in Frongoch until July 27th, 1916.

On his release from Frongoch, he became the O/C of the Fingal Brigade for the duration of the War of Independence. The town of Balbriggan was attacked by Crown Forces in retaliation for the killing of an RIC Head Constable in September 1920 and according to Colonel Joseph Lawless members of the IRA, under the command of Dan Brophy, executed a spy in the area. Soon afterwards he was arrested and interned in

Ballykinlar, County Down until December 1921. On his release, he became a member of the Active Service Unit, Dublin Brigade. He joined the Free State Army at its foundation, and resigned in September 1924, having reached the rank of Colonel.

Dan Brophy, of 3 Victoria Street, South Circular Road, died on February 25th 1961.

References:
RH; IMA, MSPC; *Irish Press*, 27th February 1961, (obit).

Eamon Bulfin: (1892 – 1968)

Lieutenant. E. Coy, 4th Batt, Dublin Brigade. Roll of Honour

Eamon Bulfin was born in Buenos Aires, in 1892. His father, William Bulfin, author of "Rambles In Éireann", was also the editor of the "Southern Cross" newspaper. After his parents returned to Ireland, he enrolled in St Enda's School, Rathfarnham, in 1908. He was sworn into the IRB in 1912. Prior to the Rising, he was engaged in manufacturing munitions at St Enda's. He was also a member of the Collegians (UCD) GAA Club. He was a lieutenant in E Company, 4th Battalion, Dublin Brigade and when he arrived at Liberty Hall with the Rathfarnham men, he was told that the insurgents had already occupied the GPO. They reached Sackville Street as the Lancers made their charge, and in the confusion were forced to gain entry to the GPO by breaking a window on Princes Street side of the building. Because he was a top marksman he spent most of the week on the roof of the GPO under constant sniper fire and took charge of the men on the roof when Lieutenant Michael Boland was wounded. He was deported to Stafford Jail on May 8th and was interned in Frongoch until Christmas, 1916.

He organised and trained Volunteers in county Offaly from 1917 until his arrest, in July 1918, in connection with the 'German Plot'. He was detained in prison in England and then deported to Argentina in 1919, where he was later appointed Irish Consul by the First Dáil. During the War of Independence he procured arms in Argentina and transported them to Ireland. He returned to Ireland in July 1922, but took no part in the Civil War. He settled in Birr, Co Offaly and became chairman of the County Council. He was also employed for many years as a tax collector with the Revenue Commissioners.

Eamon Bulfin, of Derrinlough House, Birr, died on December 24th 1968 and was buried four days later at Eglish Cemetery, Fivealley, Birr, Co. Offaly.

References:
RH; IMA, MSPC; IMA, BMH (WS 487); NLI, *Lynch Papers*, (Ms 11,131); Charles Townshend, *Easter 1916: the Irish rebellion*, (2005); *Irish Press*, 8th June 1953, (na); *Midland Tribune*, April 1966, (1916 supplement).

Bartholomew (Batt) Burke: (1882 - 1955)

E. Coy, 4th Batt, Dublin Brigade. Roll of Honour

Batt Burke, of Newbrook, Rathfarnham, was born in 1882 and was employed as a labourer in 1916. On Easter Monday morning he paraded outside Rathfarnham Church with fellow members of E. Company, 4th Battalion, Dublin Brigade, and from there they left for Liberty Hall. He was posted on the roof of the GPO for several days and was later stationed on the ground floor. After the evacuation of the GPO he and other Rathfarnham men, including Frank Burke, broke into a building known as the "White House". It had been suspected that enemy fire was coming from there, but on entering the building it was discovered to be vacant. He later played a part in boring through the walls of the houses in Moore Street as far as Hanlon's Fish Shop. After the surrender, he was deported to Knutsford Jail on May 1st and interned in Frongoch until Christmas, 1916.

After his release from Frongoch he rejoined his unit and took an active part in the War of Independence. He took the pro-Treaty side in the Civil War and was involved in the attack on the Four Courts. He was discharged from the army in 1924 and was later employed at the Stationary Office.

Batt Burke, of Whitechurch Cottages, Rathfarnham, died on November 21st 1955.

References:
IMA, MSPC; *Irish Independent*, 22nd November 1955, (dn).

Elizabeth Burke (Mrs. Elizabeth McGinty):
(1884 - 1952)

Cumann na mBan, (Central Branch). Roll of Honour

Elizabeth Burke was born in 1884 and resided at 15 North Summer Street. She was a member of the Cumann na mBan, Central Branch. On Easter Monday she reported to the GPO and was assigned to the nursing staff. The following day she was sent across the street to the Hibernian Bank, which was occupied by Volunteers and when Captain Weafer was shot dead on Wednesday, she returned under enemy fire to the GPO. She remained there for the rest of the week and administered first aid and helped with the cooking. She was part of the group that escorted the wounded to Jervis Street Hospital on Friday and, having evaded capture, she eventually made her way home safely on Saturday. She was the sister of Tom Burke, who was part of the Jacob's Garrison. She continued her role in Cumann na mBan during the War of Independence.

Elizabeth McGinty, of 5 North Great George's Street, died on Sept 17th 1952.

References:
RH; IMA, MSPC; NLI, *Lynch Papers*, (Ms 11,131); *Irish Press*, 18th September 1952, (obit).

Eva Burke (Aoife deBúrca): (1885 – 1974)
Cumann na mBan. Roll of Honour

Aoife deBúrca was born in Carbury, County Kildare, in 1885. She was a qualified nurse when she joined Cumann na mBan at its foundation. She was one of several nurses on duty in the GPO during Easter Week. Her brother, Frank, was also in the GPO Garrison. On Tuesday she was sent to Reis's Chambers and the Hibernian Bank to attend to the wounded, and attended to the mortally wounded Captain Thomas Weafer on Wednesday. When she returned to the GPO she attended to the wounded James Connolly. She left the GPO and escorted the wounded to Jervis Street Hospital on Friday. She remained in Jervis Street Hospital on Friday night and was allowed home on Saturday at the time of the surrender.

With another brother, Liam, she active in the War of Independence and she took the Republican side in the Civil War.

She was employed as a nurse for many years in the Dublin Corporation and resided at Dargle Road, Drumcondra.

Aoife deBúrca died on December 1st 1974 and was buried at Derrinturn Cemetery, Carbury, County Kildare.

References:

RH; IMA, MSPC; IMA, BMH (WS 694, *Frank Burke*); NLI, *Lynch Papers*, (Ms 11,131); *Irish Press*, 3rd December 1974, (obit).

Fergus (Frank) Burke: (1895 – 1987)
E. Coy, 4th Batt, Dublin Brigade. Roll of Honour

Frank Burke was born in Carbury, County Kildare, in 1895 and was a pupil of St Enda's College in Rathfarnham. He was in attendance as a steward at the monster meeting in 1913 when the Volunteers were formed at the Rotunda.

Under Lieutenant Michael Boland, he was one of the Rathfarnham Volunteers from E. Company, 4th Battalion, who made their way to the GPO via Liberty Hall. His first few days were spent on the roof of the GPO where he was conspicuous by his bravery and later fought at the ground floor windows of the building. After the evacuation, he manned a barricade in Moore Street under the command of J.J. Walsh. On Saturday he was part of the group in Sackville Lane, under the command of Seán McLoughlin, who were preparing to attack the British Army barricade less than thirty yards away in Parnell Street, when the decision to negotiate a surrender was made. He was deported to Stafford Jail on May 1st and interned in Frongoch, until Christmas, 1916. His sister, Aoife, was also in the GPO Garrison, while his brother, Liam, fought in the War of Independence.

During the War of Independence, Frank was detained in custody in Dublin Castle, the Curragh Camp and Arbour Hill.

He became Headmaster at St Enda's and remained in that position until the school's closure in 1935. He was one of the most outstanding all-rounders in the history of the GAA, winning two All-Ireland medals in hurling in 1917 and 1920, and three All-Ireland football medals in 1921, 1922 and 1923, all with Dublin. He also won two Junior All-Ireland medals in football with Dublin in 1914 and 1916. On Bloody Sunday, November 21st 1920, Burke was marking Mick Hogan, the captain of the Tipperary team, when Hogan was shot dead.

Frank Burke, the last Headmaster of St Enda's College, died on December 28th 1987, aged 92 and was buried at Cruagh Cemetery, Rathfarnham.

References:
RH; IMA, MSPC; IMA, BHM (WS 694); NLI, *Lynch Papers*, (Ms 11,131); *Sunday Press*, 4th, 11th, 18th & 25th February 1968, *the Frank Burke Story*, (Pádraig Purcell); *Irish Press*, 29th December 1987, (dn).

Nicholas Burke: (1896 – 1963)
Hibernian Rifles. Roll of Honour

Nicholas Burke was born on September 24th 1896 and joined the Hibernian Rifles in October 1914. Two weeks before the Rising he brought arms from Croydon Park to 28 North Frederick Street (The Hibernian Knights H/Q) in a cart. He was mobilised on Easter Monday morning at 28 North Frederick Street and then preceded to the GPO at midnight. He was sent with J.J. Scollan and another Volunteer to a house adjacent to the Evening Mail Offices in Parliament Street. He fought there until Tuesday evening when he and Irish Citizen Army man, William Egan, were forced to withdraw. They were arrested outside the Crown Alley Telephone Exchange, as they made their way to the GPO, and taken to Great Ship Street Barracks for interrogation. Because of his small stature he appeared younger than he was to his interrogators, and he and William Egan were both released from Richmond Barracks on the following Sunday. After the Rising he took no further part in the struggle.

In later years he resided at 21 Holly Road, Donnycarney and was a civilian employee of the Army Corps of Engineers, at Collins Barracks.

Nicholas Burke died on February 23rd 1963 and was buried at Glasnevin Cemetery.

References:
RH; IMA, MSPC; *Evening Herald*, 25th February 1963, (dn).

Alice Byrne (Mrs. Alice Coogan): (1889 - 1972)
Cumann na mBan, (Árd Croabh)

Alice Byrne was born in 1889 and resided at 17 North Richmond Street. She was a member of Cumann na mBan when she reported to Liberty Hall on Easter Monday. She traveled as a passenger in The O'Rahilly's car, bringing arms and ammunition to the GPO. Her sister, Catherine and brothers, Patrick, Jack and Peter, were also members of the GPO Garrison. She was sent across the street to the Hibernian Bank and Reis's Chambers later in the day with provisions. On Tuesday she delivered dispatches to the Volunteers in Fairview and Ballybough, but she was unable to return to the GPO because of the presence of the British troops in the area. After the Rising she was engaged in smuggling guns and explosives from Glasgow to Dublin with her sister, Catherine Rooney. They also brought arms from Belfast to Dublin. From 1919 she resided to Glasgow, where she married and settled. She assisted in the escape of Quartermaster Seán Flood, from Glasgow.

Alice Coogan (nee Byrne) returned to Dublin to take part in the Jubilee Celebrations in April, 1966 and passed away in Glasgow on August 23rd 1972.

References:
IMA, MSPC.

Catherine Byrne (Mrs. Catherine Rooney):
(1896 – 1971)
Cumann na mBan, (Árd Craobh). Roll of Honour

Catherine Byrne was born in 1896 and resided at 17 North Richmond Street. She joined the Árd Craobh Branch of Cumann na mBan in 1915 with her sister, Alice. On Easter Monday she entered the GPO through a window in Prince's Street, where she joined her sister, Alice and brothers, Patrick, Jack, and Peter. Shortly after arriving, she attended to the wounded Lieutenant Liam Clarke, who had been injured when a homemade bomb exploded. She also attended to a wounded British soldier who had been taken prisoner. On Easter Monday night she was sent with Leslie Price to the Hibernian Bank, located at the corner of Sackville Street and Lower Abbey Street, where Captain Thomas Weafer and seven Volunteers were stationed. She returned to the GPO on Tuesday and was sent with a dispatch that she concealed in her hair bun, to Captain Frank Fahy in the Four Courts Garrison. She then served at the North King Street outpost and in Monk's Bakery until the surrender, when she evaded capture.

After the reorganization of Cumann na mBan, she continued on active service during the War of Independence. She made several trips to Glasgow, transporting arms and gelignite back to Dublin with her sister, Alice. They also brought arms from Belfast to Dublin. She also treated many wounded Volunteers in her parents' home in North Richmond Street.

She lived at 1 de Burgh Road, Parkgate Street and was married to Patrick Rooney, who predeceased her. In later years, she became a member of the Saint John's Ambulance Brigade.

Catherine Rooney (nee Byrne) died on March 30th 1971 and was buried at Esker Cemetery, Lucan.

References:

RH; IMA, MSPC; *Evening Herald*, 13th April 1966, *The Petticoat Heroine*, (na); *Evening Herald*, 31st March 1971, (dn).

Christopher C. Byrne: (1897 – 1981)

A. Coy, 3rd Batt, Dublin Brigade. Roll of Honour

Christopher Byrne was born in 1897 and was a hairdresser by trade. A member of Fianna Éireann, he later joined A. Company, 3rd Battalion, Dublin Brigade. He spent Easter Weekend guarding an arms dump at Coleman's forge, Camden Place with Matt O'Brien, who was also a member of A. Company, 3rd Battalion and fought in the GPO throughout Easter Week. After the surrender he was deported to Stafford Jail on May 1st and interned in Frongoch until August 1916.

He rejoined his unit on the reorganisation of the Volunteers and took part in all the company's engagements in his area. On November 20th 1920, Bloody Sunday, he was involved in the operation, where a number of British agents were executed. He was arrested later that month and interned at Ballykinlar Camp until December 1921. He enlisted in the Free State Army in May 1922 and was attached to Supplies GHQ, Portobello Barracks. He resigned from the Free State Army in December 1924 with the rank of Captain, 16th Battalion.

He resided for some years at 38 St Alban's Road, South Circular Road and later at 78 The Quay, Waterford.

Christopher Byrne died in Birkenhead, England on February 8th 1981 and was buried at Deansgrange Cemetery, County Dublin.

References:

RH; IMA, MSPC; *Irish Independent* & *Irish Press*, 10th February 1981, (dn).

Edward (Eddie) Byrne: (1901 – 1922)
B. Coy, 2nd Batt, Dublin Brigade. Roll of Honour

Eddie Byrne was born in 1901 and was fifteen years old when he fought in the GPO in Easter Week. He was a member of B. Company, 2nd Battalion, Dublin Brigade and was posted to the Metropole Hotel, under the command of Lieutenant Oscar Traynor. Charles Saurin recalled that he warned him about his careless use of his rifle, while stationed at the windows of the hotel. He was in the group led by The O'Rahilly from the burning GPO into Moore Street on Friday evening. He was detained in Richmond Barracks after the surrender and was released on May 12th because of his young age.

During the War of Independence he saw service in the Dublin area and on one occasion was involved in the capture of an armored car. He escaped after the burning of the Custom House in 1921 with wounded comrade Seán Doyle, who later died from his wounds. When the Treaty was ratified by Dáil Éireann on January 7th 1922, he had risen to the rank of lieutenant of the Dublin Guards Company of the IRA.

Eddie Byrne died from the accidental discharge of a shotgun in Bodyke, County Clare, on January 14th 1922 and was buried three days later in the Republican Plot at Glasnevin Cemetery.

References:

RH; *An t-Óglach*, March 1926, (*Charles Saurin*); *Irish Independent* & *Evening Herald*, 17th January 1922, (obit).

James Byrne: (1881 -   )
Volunteer. Roll of Honour

James Byrne was born in 1881 and resided at 94 Capel Street. He was a past pupil of Synge Street, CBS and a baker by trade. Although he was a member of the IRB in 1916, he was not attached to the Volunteers when he offered his services at the GPO on Easter Monday. On Wednesday he was sent to the Metropole Hotel and remained there until the outpost was abandoned on Friday. He evacuated the GPO on Friday evening and spent the night in the houses in Moore Street. After the surrender, he was deported to Knutsford Jail on May 1st and interned in Frongoch until Christmas, 1916.

James Byrne went to live in Islington, London after his release from internment and took no part in the War of Independence.

References:

RH; IMA, MSPC; *Synge Street CBS Centenary Record, 1864-1964*, (1964); *Never a Dull Day: 150 years of Synge Street CBS, 1864-2014*, (Michael Minnock & Seán Ryan, Ed, 2014).

James Byrne: (1875 – 1945)
Irish Citizen Army

James Byrne was born in 1875 and resided at 22 Summerhill in 1916. He was employed as a labourer and was a member of the Irish Citizen Army. He reported to the GPO. on Easter Monday, and fought there until the evacuation of the building on Friday evening. After the surrender, he was deported to Knutsford Jail on May 3rd and was interned in Frongoch until Christmas, 1916.

He continued to serve with the Irish Citizen Army in the War of Independence, before taking the Republican side in the Civil War, and fought at Barry's Hotel and Vaughan's Hotel.

His health deteriorated and he was hospitalised in 1929, when he suffered a mental breakdown. James Byrne died on April 13th 1945.

References:
IMA, MSPC; NLI, *William O'Brien Papers*, (Ms 15,673).

John C. (Jack) Byrne: (1901 -   )
Fianna Éireann, (C. Coy, North Dublin Sluagh). Roll of Honour

Jack Byrne was born in 1901 and resided at 17 North Richmond Street. He was a member of Fianna Éireann, C. Company, North Dublin Sluagh, and took part in the Rising with his brothers, Patrick and Peter and his sisters, Catherine and Alice. On Easter Monday he was sent from the GPO by his brother Patrick, to monitor British troops in the north inner city area. He reported their presence in Findlater's Church and movements in other locations. He was also sent to Lemon's Sweet Shop in Sackville Street to collect tins for use in bomb making. After the surrender, he was detained in Richmond Barracks but was released on May 12th because of his young age.

During the War of Independence, he continued to serve in Fianna Éireann with his youngest brother, Frank.

Jack Byrne later moved to Limerick and resided at Lisín, North Circular Road, Limerick.

References:
RH; NLI, *Lynch Papers*, (Ms 11,131).

Louis Byrne (Junior): (1900 - 1987)
Irish Citizen Army, (Boys Corps). Roll of Honour

Louis Byrne was born in 1900 and resided at 47 Lower Gardiner Street. He was a boy scout in the Irish Citizen Army and on Easter Week he was sent out from the GPO on dispatch duty. He was sent out with Larry Corbally, who was another Irish Citizen Army boy scout, to collect scrap metal for use in making ammunition on Tuesday. On Wednesday and Thursday he was on dispatch duty, and found his route back to the GPO cut off by British troops. He spent the night in the open hall of a tenement in Waterford Street, where the body of a civilian who had been shot lay. His father, also named Louis, was killed in action in the City Hall area on April 24th. He was eventually able to return to his home and grieving mother on Saturday.

After the Rising, he served in the Irish Citizen Army during the War of Independence and took part in a number of operations. He took the anti-Treaty side in the Civil War and fought in the Hamman Hotel, in O'Connell Street and Barry's Hotel in Great Denmark Street. He joined an Irregular Column operating in County Wicklow and fought against Free State Forces at Glenasmole Lodge. He was arrested in March 1923 and interned in Tintown, at the Curragh, until December of that year.

Louis Byrne, a former employee of the Board of Works, died on August 16th 1987 and was buried at Glasnevin Cemetery.

References:
RH; IMA, MSPC; NLI, *William O'Brien Papers*, (Ms 15,673); John Heuston OP, *Headquarters Battalion, Easter Week 1916*, (1966); *Evening Herald*, 17th August 1987, (dn).

Patrick J. Byrne: (1892 – 1966)
C. Coy, 1st Batt, Dublin Brigade. Roll of Honour

Patrick Byrne was born in 1892, the eldest son of Peter Byrne, a well known coachbuilder. He attended O'Connell Schools, located across street from where he lived at 17 North Richmond Street. He joined the Volunteers in 1913 and he took part in the Howth gun running in July, 1914. He was a member of C. Company, 1st Battalion, Dublin Brigade. Early on Easter Monday morning he went with a demolition party, under the command of Captain Frank Daly, to the railway line at Cabra. He returned to the GPO and from there he was posted to the Fairview area. He was stationed at the Vitriol Works, Ballybough Bridge until Tuesday night when the Fairview contingent left for the GPO. His brothers, Peter and Jack, and sisters, Alice and Catherine, were also in the GPO Garrison. He was one of the stretcher bearers who carried the wounded James Connolly to Dublin Castle.

On his release from Frongoch, he rejoined his old unit. In 1917 he cycled to Ennis to help organize the East Clare by-election and shortly after he went to England seeking employment. On his return to Ireland, he enlisted in the Free State Army at Wellington Barracks, South Circular Road, in April 1922. He transferred to CID in July 1922, as O/C of Transport. When the CID merged with the DMP he became a member in 1923. He transferred to the Garda Síochána and for many years he was attached to the Detective Office in Dublin Castle before retiring in 1961.

Patrick Byrne, of 38 Lower Buckingham Street, passed away in December 1966 and was buried at Balgriffin Cemetery.

References:
RH; IMA, MSPC; *Irish Independent*, 10th December 1966, (obit).

Peter Byrne: (1899 - 1959)

Fianna Éireann. Roll of Honour

Peter Byrne was born in 1899 and resided at 17 North Richmond Street. He was educated at O'Connell Schools, North Richmond Street and was a member of Fianna Éireann in 1916. He spent Easter Monday in the Fairview area, where he was involved in erecting a barricade, and on Tuesday night he was in the party of Volunteers ordered to the GPO by James Connolly. His brothers, Patrick and Jack, and his sisters, Alice and Catherine, were also in the GPO Garrison. He was positioned at the ground floor windows throughout the week. He helped remove explosives from the basement of the GPO to the courtyard in Prince's Street on Friday, before the evacuation of the premises. He was in the advance party, led by The O'Rahilly, into Moore Street and spent that night at the rear of William's Provision Stores in Samson's Lane. When this group in Samson's Lane surrendered the next day, he led them out, carrying a white flag and was accompanied by a captured Connaught Ranger. After the surrender, he was detained in Richmond Barracks and released on May 11th, because on his young age.

At the re-organisation of Fianna Éireann, he was appointed Captain of 2nd Battalion, Dublin Brigade. He was later made quartermaster of Fianna Éireann, Dublin Brigade. In 1919 he was elected a member of the IRB, and the following year he was appointed to the staff of Michael Collins on fulltime duty. During the War of Independence his parent's home at North Richmond Street was used as the H/Q for Active Service Unit, under the command of Captain Paddy Daly. The house was raided on numerous occasions, but each time the Black & Tans failed to make any arrests. His three brothers and two sisters also took part in the War of Independence, while his mother, Catherine was awarded the War of Independence medal for her services.

In March 1922 he suffered injuries to his right leg in a motorbike accident while on intelligence duty for Michael Collins. He joined the Free State Army and was appointed to the rank of Captain. He was given charge of an armoured car and he took part in the fighting in the O'Connell Street vicinity in July 1922.

He later became a civil servant and resided at 7 Mount Prospect Park, Clontarf.

Peter Byrne died on August 31st 1959 and was buried at St Fintan's Cemetery, Sutton.

References:

RH; IMA, MSPC; NLI, *Lynch Papers*, (Ms 11,131); *Irish Press*, 2nd September 1959, (obit).

Thomas (Tom) Byrne: (1877 – 1962)

Captain. B. Coy, 1st Batt, Dublin Brigade. Roll of Honour

Tom Byrne was born in Carrickmacross, County Monaghan, in 1877. At the age of sixteen he emigrated to South Africa, where he worked as a miner. During the Boer War he fought with the Irish Brigade against the British, and took part in their defeat at the Battle of Dundee. He also witnessed the capture of Sir Winston Churchill, who was then a young war correspondent, at Ladysmith. When the Boer War was over and after a short period of internment, he made his way to the United States and became engaged in mining once again.

He returned to Ireland in 1914 and joined B. Company, 1st Battalion, Dublin Brigade, with the rank of Captain. On Holy Thursday he travelled to Maynooth and notified the Kildare Volunteers of the impending rising. On Easter Monday evening, after receiving a blessing from Professor Monsignor Hogan in Maynooth College, a group of fifteen Volunteers led by Tom Byrne, set out along the Royal Canal towpath towards Dublin. Shortly after leaving Maynooth, he drew his pistol and threatened to shoot two RIC men who were following them. They spent the night in Glasnevin Cemetery and he led the Maynooth Volunteers into the GPO on Tuesday morning, where they received a rousing reception and were welcomed by both P.H. Pearse and James Connolly. During the ensuing days he was involved in fighting in the Liffey Street and Parliament Street areas of the city. After the surrender he evaded capture and escaped in disguise to the north of Ireland.

On the re-organisation of the Volunteers, he was elected Commandant of the 1st Battalion, succeeding Commandant Edward Daly, one of the executed leaders of the Rising. At the end of 1919 he was arrested during a raid on his home and was interned in Brixton Prison, London. He was released five months later, after a hunger strike and was arrested again in 1921 and interned in Rath Camp, the Curragh, from where he escaped. He joined the Free State Army in 1922 and commanded several positions during the Civil War, including the one at Bolton Street Technical College.

For many years he was Captain of the Guard at Leinster House and in 1946 he was decorated by the South African Government for services rendered there. He was married to Lucy Smyth, who was also a member of the GPO Garrison and they resided at 71 Old Cabra Rd.

Tom Byrne died on September 7th 1962 and was buried at Glasnevin Cemetery.

References:
RH; IMA, MSPC; IMA, BMH (WS 564); NLI, *Lynch Papers*, (Ms 11,131); *Irish Press*, 8th September 1962, (obit).

Patrick Caddell: (1882 - 1942)
Lusk Company, Fingal Brigade. Roll of Honour

Patrick Caddell, of Collinstown, Lusk, County Dublin, was born in 1882. He was a founder member of the Lusk Branch of the Gaelic League and of the Lusk Hurling Club. He was also a drummer in the Lusk Black Raven's Pipe Band and already a member of the IRB when he joined the Lusk Company, Fingal Brigade. On Easter Tuesday he was among the group of Volunteers sent to the GPO from north county Dublin. He was then posted to Kelly's Fishing Tackle and Gunpowder Shop at the corner of Sackville Street and Bachelor's Walk. After the surrender he was deported to Knutsford Jail and interned in Frongoch.

On his release from internment in July 1916, he rejoined the Lusk Company. He was arrested in December 1920 and interned in Ballykinlar Camp until December 1921. He took no part in the Civil War.

Patrick Caddell died on April 23rd 1942 and was buried at Lusk Cemetery.

References:
RH; IMA, MSPC; NLI, *Lynch Papers*, (MS 11,131); *Irish Independent*, 25th April 1942, (obit).

John Caffrey: (1899 – 1933)
Fianna Éireann

John Caffrey was born in 1899 and was a member of Fianna Éireann. When he reported to the GPO on Easter Monday, he was sent out with dispatches. On Wednesday he was sent by Irish Citizen Army Officer, James O'Neill, to Liberty Hall with a message for any insurgents there to report to the GPO. While in this vicinity he was shot by a sniper and received a bullet in the lung. He was taken to the Mater Hospital and treated there for a month, before he was discharged.

He later joined G. Company, 1ˢᵗ Battalion, Dublin Brigade and fought in the War of Independence. He was involved in many operations and was interned in Ballykinlar Camp, from November 1920 to December 1921. While in Ballykinlar his health declined as a result of the bullet wound he received in Easter Week, and he was treated by Doctor Richard Hayes. During the Civil War he took the anti-Treaty side.

He was married with two children and resided at 14 Killarney Parade, North Circular Road. A former employee of Combridge's, Grafton Street, he was a member of the Gaelic League and was an accomplished chess player.

John Caffrey was rushed to the Mater Hospital on October 30ᵗʰ 1933 and died the following day, as a result of the bullet wound he received in 1916. He was buried at Glasnevin Cemetery on November 3ʳᵈ 1933.

References:

IMA, MSPC; *Irish Independent* & *Irish Press*, 2ⁿᵈ October 1933, (obit).

Matthew (Matt) Caffrey: (1882 – 1952)
E. Coy, 4th Batt, Dublin Brigade. Roll of Honour

Matt Caffrey, of Grove Cottage, Rathfarnham Lower, was born in 1882. He was employed as a bread van driver and was a member of the GAA club, Michael Dwyer's. He joined E. Company, 4ᵗʰ Battalion, Dublin Brigade, in 1914 and he left Rathfarnham with his unit on Easter Monday and went to the GPO via Liberty Hall. On Tuesday he left the GPO to disperse looters in the area. He was posted to the Dublin Bread Company building on Wednesday and from there fired on the Helga gunboat, moored on the River Liffey. He left the GPO at the evacuation on Friday evening and spent that night in the Moore Street houses. After the surrender he was deported to Knutsford Jail on May 1ˢᵗ and interned in Frongoch until Christmas 1916.

On its reorganisation in 1917, he re-joined his unit and during the War of Independence was assigned to intelligence duty under the command of Captain Francis Coghlan. He took the anti-Treaty side in the Civil War and served under Captain Liam Clarke.

Matt Caffrey suffered from ill health in later years and died August 7ᵗʰ 1952.

References:
RH; IMA, MSPC; *Sinn Féin Rebellion Handbook 1916, Weekly Irish Times*, (1917).

Patrick Caldwell: (1888-1972)

Liverpool Company, (Kimmage Garrison). Roll of Honour

Patrick Caldwell, a native of Carrickaboy, County Cavan, was born in 1888 and emigrated to Liverpool in 1914, where he joined the Liverpool Volunteers. He returned to Dublin in 1916 with Pádraig Supple and reported to the Volunteer Camp at Larkfield, Kimmage. He was made Volunteer Quartermaster there and on Easter Sunday morning was sent with a party of men to the De Selby quarries at Jobstown to commandeer a quantity of gelignite. On Easter Monday he was one of the 60 strong Kimmage Garrison to join the GPO Garrison. During the week he occupied a room overlooking Henry Place with two other Volunteers, and he was among the last group of eighteen to leave the burning GPO. He attempted to bring the wounded Andy Furlong to Jervis Street Hospital with assistance from Bernard Friel and Andy Carmichael, but was forced to retreat to the houses in Moore St, where he spent the night with other Volunteers, including Tom Clarke. He was deported to Knutsford Jail and later interned in Frongoch until Christmas, 1916.

On the re-organisation of the Volunteers in 1917, he joined F. Company, 1st Battalion and later the 5th Engineers Battalion. During the War of Independence he was sent to the Cavan/Monaghan area as an organiser. He joined the Free State Army in 1922 and served with the rank of captain until he was discharged in 1924. He also organised the printing and distribution of *An t-Óglach*. He was later employed as a Clerical Officer in Customs and Excise for many years.

Patrick Caldwell, of 54 Croydon Green, Fairview, died on February 4th 1972.

References:
RH; IMA, MSPC; IMA, BMH (WS 638); Max Caulfield, *The Easter Rebellion*, (1963); *Irish Press*, 5th February 1972, (dn).

Joseph Callan: (1896 - 1960)

E. Coy, 2nd Batt, Dublin Brigade. Roll of Honour

Joseph Callan was born in County Louth in 1896 and resided at 15 Clonliffe Avenue in 1916. He was employed as a motor driver and was a member of E. Company, 2nd Battalion, Dublin Brigade. On Easter Monday he in the group that occupied Lambe's Public House, Ballybough Bridge. When they arrived at the GPO on Tuesday evening, he was posted in Arnotts Stores and the Coliseum Theatre on Henry Street. After the Rising he was deported to Knutsford Jail on May 1st and interned in Frongoch until September 1916.

On his release from internment he rejoined the Volunteers and fought in the War of Independence. He was involved in many operations, including armed patrols and raids for arms. During the Civil War he took the pro-Treaty side and joined the Free State Army, becoming a captain in the Military Police. He retired from the army in 1926.

He lived at 35 Foster Terrace, Ballybough and suffered ill health in later life.

Joseph Callan passed away in James Connolly Memorial Hospital, Blanchardstown, on July 16th 1960 and was buried at St Fintan's Cemetery, Sutton.

References:
RH; IMA, MSPC; *Irish Independent*, 18th July 1960, (dn).

Daniel (Dan) Canny: (1885 - 1967)
C. Coy, 2nd Batt, Dublin Brigade. Roll of Honour

Dan Canny from Tulla, County Clare, was born in 1885 and was employed as a barman in O'Meara's Public House, 70 North Strand Road, in 1916. He was a member of the IRB and also of C. Company, 2nd Battalion, Dublin Brigade. On Easter Monday he joined the Volunteers and Irish Citizen Army men under the command of Tom Craven and Vincent Poole, that occupied the Vitriol Works, situated between Ballybough Bridge and Annesley Bridge. He arrived with this group at the GPO on Tuesday evening and he was posted to the Metropole Hotel, under the command of Lieutenant Oscar Traynor, where he was engaged in boring through the walls of the adjacent buildings. From Wednesday, the Metropole Hotel came under heavy artillery and sniper fire and on Thursday he kept rifles ready for marksman Harry Boland, while fire engulfed the roof. They were forced to retreat to the GPO on Friday and after the GPO was evacuated later that evening, he was involved in boring through the walls of the houses in Moore Street. He was part of the group, under the command of Seán McLoughlin, that was ready to charge the British Army barricades at Parnell Sreett, shortly before the surrender came. He was among the first group deported to Knutsford Jail on May 1st and was interned in Frongoch until July 26th 1916.

In 1917 he rejoined C. Company, 2nd Battalion and later transferred to D. Company, 2nd Battalion, Dublin Brigade. He fought in the War of Independence and was in the crowd at Croke Park on Bloody Sunday, November 21st 1921. During the Civil War he took the Republican side.

He was a keen hurler and was a founder member of the Young Irelands Hurling Club in 1923 and remained secretary of the club for twenty-six years.

Dan Canny, of 6 North Great Georges St, died on April 15th 1967 and was buried at Glasnevin Cemetery.

References:
RH; IMA, MSPC; NLI, *Lynch Papers*, (Ms 11,131); *Irish Press*, 16th April 1967, (obit).

Andrew Carmichael: (1897 – 1920)
Glasgow Company, (Kimmage Garrison). Roll of Honour

Andrew Carmichael was born in Glasgow, to Irish parents, in 1897. He was a carpenter by trade and joined the IRB and the Volunteers in Glasgow. He was involved in several raids to procure ammunition and weapons in that city and in 1915 he took part in a raid on a colliery in Hadingston, where a large quantity of explosives was taken. He came to Dublin, joining the Kimmage Garrison, and fought in the GPO throughout Easter Week. At the evacuation of the GPO, he attempted to carry the wounded Andy Furlong to Jervis Steet Hospital with help from Patrick Caldwell and Bernard Friel. They were unable to reach the hospital and made their way to the houses in Moore Steet. After the surrender he was deported to Knutsford Jail on May 1st and was interned in Frongoch, until Christmas 1916.

On his release he returned to Glasgow and worked as a ship's carpenter. He also became Captain of the Glasgow Company of Volunteers.

In 1920 Andrew Carmichael became ill and died. In compliance with his wishes, his remains were brought to Dublin and, in a remarkable tribute, Dublin dockers marched in military formation alongside members of the Volunteers to Glasnevin Cemetery where Andrew Carmichael was laid to rest on June 20th 1920.

References:
RH; *Evening Herald*, 30th June 1920, (obit).

Maria Winnifred (Winnie) Carney: (1887 – 1943)
Irish Citizen Army. Cumann na mBan. Roll of Honour

Winnie Carney was born in Bangor, County Down, on December 4th 1887 and later moved to the Falls Road, Belfast as a young child. She trained as a secretary and shorthand typist and during the 1913 Lockout she was involved in fundraising in Belfast for the Dublin workers. She was in charge of the women's section of the Irish Textile Workers' Union in Belfast, and became acquainted with James Connolly who was a trade union organiser in the city. She became Connolly's personal secretary at that time. On Easter Monday she was the only woman to enter the GPO carrying a gun. She accompanied James Connolly and the occupying force, armed with her typewriter and a Webley revolver, while the rest of the Cumann na mBan women arrived at the GPO at a later stage. Along with three other women, she refused to leave the burning GPO on Friday. After dictating James Connolly's final orders, she was the last woman among the final group to leave the GPO. After her arrest, she was detained in Kilmainham Jail and then deported to Aylesbury Prison, where she was interned with Nell Ryan and Helena Moloney.

She was released from internment on Christmas Eve 1916 and was later an unsuccessful Sinn Féin candidate for Belfast in the 1918 General Election. She opposed the Treaty and took the Republican side in the Civil War and was jailed in Armagh Prison. In 1924 she joined the Labour Party and continued her involvement in the trade union movement, working for the Irish Transport and General Workers' Union. She married George McBride in 1928. He was a fellow socialist and a Belfast Orangeman who fought in the Battle of the Somme in 1916.

Winnie Carney died in Belfast's Mater Hospital on November 21st 1943 and was buried at Milltown Cemetery, Belfast.

References:

RH; NLI, *William O'Brien Papers*, (Ms 15,673); Max Caulfield, *The Easter Rebellion*, (1963); Thomas Coffey, *Agony at Easter*, (1969); Ruth Taillon, *Women of 1916*, (1996); Donal Nevin, *James Connolly, a full life*, (2006); Clair Willis, *Dublin 1916, the siege of the GPO*, (2009); Ann Matthews, *The Irish Citizen Army*, (2014); Liz Gillis, *Women of the Irish Revolution*, (2015).

Peter Carpenter: (1897 – 1984)

Irish Citizen Army, (Gloucester St Section). Roll of Honour

Peter Carpenter was born to Ellen, an Irish mother and Walter, an English father of Wicklow decent, in 1897 and resided at 110 Foley Street. His father was a founder of the Irish Citizen Army, the Socialist Party of Ireland and a friend of James Connolly. Peter was employed as a plater in the Dublin Dockyard and was member of the Irish Citizen Army with his older brother, Wally. They both were part of the GPO Garrison in Easter Week. On Easter Monday he was one of a group of Irish Citizen Army men, under the command of Captain Thomas Craven, sent to the Fairview and Ballybough area. A headquarters was set up in the offices of the Vitriol Works at Annesley Bridge and he and several others then took up a position in O'Meara's Public House. They remained there until the whole unit in the area was recalled to the GPO on Tuesday evening. He then joined those fighting in the Metropole Hotel and remained there until the building was destroyed by constant shelling. He returned to the GPO and remained there until its evacuation on Friday evening. After the surrender he was deported to Knutsford Jail on May 1st and interned in Frongoch until Christmas 1916.

On his release from internment he joined H. Company, 1st Battalion, Dublin Brigade and was employed at the Midland and Great Southern Railway, Phibsborough. He fought in the War of Independence and took the anti-Treaty side during the Civil War. Towards the end of the Civil War his health broke down and he was admitted to Crooksling

Sanitorium suffering from T.B. After his release from Crooksling, he remained in poor health and was unable to work again.

Peter Carpenter died at his home at 44 Anner Road, Inchicore, on April 17th 1984.

References:
   RH; IMA, MSPC; NLI, *Lynch Papers*, (Ms 11,131) *& William O'Brien Papers*, (Ms 15, 673); *Irish Times*, 26th September 1983, *An Irishwoman's Diary*, (Eileen O'Brien, na); *Evening Herald*, 18th April 1984, (dn).

Walter (Wally) Carpenter: (1895 – 1970)

Irish Citizen Army, (Gloucester St Section). O/C I.C.A. (Boys Corps).
Roll of Honour

Wally Carpenter was born in 1895 and was the eldest son of an English socialist, also named Walter, who settled in Dublin in the 1890s. He resided at 8 Caledon Road, East Wall, when he joined the Irish Citizen Army with his brother, Peter, at its foundation. He was O/C of the Irish Citizen Army, Boys Corps that was attached to various units and acted as messengers and dispatch couriers. In 1916, at the age of twenty one, he resided at 110 Foley Street and he fought in the GPO during Easter Week with his brother, Peter. On Easter Monday he went from Liberty Hall to the GPO and was sent in a party, under the command of Frank Thornton, to assist the Irish Citizen Army men in the City Hall area. They came under sniper fire from the Crown Alley Telephone Exchange and they spent the night in a public house in Fleet Street, before making their way back to the GPO on Tuesday. He fell ill on Wednesday and was sent home from the GPO by James Connolly.

He took part in the War of Independence with the Irish Citizen Army. He was a co-founder of the Communist Party of Ireland with Roddy Connolly and Seán McLoughlin in 1921, and he fought on the Republican side in the Civil War. He was a member of the Four Courts Garrison in June 1922 and was arrested and interned in Mountjoy Jail, Gormanstown and Newbridge, until December 1923. During his internment he went on hunger strike for eleven days. During 'The Emergency' he was a sergeant in the 26th Infantry Battalion, which was made up mainly of Old IRA men. He was a former president of the Irish Trade Union Congress.

Wally Carpenter, of Linenhall Parade, died on May 18th 1970 and was buried at Deansgrange Cemetery.

References:
   RH; IMA, MSPC; NLI, *William O'Brien Papers*, (Ms 15,673); Seán O'Casey, *Drums under the Window, book 3*, (1972); Ann Matthews, *The Irish Citizen Army*, (2014); *Labour News*, 23rd October 1937, (na); *Evening Herald*, 19th May 1970, (dn).

Charles Carrigan: (1882 – 1916). Killed in Action

Glasgow Company, (Kimmage Garrison). Roll of Honour

Charles Carrigan was born in Glasgow to Irish parents in 1882, and was a tailor by trade. He was a member of Sinn Féin and became the Scottish representative of the Supreme Council of the IRB. Early in 1916 he came to Dublin with about fifty other Volunteers who formed the Volunteer Camp at the Plunkett's family farm at Larkfield, Kimmage. He fought in the GPO throughout Easter Week. At the evacuation of the building on Friday evening he was in the party led by The O'Rahilly into Moore Street. His body was later found beside the bodies of The O'Rahilly and two other Volunteers, by Seán McLoughlin.

Charles Carrigan was laid to rest at Glasnevin Cemetery on May 2nd 1916.

References:
RH; *Catholic Bulletin*, September 1916; Ray Bateson, *They Died by Pearse's Side*, (2010).

James (Jimmy) Carrigan: (1900 - 1975)

C. Coy, 1st Batt, Dublin Brigade. Roll of Honour

Jimmy Carrigan was born in 1900 and resided at North Clarence Street, North Strand. He joined Fianna Éireann in 1913 and he pushed one of the carts from Liberty Hall to Howth to offload a consignment of guns and ammunition from the Asgard on July 26th, 1914. He was employed in Pimms Department Store, South Great George's Street, at the time of the Rising. He transferred to C. Company, 1st Battalion, Dublin Brigade in early 1916. He missed the mobilisation call on Easter Monday morning and ended up with men from 2nd Battalion, operating in the Ballybough area. Later that evening he went to the GPO and was sent to the Hibernian Bank, under the command of Captain Thomas Weafer. The small group in the Hibernian Bank held their position after Weafer was killed, but were eventually forced to retreat to the GPO because of the fire and the constant bombardment. After the surrender, he spent the Saturday night with the rest of the Volunteers outside the Rotunda Hospital. He was detained in Richmond Barracks, but was considered too young to be deported and was released on May 12th.

He fought in the War of Independence and was involved in the raid on Monks Bakery, Church Street, when Kevin Barry was captured. He was also involved in the raid for arms in the King's Inns. He acted as a driver during the attack on suspected members of the Cairo Gang on Bloody Sunday, in November 1920. He became a member of the Active Service Unit and was involved in the burning of the Custom House in May 1921. He joined the Free State Army in February 1922 and served with the Transport Section of the Eastern Command, during the Civil War and the Marine Investigation Dept., until it was disbanded in December 1923.

During 'The Emergency' he served in the 26th Infantry Battalion with many of his old IRA comrades. He later resided at 3 Yellow Road, Whitehall, and was employed for many years as a driver in Dublin Corporation.

Jimmy Carrigan died on March 28th 1975 and was buried at Glasnevin Cemetery.

References:

RH; IMA, MSPC; IMA, BMH (WS 613); Donal O'Donovan, *Kevin Barry and his Times*, (1989); *Evening Herald*, 29th March 1975, (dn).

Patrick Carroll: (1898 - 1971)

Irish Citizen Army, (Boys Corps)

Patrick Carroll was born in 1898 and was a member of the Irish Citizen Army, Boys Corps. He served in the GPO during Easter Week, erecting barricades and delivering dispatches. When the order to evacuate the GPO was given, he was stationed at the ground floor windows. After the surrender he was released from Richmond Barracks on May 12th, because of his young age.

He served with the Irish Citizen Army from 1917 until the Truce, and then joined C. Company, 2nd Battalion, Dublin Brigade. He took the Republican side in the Civil War and when fighting broke out he was posted to 42 North Great George's Street. When this position came under fire from an armoured car, he and his party evacuated to Healy's Public House, Marlborough Street, and held out for a further week. He continued to serve while on the run for three weeks. He was in charge of an arms dump at 59 Capel Street and was arrested in April 1923. He was interned in Mountjoy Jail and Tintown Camp, the Curragh, from April to October 1923.

He was employed in W. D. & H. O. Wills and then in the Dept. of Social Welfare.

Patrick Carroll, of 116 Leix Road, Cabra, died on April 5th 1971 and was buried at Glasnevin Cemetery.

References:

IMA, MSPC; NLI, *Lynch Papers*, (Ms 11,131) *& William O'Brien Papers*, (Ms 15,673); John Heuston OP, *Headquarters Battalion, Easter Week* 1916, (1966); *Evening Herald*, 5th April 1971, (dn).

Peadar Carroll (O'Cearbhaill): (1893 – 1992)
Section Commander. C. Coy, 2nd Batt, Dublin Brigade. Roll of Honour

Peadar Carroll was born in 1893 and resided at 8 Lower Rutland Street. He joined C. Company, 2nd Battalion, Dublin Brigade, in 1914 and became Section Commander. On Easter Monday he reported to the GPO, and on the following day he was sent across to North Earl Street, where he was engaged in erecting a barricade. He served in the buildings between North Earl Street and the Imperial Hotel until Thursday, when the garrison was forced to evacuate because of the intensity of the fire engulfing the buildings. He retreated with a group into Cathedral Street and from there into North Cumberland Street. On Friday they were surrounded by British troops and were forced to surrender. He was deported to Knutsford Jail on May 3rd and interned in Frongoch until July 21st 1916.

He rejoined his unit and continued on active service until July 1918, when he resigned. He lived at 20 Lismore Road, Crumlin for many years, before emigrating to England.

Peadar Carroll, of Headley Court, Kingsnorton, Birmingham, died on September 5th 1992.

References:
RH; IMA, MSPC.

James Cassells: (1895 - 1934)
F. Coy, 2nd Batt, Dublin Brigade. Roll of Honour

James Cassells, the eldest son of William and Julia Cassells, was born in 1895 and resided at 42 Lower Mayor Street, North Wall. He was a clerk by profession and was a member of F. Company, 2nd Battalion, Dublin Brigade. He fought in the Fairview area on Easter Monday and Tuesday, under the command of Captain Frank Henderson. He arrived at the GPO on Tuesday night with the Fairview group and was in the party that was sent to occupy O'Neill's Public House, on the corner of Liffey Street. He returned to the GPO on Friday and left that evening at the general evacuation. After the Rising, he was deported to Knutsford Jail on May, 1st and interned in Frongoch until July 12th 1916.

On his release from internment he rejoined F. Company, 2nd Battalion and fought in the War of Independence. He took part in a number of operations, including several raids for arms and ammunitions on boats docked at North Wall. He was arrested and interned in Ballykinlar Camp between November 1920 and December 1921. He joined the Free State Army, as a Private, in 1922 and took part in the attack on the Four Courts. He served in the Pay Corps of the Army until he was discharged in 1924.

James Cassells held a position in the civil service for many years and passed away on August 4th 1934.

References:
RH; IMA, MSPC; *Irish Independent*, 2nd October 1934.

James P. Cassidy: (1878 - 1938)

B. Coy, 1st Batt, Dublin Brigade. Roll of Honour

James Cassidy, a native of Aughanagh, Letterbreen, County Fermanagh, was born in 1878. He joined the Volunteers while working in Cavan town in 1914. In 1916 he resided at 508 North Circular Road, and was a member of B. Company, 1st Battalion, Dublin Brigade. During Easter Week he fought in the GPO, manning the ground floor windows. After the evacuation he was in a group that took refuge in Samson's Lane, until the surrender was announced. He was deported to Stafford Jail on May 1st and was later interned in Frongoch until Christmas 1916.

On his release from Frongoch, he rejoined his old unit and fought in the War of Independence. He went to work in Arklow in 1917 and organised a local Volunteer Company. In June 1918 he was arrested and court-martialled at Dublin Castle. He was sentenced to twelve months imprisonment, and served the sentence in Mountjoy Jail, Belfast Jail and Strangeways Prison, Manchester. In December 1921 he moved to Cookstown, County Tyrone and was arrested in September 1922 and detained for three months. He later resided at 33 Pearse Street, Dublin and was the proprietor of a drapery concern in the city for many years.

James Cassidy died on May 5th 1938 and was buried at St Mary's Cemetery, Arney, Enniskillen, County Fermanagh.

References:
RH; IMA, MSPC; *Irish Independent*, 7th May 1938, (obit).

Maeve Cavanagh (Mrs. Maeve McDowell):
(1879- 1960)

Irish Citizen Army. Roll of Honour

Maeve Cavanagh, a milliner and trade unionist, was a prominent member of the Irish Citizen Army. She was also a poet and some of her poems were published in the *Worker's Republic*. James Connolly called her the "poetess of the Revolution". At 2.00 a.m. on Easter Monday morning she was given a dispatch by James Connolly to be delivered to Waterford, containing the message, "we fight at noon". On her return to Dublin, she was arrested and imprisoned.

Her brother, Ernest, who was a cartoonist for the Irish Worker and better known by his pseudonym, "E.K.", was shot dead on Easter Tuesday on the steps of Liberty Hall, as he tried to gain access to the building.

She was also a member of the Gaelic League and wrote two plays, performed by the Liberty Players in 1917. In 1921 she married Cathal McDowell, who fought in Boland's Mills in Easter Week, and they lived at 53 Larkfield Grove, Kimmage.

Maeve McDowell died on March 23rd 1960, and was buried in Glasnevin Cemetery.

References:

RH; NLI, *William O'Brien Papers*, (Ms 15,673); Ruth Taillon, *Women of 1916*, (1996); *Irish Independent* & *Irish Press*, 24th March 1960, (obits).

Liam Clarke: (1893 - 1941)
Lieutenant. 4th Batt, Dublin Brigade

Liam Clarke was born in 1893. He was a member of the IRB and a close friend of Con Colbert. He joined the Volunteers at its inception in 1913, and took part in the Kilcoole and Howth gun running in 1914. He was a member of the GPO Garrison, and on Easter Monday he was seriously wounded when a homemade bomb exploded in his face. He was attended to by Catherine Byrne and was later removed to the Richmond Hospital. While he was there, word was received of his possible execution and his escape was arranged. As a result of the accident he lost his left eye, received head injuries, a broken kneecap, and in the years that followed he underwent thirty six operations. He later worked with Kathleen Clarke in the National Aid and Dependents Relief Fund. He was a lieutenant in the 4th Battalion, Dublin Brigade during the War of Independence and commanded the firing party at the funeral of Thomas Ashe. Later he served on Cathal Brugha's staff and was imprisoned from May to December 1921. During this period he was allowed ten days parole to marry Dr Josephine Stallard, Danville House, Kilkenny, who was a member of Cumann na mBan. Her sister, Maisie, was married to Dr Ted O'Kelly, who was also a member of the GPO Garrison.

He fought on the Republican side in the Civil War and was temporarily in charge of the Dublin No. 2 Brigade. He fought in the areas between Blessington and Rathfarnham and, after spending some time in Kilkenny, he was arrested in Dublin and interned for twelve months.

Liam Clarke, of Dispensary House, Rathcoole, died on August 13th 1941 and was buried at Glasnevin Cemetery.

References:

RH; IMA, MSPC; NLI, *Lynch Papers*, (Ms 11,131); Max Caulfield, *The Easter Rebellion*, (1963); Thomas Coffey, *Agony at Easter*, (1969); *Irish Press*, 14th August 1941, (obit).

Thomas (Tom) Clarke: (1858 – 1916). Executed Leader
B. Coy, 1st Batt, Dublin Brigade. Roll of Honour

Tom Clarke was born on the Isle of Wight to Irish parents in March 1858. His father, a sergeant in the British Army, moved his family to South Africa for ten years before returning to Dungannon, his mother's birthplace. He was educated in Dungannon and when he was aged twenty one, he emigrated to the United States. He joined Clan na Gael, the American wing of the IRB, and in 1883 he was sent to England on a bombing mission. He was arrested and sentenced to penal servitude for life. He spent fifteen years in several British jails in extremely harsh conditions; conditions that caused other Irish prisoners to suffer physical and mental breakdowns. On his release from prison, he returned to Ireland and was made a freeman of Limerick City. In 1899 he returned to America and married Kathleen Daly from Limerick. She was daughter of the Fenian John Daly and sister of Ned Daly, who commanded the Four Courts Garrison in Easter Week and was later executed in Kilmainham Jail.

They returned to Ireland in 1907 and he opened a tobacconist's shop in Parnell Street, from where he worked in re-organising the IRB. In 1910 he published a militant, anti-British journal with Seán McDermott, entitled *Irish Freedom*. He persuaded John Devoy to return the body of Jeremiah O'Donovan-Rossa to Ireland from New York in 1915, and established a committee to organise the funeral. In the same year he became a member of the Military Council set up to plan a rising. He resided at 31 Richmond Ave, Fairview, in 1916 and was a member of St Laurence O'Toole's GAA Club and was also president of the St Laurence O'Toole's Pipe Band.

On Easter Monday he left Liberty Hall and walked to the GPO with Seán McDermott, before the main body of Volunteers departed. Both men were members of B. Company, 1st Battalion, Dublin Brigade. When he entered the GPO he ordered everyone present to leave with their hands raised and he then locked the doors and handed the Proclamation to P.H. Pearse. He was by Pearse's side as he read Proclamation outside the GPO at 12.45 p.m. Despite that fact that his arm was in a sling, the result of being accidently shot by Seán McGarry some months earlier, he was active throughout Easter Week in the GPO and was considered an inspiration by many of the Volunteers. His authority was readily accepted by the Volunteers, although he held no formal military rank and was dressed in civilian clothes. When the GPO was evacuated he spent Friday night in the Moore Street houses and when it was decided to surrender on Saturday afternoon, he opposed the decision. As Elizabeth Farrell stepped into Moore Street, carrying a white flag, he broke down sobbing. After the surrender, he was held overnight in the grounds of the Rotunda Hospital with the rest of the GPO Garrison. He and his brother-in-law, Ned Daly, were singled-out by Captain Lea-Wilson and abused and humiliated. They were strip-searched on the front steps of the hospital, apparently for the amusement of the nurses looking out the windows. This treatment was witnessed by Michael Collins, who reputedly had Captain Lea-Wilson assassinated four years later in Gorey, County Wexford.

His court-martial on May 2nd lasted about fifteen minutes and in the early hours of the next morning, Kathleen was taken from Dublin Castle, where she was a prisoner and allowed spend one hour with him in his cell.

Tom Clarke, the first signatory of the Proclamation, was the second person, after P.H. Pearse, to be executed on May 3rd 1916 and was buried in Arbour Hill, with the other executed leaders.

References:

RH; *DIB*, James Quinn, (James Quinn, Ed, 2009); Tom Clarke, *Glimpses of an Irish Felon's prison life*, (1922); Louis Le Roux, *Tom Clarke and the Irish freedom movement*, (1939); *Dublin's Fighting Story 1916 - 1921*, (1949); F.X. Martin, *Leaders and men of the Easter Rising*, (1967); Leon O'Broin, *Revolutionary Underground: the story of the Irish Republican Brotherhood 1858 – 1924*, (1976); Kathleen Clarke, *Revolutionary Woman, Kathleen Clarke 1878 – 1972: an autobiography*, (1991); Michael Foy & Brian Barton, *The Easter Rising*, (1999); Jimmy Wren, *Saint Laurence O'Toole G.A.C. Centenary History*, (2001); Ray Bateson, *They Died by Pearse's Side*, (2010); Gerard MacAtasney, *Tom Clarke: life, liberty, revolution*, (2013); Eileen McGough, *Diarmuid Lynch: a forgotten Irish patriot*, (2013); Helen Litton, *Ned Daly*, (16Lives series, 2013).

Patrick J. Clinch: (1887 – 1978)

Liverpool Company, (Kimmage Garrison). Roll of Honour

Patrick Clinch, a native of Killanny, County Louth, was born in 1887. He emigrated to England and was one of a group of Liverpool Volunteers who returned to Dublin in early 1916 to take part in the Rising. He and others from this group resided at 28 North Frederick Street, but were attached to the main group of Volunteers and IRB men who had set up camp at Larkfield, Kimmage. He fought in the GPO throughout Easter Week and on Friday he was in the group led by The O'Rahilly into Moore Street. When they came under fire, he took charge of seven Volunteers and took cover in a laneway off Cole's Lane. This group, some of whom were wounded, gained entry into stables and spent the night there before surrendering the following day. After the Rising, he was deported to Stafford Jail on May 1st and interned in Frongoch, until Christmas, 1916.

He organized and trained a Volunteer Company at Killanny, County Louth, in 1917 and was later transferred as a Staff Captain to the Meath Brigade in 1919. He opened a tobacconist shop in Navan and he was arrested and imprisoned in Mountjoy Jail in March 1920. While in Mountjoy he took part in a hunger-strike for sixteen days and on his release from prison, he spent fourteen days in the Mater Hospital. He was appointed chairman of the Republican Courts and was in charge of the Republican Police in County Meath. His shop in Navan was continuously raided by Crown Forces and he went on the run. He was also Sinn Féin Chairman of Meath County Council and, although he was opposed to the Treaty, he took no part in the Civil War.

He joined An Garda Síochána in 1923 and served as Garda Sergeant at Howth, County Dublin and at Tullaroan, County Kilkenny, before retiring in 1944.

Patrick Clinch, of 6 Bath Street, Ringsend, died on February 12th 1978.

References:

RH; IMA, MSPC; *Evening Herald*, 13th February 1978, (dn).

Seán Coade: (1898 - 1919)

Volunteer, (Unattached). Roll of Honour

Seán Coade was born in 1898 and resided at 2 Fitzgibbon Street, North Circular Road. Although he was not attached to the Volunteers, he offered his services at the GPO on Easter Monday and fought throughout Easter Week. After the Rising, he was detained at Richmond Barracks, but was released from there on May 12th because of his young age.

When the Volunteers were reorganized in 1917, he was proposed as a member of F. Company, 2nd Battalion by Liam McGinley, who lived in the same house as him and who also fought in the GPO in Easter Week. He served with F. Company until July 1919 when he caught a feverish chill while at the Volunteer Camp at Kilbarrack, County Dublin.

Seán Coade died on July 20th 1919 and was buried two days later at Glasnevin Cemetery.

References:
RH; IMA, MSPC; *Evening Herald*, 21st July 1919, (dn).

Seán Cole: (1902 - 1922)

Fianna Éireann. Roll of Honour

Seán Cole was born in 1902 and resided at 22 Buckingham Street, in the north inner-city. He was a member of Fianna Éireann and served in the GPO during Easter Week.

He took the Republican side during the Civil War. Along with fellow Fianna Éireann Officer, Alf Colley, he attended a Fianna parade at Charlemount House, Marino, at 3 o'clock on August 26th 1922 and on their return to the city, they were arrested at Newcomen Bridge. They were taken at first to Puckstown Lane (now Collins Avenue, West) and later, on reaching Yellow Lane (now Yellow Road), Whitehall, they were forced from the car. After a desperate struggle the two young men were riddled with bullets. According to the Roll of Honour for deceased members of the GPO he was 19 years old at the time of his murder, suggesting he was no more than fourteen in Easter Week. He was employed as an electrician with Dockrell's, South Great Georges St, where his father, James, worked as a clerk.

Seán Cole was buried at Glasnevin Cemetery on August 30th 1922.

References:
RH; *Freeman's Journal*, 28th August 1922, (dn) & 30th August 1922, (obit).

Patrick J. (Pat) Colgan: (1890 – 1960)

Maynooth Company, Kildare Brigade. Roll Of Honour

Pat Colgan, a native of Maynooth, was born in 1890. He was one of fifteen Volunteers from the Maynooth Company, Kildare Brigade, led by Tom Byrne and Domhnall Ua Buachalla that made their way to the GPO on Easter Monday evening. Earlier that day he was informed by a priest from Maynooth College that the Rising had begun and in Domhnall Ua Buachalla's absence, he sent word to local Volunteers to mobilize at the back of Ua Buachalla's shop. He acted as a scout on the journey along the Royal Canal towpath and, after spending the night in Glasnevin Cemetery, they arrived into the GPO on Tuesday morning to a rousing reception. He was then sent to relieve the Irish Citizen Army men who were surrounded in the Evening Mail Offices. Later he occupied the Royal Exchange Hotel in Parliament Street, before returning to the GPO. On Friday he was involved in the moving of the wounded to Jervis Street Hospital from the Coliseum Theatre in Henry Street. He was later captured in the vicinity of Liffey Street and Abbey Street with fellow Maynooth Volunteers, Tom Mangan and the Maguire brothers, Jack and Matt. Interned in Frongoch until Christmas, 1916, he was appointed Commandant of the North Kildare Battalion in 1917. He was a close friend of Michael Collins during the War of Independence. After an attack on Crown Forces at Kill, County Kildare, he was arrested in December 1920 and interned in the Curragh and later in Ballykinlar Camp. He was Commandant at Ballykinlar Camp until his release in January 1922. After the Treaty, he joined the Irish Free State Army and retired with the rank of major in 1946.

He acquired an interest in the Muckross Park Hotel in Killarney, which he managed until his death. He had a lifelong interest in the GAA and was secretary of the Kildare County Board for a period.

Pat Colgan died on September 15th 1960 and was buried at the Grange William Cemetery, Maynooth.

References:

RH; IMA, MSPC; IMA, BMH (WS 850); *An t-Óglach*, March 1926, (*Charles Saurin*); James Durney, *On the One Road: political unrest in Kildare 1913 – 1994*, (2001); *Sunday Press*, 24th April 1960, *13 Men March to Glory*, (M.L. O'Halloran, na); *Irish Independent* & *Irish Press*, 16th September 1960, (obits).

Gertrude (Gertie) Colley (Mrs. Gertrude Murphy): (1893 - 1983)

Cumann na mBan, (Fairview Branch). Roll of Honour

Gertie Colley was born in 1893 and resided at 69 Clonliffe Road. In 1915 she joined the Cumann na mBan, Fairview Branch. She reported to the GPO on Easter Monday and served there for the remainder of the week. Her brother, Harry, was also in the GPO, and was seriously wounded during the week. She later recalled the scene when Fr. Flanagan from the Pro-Cathedral gave general absolution to the Garrison on Thursday. When P.H. Pearse realised that they couldn't hold out much longer, he asked the women there to leave, and she led the first group of women that escorted the wounded to Jervis Street Hospital. This group was then taken under military escort to Broadstone Station, where they were interrogated and later released.

She helped in the reorganisation period in early 1917, and carried out anti-conscription work. She collected and distributed money for the Prisoners Dependents Fund and her house was used as a clearing station by GHQ. She took the anti-Treaty side in the Civil War and took part in the occupation of Barry's Hotel. In 1922 she was given custody of Republican funds, for which she opened a bank account in her own name.

She later married John Murphy and resided at 129 Ferguson Road, Drumcondra. Gertie Murphy died on April 21st 1983 and was buried at Glasnevin Cemetery.

References:
RH; IMA, MSPC; *Irish Press*, 23rd April 1983, (dn).

Harry Colley: (1891 – 1972)

F. Coy, 2nd Batt, Dublin Brigade. Roll of Honour

Harry Colley was born in 1891 and was a member of F. Company, 2nd Battalion, Dublin Brigade. He resided at 69 Clonliffe Road and on Easter Monday, he mobilized at their headquarters at Father Matthew Park, Fairview. He fought in the Ballybough and Fairview area and on Tuesday evening he marched with a body of Volunteers into the GPO. He was one of the defenders of the Imperial Hotel, across the street from the GPO, until they were forced to retreat from the burning building. This party then made their way to Gloucester Street (now Seán McDermott Street),

where Harry Colley was severely wounded charging a British army barricade. He received five bullet wounds, one of which entered his lung. He was detained and brought to the emergency hospital in Dublin Castle and, when he recovered, he was shipped to Frongoch.

On his release from Frongoch, he became Adjutant of the Dublin Brigade, under Oscar Traynor. He was involved in operation on Bloody Sunday in November 1920 and took part in the raid on the Custom House in 1921. He took the Republican side during the Civil War, but ill health prevented him from taking part in the fighting. He was, however, involved in organising the attack on bridges in Dublin and was arrested and interned in Gormanstown Camp until 1924.

He was employed as a rate-collector for Dublin Corporation and he resided at Malahide Road, Clontarf.

He was a founder member of Fianna Fáil, and was elected TD for Dublin North East from 1944 to 1957. He subsequently sat in the Seanad from 1957 to 1961. His son, George, was elected a Fianna Fáil TD in 1961 and held a number of Government portfolios. In 1979 he lost the Fianna Fail leadership contest to Charles Haughey.

Harry Colley died on the January 18th 1972 and was buried in Glasnevin Cemetery.

References:
RH; IMA, MSPC; IMA, BMH (WS 1687); *DIB*, Pauric Dempsey, (James Quinn, Ed, 2009); *Magill Book of Irish Politics*, Vincent Browne, Ed, (1981); *An Phoblacht*, 7th June 1930, (na); *Evening Herald*, 17th April 1936, (na); *Evening Herald* & *Irish Press*, 19th January 1972, (obits).

Michael Collins: (1890 – 1922)
London Company, (Captain. Kimmage Garrison). Roll of Honour

Michael Collins was born at Woodford, Clonakilty, County Cork, on October 16th 1890. Educated locally, he went to London at the age of 16 to work as a clerk in the Post Office and later for a stockbroker. He became a member of the Geraldines GAA Club in London and then joined the IRB there. In 1909 Collins was treasurer of the IRB in London and in the South of England and, at the same time, treasurer of the London Board of the GAA. He returned to Ireland in January 1916 and became Captain of the Kimmage Garrison. He was also Aide de Camp to Joseph Plunkett and fought in the GPO throughout Easter Week. After the Rising he was deported and interned in Frongoch. On his return to Ireland from internment, he took a leading roll in re-organising the Volunteers and Sinn Féin.

In 1919 he became Minister of Home Affairs and subsequently Minister for Finance in the First Dáil. During the War of Independence, he was Director of Intelligence of the IRA and, through his agents in Dublin Castle; he had access to the British intelligence systems. He organized the special IRA unit known as "The Squad" that was responsible for the shooting dead of 13 British Intelligence Agents in Dublin on the November 20th 1920. In retaliation, the Crown forces attacked the crowd attending a football match at Croke Park between Dublin and Tipperary, resulting in the deaths of Michael Hogan, the Tipperary captain, 13 spectators and the wounding of many others. He was a member of the delegation that negotiated the Anglo-Irish Treaty and was appointed Chairman and Minister for Finance in the Provisional Government. With the outbreak of the Civil War, he was appointed Commander in Chief of the Irish Free State Army.

Michael Collins was shot dead during an engagement with Republican forces at Béal na Bláth, near Bandon on the 22 August 1922 and, after a state funeral, his body was removed from the Pro-Cathedral, Marlborough Street, to Glasnevin Cemetery.

References:

RH; Piaras Béaslaí, *Michael Collins and the Making of a New Ireland*, (1926); Rex Taylor, *Michael Collins, the Big Fellow*, (1958); Frank O'Connor, *The Big Fellow: Michael Collins and the Irish* Revolution, (1965); Eoin Neesan, *The Life and Death of Michael Collins*, (1968); Desmond Ryan, *The Invisible Army: a story of Michael Collins*, (1968); Margery Forester, *Michael Collins, the Lost Leader*, (1972); Leon O'Broin, *Michael Collins*, (1980); Meda Ryan, *The Day Michael Collins was* Shot, (1989); Tim Pat Coogan, *Michael Collins: a biography*, (1990); Vincent MacDowell, *Michael Collins and the Brotherhood*, (1997).

Patrick Connaughton: (1889 – 1946)
B. Coy, 1st Batt, Dublin Brigade. Roll of Honour

Patrick Connaughton, a stonemason of Market Square, Longford, was born in 1899. In February 1916 he returned to Ireland from Glasgow where he had been working, and resided at 23 Nicholas Street. He joined B. Company, 1st Battalion, Dublin Brigade and reported to the GPO on Easter Monday. He was sent to an outpost on the corner of Liffey Street and Abbey Street on Monday night, and from Tuesday to Friday he guarded prisoners in the Instrument Room in the GPO. After the evacuation he spent Friday night occupying a cottage in Henry Place, until the surrender the following afternoon. He was deported to Stafford Jail on May 1st and interned in Frongoch, until November 1916.

He rejoined his unit and served in 1917 and 1918 and took no further part in the War of Independence after that.

He was later employed in the Dublin Corporation.

Patrick Connaughton died at his residence at 19 Merton Avenue, off the South Circular Road, Dublin on April 2nd 1946 and was buried at Mount Jerome Cemetery, Harold's Cross.

References:

RH; IMA, MSPC; NLI, *Lynch Papers,* (Ms 11,131); *Irish Independent* & *Irish Press*, 3rd April 1946, (dn).

Brigid Connolly: (1890 – 1981)

Cumann na mBan, (Árd Croabh Branch). Roll of Honour

Bridie Connolly was born in County Carlow, in 1890. She resided at Kilmore Cottage, Artane and was a school teacher by profession, when she joined the Árd Croabh Branch of Cumann na mBan in 1915. Prior to the Rising she stored rifles in her home. She reported to the GPO on Easter Monday and was engaged in first aid duties and also carried dispatches. Between Easter Monday and Thursday she carried dispatches from the GPO to the Four Courts on numerous occasions. Before the evacuation on Friday evening she was one of the group that was ordered to leave the GPO by P.H. Pearse, under the protection of a Red Cross flag. They were arrested by British troops and taken to Broadstone Station for interrogation, before being released.

After the Rising she was engaged in anti-conscription work and organized Cumann na mBan branches in north county Dublin. She became a member of the executive of Cumann na mBan and was clerk to the Raheny & District Sinn Féin Court. Her brother, Patrick, was a Sinn Féin Court judge. She fought on the anti-Treaty side during the Civil War and she was sent to England by Austin Stack, to send and receive telegrams to people in the United States. She served with the Barry's Hotel Garrison in 1922 and was involved in the purchase of arms in the Curragh. She was arrested in March 1923 and went on hunger strike twice while in Kilmainham Jail, before her release in November 1923

In later years she taught in Clonsaugh National School.

Bridie Connolly resided at 113 Swords Road, Whitehall and died on November 11th 1981 and was buried at Grange, Tullow, County Carlow.

References:
RH; IMA, MSPC; NLI, *Lynch Papers*, (Ms 11,131); *Irish Press*, 16th November 1981, (dn).

James Connolly: (1868 – 1916). Executed Leader

Commandant General, Dublin Division. Roll of Honour

James Connolly, socialist, trade unionist and Commandant General of the Irish Citizen Army, was born to Irish parents in the Cowgate area of Edinburgh, on June 5th 1868. Falsifying his age, he enlisted in the British Army at 14 and was stationed at the Curragh and in Dublin. He deserted the British Army and married Wicklow woman Lillie Reynolds in Edinburgh, where he worked as a carter. He became involved in socialist and trade union activities in Edinburgh and returned to Dublin as a paid organizer of the Dublin Socialist Club in 1896. With his support and approval this organization later became the Irish Socialist Republican Party. He made lecture tours of England and America in 1901 and 1902, before settling in the United States for seven years.

In 1909 returned to Ireland and became the full-time organizer of the ITGWU in Belfast, until the Lockout in Dublin in 1913. When James Larkin, the union leader in Dublin, was imprisoned, James Connolly took over as leader. He formed the Irish Citizen Army with Jack White in Liberty Hall, the headquarters of the ITGWU, to defend workers and strikers against the violence of the Dublin Metropolitan Police Force.

When the Military Council of the IRB decided on armed rebellion in 1916, the Irish Citizen Army joined with the Volunteers, and James Connolly was appointed Military Commander in Dublin. As Commandant General of the Dublin Division, he led by example.

On Thursday morning he was shot in the arm by one of a party of sharpshooters. Major Jack Morrogh of the Royal Irish Regiment stated that a sniper under his command, positioned on a rooftop in the vicinity, fired the shot. Connolly was hit while supervising the construction of a barricade in Abbey Street. Major Morrogh was credited later in the week with confiscating the green flag with the words "Irish Republic" on it from the roof of the GPO. Not long after the wound to his arm was dressed, Connolly's ankle was shattered by shrapnel as he observed Seán McLoughlin lead a party of Volunteers into the offices of the *Irish Independent* in Abbey Street. He spent the remaining time in the GPO in agony, directing operations from a stretcher. During the evacuation of the GPO on Friday evening, he was carried on a stretcher into the houses in Moore Street. After the surrender, he was taken to the emergency hospital at Dublin Castle. A few hours before his execution he was visited by his wife Lillie, one of his daughters Nora, and by Father Aloysius from the Capuchin Friary in Church St. He was then taken to Kilmainham Jail on May 12th where, due to his wounds, he was strapped to a chair and executed by firing squad.

James Connolly was buried in Arbour Hill Military Cemetery with the other executed leaders.

References:

RH; NLI, *William O'Brien Papers*, (Ms 15,673); *DIB*, Fergus D'Arcy, (James Quinn, Ed, 2009); Desmond Ryan, *James Connolly: his Life, Work & Writings*, (1924); R.M. Fox, *James Connolly: the Forerunner*, (1946); James Connolly, *Socialism & Nationalism*, (Three Candles Press, Desmond Ryan, Ed, 1948); James Connolly, *Labour & Easter Week*, (Three Candles Press, Desmond Ryan, Ed, 1949); James Connolly, *The Workers' Republic*, (Three Candles Press, Desmond Ryan, Ed,1951); ITGWU, *Fifty Years of Liberty Hall*, (1959); Desmond Greaves, *The Life and Times of James Connolly*, (1961); Ina Heron Connolly, *James Connolly: a biography*, (Liberty Magazine, 1966); Nora Connolly-O'Brien, *Portrait of a Rebel Father*, (1975); Seán Cronin, *The Young James Connolly*, (1978); WJ Whitmore-Brennan, *Dublin Burning*, (1996); Donal Nevin, *James Connolly, a Full Life*, (2006); Lorcan Collins, *James Connolly*, (16Lives series, 2012).

Roderick (Roddy) Connolly: (1901 – 1980)

Irish Citizen Army, (S.C.R. Section)

Roddy Connolly was born in 1901. He accompanied his father, Commandant General James Connolly, on the march from Liberty Hall to the GPO on Easter Monday, 1916. He was a member of the Irish Citizen Army and was assigned to scouting duties and was personal messenger to his father. On Wednesday, he was sent by his father to the house of William O'Brien in Belvedere Place. He was later arrested with O'Brien and taken to Richmond Barracks. Before the Rising, his father warned him never to reveal his identity if arrested, in case he might fall victim of a reprisal shooting. For this reason, Roddy gave a false name to  the authorities and of those in the holding cell in Richmond Barracks only Seán MacDiarmada recognised him. However, he waited until after his release to reveal Roddy's identity. He was said to have remarked that "Connolly has that boy well trained". James Connolly said to his wife, Lillie and daughter, Nora in their final meeting before his execution that "he (Roddy) was in the fight and has been imprisoned for his country and he's not yet sixteen. He has had a great start in life, hasn't he?"

After a short stay, Roddy Connolly was released from Richmond Barracks in view of his young age.

He joined the Socialist Party of Ireland in 1917 and was later a founding member, with Seán McLoughlin, Paddy Stephenson and George Pollock, of the Communist Party of Ireland. He went to Russia in 1920 and 1921 to affiliate the new party to the Communist International and while there he met Lenin and was heavily influenced by him. Although he became a member of the Labour Party in 1928, it was only after his involvement with the Bray Trade Council in 1931 that he began to take an active role in the party. As a Labour candidate he was elected TD for Louth, 1943-44 and 1948-51. He sat in the Seanad, from 1975 to 1977 and was chairman of the Labour Party from 1971 to 1978. He had a lifelong passion for chess and in later years he recorded that his first introduction to the game was made in the holding cell in Richmond Barracks, where

Seán MacDiarmada taught him the basics of the game by scratching a board on the floor and using fruit peel as chess pieces.

Roddy Connolly died in St Michael's Hospital, Dun Laoghaire on the December 16th 1980 and was buried at Glasnevin Cemetery.

References:

IMA, MSPC; NLI, *William O'Brien Papers*, (Ms 15,673); *DIB*, Lawrence White, (James Quinn, Ed, 2009); RM Fox, *History of the Irish Citizen Army*, (1943); Max Caulfield, *The Easter Rebellion*, (1963); Nora Connolly-O'Brien, *Portrait of a Rebel Father*, (1975); Uinseann MacEoin, *Survivors*, (1980); *Magill Book of Irish Politics*, Vincent Browne & Mike Farrell, Ed, (1981); Charlie McGuire, *Roddy Connolly and the Struggle for Socialism in Ireland*, (2008); Charlie McGuire, *Seán McLoughlin: Ireland's Forgotten Revolutionary*, (2011); Ann Matthews, *The Irish Citizen Army*, (2014); Diarmuid Ferriter, *A Nation and not a Rabble: the Irish Revolution, 1913-23*, (2015).

Aghna (Ina) Connolly-Heron: (1896 – 1980)

Irish Citizen Army

Ina Connolly was born in Dublin in 1896 and was the daughter of the executed leader, James Connolly. On Easter Monday she was sent with her sister, Nora, by their father with a message for Volunteers in the north to take up arms. They had difficulty in returning to Dublin and had to walk from Dundalk, arriving back after the surrender.

She lived in London, from 1918 to 1920 and was active with the Irish Determination League. She took the anti-Treaty side in the Civil War and, with Nora, set up a first aid centre in the Tara Hall in Seán McDermott Street after they raided a chemist shop for supplies.

She was married to Archie Heron, a Protestant radical, member of the IRB, and trade union organiser from Portadown, who had unsuccessfully tried to reach Dublin for the Rising in 1916.

Ina Connolly-Heron died at Ratoath Manor, Ratoath, County Meath on April 9th 1980 and was buried at Glasnevin Cemetery.

References:

IMA, MSPC; NLI, *William O'Brien Papers*, (Ms 15,673); Uinseann MacEoin, *Survivors*, (1980); Donal Nevin, *James Connolly, a Full Life*, (2006); *Irish Press*, 11th April 1980, (obit).

Nora Connolly-O'Brien: (1893 – 1981)
Irish Citizen Army

Nora Connolly, the daughter of the executed leader, James Connolly, was born in Edinburgh in 1893. The family moved to Dublin when she was three years old and six years later they moved to New York, where her father became full-time propagandist for the Labour and Nationalist movements. When the family returned to Ireland in 1910, James Connolly became organiser the ITGWU in Belfast and she became active in Fianna Éireann and Cumann na mBan in that city. In 1914 she and her sister, Ina, were involved in the Howth gun running and they returned to Belfast with two rifles. She was then sent to the United States with dispatches and later she was sent to locate Liam Mellows in Stoke and bring him back for the Rising. On Easter Monday she and Ina were sent north by their father with a message to the Volunteers there to take up arms. On their attempted return to Dublin, the train only went as far as Dundalk and they decided to walk the remainder of the journey, sleeping in a field in Balbriggan on the way. When they reached the city, they went to the Ryan's family in Clonliffe Road, where they learned that the Rising was over and that their father lay seriously wounded in emergency hospital set up in Dublin Castle. They proceeded to Countess Markievicz's cottage at Three Rock, where their mother and younger siblings were.

With her mother, Lillie, she visited her father in Dublin Castle shortly before he was taken to Kilmainham Jail and executed.

After the Rising she returned to the United States, working as a Republican propagandist. She came back to Ireland and married Seamus O'Brien in 1922. They were active on the anti-Treaty side and were both imprisoned during the Civil War.

She served as a member of the Seanad Éireann for fifteen years as the Taoiseach's nominee of both Éamon deValera and Seán Lemass.

Nora Connolly-O'Brien, of 40 Galtymore Park, Drimnagh, died on June 17th 1981 and was buried in Glasnevin Cemetery.

References:

IMA, MSPC; NLI, *William O'Brien*, (Ms 15,673); *DIB*, Lawrence White, (James Quinn, Ed, 2009); Nora Connolly-O'Brien, *Portrait of a Rebel Father*, (1975); Uinseann MacEoin, *Survivors*, (1980); Michael Foy & Brian Barton, *The Easter Rising*, (1999); Donal Nevin, *James Connolly, a Full Life*, (2006); *Irish Times*, 10th April 1978, *An Irishwoman's Diary*, (na).

Andrew (Andy) Conroy: (1892 - 1972)

Sergeant. Irish Citizen Army, (Inchicore / Crumlin Section). Roll of Honour

Andy Conroy was born in 1892, and resided at Inchicore Road in 1916. He was a sergeant in the Inchicore / Crumlin section of the Irish Citizen Army and fought in the GPO during Easter Week. On Easter Tuesday, when the outpost at Hopkins & Hopkins Jewellery Store on the corner of Eden Quay was under intense sniper fire from the roof of Trinity College, James Connolly sent him to engage the snipers. He was a top marksman and he managed to reduce the concentration of the enemy fire. The following day he moved across the street to Kelly's Gun Shop, and silenced a sniper who was positioned in McBirney's Store and who had fatally shot some civilians on the opposite side of the river. When the outpost at Hopkins & Hopkins was evacuated on Wednesday, James Connolly put him in charge of thirteen men with orders to re-occupy the building. The position was held until Friday, and as the group retreated across O'Connell Street, Conroy was shot in the abdomen. He was treated by medical student, Jim Ryan, and later carried with other wounded Volunteers from the Coliseum Theatre to Jervis Street Hospital, where he was hospitalised until June 1916.

He then helped to re-organise the Irish Citizen Army, and in 1918 he was promoted to lieutenant. He was also a full-time official in the ITGWU and during the War of Independence he was engaged in intelligence work with Joseph McGrath of the IRA.

Andy Conroy, of Pearse Square, Pearse Street, died on January 14th 1972 and was buried at Mount Jerome Cemetery, Harold's Cross.

References:

RH; IMA, MSPC; NLI, *William O'Brien Papers*, (Ms 15,673); Thomas Coffey, *Agony at Easter*, (1969);*Irish Press*, 10th April 1934, *(letter from Andy Conroy)*; *Evening Herald*, 15th January 1972, (dn).

Herbert Conroy: (1896 – 1926)

E. Coy, 2nd Batt, Dublin Brigade

Herbert Conroy was born in 1896 and resided at 3 Marino Avenue, Malahide Road. He was educated at St Joseph's CBS, Fairview, and was employed in Dublin Distillers, Jones's Road in 1916. He was a member of E. Company, 2nd Battalion, Dublin Brigade, and on Easter Monday he collected a consignment of arms hidden at Kilmore, Artane, and joined a party, under the command of Captain Thomas Weafer, that was marching to the GPO. He fought in the Hibernian Bank and later withdrew to the GPO. After the Rising he was deported and interned in Frongoch, until July 7th 1916.

On his release, he took an active part in the War of Independence and was involved in the attack on the Raheny RIC Barracks. He took part in the attack on British spies in Mount Street on Bloody Sunday, November 1920. He also took part in the attacks on the London and North Western Railway Hotel, North Wall, in April 1921; and on the Custom House the following month. He joined the Irish Free State Army in February 1922 and during the Civil War he took part in the fighting in the south of the country. He later became a detective sergeant in An Garda Síochána.

Herbert Conroy died on the March 3rd 1926 and was buried at Glasnevin Cemetery.

References:
Scoil Iósaif, Marino, 1916-1966: (a 1916 Jubilee Publication), (1966); *Irish Independent*, 6th March 1926, (obit).

James P. Conroy: (- 1981)
F. Coy, 2nd Batt, Dublin Brigade

James Conroy resided at 14 Richmond Parade, North Circular Road, and was a painter and decorator by trade. He joined the Volunteers in 1914 and took part in the Howth gun running. On Easter Monday he fought under the command of Captain Leo Henderson, at Annesley Bridge and in the East Wall Road area. At 8 o'clock on Tuesday evening he moved into the GPO with his unit under orders from James Connolly. He was then sent with a party to support the occupants in the Imperial Hotel. On Wednesday night he and David Bourke evaded capture and made their way to the north inner city. They reached Conroy's  home near Summerhill on Saturday and on the following morning the house was surrounded by troops. They were arrested and he was imprisoned in Arbour Hill Military Prison for two months. He rejoined his old unit on his release and fought in the War of Independence. He became his company's quartermaster, before transferring to ASU (the Squad) in 1920. He took part in all the Squad's major operations, until he was arrested at the Custom House attack in May 1921. After his release, he joined the Free State Army at its foundation and served as a Commandant in Cork, Kerry and Limerick. He resigned from the army and emigrated to the United States. At the time he was wanted for questioning by the police in connection with the murder of Ernest Kahn at Stamer Street, South Circular Road, in November 1923. When he returned to Ireland, there was not enough evidence available to the police to connect him to the murder. He went back to the United States, residing in New York, and was a member of the 1916 Club, New York.

James Conroy moved to California in 1966 and died in Stanton, Orange County, on July 2nd 1981.

References:
IMA, MSPC.

Seán S. (John) Conway: (1897-1959)
F. Coy, 1st Batt, Dublin Brigade. Roll of Honour

John Conway was born in 1897 and lived at 8 Moore's Cottages, Rutland Street. He joined Fianna Éireann in 1908 and transferred to F. Company, 1st Battalion, Dublin Brigade, prior to the Howth gun running. On Easter Monday he was manning a barricade in Church Street, when Captain John O'Connor sent him to mobilise other Volunteers. He then went to Ballybough and took up duty at the Vitriol Works, under the command of Captain Vincent Poole of the Irish Citizen Army. He moved into the GPO on Tuesday evening, and on Wednesday he was stationed at a window at the Henry Street side. He was posted to O'Neill's Public House in Liffey Street on Thursday, under the command of Captain Tom Byrne. When he returned to the GPO, he again manned a position at the windows, until the evacuation. He was part of the group led by The O'Rahilly into Moore Street, and he and Albert Dyas carried the wounded John Kenny to safety, despite being under heavy gunfire. He took refuge with others in a stable in Samson's Lane, where he attended to several wounded Volunteers. He was deported to Knutsford Jail on May 1st 1916, but was released after several weeks.

He rejoined his unit at its re-organisation and served until September 1919, when he emigrated to Scotland.

John Conway died at his residence at 75 Ashby Crescent, Knightswood, Glasgow, on November 6th 1959 and was buried in Glasgow.

References:
RH; IMA, MSPC; IMA, BMH (WS 1912, *Jack Kenny*); NLI, *Lynch Papers*, (Ms 11,131); *Irish Independent*, 7th November 1959, (dn).

John Dutton Cooper: (1870 – 1943)
Irish Citizen Army, (South Circular Rd Section)

John Cooper was born in 1870 and resided at 33 Lennox Street, South Circular Road. He was employed as a general labourer and he joined the Irish Citizen Army in 1915. He was not mobilised on Easter Monday 1916, but reported to the GPO on Tuesday and was involved in erecting barricades. Later he was attached to the first aid section and he also attended to the wounded in the Dublin Bread Company Building. He was in the group that carried James Connolly to the GPO when he was wounded at Abbey Street on Thursday. On Friday he escorted the Cumann na mBan women and the wounded to Jervis Street Hospital. He was arrested the following day and was deported to Wakefield Jail on May 6th. After his release from Frongoch on August 2nd, he ceased his involvement with the Irish Citizen Army.

John Cooper, of 57 Lower Mount Street, died on July 1st 1943.

References:
IMA, MSPC; NLI, *William O'Brien Papers*, (Ms 15,673).

Laurence (Larry) Corbally: (1900 – 1964)

Irish Citizen Army, (Boys Corps). Roll of Honour

Larry Corbally was born in 1900 and resided at 7 Moore's Row, Lower Gardiner Street. He was fifteen years old when he accompanied his father, Dick, to the GPO with the Irish Citizen Army contingent, at noon on Easter Monday. He spent Monday helping to make ammunition and he was sent on dispatch duty on Tuesday and Wednesday. On Thursday he was sent on dispatch duty with another ICA boy, Louis Byrne, but because of the encroaching British Troops, their route back to the GPO was blocked.

After the Rising, he continued to serve with the Irish Citizen Army and fought in the War of Independence. He took part in a number of operations, including raids for arms and the attack on the Custom House in 1921.

He was employed for many years with the Board of Works and resided at 10 North Gloucester Place, Seán McDermott Street.

Larry Corbally died on June 2nd 1964 and was buried in Glasnevin Cemetery.

References:

RH; IMA, MSPC; NLI, *William O'Brien Papers*, (Ms 15,673); John Heuston OP, *Headquarters Battalion, Easter Week 1916*, (1966).

Richard (Dick) Corbally: (1879 – 1955)

Irish Citizen Army, (North Wall Section). Roll of Honour

Dick Corbally was born in County Dublin in 1879 and resided at 7 Moore's Row, Lower Gardiner Street. He was employed as a coal porter and was a friend of James Connolly and Jim Larkin. He played a prominent part in the Howth gun running in 1914. On Easter Monday, he brought his fifteen year old son, Larry, with him to the GPO. He fought throughout the week in the GPO and after the surrender he was deported to Stafford Jail on May 1st. He was then transferred to Wandsworth Jail and interned in Frongoch, until July 14th 1916.

On his release, he was instrumental in the reforming of the Irish Citizen Army, and took part in the War of Independence. In 1920 he was involved in a raid on Richmond Barracks, Inchicore, when he drove a consignment of arms away in his lorry. These weapons were later dispersed around the country to various flying columns. He was arrested in 1921 and interned in Arbour Hill Military Prison.

For many years he was head foreman on cattle boats that sailed from Dublin Port.

Dick Corbally died in his home at 9 Poplar Row, Ballybough, on November 17th 1955 and was buried at Glasnevin Cemetery.

References:

RH; IMA, MSPC; NLI, *William O'Brien Papers*, (Ms 15,673); *Irish Press*, 18th November 1955, (obit).

Thomas Corbally: (1892 - 1959)

E. Coy, 4th Batt, Dublin Brigade. Roll of Honour

Thomas Corbally was born in 1892 and resided at 38 St Patrick's Cottages, Rathfarnham. He was employed as a labourer and was a member of the Michael Dwyer's GAA Club. He was one of the original members of the local E. Company, 4th Battalion, Dublin Brigade and was one of thirty members of the Rathfarnham unit who joined the GPO Garrison on Easter Week. As he climbed through a window into the GPO on Easter Monday, he was cut by broken glass. Catherine Byrne attended to his wound. He was stationed on the roof for most of the week, with the majority of the Rathfarnham Volunteers. After the surrender he was deported to Stafford Jail on May 1st and interned in Frongoch, until Christmas, 1916.

He re-joined his old unit in 1917, but because of ill health he ceased to be active from 1918 to 1921. He took the Republican side in the Civil War and brought food supplies to units in the Dublin Mountains and acted as a scout and guide.

Thomas Corbally was employed for many years in the Board of Works and passed away on the 11th February, 1959.

References:
RH; IMA, MSPC; *Irish Press*, 12th February 1959, (obit).

Patrick J. Corless: (1894 – 1963)

Lieutenant. B. Coy, 1st Batt, Dublin Brigade

Patrick Corless was born in Athlone, in 1894. He lived at 30 De Courcy Square, Glasnevin, and was a member of B. Company, 1st Battalion, Dublin Brigade in 1916. He was assigned to the Cabra Bridge outpost on Easter Monday, and retreated with his party to the GPO on Wednesday. He was placed on the top floor on the Henry Street side, until the withdrawal from the burning building on the Friday evening. After the surrender, he was deported to Wandsworth Jail on May 9th and interned in Frongoch, until Christmas, 1916.

On his release from internment, he helped reorganize his company and was appointed battalion quartermaster in 1918. He fought in the War of Independence and he was arrested on June 1921 and interned until December 1921. During the Civil War, he took the Republican side and fought in Parnell Square and the Fowler Hall. At this time he was quartermaster of the IRA GHQ and he was arrested in August 1922. He escaped after ten days imprisonment and remained on the run until 1923. In later life, he lived at Ben Eadar Road, Raheny, and was attached to the Accounts Dept. of the ESB.

Patrick Corless passed away on February 4th 1963 and was buried at Glasnevin Cemetery.

References:
IMA, MSPC; *Irish Press* & *Evening Herald*, 5th February 1963, (dn).

Edward Cosgrave: (1873 – 1916). Killed in Action
Irish Citizen Army

Edward Cosgrave was born in 1873 and resided at 65 Lower Dominic Street. He was employed as a rope maker, and was a member of the Irish Citizen Army prior to the Rising. He reported to the GPO on Easter Monday, but the following day he died instantly from a gunshot wound while serving there. His body was removed to Jervis Street Hospital.

Edward Cosgrave, who was married with seven children, was buried at Glasnevin Cemetery.

References:
RH; IMA, MSPC; NLI, *William O'Brien Papers*, (Ms 15,673); Ray Bateson, *They Died by Pearse's Side*, (2010).

Daniel (Dan) Courtney: (1866 - 1943)
Irish Citizen Army, (North Strand Section). Roll of Honour

Dan Courtney was born in 1866 and resided at 43 Bessboro Avenue, North Strand, when he joined the ITGWU in April 1911. He was a grain store worker and he became a member of the Irish Citizen Army in 1913 at the age of forty seven. In that year he had lived at 1 Merchants Road, East Wall, owned by his then employers, the Merchants Warehousing Company, but was evicted with over sixty other families, because of his part in the Lockout. On Easter Monday 1916, at the age of fifty, he was sent with a group from the GPO to Anncsley Bridge, Fairview, where they set up a barricade across the bridge. With word of the approach of troops from the musketry school on Bull Island, he and others in the group took up positions in the Vitriol Works and engaged the enemy, who by then had set up machine guns on the railway embankment. They were ordered back to the GPO on Tuesday evening, and he was sent to Metropole Hotel, where he was engaged in tunneling through the buildings to Mansfield's Shoe Shop on the corner of Abbey Street. He remained in the Metropole Hotel until its evacuation on Friday. He was part of the main evacuation of the GPO on Friday evening and was engaged in tunneling through the houses in Moore Street that night. After the surrender he was deported to Knutsford Jail on May 1st and later interned in Frongoch until Christmas, 1916. On his release from internment, he continued to serve with the Irish Citizen Army during the War of Independence until the Truce. He took the Republican side in the Civil War, until his wife's death in January 1923 brought his active service to an end.

His seventeen year old son, Bernard, who was a member of the St Stephen's Green Garrison in Easter Week, died in 1917. In later years Dan Courtney was active in the Old Citizen Army Comrades Association and he resided at 13 Upper Stephen Street.

Dan Courtney was the oldest surviving member of the Irish Citizen Army when he passed away on August 23rd 1943, and a guard of honour, including Walter Carpenter, Bill Oman, Joe Whelan and Vincent, Christy and Patrick Poole, attended his burial at Glasnevin Cemetery.

References:
RH; IMA, MSPC; NLI, *William O'Brien Papers*, (Ms 15,673); Hugo McGuinness, *Daniel Courtney, the Grandfather of the Irish Citizen Army*, (2015); *Irish Independent* & *Irish Press*, 25th August 1943, (obits).

Michael Cowley: (- 1960)
E. Coy, 4th Batt, Dublin Brigade. Roll of Honour

Michael Cowley from Cloncurry, County Kildare, resided at Vicarstown House, Rathfarnham in 1916. He was a member of the IRB and he was the person who swore Seán T. O'Kelly into that organisation. A member of the Gaelic League, he was also a close friend of Teresa Brayton, poet, nationalist and composer of the popular emigrant lament, *"The Old Bog Road"*. He was a member of P.H. Pearse's E. Company, 4th Battalion, Dublin Brigade and fought in the GPO during Easter Week. After the surrender, he was deported to Stafford Jail on May 1st and interned in Frongoch, until July 21st 1916. On his return to Ireland, he fought in the War of Independence. He was an original staff member of the National Land Bank and later assistant manager of National City Land Bank, Ltd.

Michael Cowley, of 3 Mayfield Road, Terenure, died on December 20th 1960.

References:
RH; IMA, MSPC; *Irish Press*, 21st December 1960, (obit).

Henry (Harry) Coyle: (1888 – 1916). Killed In Action
F. Coy, 2nd Batt, Dublin Brigade. Roll of Honour

Harry Coyle was born in 1888 and resided at 32 Leinster Avenue, North Strand. He was a slater by trade and was a member of the Davis Hurling Club. He joined his local unit, F. Company, 2nd Battalion, Dublin Brigade, in 1914. On Easter Monday he reported to the GPO and fought there throughout the Rising. On Friday, he was in the group that was led by The O'Rahilly into Moore Street. According to Thomas Leahy, he was shot by a sniper as he attempted to open the door of a shop in Moore Lane. He was twenty eight years old with a wife and baby son when he was shot dead. His brother, Thomas, a member of the Irish Citizen Army, fought at City Hall in Easter Week.

Harry Coyle was buried on May 3rd at Glasnevin Cemetery and a memorial was later erected over his grave by the National Graves Association in November, 1934.

References:
RH; *Catholic Bulletin*, August 1916; Ray Bateson, *They Died by Pearse's Side*, (2010).

Thomas (Tom) Craven: (- 1955)

Liverpool Company, (Kimmage Garrison). Roll of Honour

Tom Craven was born in Liverpool. He joined the Irish Volunteers in that city and became captain of the local battalion. His grandfather took his family to Liverpool after the failure of the Young Ireland rising in 1848 and returned to Ireland in 1865. After the Fenian collapse, he left for Liverpool once again in 1867. Tom Craven, a former British soldier who fought in the Boer War, came to Dublin in 1915 and organized the Volunteers from Britain in the camp at Kimmage. On Easter Sunday morning, he was involved in the successful raid for explosives on the De Selby quarries at Jobstown. He was one of the first to enter the GPO on Easter Monday, and later that afternoon James Connolly sent him in charge of a party to operate in the Fairview area. They occupied the Vitriol Works, Ballybough Bridge, and attempted to blow up the railway line at Fairview. The group was recalled to the GPO on Tuesday evening, and on the following day he was sent to the Metropole Hotel. He later took up a position at the corner with Abbey Street and he remained there until Friday, when returned to the GPO. After the evacuation of the GPO on Friday evening, he spent the night in a building at the corner of Moore Street and Henry Place. He was deported to Knutsford Jail on May 1st and transferred to various prisons around England, until his release from Frongoch, at Christmas, 1916.

He acted as an organiser for Sinn Féin in various parts of Ulster in 1917 and 1918. In April 1918 he was part of the unit in England, under the command of Cathal Brugha, prepared to assassinate Lloyd George and members of the British Government if conscription was introduced in Ireland. When the Liverpool Company was revived in May, 1918, he was made 1st Lieutenant of the sixty strong unit. He was sent by Harry Boland on a mission to the United States in late 1919 to purchase and transport arms back to Ireland.

Tom Craven spent many years living in the United States and died in Akron, Ohio, on February 27th 1955.

References:
RH; IMA, MSPC; NLI, *Lynch Papers*, (Ms 11,131); Eileen McGough, *Diarmuid Lynch, a forgotten Irish Patriot*, (2013).

Michael Cremen: (1882 – 1956)

F. Coy, 4th Batt, Dublin Brigade

Michael Cremen, a native of Cork City, was born in 1882. He was employed in the Postal Service in London and was active in the Irish movement from 1908. He was transferred to Dublin in 1915, and was attached to the engineering staff at Aldborough House, Portland Row. He was a member of F. Company, 4th Battalion, Dublin Brigade and of the Davis Hurling Club. In preparation for the Rising, he was engaged in the purchase of arms for transfer to Ireland. On Easter Monday he took up a snipers position on the roof of the GPO, and fought from there for the remainder of the week. After the surrender, he was deported to Stafford Jail on May 1st, but later bluffed his way to an early release.

He was dismissed from the Civil Service in 1918 for his anti-conscription activities. He fought throughout the War of Independence, and on its formation became captain of the 5th Battalion, Engineers. In advance of the attack on the Custom House in May 1921, he was responsible for the destruction of all telephone connections. He was also involved in the purchase and shipment of small arms from Germany. During the Civil War, he took the Republican side and was Director of Purchases while on the run.

In 1932, he was reinstated in the Civil Service and at various stages was private secretary to several Ministers of State. Before his retirement, he was Secretary to the Military Services Pensions Board. He also worked on behalf of IRA Veterans and was secretary to the Federation of the Old IRA and chairman of the 5th Battalion, Old IRA.

Michael Cremen died at his home at 128 Lower Kimmage Road, on March 26th 1956 and was buried at Mount Jerome Cemetery, Harold's Cross, where a memorial was unveiled in his honour, on March 24th 1958.

References:
RH; IMA, MSPC; *Irish Independent* & *Irish Press*, 27th March 1956, (obits).

Thomas (Tom) Crimmins: (1898 - 1988)

E. Coy, 2nd Batt, Dublin Brigade. Roll of Honour

Tom Crimmins was born in 1898 and resided at 49 Upper Buckingham Street, Dublin. He joined Fianna Éireann in 1910, and five years later transferred to E. Company, 2nd Battalion, Dublin Brigade. He was a piper with the Fintan Lawlor Pipe Band and a member of St Laurence O'Toole's GAA Club. On Easter Monday he was on his way to the Dublin Mountains with friends when he learned that the Rising had begun. He reported to Liberty Hall, and was put on guard outside the building. When he noticed a lorry laden with beef, he reported to O/C Frank Thornton, and the lorry was seized. He accompanied the cargo to the GPO, where he was put under the command of Diarmuid Lynch and given the task of guarding the prisoners. He was in the party led by The O'Rahilly into Moore Street, at the evacuation on Friday evening. Although already wounded in the ankle, he tried to go to the assistance of the fatally wounded O'Rahilly, who told him to look after himself. He made his way to a vacant tenement and shortly after returned to try and help O'Rahilly again. The O'Rahilly, who was on the opposite side of Moore Street, told him he was shot in the stomach and spine and that nothing could be done for him. He returned to the tenement and lay there for two days, before he was awoken by three teenagers who lived in the area. When he asked a local woman to help him get to hospital, a policeman and some high ranking British officers entered the room and he was taken prisoner to the military hospital at Dublin Castle. He spent five months in hospital and several months on crutches, afterwards.

He was active with his unit during the War of Independence, before emigrating to the United States in 1920. After 44 years living in the United States, Tom Crimmins, the last member of the GPO to surrender, returned to Dublin to retire in 1966. In his retirement, he returned to the United States periodically, before finally settling in Ireland in 1985.

Tom Crimmins died in Beaumont Convalescent Home on January 12th 1988 and his funeral took place at Glasnevin Crematorium.

References:

RH; IMA, MSPC; Marcus Bourke, *The O'Rahilly*, (1967); *Irish Press*, 2nd April 1966, (na); *Sunday Independent*, 14th April 1966, (na); *Evening Herald*, 14th January 1988, (obit).

Joseph (Joe) Cripps: (1896 - 1975)
C. Coy, 2nd Batt, Dublin Brigade. Roll of Honour

Joe Cripps was born in 1896 and resided at Hardwicke Street, Dublin. He was a druggist's assistant by profession and was a member of C. Company, 2nd Battalion, Dublin Brigade. He was also a keen photographer and was trying out a new camera on Easter Monday when the Rising began. He returned home and grabbed his rifle and first aid gear and reported to the GPO.

He was detailed for Red Cross duty, under the command of Captain Seán Doyle, before the arrival of medical students, Jim Ryan and Dan McLoughlin.

He went out raiding pharmacies in the vicinity of the GPO for medical supplies. When James Connolly was wounded, he was sent out to obtain the morphine required by the British Army Surgeon who was treating him. He had brought his camera with him to the GPO and took a few photographs while there. He escorted the wounded to Jervis Street Hospital on Friday and later evaded capture. He was eventually captured with two other Volunteers at City Quay, and was brought to Tara Street Swimming Baths where they were about to be shot, only for the timely intervention by a British Army Officer. From Tara Street they were taken to Dublin Castle, where they were surprisingly released. Before his capture he disposed of his camera and concealed the roll of film in his coat.

He rejoined his unit at its re-organisation. He became an instructor in first aid and engineering and was appointed company quartermaster in 1919. He was attached to the 5th Battalion Engineers and he was company captain in 1920 and 1921. Rory O'Connor, IRA Director of Engineering, sent him to Manchester and Liverpool to assist in activities there. He became brigade quartermaster in 1922 and took the Republican side in the Civil War. He was captured while fighting in the O'Connell Street area and was interned in Mountjoy Jail, Gormanstown and Newbridge, until his release in December 1923.

He emigrated to the United States and lived there for over forty years. While in America, he got the photographs taken in the GPO developed and they later appeared in the *Sunday Independent's* Easter Rising 50th anniversary supplement in 1966. On his retirement, he returned to Ireland and lived at 15 Johnstown Road, Cabinteely.

Joe Cripps died on December 11th 1975 and was buried at Deansgrange Cemetery.

References:
RH; IMA, MSPC; NLI, *Lynch Papers*, (Ms 11,131); Thomas Coffey, *Agony at Easter*, (1969); Clair Willis, *Dublin 1916, the Siege of the GPO*, (2009); *Irish Independent*, 12th December 1975, (obit).

Gerard Crofts: (1889 – 1934)

C. Coy, 3rd Batt, Dublin Brigade. Roll of Honour

Gerard Crofts was born in Dublin, in 1889. He was educated at Synge Street CBS. and St Mary's College, Rathmines, before embarking on a career in music. He was a member of the Gaelic League and was devoted to the Irish language. He joined C. Company, 3rd Battalion, Dublin Brigade in 1915. His father was a Papal Zouave, who fought at the famous siege of Ancona and who also identified with the Fenian movement. On Easter Monday he was sent with a party, under Captain Brennan-Whitmore, to occupy the Imperial Hotel and its adjoining buildings. Following seventy two hours of stubborn resistance, the small party was forced to abandon their position because of an incessant British artillery bombardment. He made his way to North Cumberland Street, where he was captured. He was brought to the Custom House for interrogation and detained in Richmond Barracks. Sentenced to ten years penal servitude on May 11th, this was reduced to five years and he was imprisoned in Dartmoor, Wandsworth and later in Lewes Jail. He was an organizer of a hunger strike in Lewes Jail and was later released from there on the grounds of ill-health, on June 16th 1917.

During the War of Independence he was imprisoned in Mounjoy Jail and was released, having taken part in another hunger strike. He was married to Margaret O'Callaghan and he was a gifted vocalist and as a singer of Irish ballads, who rendered great service performing at National Aid concerts throughout the country.

His health was undermined by the effects of the hunger strikes and, after a long illness, Gerard Crofts passed away at his home at Castle Avenue, Clontarf, on November 14th 1934 and, after a funeral service in Whitefriars Street Church, he was buried at Glasnevin Cemetery.

References:

RH; *Catholic Bulletin*, July 1917; *Synge Street CBS Centenary Record, 1864*-1964, (1964); W.J. Whitmore-Brennan, *Dublin Burning*, (1996); *Never a Dull Day: 150 years of Synge Street CBS, 1864-2014*, (Michael Minnock & Seán Ryan, Ed, 2014); *Evening Herald*, 14th November 1934, (obit); *Irish Independent*, 15th November 1934, (obit).

Michael Croke: (1884 – 1967)

E. Coy, 2nd Batt, Dublin Brigade. Roll of Honour

Michael Croke was born in 1884 and resided at 4 Millbourne Avenue, Drumcondra. He joined E. Company, 2nd Battlion, Dublin Brigade in 1915. He was a checker and railway porter with the LNW Railway Company and also a member of St Laurence O'Toole's GAA Club. He fought in the GPO in Easter Week, alongside his brother Thomas. He was stationed on the roof of the GPO and later manned the ground floor windows. He also commandeered materials from the Brooks Thomas premises and was posted to the junction of Abbey Street and Liffey Street. After the surrender he was deported to Stafford Jail on May 1st and interned in Frongoch until Christmas, 1916,

After his release from internment, he fought in the War of Independence. He was arrested in November 1920 and interned in Ballykinlar Camp, until December 1921. His time in prison badly impaired his health and he later received a disability pension.

Michael Croke, of 4 Millbourne Avenue, Drumcondra, died on August 3rd 1967 and was buried in Portarlington, County Laois.

References:
RH; IMA, MSPC.

Thomas Croke: (1878 - 1942)

E. Coy, 2nd Batt, Dublin Brigade. Roll of Honour

Thomas Croke was born in 1878 and resided at 4 College View Terrace, Drumcondra. He served in the Royal Irish Guards and was discharged from the British Army in February 1903. He was a member of E. Company, 2nd Battalion, Dublin Brigade. He was not mobilized until Easter Monday evening, and on arriving at the GPO he manned a window on the ground floor. On Tuesday he was part of a group that built a barricade in Abbey Street and later was sent to Reis's Chambers. He was stationed at the Hibernian Bank on Wednesday and, after the death of Captain Weafer, he returned to the GPO where he manned a window on the second floor. On Friday he helped fight the flames with his brother, Michael and they evacuated the building together later that evening. He was deported to Knutsford Jail on May 1st and interned in Frongoch, until July 13th 1916.

Like his brother, Michael, he was a member of Laurence O'Toole's GAA Club. He was employed in the Dept of Local Government and became disabled in 1935. He left his employment and he was a patient at St Kevin's Hospital for many years.

Thomas Croke died on April 19th 1942 and was buried at Glasnevin Cemetery.

References:
RH; IMA, MSPC; NLI, *Lynch Papers*, (Ms 11,131); *Irish Press*, 20th April 1942, (fr).

Mary Cullen
Cumann na mBan

Mary Cullen resided in Percy Place and was a member of Cumann na mBan. She was a member of the GPO Garrison in Easter Week, and at noon on the Wednesday she and Bridget Grace were sent to the Mount Street Bridge outpost by James Connolly, with a warning of the approach of British troops from Dún Laoghaire. Volunteer Section Commander, Seamus Grace, who was one of the defenders of 25 Northumberland Road, later recalled that his sister, Bridget and Mary Cullen arrived with food and a dispatch. They were not allowed enter the house and the dispatch was taken through the letterbox.

References:

Max Caulfield, *The Easter Rebellion*, (1963); Thomas Coffey, *Agony at Easter*, (1969); Liz Gillis, *Women of the Irish Revolution*, (2015).

William F. (Liam) Cullen: (1888 - 1942)
F. Coy, 2nd Batt, Dublin Brigade & Captain G.H.Q. Roll of Honour

Liam Cullen was born in 1888 and resided at 3 St Joseph's Terrace, Fairview. He joined F. Company, 2nd Battalion, Dublin Brigade in 1913 and was attached to the Armaments Section, GHQ. In 1915 was a member of the O'Donovan Rossa funeral committee. Before the Rising he was employed as Transport Manager of Thompson's Garage, Brunswick Street, and was also an assistant to Seán McGarry who was in charge of the transportation of munitions. He fought in the GPO in Easter Week and he was wounded while in command of the second floor. When fire spread through the building on Friday, he manned the hoses with Captain M.W. O'Reilly. During the evacuation of the GPO on Friday evening, he was wounded again, receiving bullet wounds to the knee and neck. After the surrender, he was removed to the emergency military hospital that had been set up in Dublin Castle. When he was sufficiently recovered, he was deported and interned in Frongoch.

He took part in the War of Independence and was imprisoned in Mountjoy Jail from July to September 1918. He was also imprisoned in Arbour Hill for two months in 1920. He took no part in the Civil War and formed his own company, W. F. Cullen & Sons Haulage Contractors in 1922. He resided at 3 Castle Avenue, Clontarf and was later appointed chairman of the Master Carriers Association. On the unveiling of the Cúchulainn Memorial in the GPO in 1935, he broadcast a radio commentary.

Liam Cullen died on February 18th 1942 and was buried in Glasnevin Cemetery.

References:
RH; IMA, MSPC; NLI, *Lynch Papers*, (Ms 11,131); *Irish Independent* & *Irish Press*, 19th February 1942, (obits).

Mark Joseph Cummins: (- 1943)
C. Coy, 4th Batt, Dublin Brigade

Mark Cummins resided at 49 South Great Georges Street and was a member of C. Company, 4th Battalion, Dublin Brigade prior to the Rising. He reported to the GPO on Easter Monday, and was engaged in erecting barricades and in sniping duties, throughout the week. On Friday he escorted the wounded to Jervis Street Hospital. After the surrender he was deported to Stafford Jail on May 8th and interned in Frongoch until July 14th 1916.

He transferred to F. Company, 2nd Battalion, Dublin Brigade in March 1917, and took part in numerous operations during the War of Independence. He delivered a supply of petrol to Éamon deValera in Ennis in June 1917 when he was campaigning in the East Clare by-election. Because of unemployment he emigrated to the United States in 1920, and worked for many years as a merchant seaman. He met with an accident in 1934 which prevented him from working again.

Mark Cummins died in the U.S Marine Hospital, San Francisco, California, on September 18th 1943.

References:
IMA, MSPC.

Patrick Dalton: (1900 - 1989)

G. Coy, 1st Batt, Dublin Brigade. Roll of Honour

Patrick Dalton was born in 1900 and was a member of G. Company, 1st Battalion, Dublin Brigade. Prior to the Rising, however, he had difficulty in joining the Volunteers because of his young age. He spent most of Easter Week stationed on the roof of the GPO. On Friday, he helped remove bombs from the ground floor to the basement. He was in the third party to evacuate the GPO, and spent Friday night sheltering at the rear of Williams Provision Store in Samson's Lane. After the surrender, he was detained at Richmond Barracks and was released because of his young age. When it was discovered that he took part in the Rising, he was dismissed by Dockrell's, his former employers, and soon afterwards he left the country to seek work. He travelled to London and, finding himself stranded, he joined the British Army. He was discharged from the army in June 1922 and returned to Ireland. During the Civil War, he joined the Free State Army and served as a private in the southern part of the country until March 1923. He later joined the Prison Service and worked as a warder in jails in Sligo, Cork and Dublin. He then returned to England and remained there for many years. On his return from London, he resided at Tonlegee Road, Coolock.

Patrick Dalton died on December 26th 1989, and was buried at Fingal Cemetery, Balgriffin, County Dublin.

References:
RH; IMA, MSPC; NLI, *Lynch Papers*, (Ms 11,131); *Irish Independent*, 27th December 1969, (dn).

Nora Daly Dore: (1885 – 1977)

Cumann na mBan. Roll of Honour

Nora Daly was born in Limerick, in 1885. When she learned of the commencement of the Rising, she left Limerick for Dublin by train with her sister Laura and her future husband, Eamon Dore. They were sisters of Commandant Ned Daly and Kathleen, wife of Tom Clarke. They arrived at the GPO on Tuesday night and then proceeded to Kathleen Clarke's house in Fairview, where they spent the night. Back in the GPO the following day, it was decided to send them with dispatches for the Munster Volunteers. Nora reported to Terence McSwiney in Cork, while Laura delivered her despatches to Michael Colivet in Limerick. They both managed to get back to the GPO and left with most members of Cumann na mBan on Friday. They were detained at Broadstone Railway Station for questioning, and were released after some hours.

Nora married Eamon Dore in May 1918 and they had three children. They lived in Limerick, where Eamon was involved in running the Daly family bakery in William Street.

Nora Daly Dore died on November 4th 1977 and was buried at Glin, County Limerick.

References:
RH; Kathleen Clarke, *Revolutionary Woman*, (1991); Helen Litton, *Ned Daly*, (16Lives series, 2013); *Irish Press*, 5th November 1977, (dn).

Laura Daly O'Sullivan: (1882 – 1967)
Cumann na mBan

Laura Daly was born in 1882 and was considered to be the dearest sister of Commandant Edward Daly. In 1913 when a disagreement between Ned and his uncle, the veteran Fenian John Daly, resulted in Ned leaving Limerick for good, she is reputed to have never spoken to her uncle again. She travelled from Limerick to Dublin by train with her sister Nora and Eamon Dore, on Easter Tuesday. They later spent that night win the house of their sister, Kathleen Clarke, in Fairview. Laura was sent to Limerick with dispatches from the GPO the following morning, while Nora was sent to Cork. With great difficulty they both returned to the GPO, but their attempt to garner support for the Rising in Munster failed. Both sisters left the GPO with the Cumann na mBan women before the building's evacuation. She was detained for questioning in Broadstone Railway Station and released some time later.

She married Captain Seamus O'Sullivan in 1918. He also fought with the GPO Garrison, and was Commandant Ned Daly's closest friend. He was on the run at the time and hiding in the attic of the Daly house in Limerick. They had four children, and Michael Collins was godfather to one of their sons, John. They later opened a restaurant at 3 O'Connell Street, Limerick

Laura Daly O'Sullivan passed away in 1967.

References:
Kathleen Clarke, *Revolutionary Woman*, (1997); Helen Litton, *Ned Daly*, (16Lives series, 2013).

Denis Daly: (1886 – 1965)

London Company, (Kimmage Garrison). Roll of Honour

Denis Daly was born in 1886 and was reared in Main Street, Cahirciveen, Co. Kerry. He went to England to work and, while there, became a member of the IRB and the Volunteers. He returned to Ireland with the London Volunteers and joined the Kimmage Volunteer Camp before the Rising. On Good Friday, he was in charge of a party sent to Kerry to rendezvous with Roger Casement and to collect arms from a German ship. Due to a tragic mishap, three Volunteers drowned,when their car drove off the pier at Ballykissane and Denis Daly and two other Volunteers then made their way back to Dublin. He was reputed to have fired the first shots from the GPO on Easter Monday. From Easter Monday to Wednesday, he was engaged in sniping from the ground floor windows and later from the roof of the GPO. He was in the group, led by Seán Milroy which occupied houses at the junction of Liffey Street and Abbey Street, on Thursday. On Friday, this group was recalled to the GPO, and that evening he was in the advance party under the command of The O'Rahilly, that came under fierce machine gun fire in Moore Street. He found refuge in Samson's Lane, where he spent the night. After the Rising, he was deported to Stafford Jail on May 1st and interned in Frongoch until Christmas 1916.

On his release from internment, he returned to Kerry and was appointed O/C of A. Company, 9th Battalion, No.1 Kerry Brigade. He was arrested in June 1918 and interned in Reading Jail until April 1919. Once more on his release he resumed organisational work, and became battalion quartermaster in 1920. He was appointed vice-commandant, No.3 Kerry Brigade in 1921. During the Civil War he took the Republican side, and was involved in numerous engagements. He was arrested in March 1923 and was released from St Bricin's Hospital on March 1924.

He was a Fianna Fáil TD for the Kerry Constituency, serving one term, from 1933 to 1937. In his youth he played Gaelic football for London Irish and was later chairman of the Kerry GAA County Board.

Denis Daly died on March 21st 1965 and was buried at Keelovarnogue Cemetery, Cahirciveen, County Kerry.

References:

RH; IMA, MSPC; NLI, *Lynch Papers*, (Ms 11,131); *Irish Independent*, 22nd March 1965, (dn); *Irish Times*, 23 March 1965, (obit); *The Kerryman*, 27th March 1965, (obit).

James (Seamus) Daly: (1885 – 1966)

F. Coy, 2nd Batt, Dublin Brigade. Roll of Honour

Seamus Daly was born in 1885 and resided at "Cluny", Clontarf Road. He was a member of F. Company, 2nd Battalion, Dublin Brigade, and he reported to Father Mathew Park, Fairview, on Easter Monday. He was stationed in the Ballybough Bridge area, and on Tuesday he was ordered by Frank Henderson to retrieve gelignite, which he had stored at his home, to blow up the railway bridge at Clonliffe Road. However, before he could carry out this duty, his party was ordered to return to the GPO. From there he was sent to the Imperial Hotel, where he fought until the building was evacuated on Thursday, when it was engulfed by fire.
His party made their way through Marlborough Street to Gloucester Street, and they were captured in a tenement there,on Friday. He was deported to Wakefield Jail on May 6th, and was interned in Frongoch, until July 27th, 1916. His brother, Paddy, fought in the Four Courts and another brother, Frank, saw action at Cabra Bridge and Ashbourne.

During the War of Independence, he served as adjutant of F. Company, 2nd Battalion, Dublin Brigade and later as battalion armourer. He was arrested in March 1918 and interned in Mountjoy Jail and Dundalk, where he went on hunger strike, before he was released in May 1918. He was arrested again in January 1921 and interned in Ballykinlar Camp, until December of that same year. After the Truce, he joined the Free State Army and retired from the Quartermaster General's Dept, with the rank of commandant.

Seumas Daly, of Carrig Ruadh, Howth Summit, died on February 20th 1966 and was buried at Deansgrange Cemetery.

References:
RH; IMA, MSPC; *Irish Press*, 22nd February 1966, (dn).

William (Liam) Daly: (1895 - 1966)

London Company, (Kimmage Garrison). Roll of Honour

Liam Daly was born in London in 1895, to Irish parents. He was a member of the Gaelic League and he arrived at Larkfield, Kimmage in January 1916, with other London Volunteers. He reported to the GPO on Easter Monday, and he assisted in erecting barricades in Abbey Street and in dispersing looters. Because he was a telephone operator, he was then sent by James Connolly to connect a telephone line from the roof to the ground floor of the GPO with Joe Good. Later that night he was sent across the street to Reis's Chambers Wireless School to erect an aerial. On

Wednesday morning he assisted in loading a large quantity of bread from the Dublin Bread Company and the wireless transmission apparatus on to a cart to be transported back to the GPO. He moved to the Hibernian Bank later in the day, but retreated to the GPO shortly afterwards. He was in the advance party, led by The O'Rahilly, at the evacuation of the GPO on Friday evening. He was shot through the arm and found refuge in nearby stables until his capture on Saturday morning. He was taken to the emergency hospital at Dublin Castle and then transferred to Kilmainham Jail. He was deported to Wakefield Prison on May 6th and interned in Frongoch until September, 1916.

On his release from internment, he was appointed Adjutant of E. Company, 2nd Battalion, Dublin Brigade. He fought in the War of Independence and joined the Free State Army in 1922. He served with the Eastern Division and was wounded at Bandon on August 19th 1922. He retired from the Army Corps of Engineers in 1925, with the rank of captain.

He was hon. secretary of the GPO Garrison for the Jubilee Commemorations in 1966. Liam Daly, of 1 Ossory Road, North Strand, died on June 17th 1966 and was buried in St Fintan's Cemetery, Sutton.

References:
RH; IMA, MSPC; IMA, BMH (WS 425); *Sunday Independent*, 19th June 1966, (obit).

William Darcy: (1874 – 1918)
Hibernian Rifles

William Darcy was born in Ardaghey, County Monaghan in 1874, and was a cabinetmaker by trade. He was one of the pioneers of the Sinn Féin movement in the Dundalk region, and was the IRB County Centre for County Louth. He went to work in Dublin, and resided at 51 Lower Camden Street prior to the Rising. On Easter Monday he was in a party sent to occupy Mooney's Public House and later the Ship Hotel, in Abbey Street. They were ordered to withdraw to the GPO later that evening and he was stationed on the first floor for the remainder of the week. He was deported to Stafford Jail on May 1st, and was treated by the prison doctor there after becoming ill with double pneumonia. He was later interned in Frongoch until July 18th, 1916.

After his release from internment, he was employed by Bull & Co. Suffolk Street, Dublin. On December 23rd, 1918, shortly after completing work on the altar rail of the church in Ardaghey, he suffered a fatal heart attack.

William Darcy was buried at Haggardstown Cemetery, County Louth, leaving a wife and five children.

References:
IMA, MSPC; *Dundalk Examiner*, 4th January 1919, (obit).

Daniel Davitt: (1886 – 1962)

B. Coy, 1st Batt, Dublin Brigade

Dan Davitt was born in 1886 and resided at 4 Russell Street, North Circular Road. He was a member of B. Company, 1st Battalion, Dublin Brigade and on Easter Monday he reported to the Colmcille Hall, Blackhall Street. He was in the group that went to the railway bridge on the North Circular Road, Phibsboro and, after an unsuccessful attempt to blow up the bridge, he manned the barricades on the North Circular Road until his party were withdrawn on Tuesday evening. He made his way to the GPO, where he spent the night. On Wednesday morning he was posted to the Pillar Public House, Henry Street, and remained there until Friday, when he was ordered back to the GPO. He was in advance party led by The O'Rahilly into Moore Street on Friday evening. He was near to The O'Rahilly when he was mortally wounded, and he took refuge in Cole's Lane. He spent Friday night in a stable near to Cole's Lane and after the surrender he was deported to Stafford Jail on May 1st. He was interned in Frongoch, from where he escaped and was recaptured two days later. He spent seven weeks in solitary confinement and was released from Frongoch, at Christmas, 1916.

He rejoined his unit in 1917, and served until 1918, when he ceased activities due to poor health.

Dan Davitt, of 20 Clandonagh Road, Donnycarney, died on August 18th 1962 and was buried at St Fintan's Cemetery, Sutton.

References:
    IMA, MSPC; *Evening Herald*, 18th August 1962, (dn).

Patrick (Pat) Dennany: (1877 - 1952)

C. Coy, 2nd Batt, Dublin Brigade. Roll of Honour

Pat Dennany was born in Donore, Drogheda in 1877. His grandfather fought and escaped capture at the Battle of Tara in 1798. He was a member of C. Company, 2nd Battalion, Dublin Brigade and a member of Croke's GAC. He resided at 9a Buckingham Buildings, in the north inner-city and was involved in the Kilcoole and Howth gun running. On reporting to the GPO on Easter Monday, he was put on guard duty and street patrols until Wednesday. On Thursday he was one of a party who occupied houses at the junction of Abbey Street and Liffey Street. He was one of the last to evacuate the burning GPO on Friday evening, and he was a member of the group, under the command of Seán McLoughlin, who was ready to charge the British Army barricade at the top of Moore Street, when the intention to surrender was announced on Saturday afternoon. He was deported to Stafford Jail on May 1st and interned in Frongoch, until Christmas, 1916.

On his release from internment, he rejoined his unit and served through the War of Independence as a section commander, until the Truce. He was a founder member of the Association of Easter Week Men. In the early 1940s he returned to Donore and became a member of the Local Defence Force in Drogheda, during the Emergency. He had a keen interest in the GAA and was secretary and treasurer of the local GAA club and was also involved in the Pioneer Association and the Local Amateur Dramatic Society.

Pat Dennany died on March 13th 1952 and was buried at Donore, Drogheda, County Louth.

References:

RH; IMA, MSPC; NLI, *Lynch Papers*, (Ms 11,131); *Irish Independent*, 15th March 1952, (dn); *Irish Press*, 17th March 1952, (fr); *Drogheda Independent*, 22nd March 1952, (obit).

Joseph (Joe) Derham: (1887- 1966)
F. Coy, 1st Batt, Dublin Brigade. Roll of Honour

Joe Derham was a native of Skerries, County Dublin. He resided at Hoar Rock and on leaving school he joined the Civil Service in London, where he became acquainted with Michael Collins. He returned to Dublin in 1915 and took up a position with the Land Commission. He became a member of F. Company, 1st Battalion, Dublin Brigade. He resided at 26 North Frederick Street in the lead up to the Rising.

On Easter Monday he was seeing off a friend at Kingsbridge Train Station when the first shots of the Rebellion were fired. He made his way to the GPO and fought there throughout the week. He was given the responsibility for the garrison time-keeping by Tom Clarke. He was one of the occupants of Hanlon's Shop in Moore Street shortly before the surrender. After the Rising, he was deported to Wandsworth Jail on May 9th and interned in Frongoch, where he joined his brother, Matthias, who fought at Ashbourne. He was released from Frongoch at Christmas, 1916.

During the War of Independence, he was a Captain with the North County Volunteers, Fingal Brigade. Because of his part in the Easter Rising, he had been dismissed from the Civil Service and wasn't reinstated until 1932. In the intervening years he worked as a commercial traveller and he returned to London in July 1919 to marry Annie Fitzmaurice, whom he first met while in Wandsworth Jail in 1916. She was part of a group that visited Irish prisoners in jail. They resided at 48 Hollybank Road, Drumcondra and later at 28 Iona Road, Glasnevin. For many years he was an accountant with the Commissioner of Public Works. In his youth he was a member of Skerries Harps GAA Club and in 1932, the year he was re-employed in the Civil Service, he served as a marshal at the Eucharistic Congress open-air Masses in the Phoenix Park.

Joe Derham passed away in August 1966 and was buried at Holmpatrick Cemetery, Skerries.

References:

RH; IMA, MSPC; NLI, *Lynch Papers*, (Ms 11,131); Time & Tide, *Brothers in Arms*, Frank Whearity, (Vol 7, 2010); *Irish Independent*, 13th August 1966, (obit); *Irish Press*, 15th August 1966, (obit).

Patrick Devereux: (1896 - 1955)

Irish Citizen Army, (North Strand Section). Roll of Honour

Patrick Devereux was born in Glasgow and was working as a blacksmith's helper in the Dublin Dockyard when he joined the Irish Citizen Army in 1915. He resided at 49 Summerhill, and was twenty years old when he reported to Liberty Hall on Easter Monday morning. He was sent with a party, under the command of Captain Frank Thornton, to reinforce the Irish Citizen Army Garrison at City Hall. When they reached Fleet Sreet, they came under heavy fire from British troops in the telephone exchange building, and were forced to retreat. They took up a position in Delahaunty's Public House and returned fire, before retreating to the GPO. On Tuesday morning he was in the group sent across the street to occupy the Imperial Hotel. He took up a sniping position on the roof of the hotel and held out for two days and nights. During the heavy bombardment of the hotel on Thursday, he collapsed suffering from shellshock. He abandoned the burning building with the rest of the garrison, and was among those captured on Friday morning in Marlborough Street. He was taken to the Custom House for interrogation, and later sent to Richmond Barracks. He was deported to Wakefield Prison and released on June 7th, 1916. After his release from prison, he remained an active member of the Irish Citizen Army during the War of Independence. His sister, Mary Allen, was a member of the St Stephen's Green Garrison.

He was later employed at Ross & Walpole Engineers, North Wall. He was a member of the Pro-Cathedral Confraternity and the Matt Talbot Workingman's Club. He suffered ill health for many years. In 1954 he suffered a mental breakdown and after a period in hospital, he was made a ward of court.

Patrick Deveraux died on November 4th 1955 and was buried at Glasnevin Cemetery.

References:
RH; IMA, MSPC.

Francis (Frank) Devine: (1881 - 1939)

Hibernian Rifles. Roll of Honour

Frank Devine was born in 1881. He was a painter by trade and joined the Hibernian Rifles, AOH (American Alliance), in 1915. On Easter Monday, he was in the Hibernian Rifles party that occupied houses at the corner of Dorset Street and North Frederick Street, before being ordered into the GPO on Easter Monday night. On Tuesday he was one of ten Hibernian Rifles men who proceeded to Parliament Street with the Maynooth

Volunteers. He took up a position in Henry & James Clothiers at the corner of Parliament Street opposite City Hall, and fought from there until Wednesday. When he saw no possibility of getting back to the GPO, he evaded capture and ended his activity.

He joined E. Company, 1st Battalion, Dublin Brigade in 1917 and became adjutant. He was later appointed quartermaster of E. Company, and in 1918 was forced to go on the run for three months. He took the anti-Treaty side in the Civil War and took part in the occupation of the Fowler Hall. He also fought in the O'Connell Street area and was one of the defenders of the Sackville Club.

Frank Devine, of 8 O'Donovan Road, The Tenters, South Circular Road, died on April 2nd 1939, and was buried at Glasnevin Cemetery.

References:
RH; IMA, MSPC; *Irish Independent*, 5th April 1939, (obit).

Thomas (Tom) Devine: (1898 – 1969)
E. Coy, 3rd Batt, Dublin Company. Roll of Honour

Tom Devine was born in 1898 and was a member of E. Company, 3rd Battalion, Dublin Brigade. On Easter Monday he reported to the GPO, and was stationed at the ground floor windows. He was later sent to Ballybough and was one of the Volunteers who occupied Gilbey's Stores. On Tuesday evening this group returned to the GPO, and the next day he was involved in house to house tunneling in Henry Street and Mary Street area. He was part of the group that occupied O'Neill's Public House at the corner of Liffey Street, on Thursday. While there, they came under heavy fire and when their position became untenable, they returned to the GPO. On Friday evening he was beside The O'Rahilly, when he was mortally wounded on Moore Street. He turned into Riddles Row and stayed there until the surrender on the following day. He was released from detention in Richmond Barracks on May 12th, because of his young age.

He rejoined E. Company, 3rd Battalion in 1917, but was later excused from duty by Captain Liam Tannam, because of ill health. He later made an unsuccessful claim for a Military Disability Pension, stating that he got a chill while lying in wet clothes on a roof in Mary Street and on the Rotunda lawn during Rising. As a result of this he contracted bronchitis, which later developed into tuberculosis.

Tom Devine, of 101 Larkfield Grove, Harold's Cross, died on March 16th 1969 and was buried at Mount Jerome Cemetery, Harold's Cross.

References:
RH; IMA, MSPC; NLI, *Lynch Papers*, (Ms 11,131); Marcus Bourke, *The O'Rahilly*, (1967); *Irish Press*, 17th March 1969, (dn).

James (Seamus) Devoy: (- 1982)

Section Commander, (Corporal). B. Coy, 2nd Batt, Dublin Brigade.
Roll of Honour.

Seamus Devoy, a nephew of the Fenian leader, John Devoy, resided at 25 Fairview Strand. Like his uncle before him, he attended O'Connell Schools, North Richmond Street. He was a member of the Gaelic League and joined B. Company, 2nd Battalion, Dublin Brigade in 1913, taking part in the Howth gun-running the following year.

On Easter Monday he guarded Ballybough Bridge and the following day he returned to the GPO and was stationed at the windows on the Princes Street side of the building. He was promoted to lieutenant on Wednesday by Captain Liam Breen in the presence of James Connolly. He was put in charge of sixteen men and they attempted to blow up Nelson's Pillar. After the surrender, he was one of six Volunteers who carried the wounded James Connolly through the streets to Dublin Castle. He was then sent to several British prisons, before his release from Frongoch at Christmas, 1916.

He rejoined his old unit in 1917 and was promoted to adjutant with the rank of captain in 1918. He was arrested by Black & Tans in December 1920, and detained in the North Dublin Union until January 1921. He was associated with the Gate Theatre, where he played bit parts and later he was Stage Manager there for a period. In 1941 he became a member of the High Commissioner's staff in London and he retired in 1967. He lived for many years in England and in the United States, before returning to Ireland.

Seamus Devoy, of 34 Mount Dillon Court, Artane, died on January 31st 1982 and was buried at St Fintan's Cemetery, Sutton.

References:
RH; IMA, MSPC; NLI, *Lynch Papers*, (Ms 11,131); *Irish Independent*, 3rd February 1982, (dn); *Irish Times*, 26th February 1982, (an appreciation, Dan Bryan).

William (Liam) Dickenson

Liverpool Company, (Kimmage Garrison)

Liam Dickenson came to Dublin with the Liverpool Volunteers and was stationed at Larkfield, Kimmage, before the Rising. He reported to the GPO on Easter Monday and fought there until Wednesday, when he and Volunteer, Leo (Paddy) Scullin were sent to recover arms left at a house near Finglas Bridge. They failed to retrieve the weapons and when they attempted to return to the GPO on Thursday morning, they found themselves cut off. After several unsuccessful attempts to get through the military cordon, they set out for Athenry after the surrender, but were arrested at Tyrrelspass, County Westmeath.

References:
IMA, MSPC, (*Leo Patrick Scullin*).

Brigid Dixon (Bean Uí Faoithe)

Cumann na mBan, (Central Branch). Roll of Honour

Bríd Dixon, the daughter of Henry Dixon, a lifelong nationalist and Parnellite, joined Keating Branch of the Gaelic League on leaving school. She became a member of Cumann na mBan at its foundation, and marched in the uniform of Cumann na mBan at the funeral of O'Donovan Rossa to Glasnevin Cemetery in 1915. On Easter Monday, while spending a weekend at Howth with her family, she heard news that the Rising had begun. She proceeded to Dominic Street and then on to her home at 19 Cabra Road, which was by then in the possession of Volunteers from the Cabra Bridge outpost. She then accompanied her friend, Leslie Price, from Blessington Street to the GPO on Monday afternoon. On Wednesday she was sent to the Hibernian Bank, across the street from the GPO, with her sister, Grania and friends, Leslie Price and Mary Hanley. That afternoon the firing became so severe that they moved into the house next door to the bank. Soon afterwards Captain Thomas Weafer, who was a cousin of Mary Hanley, was mortally wounded. Later on Wednesday, she crossed the street with a group, which included a wounded Volunteer on a stretcher, into the GPO. That night, under the cover of darkness, she and her friend, Leslie Price went to the Father Matthew Hall in Church Street with a parcel of ammunition and dispatches. The following day, Seán McDermott advised about twenty Cumann na mBan women to leave the GPO, and on Friday P.H. Pearse sent them to Jervis Street Hospital with the wounded, under the protection of a white flag. Bríd, her sister Grania, and several others left the hospital, but were arrested as they made their way to Summerhill. They were taken under military escort to the Broadstone Station, where they were questioned before eventually being released. Her father, Henry, was deported to Wandsworth Jail and interned in Reading and Frongoch.

Bríd Dixon married Peter Fee and they lived at 3 Royse Road, Phibsboro.

References:
RH; NLI, *Lynch Papers*, (Ms 11,131); Ruth Taillon, *Women of 1916*, (1996).

James (Seamus) Donegan: (- 1966)

Manchester Company, (Kimmage Garrison)

Seamus Donegan was born in Dublin and he joined the Irish Volunteers in Manchester. He returned to Dublin prior to the Rising, and was stationed at Larkfield, Kimmage. His parent's address at the time was 6 Wye Street, Birkenhead. He served as a medical orderly in the GPO throughout Easter Week. Upon his detention after the Rising, he gave his address as 17 Grantham Street, Dublin. He was sent Stafford Jail on the 1st May and was interned in Frongoch until Christmas, 1916.

Seamus Donegan died on April 16th 1966.

References:
Ann Matthews, *The Kimmage Garrison, 1916*, (2010); *Irish Press*, 18th April 1966, (dn).

Charles (Charlie) Donnelly: (1892 – 1964)

E. Coy, 4th Batt, Dublin Brigade. Roll of Honour

Charlie Donnelly was born in 1892 and resided at 10 Willsbrook Terrace, Rathfarnham. He was employed as a grocer's assistant and he was sworn into the Fintan Lalor Circle of the IRB by Seán McDermott in 1912. He became a member of E. Company, 4th Battalion, Dublin Brigade in 1913, and was appointed a section commander in 1916.

On Easter Monday he left a wedding breakfast to cycle to Liberty Hall with twelve others, while the bulk of his Company travelled into the city later by tram. Included in this group was his brother-in-law, Jack Kealy, who was fatally wounded as he entered the GPO through a window in Princes Street. On Easter Monday he was engaged in erecting barricades both outside and inside the GPO under the supervision of The O'Rahilly. He then manned the barricades for the remainder of the week. On Friday, he was initially involved in moving explosives to the basement, but as the fire intensified and spread through the roof, he was part of the group who removed the explosives from the basement again. After the surrender, he was deported to the Knutsford Jail on May, 1st and was interned in Frongoch, until Christmas, 1916.

He rejoined his unit after his release and was appointed lieutenant. He was involved in many engagements during the War of Independence, and was arrested and interned in Mountjoy Jail in June 1919. He was in charge of the political prisoners there when the outbreak of cell-breaking and a hunger strike took place. He was a rate collector for Dáil Éireann during the War of Independence. He didn't take part in the Civil War.

He had a keen interest in Gaelic games and played football for Michael Dwyer's GFC and Geraldine's GFC, for many years. Later in life, he was a rates collector with Dublin County Council. Charlie Donnelly resided at Glenamoy, Grange Road, Rathfarnham, at the time of his death on June 29th 1964.

References:
RH; IMA, MSPC; *Sinn Féin Rebellion Handbook 1916*, Weekly Irish Times, (1917); *Irish Independent*, 30th June 1964, (obit).

Patrick (Paddy) Donnelly: (1873 - 1958)

E. Coy, 4th Batt, Dublin Brigade. Roll of Honour

Paddy Donnelly was born in Wexford in 1873, and he spent over 40 years living in Rathfarnham. He worked as a gardener for P.H. Pearse at St Enda's, and joined the Volunteers at its foundation in 1913. He was a member of E. Company, 4th Battalion, Dublin Brigade and fought in the GPO throughout Easter Week. After the surrender, he was deported to Stafford Jail on May 1st and then interned in Frongoch.

In 1917 he was made quartermaster of E. Company and his home at Whitechurch Cottages, Rathfarnham, was often raided during the War of Independence as a consequence. He took part in armed patrols in the city and the Rathmines area, and was involved in an ambush on Crown Forces at Kenilworth Square, Rathmines. During the Civil War he took the Republican side and was attached to the Intelligence Section of 4th Battalion, IRA.

In his early life, he was renowned for training Tug O' War teams, including All-Ireland Championship winners. Later in life, he was the green-keeper at the Grange Golf Club, Rathfarnham.

Paddy Donnelly died on January 8th 1958, and was buried in Mount Jerome Cemetery, Harold's Cross.

References:
RH; IMA, MSPC; *Irish Press*, 9th January 1958, (obit).

Eamon Dore: (1896 - 1972)

Limerick Volunteers. Roll of Honour

Eamon Dore was born in Glin, County Limerick, in 1896 and was educated at Rockwell College. He was initiated into the IRB by local organizer P.C. O'Mahony, while at Rockwell. In 1914, he was studying medicine in UCD and he became courier for the Supreme Council of the IRB.

He was in Limerick on Easter Monday and, on learning of the Rising, he travelled by train to Dublin with Laura and Nora Daly, the sisters of Commandant Ned Daly and Kathleen Clarke, wife of Thomas Clarke. He escorted Laura and Nora through the city streets to Kathleen's house in Fairview, and then returned to the GPO late on Tuesday night. In the GPO he was made bodyguard to Seán McDermott and on Wednesday he escorted Laura and Nora through the streets again. The sisters had been given dispatches for Volunteer Leaders in Munster and they bluffed their way through British Army lines to reach Kingsbridge Railway Station. He immediately re-traced his steps to the GPO, making a dash under gun-fire into the building. When the incendiary bombs descended on the GPO on Friday, the garrison was forced to move from floor to floor as the flames spread. He and a handful of Volunteers went into the cellar and removed a stash of homemade bombs to safety before they exploded. He was in the group, led by The O'Rahilly into Moore Street. He was not far from O'Rahilly when he was shot and he witnessed him fall. He was later deported to Stafford Jail on May 1st and was interned in Frongoch until Christmas, 1916. A year later, he married Nora Daly in their native city and for many years, they ran the family bakery and confectionary business in William Street in Limerick until it closed in 1959. Eamon Dore passed away in 1972, aged seventy six.

References:
RH; *Capuchin Annual*, 1966; Kathleen Clarke, *Revolutionary Woman*, (1991); Padraic O'Farrell, *Who's Who in the Irish War of Independence, 1916-1921*, (1997); Helen Litton, *Ned Daly*, (16Lives series, 2013).

Michael Dowling: (1898 - 1948)
F. Coy, 4th Batt, Dublin Brigade. Roll of Honour

Michael Dowling was born in 1898 and was part of a well known Republican family. He was a member of F. Company, 4th Battalion, Dublin Brigade and was involved in the Howth gun-running in 1914. He arrived at the GPO at midnight on Easter Monday with a party from F. Company, 4th Battalion, Dublin Brigade, from Larkfield, Kimmage. He was stationed in the GPO while a section of the group was sent to the Four Courts. He fought there throughout the week and was wounded in the foot in Moore Street after the evacuation on Friday evening. He was taken to the hospital at Dublin Castle, and the big toe on his left foot was amputated. He was later deported and interned in Frongoch until September 1916. His brothers, Andrew and John, were members of the Four Courts Garrison in Easter Week.

He rejoined his unit in 1917 and took part in many operations during the War of Independence. He was appointed lieutenant and was captured and interned from May to July, 1921. He fought on the Republican side in the Civil War and was a member of the Barry's Hotel Garrison. He continued fighting until his capture in October 1922 and was imprisoned in Mountjoy Jail and Tintown, the Curragh until September 1923.

Michael Dowling died on April 17th 1948 and was buried at Mulhuddart Cemetery, County Dublin.

References:
RH; IMA, MSPC; *Irish Press*, 20th April 1948, (obit).

Margaret (Peggy) Downey (Mrs. Peggy Viant)
Cumann na mBan, (Liverpool Branch)

Peggy Downey, her sister, Frances and a number of Cumann na mBan members, including Anastasia O'Loughlin and Kathleen Lynch, arrived in Dublin from Liverpool a few days before the Rising. On Easter Monday she was assigned to cooking duties in the charge of Desmond Fitzgerald. The Liverpool native, who had experience in catering, advised that the food stocks in the GPO would last three weeks. On Friday she escorted to the wounded to Jervis Street Hospital and spent the night there. She accompanied Louise Gavan-Duffy and Mae Murray to the Jacob's Garrison on Saturday, to inform Thomas McDonagh and Major McBride of the surrender.

She returned to Liverpool in May 1916, and when she moved to London a year later, she ceased her association with Cumann na mBan.

Peggy Viant, of 21 Belleview Close, Twickenham, Middlesex, surrendered her 1916 Military Service Pension in October 1962.

References:
IMA, MSPC; Max Caulfield, *The Easter Rebellion*, (1963); Thomas Coffey, *Agony at Easter*, (1969).

John J. Doyle: (1881 – 1972)

Commandant. G.H.Q. Brigade Medical Officer. C. Coy, 2nd Batt, Dublin Brigade. Roll of Honour

John J. Doyle was born in Dun Laoghaire, in 1881. His father was a painting contractor and chairman of the Bray Branch of the Land League, and was imprisoned for his Land League activities. After his father was jailed for one month, the family moved to Dublin, where John took a first aid course with the Catholic Boys Brigade, Church Street. He later became an instructor with the City of Dublin St John's Ambulance Association. In 1912 the Dublin St John's Ambulance Brigade became associated with the British Naval Auxiliary Medical Service and he attended a number of training courses with the Navy. When World War One broke out in 1914, he saw service as a member of the British Naval Auxiliaries, on ships transporting the wounded back to England. He was already a member of C. Company, 2nd Battalion, Dublin Brigade, and when he returned to Dublin in 1915 he was appointed Dublin Brigade Medical Officer of the Volunteers and he organised and trained a number of Volunteers and Cumann na mBan women in first aid. On Easter Monday he organized the commandeering of a lorry at Fairview to transport medical supplies from Father Mathew Park to the GPO, and he followed on afterwards with a party of fifty or so men, arriving there at five o'clock. He attended to a number of wounded men in the GPO with the help of his orderly, Tom Mason and some Cumann na mBan nurses. When James Connolly received a serious ankle wound on Thursday, he performed an operation with Jim Ryan (then still a medical student) and Dr. M. O'Mahony of the Indian Medical Service, who was a prisoner. On Friday he led the party carrying the wounded from the Coliseum Theatre to Jervis Street Hospital, under the protection of a Red Cross flag and as he and his party returned to Henry Street, they were taken prisoner. He was interrogated in Dublin Castle and on Sunday morning he and five or six other Red Cross men were released.

When the Volunteers were reorganised after the Rising, he formed a medical unit and served through the War of Independence. He attended the wounded Dan Breen and Commandant Paddy Daly, after the Ashtown Ambush in 1919. He took the Republican side in the Civil War and he was imprisoned in Wellington Barracks, South Circular Road and Mountjoy Jail after the fall of the Four Courts and Moran's Hotel.

John J. Doyle, of 48 Cabra Drive, died on December 19th 1972 and was buried at Glasnevin Cemetery.

References:
RH; IMA, MSPC; NLI, *Lynch Papers*, (Ms 11,131); *Evening Herald*, 20th December 1972.

John Doyle: (1894 - 1952)

C. Coy, 2nd Batt, Dublin Brigade. Roll of Honour

John Doyle was born in 1894 and resided at Mountpelior Hill, Arbour Hill. He was a member of C. Company, 2nd Battalion, Dublin Brigade and fought in the GPO during Easter Week. He was later deported and interned in Frongoch, until July 25th 1916.

He rejoined his unit in 1917, and served through the War of Independence. In April 1918 he was arrested following a raid for arms in Rathmines. He was court-martialed and sentenced to five years penal servitude. He was released in 1919, and took part in the attack on the Customs House in May, 1921. After the Truce, he joined the CID and was wounded during the Civil War. He was attached to the Special Branch in Dublin Castle for a period and was later appointed to the Rathmines District and served there until his retirement in August 1949.

John Doyle, of 137 McDowell Avenue, Mount Brown, died on January 14th 1952 and was buried at Mount Jerome Cemetery, Harold's Cross.

References:
RH; IMA, MSPC; *Irish Independent* & *Irish Press*, 15th January 1952, (obits).

John J. Doyle: (1889 - 1961)

E. Coy, 2nd Batt, Dublin Brigade. Roll of Honour

John Doyle was born in 1889 and resided at 8 Harbour Road, Bullock, Dalkey. He was a member of E. Company, 2nd Battalion, Dublin Brigade, and on Easter Monday he was posted to Fairview and was placed as a sentry at Ballybough Bridge. The following day he was part of the group that destroyed the railway tracks at Fairview. The noise from the resulting explosion brought British troops from Amiens Street to investigate. The British suffered a number of casualties when they came under fire from the Volunteers. He marched into the GPO on Tuesday in a party led by Captain Vincent Poole of the Irish Citizen Army. On Wednesday he was stationed at the first floor windows in the GPO and the following day, took up a position on the roof, where he engaged with an enemy sniper in one of the buildings overlooking O'Connell Bridge. He left the burning GPO on Friday and spent the night in the houses in Moore Street. After the surrender, he was deported to Stafford Jail on May 1st and then interned in Frongoch, until Christmas, 1916.

After his release from internment, he joined B. Company, 3rd Battalion, Dublin Brigade, and in January 1919 he was interned at Mountjoy and later Maryborough Jail, where he went on hunger strike. He was released from prison in October 1919 and GHQ of the IRA sent him to the United States to work with the Irish Republican Mission. He worked his passage on board a ship back to Ireland in September 1920, and was appointed lieutenant with B. Company, 3rd Battalion. He was involved in numerous attacks on British Forces in the area known as the "Dardenelles", around Camden Street and Aungier Street, and took part in the operation on Bloody Sunday, November 21st 1920, when a number of British Agents were shot. Arrested in April 1921, he was deported to Dartmoor Prison, where he was badly beaten by prison warders and hospitalised for several weeks. He was released from prison on January 1922 and returned to Ireland. He didn't take part in the Civil War.

John Doyle, of 4 Summerhill Avenue, Dun Laoghaire, died on November 26th 1961 and was buried at Deansgrange Cemetery.

References:

RH; IMA, MSPC; NLI, *Lynch Papers*, (Ms 11,131); *Irish Independent* & *Irish Press*, 27th November 1961, (obits).

John Doyle: (1897-   )

Hibernian Rifles. Roll of Honour

John Doyle lived at 8 Church Lane, Lower Kevin Street, and was a member of the Hibernian Rifles. On Easter Monday he was in the group of thirty Hibernian Rifle men, under the command of Captain J. J. Scollan, held in reserve at their headquarters at 28 North Frederick Street. They were given orders to proceed to the GPO at midnight, and they immediately set about breaking and barricading the upper windows. He was photographed with Tom McGrath on Tuesday by Joe Cripps on the ground floor of the building. This photograph is one of two widely published photographs taken in the GPO in  Easter Week. He was deported to Stafford Jail on May 1st and later interned in Frongoch, until July 15th 1916.

Later in life, John Doyle resided at 39 Cuffe Street.

References:
RH.

Edward Doyle: (1883 – 1948)

Irish Citizen Army

Edward Doyle was born in County Wicklow in 1883. He was employed as a labourer in an ironworks foundry, when he joined the Irish Citizen Army in 1915. He left Liberty Hall on Easter Monday and reported to the GPO, where he served until Tuesday. He was posted to Hopkins & Hopkins, Eden Quay and fought there and in the Dublin Bread Company until Thursday, and spent that night in the houses in Moore Street. After the surrender, he was deported to Knutsford Jail on May 1st, and was interned in Frongoch until July 16th, 1916.

He rejoined the Irish Citizen Army after his release from internment and served throughout the War of Independence.

Edward Doyle, of 13 Broadstone Avenue, Phibsboro, died on January 12th 1948 and was buried at Avoca, County Wicklow.

References:
    IMA, MSPC; *Irish Independent*, 13th January 1948.

Peter (Peadar) Doyle: (1887 - 1976)

B. Coy, 1st Batt, Dublin Brigade. Roll of Honour

Peadar Doyle, of 74 Summerhill, Dublin, was born in 1887 and was a bricklayer by trade. He was sworn into the IRB in 1907, and joined the Volunteers in 1913. He was a member of B. Company, 1st Battalion, Dublin Brigade and was involved in the Howth gun-running in 1914. On Easter Monday he was mobilised at his home by Lieutenant Frank Daly. He proceeded with a small party under Frank Daly's command, to the railway bridge at Connaught Street, Phibsborough, before reporting to the GPO. He was engaged in barricading the ground floor windows and later spent the week stationed at the Princes Street entrance, where he allowed couriers in and out through the barricade. After the evacuation, he spent Friday night in the houses in Moore Street. He was deported to Knutsford Jail on May 3rd and interned in Frongoch, until July 14th, 1916.

He rejoined his unit at its reorganization, and served through the War of Independence. He took part in many operations, including an ambush at the Rotunda Hospital, Parnell Street, and an arms raid at Findlater's Place. He took the anti-Treaty side in the Civil War and was involved in the taking over of the Fowler Hall. He later fought at Barry's Hotel and at the Hamman Hotel, O'Connell Street. For many years he was an employee of the Gas Company, Ringsend and lived at 114 St Declan's Road, Marino and later at 65 Blarney Park, Crumlin.

Peadar Doyle died on December 14th 1976 and was buried at Kilbarrack Cemetery.

References:
    RH; IMA, MSPC; NLI, *Lynch Papers*, (Ms 11,131); *Evening Herald*, 15th December 1976, (dn).

Patrick (Paddy) Drury: (1892 – 1977)
Irish Citizen Army

Paddy Drury was born in 1892 and resided at 9 Annesley Square, North Strand. He was a printer by trade, and was a member of the Irish Citizen Army. On Easter Monday he was engaged in conveying ammunition and supplies from Liberty Hall to the GPO. He was in the group under the command of Captain Frank Thornton, sent to reinforce the garrison at City Hall on Monday evening. As they approached the Crown Alley Telephone Exchange, they came under heavy enemy fire and were forced to retreat to positions in the Fleet Street and Westmoreland Street area. They were ordered to return to the GPO on Tuesday morning and he was sent to the Imperial Hotel. He fought there until Thursday night, when the burning building was evacuated and he made his way back to the GPO. After the evacuation of the GPO on Friday evening, he evaded capture.

He joined F. Company, 1st Battalion, Dublin Brigade, in 1917 and was transferred to the Active Service Unit in April 1920. He became Michael Collins's chief courier and took part in many engagements during the War of Independence. He joined the Free State Army in July 1922, and was demobilised in March 1924 with the rank of lieutenant.

Paddy Drury, of 20 Marino Park Ave, died on May 21st 1977 and was buried at Glasnevin Cemetery.

References:
  IMA, MSPC.

Edward Duffy: (1898 - 1951)
F. Coy, 4th Batt, Dublin Brigade. Roll of Honour

Edward Duffy was born in 1898 and resided at River Road Cottage, Castleknock, in 1916. He was a member of F. Company, 4th Battalion, Dublin Brigade and on Easter Monday he reported to Larkfield, Kimmage, with his father, Christopher. They proceeded to the GPO at midnight and he served there throughout the week, while his father was sent with some of F. Company to the Four Courts. After the surrender, he was deported to Stafford Jail on May 1st and interned in Frongoch, until July 21st 1916. When the Volunteers re-organised in 1917, he rejoined his unit and served in the War of Independence. He fought in the Civil War on the Republican side in the Dublin city area.

During the Emergency he was a member of the Irish Army.

Edward Duffy, of 2 Convent View, Cabra, died on August 20th 1951.

References:
  RH; IMA, MSPC; *Irish Press*, 21st August 1951.

Joseph (Joe) Duffy: (1892 - 1972)

Liverpool Company, (Kimmage Garrison). Roll of Honour

Joe Duffy was born in 1892 and lived in Liverpool. He became a member of the IRB in Liverpool in 1910, and joined the Volunteers in that city in 1913. He travelled to Dublin in February 1916 and joined the Volunteer Camp at Larkfield, Kimmage, where he was engaged in making munitions. He left Larkfield for the GPO on Easter Monday morning with the Kimmage Garrison, and that night he was sent with a detachment to Fairview. He served there, under Captain Frank Henderson, until Tuesday evening, when the column marched into the GPO. He was stationed on the roof of the GPO until forced down later in the week by the bombardment. After the surrender he was deported to Stafford Jail on May 1st and interned in Frongoch until Christmas, 1916.

He joined F. Company, 2nd Battalion in 1917, but shortly after he went to England seeking employment and took no further part in IRA activities.

Joe Duffy, of 132 Cooley Road, Drimnagh, died on May 13th 1972 and was buried at Deansgrange Cemetery.

References:
RH; IMA, MSPC; NLI, *Lynch Papers*, (Ms 11,131); Ann Matthews, *The Kimmage Garrison, 1916*, (2010); *Evening Herald*, 15th May 1972, (dn).

Louise Gavan Duffy: (1884 – 1969)

Executive Member, Cumann na mBan

Louise Gavan Duffy was born in Nice, France, in 1884. She was daughter of Charles Gavan Duffy, the Young Irelander, and one of the founders of the Nation newspaper. Her brother George, who defended Roger Casement in Court, was a signatory of the Anglo-Irish Treaty and was later Minister for Foreign Affairs in the 1st Dáil. When her father died in 1903, Louise returned to Ireland. She entered UCD, graduating with a Bachelor of Arts in 1911 and later with a Master of Arts in 1916. She was a founder member of Cumann na mBan and was an Executive Member in 1916. During

Easter Week she was in charge of the Cumann na mBan members in the GPO and worked day and night in the kitchen and first aid centre. She was one of a small group of women who refused P.H. Pearse's order to vacate the burning building on Friday. She was sent to Jacob's on the Saturday to notify the garrison there of the surrender and later evaded arrest.

She was renowned for her promotion of the Irish language and she founded Scoil Bhríde, the first all-girl's school in Dublin, in 1917. She served with Cumann na mBan throughout the War of Independence and at the outbreak of the Civil War she supported the pro-Treaty side, but took no further active part in politics. She was awarded an Honorary Degree of Doctor of Law by UCD in 1948.

Louise Gavan Duffy, of 24 Cabra Road, Phibsboro, died on October 12th 1969 and was buried at Glasnevin Cemetery.

References:

NLI, *Lynch Papers*, (Ms 11,131); Thomas Coffey, *Agony at Easter*, (1969); Clair Willis, *Dublin 1916, the Siege of the GPO*, (2009).

Francis (Frank) Dunne: (1894 - 1965)
E. Coy, 2nd Batt, Dublin Brigade. Roll of Honour

Frank Dunne was born in 1894 and resided at 1 Clonmore Road, Ballybough. He was a bookbinder by trade, and joined the Volunteers at the Rotunda in 1913. He was a member of E. Company, 2nd Battalion, Dublin Brigade, and on Easter Monday he reported to Father Mathew Park, Fairview and served in the Annesley Bridge area. He moved into the GPO on Tuesday evening with the Fairview contingent, and fought there until the evacuation on Friday evening. He was deported to Wakefield Prison on May 6th and interned in Frongoch, until July 25th, 1916. He rejoined his unit in 1917 and served until 1919, when he ceased activities because of his failing health.

Frank Dunne, of 149 Clonliffe Avenue, Ballybough, died on October 12th 1965 and was buried at Glasnevin Cemetery.

References:

RH; IMA, MSPC; *Evening Herald*, 12th October 1965.

John Dunne: (1898 - 1960)
D. Coy, 2nd Batt, Dublin Brigade. Roll of Honour

John Dunne was born in 1898 and, in 1916, was employed as a barman at J.J. Healy's Public House, 93 Parnell Street. He a member of D. Company, 2nd Battalion, Dublin Brigade and he reported to the GPO on Easter Monday with Richard Healy, the nephew of J.J. Healy. He was sent across the street to take up guard-duty at Reis's Chambers. The next day he was engaged in clearing looters from the vicinity, before returning to Reis's until Thursday. He left the GPO on Friday evening at the evacuation. After the surrender he was detained in Richmond Barracks but was released on May 22nd because of his young age.

He later went to work in County Tipperary and for many years resided at Denis Lacey Terrace, Templemore.

John Dunne died on February 27th 1960 and was buried in Templemore, County Tipperary.

References:

RH; NLI, *Lynch Papers*, (Ms 11,131); *Irish Independent* & *Irish Press*, 1st March 1960, (obits).

Joseph Dunne: (1891 - 1967)

B. Coy, 1st Batt, Dublin Brigade. Roll of Honour

Joseph Dunne was born in 1891 and resided at 14 Upper Liffey Street, Dublin. He joined the Volunteers in 1914 and was a member of B. Company, 1st Battalion, Dublin Brigade. He was employed as a taxi driver with Thompson's Motors, North Brunswick Street, in 1916. On Easter Sunday he was sent by P.H. Pearse with a dispatch to Seamus Rafter in Enniscorthy, County Wexford. On his return the next day, he went to the Fairyhouse Races and from there he reported to the GPO. He fought in the GPO alongside his brother, Thomas, until the evacuation. He was deported to Stafford Jail on May 1st and interned in Frongoch until Christmas 1916.

After his release from internment, he rejoined B. Company, 1st Battalion in early 1917, providing transport for the movement of arms and ammunition in the Dublin area. He found employment as a chauffeur in 1918, which necessitated leaving Dublin and he ceased to take part in Volunteer activity.

He later lived at 7 Grace Park Avenue, Drumcondra and was an employee of the B&I Steampacket Company, North Wall.

Joseph Dunne died on June 20th 1967 and was buried at St Fintan's Cemetery, Sutton.

References:
RH; IMA, MSPC; IMA, BMH (WS 329, *Garry Holahan*); *Evening Herald*, 21st June 1967, (dn).

Thomas Dunne: (1894 - 1961)

B. Coy, 1st Batt, Dublin Brigade. Roll of Honour

Thomas Dunne was born in 1894 and resided at 14 Upper Liffey Street. He was employed in the Dublin Corporation Waterworks Dept, in 1916. He fought alongside his brother, Joseph, in the GPO on Easter Week. He was engaged in erecting barricades in Middle Abbey Street on Easter Monday, and was later stationed at the ground floor windows in the GPO. He was deported with Joseph to Stafford Jail on May 1st and interned in Frongoch, until Christmas, 1916.

He rejoined his unit in March 1917 and was involved in anti-conscription activity in 1918. He took no further part with Volunteers after 1918.

He was a former employee of Dublin Corporation and resided at 60 Gledswood Park, Clonskeagh and later at 56 Casino Road, Marino.

Thomas Dunne died on August 15th 1961 and was buried at St Fintan's Cemetery, Sutton.

References:
RH; IMA, MSPC; *Irish Independent*, 16th August 1961, (dn).

Michael Dwyer: (1899 - 1943)
Irish Citizen Army, (Gloucester St Section). Roll of Honour

Michael Dwyer was born in 1899 and resided at 20 Rutland Cottages, Lower Rutland Street. He was the son of Patrick Dwyer, who was born in Capetown, South Africa and was a timber sawyer by trade. He joined the Irish Citizen Army before the Rising and was attached to the Gloucester Street Section. On Easter Monday he was in a party sent from Liberty Hall to take control of Harcourt Street Railway Station. He was later stationed at a barricade at Hatch Street and was sent to the College of Surgeons on Wednesday. He was then sent with a dispatch to an address at Henrietta Street. He could not get back to the College of Surgeons, so he joined the GPO Garrison and remained there until the evacuation on Friday evening. After the surrender, he was detained at Richmond Barracks and released on May 24th, because of his youth.

He served with the Irish Citizen Army from 1917 until the Truce. He joined the Free State Army in 1922 and served with the Dublin Guards until his discharge in September 1923, with the rank of sergeant major.

He later lived at 32 Glencorp Road, Ellenfield, Whitehall and was a member of the 1916 Veterans Association.

Michael Dwyer died on April 3rd 1943 and was buried at Mount Jerome Cemetery, Harold's Cross.

References:
RH; IMA, MSPC; *Irish Independent*, 6th April 1943, (dn).

Albert Dyas: (1899 – 1960)
Fianna Eireann, Céad Sluagh. Roll of Honour

Albert Dyas was born in 1899 and resided at 96 Haddington Road. He became a member of Fianna Éireann, Céad Sluagh, at Camden Street, in 1912. He fought throughout Easter Week in the GPO, and was in the party led by The O'Rahilly into Moore Street on Friday evening. When John Kenny was shot several times, Dyas and Seán Conway carried their wounded comrade to safety while under intense gunfire themselves. After the surrender, he was detained in Richmond Barracks and later released from their on May 12th, because of his young age.

In 1917 he helped re-organise his company of Fianna Éireann and served until his transfer to the Volunteers later that year. He took no part in War of Independence or the Civil War. For many years he worked, as a foreman compositor, in Monson & Robinson Printers, Talbot Street, Dublin.

Albert Dyas, of 33 Seafort Avenue, Sandymount, died on July 11th 1960 and was buried at Deansgrange Cemetery.

References:
RH; IMA, MSPC; *Irish Press*, 13th July 1960, (dn).

John (Jack) Early: (1896 - 1966)
C. Coy, 2nd Batt, Dublin Brigade. Roll of Honour

Jack Early was born in 1896 and joined C. Company, 2nd Battalion, Dublin Brigade, in March 1916. He was not mobilised on Easter Monday and reported to the GPO later that day. He was in front of the GPO when the Lancers charged down Sackville Street. On Tuesday he was sent to outposts in Henry Street and Liffey Street, and later that evening he was sent with a dispatch to Commandant Ned Daly in the Four Courts. He remained with the Four Courts Garrison and was at a barricade at Mary's Lane until Saturday, when he was sent to North King Street. After the surrender he was deported to Stafford Jail on May 1st and interned in Frongoch until July 28th 1916.

On his release from internment, he settled in Liverpool and took part in numerous operations with the local Volunteers there, before returning to Ireland in 1921. He rejoined C. Company and served through the War of Independence. He fought on the anti-Treaty side in the Civil War and was a member of the Four Courts Garrison. After the surrender he was interned until October 1922. He was a civil servant, based at the labour exchange on Gardiner Street, for over thirty years.

Jack Early, of 49 Shelmartin Avenue, Marino, died on November 24th 1966 and was buried in Glasnevin Cemetery.

References:
RH; IMA, MSPC; *Irish Independent*, 25th November 1966, (obit); *Irish Press*, 26th November 1966, (obit).

William Egan: (1898 - 1985)
Irish Citizen Army, (Capel St Section)

William Egan was born in 1898 and resided at 98 Capel Street. He was a member of the Irish Citizen Army and was attached to Capel Street, No.4 Section. He was part of the GPO Garrison in Easter Week. He was sent to a house adjacent to the Evening Mail Offices in Parliament Street on Easter Monday. On Tuesday evening he was forced to withdraw with Nicholas Burke of the Hibernian Rifles. As they attempted to return to the GPO, they were both arrested near Crown Alley Telephone Exchange and taken to Great Ship Street Barracks for interrogation.

He was released from Richmond Barracks on May 12th, because of his young age.

He served with the Irish Citizen Army during the War of Independence, and joined the Free State Army in May 1922. He served in Kerry during the Civil War and was discharged in 1924.

He emigrated to the United States, sometime later in the 1920s. In April 1979, while attending the unveiling of a statue outside the Nassau City Courthouse in New York, he stated that when the Volunteers broke into the GPO, they had made their confession and received communion, and were ready to die.

William Egan passed away in New York on April 26th 1985.

References:

IMA, MSPC; *Irish Independent*, 14th August 1976, (*Dublin visit,* na); *Evening Herald*, April 1979, (*1916 monument unveiling in New York,* na).

Marie English: (1887 – 1968)

Cumann na mBan, (Árd Craobh Branch). Roll of Honour

Marie English was born in 1887 and joined the Árd Craobh Branch of Cumann na mBan, one week before the Easter Rising. She assisted the Volunteers who restored the wireless equipment in Reis's Chambers, at the corner of Sackville Street and Lower Abbey Street on Easter Tuesday. The first message was sent at 5.30 p.m. on Tuesday. She also helped to prepare a field hospital next door to the Hibernian Bank. On Wednesday, when the wireless equipment was removed from Reis's, she carried supplies under fire across the street to the GPO. She returned to the field hospital and later that evening was ordered to go home for some rest. On Thursday morning she was arrested on the North Circular Road as she returned to the GPO, but was released shortly afterwards. Paddy Belton sent her to collect AOH money and ammunition and deliver them to Thomas Ashe in Ashbourne on Friday, and she returned to the GPO with a message from Ashe to James Connolly.

During the War of Independence she was involved in the Prisoners Dependents Fund and anti-conscription work. She took the Republican side in the Civil War. She brought medical supplies to the Four Courts Garrison and supplied and cooked food for those in the Hickey's, North Earl Street headquarters. She also assisted men on the run.

Marie English, of 12 Wigan Road, Drumcondra, died at her residence on January 2nd 1968, and was buried at Glasnevin Cemetery.

References:

RH; IMA, MSPC; *Evening Herald*, 3rd January 1968, (dn).

Patrick (Paddy) English: (1894 – 1970)

F. Coy, 4th Batt, Dublin Brigade. Roll of Honour

Paddy English was born in 1894 and lived at Dunsink Cottages, Castleknock. He was employed as a gardener on Lord Holmpatrick's estate, at Abbotstown. He was a member of F. Company, 4th Battalion, Dublin Brigade and fought in the GPO during Easter Week. After the surrender he was deported to Stafford Jail on May 1st. He was later transferred to Wormwood Scrubs and then interned in Frongoch until Christmas, 1916.

After his release from Frongoch, he lost his job and he and his parents were evicted from their home because he had taken part in the Rising. He was a keen Gaelic footballer and played for St Margaret's before the Rising. When Erin's Isle was formed in Finglas in 1917, he became a prominent member and togged out for the club throughout the 1920s.

Paddy English, of 16 Dubber Cross, Finglas, died on January 27th 1970 and was buried at Glasnevin Cemetery.

References:
RH; IMA, MSPC; John Campbell & Liam Casey, *A History of Erin's Isle GAA Club*, (2000); *Evening Herald*, 28th January 1970, (dn).

Patrick Francis English: (1879 – 1949)

F. Coy, 1st Batt, Dublin Brigade. Roll of Honour

Patrick English was born in 1879 and was a member of F. Company, 1st Battalion, Dublin Brigade. He had been in Ballinasloe on Easter Saturday, before returning to his home in Sutton. He didn't receive any mobilisation notice, and was unsuccessful in getting in touch with his company, so he decided to walk into the city on Easter Monday. After he spent Tuesday at a friend's house, he reported to the Imperial Hotel on Wednesday morning. He fought there, under the command of Captain Frank Thornton, until fire forced the Volunteers to evacuate the building on Thursday night. He escorted a group of Cumann na mBan women to the Pro-Cathedral on Friday and was captured and taken to the Custom House, where he was detained until Saturday. He convinced his interrogators that he had been engaged in first aid work in the Imperial Hotel and was released on Sunday. After the reorganization of the Volunteers in 1917, he rejoined his unit and served until October 1918, when he contracted pneumonia and was declared unfit for further service.

For many years, he was manager of the National Bank, 32 Main Street, Blackrock, County Dublin.

Patrick English died at his residence at 18 Temple Crescent, Blackrock, on March 24th 1949.

References:
RH; IMA, MSPC; NLI, *Lynch Papers*, (Ms 11,131); *Irish Press*, 25th March 1949, (dn).

Thomas (Tom) Ennis: (1892 - 1945)

E. Coy, 2nd Batt, Dublin Brigade. Roll of Honour

Tom Ennis was born in 1892 and resided at 3 Richmond Cottages, North Circular Road. He was employed as a checker with the M.G.W. Railway. In 1913 he joined the Volunteers, and a year later he became a member of E. Company, 2nd Battalion, Dublin Brigade. He was part of the GPO Garrison in Easter Week. He was stationed in the tower of the Dublin Bread Co. early in the week, and only reluctantly left his position after being ordered to do so by James Connolly. From there, he joined the Volunteers in North Earl Street, before he withdrew to the GPO. After the surrender he was deported to Stafford Jail on May 1st and interned in Frongoch until Christmas, 1916.

He rejoined his old unit on his release from internment and fought in the War of Independence. In 1921, men from 2nd Battalion under his command, were responsible for the destruction of the Custom House. He was severely wounded in the leg during this operation, but evaded capture. In 1922 he joined the Free State Army with the rank of major general, and he led the attack on the Republican forces in the Four Courts. When Cork was taken by pro-Treaty forces, he refused to have any Republicans in the area executed and he was generally considered a good soldier by the anti-Treaty side. He retired from the army in 1924 and later became a park superintendent, based in the Phoenix Park.

He was an accomplished footballer and hurler and was on the panel of the Dublin Junior All-Ireland Championship winning side in 1916. He captained St Laurence O'Toole's to their first Dublin Senior Football Championship title in 1918 and played on a further three championship winning sides, before the Custom House injury ended his career. In later years he became a well known golfer and was captain of Elm Park Golf Club.

Tom Ennis died on March 10th 1945 and was buried at St Fintan's Cemetery, Sutton.

References:
RH; IMA, MSPC; *Dublin's Fighting Story*, (1949); Thomas Coffey, *Agony at Easter*, (1969); Calton Younger, *Ireland's Civil War*, (1970); Michael Hopkinson, *Green Against Green: the Irish Civil War*, (1988); Michael Foley, *The Bloodied Field*, (2014); *Sunday Independent*, 11th March 1945, (obit); *Irish Press*, 12th March 1945, (obit).

Robert Eustace: (1895 – 1918)

Irish Citizen Army

Robert Eustace was born in 1895 and resided at 24 Gloucester Street. He was a carpenter by trade and a member of the Irish Citizen Army.

On Easter Monday he fought at the Vitriol Works, Ballybough, under the command of Captain Vincent Poole. He moved to the GPO on Tuesday evening with the main body of men from the Fairview area and fought there throughout Easter Week.

Robert Eustace died on August 23RD 1918 and was buried at Glasnevin Cemetery.

In 1925 Mrs Margaret Eustace made an unsuccessful pension claim, stating that her son, Robert, had supported her financially during his lifetime and that he had been wounded in the neck during Easter Week. Colonel Michael Costello, Director of Intelligence, GHQ, stated in October 1925 that "Robert Eustace fought with the Irish Citizen Army at Clontarf (*Vitriol Works, Ballybough*) and later at the GPO in Easter 1916. He was a first-class soldier who fought with bravery and determination in 1916." He also stated that he was not wounded during that period, but died of natural causes, described as a disease of the throat.

References:
IMA, MSPC.

Margaret Fagan (Mrs. Margaret MacSherry): (1899 – 1964)

Clan na nGael Girl Scouts. Roll of Honour

Margaret Fagan was born in 1899 and was a member of Clan na nGael Girl Scouts, who were attached to the Hibernian Rifles. She reported to the GPO on Easter Monday, and helped with cooking and other duties, including carrying dispatches. James Connolly sent her to the College of Surgeons with a dispatch for Countess Markievicz on Wednesday. On Thursday she was sent to the North Dublin Union and returned to the GPO with a message from Commandant Ned Daly in the Four Courts. On Friday she among a group of women arrested at North Circular Road after they had escorted the wounded Volunteers to Jervis Street Hospital. She was taken to Broadstone Station for interrogation and was released shortly afterwards.

In September 1917 she joined the Ranelagh Branch of Cumann na mBan and was engaged in collecting for the Prisoners Dependents Fund and in election work. In October 1920 she went to Mountmellick, County Laois and set up a branch of Cumann na mBan. During the Civil War she took the anti-Treaty side and was involved in the occupation of 11 Harcourt Street. She joined the Republican ASU under the command of Peadar White, and her home was used as an arms dump and wounded IRA men were treated there. She later joined the IRA. column at Blessington, County Wicklow. She was married to James MacSherry, who was interned in the Civil War. Her brother, Brian Fagan, was badly wounded at the South Dublin Union during the Easter Rising.

Margaret MacSherry died on July 26th 1964 and was buried at Glasnevin Cemetery.

References:
RH; IMA, MSPC; *Irish Independent*, 27th July 1964, (dn).

Michael Finnegan: (1874 – 1945)
Irish Citizen Army, (Church St Section). Roll of Honour

Michael Finnegan was born in 1874 and resided at 4 Usher's Lane, Ushers's Quay. He joined the Irish Citizen Army at its formation in 1914, and was a member of the Church Street Section. He escorted a dray full of arms from Liberty Hall to the GPO on Easter Monday. He was part of the group, under the command of Captain Frank Thornton that was sent from the GPO to reinforce the Irish Citizen Army Garrison at City Hall. When they came under enemy fire, they retreated and occupied Delahunty's Public House in Fleet Street. They remained there that night and returned to the GPO the following morning. He was then sent to the Imperial Hotel and fought there until the evacuation on Thursday night. He was later arrested in the Pro-Cathedral, Marlborough Street and detained in the Custom House. He convinced his interrogators that he had been on his way to work when he was arrested, and was released after a week. He did not take part in the War of Independence.

Michael Finnegan, of 2 White's Cottages, Summerhill, died in 1945.

References:
RH; IMA, MSPC.

Desmond Fitzgerald: (1888 – 1947)
Staff Captain. G.H.Q. Roll of Honour

Thomas Joseph Fitzgerald was born in London, on February 13th 1888. He changed his name to Desmond in his teens, because he considered the name more romantic. He travelled to Brittany at the age of twenty and was fluent in many languages. He first visited Ireland in 1910, and the following year he married Mabel McConnell from Belfast in London. They shared an interest in the Irish language, and after their marriage they lived in Brittany. On returning to live in Kerry in 1913, he organised the Volunteers in the county. At this time he was also involved with the Imagist group of poets. He was arrested in 1915, sentenced to six months imprisonment and expelled from Kerry for making a political speech. As a result, the family moved to Bray, County Wicklow.

During Easter Week he was in charge of the commissariat in the GPO. Mabel also served in the GPO. After the Rising he was sentenced to life imprisonment, which was commuted to twenty years penal servitude. He spent two years in English prisons, including Lewes Jail, and after his release, he was elected Sinn Féin MP for the Dublin Pembroke constituency in 1918. He was appointed Director of Publicity for Dáil Éireann in 1919 and was also editor of the *Irish Bulletin*. He was again imprisoned in 1921, but was released at the time of the Truce.

He supported the Anglo Irish Treaty and became Minister for External Affairs in the Free State Government from 1922 to 1927. From 1927 to 1932, he was Minister for Defence and was Ireland's representative at the League of Nations and at Imperial Conferences. He was TD for Dublin County from 1922 to 1932 and following the defeat of the Cumann na nGaedheal, he was TD for Carlow County from 1932 to 1937. He was a member of the Seanad from 1938 to 1943, the year he retired from politics.

He had a play, *"The Saints"*, produced by the Abbey Theatre in 1919 and he published books on poetry and the philosophy of politics.

He had four sons, Desmond, Pierce, Fergus and the youngest Garrett, who was Minister for Foreign Affairs in the 1970's and served two terms as Taoiseach in the 1980s. Desmond Fitzgerald died in Dublin on April 9th 1947 and was buried at Glasnevin Cemetery.

References:

RH; *DIB*, (James Quinn, Ed, (2009); Max Caulfield, *The Easter Rebellion*, (1963); Thomas Coffey, *Agony at Easter*, (1969); Michael Foy & Brian Barton, *The Easter Rising*, (1999); Desmond Fitzgerald, *Desmond's Rising: memoirs, from 1913 to Easter 1916*, (2006); Charles Townshend, *Easter 1916: the Irish Rebellion*, (2006); Clair Willis, *Dublin 1916, the Siege of the GPO*, (2009); Diarmaid Ferriter, *A Nation and not a Rabble: the Irish Revolution, 1913-23*, (2015); *Irish Independent* & *Irish Press*, 10th April 1947, (obits).

John Fitzharris: (1894 - 1944)
E. Coy, 2nd Batt, Dublin Brigade. Roll of Honour

John Fitzharris was born in 1894 and resided at 2 Oriel Place. He joined E. Company, 2nd Battalion, Dublin Brigade, in 1914. On Easter Monday he went with members of E. Company, 2nd Battalion, to St Stephen's Green. He was sent to a house in Kevin's Street, where he covered the main group entering Jacob's Factory. He returned home that night and reported to the GPO early on Tuesday morning. He was posted to Henry Street and fought there and from the GPO until the evacuation on Friday evening. He spent Friday night in the houses in Moore Street, before the surrender on Saturday afternoon. He was deported to Stafford Jail on May 1st and interned in Frongoch until Christmas 1916.

In 1917 he rejoined his unit but took no further active part. A fine hurler, he was a lifelong supporter of St Laurence O'Toole's. He played on their minor teams in 1910 and 1911 and still figured on the senior team in the early 1920s. He was employed in the Woollen Mills for over thirty years.

John Fitzharris died on October 18th 1944 and was buried at Glasnevin Cemetery.

References:

RH; IMA, MSPC; *Irish Independent*, 19th October 1944, (dn).

Andrew J. (Andy) Fitzpatrick: (1874 - 1936)
A. Coy, 1st Batt, Dublin Brigade. Roll of Honour

Andy Fitzpatrick was born in 1874 and resided at 1 Chatworth Terrace, Hanbury Lane, in the Coombe. He was employed as a foreman in the Engineering Department of the Department of Posts and Telegraphs and was a member of A. Company, 1st Battalion, Dublin Brigade. He was involved in the gun running at Kilcoole and Howth, in 1914.

On Good Friday he and Martin King, a member of the Irish Citizen Army who also worked in the Engineering Department, were given a detailed plan to destroy the telephone system in Dublin. However, because of the countermanding order and the confusion over mobilisation, the plan was never carried out. From noon on Easter Monday until Wednesday night he fought in Hopkins & Hopkins, on the corner of Eden Quay and Sackville Street. He then moved to Noblett's, North Earl Street and fought there until this outpost was evacuated on Thursday night. He was captured the following day in Waterford Street. After the surrender he was deported to Knutsford Jail on May 3rd and interned in Frongoch until July 17th 1916.

After his release from internment he lost his job because of his participation in the Rising. In 1918 he was elected Sinn Féin Councillor for the Usher's Quay Ward. He was reinstated in his job in January 1924 by the Free State Government and was appointed a Post & Telegraph Engineering Department Inspector.

Andy Fitzpatrick died on January 16th 1936, a year after his retirement and was buried at Glasnevin Cemetery.

References:
RH; IMA, MSPC; *Irish Independent*, 17th January 1936, (obit); *Irish Press*, 18th January 1936, (obit).

Maurice Fitzsimons: (1895 - 1963)
F. Coy, 1st Batt, Dublin Brigade

Maurice Fitzsimons, of Conquer Hill Road, Clontarf, was born in 1895 and educated at St Joseph's CBS, Marino. He began his working life as a messenger boy with the DUC Tramway Co and joined F. Company, 1st Battalion, Dublin Brigade, in 1914. In 1916 he was working for Messer's Films, Belfast and he assisted James Connolly in organising cinema workers for the labour movement. He reported to the GPO on Easter Monday and offered his services. He was engaged in building barricades, commandeering food for the garrison and in preventing looting in the vicinity of the GPO. Towards the end of the week his manned the hoses on the upper floors of the burning building. After the surrender he was deported to Stafford Jail on May 1st and was interned in Frongoch until Christmas 1916.

He rejoined his unit in 1917 and took part in many operations. In March 1919 he was involved in a raid for arms at Collinstown Aerodrome and was given charge of some of the rifles captured, there. He was arrested in December 1920 and interned in Ballykinlar until December 1921. He took the Republican side in the Civil War. He was involved in the defence of the Fowler Hall, Parnell Square and Barry's Hotel and evaded capture.

He lost his job with Messer's Films after the Rising and in 1919 he joined the Laskey Film Co., which later became Paramount Films. He worked for them as despatch manager for forty four years until 1963.

Maurice Fitzsimons, of 39 Londonbridge Road, Sandymount, died on July 29th 1963 and was buried at Glasnevin Cemetery.

References:
RH; IMA, MSPC; *Irish Independent* & *Evening Herald*, 30th July 1963, (obits); *Irish Press*, 31st July 1963, (obit).

James Flanagan: (1877 – 1950)
G. Coy, 2nd Batt, Dublin Brigade

James Flanagan was born in Killoghteen, County Limerick, in 1877. He was employed as an insurance agent and resided at 40 Belvedere Road, North Circular Road, in 1916. He was a member of G. Company, 2nd Battalion, Dublin Brigade and he reported to the GPO on Easter Monday and served there throughout the week. After the surrender he was deported to Knutsford Jail on May 1st and interned in Frongoch until Christmas 1916.

He transferred to D. Company, 2nd Battalion, Dublin Brigade, in 1917 and was involved mainly in intelligence work, during the War of Independence. In 1919 he married Marie Perolz, a member of Cumann na mBan and of the Irish Citizen Army, who delivered dispatches to Cork on Easter Monday 1916. He enlisted in the Free State Army in June 1922 and was attached to the Army Pay Corps. He was demobilised in March 1924 and he was placed in service custody in connection with an alleged fraud in the Dependent's Branch of the Army Pay Branch, in December 1923. In April 1927 the Attorney General, John A. Costello directed that "no useful purpose would be served by the institution of a criminal proceeding".

James Flanagan, of St Laurence Cottages, Strand Rd, Sutton, died on April 30th 1950 and was buried at Mount Jerome Cemetery, Harold's Cross.

References:
IMA, MSPC; *Limerick's Fighting Story, 1916-1921*, (Brian Ó'Conchubair, Ed, 1948).

Father John Flanagan: (1872-1935)
Roll of Honour

During the Easter Week fighting, Father John Flanagan received a call to go to the GPO on Thursday afternoon and attend to wounded Volunteers. According to Max Caulfield, he set off with a friend towards the GPO and on reaching Moore Street, his companion was shot dead beside him. Leslie Price (Mrs. Tom Barry), who was sent by Tom Clarke to the Pro-Cathedral with that request and who accompanied Fr. Flanagan back to the GPO recalled, "Further down Moore Street a white-haired man was shot but not dead. He was lying, bleeding on the kerb. I remember the priest knelt down to give Absolution". She also recalled he had earlier passed a dying impoverished looking man, who had been shot.

When Fr. Flanagan reached the GPO, he found a number of wounded Volunteers and he administered to them until the evacuation, with the utmost disregard for his own safety. He also accepted letters and last wills from Volunteers for delivery to their families.

Fr. Flanagan, a native of Dublin, who is sometimes confused with Father Michael Flanagan, a vice-president of Sinn Féin, was transferred to the parish of Fairview as administrator. He was created a parish priest in 1928 and a canon in 1933.

Canon John Flanagan died suddenly on December 16th 1935 and was buried in Glasnevin Cemetery.

References:

RH; IMA, BMH (WS 1,754, *Mrs. Tom Barry*); Max Caulfield, *The Easter Rebellion*, (1963); Thomas Coffey, *Agony at Easter*, (1969); Michael Foy & Brian Barton, *The Easter Rising*, (2000); *Irish Press*, 1st June 1938, (na, *profile & memorial*).

Matthew (Matt) Flanagan: (1891 -   )
F. Coy, 2nd Batt, Dublin Brigade. Roll of Honour

Matt Flanagan was born in Monagea, County Limerick, in 1891. He was employed in the Civil Service and resided at 14 St Clements Road, Drumcondra, in 1916. He was a member of F. Company, 2nd Battalion, Dublin Brigade and fought and a member of the Davis Hurling Club. He fought in the GPO throughout Easter Week with his cousin, James Flanagan. He was deported to Stafford Jail on May 1st and was later interned in Frongoch until Christmas, 1916.

Matt Flanagan's last known residence in the late 1930s was the Top Lodge, in the Phoenix Park.

References:

RH; *Limerick's Fighting Story*, (Brian Ó'Conchubhair, Ed, 1948).

Maurice Flanagan: (1896 - 1934)
F. Coy, 1st Battalion, Dublin Brigade

Maurice Flanagan was born in County Clare, in 1896. He resided at 36 Blessington Street and in 1916 he was employed as a clerk at a shipping office at North Wall. He was a member of F. Company, 1st Battalion, Dublin Brigade. IRB man, Kevin McCabe, recalled recommending Maurice, the son of a retired RIC Inspector, to be sworn into the organisation, but his membership was dropped because of an objection by the Branch Centre. On Easter Monday he received telephone messages from England of troop movements by ship. He brought the messages to the GPO and was sent across the street to the houses between Noblett's and Lloyd's Public House, North Earl Street, where he served with Kevin McCabe. He remained there until Thursday night when the outpost was evacuated. He made his way in a party along Cathedral Street into Gloucester Street, where he was wounded by machine gun fire. He was picked up by the British Military and taken to the hospital in Dublin Castle. After being held in Dublin Castle for some time, he was interned in Frongoch until July 27th 1916. On his release he returned to his employment at the North Wall. He suffered pneumonia during his internment in Frongoch and later contracted tuberculosis as a result of the gunshot wound to his right lung.

His right lung was operated on in Richmond Hospital on February 1934 and Maurice Flanagan died there on September 20th 1934.

References:
IMA, MSPC; Derek Molyneux & Darren Kelly, *When the Clock Struck in 1916: Close-Quarter Combat in the Easter Rising*, (2015).

James (Jimmy) Fleming: (1900 – 1961)
Fianna Éireann

Jimmy Fleming was born in 1900 and resided at 9 Hamilton Row, Westland Row. He was a member of Fianna Éireann and was fifteen and a half years of age at the time of the Rising. He was involved in carting arms and ammunition from Liberty Hall to the GPO on Easter Monday. He also assisted in holding up a number of bread and milk vans and commandeering their contents. While he was in the GPO, he assisted at the fist aid station. Tom Clarke sent him home on Wednesday because of his young age. His older brother, Michael, fought in Boland's Mills in Easter Week.

He became a member of B. Company, 3rd Battalion, Dublin Brigade at its reorganisation in 1917 and took part in an unauthorised raid on Westland Row Railway Station. As a result, he was court-marshalled by the IRA and was ordered to carry out certain duties, which he failed to do. He was suspended and was reinstated during the Truce. He joined the Free State Army in May 1922 and during the attack on the Four Courts, he manned an eighteen-pounder gun and suffered a perforated eardrum. He was discharged from the army in September 1924. He rejoined the army in 1940 and served until 1945.

Jimmy Fleming, of 114 Broombridge Road, Cabra, died on June 1st 1961 and was buried at Deansgrange Cemetery.

References:
IMA, MSPC.

Ignatius Flynn: (1895 - 1922)
E. Coy, 2nd Batt, Dublin Brigade. Roll of Honour

Ignatius Flynn was born in 1895 and resided at 1 Rose Terrace, Wharf Road, East Wall. He was a carpenter by trade and was employed in Kennedy's Bakery, Parnell Street. He was a member of E. Company, 2nd Battalion, Dublin Brigade and on Easter Monday he left Ballybough in the group under the command of Captain Thomas Weafer. They proceeded along Summerhill towards the GPO and arrived there about 4 o'clock with military and medical supplies. While fighting in the Imperial Hotel, he was severely wounded in the foot and was taken to Jervis Street Hospital. He was transferred to the hospital at Dublin Castle, where his big toe was amputated.

In 1917 he returned to work at Kennedy's Bakery and remained there until his health deteriorated in February 1922. He never to recovered from the wounds he received in the Rising and died of meningitis in the Mater Hospital on March 14th 1922 , while being treated for gangrene to his foot.

Ignatius Flynn was survived by his widowed mother, four sisters and two brothers and was buried in Glasnevin Cemetery.

References:
RH; *Evening Herald*, 16th March 1922, (obit).

Patrick Flynn: (1900 – 1970)
Volunteer, (Unattached)

Patrick Flynn was born in 1900 and resided at Royal Canal Bank, Broadstone. He was sixteen years old and employed as a hairdresser's apprentice, when he went to the GPO on Easter Monday and volunteered his services. He was sent across to the corner of North Earl Street, where he received a gunshot wound to the side of his head. He was taken to the GPO where the wound was dressed and he was then brought to Jervis Street Hospital for further treatment. He then returned to the GPO and remained there until the evacuation. He was detained at Richmond Barracks and was released on May 12th because of his young age.

He joined C. Company, 1st Battalion, Dublin Brigade in 1917 and at one stage was excused duties because of a breakdown in his health. He took the Republican side in the Civil War and was one of the occupiers of the Fowler Hall, Parnell Square and of Hughes Hotel. In 1934 he was married with a young family, when he was hospitalised with both a physical and mental breakdown and spent many years in St Ita's Hospital, Portrane, County Dublin.

Patrick Flynn died on October 16th 1970 and was buried at St Patrick's Cemetery, Donabate, County Dublin.

References:
IMA, MSPC; *Irish Independent*, 17th October 1970, (dn).

Thomas Fogarty: (1898 – 1962)
B. Coy, 1st Batt, Dublin Brigade. Roll of Honour

Thomas Fogarty was born in 1898 and resided at 79 Fitzroy Avenue, Drumcondra. He was a tailor by trade and he joined B. Company, 1ˢᵗ Battalion, Dublin Brigade, in 1915. On Easter Monday he was mobilised for Blackhall Street and he made his way to the GPO. He was sent to Reis's Chambers, where he was engaged in erecting an aerial on the roof of the building. He spent Tuesday in the Dublin Bread Company Building and Wednesday in the Hibernian Bank. After Captain Tom Weafer was killed on Wednesday, he crossed the street to the GPO under heavy sniper fire. On Thursday morning he was posted to the Metropole Hotel and fought there until the building was evacuated on Friday. He was in the advance party that was led by The O'Rahilly into Moore Street on Friday evening. After the surrender, he was deported to Knutsford Jail on May 1ˢᵗ and interned in Frongoch until July 17ᵗʰ 1916. His brother, Patrick, was a member of the Four Courts Garrison in 1916 and he died in 1920.

Thomas Fogarty, of 34 Mountjoy Square, died on September 9ᵗʰ 1962 and was buried at Kilmacanogue Cemetery, County Wicklow.

References:
RH; IMA, MSPC.

Bridget Foley (Mrs. Bridget Martin): (1887 -   )
Cumann na mBan

Bridget Foley was born in 1887 in Cork. In 1920 she came to Dublin and joined the Keating Branch of the Gaelic League, where her brothers and sisters were members. In 1915 she joined the Central Branch of Cumann na mBan and carried guns and dispatches to various parts of the city. In the week preceding the Rising, she made three trips to Cork with dispatches. The last of these was on Easter Sunday, when she travelled there and returned to Dublin the following morning. On Easter Tuesday, she crossed Sackville Street to the outpost at the Hibernian Bank, where her sister Vera was stationed. Captain Thomas Weafer sent the Foley sisters and fellow Cumann na mBan member Mary Lawless to a vacant shop premises in Sackville Street, to set up a first aid centre and she later assisted Dr John Tuohy there.

On Thursday with Vera and another sister, Kate they made their way to Church Street to see Michael, their brother, who was involved in the fighting there. They spent the night in the Church Street area, before returning to the GPO. When it was decided to send the women away from the GPO on Friday, she evaded capture and went to Phibsboro with Mary Lawless. She was later arrested and kept in detention in appalling conditions in Ship Street Barracks. She was moved to Kilmainham Jail and then on to Lewes Prison.

She continued her involvement in Cumann na mBan after her release from prison and in 1918 married Joseph Martin. Their business premises at College Green, was regularly raided by the Black and Tans and their home in Leeson Park Avenue was a refuge for people on the run.

In her Bureau of Military History Witness Statement she stated that she applied for 1916 and War of Independence medals, which were "only granted four years ago". On principle, Bridget Martin never applied for a pension.

References:
IMA, BMH (WS 398).

Michael P. Foley: (1893 – 1960)
D. Coy, 2nd Batt, Dublin Brigade

Michael Foley was born in Edenderry, County Offaly in 1893 and was employed as a grocer's assistant in a public house at 62 Talbot Street, Dublin, in 1916. He was a member of D. Company, 2nd Battalion and on Easter Monday he was mobilised by Seán Milroy. He was put in charge of a group of six or seven men in the GPO including, Maynooth Volunteers, Joe Ledwith and Michael O'Raogan and Dick Healy, who also was a Parnell Street barman, At the evacuation of the GPO he was engaged at the barricade at Henry Place and Moore Lane. He was deported to Knutsford Jail on May 1st and interned in Frongoch until August 1916.

In 1917 he was sent to Edenderry by Michael Collins, to assist in the reorganisation of the Volunteers in Offaly. Ernie O'Malley was sent to replace him when he was arrested in September 1918 and imprisoned in Belfast Jail. He was released three months later and was arrested again in December 1920 and interned at Rath Camp, until December 1921. He took no further part when the Civil War broke out in 1922.

Michael Foley, of 13 Gledswood Park, Clonskeagh, died on July 19th 1960 and was buried at Deansgrange Cemetery.

References:
IMA, MSPC; *Sinn Féin Rebellion Handbook 1916*, Weekly Irish Times, (1917); *Evening Herald*, 19th July 1960, (dn).

Nora Foley (Nóra Ní Foghludha): (1891-)

Cumann na mBan. Roll of Honour

Nora Foley was a member of Cumann na mBan and was a sister of Bridget, Vera and Kate of the GPO Garrison, and Michael, who fought in the Four Courts Garrison.

On Easter Sunday, she accompanied Bridget to Cork with a dispatch for Tomás McCurtain and they arrived back in Dublin on the following morning. She remained in the GPO until noon on Friday. Nora Foley then left with the majority of women and evaded capture.

References:
   RH; IMA, BMH (WS 398, *Brigit Martin, nee Foley*).

Michael (Mick) Fox: (1891 – 1982)

F. Coy, 4th Batt, Dublin Brigade. Roll of Honour

Mick Fox was born on October 27th 1891 and resided at the Brass Castle, Chapelizod. He was a member of F. Company, 4th Battalion, Dublin Brigade, under the command of Captain Con Colbert and initially he saw action in the South Dublin Union in Easter Week. He then made his way to the GPO and served there until the building was evacuated on Friday evening. After the surrender, he was deported to Stafford Jail on May 1st and interned in Frongoch until August 1916.

When he was released from internment and returned to Dublin, he discovered that he had lost his job as a coach painter in the Inchicore Railway Works, as a consequence of his involvement in the Rising. He resumed active service during the War of Independence and in 1921 he took part in the ambush of Crown Forces at the Red Cow, Clondalkin. He took the pro-Treaty side during the Civil War and joined the Free State Army in 1922, with the rank of Private. After his demobilization from the army in 1924, he returned to his old job in the Inchicore Railway Works.

Mick Fox died on New Year's Day, 1982 at St Mary's Hospital, in the Phoenix Park and was buried in Mulhuddart Graveyard.

References:
   RH; IMA, MSPC; NLI, *Lynch Papers*, (Ms 11,131); *Evening Herald*, 4th January 1982, (dn).

Bernard Friel: (1895 – 1949)

Glasgow Company, (Kimmage Garrison). Roll of Honour

Bernard Friel was born in Glasgow, in 1895. He was a plumber by trade and a member of the Fianna in that city. Prior to the Rising he travelled to Dublin with a group of fellow Glaswegians, and joined the Kimmage Garrison at Larkfield.

Early in Easter Week he was sent with two other Volunteers to occupy The Arch Public House, Henry Street and they dispersed a number of looters from the street by drenching them with water from the roof. He returned to the GPO and served there throughout the week. At the evacuation of the GPO on Friday evening, along with Andrew Carmichael and Patrick Caldwell, he attempted to carry the wounded Volunteer Andy Furlong to Jervis Street Hospital. They were unable to reach the hospital and returned to the houses in Moore Street. He was deported to Knutsford Jail on May 1st and was interned in Frongoch.

On his release from internment, he returned to Glasgow and continued to serve in the War of Independence. He was sentenced to three years penal servitude for conspiracy to export explosives to Ireland and served his sentence in full in Peterhead Prison.

Bernard Friel continued to live in Glasgow after his release from jail and died there, in November 1949.

References:
RH; IMA, MSPC; *An t-Óglach*, 1st May 1926.

Andrew (Andy) Furlong: (1891 – 1922)

E. Coy, 2nd Batt, Dublin Brigade. Roll of Honour

Andy Furlong was born in 1891. He was an Irishman residing in London and he returned to Dublin in 1915. He joined the Kimmage Garrison at Larkfield, and later he became a member of E. Company, 2nd Battalion, Dublin Brigade. He was posted to the Metropole Hotel during Easter Week. On Friday evening, while waiting in the sorting office in the GPO with others from the Metropole Garrison for orders to evacuate, his ammunition pouch exploded. He was wounded in the knee and several others in the vicinity were also injured. Arthur Wicks, who was standing beside him, was seriously wounded and died the following night. Patrick Caldwell, Andrew Carmichael and Bernard Friel were among the last group to leave the GPO and they attempted carry Furlong to Jervis Street Hospital. When they realised their task was impossible, they returned with him to the occupied houses in Moore Street.

He took part in the War of Independence and supported the Treaty side during the Civil War. He joined the Free State Army at its inception and for a time was Staff Captain attached to General Michael Collins. On October 13th 1922 he was wounded while stationed in Roscrea and died two days later in the Mater Hospital, Dublin.

Andy Furlong was identified at the inquest by his brother, Walter, from Acton, London, and was buried in Glasnevin Cemetery.

References:
RH; *Irish Independent*, 18th & 19th October 1922, (fr); *Evening Herald*, 18th October 1922, (obit).

Joseph (Joe) Gahan: (1895 - 1969)

Kimmage Garrison. Roll of Honour

Joe Gahan was born in 1895 and resided at 19 Nicholas Street, near Christchurch Cathedral. He was the son of Robert Gahan, who emigrated to Canada as a young man and spent some time in the Northwest Mounted Police. Prior to the Rising, Joe was attached to the Kimmage Garrison, where he made canister bombs and buckshot. When he arrived at the GPO on Easter Monday with the Kimmage Garrison, he was put in charge of six men and sent to occupy the Ship Inn, in Abbey Street. He later returned to the GPO and fought there as a sniper, until Thursday. He and Seamus Brennan then occupied the Pillar House in Henry Street. He returned to the GPO on Friday evening and was part in the advance party led by The O'Rahilly that came under machine-gun fire in Moore Street. He was deported to Wandsworth on May 9th and later interned in Frongoch, where he joined his brother, Matt, who was a member of the Four Courts Garrison. He was released from internment in Frongoch on July 17th 1916. His sister, May, was also a member of the GPO Garrison. He joined C. Company, 1st Battalion, in January 1918 and later that year he went to England. He returned to Ireland in 1919 and spent six months in Newcastle Sanatorium, suffering with lung problems. Early in 1921 he was transferred to the 3rd Engineer's Company, IRA and served until the Truce.

Joe Gahan, of 6 Westbrook Road, Dundrum, who attended the Easter Commemorations in 1966 in a wheelchair, died on July 30th, 1969.

References:
RH; IMA, MSPC.

Mary (May) Gahan (Mrs. May O'Carroll):
(1899 – 1988)

Cumann na mBan

May Gahan was born in 1899 and resided at Nicholas Street. She joined Cumann na mBan in 1915 and reported to St Stephen's Green on Easter Monday, 1916. She was sent from there to the GPO with dispatches, and then served across the street in the Imperial Hotel. After the surrender, she was among the women who were imprisoned in Kilmainham Jail until she was released on May 22nd. Her brother Joe was a member of the GPO Garrison, while another brother, Matt, fought in the Four Courts.

During the War of Independence she was arrested for collecting for the National Aid Organisation. She was later involved in purchasing arms and ammunition from British soldiers, and on one occasion, secured a Lewis machine gun for H. Company, 1ˢᵗ Battalion. In the Civil War she took the Republican side, and was arrested in May 1923 and interned in Kilmainham Jail, where she went on hunger strike. She was transferred to the North Dublin Union, where she again went on hunger strike for sixteen days and when she was released, her health suffered as a result of the hardship she endured.

She married and emigrated to Australia and raised ten children.

May O'Carroll died in Sydney, on April 29ᵗʰ 1988.

References:

IMA, MSPC; Sinéad McCoole, *No Ordinary Women: Irish Female Activists in the Revolutionary Years, 1900-1923*, (2004).

Patrick (Pat) Gallagher: (– 1960)

E. Coy, 4th Batt, Dublin Brigade. Roll of Honour

Pat Gallagher was a cattle dealer, from Edmondstown, Rathfarnham and a member of Ballyboden Wanderers GAA Club. He joined E. Company, 4ᵗʰ Battalion, Dublin Brigade, in 1915. On Easter Monday he was sent from the GPO with some other members of E. Company to the Fairview area. He was involved in the attempt to blow up the GNR railway bridge at East Wall Road, and he fought in the Annesley Bridge area, until ordered back to the GPO on Tuesday evening. He fought from the roof of the GPO throughout Easter Week. He was considered a top marksman and he silenced a British Army sniper on the roof of Trinity College. After the surrender he was deported to Stafford Jail on May 1ˢᵗ and interned in Frongoch, until Christmas, 1916.

In 1917 he helped to reorganize the Rathfarnham Volunteers. He took part in a number of operations during the War of Independence, including the burning of Rockbrook RIC Barracks and the ambushing of a military lorry at Templeogue. He was later arrested by the Black and Tans, but managed to escape.

Pat Gallagher, of 4 Eglinton Road, Bray, County Wicklow, died on August 10ᵗʰ 1964 and was buried at Croagh Cemetery, Edmondstown, Rathfarnham.

References:

RH; IMA, MSPC; *Irish Press*, 11ᵗʰ August 1964, (dn).

Peter Paul Galligan: (1888 - 1966)

Vice-Commandant. Enniscorthy Volunteers. Roll of Honour

Paul Galligan was born in Cavan, in 1888 and educated at St Patrick's College. He came to Dublin in 1907 to be apprenticed to the drapery trade, and he joined the IRB in 1912. He became a member of the Volunteers in 1913 and was later involved in the Howth gun-running in 1914. In 1916 he was working in Enniscorthy, as a drapery assistant and was Vice-Commandant of the Enniscorthy Volunteers. On Easter Monday, he attended the Fairyhouse Races and then travelled to the GPO when he heard that the Rising had begun. On Tuesday, he cycled to Enniscorthy with orders from James Connolly to prevent British troops passing through the district by train to Dublin. He took control of Volunteer operations in Enniscorthy and his group was the last to surrender after the Rising. He was sentenced to death for his part in the Rising, but this was later commuted to five years penal servitude. He was imprisoned in Dartmoor and Lewes Jail and was released in June 1917 from Pentonville Prison.

In the following year, at the time of the German Plot, he was held prisoner in Reading Jail. He was elected as the Sinn Féin candidate for West Cavan, in 1918 and was a member of the 1st Dáil, in 1919. He spent time in solitary confinement in Belfast Jail later that year and he spent a further time in British prisoners, before finally being released in 1921. He supported the Treaty, but took no active part in the Civil War.

In his early days in Dublin, he was a member of the Kickhams GAA Club and he later became one of Dublin's leading drapers.

Paul Galligan died on December 15th 1966 and was buried at Deansgrange Cemetery.

References:
RH; IMA, MSPC; *Irish Press*, 16th December 1966, (obit).

Henry (Harry) Gannon: (1880 - 1939)

E. Coy, 4th Batt, Dublin Brigade. Roll of Honour

Harry Gannon was born in 1880 and resided at 10 Main Street, Rathfarnham. He was a painter by trade. He joined the Volunteers in 1914 and was a member of E. Company, 4th Battalion, Dublin Brigade. P.H. Pearse appointed him armourer of E. Company, in 1915. He reported to the GPO on Easter Monday with his fellow Rathfarnham Volunteers and fought there throughout the week. He was deported to Knutsford Jail on May 1st and was interned in Frongoch, until Christmas, 1916. In 1917 he rejoined his unit and served through the War of Independence. He was engaged as an armourer and in intelligence duties, reporting RIC movements in his area. He took no part in the Civil War.

Harry Gannon died on October 29th 1939 and was buried in St Nahi's Graveyard, Dundrum, County Dublin.

References:
RH; IMA, MSPC; *Irish Press*, 1st November 1939, (obit).

Patrick (Paddy) Garland: (1897 – 1963)
Hibernian Rifles. Roll of Honour

Paddy Garland was born in 1897 and resided at 27 Lower Kevin Street. He was an apprentice bricklayer by trade and he joined the Hibernian Rifles in 1915. He reported to the GPO on Easter Monday and was stationed on the top floor, guarding prisoners. On Tuesday and Wednesday, he manned the ground floor windows, under the command of Captain Diarmuid Lynch. He was part of the group under the command of Seán McLoughlin that took control of Independent House in Abbey Street on Thursday. They were ordered to return to the GPO on Friday and he was in the main group that evacuated the building later that evening. On Friday night and Saturday morning, he was with a group led by Captain Jim O'Sullivan that held a position in Samson's Lane, until the surrender was called. He was deported to Stafford Jail on May 1st and interned in Frongoch, until July 26th 1916.

After his release from internment, he joined E. Company, 1st Battalion, Dublin Brigade and was appointed captain, during the War of Independence. During the anti-conscription campaign in 1918, he was jail for a month and was later interned in Ballykinlar Camp, from November 1920 to December 1921. He took the Republican side in the Civil War and among those who seized the Fowler Hall, in March 1922. He fought in Hughes Hotel, Gardiner Street and in the Sackville Club, O'Connell Street. He was arrested in July 1921 and interned in Mountjoy Jail and in Tintown, the Curragh, until December 1923. During the emergency years, he was a Lieutenant in the Construction Corps, 26th Battalion.

He resided at 171 Ceannt Fort, Mount Brown, and was employed as a bricklayer in Dublin Corporation's Sewers Dept.

Paddy Garland died on January 28th 1963 and was buried at Glasnevin Cemetery.

References:
RH; IMA, MSPC; NLI, *Lynch Papers*, (Ms 11,131); *Irish Press*, 29th January 1963, (obit).

John James Gavan: (1892 - 1945)
F. Coy, 2nd Batt, Dublin Brigade. Roll of Honour

James Gavan was born in Dublin, in 1892. He was a barman by trade and a member of F. Company, 2nd Battalion, Dublin Brigade. On Easter Monday, when his place of employment, Lambe's Public House near Ballybough Bridge, was taken over by Volunteers, he decided to join them and take part in the Rising. He was in the party, led by Seán Russell, that engaged with British Forces at North Strand on Tuesday. Later that evening was ordered back to the GPO with the Fairview contingent. On Wednesday, he and three other Volunteers were involved in boring through the walls of the Henry Street buildings and bringing provisions back from the Henry Street warehouse. He was in the group, led by Lieutenant Patrick Shortis that occupied O'Neill's Public House, on the corner of Liffey Street and Abbey Street, on Thursday. They were forced to return to the GPO on the following day when their position became untenable due to the constant bombardment directed at them. He left the GPO on Friday evening in the advance group with Captain Liam Breen and witnessed The O'Rahilly fall in Moore Street. He spent that night in buildings in Riddles Row, off Moore Street and was arrested the next morning. He was put up against a wall to be shot, but a British Officer intervened and beat him badly around the head with a riding crop. After the surrender, he was sent to Stafford Jail on May 1st, where he spent six weeks in solitary confinement and was then interned in Frongoch, until August 1916. His nerves and health suffered after his release from internment and he spent two months in Richmond Asylum. He also was treated for tuberculosis in 1918.

In later life, he lived with his family in Clonmellon, County Westmeath.

James Gavan died on July 21st 1945 and was buried in Kilbarrack Cemetery, Dublin.

References:

RH; IMA, MSPC; NLI, *Lynch Papers*, (Ms 11,131).

John J. Geoghegan: (1897 – 1977)
F. Coy, 1st Battalion

John Geoghegan was born in Limerick, in 1897. He worked in the Dublin Dockyards and joined F. Company, 1st Battalion, Dublin Brigade, in 1914. He was not mobilised on Easter Monday and he went to Annesley Bridge, where he served on Monday and Tuesday. On Tuesday evening he proceeded to the GPO with the Fairview contingent and he posted to the Metropole Hotel. He fought in the hotel until Friday, when the garrison there retreated to the GPO. He was part of the main body to evacuate the GPO on Friday evening and spent the night in the houses in Moore Street. After the surrender he was deported to Stafford Jail on May 1st and interned in Frongoch until August 1916.

In 1917 he returned to his native Limerick and rejoined the Volunteers there. He returned to Dublin in 1919 and again worked in the Dublin Dockyards, where he gathered intelligence for Michael Collins. He went to Sligo in December 1921 and joined up with his brother, who was an IRA officer there. During the Civil War he fought on the Republican side and was involved in attacks on the Ulster Bank and the Town Hall in Sligo Town and the RIC Barracks, at Collooney. His brother was killed in September 1921 and he was arrested in April 1923. He was interned at Newbridge, where he took part in a hunger strike and he was released in December 1923.

John Geoghegan, of 39 Waverley Avenue, Fairview, died on April 21st 1977 and was buried at St Fintan's Cemetery, Sutton.

References:

IMA, MSPC.

Lucy Gethings (Mrs. Lucy Grimley): (1899 - 1954)

Irish Citizen Army. Cumann na mBan. Roll of Honour

Lucy Gethings was born in 1899 and resided at 6 Eden Gardens, South Dock. She was a member of the Irish Citizen Army and she later joined Cumann na mBan. After reporting to Liberty Hall on Easter Monday, she was sent to the GPO and worked in the kitchen assisting Louise Gavan Duffy, until she was sent home on Tuesday because of her young age.

In 1920 she married Michael Grimley, who fought in the Four Courts in 1916. She was active in the War of Independence, along with her mother Ellen and her sister Eleanor, who were also members of the Irish Citizen Army. They all took the Republican side in the Civil War.

Mrs Lucy Grimley, of 86 Sundrive Road, Crumlin, died on January 29th 1954 and was buried in Glasnevin Cemetery.

References:
RH; NLI, *Lynch* Papers, (Ms 11,131); & NLI, *William O'Brien Papers*, (Ms 15,673); *Irish Press*, 30th January 1954, (dn).

Marie (May) Gibney (Mrs. Marie O'Neill): (1898 - 1984)

Volunteer, (Unattached). Roll of Honour

May Gibney was born in 1898. She arrived at the GPO on Easter Monday and volunteered her services. She stayed in the GPO throughout Easter Week and was engaged in cooking duties and delivering dispatches. On Friday she left the GPO with Brigid Connolly and some wounded Volunteers, but failed to gain entry to Jervis Street Hospital. They were later arrested in Summerhill and taken to the Broadstone Station, where they were interrogated and then released.

After the Rising she joined Cumann na mBan and was an active member during the War of Independence. She was engaged to be married to Dick McKee, who was shot and killed, allegedly trying to escape from Dublin Castle in November 1920. Her home at 31 Temple Street was used to provide accommodation for Volunteers on the run. She was a member H/Q Staff up to the Truce. She fought during the Civil War on the anti-Treaty side and was imprisoned in Kilmainham Jail, in 1923. She later married Lawrence O'Neill, who was commander of the Carlow Brigade of the IRA.

Mrs May O'Neill, of 16 Lennox Street, South Circular Road, died on February 13th 1984 and was buried at Balgriffin Cemetery.

References:
RH; IMA, MSPC; *Evening Herald*, 14th February 1984, (dn).

Richard Gibson: (1899 - 1977)
F. Coy, 1st Batt, Dublin Brigade. Roll of Honour

Richard Gibson was born in 1899 and resided at 6 Temple Street. He worked in the Midland Railway and was a member of F. Company, 1st Battalion, Dublin Brigade. On Easter Monday he was engaged in bringing supplies from Liberty Hall to the GPO. He was then sent to Annesley Bridge and was posted to the Vitriol Works. He was stationed there until recalled to the GPO on Tuesday evening. He fought throughout the week in the GPO and was wounded in Moore Street on Friday, when in the advance party led by The O'Rahilly. After the surrender he was removed to the hospital in Dublin Castle and later deported to Knutsford Jail. He was released from internment in Frongoch on July 27th 1916. He rejoined his unit and served until 1919, when ill health forced him to cease active service.

Richard Gibson, of 47 Harold Road, Manor Place, Stoneybatter, died on February 4th 1977 and was buried at Glasnevin Cemetery.

References:
RH; IMA, MSPC; *Irish Independent*, 5th February 1977, (dn).

Michael Giffney: (1890 – 1951)
F. Coy, 1st Batt, Dublin Brigade. Roll of Honour

Michael Giffney was born in New Ross in 1890. He came to Dublin at a young age and lived at 10 Seville Place Cottages. He was educated at St Laurence O'Toole's CBS and later O'Connell Schools CBS. He joined F. Company, 1st Battalion, Dublin Brigade in 1914. On Easter Monday he joined up with the 2nd Battalion Volunteers, at Fairview. He was detailed with six Volunteers to occupy a house at the corner of Clonliffe Road and Ballybough Road, and was later posted to a house at the corner of Portland Row and Summerhill. Later that evening he set out with his party for the GPO and was sent out from there to disperse looters from the premises in the area. Later in the week he guarded British soldiers held captive in the GPO. During the evacuation he was wounded in the knee in Henry Place, and he was removed to the hospital at Dublin Castle after the surrender on Saturday. He was deported to Wakefield Prison on May 6th and interned in Frongoch, until July 15th 1916.

He later resided at 22 East Road, East Wall and was employed as a joiner with T. & C. Martin's.

Michael Giffney died on April 23rd 1951 and was buried in Rathnew Cemetery, County Wicklow.

References:
RH; IMA, MSPC; NLI, *Lynch Papers*, (Ms 11,131); *Irish Independent*, 24th April 1951, (dn).

Joseph Gleeson: (1889 - 1959)

Liverpool Company, (Kimmage Garrison). Roll of Honour

Joseph Gleeson was born in Liverpool, to Irish parents, in 1889. He joined the IRB in 1915 and was a member of the Supreme Council, representing the North of England. He came to Dublin before the Rising with his brother, Martin and joined the Kimmage Garrison. They both fought in the GPO in Easter Week and were later interned in Frongoch.

After his release from internment, he served with the Dublin and Meath Brigades in the War of Independence. He was arrested in December 1920 and interned in Ballykinlar Camp, until December 1921. His younger brother, Aidan (a.k.a. Redmond), died on hunger strike in Mountjoy Jail, in 1920. During the 1920/21 period, *An t-Óglach* was secretly printed at the Gleeson's family tobacconist's shop in Aungier Street, by Oscar Traynor, who was a printer by trade. Gleeson joined the Free State Army at its inception with the rank of lieutenant and served with the Printing and Stationary Dept. of the Quartermaster General's Staff and was demobilized in March 1924.

Joseph Gleeson, of 10a Aungier Street, died on December 18th 1959 and was buried at Mount Jerome Cemetery, Harold's Cross.

References:
RH; IMA, MSPC; *Irish Independent*, 19th December 1959, (dn).

Martin Gleeson: (1882 - 1947)

Liverpool Company, (Kimmage Garrison). Roll of Honour

Martin Gleeson was born in Liverpool in 1882. He joined the IRB and the Volunteers there, and came over to Dublin with his brother, Joseph, prior to the Rising. They both joined the Volunteer Camp in Kimmage. He fought in the GPO throughout Easter Week. He was deported to Wakefield Prison on May 9th and was later interned in Frongoch until Christmas 1916.

He became a member of A. Company, 4th Battalion, Dublin Brigade, during the War of Independence. He was sent to London in 1918 with a group of Volunteers, including Joe Good, with orders to assassinate members of the British Cabinet if conscription was introduced in Ireland. In February 1920 he was arrested with his younger brother, Aidan (a.k.a. Redmond) and imprisoned in Mountjoy Jail. They went on hunger strike and Aidan died as a result. He joined the Free State Army in 1922 and served as an Accounts Officer with the Quartermaster General's Dept, until his demobilization in 1924.

In later life, he was employed as a clerical officer in the Revenue Commissioner's Office and resided at 3 Galtymore Close, Drimnagh.

Martin Gleeson died on November 12th 1947 and was buried at Mount Jerome Cemetery, Harold's Cross.

References:
RH; IMA, MSPC; Clair Willis, *Dublin 1916, the Siege of the GPO*, (2009); *Irish Independent*, 15th November 1947, (obit); *Irish Press*, 17th November 1947, (obit).

Richard Gogan: (1899 – 1982)

B. Coy, 1st Batt, Dublin Brigade. Roll of Honour

Richard Gogan, was born in 1899 and resided at 184 Parnell Street. The son of a Fenian, he joined the Volunteers at the inaugural meeting in the Rotunda in 1913. He and his brother, Vincent, were assigned to B. Company, 1st Battalion, Dublin Brigade, under Commandant Edward Daly. On Easter Monday, he was sent to the Volunteer outpost at Cabra Bridge and the following day they were ordered to retreat when they came under artillery fire. Their escape route took them through Glasnevin Cemetery and they spent that night in the loft of an outhouse in the Glasnevin locality. On Wednesday the party decided to divide in two and while some set out to join up with Thomas Ashe in North County Dublin, he proceeded to the GPO with P.J. Corless and Seán Price. During the evacuation of the GPO on Friday evening, he was one of the stretcher-bearers who carried James Connolly into Henry Place. He was held in Richmond Barracks after the surrender, but was released two weeks later because of his young age. He then resumed his education at O'Connell Schools, North Richmond Street.

He took the Republican side during the Civil War and the family home in Parnell Street was used as an arms dump. He fought in the defence of the Hamman Hotel and the CYMS Building, North Frederick Street, and he was detained for three months in Mountjoy Jail. In 1926 he was a founder member of Fianna Fáil and was elected TD, serving for 23 years in Dáil Éireann for the Dublin North-West Constituency between 1954 and 1977.

Richard Gogan, of 122 Nephin Road, Cabra, died on May 28th 1982 and was buried at Glasnevin Cemetery.

References:
RH; IMA, MSPC; NLI, *Lynch Papers*, (Ms 11,131); *Irish Press*, 29th May 1982, (obit).

David (Davy) Golden:
(1899 - 1967)

E. Coy, 2nd Batt, Dublin Brigade

Davy Golden was born in 1899 and resided at Richmond Road, Fairview. He was educated at St Joseph's CBS, Marino and he joined E. Company, 2nd Battalion, Dublin Brigade, in 1915. One of his grandfathers, David Golden, was a Fenian who was imprisoned in Cork Jail, while the other, Thomas Whelan, was a member of the Invincibles. On Easter

Monday, he was mobilized at Father Mathew Park, Marino and later that day he proceeded to the GPO with a group, under the command of Captain Thomas Weafer. He was assigned to the high sniping post in the Dublin Bread Company Building in Sackville Street and later moved to the Hibernian Bank before it was evacuated. He spent the rest of the week in the GPO and after the surrender he was released because of his young age.

After the re-organisation of the Volunteers in 1917, he was transferred to H. Company, 1st Battalion, Dublin Brigade, and in 1919 he became a member of the Active Service Unit. He was interned in Ballykinlar Camp from February to December, 1921. When the Treaty was signed he enlisted in the Free State Army and was one of the first Irish soldiers to take over Beggar's Bush Barracks.

He resigned in 1924 with the rank of lieutenant. He emigrated to the United States in 1926 and worked there for the Bell Telephone Co. for forty years.

Davy Golden came back to Ireland for the 1916 Commemoration Ceremony in 1966, before returning to Chicago, where he passed away on September 22nd 1967.

References:
IMA, MSPC; *Scoil Iósaif, Marino, 1916-1966, (a 1916 Jubillee Publication)*, (1966).

Alfred Joseph (Joe) Good: (1895 – 1962)
London Company, (Kimmage Garrison). Roll of Honour

Joe Good, an electrician by trade, was born in Soho, London in 1895. He joined the same company of Volunteers in London as Michael Collins. He came across to Dublin prior to the Rising and joined the Kimmage Camp. On Easter Monday he was initially assigned to O'Connell Bridge and was later stationed at Kelly's Gun Shop, at the corner of Bachelor's Walk, with some other Volunteers under the command of crack shot Peadar Bracken. They held out against the heavy machinegun fire until Wednesday, when they withdrew to the GPO. On Thursday he was put in charge of the top-floor of the Metropole Hotel until the building was evacuated on Friday. He was in main group that evacuated the GPO on Friday evening and spent the night in the houses in Moore Street. After the surrender he was deported to Knutsford Jail on May 1st and interned in Frongoch until Christmas 1916.

On the re-organisation of the Volunteers in 1917, he became a member of C. Company, 2nd Battalion, Dublin Brigade. He was also an organiser for the Volunteers at various times with the East Mayo, West Limerick and Mid Clare Brigades. He worked closely with Michael Collins and was sent to London in 1918 with a party of Volunteers with orders to assassinate British MP's, if conscription was passed for Ireland. He later joined the Free State Army, but resigned his commission when Civil War broke out. However, he rejoined the army on the death of Michael Collins. After the Civil War ended he again resigned his commission and returned to civilian life. He married Mary Ellen Donovan, a London–Irish girl, and they resided at 109 Richmond Road, Drumcondra. They reared four children and he later settled with his family in Templeogue village. He was employed for many years as an electrician in the College of Science. His wife predeceased him and late in life he married the poet Pamela Heal.

Joe Good, of Butterfield Avenue, Templeogue, died on July 21ˢᵗ 1962 and was buried in Bohernabreena Cemetery, County Dublin.

His memoir, entitled, "Enchanted By Dreams", was published in 1996 by his son Maurice, an actor, playwright and theatre director, who passed away in Canada, in 2013.

References:
RH; IMA, MSPC; Thomas Coffey, *Agony at Easter*, (1969); Joe Good, *Enchanted by Dreams*, (1996); Michael Foy & Brian Barton, *The Easter Rising*, (2000); Charles Townshend, *Easter 1916, the Irish Rebellion*, (2006); Charlie McGuire, *Seán McLoughlin, Ireland's Forgotten Revolutionary*, (2011); *Sunday Times*, 20ᵗʰ October 1996, (na).

Bridget Grace: (1896 -   )
Cumann na mBan

Bridget Grace resided at 3 Stanley Cottages, Mespil Road and was a member of Cumann na mBan in 1916. She was a member of the GPO Garrison in Easter Week, and on Wednesday morning James Connolly sent her and May Cullen to Boland's Mills to warn the garrison there that British troops had landed at Dun Laoghaire, and were approaching their position. At noon they arrived at the 25 Northumberland Road outpost, where her brother Seamus Grace was stationed, with food and a dispatch. They were not allowed enter the barricaded building and passed the dispatch through the letterbox, instead.

References:
IMA, BMH (WS 310, *Seamus Grace*); Max Caulfield, *The Easter Rebellion*, (1963); Thomas Coffey, *Agony at Easter*, (1969); Liz Gillis, *Women of the Revolution*, (2015),

John (Jack) Graves: (1893 - 1971)
Maynooth Company, Kildare Brigade

Jack Graves was born in 1893 and was a native Irish speaker from Ring, County Waterford. He was an assistant in Dómhnall Ó Buachalla's shop in Main Street, Maynooth, County Kildare, at the time of the Easter Rising. He was among the Maynooth Volunteers who traveled to Dublin along the Royal Canal towpath on Easter Monday. They arrived in the GPO on Tuesday morning, having spent Monday night in Glasnevin Cemetery. He was sent to Parliament Street with other Maynooth Volunteers, to support a party of Irish Citizen Army men who were holding the Evening Mail Offices. He was next to Volunteer Edward Walsh on the roof of the Royal Exchange Hotel in Parliament Street, when he was mortally wounded. With Pat Weafer and Joe Ledwith, he evaded capture and returned to Maynooth, where they were promptly arrested. He was court-martialled and sentenced to two years on May 15th, which was later commuted to six month's hard labour. In 1917 he rejoined the Maynooth Company before transferring to the Rathdrum Company, County Wicklow, in 1919. He helped to set up the Rathdrum Sinn Féin Court and was appointed the Court Clerk in 1921. He took the Republican side in the Civil and was Intelligence Officer with the Rathdrum Company.

He joined the Garda Síochána in 1933 and was stationed at Killorglin, County Kerry, when he retired in 1954.

Jack Graves, of Ring, County Waterford, died in Waterford hospital on July 31st 1971.

References:
IMA, MSPC.

Julia Grenan: (1884 - 1972)
Cumann na mBan

Julia Grenan was born in 1884 and was reared in Lombard Street, Dublin. She was educated in the local convent school and later became a member of the Gaelic League and hIghinidhe na hÉireann. She attended the Rotunda for the formation of the Volunteers and joined Cumann na mBan with her school friend and neighbour, Elizabeth O'Farrell. On Easter Saturday, Roddy Connolly notified her that she was required at Liberty Hall by his father, James Connolly. Although she was a member of Cumann na mBan, James Connolly attached her to the Irish Citizen Army. She was sent with dispatches, by train, to Dundalk and Carrickmacross early on Easter Monday morning. Also on the train was Nora Connolly, who was also northward bound with dispatches. On her return to Dublin, she reported to the GPO and was engaged in delivering dispatches to various locations throughout the city, including the Four Courts, the College of Surgeons and she made an unsuccessful attempt to reach the Mendicity Institute. She was one of the last women to leave the burning GPO. and remained with the garrison in Moore Street. There she helped attend to the many wounded, including James Connolly, throughout Friday night, and she witnessed James Connolly give Seán McLoughlin his command. After the surrender on Saturday afternoon, she spent Saturday night beside Winnie Carney on the green plot outside the Rotunda Hospital. She was detained in Kilmainham Jail until May 9th and while there she heard the shooting of the 1916 Leaders from her cell.

During the War of Independence she was involved, along with other Cumann na mBan members, in collecting for the Republican Prisoners' Dependents Fund. She worked as a furrier in Dublin and in later years was employed with the Irish Hospitals Trust.

She shared a house at 27 Lower Mount Street, with Elizabeth O'Farrell for many years.

Julia Grenan died on January 6th 1972, in St Monica's Nursing Home, Belvedere Place and was buried at Glasnevin Cemetery.

References:

Catholic Bulletin, June 1917; Desmond Ryan, *The* Rising, (1949); Max Caulfield, *The Easter Rebellion*, (1963); Thomas Coffey, *Agony at Easter*, (1969); Donncha Ó'Dúlaing, *Voices of Ireland*, (1984); Ruth Taillon, *Women of 1916*, (1996); Michael Foy & Brian Barton, *The Easter Rising*, (2000); *Irish Press*, 7th January, 1972, (obit); *Evening Herald*, 8th January 1972 (obit).

Gerald J. Griffin: (1879 – 1960)

Quartermaster. 1st Batt, Dublin Brigade. Roll of Honour

Gerald Griffin was born in Mayo, in 1879. He moved to Dublin and was a pupil of O'Connell Schools, North Richmond Street, before becoming a Civil Servant. He was a prominent member of the McHale Branch of the Gaelic League, which was comprised mainly of Connaught men, and was also a member of the IRB. He joined the Volunteers after the inaugural meeting in 1913 and was appointed Quartermaster of 1st Battalion, Dublin Brigade. On Easter Monday he supplied a bundle of dynamite that was hidden locally, to a party led by Captain Seamus O'Sullivan, who had orders to blow up bridges on the North Circular Road, at Phibsboro and at Cabra. However the quantity supplied was insufficient to cause any serious damage. On Easter Tuesday, he left the GPO and was accompanied by Piaras Beasley to Mountjoy Square and Parnell Square, to obtain AOH rifles. He was also given £60 to hire some lorries from various haulage companies throughout the city and, although deposits were paid on several, none were ever called upon. He was sent out on several missions from the GPO on Wednesday and Thursday by James Connolly. On Friday he was unable to break through the military cordon and return to the GPO, despite several attempts. He evaded capture after the surrender.

After the Rising, he was employed as general secretary of the Clerical Workers' Union and because of his work commitments he was unable to continue as an active Volunteer.

His wife Florence, nee Meade, and her brothers, Henry and William were all members of the Four Courts Garrison in Easter Week.

Gerald Griffin, of Glenburn, Sutton Road, Sutton, died on May 8th 1960 and was buried at St Fintan's Cemetery, Sutton.

References:

RH; IMA, MSPC; IMA, BMH (WS 201, *Nicholas Laffin*), BMH (WS 278, *Frank Daly*), BMH (WS 411, *Eamon Morkan*), BMH (WS 926, *Kevin McCabe*); *Irish Press*, 10th May 1960; *Irish Press*, 10th November 1960, (obit).*
*newspaper strike.

John Griffin. (1872-   )
C. Coy, 2nd Batt, Dublin Brigade

John Griffin was a tailor by trade and resided at 3 Grenville Lane, Gardiner Place. He was a member of C. Company, 2nd Battalion, Dublin Brigade. On Easter Monday he reported to Father Mathew Park and took up a position at Gilbey's Wine Shop, Ballybough Bridge, before moving into the GPO on Tuesday evening. He remained in the GPO for the rest of the week.

John Griffin was deported to Knutsford Jail on May 3rd and then interned in Frongoch.

References:

NLI, *Lynch Papers, (Patrick McGinley refers to John Griffin)*, (Ms 11,131).

John Halpin: (1892- 1938)
B. Coy, 1st Batt, Dublin Brigade. Roll of Honour

John Halpin resided at 2 Lower Dominic Street and was employed as a draper's porter, in 1916. He joined the Volunteers in 1913 and was a member of B. Company, 1st Battalion, Dublin Brigade. He was stationed at Cabra Bridge on Easter Monday and Tuesday, and later served in the Four Courts. Volunteer Tom Grath, who lived on the same street as him, stated that he was also with him in the GPO on Wednesday and Thursday. After the surrender he was detained at Richmond Barracks and was released on May 22nd because of his young age.

A month after the Rising, he received severe head injuries in a police baton charge while taking part in a Republican procession in Westmoreland Street. His injuries were so serious that he required continued medical attention. During the War of Independence he was interned in Ballykinlar Camp for a year. He was an early member of St Laurence O'Toole's.

John Halpin, of 140 Parnell Street, died in a Dublin hospital on April 12th 1938 and over three hundred IRA volunteers attended his funeral.

References:

RH; IMA, MSPC; *Irish Press*, 13th & 14th April 1938, (obits); *Irish Independent*, 14th April 1938, (obit).

Patrick (Paddy) Halpin: (1899 -   )
Volunteer, (Unattached)

Paddy Halpin was born in 1899 and resided at 24 Lower Summerhill. On Easter Monday he went to the GPO with two friends, James Wren and Tommy Mahon and offered his services. He was given a double-barrelled shotgun and fought there through the week. On Thursday he was one of a party, under the command of Seán McLoughlin, who occupied the Independent Newspaper Offices in Abbey Street. He was part of the main evacuation of the GPO on Friday evening. After the surrender he was deported to Knutsford Jail on May 1st and was released after a short period, because of his young age.

On the reorganisation of the Volunteers in 1917, he joined 1st Battalion, Dublin Brigade and served through the War of Independence. He was a G.H.Q. sharpshooter and in 1920 was involved in a failed attempt to rescue Kevin Barry from Mountjoy Jail. The rescue party was withdrawn at the last minute, when a large military reinforcement arrived at the prison. His older brother, Robert, who served with the British Army in the Middle East during Easter Week, returned to Dublin and also fought in the War of Independence. Both brothers fought on opposite sides in the Civil War. He emigrated to the United States in 1925, and retired as a civilian foreman with the US Navy, at Long Beach, California, many years later.

Paddy Halpin returned to Dublin in 1965 and visited his brother, William, who resided at Rathmines Road.

References:
Irish Independent, 7th June 1965, (na, *Dublin visit from the USA*).

Arthur (Art) Hannon: (1899 – 1973)
Volunteer, (Unattached)

Art Hannon was born in 1899 and resided at 12 Saint Laurence Street, North Wall. He was employed as an office-boy for Hugh Moore & Alexander. Although not a member of the Volunteers, he offered his services in Fairview on Easter Monday and was posted to the Vitriol Works, Ballybough. Later that day, he was sent to report on troop movements in the North Wall area. He encountered some troops on Saint Laurence Street, where he lived. He engaged them in conversation and followed them by bicycle to Oriel Street, where he was forced to make a hasty retreat when a local woman shouted to the soldiers that he was a Sinn Féiner. He returned to the Vitriol Works and was sent to the GPO on three occasions with despatches. He then guided some of the Volunteers, who were unfamiliar with the north inner-city, into the GPO on Tuesday evening. From the GPO he was sent with three other Volunteers to deal with looters in the area, and was later sent to the Four Courts twice with despatches. He was stationed at the door of the GPO on Thursday when James Connolly escorted a group, under the command of Seán McLoughlin, towards Abbey Street. He then opened the door when James Connolly was carried in after his ankle was shattered. At the evacuation of the GPO on Friday evening, he helped erect the barricade at the top of Moore Lane, enabling the Volunteers to get from Henry Place into the houses in Moore Street. After the surrender, he spent Saturday night outside the Rotunda and was then detained at Richmond Barracks until May 12th, when he was released because of his young age. His older brother, James, was a member of the Jacob's Garrison during Easter Week. He lost his job after the Rising and later became a merchant seaman.

In 1917 he set the Union Jack alight on the roof of the GPO ruins and replaced it with the Tricolour.

He emigrated to the United States and lived at various locations around Philadelphia for over thirty years, before settling in California in the 1960's.

Art Hannon, of 1168 13th Street, San Diego, died on June 5th 1973.

References:
IMA, MSPC.

Thomas (Tom) Harris: (1895 – 1974)

Maynooth Company, Kildare Brigade. Roll of Honour

Tom Harris, a native of Cloncurry, County Kildare, was born in 1895. He was a farmer and a member of the Maynooth Company, Kildare Brigade. On Easter Monday he left Maynooth with fifteen other local Volunteers for the GPO. They travelled by the Royal Canal towpath towards the city and spent that night in Glasnevin Cemetery, before arriving at the GPO on Tuesday morning. He was in the group that was sent to relieve the Irish Citizen Army men, who were surrounded in the Evening Mail Offices, across from City Hall. He fought in the Royal Exchange Hotel in Parliament Street, until his party was forced to retreat to the GPO. Having been wounded in the evacuation of the GPO on Friday evening, he was later detained in the emergency hospital in Dublin Castle for three months, before being deported and interned in Frongoch until August 15th 1916.

He fought in the War of Independence and was appointed Commandant of No.2 Kildare Brigade in 1920. As leader of the Kill Company, he orchestrated an attack on the local RIC Barracks in a search for arms in which two policemen were killed. He took the anti-Treaty side in the Civil War and was interned in Newbridge Barracks until October 1922.

Having been first elected to Kildare County Council in 1920, Harris was a Fianna Fail TD for County Kildare from 1927 to 1937 and for Carlow /Kildare from 1937 to 1948.

Tom Harris, of Caragh, Naas, County Kildare, died on February 19th 1974.

References:
RH; IMA, MSPC; James Durney, *On the One Road*, (2001); *Irish Press*, 20 February 1974, (obit).

James J. (Seamus) Hayes: (1888 – 1941)

C. Coy, 2nd Batt, Dublin Brigade. Roll of Honour

Seamus Hayes was born in 1888 and resided at 5 Marino Avenue, Malahide Road. An upholsterer by trade, he joined Sinn Féin at its inception and was also a member of both the McHale Branch of the Gaelic League and of the Celtic Literary Society. He joined the Volunteers in 1913 and took part in the Howth gun running in 1914. On Easter Monday he reported to the volunteer post at Annesley Bridge and took part in the engagement with British Troops there. He later took up a position in Gilbey's shop, Fairview Strand, until ordered into to the GPO on Tuesday evening.

From the GPO, he went to the Imperial Hotel and remained there until the building was evacuated. After the surrender he was deported to Stafford Jail on May 1st and interned in Frongoch until July 25th 1916.

He rejoined his unit after his release from internment. In 1919, he resigned from the Volunteers because of ill health and took no further part in the War of Independence.

Seamus Hayes, of 41 Holly Road, Donnycarney, died on April 27th 1941 and was buried at Glasnevin Cemetery.

References:

RH; IMA, MSPC; *Irish Press*, 28th April 1941, (obit).

Seán Hayes: (1884 – 1928)

F. Company, 1st Battalion, Dublin Brigade

Seán Hayes was born in Glandore, West Cork, in 1884 and entered the Civil Service in London in 1904. He joined the Volunteers at its formation. He returned to Dublin in early 1916 and joined F. Company, 1st Battalion, Dublin Brigade. Having served with the GPO Garrison throughout Easter Week, he was deported to Stafford Jail on May 1st and interned in Frongoch until Christmas 1916.

On his release from internment he returned to Cork. He was elected TD for West Cork, in 1918 and was a member of Dáil Éireann, until 1923. He was deported several times and took part in a hunger strike in Wormwood Scrubs, which caused a breakdown of his health. He was a close friend of Michael Collins and he voted in favour of the Treaty. During the Civil War he was military governor of Newbridge Internment Camp. He resigned from the Free State Army in 1924 with the rank of commandant.

He later resided at 28 Seafield Road, Clontarf and was Executive Officer of the Stores Branch of the GPO.

Seán Hayes died on January 24th 1928 and was buried at Glasnevin Cemetery.

References:

IMA, MSPC; *Irish Independent*, 25th January 1928, (obit).

Richard (Dick) Healy: (1894 – 1982)

D. Coy, 2nd Batt, Dublin Brigade. Roll of Honour

Dick Healy was born in Kilkenny in 1894. He was employed as a grocer's assistant and resided at 93 Parnell Street in 1916. He was a member of D. Company, 2nd Battalion, Dublin Brigade, which included barmen and night workers. On Easter Week he reported to the GPO and was sent across the street to Reis's Chambers. From there, he was posted to the Imperial Hotel and when Captain Tom Weafer was mortally wounded in the Hibernian Hotel, he helped fellow Kilkenny man Paddy McGrath carry him out of the line of fire. He was later in the group, led by Paddy McGrath, that made their way back across to the GPO under heavy fire. After the surrender he was deported to Knutsford Jail on May 1st and interned in Frongoch until the end of August 1916.

When the Volunteers reorganised in 1917, he rejoined his old unit and was promoted to lieutenant. He was involved in raids for arms and in the purchase of arms. He was in charge of armed patrols that operated from the Banba Hall, Parnell Square and was present when Auxiliaries raided the premises and killed Volunteer Henry Kelly. When the Civil War broke out he ceased to be active and took no further part in the fighting.

Dick Healy, of 4 Ormond Road, Drumcondra, died on June 13th 1982 and was buried at Glasnevin Cemetery.

References:
RH; *Banba Review,* January 1963; *Irish Press,* 14th June 1963, (dn).

James Heery: (1892 - 1967)

C. Coy, 2nd Batt, Dublin Brigade

James Heery, the son of John Heery, the sub postmaster of Garristown, County Dublin, was born in 1892. In 1916 he was employed as a clerical assistant in the Post Office Engineering Dept, of the GPO. He resided at Fitzroy Avenue, Drumcondra and was a member of C. Company, 2nd Battalion, Dublin Brigade. He fought in the GPO during Easter Week, and was deported to Stafford Jail on May 1st. After his release on June 14th, he applied unsuccessfully to be reinstated to his former position in the Civil Service. In his application he stated that he was forced into the GPO by armed men and held there against his will throughout the building's occupation.

In December 1920 he was one those Volunteers who were chosen to join the Active Service (A.S.U.) as a full-time, paid soldier. He took part in many engagements, including the attack on Black and Tans in Beresford Place. He was involved in the burning of the Custom House and he was captured and imprisoned. He was released shortly before the Truce, owing to his failing health.

After Independence, he returned to his former position in the Engineering Dept in the Civil Service, but he was forced to retire in 1936 on medical grounds, due to failing eyesight. In 1966 he suffered a stroke, while residing at Clonturk House, a home for blind men in Drumcondra.

James Heery, of Ely Place, Dublin, died on February 10th 1967.

References:

IMA, MSPC; IMA, BMH (WS 390, *Joseph Gilhooly*); Keith Jeffery, *The GPO and the Easter Rising*, (2006); *Irish Independent*, 11th February 1967, (obit).

Michael Heffernan: (1889 - 1954)

B. Coy, 3rd Batt, Dublin Brigade. Roll of Honour

Michael Heffernan was born in 1889 and resided at Myra Lodge, Emmet Road, Inchicore. He was a member of B. Company, 3rd Battalion and in 1916 was employed in the boiler shop at the Inchicore Railway Works. He reported to the GPO on Easter Tuesday and helped erect barricades. He was then stationed at the ground floor windows until Friday, when he relieved the guard on the prisoners. He was later injured in an accident at one of the barricades, and he was taken to Jervis Street Hospital with other wounded volunteers on Friday. On Sunday morning he was taken from the hospital to the Rotunda and then transferred to the emergency hospital in Dublin Castle. He was deported to Stafford Jail on May 8th and interned in Frongoch, until July 15th 1916.

On his release from internment, he joined F. Company, 4th Battalion, Dublin Brigade and was involved in many operations during the War of Independence. He took part in the escape of Frank Teeling, Ernie O'Malley and Simon Donnelly, from Kilmainham Jail in February 1921. During the Civil War he fought on the anti-Treaty side, and was involved in the defence of 44 Parnell Square in June 1922. He was a member of the 26th Infantry Battalion, based at Collins Barracks from 1939 to 1945.

Michael Heffernan, of Nash Street, Inchicore, died on June 9th 1954 and was buried in Tay Lane Cemetery, Church Road, Celbridge, County Kildare.

References:

RH; IMA, MSPC; NLI, *Lynch Papers*, (Ms 11,131); *Irish Independent*, 7th June 1954, (obit); *Irish Press*, 7th June 1954, (obit).

Seán Hegarty: (1893 – 1933)

Glasgow Company, (Kimmage Garrison). Roll of Honour

Seán Hegarty was born in Dublin in 1895. He went to work in Glasgow, where he joined the Volunteers and took part in raids for explosives and detonators at Scottish collieries. He returned to Dublin in January 1916 and joined the Kimmage Garrison. On Easter Monday he was stationed on the roof of the GPO and hoisted the flag of the Irish Republic at the Prince's Street corner of the building with the Fianna Officer Harry Walpole. After the surrender he was deported to Knutsford Jail on May 1st and interned in Frongoch.

He fought in the War of Independence and took the anti-Treaty side in the Civil War. He was one of the defenders of the Gresham Hotel and when he was interned in October 1923, he went on hunger strike, which had a permanent impact on his health.

He resided at 5 Hogan Place in later years, and was a founder member of Fianna Fáil.

Seán Hegarty died on September 23rd 1933, and was buried in the Republican Plot at Glasnevin Cemetery.

References:
RH; *Irish Press*, 23rd September 1933, (obit); *Irish Independent*, 24th September 1933, (obit).

Francis (Frank) Henderson: (1886 – 1959)

Captain. F. Company, Dublin Brigade. Roll of Honour

Frank Henderson was born in 1886 and resided at 21 Northbrook Avenue, North Strand. He was educated at St Joseph's CBS, Fairview, where he became a keen student of the Irish language. He joined the Árd Craobh Branch of the Gaelic League in 1903, and played hurling for the Árd Craobh hurling team. In 1909 he joined St Laurence O'Toole's GAA Club and the following year he formed the O'Toole's Pipe Band with his friend, the playwright, Seán O'Casey. On Easter Monday he was in charge of Volunteers at Gilbey's Shop and Lambe's Public House, Ballybough Bridge, while his brother, Leo, was in charge of the party that engaged British troops at Annesley Bridge, Fairview. After arriving at the GPO on Tuesday evening, he took over buildings in Henry Street and organised the erection of a barricade at Moore Street. He was deported to Stafford Jail on May 1st and interned in Frongoch until Christmas 1916.

He rejoined his unit and in 1918 he was appointed Vice-Commandant of 2nd Battalion. He took over as commandant of the 2nd Battalion, when Tom Ennis was wounded during the attack on the Custom House in May 1921. He was imprisoned in Mountjoy and Dundalk Jails during this period. During the Civil War he took the Republican side, and fought in the O'Connell Street area. After Oscar Traynor was arrested in August 1922, he became Commanding Officer of the Dublin Brigade, IRA. He was captured in March 1923 and interned until 1924.

When the last Civil War prisoners were released, he founded Fodhla Printing Works with Oscar Traynor. During the emergency years he was Commandant of 26th Infantry Battalion. He was a Dublin Corporation Councillor in 1934.

Frank Henderson, of 83 St Mobhi Road, died on January 13th 1959 and was buried at Glasnevin Cemetery.

References:

RH; IMA, MSPC; IMA, BMH (WS 249 & 821); *Scoil Iósaif, Marino, 1916-1966, (a 1916 Jubilee Publication),* (1966); *Dublin's Fighting Story 1916-1921,* (1949); Michael Hopkinson, *Frank Henderson's Easter Rising Recollections of a Dublin Volunteer,* (1998); Jimmy Wren, *Saint Laurence O'Toole's GAC Centenary History,* (2001); Charles Townshend, *Easter 1916 and the Irish Rebellion,* (2006); *Irish Press,* 19th January 1959, (obit).

Leo Henderson: (1893 - 1973)

Captain. B. Coy, 2nd Batt, Dublin Brigade

Leo Henderson, of 5 Windsor Villas, Fairview, was born in 1893 and was one of three brothers, who joined the Volunteers in 1913. He was a member of B. Company, 2nd Battalion, Dublin Brigade and took part in the Howth gun running, in 1914. Early in Easter Week he fought in the Fairview and Ballybough area, before withdrawing to the GPO on Tuesday evening. He fought in the GPO and Henry Street area during Easter Week. After the surrender, he was deported to Wakefield Prison on May 6th and interned in Frongoch until Christmas 1916.

On the reorganisation of the Volunteers he took part in many operations in Dublin. He was with Dick McKee and Seán Treacy, when they were surprised by British Secret Service agents in Talbot Street, in October 1920. In the shootout that followed, he was captured and Seán Treacy was shot dead. He was then interned in Ballykinlar Camp, where he was appointed commandant. After his release he took the Republican side in the Civil War and was a member of the Four Courts Garrison in 1922. At that time the pogroms were taking place in Belfast and the IRA decided to send men to the north to defend the Nationalists. He was arrested while raiding a garage in Baggot Street for lorries to transport the men to Belfast and held in Kilmainham Jail. In retaliation, General "Ginger" O'Connell, of the Free State Army was arrested and taken to the Four Courts. Two days later the Civil War began with the attack by the Free State Army on the Republicans in the Four Courts. He was released from Kilmainham Jail in November 1923, after taking part in a hunger strike lasting thirty days. His brother, Frank, also fought in the GPO in 1916 and with the Four Courts Garrison in 1922.

He later became secretary of the Irish Local Government Officials' Union and was also secretary of the Dublin Board of Assistance.

Leo Henderson, of Rosslea, Millbrook Road, Rathfarnham, died on October 28th 1973.

References:

RH; IMA, MSPC; *An Phoblacht,* 29th December 1930; *Scoil Iósaif, Marino, 1916-1966, (a 1916 Jubilee Publication),* (1966); Calton Younger, *Ireland's Civil War,* (1980); Michael Hopkinson, *Green Against Green: Irish Civil War,* (1992); David Fitzpatrick, *Harry Boland's Irish Revolution,* (2004); *Evening Herald,* 29th October 1973, (dn); *Irish Press,* 8th November 1973, (obit).

James J. Heron: (1898 – 1975)
F. Coy, 1st Batt, Dublin Brigade

James Heron was born in Carlow in 1898, and was a victualler by trade. He resided at 23 Bessborough Avenue, North Strand, and joined F. Company, 1st Battalion in 1915. On Easter Monday he attended the Fairyhouse Races and made his way to the GPO when he discovered the Rising had begun. On Tuesday he was sent to the Imperial Hotel under the command of Captain Frank Thornton. When the garrison were forced to retreat from the burning building, he spent Friday night in a tenement house in the vicinity of Marlborough Street and North Cumberland Street, with a party that included Captain Brennan-Whitmore and Noel Lemass. The house was surrounded the following morning by British troops, and he was taken prisoner to the Custom House. He was detained in Richmond Barracks and deported to Knutsford Jail on May 3rd. After his release from internment in Frongoch on July 17th 1916, he rejoined his old unit.

He was arrested on Christmas Eve, 1920 and was interned in Ballykinlar Camp for twelve months. During the emergency years, he served with the Local Defence Force in the Swords area.

James Heron, of Malahide Road, Swords, died on January 24th 1975 and was buried at St Colmcille Cemetery, Swords.

References:
IMA, MSPC; *Evening Herald*, 25th January 1975, (dn).

Richard Hickey: (1892 – 1969)
C. Coy, 3rd Batt, Dublin Brigade

Richard Hickey was born in 1892 and resided at 2 Wharton Terrace, South Circular Road. He was employed as a cabinet maker and he joined C. Company, 3rd Battalion, Dublin Brigade, in 1913. On Easter Monday morning, as his unit moved off from Camden Row, he was detailed to keep watch on Portobello Barracks, Rathmines Road. He remained at his post until four o'clock and then went to Larkfield, Kimmage. He left Kimmage at midnight and proceeded to the GPO. He served in the GPO until the evacuation on Friday evening. Throughout Friday night he was engaged in boring through the walls in the houses in Moore Street. Following the surrender, he was deported to Knutsford Jail on May 1st and interned in Frongoch until Christmas 1916.

He rejoined his unit in 1917 and served until a serious illness to a member of his family prevented him from taking any further active part. However, he was later arrested in January 1921 and interned in Ballykinlar until December 1921.

Richard Hickey, of 9 Harrington Street, South Circular Road, died on March 11th 1969 and was buried in Mount Jerome Cemetery, Harold's Cross.

References:
IMA, MSPC.

Frederick P. (Fred) Higgins: (1896 – 1952)
C. Coy, 2nd Batt, Dublin Brigade. Roll of Honour

Fred Higgins was born in 1896 and resided at Belvedere Place. He was an electrician by trade and he was a member of C. Company, 2nd Battalion, Dublin Brigade, in 1916. He was not mobilised on Easter Monday and he made his own way to the GPO. He fought in the GPO, and during the week he was posted to the Freeman's Journal premises in Middle Abbey Street. On Friday he returned to the GPO and while moving sandbags to the yard, he was shot in the back. The bullet narrowly missed his spine and he was taken to Jervis Street Hospital. From there, he was taken to the hospital in Dublin Castle and was released in early June 1916.

He transferred to 1st Company, 5th Battalion, Dublin Brigade in 1918 and fought in the War of Independence. In 1919 he put a crane that the British Army was using to unload arms out of action, and he took part in an attempt to derail a troop train at Drumcondra. He fought on the Republican side in the Civil War and was a member of the Four Courts Garrison in 1922.

In his later life he resided at 37 Seafield Road, Clontarf, and was employed as an engineer with the Dublin Port and Docks Board.

Fred Higgins died on December 3rd 1952 and was buried at Glasnevin Cemetery.

References:
RH; IMA, MSPC; *Irish Press*, 4th December 1952, (dn).

Peter Higgins: (1879 - 1966)
Irish Citizen Army. Roll of Honour

Peter Higgins was born in 1879. He lived at 9 Horseman's Row and was a father of four children in 1916. On Easter Monday he went to Liberty Hall and joined the Irish Citizen Army. He marched to the GPO with the main body of men and was stationed at the rear of the building throughout Easter Week. On Thursday he noticed the wounded James Connolly, dragging himself along the wall in Prince's Street and went for help. After the evacuation on Friday evening, he left Moore Street and made his way to Dominic Street, where he was stopped by British troops. He was allowed through the cordon and evaded capture by convincing them that he was separated from his wife and family during the fighting and was attempting to return home. He took no further part in the struggle after Easter Week.

Peter Higgins, of 9 Horseman's Row, died on May 7th 1966 and was buried at Glasnevin Cemetery.

References:
RH; IMA, MSPC; NLI, *Lynch Papers*, (Ms 11,131); *Evening Herald*, 8th Mat 1966, (dn).

Patricia Hoey: (- 1930)

Cumann na mBan. Roll of Honour

Patricia Hoey was a member of Cumann na mBan and served with the GPO garrison, throughout Easter Week.

She was a close confidante of Michael Collins and other leaders. During the War of Independence she was a member of Collins' staff and her home in Mespil Road was used as a place of refuge for Volunteers on the run. She was imprisoned in Mountjoy Jail in July 1921 and was released after the Truce.

In her later life she was the Dublin correspondent of the American News Agency.

Patricia Hoey died on November 9th 1930 and was buried at Glasnevin Cemetery.

References:
RH. *Evening Herald*, 10th November 1930, (obit).

Hugh Holahan: (1899 -)

A. Coy, 1st Batt, Dublin Brigade

Hugh Holahan was born in 1899 and was the son of Sinn Féin activist, Aogh Holahan. The family home, a tobacconist's shop at 77 Amiens Street, was formerly in the possession of Tom Clarke. He joined A. Company, 1st Battalion with his brother Patrick, who fought at Ashbourne in Easter Week. His cousins, Gary and Patrick Holohan, also fought in the Rising. On Easter Monday, with Sam O'Reilly and other Volunteers, he attempted to blow up the railway line near Phibsboro and they then sent an engine down the tracks to block the railway line. They defended the barricade at Phibsboro Bridge, until

they came under artillery fire and were forced to retreat to the GPO. He fought there for the remainder of the week. After the surrender he was deported to Knutsford Jail on May 1st and interned in Frongoch until August 1916. Early in 1917 he went to the United States, where he raised money for the Prisoners Dependents Fund. He returned to Ireland in September 1917 with dispatches from John Devoy and with a quantity of arms. He joined 3rd Battalion Engineers and served with the East Wicklow Brigade. In February 1920 he was arrested at his home, 34 Cadogan Road, Fairview and interned in Mountjoy Jail. He took part in a hunger strike on April 6th 1920 with eighty other prisoners and was released ten days later. Because of his poor health he was admitted to Jervis Street Hospital. He sailed to the United States in December 1920 and remained there for the remainder of his life.

Hugh Holahan died in New York, in the mid 1960's.

References:
IMA, MSPC.

John J. Horan: (1897- 1934)
Volunteer, (Kimmage Garrison)

John J. Horan resided at 4 Francis Street, Tralee, Co. Kerry and joined the Volunteers in 1913. He moved to England to work, but returned to Ireland early in 1916 when he received his conscription notice. On Easter Monday he reported to the GPO with the Kimmage Garrison and was posted to Hoyte's Chemist and Oil Warehouse, near the Imperial Hotel, in Sackville Street. He returned to the GPO before Hoyte's was destroyed later in the week, and was prominent during the fighting in the Moore Street area after the evacuation. He was deported to Stafford Jail on May, 1st and later interned in Frongoch, until Christmas, 1916.

From 1917 until the Truce, he served as Lieutenant with the Kerry No.1 Brigade, Southern Division, IRA. He joined the Free State Army in August 1922 and served with the Kerry Command. He was demobilised in 1924 with the rank of lieutenant. He moved to Dublin and was employed by the Office of Public Works.

John Joseph Horan, of 60 Oak Road, Donnycarney, died on July 29th 1934 and left a wife and five young children.

References:
IMA, MSPC; *Sinn Féin Rebellion Handbook* 1916, Weekly Irish Times, (1917); *Irish Independent*, 3rd October 1934, (obit).*
* *newspaper strike.*

Martin Hore: (1884 – 1961)
B. Coy, 2nd Batt, Dublin Brigade

Martin Hore was born in 1884 and resided at 1 Dean Swift Square. He was a member of B. Company, 2nd Battalion, Dublin Brigade and he served in the GPO during Easter Week. He left the GPO at the evacuation on Friday evening and spent the night in the Moore Street houses. Following the surrender he was arrested and later released.

In 1917 he was transferred to A. Company, 3rd Battalion, Dublin Brigade, and was appointed a section commander. He took part in armed patrols and was involved in a number of attacks on British Forces in the Camden Street and Bishop Street area, often referred to as the "Dardenelles". In June 1921 he was arrested and sentenced to five years penal servitude. He was released from prison in December 1921 and joined the Criminal Investigation Dept in February 1922. Based in Oriel House, at the corner of Fenian Street and Westland Row, and served through the Civil War until October 1923 when the CID was disbanded. He retired with the rank of Inspector and later became a Detective Officer with An Garda Síochana.

Martin Hore, of 33 Cabra Drive, North Circular Road, died on November 9th 1961 and was buried at Glasnevin Cemetery.

References:
IMA, MSPC; *Irish Press*, 10th November 1961, (dn).

Patrick Hughes: (1875 - 1955)

C. Coy, 1st Batt, Dublin Brigade. Roll of Honour

Patrick Hughes was born in 1875 and resided at 30 Little Denmark Street. He was employed as a carpenter by Dublin Corporation and was a member of the Sheares Club IRB, when he joined C. Company, 1st Battalion, Dublin Brigade, in 1914. He was arrested in 1915 and charged with attempting to purchase arms from British soldiers. On Easter Monday he reported to the GPO and was sent out on Tuesday with a group to clear looters from William's Stores, Henry Street. He spent Wednesday in the GPO and the following day was sent to O'Neill's Public House at the corner of Liffey Street and Henry Street, under the command of Captain Patrick Shortis. The post came under attack from a British armoured car that poured continuous volleys into the building and he was wounded in the throat. When his party was withdrawn to the GPO on Friday morning, his wound was dressed by Dr James Ryan. After the surrender he was deported to Knutsford Jail on May 1st and then interned in Frongoch, until Christmas 1916.

On the reorganisation of the Volunteers, he continued to purchase arms from British soldiers with the aid of a soldier named Collins, who was a deserter and a former member of Fianna Éireann. He served in the War of Independence and took part in armed patrols. He was a member of the IRA until June 1922 when he refused to take part in the Civil War.

He was employed in the Dublin Corporation Housing Dept, as a caretaker at Corporation Buildings, Foley Street, for many years.

Patrick Hughes, of 110 Clonard Road, Crumlin, died on December 18th 1955 and was buried at Glasnevin Cemetery.

References:
RH; IMA, MSPC; NLI, *Lynch Papers*, (Ms 11,131); *Evening Herald*, 19th December 1955, (dn).

Thomas Hughes: (1896 – 1983)

B. Coy, 2nd Batt, Dublin Brigade. Roll of Honour

Thomas Hughes was born in 1896 and resided at 8 Summerhill. He joined the Volunteers at the Rotunda in November 1913 and became a member of B. Company, 2nd Battalion, Dublin Brigade. An electrician by trade, he was working in Chester, England, before returning to Dublin a week before the Rising.

He reported to the GPO and fought under the command of John Plunkett. Later in the week he was attached to the section under the command of Captain John O'Neill of the Irish Citizen Army.

During the evacuation of the GPO on Friday evening, he had a lucky escape in Moore Street when a bullet pierced his hat. He was deported to Stafford Jail on May 1st and was interned in Frongoch until July 1916.

On his release from internment, he went to work in Belfast and was attached to the Belfast Brigade before returning to Dublin in 1918. During the War of Independence he was active with B. Company, 2nd Battalion and took part in a number of operations. While on armed patrol on Grafton Street in March 1920 he held up an Auxiliary Officer and took away his weapon. He served until the Truce and took no part in the Civil War.

In later years he was an employee of the Board of Works and worked in Government Buildings, Leinster House, as Head Electrician.

Thomas Hughes, of 40 Belton Park Avenue, Donnycarney, died on May 29th 1983 and was buried at St Fintan's Cemetery, Sutton.

References:

RH; IMA, MSPC; *Evening Herald*, 30th May 1983, (dn).

Richard (Dick) Humphries: (1898 - 1968)

B. Coy, 3rd Batt, Dublin Brigade. Roll of Honour

Dick Humphries, the nephew of The O'Rahilly, was born in 1898 and resided at 54 Northumberland Road. He was one of the first pupils of P.H. Pearse at St Enda's, Rathfarnham. He was a member of B. Company, 3rd Battalion, Dublin Brigade and he drove a car laden with guns and ammunition at the Howth gun running in 1914. He was a member of the GPO Garrison in Easter Week. On Easter Monday and Tuesday he made many trips by car to retrieve supplies. On Tuesday night P.H. Pearse sent him home, but he returned on Wednesday morning and was posted to the GPO roof. After the surrender he was deported to Wakefield Prison on May 6th, but was soon released because of his young age.

He took part in the War of Independence, going on hunger strike and other activities. His mother's home at 36 Ailesbury Road, was used as meeting place for the Dáil Cabinet. He signed the Roll of Honour with members of B. Company, 3rd Battalion, for the Boland's Mills Garrison.

Dick Humphries died on September 20th 1968 and was buried at Saggart Cemetery, County Dublin.

References:

RH; *Evening Herald*, 20th September 1968, (obit); *Irish Press*, 21st September 1968, (obit); *Sunday Press*, 22nd September 1968, (obit).

James Hunter: (1876 – 1947)

E. Coy, 2nd Batt, Dublin Brigade

James Hunter, of 13 Sackville Avenue, Ballybough, was born in 1876 and was a carpenter by trade. He was a member of the IRB and a founder member of the Celtic Hurling Club, an early North Dublin hurling club. He joined E. Company, 2nd Battalion, Dublin Brigade, in 1915. On Easter Monday he was posted to Lambe's Public House, Ballybough, under the command of Captain Frank Henderson. He remained there until Tuesday evening, when the main body of men in the Fairview area marched to the GPO. From Wednesday to Friday he was engaged in boring through the walls of buildings in Henry Street. After the surrender he was deported to Knutsford Jail on May 1st and interned in Frongoch until July 27th 1916.

Because of his role in the Rising he lost his job as foreman carpenter with the Dublin Port & Docks on his return to Dublin. He rejoined his old unit at its reorganisation in 1917, and later transferred to the 5th Battalion, Engineers. His home at Sackville Avenue was raided continually by the British Army and the Black & Tans and he was forced to go on the run. He served up to the Truce, and took no part in the Civil War.

James Hunter died on March 24th 1947 and buried at Glasnevin Cemetery.

References:
IMA, MSPC; Michael Hopkinson, *Frank Henderson's Easter Rising Recollections as a Dublin Volunteer*, (1998); *Evening Herald*, 25th March 1947, (dn).

Joseph (Joe) Hutchinson: (1887 – 1970)

F. Coy, 2nd Batt, Dublin Brigade. Roll of Honour

Joe Hutchinson was born in 1887 and resided at 12 Summerhill Parade. He was a printer by trade and joined the Volunteers in 1913. He was a member of F. Company, 2nd Battalion, Dublin Brigade, and a week before the Rising he joined other members of his unit in defending against a police raid on Fr Mathew Park in Fairview, where the 2nd Battalion arms were located.. On Easter Monday he was posted at Lambe's Public House, Ballybough Bridge and remained there until the men in the Fairview area left for the GPO on Tuesday evening. He was then stationed in the Imperial Hotel until forced to withdraw when the buildings on that block were engulfed in flames. He was arrested in Gloucester Street on Thursday and taken to the Custom House for interrogation. He was transferred to Richmond Barracks and then deported to Knutsford Jail on May 3rd.

After his release from internment in Frongoch in August 1916, he rejoined his unit at its reorganisation in 1917. He fought in the War of Independence and took part in many operations, including participating in armed patrols in the Ballybough and North Strand area. He served until the Truce and took no part in the Civil War.

Joe Hutchinson, of 13 Offaly Road, Cabra, died on March 23rd 1970 and was buried at Glasnevin Cemetery.

References:
RH; IMA, MSPC; *Evening Herald*, 24th March 1970, (dn).

John F. Hynes: (1892 - 1975)
Lusk Coy, 5th Batt, Dublin Brigade. Roll of Honour

John Hynes was born in the United States in 1892 and his parents returned to Ireland when he was a child. He was employed as a farm worker in Lusk and joined the Volunteers in 1913. He was a member of the Lusk Company that blew up the railway bridge at Rogerstown, situated between Donabate and Rush, on Easter Monday. On Tuesday he was in the group of twenty Volunteers sent from the Fingal area to the GPO. While the majority went on to reinforce the Mendicity Institute Garrison, he was sent to Kelly's Gun Shop at the corner of Bachelor's Walk, under the command of Peadar Bracken, and fought there until Wednesday. He then crossed over to Reis's Chambers,  on the opposite side of the street, and was wounded in the leg during the retreat from there to the GPO on Thursday. He was evacuated with other wounded Volunteers to Jervis Street Hospital on Friday, and from there was transferred to Dublin Castle. He was deported to Wakefield Prison on May 1st and interned in Frongoch, until August 1916.

He went to Liverpool in 1918, where he joined the Liverpool Company of the IRA and took part in a raid for arms in the Territorial Army Training Hall in the Everton Valley. Returning to Ireland, he served with the Lusk Company, 2nd Battalion, Fingal Brigade, from 1920 to 1921. In later years his claim for a pension because of the wound he received in Easter Week was rejected.

John Hynes, of North Commons, Lusk, County Dublin, died on August 23rd 1975 and was buried at St MacCullins Cemetery, Lusk.

References:
RH; IMA, MSPC; NLI, *Lynch Papers*, (Ms 11,131).

P. Jackson
Hibernian Rifles. Roll of Honour

P. Jackson was a member of the Hibernian Rifles and fought in the GPO in Easter Week.

References:
RH.

Thomas Jones: (– 1928)

B. Coy, 3rd Batt, Dublin Brigade. Roll of Honour

Thomas Jones was entered on the Roll of Honour of the deceased members of the GPO Garrison. According to the roll compiled by Brother Allen, O'Connell Schools, North Richmond Street; Thomas Jones, B. Company, 3rd Battalion, died on February 16th 1928. Death notices of Thomas Jones, a sailor, who died at the residence of his brother-in-law, James Geoghegan, at 3 Seapoint Terrace, Irishtown, appeared in the *Evening Herald* and the *Irish Independent* on April 22nd 1928. An Irish Military History Archive list comprising of members of B. Company, 3rd Battalion, who took part in the Easter Rising, included a John Jones. There is a Thomas Jones, of 15 Emmet Street, Harold's Cross, on a list that will be released at Easter 2016 by the Irish Military History Archive. Both Irishtown and Harold's Cross were within the catchment area of the 3rd Battalion.

References:
RH; IMA; O'Connell Schools, (*Brother Allen Archive*); *Irish Independent* & *Evening Herald*, 23rd April 1928, (dn). *Irish Independent* & *Evening Herald*, 23rd April 1928, (dn).

Brian Joyce (Seoige): (1896 - 1980)

E. Coy, 4th Batt, Dublin Brigade. Roll of Honour

Brian Joyce, a native of Inisheer, was one of two natives of the Aran Islands who fought in the Easter Rising; the other was Seán O'Brien. He was a student at St Enda's, Rathfarnham and later at UCD. He was a member of E.Company, 2nd Battalion, Dublin Brigade and fought in the GPO throughout Easter Week. After the surrender he was deported to Stafford Jail on May 1st and interned in Wormwood Scrubs and Frongoch until July 27th 1916.

On his release from internment he took part in the War of Independence. A lifelong member of the GAA he won the 1916 Junior All-Ireland Football medal with Dublin, although the final was played in 1917. He played hurling and football with Dublin at senior level and won several Dublin Senior Championship medals with Collegians, UCD.

He later taught at St Enda's until its closure in 1935 and then took up a teaching position at St Vincent's, Glasnevin.

Brian Joyce, of 443 Griffith Avenue, died on July 18th 1980 and buried at Cruagh Cemetery, Rathfarnham.

References:
RH; IMA, MSPC; *Irish Press*, 12th December 1958, (na); *Evening Herald*, 18th July 1980, (dn).

Michael Kavanagh
C. Coy, 3rd Batt, Dublin Brigade

Michael Kavanagh resided at 10 Upper Bride Street, and was already a member of the O'Growney Branch of the Gaelic League when he joined C. Company, 3rd Battalion, Dublin Brigade with his brother Seamus in 1913. On Easter Monday he reported to the GPO with Seamus and was designated scouting duties. He moved constantly to and from the GPO throughout the week, and on Thursday he was sent on a foray to Liffey Street. On Friday was sent with a message for Thomas McDonagh in the Jacob's Biscuit Factory, and because of the difficulty getting out of Bishop Street he remained with the Jacob's Garrison.

Michael Kavanagh evaded capture after the surrender.

References:
IMA, BMH (889, *Seamus Kavanagh*).

Seamus Kavanagh: (1880 – 1955)
C. Coy, 3rd Batt, Dublin Brigade. Roll of Honour

Seamus Kavanagh was born in 1880 and resided at 10 Upper Bride Street. He was educated at Francis Street CBS, and was later employed as a junior clerk in the Board of Works, Dublin Castle. He was a member of the O'Growney Branch of the Gaelic League and later joined the Keating Branch. In 1913 he became a member of C. Company, 3rd Battalion, Dublin Brigade and was appointed secretary of the Defence of Ireland Fund that purchased arms and ammunition for the Volunteers. He took part in the Howth gun running in 1914. On Easter Monday he reported to the GPO with his brother, Michael. From Monday to Wednesday he was engaged in delivering dispatches. On Friday he went to the top floor of the GPO with The O'Rahilly and hosed the fire on the roof. After the surrender he was deported and interned in Frongoch until Christmas 1916. Two other brothers, Patrick and Peter, served with the Boland's Mills Garrison, while another, Seán, fought at Marrowbone Lane.

In later years he resided at 302 Howth Road and was attached to the Dept. of Local Government until his retirement in 1945.

Seamus Kavanagh died on June 8th 1955 and was buried at St Fintan's Cemetery.

References:
RH; IMA, BMH (WS 889); *Irish Press*, 10th June 1955, (dn).

John (Jack) Kealy: (- 1916). Killed in Action
E. Coy, 4th Batt, Dublin Brigade. Roll of Honour

Jack Kealy, a native of Dun Laoghaire, was educated at the local Christian Brothers School. He joined the Glasthule Branch of the Gaelic League while still a boy and became a fluent Irish speaker. While working as a printer in Rathfarnham, he joined E. Company, 4th Battalion, Dublin Brigade. On Easter Monday he set off from Rathfarnham Church with his company to the GPO. When they arrived there, they found the doors locked and they proceeded to enter the building through a side window in Prince's Street. As he climbed through the window he was shot and wounded. According to Captain Eamon Bulfin, he was shot by a sniper from the Metropole Hotel direction. He was carried to Jervis Street Hospital and died there from his wounds early on Tuesday morning.

Jack Kealy, the first casualty at the GPO, was buried at Deansgrange Cemetery.

References:
RH; *Catholic Bulletin*, July 1916; Max Caulfield, *The Easter Rebellion*, (1963); Ray Bateson, *They Died by Pearse's Side*, (2010).

Thomas (Tom) Kearney: (1896 – 1969)
E. Coy, 4th Batt, Dublin Brigade. Roll of Honour

Tom Kearney, from Ballyboden, was born in 1896 and joined E. Company, 4th Battalion, Dublin Brigade, in 1915. He was a member of Ballyboden Wanderers, GAA Club. On Easter Monday he left Rathfarnham with the local Volunteers and travelled to Liberty Hall and then on to the GPO. He was sent to Annesley Bridge and was in the party that attempted to blow up the railway line at Fairview. Having fought at Annesley Bridge until Tuesday evening, the Fairview men were ordered into the GPO. He remained in the GPO until the evacuation on Friday evening, after which he was deported to Stafford Jail on May 1st and interned in Forngoch until August 1916.

He rejoined his unit and fought in the War of Independence, taking part in many operations including the blowing up of Rockbrook RIC Barracks in 1919, and ambushes at Harold's Cross, Templeogue Road and Kenilworth Square. He joined the Free State Army in August 1922 and served with the Army Corps of Engineers until he was discharged from the army in 1924.

He later resided at 52 Barton Road, Rathfarnham and was an employee of the Architects Dept. in Dublin Corporation.

Tom Kearney died on December 18th 1969 and was buried at Mount Jerome Cemetery, Harold's Cross.

References:
RH; IMA, MSPC; *Evening Herald*, 19th December 1969, (dn).

Hubert (Hugh) Kearns: (1898 – 1955)

G. Coy, 2nd Batt, Dublin Brigade. Roll of Honour

Hugh Kearns was born in 1898 and resided at 13 Saint Clements Road, Drumcondra. He was one of five brothers who fought in the Easter Rising. His brothers, Frank, Joe, John and Tom, were part of the Jacob's Garrison. On Easter Tuesday he took arms from his home and the home of Volunteer neighbours, the Cotter family, to the GPO. Although he was suffering from the measles, he served in the GPO until Friday, when he was sent home by Seán McDermott.

On the reorganisation of the Volunteers he transferred to E. Company, 2nd Battalion, Dublin Brigade and in 1918 he became a full time Volunteer, attached to the Quartermaster General's Staff of the IRA. In 1919 he took part in the attack on Sallins RIC Barracks. He worked on the distribution and despatching of munitions to country units. In August 1922 he joined the Free State Army and became Chief Courier to General Michael Collins. He resigned from the army in 1924 with the rank of lieutenant.

Hugh Kearns, of Mont Alto, Sorrento Road, Dalkey, died on March 10th 1955.

References:
RH; IMA, MSPC; *Irish Press*, 11th March 1955, (dn).

Linda Kearns McWhinney: (1889 – 1951)

Nurse

Linda Kearns, a native of Dromard, County Sligo, was born in 1889. She trained as a nurse in Baggot Street Hospital, Dublin, in 1907. In Easter Week she set up a Red Cross Field Hospital in a house in North Great Georges Street. When the British Military ordered her to attend to British Troops only, she refused and closed down the hospital. She then moved into the GPO and tended to the wounded there. She also did dispatch duties and was in Moore Street, soon after The O'Rahilly was mortally wounded. After the surrender, she evaded capture.

During the War of Independence she had many narrow escapes, before being arrested in Sligo in 1920. She was interned in Walton Prison, Liverpool and later transferred to Mountjoy Jail, from where she made a sensational escape in 1921. She took the anti-Treaty side in the Civil War and tended to the wounded in the Republican Garrisons, including Cathal Brugha when he was mortally wounded on July 5th 1922.

She was a founder member of Fianna Fáil and became a Senator. In 1929 she married Charles McWhinney, O/C of the Derry Brigade during the War of Independence. She was a member of the National Council of Nurses for many years and in 1946 she set up Kilrock Nurses Convalescent Home, Howth.

Shortly before she died on June 5th 1951 at Kilrock, she was awarded the Florence Nightingale Medal by the Red Cross for meritorious service.

Linda Kearns McWhinney was buried on June 7th at Glasnevin Cemetery.

References:

Dublin's Fighting Story, (1948); Ruth Taillon, *Women of 1916*, (1996); Sinéad McCoole, *No Ordinary Women, Irish Female Activists in the Revolutionary Years 1900-1923*, (2004); Proinnsíos Ó'Duigneáin, *Linda Kearns, a Revolutionary Irish Woman*, (2006); Liz Gillis, *Women of the Irish Revolution, 1913-1923*, (2014); *Irish Press*, 8th June 1951, (app).

Cornelius (Con) Keating: (1873 - 1947)

C. Coy, 1st Batt, Dublin Brigade. Roll of Honour

Con Keating was born in 1873 and educated at O'Connell Schools, North Richmond Street. He played Gaelic football for Keating's GFC. In 1916 he was residing at 14 Rutland Place, the home of his brother-in-law John E. Lyons, and nephew Charles, who both fought with the Four Courts Garrison. He was a member of C. Company, 1st Battalion, Dublin Brigade and should not be confused with his namesake, who was drowned a couple of days before the Rising at Ballykissane Pier, in County Kerry. He reported to the GPO on Easter Monday and the following day he was ordered by The O'Rahilly to confiscate mattresses and other items from Clery's. On Wednesday he was sent out by James Connolly to prevent looting in the Henry Street area. On Thursday he was posted to the Lucas Cycle Shop at the corner of Abbey Street and Liffey Street, under the command of Seán Milroy. After the surrender he was deported to Stafford Jail on May 1st and interned in Frongoch until July 26th 1916.

He rejoined his unit at its reorganisation and served until 1918. He took no further part because he suffered with rheumatism.

Con Keating, of 46 Richmond Road, Drumcondra, died on May 26th 1947 and was buried at Deansgrange Cemetery.

References:

RH; IMA, MSPC; NLI, *Lynch Papers*, (Ms 11,131); *Evening Herald*, 26th May 1947, (dn).

Christopher (Chris) Keeling
Hibernian Rifles. Roll of Honour

Chris Keeling resided at 13 Hardwicke Street and was a member of the Hibernian Rifles. On Easter Monday he mobilised at 28 North Frederick Street, under the command of Captain John Scollan. They were instructed to remain in reserve by James Connolly, before eventually receiving orders to proceed to the GPO at midnight. Soon after arriving at the GPO, he was sent with ten other Hibernian Rifles and members of Maynooth Company to reinforce the Citizen Army men in the City Hall area. He was in the party that occupied the Royal Exchange Hotel in Parliament Street, under the command of Captain Tom Byrne. On Thursday they unsuccessfully attempted to return to the GPO and after this group disbanded, he evaded capture.

Chris Keeling lived at 4 Yellow Road, Whitehall, in later years.

References:
RH.

Edward Kelly: (1892 – 1963)
Hibernian Rifles. Roll of Honour

Edward Kelly, a native of County Westmeath, was born in 1892. He was a member of the IRB and joined the Hibernian Rifles in 1914. On Easter Monday he and eight others accompanied J.J. Walsh from Blessington Street to the GPO. Early on Tuesday morning he was sent to the Royal Exchange Hotel, Parliament Street, under the command of Captain Tom Byrne. He fought there until Wednesday evening, when he and several others were separated from the main body returning to the GPO. They unsuccessfully tried to make it to Sackville Street and on Thursday the group disbanded. He later evaded capture.

He joined C. Company, 1st Battalion, Dublin Brigade, at the reorganisation of the Volunteers and took part in a number of operations. In 1919 he transferred to 5th Battalion, Engineers and was promoted to lieutenant. He took part in attacks on British Forces in Dorset Street and North Frederick Street and was involved in cutting communications to the Custom House, prior to its burning on May 25th 1921. He joined the Free State Army in May 1922 and was discharged in 1928 with the rank of captain.

He was proprietor of a bicycle business in Townsend Street and later an employee of McQuillan's Toolmakers, Capel Street.

Edward Kelly, of 16 Lower Mount Street, died on October 9th 1963.

References:
RH; IMA, MSPC; IMA, BMH (WS 1094); *Irish Independent* & *Irish Press*, 10th October 1963, (obits).

Francis W. (Frank) Kelly: (1888 – 1971)

London Company, (Kimmage Garrison). Roll of Honour

Frank Kelly was born to Irish parents in London, in 1888. He joined the IRB and the Volunteers in London, and came to Dublin early in 1916 to take part in the Rising. He joined the Volunteer Camp at Kimmage, where he was engaged in making munitions.

On Easter Monday he reported to the GPO with the Kimmage Garrison and fought there throughout Easter Week. After the surrender he was deported to Stafford Jail and then interned in Frongoch, until Christmas 1916.

At the reorganisation of the Volunteers in 1917, he joined C. Company, 2nd Battalion, Dublin Brigade. He moved to Dundrum in early 1918 and transferred to the Ticknock Company. In May 1918 he was posted to the Sinn Féin headquarters at 6 Harcourt Street and then transferred to the Dept of Local Government early in 1919. He was sent by Michael Collins to England to aid in the escape of Éamon deValera from Lincoln Jail in February 1919. In 1921 he transferred to the Dept. of Foreign Affairs and put in charge of foreign communications. He took the Republican side in the Civil War and joined the 3rd Battalion, Dublin Brigade, reporting to 51 York Street. In October 1922, he was arrested and interned for his work on the Republican newspaper, *War News*. While interned in Hare Park in the Curragh, he went on hunger strike for two weeks and was released in 1924.

He joined the Dept of Local Government and retired as Principal Officer, after twenty five years' service.

Frank Kelly, of 17 Rathgar Avenue, died on January 3rd 1977 and was buried at Mount Jerome Cemetery, Harold's Cross.

References:

RH; IMA, MSPC; *Irish Press*, 8th & 9th January 1936, (*na, Frank Kelly's account of deValera's escape from Lincoln Jail*); *Irish Press*, 4th January 1971, (obit).

John (Jack) Kelly: (1879 – 1939)

Swords Coy, 5th Battalion, Dublin Brigade. Roll of Honour

Jack Kelly was born in 1879 and resided at Commons West, Swords. He joined the Volunteers in 1914 and was a member of the Swords Company, 5th Battalion, Dublin Brigade. He was mobilised on Easter Monday and spent the night at the Volunteer Camp at Finglas. On Tuesday morning he was in the group, under the command of Captain Richard Coleman that was sent by Thomas Ashe to the GPO. He fought in Kelly's Gunshop at the corner of Bachelor's Walk until Wednesday, and then served in the Metropole Hotel. On Friday evening he was one of twelve Volunteers who covered the evacuation of the GPO. After the surrender he was deported to Knutsford Jail on May 1st and interned in Frongoch until Christmas 1916.

He rejoined his unit at the reorganisation of the Fingal Brigade in 1917 and took part in the attack on Rush RIC Barracks. He was involved in the attempted ambush of the Military at Lissenhall, Swords and was arrested, while on the run. Interned from December 1920 until 1921, he took no part in the Civil War. In 1938 he hoisted the Tricolour at the official opening of the Sluagh Hall, Swords that was attended by Éamon deValera. He was a County Council employee and resided at Rathbeal Road, Swords.

Jack Kelly died, as a result of a car accident, on August 7th 1939 and was buried at Swords Cemetery.

References:
RH; IMA, MSPC; *Irish Independent*, 8th August 1939, (dn); *Irish Press*, 9th August 1939, (inq).

Joseph (Joe) Kelly: (1900 – 1969)

Volunteer, (Unattached). Roll of Honour

Joe Kelly was born in 1900 and resided at Lombard Street East. Although he was unattached to the Volunteers, he arrived at the GPO on Easter Monday and offered his services. He was given a shotgun and sent to the *Freeman's Journal* Offices, Abbey Street. He later returned to the GPO and served there until the evacuation on Friday evening. He was held in Richmond Barracks for a week after the surrender and was then released because of his young age.

After the reorganisation of the Volunteers he joined B. Company, 3rd Battalion, Dublin Brigade, and took part in armed patrols and in raids for arms. In 1919 he was transferred to B. Company's munition workshop and April 1921 he was arrested at the workshop in Sandwith Place. He was sentenced to five years penal servitude in Dartmoor Prison and was released in 1922. At the outbreak of the Civil War, he took the anti-Treaty side. He was an Intelligence Officer, attached to the Republican Active Service Unit and took part in a number of operations. His unit were involved in the operation that resulted in the killing of Seán Hales TD and the wounding of Pádraig Ó'Máille in December 1922. He remained on active service and stayed on the run until 1925.

As a result of his military service, he contracted tuberculosis. He later was an employee of the Dept of Posts & Telegraphs and worked as a porter in the GPO.

His brother, Thomas, was a member of the Boland's Mills Garrison in Easter Week and was seriously wounded in an ambush in Pearse Street in 1921.

Joe Kelly, of 36 Larkfield Grove, Kimmage, died on February 4th 1969 and was buried at Deansgrange Cemetery.

References:

RH; IMA, MSPC; *Sunday Independent*, 21st April 1957, (na, *Joe Kelly's recollections*); *Evening Herald*, 5th February 1969, (dn).

Martha Kelly (Mrs. Martha Murphy): (1897 - 1943)

Irish Citizen Army. Roll of Honour

Martha Kelly was born in 1897 and resided at Kilmainham. She was employed as a laundry worker and joined the Irish Citizen Army in 1913. She reported to the GPO on Easter Monday, and on Tuesday she and Mary Gahan were sent across the street to the Imperial Hotel. While she was there, she met her future husband, Michael Murphy, who was also a member of the GPO Garrison. During the evacuation of the Imperial Hotel on Thursday she attended the wounded Volunteers, Paddy Mahon and Noel Lemass. She was arrested on Friday morning and taken to the Custom House for interrogation, after which she was detained in Kilmainham Jail until May 22nd 1916.

Because of her involvement in the Rising she lost her job and worked for a while in JJ Walsh's shop in Blessington Street in 1917. She served through the War of Independence and she married Michael Murphy in April, 1919. They resided at 1 Leinster Avenue, North Strand, and after Frank Teeling escaped from Kilmainham Jail in February 1921, he stayed at their home. When her husband was arrested after the attack on the Custom House, she continued collecting and moving arms to the company's arms dump in Ballybough. She took the Republican side in the Civil War and reported to Barry's Hotel. She also served in the Minerva Hotel during the fighting.

Martha Murphy, the mother of sixteen children, died on September 15th 1943 and was buried at Glasnevin Cemetery.

References:

RH; IMA, MSPC; IMA, BMH (WS 1687, *Harry Colley*); NLI, *William O'Brien Papers*, (Ms 15,673); *Irish Press*, 16th September 1943, (obit).

Mary (May) Kelly (Mrs. Mary Chadwick):
(1900 - 1964)
Captain. Clann na nGaedhael. Cumann na mBan

May Kelly was born in 1900. She was a founder and Commandant of the Clann na nGaedhael girl scouts that was attached to the Hibernian Rifles and later amalgamated with Cumann na mBan. She reported to the GPO on Easter Monday and carried supplies to the various outposts in the Sackville Street vicinity. She also tended to the wounded in the GPO until Tuesday, when she was sent to report on troop movements at the Royal Barracks (later Collins Barracks), near to Arbour Hill. She was sent with dispatches to the Jacob's Garrison later on Tuesday and she remained there for the remainder of the week. She was arrested in August 1916 while participating in a parade to Glasnevin Cemetery, and detained for a week.

During the Civil War she organised Clann na nGaedhael branches in Cork and Athlone, and also served in south county Dublin. She took the Republican side in the Civil War, and served in the Gresham Hotel, Barry's Hotel, the C.Y.M.S. North Frederick Street and Healy's Public House, Parnell Street. She was arrested on Easter Sunday 1923, and taken to Oriel House. She was later interned in Kilmainham Jail and the South Dublin Union until October 1923. As a result, she lost her job in Forrest's, Grafton Street, where she worked for many years. She was married to Commandant Mick Chadwick of the 6th Battalion, Dublin Brigade and they lived at 59 Belton Park Road, Donnycarney.

May Chadwick died suddenly on March 31st 1964 and was buried at Deansgrange Cemetery.

References:
   RH; IMA, MSPC; NLI, *Lynch Papers*, (Ms 11,131); Ann Matthews, *Renegades*, (2010).

Austin Kennan: (1890 – 1979)
London Company, (Kimmage Garrison). Roll of Honour

Austin Kennan was born in 1890 and was originally from North Strand, Dublin. In 1913 he was living in London when he joined the IRB and the Volunteers. He returned to Dublin on Good Friday 1916 with Michael Mulvihill and Seán McGrath and joined the Kimmage Garrison. On Easter Monday he was posted to the roof of the GPO with Mulvihill, beside the Volunteers from Rathfarnham. He remained there until Wednesday evening when he was moved to the ground floor. On Thursday he manned a window beside the Henry Street corner. He left the GPO on Friday in the group led by The O'Rahilly into Moore Street, and spent that night sheltering in a house there. At the time of the surrender, he evaded capture by mingling among the people in the neighbourhood, before escaping from the area and then returning to London.

In December 1966 he was present at the unveiling of a memorial to his brother-in-law, Michael Mulvihill, who was killed at the junction of Henry Place and Moore Lane, following The O'Rahilly after the evacuation of the GPO.

Austin Kennan died at the home of his daughter, Mrs O'Neill, of 46 Blackheath Park, Clontarf, on November 27th 1979 and was buried at Balgriffin Cemetery.

References:

RH; IMA, MSPC; NLI, *Lynch Papers*, (Ms 11,131); Clair Willis, *Dublin 1916, the Siege of the GPO*, (2009); *Irish Press*, 29th November 1979, (dn).

Luke Kennedy: (1867 - 1950)

Executive Council, Volunteers. Roll of Honour

Luke Kennedy was born in the United States, in 1867. In 1911 he was a widower and lived at 12 Grenville Street, and was employed as a mechanical engineer. By 1916 he was residing at 58 North Great Charles Street and was a member of the Supreme Council of the IRB and also of the Executive Council of the Volunteers. On Easter Sunday he was in charge of a group of Volunteers, who commandeered several lorries, for the purpose of collecting arms and ammunition from the German ship, The Aud, at Fenit, County Kerry. When they reached Limerick they were informed of Roger Casement's capture and so returned to Dublin. He had previous experience of gun-running, having participated in the landing of arms at Kilcoole, County Wicklow in 1914. On Easter Monday he reported to the GPO and he spent some time in the armory. On Tuesday he was called to the wireless station in Reis's Chambers where, after some difficulty, he got the radio apparatus to work. The following day he helped bring the radio equipment back across the street under heavy gunfire. He made several further crossings to the wireless station and, on one occasion, silenced a sniper in Wynn's Hotel. Later on Wednesday, under heavy gunfire, he drove J.J. Walsh in a car to the College of Surgeons with a dispatch. On their return journey they drove to an engineering works in Bride Street and confiscated some wire and detonators. By the time of the evacuation on Friday, he had been wounded three times during the various crossings of Sackville Street. He sought shelter in a house in Moore Street with four other Volunteers, before the surrender on Saturday afternoon. Lieutenant King, one of the British Officers held prisoner in the GPO by the Volunteers, identified him as having made grenades there. He was deported and interned in Frongoch until Christmas, 1916. During the War of Independence, he was a member of the Executive Committee of the Volunteers. He was Chairman of the Dublin Arms Committee that organized the purchase and distribution of arms. He was also involved in intelligence work. He was described as a "whitesmith, with an engineering genius" and was also a fine amateur actor. He was employed as an electrician in the *Irish Press*, from its formation in 1931.

Luke Kennedy died at his grand-daughter's residence at 22 Millmount Avenue, Drumcondra, on Christmas Day, 1950 and was buried in Glasnevin Cemetery.

References:

RH; IMA, MSPC; NLI, *Lynch Papers*, (Ms 11,131); Seamus deBurca, *The Soldier's Song, the story of Peadar Ó'Cearnaigh*, (1955); *Irish Press*, 27th December 1950, (obit).

Henry V. Kenny: (1895 - 1968)

A. Coy, 4th Batt, Dublin Brigade. Roll of Honour

Henry Kenny was born in 1895. He was a printer by trade and a member of A. Company, 4th Battalion, Dublin Brigade. Because he didn't live in the vicinity of the 4th Battalion area, he was told in advance of the Rising to link up with the nearest battalion in an emergency. On Easter Monday he reported to Liberty Hall and was instructed to commandeer a car to transport weapons and supplies to the GPO. From Monday to Wednesday he was sniping from the windows of the GPO. Along with Tom McGrath, he volunteered to go to Arnott's, Henry Street on the Thursday, to obtain red and white material for use in

making a Red Cross flag to be carried in front of the wounded that were about to be brought to Jervis Street Hospital. After the evacuation on Friday evening, he spent the night in Price's shop in Moore Street. He was deported to Knutsford Jail on May 1st and interned in Frongoch until Christmas 1916.

After his release from internment he was transferred to A. Company, 3rd Battalion and was later attached to the 5th Battalion, Engineers. He took part in raids for arms and in the burning of Stepaside RIC Barracks. He served on the staff of Rory O'Connor and was sent to Belfast for a short time. In February 1922 he joined the Free State Army and resigned a month later, only to rejoin in April and serve in the Civil War. He resigned from the army in 1927 with the rank of captain and was later a civilian employee of the Army Corps of Engineers.

Henry Kenny died, while in the care of the Little Sisters of the Poor, Roebuck Road, on August 2nd 1968 and was buried in Glasnevin Cemetery.

References:
    RH; IMA, MSPC; NLI, *Lynch Papers*, (Ms 11,131); *Irish Independent* & *Evening Herald*, 3rd August 1968, (dn).

James Kenny: (1897 - 1981)

E. Coy, 4th Batt, Dublin Brigade. Roll of Honour

James Kenny was born in 1897 and was employed as a grocer's assistant. He left Rathfarnham on Easter Monday morning with members of E. Company, 4th Battalion, Dublin Brigade and reached the GPO at 2 o'clock in the afternoon. At 4 o'clock he volunteered to bring a dispatch to Captain Tom Weafer at Ballybough Bridge, before returning to the GPO. After being accidently shot in the foot by Antti Makalpaltis, a Finnish seaman, he was attended to by Dr James Ryan, who removed the shot and cleaned the wound. He returned to his post and fought there throughout Easter Week, and he was among the last group to vacate the blazing building on Friday evening. He was deported to Knutsford Jail, on May 3rd and interned in Wandsworth Prison and Frongoch, before being released in July, 1916.

After E. Company was reorganized, he was appointed lieutenant and took part in many operations, including the burning of Rockbrook RIC Barracks and an ambush at Templeogue. He was in the group sent to execute British Agents on Bloody Sunday, November 21st 1920. He was appointed of K. Company, 4th Battalion in December 1921 and fought on the anti-Treaty side in the Civil War. He was arrested in the attempt to rescue Tom Barry from Mountjoy Jail in August 1922. He was interned in Newbridge Barracks and escaped from there, in November 1922.

He joined An Garda Síochana in 1933 and was attached to the Special Branch, Dublin Castle. James Kenny, of 1 Whitehall Road, Churchtown, died on January 26th 1981 and was buried at Cruagh Cemetery, Rathfarnham.

References:
RH; IMA, MSPC; IMA, BMH (WS 141); *Irish Independent*, 27th January 1981, (dn).

John (Jack) Kenny: (1897 - 1978)
F. Coy, 1st Batt, Dublin Brigade. Roll of Honour

Jack Kenny was born on March 5th 1897 and, in 1916 he was living at 16 Belvedere Place, North Circular Road. He joined the Volunteers at the inaugural meeting in the Rotunda in 1913 with his brother, Michael. Both were members of F. Company, 1st Battalion, Dublin Brigade and were previously members of the Irish National Guard, a branch of Fianna Éireann. On Easter Monday he escorted Seán T. O'Kelly with the National Flag to the GPO before reporting to the Fairview outpost. On Tuesday evening he, along with his brother Michael, was among the men fighting in the Fairview area that were ordered back to the GPO, taking prisoners with them. He was posted at the windows in the GPO, and later on Wednesday he moved to the roof. On Thursday he was in the group, who occupied a warehouse in Henry Street, and met up with Volunteers there, led by Tom Byrne and Seán McGrath, who were coming from the direction of Capel Street. They were ordered to return to the GPO and on Friday he helped fight the fire. He was in the group, led by The O'Rahilly, who came under a storm of machinegun fire in Moore Street. He was only thirty yards into Moore Street when he was shot in the foot and when he got to his feet again, he was wounded a second time. His life was saved by Albert Dyas and Seán Conway, who pulled him out of the line of fire. After eight weeks in Jervis Street Hospital, he was arrested and sent to Kilmainham Jail. He was deported to Knutsford and Wandsworth Jails and interned in Frongoch.

On his release from internment, he rejoined F. Company and fought in the War of Independence. He joined the Free State Army at its formation with rank of Sergeant and took part in the fighting at the Four Courts during the Civil War. After he was discharged from the army, he was employed as an usher in Dáil Éireann for many years.

Jack Kenny, of 106 Tyrconnell Park, Inchicore, died on May 2nd 1978.

References:
RH; IMA, MSPC; IMA, BMH (WS 1693); *Irish Independent*, 3rd May 1978, (dn).

Michael Kenny: (1898 - 1972)

F. Coy, 1st Batt, Dublin Brigade. Roll of Honour

Michael Kenny was born in 1898 and resided at 16 Belvedere Place, North Circular Road. He joined the Irish National Guard, a branch of Fianna Éireann, in 1912 with his brother, Jack. The following year he joined the Volunteers at the inaugural meeting in the Rotunda and became a member of F. Company, 1st Battalion, Dublin Brigade. On Easter Monday he was stationed at Annesley Bridge, Fairview and was in the party that blew up the railway track at the sloblands in Fairview. He moved to the GPO on Tuesday evening with the main group from the Fairview area, including his brother Jack, and was posted at a window, facing Henry Street. He manned the windows on Wednesday and Thursday and on Friday he moved explosives to the basement. After the evacuation, he went with a party led by Seán McEntee to Samson's Lane where they remained overnight. He was detained and freed early from Richmond Barracks after the surrender, because of his young age.

He took an active part in the War of Independence. In 1922 he joined the Free State Army with the rank of company sergeant and served with the Army Air Corps, Baldonnell until 1940, when he became a civilian employee of the Dept of Transport, Power & Aviation. Michael Kenny, of 27 Knockmanagh Road, Clondalkin, died on February 21st 1972 and was buried at Esker Cemetery, Lucan.

References:
RH; IMA, MSPC; NLI, *Lynch Papers*, (Ms 11,131); *Evening Herald*, 22nd February 1972, (dn).

Bernard Keogh: (1896 - 1949)

F. Coy, 2nd Batt, Dublin Brigade. Roll of Honour

Bernard Keogh was born in 1896 and resided at 2 Richmond Parade, North Circular Road, in 1916. He was a Section Commander with F. Company, 2nd Battalion, Dublin Brigade and fought as a sniper in the GPO throughout Easter Week. After the evacuation on Friday evening, he was in charge of a party that erected a barricade in Henry Place, while under heavy enemy fire. He was deported to Knutsford Detention Barracks on May 1st and interned in Frongoch, until July 15th 1916.

On his release from internment, he rejoined his old unit and took part in many operations, including the burning of Raheny RIC Barracks, an attack on a British munitions train at Newcomen Bridge and other raids for arms. He was arrested in January 1921 and interned in Ballykinlar Camp, until December 1921. He joined the Dublin Guards, No. 1 Brigade, Free State Army, in April 1922 and served through the Civil War. He was demobilized in 1924 with the rank of captain.

In 1949 he was admitted to a sanatorium, after his health deteriorated.

Bernard Keogh, of 154 Larkhill Road, Whitehall, died on October 8th 1949 and was buried at Glasnevin Cemetery.

References:
RH; IMA, MSPC; *Irish Independent*, 10th October 1949, (dn).

Francis (Frank) Keogh: (1889 -   )
D. Coy, 4th Batt, Dublin Brigade

Frank Keogh was born in 1889 and resided at 25 Elmsgrove, Ranelagh, in 1916. He was a member of D. Company, 4th Battalion, Dublin Brigade. He reported to the GPO on Monday afternoon with the Rathfarnham Volunteers. Included in the Rathfarnham Volunteers was his brother, Gerald, who was killed in action during Easter Week. His other brother, Cyril, was a member of the St Stephen's Green Garrison. After the Rising, he was held captive in Dublin Castle, from where he made a dramatic escape.

Frank Keogh emigrated to England and lived in Liverpool.

References:
Irish Independent, 16th April 1964, (obit *of Cyril Keogh*).

Gerald Keogh: (1894 – 1916). Killed in Action
D. Coy, 4th Batt, Dublin Brigade. Roll of Honour

Gerald Keogh was born in 1894 and resided at 25 Elmsgrove, Ranelagh. He was educated at Synge Street CBS and at St. Enda's, Rathfarnham. He was a member of D. Company, 4th Battalion, Dublin Brigade. His father, James had been a Fenian and two of his brothers fought in the Rising; Cyril was with the St Stephen's Green Garrison and Frank was in the GPO. Another brother, Leo took part in the War of Independence. On Easter Monday he was sent by P.H. Pearse to the St Stephen's Green Garrison with dispatches. As he passed Trinity College while cycling back to the GPO early the following morning, he was shot dead by one of the Colonial soldiers who were stationed there.

Gerald Keogh was initially buried in the grounds of Trinity and was later interred in Glasnevin Cemetery.

References:
RH; IMA, MSPC; *Catholic Bulletin*, November 1916; HI, March/April 2009; Max Caulfield, *The Easter Rebellion*, (1963); *Synge Street CBS Centenary Record, 1864-1964*, (1964); Ray Bateson, *They Died by Pearse's Side*, (2009); *Never a Dull Day: 150 years of Synge Street CBS, 1864-2014*, (Michael Minnock & Seán Ryan Ed, 2014).

Joseph J. (Mike) Keough: (1896 - 1966)
B. Coy, 1st Batt, Dublin Brigade. Roll of Honour

Joseph Keough, who was known as Mike, was born in 1896 and resided at 18 Synge Street. In 1916 he was an employee of McQuillan's, Capel Street. As a member of B. Company, 1st Battalion, Dublin Brigade and he reported to the 2nd Battalion HQ, at Father Mathew Park, Fairview on Easter Monday. He was stationed at Gilbey's Shop, Ballybough Bridge and fought in the Fairview area until Tuesday evening, when he withdrew to the GPO. He was sent to the Imperial Hotel and fought there until Thursday when the building was evacuated, because of fire. He left with a group that made their way into the north inner city and he spent that night in a cellar of a tenement in Gloucester Street. The following morning he was arrested and taken to the Custom House for interrogation, after which he was deported to Wandsworth Jail on May 9th, but was released from there at the end of May suffering from pleurisy.

He rejoined his unit and fought in the War of Independence. During the Truce period he took part in the occupation of the Fowler Hall, Mountjoy Square. He fought on the Republican side in the Civil War and was posted in Barry's Hotel, where he was injured, but evaded capture.

He later lived at 33 Haverty Road, Marino and was employed for over thirty years in the Botanic Gardens, Glasnevin.

Mike Keough died on November 24th 1966 and was buried at Balgriffin Cemetery.

References:
RH; IMA, MSPC; *Irish Press*, 26th November 1966, (dn).

John (Seán) Kerr: (- 1979)
F. Coy, 2nd Batt, Dublin Brigade. Roll of Honour

Seán Kerr was a member of a Republican family from Armagh, who emigrated to Liverpool. His father, Neil Kerr, was a prominent member of the IRB in Liverpool. In 1913 he returned to Dublin and joined F. Company, 2nd Battalion the following year. On Easter Monday he reported to the 2nd Battalion's HQ at Father Mathew Park, and took part in the attack on British Troops at Wharf Road, East Wall. He was stationed at Gilbey's Shop, Ballybough Bridge until Tuesday evening when he was ordered into the GPO. On Wednesday he was part of the group that occupied O'Neill's Public House, at the corner of Liffey Street. Despite coming under intense fire from a British armoured car, they held out until Friday when they withdrew to the GPO. His brothers, Niall and Tom, were part of the Kimmage Garrison in the GPO. After the surrender he was deported to Stafford Jail on May 1st and interned in Frongoch until Christmas 1916.

Following his release, he rejoined his old unit and in 1918 he was sent to Ulster by the GHQ to organize the Sinn Féin and Dáil Loans there. He was sent to Liverpool, in 1920 and took part in an arson attack on a cotton warehouse. He worked as a purser on a shipping line, which enabled him to transport arms and ammunitions and act as an agent for Michael Collins. Like his brother Tom, he was arrested and imprisoned in 1920 for these activities. He had been a member of the GAA in Liverpool. On his release from prison, he returned to Dublin and later became a member of St Laurence O'Toole's GAA Club. He emigrated to the United States, before returning to Ireland in 1930.

Seán Kerr died at the Holy Family Home, Roebuck, on April 12th 1979.

References:
RH; IMA, MSPC; Michael Hopkinson, *Frank Henderson's Easter Rising Recollections of a Dublin Volunteer*, (1998); Jimmy Wren, *Saint Laurence O'Toole's GAC Centenary, 1901-2001*, (2001).

Niall Kerr, Junior: (1896 - 1920)
Liverpool Company, (Kimmage Garrison)

Niall Kerr was born in 1896 and came to Dublin from Liverpool in 1916, shortly before the Rising with his brother, Tom. They joined the Kimmage Garrison and fought in the GPO. Another brother, Seán, also fought in the GPO, while their father, Neil Kerr Senior, had intended joining his sons at Kimmage, but due to a misunderstanding he arrived in Dublin towards the end of Easter Week. Neil (Sr.) was involved in many exploits during the War of Independence, including some important jail rescues. He passed away in June, 1936.

Niall Kerr, Junior was deported to Knutsford Jail on May 3rd and was interned in Frongoch, until Christmas 1916.

On his release, he returned to Liverpool and worked as a seaman.

Niall Kerr died in an accident in Liverpool on September 7th 1920 and his remains were brought to Dublin for burial. His coffin was accompanied by a large rally of Volunteers in a slow march through the streets of the city to Glasnevin Cemetery.

References:
Evening Herald, 8th September 1920, (obit); *Freeman's Journal* & *Irish Independent*, 9th September 1920, (obits).

Thomas (Tom) Kerr: (- 1973)
Liverpool Company, (Kimmage Garrison)

Armagh born Tom Kerr arrived in Dublin with his brother, Neil, from Liverpool, shortly before the Easter Rising. They joined the Kimmage Garrison and fought in the GPO throughout Easter Week. Another brother, Seán, also fought in the GPO. He was deported to Knutsford Jail on May 3rd and interned in Frongoch.

After his release from internment, he returned to Liverpool where he found employment, working as a docker. Like his father before him, he was a member of the IRB and on his return home he was made captain of the Liverpool Volunteers. He was responsible, on Michael Collins's instructions, for the gathering of weapons and ammunition throughout the North of England and Scotland, and for their transportation by boat to Dublin. On many occasions he was lucky to escape capture, but was finally arrested and imprisoned. He returned to Dublin on his release prison and lived at 44 West Road, East Wall.

Tom Kerr died on January 9th 1973 and he was buried at Glasnevin Cemetery.

References:
John A. Pinkman, *In the Legion of the Vanguard*, (1998); *Irish Press*, 23rd January 1973, (obit).

Thomas Kilcoyne: (1898 – 1971)
Fianna Éireann

Thomas Kilcoyne was born in 1898 and resided at 4 St Joseph's Parade, Philipsburgh Avenue, Fairview. In 1916 he was an apprentice baker by trade and was a member of Fianna Éireann. On Easter Monday he reported to Father Mathew Park, Fairview and he was in the party that occupied Gilbey's Wine Shop, Ballybough Bridge. He served there until Tuesday, when the withdrawal to the GPO took place. He was sent to the Imperial Hotel and fought there until Thursday when the building was evacuated because of the intense fire. He was in a group that attempted to escape into the north inner city. They were intercepted in Gloucester Street and were captured twelve hours later. He was taken to the Custom House for interrogation and then transferred to Richmond Barracks, but was released on account of his young age.

In 1917 he joined B. Company, 2nd Battalion, Dublin Brigade and took part in a number of operations, including the attempted assassination of Lord French at Ashbourne in 1919 and the attack on the Custom House, in May 1921. He was arrested shortly after the burning of the Custom House, and was interned until December 1921. He joined the Free State Army with the rank of commandant, in 1922 and took part in the fighting in

Dublin, Cork and Waterford, during the Civil War. In March 1923 he resigned his post because he refused to take orders from former British Army Officers serving in the Free State Army, and also in protest against the treatment former IRA members in the army.

Thomas Kilcoyne, late of 10 Rostrevor Road, Rathgar and of 7 Mountpellier Parade, Cheltenham, Gloucestershire, died on August 2nd 1971 and was buried at Deansgrange Cemetery.

References:
    IMA, MSPC; *An t-Óglach*, January 1926, (W.J. Brennan-Whitmore); *Irish Press*, 4th August 1971, (dn).

John Kilgallon: (1893 – 1972)
E. Coy, 4th Batt, Dublin Brigade. Roll of Honour

John Kilgallon was born in the village of Far Rockaway, New York, United States, in 1893. His parents were from County Mayo and his father, Luke, was a blacksmith by trade. They built a prosperous auto repairs business and patented a safety device for removing tyres. In 1914 he was sent to be educated at St Enda's, Rathfarnham, and joined E. Company, 4th Battalion, Dublin Brigade, with other St Enda's students. On Easter Monday morning he left Rathfarnham with his unit for the GPO and fought on the roof of the building. When the fire took hold, he helped fight the flames. Much to the amusement of his beleaguered comrades, he appeared on Friday dressed in a postman's trousers and puttees, a fur-lined coat and an Australian hat, complete with dangling corks. He had returned from the Dublin Waxworks, Henry Street, where he had relieved some of the wax figures of their clothing.

He was deported to Stafford Jail on May 1st and interned in Frongoch, until Christmas, 1916.

On his release from internment, he was deported to the United States. He later enlisted in the US Airforce as a mechanic and fought in World War 1. He was still running the family auto repair business in the 1940's.

John Kilgallon, of 1502 Mott Avenue, Far Rockaway, Long Island, New York, died on January 30th 1972.

References:
    RH; IMA, MSPC; Michael Foy & Brian Barton, *The Easter Rising*, (2000); *Irish Press*, 4th August 1972, (dn).

Robert (Bob) Killeen: (1878 - 1938)

Irish Citizen Army, (Dorset St Section). Roll of Honour

Bob Killeen was born in 1878 and resided at 14 St Joseph's Parade, Dorset Street. He was employed as a float driver by Boileau & Boyd's, and joined the Irish Citizen Army in 1914. He was part of the guard duty in Liberty Hall for several weeks, prior to the Rising. On Easter Monday morning he was selected by James Connolly to take part in the attack on the Magazine Fort in the Phoenix Park. After the attack, he made his way to the GPO. and later that evening he was one of a party detailed to reinforce the garrison in the City Hall area. As they approached Crown Alley, they came under attack from British forces who occupied the telephone exchange buildings. On Tuesday morning his party returned to the GPO, and he was sent with a group under the command of Captain Frank Thornton to occupy the Hibernian Bank. He fought there until Thursday, when they were forced out by the fire. On Saturday morning he was arrested in the basement of a house in Gloucester Street. He was taken to the Custom House for interrogation and deported to Knutsford Jail on May 3rd. He was interned in Frongoch until Christmas 1916 and on his release he lost his job because of his involvement in the Rising.

He rejoined his unit in early 1917 and was employed from 1917 to 1920 by J.J. Walsh, later Minister of Posts & Telegraphs. He was attached to the GHQ dispatch service and was involved in purchasing arms from British soldiers. In February 1920 he was arrested and sent to Wormwoods Scrubs Prison where he took part in the Republican prisoner's hunger strike and was released in June 1920.

Bob Killeen, who later was employed as a postman, died on May 2nd 1938 and was buried at Glasnevin Cemetery.

References:

RH; IMA, MSPC; *Irish Independent* & *Irish Press*, 5th May 1938, (obits).

Patrick J. (Paddy) Kilmartin: (1895 – 1976)

D. Coy, 1st Batt, Dublin Brigade. Roll of Honour

Paddy Kilmartin was born in 1895 and resided at 23 Stoneybatter, where his family had a florist's shop. He was a member of D. Company, 1st Battalion, Dublin Brigade and on Easter Monday he was posted to the railway bridge on the North Circular Road, near Phibsboro. A barricade was erected at the bridge and *Mountain View*, a house close by, was occupied. Later he drove a Ford car to the GPO and collected dynamite and materials and brought them back to Phibsboro. He fought at the North Circular Road on Monday and Tuesday, until the barricade was destroyed by artillery

153

fire and shrapnel. He was arrested on Wednesday morning at *Mountain View* and taken to Arbour Hill Military Prison and then Richmond Barracks. He was deported to Wakefield Prison on May 6th and interned in Frongoch, until June 1916.

He rejoined his unit at the reorganisation of the Volunteers and was engaged in buying arms from British soldiers. In 1917 his sister, Mary, who was a member of the Four Courts Garrison in the Rising, married Paddy Stephenson, who fought in the Mendicity Institute in Easter Week. Kilmartin took no part in the Civil War. He joined the army in the emergency years and served as lieutenant in the 2nd Field Company, Transport Section, until March 1946. He was involved in amateur boxing and in his youth fought under the name, "*Young Knox*". Two of his sons later represented Ireland in amateur boxing.

Paddy Kilmartin died on October 18th 1976.

References:
RH; IMA, MSPC; *Irish Independent* & *Irish Press*, 19th October 1976, (dn).

George King: (1896 - 1922)
Liverpool Company, (Kimmage Garrison). Roll of Honour

George King, of 61 Orwell Road, Kirkdale, Liverpool, was born in 1896. He came to Dublin with his two brothers, Patrick and John, before the Rising and joined the Volunteer Camp at Kimmage. He fought in the GPO and the Metropole Hotel during Easter Week. After the surrender he was deported to Stafford Jail on May 1st and later interned in Frongoch until Christmas 1916. On his release he returned to Ireland and fought in the War of Independence. He took the Republican side in the Civil War, while his brother, Patrick, became an officer in the Free State Army. He resided at Tallaght, County Dublin and was employed as an insurance agent.

On February 5th 1923 an attack took place at 135 Leinster Road, Rathmines, the home of the State Solicitor. George King was wounded attempting to disarm a sentry and was admitted to the Meath Hospital, where he later died from his wounds.

References:
RH; IMA, BMH (WS 889, *Seamus Kavanagh*); *Irish Independent*, 9th & 10th February 1923, (obits); *Irish Times*, 9th February 1923, (obit).

John King: (1890 - 1969)
Liverpool Company, (Kimmage Garrison). Roll of Honour

John King was born in 1890 and was one of three brothers from Liverpool who fought with the GPO Garrison in 1916. He was severely wounded when he was shot in the hip during the evacuation from the GPO. Seamus Donegan, the Kimmage Garrison Red Cross man, attended to him, bandaging his wounds as he lay in one of the houses in Moore Street. After the surrender, he was removed to the hospital in Dublin Castle and on his discharge was interned in Frongoch until Christmas, 1916.

After his release from internment he took no further part in fight for independence. He later resided at 113 Home Farm Road and became a Director of Davis, King & Co Ltd, South Leinster Street, Dublin, 2.

John King died on August 12th 1969 and was buried at Glasnevin Cemetery.

References:
RH; IMA, MSPC; *Irish Press*, 16th August 1969, (obit).

Patrick King: (- 1979)
Liverpool Company, (Kimmage Garrison). Roll of Honour

Patrick King was a member of the Liverpool Volunteers and he came to Dublin with his brothers, John and George, to take part in the Rising. They joined the Kimmage Garrison and fought in the GPO during Easter Week. After the surrender, he was deported to Stafford Jail on May 1st and interned in Frongoch. While in Frongoch he was called for military service, but refused to wear the uniform and as a result was not released until April 1917. On his release he fought in the War of Independence. He was arrested and interned in Rath Camp in 1921. He joined the Free State Army in 1922, attaining the rank of major and he served for a second time during the emergency years, 1939-45.

Patrick King died in November 1979.

References:
RH; IMA, MSPC; *Irish Independent*, 20th November 1979, (dn).

Samuel (Sam) King: (1882 - 1945)

Irish Citizen Army, (Dorset St Section). Roll of Honour

Sam King was born in 1882 and lived at 25 St Ignatius Road, Glasnevin. He was a member of the Irish Citizen Army and was one of four brothers who fought in the Easter Rising. On the evening of Easter Monday he was sent from the GPO to re-enforce the insurgents in the City Hall area. He was detailed to Henry & James shop, opposite to City Hall, that came under a heavy onslaught from British troops. On Tuesday this small detachment successfully withdrew to the GPO. He was sent across the street to the Imperial Hotel, where he hoisted the ICA flag, *The Starry Plough*, on the roof. He then laid a telephone line from the hotel to be connected to the GPO and when the building took fire, he escaped into the north inner city with his comrades. He was arrested in Waterford Street on Saturday morning and was taken to the Custom House for interrogation. He escaped from the Custom House with the help of a British Army Officer, who was a former neighbour and who knew him well.

His brothers, George and Arthur were in the City Hall Garrison, while Martin was in the St Stephen's Green Garrison. He took part in the reorganization of the Irish Citizen Army and fought through the War of Independence.

Sam King, of 18 Berkeley Street, died on December 18th 1945 and was buried at Glasnevin Cemetery.

References:
RH; IMA, MSPC; NLI, *William O'Brien Papers*, (Ms 15, 673); *Irish Independent*, 19th December 1945, (dn).

Patrick Kirwan: (1871 – 1959)

Maynooth Company, Kildare Brigade. Roll of Honour

Patrick Kirwan was born in 1871 and was a Volunteer in the Maynooth Company, Kildare Brigade. He left Maynooth, his home town, with his company on Easter Monday evening and travelled by the Royal Canal towpath to Dublin. They slept in Glasnevin Cemetery that night and arrived at the GPO on Easter Tuesday morning to a rousing reception from the garrison there. He and other members of Maynooth Company were sent to re-enforce the group of Irish Citizen Army men and Volunteers in the vicinity of City Hall. He was stationed in the *Evening Mail*

Offices in Parliament Street and fought there until Tuesday evening when he returned to the GPO. On the Thursday and Friday, he was posted on the roof and at the windows of the GPO. On May 1st, Kirwan, the father of six young children, was deported to Stafford Jail, and interned in Frongoch. While in Stafford Jail, Michael Collins wrote to his cousin Susan, to seek Cumann na mBan aid for Patrick's wife and children. He was released from Frongoch on July 22nd 1916.

He rejoined the Maynooth Company in 1917 and took part in many operations during the War of Independence. He took the anti-Treaty side in the Civil War and was arrested in July 1922. He was interned in Dundalk Jail and took part in a hunger strike, after he was badly beaten. He was freed from Dundalk Jail by Republican Forces, but was arrested again and interned in Gormanstown, until February 1923.

Patrick Kirwan, of Double Lane, Maynooth, died on November 7th 1959 and was buried in Laraghbryan Cemetery, Maynooth.

References:

RH; IMA, MSPC; NLI, *Lynch Papers*, (Ms 11,131); *Irish Press*, 9th April 1959, (dn).

Michael Knightly: (1888 - 1965)

F. Coy, 1st Batt, Dublin Brigade. Roll of Honour

Michael Knightly born in 1888 and was a native of Tralee, County Kerry. He resided at 16 Gardiner's Place and was working as a reporter for the *Irish Independent* newspaper in 1916. He was also a member of F. Company, 1st Battalion. When the Rising started he was sent to investigate by the newspaper, but on entering the GPO was handed a shotgun instead. He spent the next few days manning ground floor windows in the GPO and also the Coliseum Theatre in Henry Street, until he received treatment for a carbuncle on his throat on Thursday. He was among the wounded transferred to Jervis Street Hospital, but he was detained there and deported to Wakefield Prison on May 6th. He was later interned in Frongoch until July 17th 1916.

He was arrested during the War of Independence and was imprisoned in Mountjoy Jail when Kevin Barry was hanged. In 1921 he worked as a reporter covering the Treaty Debate negotiations. The following year, he was appointed editor of the Dáil Debates in Dáil Éireann. During the Emergency years he was Official Censor of Newspapers.

Michael Knightly retired to Dunmore, County Galway and died on December 20th 1965.

References:

RH; IMA, MSPC; IMA, BMH (WS 833-835); *Irish Press*, 21st December 1965, (dn).

John Lafferty: (1894 – 1958)
Glasgow Company, (Kimmage Garrison)

John Lafferty was born in Magilligan, County Derry, in 1894. In 1915, while an apprentice engineer, he joined the Volunteers and the IRB in Glasgow. He came to Dublin and joined the Volunteer Camp at Larkfield, Kimmage, in March 1916. On Easter Monday morning he left Kimmage for Liberty Hall with a group of Volunteers and reported to the GPO and fought there throughout Easter Week. After the surrender he was deported to Knutsford Jail on May 1st and interned in Frongoch until Christmas 1916.

He was sent north by Michel Collins in September 1917 and assisted in founding a Sinn Féin Club and a Volunteer Company in Derry City. He served through the War of Independence and he enlisted the Free State Army at Moville Barracks, County Donegal, in June 1922, where he was appointed Barrack's quartermaster. He lived for many years in the United States and was employed as a clerk with Express Railway, Chicago.

John Lafferty died in Chicago on October 6th 1958 and was buried there.

References:
IMA, MSPC.

Brigid Lambert (Mrs. Brigid Doran): (1897 – 1961)
Irish Citizen Army. Roll of Honour

Brigid Lambert was born in 1897 and lived at Old Bridge House, Milltown. She was employed in the Manor Mill Laundry with her father, Thomas, her sister, Ellen and her aunt, Ellen Hartnett, and was a member of the Irish Citizen Army. On Easter Monday she went to Liberty Hall with her sister, Ellen, with a message for their father, who was also in the Irish Citizen Army. When he was posted to City Hall, they reported to the GPO where they offered their services and were detailed to work in the kitchen. On Easter Monday night she returned home to inform her mother of what had happened and then returned to the GPO with her aunt, Ellen Noone nee Hartnett. She remained in the GPO throughout Easter Week. On Friday, when the thirty four women present were ordered to leave the GPO by P.H. Pearse, she was in the group that was arrested and taken to Broadstone Station for interrogation. She was released shortly afterwards and went to the night refuge in Henrietta Street with her sister and her aunt, before they made her way home the following day.

She joined the Cumann na mBan, Dundrum Branch, in 1917. During the War of Independence she and her sister, Ellen, were engaged in collecting funds, carrying dispatches and distributing arms and ammunition. She took the anti-Treaty side in the Civil War, and was on duty at Rathfarnham Castle during the attack on the Four Courts. She acted as a scout for the Republican Forces at Blessington in July 1922 and her home at Milltown was used as a safe house. In the 1930s Brigid Lambert and her sister, Ellen, regularly attended Old ICA functions and funerals and they were among the guard of honour at Kathleen Barrett's funeral. In later years she and her husband emigrated to England.

Brigid Doran, of 16 Bowman's Green, Garston, Watford, died on January 17th 1961.

References:
RH; IMA, MSPC; NLI, *William O'Brien Papers*, (Ms 15,673).

Ellen Lambert (Mrs. Ellen Stynes): (1899 - 1980)
Irish Citizen Army. Roll of Honour

Ellen Lambert was born 1899 and resided at Old Bridge House, Milltown. She worked in the Manor Mill Laundry with her father, Thomas, her sister, Brigid and her aunt, Ellen Noone nee Hartnett. She went with her sister, Brigid, to Liberty Hall on Easter Monday morning, seeking their father and they then proceeded to the GPO, while he was posted to the City Hall. She was engaged delivering despatches on Monday and Tuesday and she worked in the kitchen on Wednesday and Thursday. At noon on Friday, when P.H. Pearse ordered the majority of women to leave the GPO, she was in the group with her sister and aunt that was detained at Broadstone Railway Station for interrogation, before being released shortly afterwards. They spent the night in the night refuge in Henrietta Street and returned to Milltown the following morning.

After the Rising she joined Cumann na mBan, Dundrum Branch and served in the War of Independence. She fought on the Republican side in the Civil War and carried dispatches and ammunition to the Four Courts. She was also attached to the first aid section at Rathfarnham Barracks, and she was arrested in February 1923. She was interned in Kilmainham Jail and released from the North Dublin Union in September 1923. She later married John Stynes.

Ellen Stynes, of 29 Cornamona Court, Kylemore Road, Ballyfermot, died on November 7th 1980 and was buried at Palmerstown Cemetery.

References:
RH; IMA, MSPC; NLI, *Lynch Papers*, (Ms 11,131); *Evening Herald*, 7th November 1980, (dn).

Seamus Landy
Liverpool Company, (Kimmage Garrison)

Seamus Landy came to Dublin from Liverpool before the Rising and joined the Volunteer Camp at Larkfield, Kimmage. During Easter Week he was sent from the GPO to Hopkins and Hopkins at the corner of Eden Quay. There he joined Seamus Robinson and Cormac Turner, who were also part of the Kimmage Garrison, and Irish Citizen Army marksman, Andy Conroy.

After the surrender Seamus Landy was deported to Stafford Jail on May 1st and interned in Frongoch, until Christmas 1916.

References:
IMA, BMH (WS 156, *Seamus Robinson*); Thomas Coffey, *Agony at Easter*, (1969); Ann Matthews, *The Kimmage Garrison 1916*, (2010).

Michael Largan: (1889 - 1946)

Irish Citizen Army, (Gloucester St Section)

Michael Largan was born in 1889 and resided at 12 Waterford Street. He was employed as a labourer in the Dublin Market. He was a member of the Irish Citizen Army, Gloucester Street Section, and on Easter Monday he was posted at a window on the Prince's Street side of the GPO. He crossed the street to the Imperial Hotel on Tuesday, where he was posted as a sniper at the front windows, under the command of Frank Thornton. On Wednesday he volunteered to take a dispatch across to the GPO and return to the Imperial Hotel with the reply, while under heavy fire. The next day the burning Imperial Hotel was evacuated and he made his escape to the north inner city tenements. He was captured the following morning in Marlborough Street and taken to the Custom House for interrogation. He was then transferred to Richmond Barracks and deported to Wakefield Prison on May 6th. He was later interned in Frongoch.

He joined the Free State Army in 1922 and served as a private until 1924, when he was discharged. Because he could not get regular employment he sold newspapers and he was living in poor circumstances when his health broke down. When he was admitted to the Pigeon House Sanitorium in 1945 his clothes had to be destroyed.

Michael Largin died on February 27th 1946 and was buried at Mount Jerome Cemetery, Harold's Cross.

References:

IMA, MSPC; NLI, *Lynch* Papers, (Ms 11,131) & *William O'Brien Papers*, (Ms 15,673); Ann Matthews, *The Irish Citizen Army*, (2014).

Patrick Lawler: (1900 – 1969)

A. Coy, 2nd Batt, Dublin Brigade

Patrick Lawler was born in 1900 and resided at 16 Fitzwilliam Lane. He was a member of Fianna Éireann and he joined A. Company, 2nd Battalion, Dublin Brigade, prior to the Rising. On Easter Monday he reported to Larkfield, Kimmage and he remained there until midnight, before proceeding to the GPO. On Tuesday he was sent to Henry Street on sentry duty. He and two other Volunteers later delivered supplies and provisions to the Imperial Hotel. When the hotel was evacuated on Thursday night, he made his way to Marlborough Street, where he was captured. He was taken to the Custom House for interrogation and transferred to Richmond Barracks. He was detained there for a week and released because of his young age.

He rejoined A. Company, 2nd Battalion, Dublin Brigade in 1917 and fought in the War of Independence. He took part in armed patrols and raids for arms, and was involved in an attack on British forces at Harold's Cross and served up to the Truce. He took no part in the Civil War.

Patrick Lawler, of 13 Clonfert Road, Crumlin, died on March 25th 1969 and was buried at Glasnevin Cemetery.

References:

IMA, MSPC; *Irish Independent*, 27th March 1969, (dn).

Edward Lawless: (1876 - 1952)

Swords Company, Fingal Brigade. Roll of Honour

Edward Lawless, a farmer from Rathbeale, Swords, was born in 1876 and, by 1916, was father of a young family. On Easter Monday he left Knocksedan and went to the Volunteer Camp at Finglas, where he spent the night. He arrived at the GPO on Easter Tuesday with a party of twenty Volunteers from North County Dublin, under the command of Captain Richard Coleman. On Tuesday and Wednesday he fought in Kelly's Gunpowder Shop at the corner of Bachelor's Walk and later returned to the GPO. After the surrender he was deported to Knutsford Jail on May 1st and interned in Frongoch, until Christmas, 1916. His sister, Mary, was also a member of the GPO Garrison and his brother

Frank, who was quartermaster of the Fingal Brigade, fought at Ashbourne with another brother, James.

He served with the Swords Company, Fingal Brigade, during the Civil War and took part in a number of operations, including the attack on Rush RIC Barracks and the attempted ambush at Lissenhall, Balbriggan. He was imprisoned in Arbour Hill from December 1920 to April June 1921. On his release he went on the run until the Truce.

Edward Lawless, of Rathbeale, Swords, died on July 13th 1952.

References:
RH; IMA, MSPC.

Mary Lawless: (- 1924)

Cumann na mBan (Central Branch). Roll of Honour

Mary Lawless, of Saucerstown, Swords, was a sister of Frank and James Lawless, who fought at Ashbourne, and of Edward who was in the GPO during Easter Week. Her nephews, Joseph and Colm Lawless, were in the Fingal Brigade and fought at Ashbourne. She was a member of the Gaelic League and of the Central Branch of Cumann na mBan. She reported to the GPO on Easter Monday and on Tuesday she was sent across the street to the Hibernian Bank, where Captain Thomas Weafer was in command. Captain Weafer sent her and the Foley sisters, Brigid and Vera, to an empty shop premises nearby to set up a first aid centre. There, she assisted Dr. JJ Touhy, who did splendidly in attending to the wounded. She was in the GPO when it was decided to evacuate all the women present, and she evaded capture by making her way to Phibsboro with Brigid Foley.

Mary Lawless passed away at Wyanstown House, Oldtown, County Dublin, on July 24th 1924 after a long illness, and her funeral at Killossery, was one of the largest seen in the Fingal area for many years.

References:

RH; *Drogheda Independent*, 26th July 1924, (obit); *Sunday Independent*, 30th July 1924, (obit).

Thomas (Tom) Leahy: (- 1958)
E. Coy, 2nd Batt, Dublin Brigade. Roll of Honour

Tom Leahy, of 14 Lower Buckingham Street, was a riveter in the Dublin Liffey Dockyard and joined E. Company, 2nd Battalion, Dublin Brigade in 1914. He was also a member of St Laurence O'Toole's GAA Club. On Easter Monday he was sent from Liberty Hall to take part in the attack on the Magazine Fort in the Phoenix Park. After the raid he made his way to the GPO and from there, he was sent to Fairview under the command of Captain Frank Henderson. On Tuesday evening this group was ordered to return to the GPO. He was then sent to the Metropole Hotel, where Oscar Traynor was in charge. The men in the Metropole came under heavy sniper fire and he and Irish Citizen Army man, Vincent Poole, a former British soldier and Boer War veteran, felled many of the enemy snipers with their accurate marksmanship. The party in the Metropole held out desperately until Friday, before returning to the GPO. After the surrender, he was deported to Knutsford Jail and interned in Frongoch, until July 26th 1916.

He was a member of the Irish Citizen Army from 1917 to 1923. A shipyard worker, he contested the municipal elections in 1920 for Labour. He took the Republican side in the Civil War and fought in Barry's Hotel and the Hamman Hotel in Sackville Street. After his release from prison, he left for Glasgow in 1924 and resided at 657 Dumbarton Road.

Tom Leahy died on February 13th 1958 and was buried at Glasnevin Cemetery.

References:

RH; IMA, MSPC; IMA, BMH (WS 660); NLI, *Lynch Papers*, (Ms 11,131); Jimmy Wren, *Saint Laurence O'Toole's GAC Centenary History, 1901-2001*, (2001); *Irish Press*, 15th February 1958, (obit).

Joseph (Joe) Ledwith: (1894 – 1970)

Maynooth Company, Kildare Brigade. Roll of Honour

Joe Ledwith was born in 1894 and was a member of the Maynooth Company, Kildare Brigade. He mobilized at the back of Domhnall Ó Buachalla's shop in Maynooth on Easter Monday. After receiving a blessing from Professor Monsignor Hogan at Maynooth College, the fifteen Maynooth Volunteers made their way to Dublin by the Royal Canal towpath. They spent Monday night in Glasnevin Cemetery and arrived at the GPO on Tuesday morning. He was in the party sent to relieve the Irish Citizen Army men and Volunteers, surrounded in the Evening Mail office across from City Hall. He took up a position on the roof of Shortall's in Parliament Street and he later moved to the Royal Exchange Hotel, until this group was ordered to return to the GPO on Tuesday evening. From Wednesday he was posted on the roof of the GPO and on Friday he was stationed in the Coliseum Theatre, in Henry Street. He evaded capture after the surrender and returned to Maynooth with Pat Weafer and Jack Greaves. He was promptly arrested, court-martialled and sentenced to two years hard labour, which was reduced to six months imprisonment.

He rejoined the Maynooth Company after his release from prison and took part in a number of operations during the War of Independence. He was arrested in January 1921 and interned in Rath Camp, the Curragh, until December of the same year. During the Civil War he took the pro-Treaty side. He served with the 4th Battalion, 1st Eastern Division, Meath Brigade and the Free State Army Air Service, with the rank of Lieutenant.

Joe Ledwith, of Blanchardstown, County Dublin, died on April 18th 1970 and was buried at Laraghbryan Cemetery, Maynooth.

References:
  RH; IMA, MSPC; NLI, *Lynch Papers*, (Ms 11,131); *Irish Independent*, 20th April 1970, (dn).

Hugh Lee: (1899 - 1964)

E. Coy, 4th Batt, Dublin Brigade. Roll of Honour

Hugh Lee was born in 1899 and resided at 29 St Patrick's Cottages, Rathfarnham. He was a member of E. Company, 4th Battalion, Dublin Barracks and fought in the GPO during Easter Week beside his father, Joe. He was wounded in the leg and after receiving first aid treatment, he remained in action throughout the week. After the evacuation of the GPO on Friday evening, he spent the night in Hanlon's Shop in Moore Street. He was detained in Richmond Barracks until May 24th when he was released because of his young age.

He rejoined E. Company, 4th Battalion, in 1917, and was imprisoned in Mountjoy Jail in August 1919 for pulling down a Union Jack at the Armistice Celebrations. In 1920 he transferred to the South County, Irish Citizen Army and took part in the War of Independence. He was arrested and interned in the Curragh Camp, from December 1920 to December 1921. In 1922 he joined the Free State Army and served with the rank of Sergeant, until he was discharged in 1924.

Hugh Lee, of 3 Ballyboden Road, Rathfarnham, died on January 21st 1964 and was buried in Churchtown Cemetery.

References:
RH; IMA, MSPC; *Evening Herald*, 23rd January 1964, (dn).

Joseph (Joe) Lee: (1863 - 1938)
E. Coy, 4TH Batt, Dublin Brigade. Roll of Honour

Joe Lee was born in 1863 and resided at 29 St Patrick's Cottages, Rathfarnham. He was a member of E. Company, 4th Battalion, Dublin Brigade and on Easter Monday he travelled by tram with members of his company to Liberty Hall. From there he went to the GPO where he spent the week along with his son, Hugh, sniping from the roof. He was severely wounded and was brought to Jervis Street Hospital. Despite his wounds, he was deported to Knutsford Jail on May 1st and was interned in Frongoch, until July 31st 1916.

He had two other sons, Thomas and Patrick, who fought in the War of Independence.

At his passing on May 17th 1938, Joe Lee was the oldest surviving member of E. Company, 4th Battalion from the Rising, and he was buried two days later at Churchtown Cemetery.

References:
RH; IMA, MSPC; NLI, *Lynch Papers*, (Ms 11,131); *Irish Independent* & *Irish Press*, 18th May 1938, (obit).

Noel Lemass: (1897 – 1923)
A. Coy, 3rd Batt, Dublin Brigade. Roll of Honour

Noel Lemass was born in 1897 and resided at 2 Capel Street, Dublin. He was the son of a well known hat manufacturer and Parnellite. A member of A. Company, 3rd Battalion, Dublin Brigade, he reported to the GPO on Easter Tuesday morning with his brother, Seán. On Wednesday he was in the Imperial Hotel, and volunteered to take a dispatch to the GPO. He came under heavy machinegun and sniper fire as he dashed across the street and on his return from the GPO he was shot in the ankle. Despite the fusillade, Ned Boland, brother of Harry, and an Irish Citizen Army man Joe Whelan, managed to drag him to the safety of the hotel. He was carried by stretcher from the Imperial Hotel, as it was abandoned, and he was captured in a tenement in Marlborough Street on Friday morning with Harry Manning, who was also wounded. He was brought to the hospital in Dublin Castle with the other wounded prisoners, but was later released because of his young age.

In 1917 he resumed his activities with his old battalion and was sentenced to 6 months for illegal drilling. He was put in charge of E. Company, 3rd Battalion, when Captain Michael Tannam was arrested and imprisoned. In February 1921 he was in charge of the ambush at Mespil Road, and in April he was arrested and imprisoned at Collinstown, Kilmainham Jail and Rath Camp. He was released in the general amnesty in December, 1921. Like his brother, Seán, he took the Republican side in the Civil War and escaped from Gormanstown Camp, where he was being held. He was captured and brutally murdered after the ceasefire in July 1923. His decomposed body was found on the Featherbed Mountain, just south of Dublin, on October 12th 1923. Several people were suspected of his killing, including the notorious Captain James Murray who was later imprisoned for another murder and died in captivity in Maryboro Prison in 1929. Noel Lemass's remains were identified by optical records supplied by Jimmy O'Dea. O'Dea, the famous comedian, had trained as an optician and was a family friend. Seán Lemass was Jimmy O'Dea's best man at his wedding.

Noel Lemass was buried in the family plot in Glasnevin Cemetery.

References:

RH; *DIB*, Anne Dolan, (James Quinn, Ed, 2009); Max Caulfield, *The Easter Rebellion*, (1963); W.J. Brennan-Whitmore, *Dublin Burning*, (1996); Diarmaid Ferriter, *A Nation and not a Rabble: the Irish Revolution, 1913-1923*, (2015); *Irish Independent*, 23rd October 1923, (inq).

Seán Lemass: (1899 – 1971)

A. Coy, 3rd Batt, Dublin Brigade. Roll of Honour

Seán Lemass, the son of a Capel Street hat manufacturer, was born in Norwood Cottage, Ballybrack, on July 15th 1899. At the age of 15, and while still attending O'Connell Schools, North Richmond Street, he joined A. Company, 3rd Battalion, Dublin Brigade. He joined the GPO Garrison on Easter Tuesday morning with his brother, Noel and was given a shotgun and some homemade bombs and sent to the roof of the building. He remained there until Thursday and was then moved to the ground floor. After the evacuation he helped bore through the walls of houses in Moore Street. On Saturday, he was part of the group under the command of Seán McLoughlin, who were ready to charge the British Army barricade in Great Britain Street. However, the surrender was announced before the attack occurred. He was later released from Richmond Barracks on May 12th, because of his young age.

After the Rising he fought in the War of Independence and it is believed that he took part in the assassination of 14 British agents in November, 1920.

During the Civil War he took the Republican side and fought in the Four Courts in 1922. He was captured and interned in the Curragh Camp and Mountjoy Jail from December, 1922 to December, 1923. In 1924 he was elected a Sinn Féin TD, but didn't take his seat. When the Fianna Fáil party was formed, he became secretary. The party entered the Dáil in 1927, and he became Minister for Industry and Commerce in 1932. Except for a brief spell in opposition, he held this post until 1959. During this time he established semi-state bodies, such as Aer Lingus and Bórd na Móna. In 1959 he succeeded Éamonn deValera as Taoiseach and pursued a policy of economic and industrial development. He also developed cross-border co-operation with the Prime Minister for Northern Ireland, Captain Terence O'Neill, they met in Belfast in January 1965 and the following month in Dublin. He resigned as Taoiseach in 1966 and as a TD in 1969. While attending a rugby match at Lansdowne Road in February 1971, he became unwell and was rushed to hospital.

Seán Lemass died on May 11th 1971 in the Mater Hospital and was buried at Deansgrange Cemetery.

References:

RH; *DIB*, Ronan Fanning, (James Quinn, Ed, 2009); Brian Farrell, *Seán* Lemass, (1988); Michael O'Sullivan, *Seán Lemass, a Biography*, (1994); John Horgan, *Seán Lemass, an Enigmatic* Patriot, (1997); Diarmaid Ferriter, *A Nation and not a Rabble: the Irish Revolution, 1913-1923*, (2015); *Irish Press*, 18th February 1969, (na, Michael Mills, *Seán Lemass, a Profile*); *Irish Independent, Irish Press* & *Irish Times*, 12th May 1971, (obits).

Diarmuid Lynch: (1878 – 1950)

Staff Captain, G.H.Q. Roll of Honour

Diarmuid Lynch was born in Tracton, County Cork in 1878. The son of a farmer, he became a sorting clerk in the GPO in Cork, before taking up a position in the Post Office in London. In 1896 he emigrated to the United States and became an American citizen in 1901.

He was involved in the Irish language movement in America and by 1905 he was president of the Gaelic League in New York State. He returned to Ireland in 1907 and the following year he became a member of the IRB in Dublin. He returned to his native Cork in 1910 and became Divisional Centre for South Munster on the IRB Supreme Council. In 1914 he toured America as a representative of the Gaelic League and raised funds for the Volunteers. He was designated aide-de-camp to James Connolly in Easter Week. On entering the GPO on Easter Monday, he organized the smashing of the partition that divided the main public office and the primary sorting office. He was put in charge of the main floor front and side windows and on Tuesday he led a squad to disperse the looters who had set Lawrence's shop on the corner of Earl Street alight. On Wednesday, he led the party that broke through the walls of the adjoining Coliseum Theatre in Henry Street. Early on Friday morning he succeeded in bringing the men in the outposts in the Liffey

Street and Abbey Street area safely back to the GPO. He organized the erecting of an "L" shaped barricade on the ground-floor of the post office and when the building was burning out of control, organized the removal of munitions and the British prisoners from the basement. He was also one of the last people to vacate the GPO. After the surrender, he was in charge of the six men who carried James Connolly's stretcher to Dublin Castle. Diarmuid Lynch, with an address at 11 Mountjoy Square, was sentenced to death for his part in the Rising, but his sentence was later commuted to 10 years penal servitude in Pentonville Prison and Lewes Jail.

He was released on June 16th 1917 and became a member of the re-organised Supreme Council of the IRB. In 1918 he was arrested and imprisoned in Dundalk Jail. While in prison, Sinn Féin arranged for his fiancée Kathleen Quinn to be smuggled into the prison, where they married. He was a TD in the 1st Dáil, representing South Cork.

He resided in the United States from 1918 to 1932 and was national secretary of the Friends of Irish Freedom. In 1932 he returned to Dublin and undertook the compilation of a record of the GPO Garrison during Easter Week.

Diarmuid Lynch died in his native, Tracton, County Cork, on November 10th 1950 and was buried at Tracton Abbey.

References:

RH; IMA, MSPC; IMA, BMH (WS 4); NLI, *Lynch Papers*, (Ms 11,131); Diarmuid Lynch, *The IRB and the 1916 Insurrection*, (1959); Max Caulfield, *The Easter Rebellion*, (1963); W.J. Brennan-Whitmore, *Dublin Burning*, (1996); Charles Townshend, *Easter 1916, the Irish Rebellion*, (2006); Clair Willis, *Dublin 1916, the Siege of the GPO*, (2009); Eileen McGough, *Diarmuid Lynch, a Forgotten Irish Patriot*, (2013); *Irish Independent*, 10th November 1950, (obit); *Irish Press*, 11th November 1950, (obit).

John Lynch: (1875 – 1950)
C. Coy, 1st Batt, Dublin Brigade. Roll of Honour

John Lynch, of 5 St Joseph's Terrace, North Circular Road, was born in 1875 and became a member of the IRB in 1902. He was employed as a carter and joined C. Company, 1st Battalion, Dublin Brigade, in 1913. Before the Rising he was involved in distributing arms and ammunition and on Easter Sunday he delivered ammunition between Liberty Hall and the Columcille Hall, Blackhall Street, which was the headquarters of 1st Battalion. When he left Summerhill on Easter Monday and proceeded to the GPO he was sent to Reis's Chambers. He fought in the Dublin Bread Company building and later took up a position between Abbey Street and North Earl Street, under the command of Captain Brennan-Whitmore. Later when this position was abandoned, he was taken prisoner in Parnell Street, as he attempted to get back home. He was deported to Wandsworth Prison on May 9th and then transferred to Woking Jail. He was later interned in Frongoch until Christmas 1916.

After his release from internment, he rejoined his old unit and served until 1919, when he ceased activities due to ill health.

John Lynch, of 12 Shamrock Cottages, North Strand, died on July 30th 1950.

References:
RH; IMA, MSPC.

Martin Lynch: (1894 -   )

Section Commander, C. Coy, 2nd Batt, Dublin Brigade. Roll of Honour

Martin Lynch was born in 1894 and resided at 7 St Brigid's Avenue, North Strand. He was a Section Commander in C. Company, 2nd Battalion, Dublin Brigade. On Easter Monday, he reported to Captain Paddy Daly and then proceeded to the Magazine Fort in the Phoenix Park. After the sentries on guard at the fort were disarmed and the explosives detonated, he made his way with some members of the raiding party to the GPO, while the remainder went to the Four Courts. He was detailed to man the front windows of the GPO on Monday afternoon. On Tuesday he went to Kennedy's Bakery, Parnell Street and returned with several van loads of bread, before resuming his position manning the front windows. He was detailed to establish contact with the St Stephen's Green Garrison on Wednesday, and returned from there in a commandeered car while under enemy fire. Along with four others, he occupied the premises of Hoyte's Oil Works across the street from the GPO on Thursday, but was forced to evacuate this position when the shop was burnt out. The small group dashed back across the street to the GPO under heavy machinegun fire unscathed, where their act of bravery was applauded by Tom Clarke. He guarded the ground floor windows on Friday and when the GPO was evacuated, he covered the garrison's retreat from the burning building with Seán Russell.

He spent Friday night in Moore Street and he was part of the group commanded by Seán McLoughlin, who volunteered to charge the British Army barricade at Parnell Street, when the surrender order was announced. He was deported to Stafford Jail on May 1st and interned in Frongoch, until Christmas, 1916.

Martin Lynch joined the Garda Síochána at its inception and was later to become Chief Superintendent for Wexford.

References:
RH; NLI, *Lynch Papers*, (Ms 11,131).

Patrick Lynch: (1895 - 1948)

C. Coy, 2nd Batt, Dublin Brigade. Roll of Honour

Patrick Lynch, of John's Brook, Kells, County Meath, was born in 1895 and, prior to the Rising, was employed in the licensed trade in Dublin. He resided at 14 Nelson Street and was a member of the IRB and C. Company, 2nd Battalion, Dublin Brigade. On Easter Monday he carried supplies from Liberty Hall to the GPO, and was then posted to the Fairview area. He fought at Annesley Bridge until ordered back to the GPO on Tuesday evening. On Wednesday he was in the party led by James Connolly that went to dislodge British troops in buildings in the Liffey Street area. After the Rising he was deported to Stafford Jail on May 1st and interned in Frongoch until Christmas 1916.

On his release from internment, he rejoined his unit and took part in a number of engagements during the War of Independence. He took the Republican side in the Civil

War and took part in the fighting in O'Connell Street. He was interned in Newbridge Barracks in December 1922, and released after a twenty eight day hunger strike in December 1923. In later years he was the proprietor of a licensed premises, at 144 Thomas Street, Dublin.

Patrick Lynch died on June 2nd 1948 and was buried at Martry Cemetery, Kells, County Meath.

References:

RH; IMA, MSPC; *Irish Press*, 3rd June 1948, (obit).

Rory MacDermott: (1892 - 1942)
C. Coy, 1st Batt, Dublin Brigade. Roll of Honour

Rory McDermott was born in 1892 and resided at 58 Harcourt Street. He was the son of HR McDermott, County Inspector of the RIC, and he joined C. Company, 1st Battalion, Dublin Brigade, while still a student. When he reported to the GPO at 1.00 pm on Easter Monday and was sent across the street to Reis's Chambers. On Tuesday he helped erect a barricade across Abbey Street with Con Keating. When the fire took hold in Reis's on Wednesday, he returned to the GPO and took up a position at the ground floor windows. After the evacuation from the GPO on Friday evening, he found shelter in Price's Stores in Moore Street, with a number of other Volunteers. He was in the first batch of Volunteers deported to Knutsford Jail on May 1st and was interned in Frongoch, until Christmas 1916.

After his release from internment he rejoined C. Company, 1st Battalion and in 1918 he transferred to the Blackrock Company, 6th Battalion, with the rank of lieutenant. He took part in a number of raids and ambushes and was arrested in January 1921. He was interned until January 1922 and suffered lung problems due to his prison conditions. The following June he joined the Free State Army, and served in Dublin, Wicklow, Carlow, the Curragh and GHQ, Parkgate Street. He was demobilised in December 1923 with the rank of captain.

He later resided at 1 Eaton Square, Monkstown and was employed as a commercial traveller and a journalist.

Rory MacDermott died on February 23rd 1942, and was buried at Deansgrange Cemetery.

References:

RH; NLI, *Lynch Papers*, (11,131); *Irish Press*, 25th February 1942, (obit).

John MacDonnell: (1888 - 1973)

F. Coy, 2nd Batt, Dublin Brigade. Roll of Honour

John MacDonnell was born in 1888 and resided at 6 St Brigid's Avenue, North Strand in 1916. He joined the Volunteers in 1913 and took part in the Howth gun running in 1914. He was a member of F. Company, 2nd Battalion, Dublin Brigade, and on Easter Monday he reported to Father Mathew Park and escorted the transport bringing supplies to the GPO. He was in the group that returned to Fairview and he was stationed at the Vitriol Works, Annesley Bridge and Gilbey's, until Tuesday. This group, led by Captain Frank Henderson, was ordered to go to the GPO on Tuesday evening and from then until Thursday he was stationed in the Imperial Hotel, until the occupants were forced to evacuate because of the intensity of the fire. They made their way through Cathedral Street into Gloucester Street, where they took shelter in a tenement house on Friday night. Troops from the Royal Irish Guards arrested them there on Saturday morning, and they were taken to the Custom House for interrogation. He was later detained in Richmond Barracks and deported to Knutsford Jail, on May 3rd. After his release from internment in Frongoch at Christmas 1916 he rejoined his unit.

He was active in the War of Independence and took part in armed patrols and raids in the 1920-21 period. He took no part in the Civil War.

In September 1962 he retired from the Independent Newspaper Group, after many years service as a linotype operator.

John MacDonnell, of 21 Croydon Green, Marino, died on July 3rd 1973 and was buried in Glasnevin Cemetery.

References:
  RH; IMA, MSPC; NLI, *Lynch Papers*, (Ms 11,131); *Irish Independent*, 4th July 1973, (dn).

Seán McDermott (Seán MacDiarmada):
(1884 – 1916). Executed Leader
Military Council, IRB. Roll of Honour

Seán McDermott was born in Kiltyclogher, County Leitrim, on February 28th 1884. At the age of sixteen he emigrated to Glasgow and worked there for six years. He returned to Belfast, where he joined the Gaelic League becoming a fluent Irish speaker. He became organizer of the Dungannon Clubs that were founded by the IRB to promote republicanism in Ulster. He was a member of the Belfast circle of the IRB, and became president of its Supreme Council and later was appointed full-time organiser of Sinn Féin. In 1908 he was appointed National Organiser of the IRB and at this time he also formed a close friendship with Tom Clarke, who had spent fifteen years in penal servitude in English prisons and who had recently returned from America.

In 1910 he became manager of *Irish Freedom*, a journal edited by Dr Pat McCartan from County Tyrone. He also associated with Saint Laurence O'Toole GAA Club and the Saint Laurence O'Toole Pipe Band. Two years later he suffered an attack of polio which crippled him and made movement very difficult. Despite this, he continued his work for the Republican cause and was elected on to the Provisional Committee of the Irish Volunteers in 1913. In 1915 he became a member of the secret military council set up by the IRB to plan for the Rising. When Eoghan MacNeill called off the Rising and issued the countermanding order, Seán MacDiarmada sent dispatch carriers throughout the country advising Volunteers to prepare to take action on Easter Monday. At noon on Easter Monday, the selfless, ill and exhausted Seán MacDiarmada, joined the Headquarters Garrison in the GPO. During the week he organised the field hospital at the back of the building and when James Connolly was wounded, he asserted greater control. Early on Friday morning he sent orders to several out-lying posts to withdraw to the GPO and, as the fire spread from the roof of the building, he helped with the firefighting. While being held captive at the Rotunda after the surrender, he was the recipient of some harsh treatment from Captain Lee-Wilson, who confiscated his walking stick. This caused him immense hardship as he made his way to Richmond Barracks on the following morning, accompanied by Julia Grenan and Winnie Carney. Totally exhausted, he arrived there one hour after the main body of Volunteers. Initially he was detained with a group of prisoners about to be deported to an English prison, before he was identified by Detective Hoey, G Division, DMP, and returned to the holding cell. He was then court-martialed on May 8th and sentenced to death.

Seán MacDiarmada was executed by firing-squad in Kilmainham Jail on May 12th and his remains lie in Arbour Hill.

References:

RH; *Capuchin Annual*, 1966; Dorothy Macardle, *The Irish Republic*, (1937); *Dublin's Fighting Story*, (1948); Max Caulfield, *The Easter Rebellion*, (1963); F.X. Martin, *The Irish Volunteers 1913-1915:Recollections and Documents*, (1963); Seamus G. O'Kelly, *The Glorious Seven*, (1966); Thomas Coffey, *Agony at Easter*, (1969); Tom Garvin, *Nationalist Revolutionaries in Ireland, 1858-1928*, (1987); Gerard MacAtasney, *Seán MacDiarmada, the Mind of a Revolution*, (2004); Ray Bateson, *They Died by Pearse's Side*, (2010); Helen Litton, *Ned Daly*, (16Lives series, 2013).

Seán MacEntee: (1899 – 1984)

Adjutant. Dundalk Battalion, Louth Brigade. Roll of Honour

Seán MacEntee was born in College Square, Belfast, in 1899 and was a relative of Charles Gavan Duffy. He was educated at St Malachy's and the Belfast Municipal College. He qualified as an electrical engineer, as an apprentice to the Belfast City Engineer. He joined the Gaelic League, and in 1914 became a member of the Irish Volunteers and became adjutant of the Dundalk Battalion, Louth Brigade. Because of the confusion over McNeill's countermanding orders, he decided to come to Dublin on Easter Monday where he met P.H. Pearse, who told him to return to Louth with the order "to strike at once". It was planned for Volunteer columns from Louth, Meath and units from the North to mobilise at Tara and to link up with Volunteers from North County Dublin and Kildare. When this plan did not materialise, he decided to return to Dublin and he made his way back to the GPO, overcoming many obstacles and difficulties, before he reached the city on Wednesday morning. He joined the garrison in the Imperial Hotel and remained there until Thursday night when the decision to evacuate the burning building was made. He made a dash across the street to the GPO under heavy fire. At 7.00 o'clock on Friday, he left the GPO in the group led by The O'Rahilly into Moore Street. He retreated into an adjoining laneway with others of this group and spent the night in stables there. After the surrender, he was court-martialed and sentenced to death, which was later commuted to life imprisonment.

He was released from Lewes Jail in June 1917 and was elected a Sinn Féin MP in the General Election of 1918. He took the anti-Treaty side during the Civil War and was O/C in the former Marlborough Street Post Office, at the rear of the Hamman Hotel. On his arrest he was interned in Kilmainham Jail and Gormanstown, before being released in 1923. After the Civil War he became a partner with Fergus O'Kelly in a firm of consultant engineers. He was a founding member of Fianna Fáil in 1926, and was a TD from 1927 to 1969. In that time he held the posts of Minister of Industry & Commerce, Minister for Local Government & Public Health, Minister for Finance, Minister for Social Welfare, Minister for Health and in 1959 he became Tánaiste to Seán Lemass. When he retired in 1969 at the age of 80, he was the oldest TD to serve in the history of the State.

He was also a poet of some quality, as his collection entitled *"Poems"* (1918) testifies. He was married to Tipperary woman, Margaret Browne and their daughter is poet, Máire Mhac An tSaoi, who was married to Conor Cruise O'Brien. He resided at 30 Trimleston Avenue, Booterstown and at the time of his passing, he was the sole remaining member of the 1st Dáil. Seán MacEntee died on 9th January 1984, aged 94 and was buried in Glasnevin Cemetery.

References:

RH; IMA, MSPC; Seán MacEntee, *Episode at Easter*, (1966); Tom Feeney, *Seán MacEntee, a Political Life*, (2009); *Irish Times*, 22nd – 25th July 1974, (na, *Seán MacEntee, Republican Leader*, Michael Mills); *Irish Times*, 10th January 1984, (obit).

Francis Macken: (1887 – 1916). Killed In Action

E. Coy, 4th Batt, Dublin Brigade. Roll of Honour

Francis Macken was born in York Steet, Dublin, in 1887. He joined the Volunteers at its inception in 1913, and by 1916 he was working in his father's hairdresser's shop in Rathfarnham Village. He was a member of the Gaelic League and he established a branch in Rathfarnham. He was a section commander in E. Company, 4th Battalion, Dublin Brigade, and always issued commands to his section in Irish. On Easter Monday, he left Rathfarnham with E Company and fought throughout the week in the GPO. On Friday, he was part of the group led by The O'Rahilly into Moore Street. He fell under heavy enemy fire and his body was later found lying beside The O'Rahilly.

Francis Macken was buried in the 1916 Plot in Glasnevin Cemetery on May 4th 1916.

References:

RH; *Catholic Bulletin*, August 1916; Ray Bateson, *They Died by Pearse's Side*, (2010).

Lawrence (Larry) Mackey: (1886 - 1958)

E. Coy, 2nd Batt, Dublin Brigade. Roll of Honour

Larry Mackey was born in 1886 and resided at 23 North William Street. He was blacksmith by trade, and he joined E. Company, 2nd Battalion, Dublin Brigade, in 1914. On Easter Monday he reported to 2nd Battalion's HQ at Father Mathew Park, with his younger brother Michael. He served at Ballybough and Annesley Bridge until Tuesday evening when he withdrew with the Fairview men to the GPO. He was posted to the Imperial Hotel and fought there until Thursday night when the building was engulfed in fire. The majority of the Volunteers made their way through the north inner city, and he was later captured in Gloucester Street, taken to the Custom House and detained at Richmond Barracks. He was deported to Knutsford Jail on May 3rd and interned in Wandsworth Jail and Frongoch until July 18th 1916.

On his release from internment he rejoined his unit, but because of poor health he unable to continue activities. Because of his skill as a blacksmith, he was involved in making munitions under the command of Seán Russell during the War of Independence. He was a prominent hurler with St Laurence O'Toole's in their early successes and remained a lifelong supporter.

Larry Mackey, Richmond Crescent, North Circular Road, died on February 20th, 1958 and was buried in Glasnevin Cemetery.

References:

RH; IMA, MSPC; Jimmy Wren, *Saint Laurence O'Toole GAC Centenary History, 1901-2001*, (2001); *Irish Press*, 22nd February 1958, (obit).

Michael Mackey: (1895 - 1954)

C. Coy, 2nd Batt, Dublin Brigade. Roll of Honour

Michael Mackey was born in 1898 and resided at 23 North William Street. Like his brother Larry, who also fought in the GPO, he was a blacksmith by trade. He was a member of C. Company, 2nd Battalion, Dublin Brigade. Initially on Easter Monday he was engaged in activity in the Ballybough area, under the command of Captain Tom Weafer, before moving into the GPO. He was posted to the Imperial Hotel on Tuesday and remained there until the burning building was evacuated on Thursday night. He made his way to North Cumberland Street, where he took cover with a group of Volunteers, who were sheltering in a tenement. The following day they were captured and taken to the Custom House. He was deported to Knutsford Jail on May 3rd and he was interned in Frongoch, until July 25th 1916.

He rejoined his unit on his release from internment and fought in the War of Independence. In 1922 he joined the anti-Treaty side, and was part of a group who occupied Healy's Public House at the corner of Marlborough Street, and later occupied Bridgeman's Public House and Findlater's. He fought in the O'Connell Street area until the dispersal of the Republican forces. In October 1922 he was in a party that was ambushed by Free States forces at The Thatch, Whitehall and was he was later arrested and interned until November 1923.

He was a lifelong member of Lawrence O'Toole's GAA club, who were then based in the North Wall area.

Michael Mackey, of 40 Clancy Road, Finglas, died on May 1st 1954 and was buried at Glasnevin Cemetery.

References:
RH; IMA, MSPC; NLI, *Lynch Papers*, (Ms 11,131); *Sunday Press*, 2nd May 1954, (dn).

Francis (Frank) MacPartland

Hibernian Rifles. Roll of Honour

Frank MacPartland, of 32 St Joseph's Parade, off Dorset Street, was a gas fitter by trade. He was a member of the Hibernian Rifles and on Easter Monday he reported to the North Circular Road barricade, which was an outpost of the Four Courts Garrison. On Tuesday Volunteers at this outpost, as well as the one at Cabra Bridge, were forced to retreat because of the heavy British artillery fire directed at them. He went to the GPO with others, where he served for the remainder of the week. He was deported to Stafford Jail on May 1st and interned in Frongoch after the surrender.

Frank MacPartland lived at Millbank, Rush, County Dublin, in later years.

References:
RH.

Micheál MacRuaidhrí, (Rogers): (1862 – 1936)

E. Coy, 4th Battalion, Dublin Brigade. Roll of Honour

Micheál MacRuaidhrí was born in 1862 and was a native of Fohill, Lacken, Co. Mayo. He was a prominent worker in the Irish language movement for many years, and was dubbed the "Mayo Poet", by Douglas Hyde. From 1908, he was employed primarily as a gardener at St Enda's, Rathfarnham, but taught horticulture to the pupils as well. He was also a teacher of the Irish language at the Árd Branch of the Gaelic League. He was a member of E. Company, 4th Battalion, Dublin Brigade from Rathfarnham. Fifty four years old when he took part in the Rising, he was standing beside P.H. Pearse in the street outside the GPO when he read the Proclamation on Easter Monday. After the surrender, he was deported to Stafford Jail on May 8th and interned in Frongoch until July 21st 1916. While in Frongoch, he taught the Irish language to his fellow internees. He was one of the last of the traditional storytellers, winning eight Oireachtas gold medals for oratory and storytelling, and he also wrote under the pseudonym of Meartóg Ghuill.

Michael MacRuaidhrí passed away on June 1st 1936 and was buried at Glasnevin Cemetery.

References:

RH; Brian Cleeve, *Dictionary of Irish Writers*, (1971); C.S. Andrews, *Dublin Made Me*, (1979); Michael Hopkinson, *Frank Henderson's Easter Rising Recollections as a Dublin Volunteer*, (1998); *Irish Press*, 1st June 1936, (obit); *Irish Independent*, 2nd June 1936, (obit).

John Madden: (1895 - 1946)

C. Coy, 1st Batt, Dublin Brigade. Roll of Honour

John Madden was born in 1895 and resided at 27 Clonliffe Avenue. He joined C. Company, 1st Battalion, Dublin Brigade, in 1915. On Easter Monday, he manned a window at the Prince's Street corner of the GPO. That evening he was sent across the street to Tyler's Boot Manufacturer's shop at the corner of North Earl Street to clear out looters. He threw a drunken British soldier in full uniform, who was found among the looters there, through the window onto the pavement. On Tuesday he remained manning a ground floor window in the GPO and at noon on Wednesday he left with a party under the command of Seán Milroy, to occupy the Lucas Bicycle shop at the corner of Liffey Street and Abbey Street. He remained on the top floor of this building until his recall to the GPO on Thursday. He was one of the rear-guard at the evacuation of the GPO. In Henry Place he broke into a stable and released some horses that had been locked in there all week. He spent Friday night in the Moore Street houses. He was deported to Stafford Jail on May 1st and interned in Frongoch, until Christmas, 1916.

On his release he rejoined his unit, and fought until the Truce. In 1922, he joined the Free State Army with the rank of lieutenant. He served with the Corps of Engineers and with the Infantry Corps, before retiring on medical grounds in April 1946, with the rank of captain.

Captain John Madden, of 35 Seapark Road, Dollymount, died on December 23rd 1946 and was buried at Glasnevin Cemetery.

References:

RH; IMA, MSPC; NLI, *Lynch Papers*, (Ms 11,131); *Irish Independent* & *Irish Press*, 27th December 1946, (obits).

John (Jack) Maguire: (1886 – 1968)

Maynooth Company. Roll of Honour

Jack Maguire, from Crew Hill, Maynooth, was born in 1886. He was a member of Maynooth Company and was among the local Volunteers, who set out for the GPO on Easter Monday evening, by way of the Royal Canal towpath. They spent Monday night in Glasnevin Cemetery and on arriving in the GPO on Tuesday morning, he was sent with a group, including his brother, Matt, to relieve those who were besieged in the City Hall area. He took a position in the Evening Mail Offices, Parliament Street, where heavy losses were inflicted on the British Troops. After his group was recalled to the GPO, he spent Wednesday and Thursday manning the windows. On Friday he helped carry the wounded to Jervis Street Hospital and was captured in Liffey Street on Saturday with his brother, Matt, and another Maynooth man, Tom Mangan. He was deported and later interned in Frongoch until Christmas 1916. On his release he rejoined his unit and fought in the War of Independence. He was an accomplished Gaelic footballer, he played for Maynooth and represented his native County Kildare.

Jack Maguire, of 2 Leinster Cottages, Maynooth, passed away on August 8th 1968, at the age of 82.

References:

RH; IMA, MSPC; NLI, *Lynch Papers*, (Ms 11,131); *Irish Press*, 17th August 1968, (obit).

Matthew (Matt) Maguire: (1884 - 1947)

Maynooth Company. Roll of Honour

Matt Maguire, of Crew Hill, Maynooth, was born in 1884 and was a member of the Maynooth Company. On Easter Monday he helped in the mobilisation of the local Volunteers at the back of Domhnall Ua Buachalla's shop in Maynooth. After a brief detour to Maynooth College, where they received a blessing from Professor Monsignor Hogan, they set out along the Royal Canal towpath towards Dublin at seven o'clock on Easter Monday evening, and spent the night in Glasnevin Cemetery on the way. He was the company's tallest man and was a prominent midfielder on the local GAA team. On arriving in the GPO on Tuesday morning, he was sent with a group, including his brother Jack, to relieve the Irish Citizen Army men in the City Hall area. He was positioned in the Royal Exchange Hotel and in Shorthall's shop. When recalled to the GPO, he took up a position at the rear of the building. On Friday he manned the ground floor windows, before escorting the wounded to Jervis Street Hospital. He was captured on Saturday in Liffey Street with his brother Jack and another man from the Maynooth Company, Tom Mangan. He was deported to Stafford Jail on May 8th and interned in Frongoch until Christmas 1916.

On his release he fought in the War of Independence. Like his brother, Jack, he played for Maynooth GAA Club and also represented County Kildare.

Matt Maguire died at his residence at Brownstown, Dunboyne, on May 11th 1947 and was buried at Moyglare Cemetery.

References:

RH; IMA, MSPC; NLI, *Lynch Papers*, (Ms 11,131); *Irish Independent*, 12th May 1947, (dn).

Patrick J. Maguire (alias White)

Glasgow Company, (Kimmage Garrison)

Patrick Maguire came to Dublin with a group of Volunteers from Glasgow prior to the Rising, and joined the Volunteer Camp at Larkfield, Kimmage. He fought throughout Easter Week in the GPO, and after the surrender he was deported to Wandsworth Jail on May 9th, under the alias of Patrick White.

Patrick Maguire returned to Glasgow on his release from internment.

References:

John Heuston OP, *Headquarters Battalion, Easter Week 1916*, (1966); Ann Matthews, *The Kimmage Garrison 1916*, (2010).

Patrick Mahon: (1896 - 1962)

C. Company, 2nd Battalion, Dublin Brigade. Roll of Honour

Patrick Mahon was born in 1896 and was working in a Scottish Steelworks prior to 1916. He joined the IRB and the Volunteers in Scotland, and following his Republican activity in that country, he came under police suspicion. He travelled to Dublin at Christmas 1915 and transferred to C. Company, 2nd Battalion, Dublin Brigade. On Easter Monday he joined the GPO Garrison and was sent on armed patrol in the Henry Street area. When he returned to the GPO, he was posted to the instrument room in the building. He manned the hoses and fought the fire on Friday until the GPO was evacuated that evening. He was one of the Volunteers, who then took up a position in Henry Place and covered the withdrawal of the GPO Garrison. After the surrender he was deported to Knutsford Jail on May 1st and interned in Frongoch.

On his release from internment he transferred to C. Company, 1st Battalion, Dublin Brigade. He was involved in the transportation of arms and ammunition, under the command of Frank Harding, the Dublin Brigade quartermaster. During the Civil War, he took the Republican side, and was part of the garrison that occupied Hughes Hotel, Gardiner Street, in 1922. He was arrested in July 1922 and after a thirteen day hunger strike in October 1923, was released from Gormanstown Camp in December 1923.

In later years he ran a grocery business at 37 Upper Rathmines Road.

Patrick Mahon died on May 19th 1962 and was buried at Deansgrange Cemetery.

References:
RH; IMA, MSPC; *Sunday Press*, 20th May 1962, (dn).

Patrick J. (Paddy) Mahon: (1896 - 1965)

Section Commander. F. Coy, 2nd Batt, Dublin Brigade. Roll of Honour

Paddy (P.J.) Mahon Junior was born in 1896 and he resided at 71 Summerhill. He was educated at O'Connell Schools, North Richmond Street, and was the eldest son of City Councilor, Patrick Mahon. His father was also the printer of *An t-Óglach* and friend of Tom Clarke, Seán MacDiarmada, Arthur Griffith and Michael Collins, and leading member of the Mountjoy Ward Branch of the United Irish League. PJ became Secretary of the branch at the age of seventeen, and joined the Volunteers in 1913. He was a Section Commander in F. Company, 2nd Battalion, Dublin Brigade, when he reported to the Battalion's HQ at Father Mathew Park, Fairview, on Easter Monday. He was one of a group of Volunteers located in O'Meara's Public House, North Strand that engaged with British machine gunners at Annesley Bridge. He was a top marksman and he put a machine gun out of action, forcing its crew to flee down the East Wall Road. He was one of the occupants of Gilbey's Wine Shop, Ballybough Bridge, when they were recalled to the GPO on Tuesday evening. He was posted to the Imperial Hotel and fought there until the garrison was forced out by fire on Thursday night. He was badly hurt when his party came under heavy fire, while retreating into Cathedral Street. ICA man, Joseph McDonagh, carried him into the Pro-Cathedral Presbytery, where he was later arrested.

He was deported to Stafford Jail and interned in Frongoch until Christmas 1916. On his release, he rejoined his unit and took an active part in the War of Independence and was attached to Battalion Machine Gun Section. During 1919 and 1920, he helped Dick McKee print *An t-Óglach*, in Aungier Street. He was arrested in November 1920 and was interned in Bedford Jail until May 1921. A physical disability prevented him from taking any further active in the War of Independence.

He was employed for many years in the Dept of Education.

Paddy Mahon, of 10 Fairfield Road, Glasnevin, died on 20th July 1965 and was buried in Glasnevin Cemetery.

References:
RH; IMA, MSPC; IMA, BMH (WS 288, *Charles Saurin*), BMH (WS 1687, *Harry Colley*); *Irish Independent*, 21st September 1965, (na, *acknowledgement*).

Thomas (Tommy) Mahon: (1898 – 1959)
Volunteer, (Unattached). Roll of Honour

Tommy Mahon was born in 1898 and resided at 71 Summerhill. He was educated at O'Connell Schools, North Richmond Street. After the GPO was occupied on Easter Monday, he presented himself at the building with his cousin Jimmy Wren and friend Paddy Halpin, and offered his services. Although the three youths were not members of the Volunteers, they were admitted and given a shotgun each. He fought in the GPO throughout the week. After the surrender he was detained in Richmond Barracks, but was later released after a week, because of his young age.

His older brother, Paddy, fought in the Fairview area early in Easter Week and was a member of the GPO Garrison from Tuesday evening onwards. His younger brother, Ross, was a Captain in F. Company, 1st Battalion, during the War of Independence and later a Captain in the Free State Army. His father, nationalist Councillor Patrick Mahon, a printer by trade, was sentenced to three years hard labour, reduced to six months, in the aftermath of the Rising.

In 1917 Tommy joined F. Company, 2nd Battalion and was appointed assistant battalion quartermaster to Mick McDonnell. He took part in many operations, including the capture of the Dublin Castle mail in Dominic Street, the raid on the B&I Stores in North Wall, and the burning of the Custom House in May 1921. He joined the Free State Army with the rank of lieutenant in February 1922, but resigned just before the split and took no part in the Civil War.

He was employed as a water mains inspector with Dublin Corporation for many years and resided at 180 Collins Avenue West.

Tommy Mahon died on September 30th 1959 and was buried at Glasnevin Cemetery.

References:
RH; IMA, MSPC; *Irish Press*, 1st October 1959, (dn).

Antil (Antii) Makapaltis: (1884 – 1955)
Volunteer, (Unattached)

Antti Makapaltis was born in Finland in 1884 and emigrated to the United States in 1905. He found employment as a merchant seaman, and on Easter Monday he, and an unnamed Swedish seaman, presented themselves at the GPO and offered their services until Thursday, when their ship was to due to depart. Although neither spoke much English, they were allowed to enter, and captain Liam Tannam provided him with a shotgun and the Swede, with a rifle. When the shotgun was accidentally discharged, slightly wounding Volunteer James Kenny, they were transferred to the bomb making section. They were later posted to the roof and remained in the GPO until the evacuation. He was deported to Knutsford Jail on May 2nd and interned in Frongoch until Christmas 1916. The day after his release from internment he boarded a ship to the United States.

Because he was a Russian Finn and the Russian Revolution had just taken place, when he arrived in Philadelphia he was declared an enemy alien, and was given the option of returning to Finland or of joining the United States Army. Although he enlisted in the army in 1917, he was not sent to fight in Europe instead remaining in America. He later settled in Detroit and was employed as a toolmaker.

Antti Makapaltis died in Detroit, in 1955.

References:
IMA, BMH (WS 232, *Liam Tannam*); *An t-Óglach*, 23rd January 1926, (*Michael Staines*); *Sinn Féin Rebellion Handbook, Easter 1916*, Weekly Irish Times, (1917).

Jerome Joseph (Jerry) Malone (a.k.a Joseph Coughlan): (1896 – 1958)

D. Coy, 3rd Batt, Dublin Brigade, (Kimmage Garrison). Roll of Honour

Joseph Coughlin was born in 1896. He returned from London to Dublin and joined D. Company, 3rd Battalion, Dublin Brigade. In February 1916 he joined the Volunteer Camp at Larkfield and became a member of the Kimmage Garrison. On Easter Monday he travelled with his company from Kimmage to Liberty Hall by tram and then marched to the GPO. He was then posted to the Ship Hotel, Abbey Street, for a few hours, before returning to the GPO. He remained there for the remainder of the week and during the evacuation on Friday evening he found shelter in Price's Store, Moore Street. He was in a party of Volunteers that surrendered from Price's on Saturday afternoon. Deported to Stafford Jail on May 1st, he was interned in Frongoch until Christmas 1916.

After his release from internment he took no further part in the Volunteers. On December 6th 1930, while living in Limerick, he changed his name by deed pole to Jerome Joseph Malone.

Jerry Malone, a retired commercial traveller, of 176 Home Farm Road, Drumcondra, died on August 29th 1958.

References:
RH; IMA, MSPC; Ann Matthews, *The Kimmage Garrison, 1916*, (2010); *Irish Independent*, 30th August 1958, (dn).

Thomas (Tom) Mangan: (1887 - 1968)

Maynooth Company, Kildare Brigade. Roll of Honour

Tom Mangan, of Convent Lane, Maynooth, was born in 1887. He left Maynooth on Easter Monday evening with members of the Maynooth Company, Kildare Brigade and travelled by the Royal Canal towpath to Dublin. After sleeping that night in Glasnevin Cemetery, they arrived at the GPO early on Tuesday morning. He was sent with a party of Volunteers and Hibernian Rifles to relieve the besieged Irish Citizen Army men in the Parliament Street area. He fought in the premises of Henry & James Clothiers and the Royal Exchange Hotel, before returning to the GPO that evening. On Wednesday and Thursday he manned  the windows in the GPO, and the following day he was ordered to the Coliseum Theatre. He assisted in bringing the wounded from there to Jervis Street Hospital, and on Saturday he was arrested in the Liffey Street and Abbey Street area with Jack and Matt Maguire, who were also from Maynooth.. He was deported to Stafford Jail on May 8th and was interned in Frongoch until Christmas, 1916.

After his release from internment he rejoined the Maynooth Company and took part in a number of operations during the War of Independence. He took the Republican side in the Civil War and was involved in an attack on Free State Troops in Maynooth. He went on the run and was arrested on August 3rd 1922, but escaped from Dundalk Prison two weeks later. Later he took part in the destruction of the railway bridge at Dunleer, County Louth and was recaptured. He was interned at Newbridge Barracks, County Kildare and was released in December 1923 after taking part in a hunger strike. He played Gaelic football for his local club, Maynooth, and represented County Kildare.

Tom Mangan, of Rail Park, Maynooth, died in St Dymphna's Hospital, Carlow, on May 29th 1968 and was buried at Grangewilliam Cemetery, Maynooth.

References:

RH; IMA, MSPC; NLI, *Lynch Papers*, (Ms 11,131); *Irish Press*, 30th May 1968, (dn).

Henry (Harry) Manning: (1888 – 1959)
C. Coy, 1st Batt, Dublin Brigade. Roll of Honour

Harry Manning was born in 1888 and resided at 5 St Joseph's Terrace, North Circular Road. He was employed as a railway checker and joined the Volunteers at its inception in 1913. He was a member of C. Company, 1st Battalion, Dublin Brigade and took part in the Howth gun running in 1914. On Good Friday 1916, he was one of the Volunteers, ordered to guard Bulmer Hobson in Martin Conlon's house at Cabra Road. He was not mobilised on Easter Monday and joined Captain Tom Weafer's party as they marched to the GPO from the Fairview area. He was sent to Reis's Chambers across the street and later served in the Imperial Hotel. After the evacuation of the Imperial Hotel on Thursday night, he made his into the north inner city. He was wounded in the instep of his left foot in Waterford Street and was dragged into a nearby house in Marlborough Street, where Noel Lemass lay wounded. They were captured the following morning, and taken to the Custom House for interrogation, before they were moved to the hospital at Dublin Castle. He was deported to Knutsford Jail and interned in Frongoch until August 1916.

After his release from internment, he rejoined his unit and was caretaker of the Seán McDermott Club, Margaret Place, North Circular Road, which was a Volunteer meeting place. Despite his leg injury, he served throughout the War of Independence until the Truce.

In later years he resided in Shelmartin Avenue, Marino and was employed in the Department of Defence.

Harry Manning passed away on the June 14th 1959 and was buried in Mount Jerome Cemetery.

References:

RH; IMA, MSPC; *An t-Óglach*, 30th January 1926, (*W.J. Brennan-Whitmore*); W.J. Brennan-Whitmore, *Dublin Burning*, (1996); *Irish Independent*, 18th June 1959, (obit).

Marie Mapother: (1891 – 1979)

Cumann na mBan, (Árd Croabh Branch). Roll of Honour

Marie Mapother was born in 1891 and resided at 18 Drumcondra Park. She joined the Cumann na mBan, Árd Croabh Branch, in 1914. She was not mobilised on Easter Monday and had intended going on an outing on the bank holiday. When she heard that the Rising had begun, she made her way to the GPO and was sent to Reis's Chambers. She moved to the Hibernian Bank on Tuesday morning and was attached to the first aid section there. She was standing close to Captain Tom Weafer, when he was fatally shot on Wednesday, and assisted Aoife Burke and Leslie Price who attended him. After the evacuation of the Hibernian Bank, she retreated across Sackville Street to the GPO with Aoife Burke and Leslie Price, under heavy enemy fire. Having left the GPO she evaded capture and got home.

After the Rising she joined the National Aid Association and was engaged involved in collecting for the Prisoners Dependents Fund.

Marie Mapother, of 18 Drumcondra Park, died in St Monica's Nursing Home, Belvedere Place, on November 16th 1979 and was buried at Glasnevin Cemetery.

References:
RH; IMA, MSPC; *Evening Herald*, 16th November 1979, (dn).

Louis Marie: (1900 - 1957)

Fianna Éireann. F. Coy, 3rd Batt, Dublin Brigade. Roll of Honour

Louis Marie, the son of a French father, was born in 1900 and resided at 17 Grantham Street. He joined Fianna Éireann at its foundation and was also a member of F. Company, 3rd Battalion, Dublin Brigade. His mother, Brigid (nee O'Connor), was from Limerick and was an early member of Sinn Féin. He was educated at O'Connell Schools, North Richmond Street, and took part in the Howth gun running in 1914. He also became a member of the Irish Citizen Army and was attached to the South Circular Road Section. On Easter Monday he was among the group that raided the Magazine Fort in the Phoenix Park. On returning to the GPO, he was then posted to Annesley Bridge. On Tuesday evening he was ordered into the GPO with the main body of insurgents from Fairview area, and fought there for the remainder of Easter Week. He was one of the stretcher-bearers, who carried James Connolly from the GPO at the evacuation on Friday evening. He was deported to Stafford Jail on May 1st, but was later released because of his young age. During the War of Independence he was employed on an ocean liner and acted as a liaison officer between the IRA in Ireland and its American contacts.

In March 1920 he was conscripted into the French Army, and served until December 1921. He joined the Free State Army in 1922 and was a staff officer, attached to the quartermaster general's staff. He retired in 1929 with the rank of captain adjutant. He rejoined the army in 1940, during the emergency years and retired in 1946. In that same year, he was appointed Assistant Manager of the Theatre Royal. He later managed the De Luxe Cinema, Camden Street and the Grande Cinema, Cabra, before returning to the Theatre Royal as Manager.

Commandant Louis Marie, of 3 Oakley Park, Blackrock, died on September 1st 1957 and was buried at Deansgrange Cemetery.

References:

RH; IMA, MSPC; IMA, BMH (WS 218, *Harry Walpole*) & BMH (WS 800, *Michael O'Flanagan*); *Irish Press*, 2nd September 1957, (obit).

Thomas Mason

B. Coy, 2nd Batt, Dublin Brigade. Roll of Honour

Thomas Mason lived in St James's Avenue, Clonliffe Road and joined B. Company, 2nd Battalion, Dublin Brigade, as a medical orderly. On Easter Monday, he assisted Captain John J. Doyle, who was in charge of first aid in the GPO, before the arrival of final year medical student James Ryan. During the week, he attended many of the wounded, including James Connolly. On the Friday, he was among the group that left with the wounded for Jervis Street Hospital and included in this group was Father John Flanagan from the Pro-Cathedral, the captured British Army Doctor, Captain Mahony, medical students James Ryan and Dan McLoughlin, and over thirty Cumann na mBan women. He was deported to Knutsford Jail on June 2nd and was interned in Frongoch until July 27th 1916.

For many years, Thomas Mason had a newsagent and confectionary shop at 2 Clonliffe Road, Ballybough Bridge, which was a rebel outpost on Easter Monday and Tuesday 1916.

References:

RH; IMA, BMH (WS 748, *John J. Doyle*); *Sinn Féin Rebellion Handbook, Easter 1916*, Weekly Irish Times, (1917).

Garrett McAuliffe: (1886- 1952)

Manchester Company, (Kimmage Garrison). Roll of Honour

Garrett McAuliffe, a native of Newcastle West, County Limerick, was living in Manchester, before the Rising. He was one of the Manchester Volunteers that returned to Dublin prior to Easter Week and took up residence at Larkfield, Kimmage. On Easter Monday he was manning the windows in the GPO when Lancers from the 6th Reserve Cavalry Regiment came under fire. He was in a group that included Brendan Friel, a fellow Kimmage Garrison member, which took over the Arch Bar, Henry Street. They bored through the walls of a number of houses in the street, before they were recalled to the GPO on Friday. He took part in the general evacuation, and spent Friday night in the houses in Moore Street. After the surrender he was deported to Knutsford Jail on May 1st and interned in Frongoch.

On his release from internment, he continued in the fight for Independence and was arrested in 1918. He took part in the revolt in Belfast Jail with Austin Stack and other prisoners. After the Knocklong train rescue of Seán Hogan in 1919, he brought Seán Treacy, Seamus Robinson and Dan Breen to safety in Newcastle West. He became Second-in-Command of the West Limerick Brigade and took part in the attack on Kilmallock RIC Barracks in May 1920. In 1922 he took the Republican side and continued to serve with the West Limerick Brigade up to the end of the Civil War in 1923.

In later years he was employed in the Limerick Health Board.

Garrett McAuliffe, of Woodlawn, Newcastle West, died on June 3rd 1952 and was buried in Newcastle West.

References:

RH; IMA, MSPC; NLI, *Lynch Papers*, (Ms 11,131); *Irish Independent* & *Irish Press*, 4th June 1952, (obits).

Kevin J. McCabe: (1890 - 1970)

F. Coy, 2nd Batt, Dublin Brigade. Roll of Honour

Kevin McCabe, of 559 North Circular Road, was born in 1890 and was a watchmaker by occupation. In 1911 he joined the IRB at 41 Parnell Square. He was also a member of the Archbishop McHale Branch of the Gaelic League and in 1913 he joined F. Company, 2nd Battalion, Dublin Brigade. Two days before the Rising, he was sent with Luke Kennedy in a hired lorry to collect German arms at Fenit, County Kerry, but because of the failure to land the arms they returned empty-handed. He arrived at the GPO at 1.00 pm on Easter Monday, and was sent across the street to

Noblett's Sweet Shop at the corner of North Earl Street. While there, the Volunteers broke through interior walls towards the Imperial Hotel in one direction and Lloyd's Public House in the other. On Wednesday, the post came under heavy sustained military fire. The following day the garrison was ordered to evacuate the blazing building and they made their way through Cathedral Street into Gloucester Street. He found refuge along with 10 other Volunteers in the basement of a tenement and they were all captured there on Friday morning. They were taken to the Custom House, where they were interrogated and sent to Richmond Barracks. He was deported to Knutsford Jail on May 3rd and interned in Frongoch until Christmas, 1916.

On his release, he rejoined his unit and fought in the War of Independence. He later resumed employment as a watchmaker and resided at 5 Valentia Road, Drumcondra. During the emergency years, he was a member of the 26th Infantry Battalion.

Kevin McCabe died on October 4th 1970 and was buried at Glasnevin Cemetery.

References:
RH; IMA, MSPC; IMA, BMH (WS 926); *Evening Herald*, 5th October 1970, (dn).

James McCarra: (1895 – 1986)

Glasgow Company, (Kimmage Garrison)

James McCarra was born in Monaghan and emigrated to Glasgow in 1914, where he became a member of the IRB. He also joined 1st Battalion, Scottish Brigade and took part in several operations in Glasgow, including raids for arms and explosives. He came to Dublin in February 1916 and joined the Volunteer Camp, at Kimmage. He was sent to Galway, shortly before the Rising. He was mobilised on Easter Tuesday at Carnmore crossroads and took part in an attack on a lorry conveying armed RIC men. He was also involved in action at Moyode and evaded capture. In 1917 he went to Belfast, where he joined the Belfast Brigade and took part in a number of engagements. He returned to Scotland in 1920 and was placed in charge of collecting munitions with the Glasgow Company. In May 1921 he was arrested on a charge of killing a Police Constable, but the case was not proven and he was released in August 1921. He returned to Ireland and took no part in the Civil War. He later resided at Rahoon House, Rahoon, County Galway.

James McCarra, of Ballinode, County Monaghan, died on January 13th 1986 and was buried at St Oran's Cemetery, Urbleshanny, County Monaghan.

References:
IMA, MSPC.

William J. McCleane: (1899 - 1941)

E. Coy, 1st Batt, Dublin Brigade. Roll of Honour

William McCleane was born in Wexford in 1899. He was a painter and decorator by trade and resided at 4 Upper Fownes Street in 1916. A member of E. Company, 1st Battalion, Dublin Brigade, he served with the GPO Garrison during Easter Week. After the surrender he was released from Richmond Barracks on May 24th 1916, because of his young age.

He took part in the War of Independence with the 1st Battalion in Dublin and in later years he resided at 11 East Arran Street. He was a member of the Amalgamated Society of Painters and the National Association of the IRA.

William McCleane died on July 4th 1941 and was buried at Glasnevin Cemetery.

References:
RH; *Evening Herald*, 5th July 1941, (dn).

Mabel McConnell (Mrs. Mabel Fitzgerald): (1884 – 1958)

Cumann na mBan

Mabel McConnell was born in Belfast in 1884, into an Ulster Scots Presbyterian family. She was educated at Queen's College, where she became an Irish language enthusiast. She was deeply interested in literature, and when she moved to London, she was secretary to George Bernard Shaw and George Moore. In 1911 she married Desmond Fitzgerald and they moved to Brittany. Two years later they returned to live in Ireland, residing in County Kerry and later Bray, County Wicklow.

As a member of Cumann na mBan, she joined her husband in the GPO in Easter Week. She made several trips as courier, and on Tuesday P.H. Pearse sent her to City Hall with a replacement tricolor for one he mistakenly thought had been captured. When she discovered this mistake, she promptly returned to the GPO. As a mother of two young children, she was then ordered to return to her home in Bray.

She worked tirelessly in the Republican cause after the surrender and she favoured continuing the struggle when the Treaty was signed, despite her husband supporting it. However, she took no active part in the Civil War.

Mabel Fitzgerald resided at Airfield, Donnybrook, and passed away on April 24th 1958. She was buried at Glasnevin Cemetery.

References:
Padraic Colum, *Arthur Griffith*, (1959); Sinéad McCoole, *No Ordinary Women: Irish Female Activists in the revolutionary years, 1900-1923*, (2004); Desmond Fitzgerald, *Desmond's Rising: memoirs, from 1913 to Easter 1916*, (2006); Ann Matthews, *Renegades: Irish Republican Women, 1900-1923*, (2010); *Irish Press*, 25th April 1958, (obit); *Irish Independent*, 26th April 1945, (obit).

James McCormack: (1879 – 1916). Killed In Action
Irish Citizen Army, (Baldoyle Section). Roll of Honour

James McCormack was born in Gormanstown, County Meath, in 1879. He was employed at Baldoyle Racecourse and in 1916 he resided at 13 Sutton Cottages, Baldoyle with his wife and four children. He was a member of the Irish Citizen Army and although he was attached to the GPO Garrison, it is uncertain where he was killed. Several different locations were given; including Fairview, Beresford Place and the College of Surgeons.

James McCormack was buried in Glasnevin Cemetery on May 5th 1916. In later years, James McCormack Gardens in Baldoyle was named in his memory.

References:
RH; NLI, *William O'Brien Papers*, (Ms 15, 673); *Catholic Bulletin*, September 1916; Ray Bateson, *They Died by Pearse's Side*, (2010).

Patrick (Pat) McCrea: (1885 - 1964)
Section Commander. B. Coy, 2nd Batt, Dublin Brigade. Roll of Honour

Pat McCrea was born in 1885 and was a native of Carnew, County Wicklow. He was employed as a tram conductor with the Dublin United Tramway Co., and he took part in the strike led by Jim Larkin in 1913. He also joined the Volunteers and the IRB that same year, and became a Section Commander of B. Company, 2nd Battalion, Dublin Brigade. He was sworn into the IRB by Tom Hunter. On Easter Monday he travelled to Wicklow by train, but returned to Dublin on hearing that the Rising had begun and reported to the GPO in civilian clothes. He accompanied Captain MW O'Reilly to Parnell Square on Tuesday and commandeered rifles for the Volunteers and the Hibernian Rifles from there. After his return to the GPO he was involved in a skirmish in Jervis Street and received a wound to his hand. On Wednesday he was wounded again, this time in Marlborough Street, and was taken to the Mater Hospital. While in the hospital, he was identified by a policeman, but escaped with the help of the nuns before he could be arrested. He was taken by car to Carnew, but gave himself up when the authorities threatened to arrest his wife. He was deported to Wakefield Jail and was released two months later.

In 1917 he was transferred to the Dublin Brigade Transport Section and was detailed to assist in Active Service Unit operations in 1918. He took part in the successful raid on Collinstown Aerodrome in 1919 and later became a member of Michael Collins's "Squad". He took part in several ambushes and raids for arms. On Bloody Sunday he drove the getaway car for several of the unit members who had executed the British agents. He also drove the car in the attempt to rescue Seán McEoin from Mountjoy Jail on Whit Sunday, 1921.

During the Civil War he supported the Treaty and joined the Free State Army with the rank of colonel commandant. He took part in the principal engagements around Dublin and was wounded at Baltinglass. He was also involved in the taking of Cork by sea.

During the 1939-45 Emergency, he was captain of the 26th Rifle Battalion, of which members of the Old Dublin Brigade formed the nucleus.

In later years he became a Director of New Ireland Assurance Company and resided at 376 Clontarf Road.

Pat McCrea died on February 3rd 1964 and was buried at Clontarf Cemetery, Castle Avenue.

References:

RH; IMA, MSPC; IMA, BMH (WS 413); *Irish Independent* & *Irish Press*, 4th February 1964, (obits).

Patrick McDermott: (1889 – 1977)

Liverpool Company, (Kimmage Garrison).

Patrick McDermott was born in 1889 and was a native of Drumcliffe, County Sligo. He emigrated to England to work and joined the Volunteers in Liverpool in 1915. He returned to Dublin in February 1916, and joined the Volunteer Camp at Larkfield, Kimmage. On Easter Sunday he was in the party that raided the De Selby Quarry at Tallaght for explosives and he was part of the Kimmage Garrison that reported the GPO on Easter Monday. Later on Easter Monday evening he was in the group sent to blow up the railway bridge at Cabra. Their position was surrounded by British Troops on Tuesday evening, and he was arrested and detained in Arbour Hill. He was deported to Wakefield Prison on May 6th and interned in Frongoch until June 16th 1916.

He joined B. Company, 3rd Battalion in 1917 and took part in a number of operations. He was mobilised on Bloody Sunday, November 21st 1920, for the attack on British agents, but the intended target was not present when his party raided the premises. In March 1921 he was involved in the Pearse Street attack, in which Volunteer Leo Fitzgerald was killed. He took no part in the Civil War and returned to live in Sligo.

Patrick McDermott, of Strand Road, Sligo, died on October 15th 1977 and was buried at Carrigan's Cemetery, County Sligo.

References:

RH; IMA, MSPC; *Sunday Press*, 16th October 1977, (dn).

Joseph McDonagh: (1877 - 1950)
Irish Citizen Army, (Baldoyle Section). Roll of Honour

Joseph McDonagh was born in 1877. He was one of three Irish Citizen Army men from Baldoyle, who fought in the GPO in 1916; Michael Nolan and James McCormack, who was killed in action, were the others. On Easter Monday he walked from Baldoyle to the GPO, leaving a wife and young family, to take part in the Rising. Initially, he was stationed at the front ground floor windows and Volunteer Liam McGinley later recalled seeing him in the Dublin Bread Company Building. On Thursday, when the Imperial Hotel was burned, he withdrew into the north inner city, he carried the injured Volunteer Paddy Mahon into the Pro-Cathedral Presbytery. He was wounded in the right hand during the retreat. After his arrest he was deported to Stafford Jail on May 1st and interned in Frongoch until Christmas 1916.

He reorganised the Irish Citizen Army in Baldoyle after his release from internment, and co-operated with the IRA in the area during the War of Independence. He took the anti-Treaty side in 1922 and reported to Barry's Hotel at the outbreak of the Civil War. He also occupied a post at Raheny and was interned for a short term. He later had a breakdown in health as a result of the hardship of internment and of active service.

Joseph McDonagh, of 18 Station Road, Baldoyle, died on May 26th 1950 and was buried at Kinsealy Cemetery, County Dublin.

References:
RH; IMA, MSPC; NLI, *William O'Brien Papers*, (Ms 15,673); Ann Matthews, *The Irish Citizen Army*, (2014); *Irish Press*, 29th May 1950, (dn).

James J. (Jimmy) McElligott: (1893 – 1974)
B. Coy, 2nd Batt, Dublin Brigade. Roll of Honour

Jimmy McElligott was born in Tralee, County Kerry, on July 26th 1893, and graduated from UCD with honours in Economics and the Classics in 1913. He entered the Civil Service and was assigned to the Irish Local Government Board. He also joined B. Company, 2nd Battalion, Dublin Brigade in 1913, and was part of the GPO Garrison in Easter Week. He was in the group of Volunteers who occupied the Imperial Hotel until Thursday, when the building was engulfed in fire. He returned to the GPO by making a dash across the bullet swept street. After the surrender, he was deported to Stafford Jail on May 1st and interned in Frongoch until November 25th 1916.

He lost his job in the Civil Service on his release from internment because of his involvement in the Rising. He completed a Postgraduate Degree course in UCD and in 1919 became a journalist in London, eventually becoming Editor of *"The Statist"*, a financial weekly journal. In 1923, he returned to Ireland and became Financial Adviser to the Government. Four years later he was appointed Secretary of the Dept. of Finance and head of the Civil Service. He married Anne Fay from Edenderry, County Offaly, in 1927. He acted as chairman of the committee for the Eucharistic Congress in Dublin in 1932 and was also on the Irish delegation to the World Economic Conference in London in 1933. He resigned as Secretary of the Dept of Finance in 1953 to become Governor of the Central Bank, a position he held until 1960.

Jimmy McElligott died suddenly at his home at Oak Lodge, South Hill, Blackrock, on January 23rd 1974 and was buried in Deansgrange Cemetery.

References:

RH; IMA, MSPC; *DIB*, Seán Cromien, (James Quinn, Ed, 2009); Seán MacEntee, *Episode at Easter*, (1966); Louis McRedmond, *Modern Irish Lives: Dictionary of 20th century Irish Biography*, (1998); *Irish Press*, 26th January 1974, (na, *an appreciation*).

John McEntagart: (1883 – 1963)

Section Commander, A. Coy, 3rd Batt, Dublin Brigade. Roll of Honour

John McEntagart, a native of Mullaghbawn, Dunsany, County Meath, was born in 1883. He joined the Purveyors' Branch of the Gaelic League in 1905, and in 1910 he moved from Dublin to Wexford where he became a member of the IRB. He joined the Volunteers in Wexford in 1914, and was transferred to A. Company, 3rd Battalion, Dublin Brigade, in 1915 as a section commander. On Easter Monday, he was attending the races at Fairyhouse when he heard the Rising had begun. He made his way to the GPO and he was put in charge of a group guarding the windows facing Henry Street. He fought in the GPO throughout the week, and he was in the party led by The O'Rahilly into Moore Street on Friday evening. On Saturday morning he was seriously wounded in the left thigh, while trying to escape from a house in Moore Lane. He was taken to Jervis Street Hospital and held as a patient under arrest, but managed to escape in a very weak condition. A general breakdown in his health rendered him unfit for any further active service and he was unable to work. He later left Dublin to live in Drogheda.

John McEntagart, of Sienna Lodge, Chord Road, Drogheda, died in St Mary's Hospital, Drogheda on October 17th 1963 and was buried in St Peter's Cemetery, Drogheda, County Louth.

References:

RH; IMA, MSPC; *Irish Press*, 19th October 1963, (dn).

James McEvoy: (1892 – 1965)
F. Coy, 1st Batt, Dublin Brigade

James McEvoy, the son of a Fenian, was born in 1892 and resided at 33 Lower Erne Street. He was employed as a cinematograph operator and was a member of F. Company, 1st Battalion, Dublin Brigade. On Easter Monday he reported to the GPO and was sent across the street to Reis's Chambers by James Connolly. He was one of six Volunteers who carried the wireless apparatus back across Sackville Street to the GPO on Wednesday. He fought in the GPO until the evacuation on Friday evening. He was one of the four stretcher bearers who carried the wounded James Connolly into Henry Place. After the surrender he was brought to the Custom House for interrogation, and then transferred to Richmond Barracks. He was then deported to Knutsford Jail on May 3rd and interned in Frongoch.

On his release from internment in July 1916 he rejoined his old unit. He served in the War of Independence and took part in many operations. He supported the Treaty and joined the Free State Army in 1922. He served through the Civil War and was demobilised in April 1924. His brother, Patrick, was a member of the Jacob's Garrison in 1916, while another brother, Commandant Michael McEvoy, served in the War of Independence.

James McEvoy, of 128 Kehoe Square, Inchicore, died on the March 28th 1965.

References:
IMA, MSPC; *Irish Press*, 29th March 1965, (dn).

Thomas McEvoy: (1898 – 1970)
C. Coy, 1st Batt, Dublin Brigade. Roll of Honour

Thomas McEvoy was born in 1898 and resided at 2 Sampson's Lane, off Moore Street. He was employed as a grocer's assistant. He was a member of Fianna Éireann, and he joined C. Company, 1st Battalion, Dublin Brigade, several weeks before the Rising. He set off from home on Easter Monday morning, assuming he was going on a route march, but instead ended up in the GPO. He was one the Volunteers who fired at the Lancers as they approached the GPO, and he was later sent out in a party to disperse looters in the area. On Tuesday he escorted Mrs Sheehy Skeffington and May McLoughlin from the GPO to the College of Surgeons, laden down with a large sack of foodstuffs and dispatches. He spent the week delivering dispatches to other outposts, including the Four Courts. His father, Andrew, fought in the Boer War and was serving in British Army in the First World War at the time of the Rising. After the surrender Thomas was used as a human shield by

British soldiers, as they searched for Volunteers in the Moore Street area, but was released and told to go home shortly afterwards.

He transferred to C. Company, 3rd Battalion, Dublin Brigade, in 1917 and later that year he escaped from British Forces during a raid at Rathfarnham. In 1918 he was promoted to lieutenant with the 5th Battalion Engineers (Machine Gun Section) and took part in many operations during the War of Independence, including the attack on the Independent Newspaper Offices in December 1919 and the destruction of Stepaside RIC Barracks in 1920. In November 1920 he prepared the explosives for the attempted rescue of Kevin Barry, and took part in the burning of the Custom House in May 1921. He took the anti-Treaty side in the Civil War and was involved in the fighting in the O'Connell Street area. He was arrested in November 1922 and took part in a sixteen day hunger strike in Newbridge Barracks before his release in 1923.

In later years, he was a member of Our Lady's Choral Society.

Thomas McEvoy, of 47 East Wall Road, died on September 7th 1970 and was buried at Kenure Cemetery, Rush, County Dublin.

References:

RH; IMA, MSPC; *Evening Herald*, 7th September 1970, (dn); *Irish Press*, 8th September 1970, (dn).

James McGallogly: (- 1924)
Glasgow Company, (Kimmage Garrison). Roll of Honour

James McGallogly was born to Irish parents, in Lanarkshire, just outside Glasgow. He joined the Glasgow Volunteers with his brother, John. Both brothers were active in Scotland, and were involved in raids to procure explosives from the many coalmines in the area. This brought them to the attention of the authorities and both brothers were questioned by detectives in the days before they came to Ireland in January 1916. They joined the Volunteer Camp at Larkfield, Kimmage, having travelled there, via Belfast.

James joined his Kimmage Exiles on Easter Monday in the GPO and fought there for the week.

He returned to Glasgow after his release from detention. At the beginning of 1920 he went to Manchester with his brother, John and they joined the Volunteers there, through their acquaintance with Larry Ryan, who had been with them in Kimmage. James was sent back to Glasgow to escort a lorry load of guns and ammunitions to Liverpool and Manchester in autumn 1920, but on his arrival he took ill.

James McGallogly never recovered from his illness and passed away in 1924.

References:

RH; John Heuston OP, *Headquarters Battalion, Easter Week 1916*, (1966); Ann Matthews, *The Kimmage Garrison 1916*, (2010).

John McGallogly: (1898 - 1989)

Glasgow Company, (Kimmage Garrison). Roll of Honour

John McGallogly was born about 10 miles outside Glasgow, to Donegal parents. With his older brother, James, he was being sought by the police when they left Scotland for Dublin, via Belfast, in January 1916. They initially made contact with Countess Markievicz on their arrival, and later joined the Volunteer camp at Larkfield, Kimmage, under the command of George Plunkett. They were sent to work at the de Selby Quarries in Brittas, County Dublin, using the false name of Doherty. On Easter Monday, John was sent to a position on the corner of Sackville Street and Middle Abbey Street. While on one of many sorties to get provisions for the garrison, he captured a British Officer, Lieutenant King, and brought him back to the GPO. On Wednesday, he manned a ground floor window in the GPO and the following day he took up guard duty at the Princes Street entrance. After the surrender, he was taken to Richmond Barracks where he was court-martialed on the evidence of Lieutenant King, and sentenced to death. From there, he was brought to Kilmainham Jail with eighteen others, and each person was given an individual cell. However, his sentence was commuted to ten years penal servitude.

He was released in 1917 after serving time in various English Jails and returned to Scotland. In 1920, he moved to Manchester with his brother James, where they were engaged in collecting arms and sending them to Ireland. At this time, he also suggested reprisal actions in Britain for the Black and Tan atrocities in Ireland. Among his suggestions was the destruction of the Power Station in Manchester and the locks on the Manchester Canal, and the burning of warehouses in the region. The plans were discovered in Dick Mulcahy's home on the South Circular Road, Dublin and the whole operation was scrapped. Occasionally however, he was involved in the starting of fires in warehouses in the area. Shortly after, he was arrested with Frank Breen at a weapons dump containing two cwt of gelignite by police who had been laying in wait for two days. He was sentenced to five years in Dartmoor Prison, but was released in February, 1922.

On his release, he returned to Ireland and entered the Civil Service, serving in the Depts of Post & Telegraphs, Industry & Commerce, and Social Welfare.

John McGallogly, of 46 Eglington Road, Donnybrook, died on February 2nd 1989 and was buried at Shanganagh Cemetery, Shankill, County Dublin.

References:
RH; IMA, MSPC; NLI, *Lynch Papers*, (Ms 11,131);
John Heuston OP, *Headquarters Battalion, Easter Week 1916*, (1966); Ann Matthews, *The Kimmage Garrison 1916*, (2010); *Irish Independent*, 3rd February 1989, (dn).

Seán McGarry: (1886 - 1958)

Honorary Secretary, Volunteers. Roll of Honour

Seán McGarry was born in 1886 and was a native of Dundrum, County Dublin. He was a founder member and Honorary Secretary of the Irish Volunteers. He was also involved in the founding of Fianna Éireann, with Countess Markievicz and in the publication of *"Irish Freedom"*, with Seán MacDiarmada. He was also a member of the IRB. He was an electrician by trade and in 1916 was living at 24 Ballybough Road, Dublin. During Easter Week he was aide-de-camp to Tom Clarke. On Easter Monday he was in charge of the party that was sent by Joseph Plunkett to the School of Telegraphy in Reis's Chambers, to set up a radio transmitter. When the GPO was evacuated on Friday evening, he was one of the last to leave the burning building. After the surrender, he was sentenced to death, which was later commuted to six years penal servitude in Lewes Jail.

On his release on June 16th 1917, he was made general secretary of the Irish Volunteers.

He was arrested in connection with the "German Plot" allegation, and was once again deported. In February 1919 he made a famous escape from Lincoln Jail with Éamon deValera and successfully returned to Ireland. He was elected to the first Dáil in 1918 and sat as a Sinn Féin TD. He took the pro-treaty side in 1922 and joined the Free State army, retiring with the rank of Captain in August 1923. A fire caused by a landmine planted at his home in Ballybough by Republican forces on December 10th 1922, resulted in the death of his seven year old son. His electrical fittings shop in St Andrew's Street was also bombed in February 1923. Later in 1923, he was re-elected to the Dáil as a Cumann na nGaedheal TD for the constituency of Dublin North. He resigned from Cumann na nGaedheal after the Irish Army Mutiny affair, citing the lack of progress in the unification of a 32 County Ireland as the reason, and joined the National Party, set up by Joseph McGrath, which was a splinter group of nine Cumann na nGaedheal TDs. He resigned from the Dáil in 1924.

Seán McGarry, of 44 Richmond Avenue, Monkstown, died on December 9th 1958 and was buried at Deansgrange Cemetery.

References:

RH; IMA, MSPC; IMA, BMH (WS 386); *DIB*, Lawrence White, (James Quinn, Ed, 2009); *Catholic Bulletin*, July 1916; Dorothy Macardle, *The Irish Republic*, (1937); Max Caulfield, *The Easter Rebellion*, (1963); Anne Marreco, *The Rebel Countss, the life and times of Constance Markievicz*, (1969); Calton Younger, *Ireland's Civil War*, (1970); *Irish Independent* & *Irish Press*, 10th December 1958, (obits).

Michael McGarvey: (1882 – 1949)
Liverpool Company, (Kimmage Garrison)

Michael McGarvey, a native of Blackrock, Dundalk, County Louth, was born in 1882. He joined the IRB in Dundalk, before he went to work in Liverpool. While he was in Liverpool, he joined the Volunteers and he returned to Dublin in March 1916. He joined the Volunteer Camp at Larkfield, Kimmage and on Easter Monday he travelled to Liberty Hall with the Kimmage Garrison. He proceeded to the GPO with the main body of Volunteers and he took part in the attack on the Lancers as they approached the GPO. He fought throughout the week, and after the surrender he was deported to Stafford Jail on May 1st and interned in Frongoch until Christmas 1916. On his release from internment he returned to Liverpool and then emigrated to the United States in June 1917. He joined the 1916 Club in New York and was engaged in securing and shipping arms to Ireland for the IRA.

Michael McGarvey, of 249 West 15th Street, New York, died on October 29th 1949 and was buried at Calvary Cemetery, New York.

References:
IMA, MSPC; John Heuston OP, *Headquarters Battalion, Easter Week 1916*, (1966); Ann Matthews, *The Kimmage Garrison 1916*, (2010).

Conor McGinley: (1897 – 1975)
E. Coy, 4th Batt, Dublin Brigade. Roll of Honour

Conor McGinley was born in 1897 and was a native of Letterkenny, Co Donegal. He was the eldest of the twelve children of Peadar McGinley, the author and Irish language playwright, better known as *Cú Uladh* and was educated at P.H. Pearse's school, Scoil Éanna, in Rathfarnham. He was a nineteen year old architectural student in UCD and a member of the Collegians (UCD) GAA Club, at the time of the Rising. He fought throughout the week in the GPO along with the 38 Volunteers of E. Company, 4th Battalion, including his younger brother, Eunan, who left Rathfarnham on Easter Monday. After the surrender, he was sentenced of 10 years penal servitude, which was commuted to 3 years.

He was released under the general amnesty on June 16th 1917 and resumed his part in the War of Independence. He was re-arrested in 1920 and wasn't released from Ballykinlar Camp until the Truce. He was appointed Assistant Dublin City Architect in 1924 and held the post of Dublin City Architect from 1936 until his retirement in 1959. After retirement he continued in practice as a consultant with his son, Cian, a Dublin architect.

Conor McGinley died on March 27th 1975 and was buried in Mount Jerome Cemetery.

References:
RH; *Catholic Bulletin*, August 1916; *Irish Independent* & *Irish Press*, 31st March 1975, (obits).

John Eunan McGinley: (1899 - 1923)
E. Coy, 4th Batt, Dublin Brigade

Eunan McGinley was born in 1899 and the son of Peter McGinley (Cú Uladh), the President of the Gaelic League. In 1916 he was a seventeen year old student at Scoil Éanna, Rathfarnham and a member of E. Company, 4th Battalion, Dublin Brigade. He lived at 108 Drumcondra Road, and was a member of the Collegians (UCD) GAA Club. On Easter Monday he marched with his company that included his brother, Conor, to the GPO and served throughout Easter Week, there. After the surrender, was deported to Stafford Jail on May 1st 1916 and interned in Frongoch until July 15th 1916.

He was later employed as a Local Government Dept Auditor. On May 11th 1923 he was fatally injured when his motorcycle was in collision with a military lorry, near Balbriggan.

Eunan McGinley was buried at Glasnevin Cemetery on May 15th 1923 and Mrs Margaret Pearse was among the large attendance at the funeral.

References:
    Freeman's Journal & *Irish Independent*, 15th May 1923, (na, *accident reports*).

Patrick McGinley: (1886 - 1959)
F. Coy, 2nd Batt, Dublin Brigade. Roll of Honour

Patrick McGinley was born in 1886, resided at 2 Fitzgibbon Street and was a tailor by trade. He and his younger brother, Liam, were members of F. Company, 2nd Battalion, Dublin Brigade and on Easter Monday he left Fr Mathew Park, Fairview, with a party led by Captain Leo Henderson. They entered O'Meara's Public House at the junction of Spring Garden Street and Annesley Place and took up positions at the first floor windows. An enemy machine gun was silenced while the retreating British troops then came under fire from Volunteer positions along Leinster Avenue.

He then joined those holding Gilbey's Shop, Ballybough Bridge and remained there until Tuesday evening, when they were ordered into the GPO. On arriving at the GPO, he was sent across the street to report to Captain Frank Thornton in the Imperial Hotel. He hoisted the Starry Plough flag on the hotel's roof on Wednesday and when the outpost was evacuated on Thursday because of the raging fire, he made his way with five others to 42 Lower Gloucester Street where they remained until their arrest on Saturday morning by troops from the Royal Irish Regiment. He and his brother, Liam, who was also in the GPO, were deported to Knutsford Jail on May 1st and he was interned in Frongoch until August 3rd 1916.

He resumed active service in the War of Independence and his family home in Fitzgibbon Street was regularly used as a place of refuge for the IRA. In 1922 he joined the Free State Army and two years later he joined the Customs & Excise, and was the Excise Officer for Howth for the next 30 years.

Patrick McGinley of West Pier, Howth, died on April 29th 1959 and was buried at St Fintan's, Sutton.

References:

RH; IMA, MSPC; NLI, *Lynch Papers*, (Ms 11,131); *Irish Independent*, 30th April 1959, (dn); *Irish Press*, 1st May 1959, (obit).

William (Liam) McGinley: (1894 - 1963)
F. Coy, 2nd Batt, Dublin Brigade. Roll of Honour

Liam McGinley was born in 1894 and resided at 2 Fitzgibbon Street. He was a tailor by trade and a member of F. Company, 2nd Battalion, Dublin Brigade, in 1916. He was mobilized with his older brother, Patrick, at Father Mathew Park, Fairview on Easter Monday, and spent the first two days in positions in the Ballybough and Fairview area. On Tuesday he was ordered into the GPO with the rest of the Fairview men, and as they approached the GPO the Volunteers in the Imperial Hotel fired on them, mistaking them for the enemy. As a result, Liam McGinley received shrapnel injuries and this attack only ceased when James Connolly ran into the street shouting for the firing to stop. His wounds were dressed by John J. Doyle, the brigade medical officer and afterwards he took up a new post in the GPO, where he remained for the rest of the week. After the surrender, he was deported to Knutsford Jail on May 1st and was released in June, 1916.

He rejoined his unit on the reorganization of the Volunteers and was interned in Crumlin Road Jail, Belfast, in 1918. He took no part in the Civil War. Three of his children entered religious life, Brother Louis, OCSC Roscrea; Sister Philomena, Irish Sisters of Charity, Bristol and Sister Margaret, Irish Sisters of Charity, Waterford.

Liam McGinley, of 27 Ratoath Road, Cabra, died on October 23rd 1963 and was buried in St Joseph's Monastery Cemetery, Roscrea.

References:

RH; IMA, MSPC; *Irish Independent*, 24th October 1963, (obit).

Michael Conway (Con) McGinn: (1897 - 1960)
F. Coy, 2nd Battalion, Dublin Brigade. Roll of Honour

Con McGinn was born in Omagh, in 1897 and was the son of Michael McGinn, the Fenian Head Centre for County Tyrone. He was reared in Dublin and resided at 6 Strandville, Strand Road, Clontarf, where his father had become the caretaker for the Clontarf Town Hall. He was a member of F. Company, 2nd Battalion, Dublin Brigade and on Easter Monday he joined others from F. Company at Ballybough Bridge, where they held defensive positions. As well as taking part in action in the area, he was also in the group that occupied Gilbey's Shop, opposite the bridge. On Tuesday evening his company was ordered back into the GPO and on their arrival P.H. Pearse addressed and congratulated them. They were then divided into three sections, and Con was among the group sent to reinforce the outpost across the street in the Imperial Hotel. He remained there until Thursday evening when fire took hold of the building. He evacuated with a party into Marlborough Street and was eventually captured in Gloucester Street. He was deported to Wakefield Prison on May 6th, and interned in Frongoch until July 17th 1916.

On his release, he continued to serve in the War of Independence, with his brother, Ron.

After the Truce, he joined the Free State Army and was demobilized in 1924 with the rank of captain. During the emergency years he was in charge of the Local Defence Force in North County Dublin. He became a Customs & Excise Officer at Dublin Airport and lived at Clonvilla, Dublin Road, Sutton.

Con McGinn died on October 2nd 1960 and was buried at St Fintan's Cemetery, Sutton.

References:
RH; IMA, MSPC; *Irish Press* & *Evening Herald*, 3rd October 1960, (obits).

Seamus McGowan: (1875 - 1955)

Captain. Irish Citizen Army, (Dorset Street Section). Roll of Honour

Seamus McGowan was born in 1875 and resided at 93 Victoria Lane, Botanic Avenue, Drumcondra. He became a council member of the Irish Citizen Army at the inaugural meeting on March 22nd 1914. When Liberty Hall became a social as well as military centre, he became active in the dramatic group, the Liberty Players. He also organized large open air meetings in Croydon Park on summer evenings, which were very popular, with mock battles and participants dressed as Red Indians. In 1915, as sergeant and assistant quartermaster, he was in charge of bomb making in Liberty Hall, where large quantities of homemade bombs were made and stored. He was ranked as captain before the Rising, but didn't take any command leading up to Easter Week, as he was in charge of the distribution of arms. When the general body of men left Beresford Place on the morning of Easter Monday, he remained behind with a small contingent in Liberty Hall. By that afternoon, they had commandeered some vehicles and the remainder of the ammunition, weapons and stores were brought to the GPO. He was assistant to Captain James O'Neill, Irish Citizen Army, in the distribution of arms and ammunition in the GPO. After the surrender, he shared the holding cell in Richmond Barracks with Tom Clarke and Seán MacDiarmada. He was deported to Stafford Jail on May 8th and interned in Frongoch, until Christmas, 1916.

During the Civil War, he took the anti-Treaty side and with a group of Irish Citizen Army men, he occupied Findlater's Stores and was interned, as a consequence.

In 1934 he was part of the unsuccessful attempt to form a New Citizen Army, within the trade union movement. Two years later, in 1936, he contested the Dublin Municipal elections as a Labour candidate.

Seamus McGowan died on March 7th 1955 and was buried in the graveyard at St John the Baptist, Church of Ireland, Drumcondra.

References:
RH; IMA, MSPC; NLI, *William O'Brien Papers*, (Ms 15,673); R.M. Fox, *History of the Irish Citizen Army*, (1943); Frank Robbins, *Under the Starry Plough: Recollections of the Irish Citizen Army*, (1977); Ann Matthews, *The Irish Citizen Army*, (2014); *Irish Press*, 9th March 1955, (dn).

Christopher (Christy) McGrane: (1898 – 1966)

Fianna Éireann. C. Coy, 1st Batt, Dublin Brigade. Roll of Honour

Christy McGrane was born in 1898 and resided at 99 Lower Gardiner Street. He joined Fianna Éireann in 1912 and also became a member of the Fianna Pipe Band. In 1914 he took part in the Howth gun running. He was among the group assigned to push the fully laden carts of guns and ammunition back to Dublin and when they were about to be intercepted near Fairview, they made their back up the Malahide Road and escaped across country. Later in the same year, he joined C. Company, 1st Battalion, Dublin Brigade. On Easter Monday arrived at the GPO with his Mauser rifle and fought there throughout Easter Week. After the surrender, he was released at the Rotunda, because of his young age.

He joined E. Company, 2nd Battalion, Dublin Brigade and served as an armed guard at the convention, held in Croke Park in 1917. He was transferred to H. Company, 1st Battalion and in September 1917 he was part of the guard of honour at the funeral of Thomas Ashe. In 1918 he was appointed Section Commander of H. Company and he was involved in at least two abortive attempts to rescue Kevin Barry from Mountjoy Jail. He was on armed guard duty in Croke Park on Bloody Sunday, November 21st 1920, when Crown Forces raided the ground in retaliation to the assassinations of members of the Cairo Gang. When the firing began, he temporarily dumped his revolver and escaped among the crowd, returning the following day to retrieve his firearm. He was arrested in April 1921, while visiting his family home in Lower Gardiner Street, and was interned in Collinstown. He was later transferred to Arbour Hill and Ballykinlar and wasn't released until after the Treaty was signed. He took no part in the Civil War. He was later an active member of various old comrade associations. In 1935 he was part of the armed guard that led the march of veterans past the GPO for the unveiling of the statue of Cuchulain.

Christy McGrane, of 163 Crumlin Road, died on March 6th 1966 and was buried at Glasnevin Cemetery.

References:
RH; IMA, MSPC; *The McGrane family private papers*, (ref Pádraig McGrane); *Irish Press*, 9th March 1966, (obit).

Michael McGrath: (1884 – 1966)

London Company, (Kimmage Garrison). Roll of Honour

Michael McGrath was born in Keenagh, County Longford, in 1884. He emigrated to London, where he worked as a railway clerk. He also joined the London Company of Volunteers and returned to Dublin before the Rising. He joined the Volunteers at Larkfield, Kimmage and on reporting to the GPO on Easter Monday, he was sent to Ballybough. He returned to the GPO with the Fairview men on the Tuesday evening, and he spent Wednesday and Thursday occupying a post in a small public house at the corner of Henry Street and Sackville Street. On Friday he was back to the GPO, and when fire spread from the roof he was sent with two other London Volunteers, Michael Collins and "Blimey" O'Connor, to fight the flames. He was later injured during the evacuation of the GPO. He was deported to Stafford Jail on May 1st and interned in Frongoch until Christmas 1916.

On his release from internment he moved to Athlone and became instructor to the Drumraney Company of Volunteers. He later returned to London, but was arrested and interned in Ballykinlar Camp, from March to December 1921. He joined the Free State Army with the rank of private in January 1923, and was demobilised in April 1924. He joined the Civil Service in 1925 and was employed in the Employment Exchange in Tralee, County Kerry.

Michael McGrath, of Lyranes, Glencar, County Kerry, died on April 24th 1966 and was buried at Incharue Cemetery, Glencar.

References:
RH; IMA, MSPC; NLI, *Lynch Papers*, (Ms 11,131); Ann Matthews, *The Kimmage Garrrison, 1916*, (2010); *Irish Press*, 26th April 1966, (dn).

Patrick (Paddy) McGrath (Junior): (1895 – 1967)

F. Coy, 2nd Batt, Dublin Brigade. Roll of Honour

Paddy McGrath Junior was born in 1895 and resided at 3 Northbrook Avenue Upper, North Strand. He was a member of F. Company, 2nd Battalion, Dublin Brigade and was a member of the guard of honour at the lying in state of O'Donovan Rossa in 1915. On Easter Monday he reported to Father Mathew Park, Fairview, and joined up with his unit, under the command of Captain Frank Henderson. He took up a position at the junction of Ballybough Road and the North Circular Road, until proceeding to the GPO on Tuesday evening. He was then sent across the street to the North Earl Street junction and later to the Reis's Chambers, where he joined his father, also named Paddy. At the wireless school in Reis's Chambers, he assisted in erecting the wireless equipment on the roof under heavy fire. On Wednesday he was in the party led by his father that transferred the wireless equipment to the GPO, before he returned to the Hibernian Bank at the corner of Abbey Street. He was on the roof of the GPO on Thursday evening when he was seriously wounded. He was shot in the chest and head and lost an eye. He was attended to by Dr. Jim Ryan, then a medical student and was conveyed to Jervis Street Hospital. He was later transferred to the Royal Victoria Eye and Ear Hospital, Adelaide Road and was discharged in June 1916.

During the War of Independence he was a member of the Active Service Unit. He was arrested in 1920 and released from Rath Camp, the Curragh, in December 1921. He joined the Free State Army on April 1st 1922 with the rank of Sergeant, and was demobilised on October 27th 1924. He was resided at 28 Killarney Street, North Strand and originally employed as a hairdresser, but in later years he worked for the *Irish Press*.

Paddy McGrath, who survived with a bullet lodged in his skull after 1916 that caused epileptic fits, died on November 27th November 1967 and was buried at Glasnevin Cemetery.

References:

RH; IMA, MSPC; NLI, *Lynch Papers*, (Ms 11,131); *Irish Independent* & *Irish Press*, 28th November 1967, (obits).

Patrick (Paddy) McGrath, (Senior): (1876 - 1940)

D. Coy, 2nd Batt, Dublin Brigade. Roll of Honour

Paddy McGrath was born in 1876 and left his native Kilkenny city at a young age to come to Dublin. He resided at 3 Northbrook Avenue Upper, North Strand and, like his older brother Martin, who was a Fenian, he worked as a compositor in the printing trade. He joined the Volunteers at the Rotunda in 1913 and became a member of D. Company, 2nd Battalion, Dublin Brigade. He reported to the GPO on Easter Monday and was sent with a group to the wireless school in Reis's Chambers, at the corner of Lower Abbey Street, where they transmitted news that the Irish Republic had been declared. When Captain Thomas Weafer was mortally wounded in the Hibernian Bank, he helped Richard Healy move him out of the line of fire. He then took charge of the group in Reis's and led them back to the GPO carrying the wireless equipment with them, while under heavy fire. He fought for the remainder of the week in the GPO. His son, Paddy (Junior), was also in the GPO, and was badly wounded on the parapets on Thursday evening. After the surrender he was detained in Richmond Barracks and was released from detention after a short period, because of the influence of his employer, Michael Martin Murphy, proprietor of Independent Newspapers.

He was involved in the reorganisation of the Volunteers in 1917 and became quartermaster of D. Company, 2nd Battalion. He was one of Michael Collins's most trusted lieutenants during the War of Independence. He took the pro-Treaty side in the Civil War, and joined the Free State Army with the rank of staff captain, retiring in 1924.

When the *Irish Press* newspaper was founded in 1931, he became Works Manager until his retirement in June 1939.

Paddy McGrath, of 32 Lindsay Road, Glasnevin, died on September 24th 1940 and was buried at Glasnevin Cemetery.

References:

RH; IMA, MSPC; NLI, *Lynch Papers*, (Ms 11,131); *Irish Independent* & *Irish Press*, 25th September 1940, (obits).

Seán McGrath: (1883 – 1950)

London Company, (Kimmage Garrison)

Seán McGrath, the son of a Fenian, was born in Keenagh, County Longford, in 1883. He emigrated to London in 1908 and found employment as a clerk in the British Rail Company. He joined the Gaelic League in London and was later sworn into the IRB. After he joined the Volunteers he was involved in the purchase of arms for shipment to Ireland. Prior to the Rising he returned to Dublin with twenty five Volunteers and one Cumann na mBan member from London, and joined the Kimmage Garrison. He fought throughout Easter Week in the GPO and was later deported and interned. After his release, he was interned a second time for a year in 1918.

He was a founder member of the Irish Self-Determination League of Britain and he opposed the Treaty. He was among those League members who were deported in 1923, but when the House of Lords declared the deportation to be illegal, he returned to England and subsequently was sentenced to one year imprisonment on a charge of conspiracy.

He resided at 148 St John's Way, London, N19 and was honorary secretary of the Anti-Partition League in Britain. In early June 1950 he took ill while returning from an Anti-Partition League meeting.

Seán McGrath died on July 22nd 1950 and was buried at Leytonstone Cemetery. His funeral was attended by representatives of many Irish organisations in Britain and was led by the Irish Ambassador to the United Kingdom, JW Dulanty.

References:

DIB, (James Quinn, Ed, 2009); John Heuston OP, *Headquarters Battalion, Easter Week 1916*, (1966); Denis Hickey & James Doherty, *Dictionary of Irish* History, (1980); Ann Matthews, *The Kimmage Garrison 1916*, (2010); *Sunday Independent*, 23rd July 1950, (obit); *Irish Independent*, 25th July 1950, (dn).

Thomas (Tom) McGrath: (1883 - 1948)

C. Coy, 2nd Batt, Dublin Brigade. Roll of Honour

Tom McGrath was born in 1883 and resided at 13 Grenville Street, off Mountjoy Square. He was employed as a vanman, and joined the Irish Citizen Army in 1913. He later became a member of C. Company, 2nd Battalion, Dublin Brigade. He fought throughout Easter Week in the GPO, and was photographed with Jack Doyle by Joe Cripps. This photograph, and another of a group of Volunteers taken by Joe Cripps were the only photographs from inside the GPO during Easter Week. After the surrender he was deported to Knutsford Jail on May 1st and later interned in Frongoch until July 15th 1916.

He rejoined his unit in 1917 and was engaged in buying arms from British soldiers. He was arrested and imprisoned in Arbour Hill. In 1919 he was arrested again and spent two months in Mountjoy Jail. On his release he joined H. Company, 1st Battalion, and in 1920 he became a member of the Active Service Unit. In January 1921, he was wounded in an attack on Auxiliaries at Bachelor's Walk, and in July of that year he was wounded in the leg in an ambush at Liberty Hall. He took the Republican side during the Civil War and fought at Healy's Public House, Parnell Street and Findlater's, O'Connell Street. He was arrested in July 1922 and interned until 1923.

Tom McGrath, of 4 Library View, Phibsboro, died on October 23rd 1948 and was buried at Glasnevin Cemetery.

References:
RH; IMA, MSPC; *Irish Independent*, 25th October 1948, (obit); *Irish Press*, 27th October 1948, (obit).

Dr. Daniel (Dan) McLoughlin: (1891 – 1958)
Volunteer, (Unattached). Roll of Honour

Dan McLoughlin, a native of Coleraine, County Derry, was born in 1891. He was educated at St Columba's College, Derry and UCD. He was studying medicine in Dublin when the Rising began in 1916. Although not attached to the Volunteers, he offered his services at the GPO on Easter Monday and assisted the medical team there throughout the week. He attended to James Connolly when he was initially wounded in the arm on Thursday while in Princes Street, and Connolly warned him not to disclose that he had been shot. He also attended to Connolly when he received the more serious leg wound, shortly after, on Abbey Street. On Friday, he was in charge of the wounded that were conveyed to Jervis Street Hospital. He was sent back to the GPO from the hospital with some Volunteers, but they could only get as far as Arnott's, Henry Street and the next morning they took refuge in a house in Abbey Street. He was later captured and taken to Trinity College, where he was interrogated and later released.

He qualified at UCD in 1930 and worked in several Dublin hospitals, including the South Dublin Union Hospital, James's Street. He also practiced, as a GP in Rathmines and in Cabra for the last fifteen years of his life.

Dr. Dan McLoughlin, of 61 Cabra Road, who was unmarried, died on December 29th 1958 and was buried at the family burial ground at St John's, Killowen, Coleraine, County Derry.

References:
RH; IMA, MSPC; Max Caulfield, *The Easter Rebellion*, (1963); Thomas Coffey, *Agony at Easter*, (1969); *Irish Press* & *Irish Times*, 30th December 1958, (obits); Coleraine Chronicle, 3rd January 1959, (dn).

Mary (May) McLoughlin: (1901 – 1954)

Clan na nGael Girl Scouts. Roll of Honour

May McLoughlin was born in 1901 and resided at 4 North King Street. She became a member of Clan na nGael Girl Scouts (American Alliance) in 1915 and was employed as a trainee tailoress in Arnott's, Henry Street, in 1916. On Easter Monday she was mobilised by her captain, May Kelly (Mrs Chadwick) for a route march to the Dublin Mountains. When they heard that the Rising had begun, they made their way to St Stephen's Green. She was sent from there to a house in Drumcondra to collect revolvers and ammunition, and she spent that night in the College of Surgeons. On Tuesday morning she was sent to the GPO where she met James Connolly, who sent her back to the College of Surgeons with a dispatch and food. On her return to the GPO on Tuesday, she made a second trip to the College of Surgeons, accompanying Hannah Sheehy Skeffington and Volunteer Thomas McEvoy with a large sack of food. On the following day, she was sent to Jacob's and was told to swallow the dispatch note she was carrying, if stopped by the military. On Thursday, she met her brother Seán in the GPO, and he told her to return to the family home in North King Street. May was again given dispatch notes for Jacob's and on her return decided to call home to re-assure her mother of her well-being. When she got there her mother locked her in her bedroom while she prepared a hot meal for her, but May escaped out the window and returned to the GPO. Later on Thursday she was sent to Arnott's, Henry Street, where she collected items of clothing for the Volunteers. P.H. Pearse gave her a dispatch for Thomas McDonagh in Jacob's on Friday morning and while returning to the GPO, she was stopped by a British soldier. Unaware that she was a courier for the Volunteers, he brought her to the house of another soldier for her safety, where she was fed and given a bed for the night by the soldier's wife. On Saturday she joined her family at Bolton Street Technical College, where they had been evacuated to from their North King Street home.

She rejoined Clan na nGael Girl Scouts after the Rising, and became a member of Cumann na mBan in 1918. She took the Republican side in the Civil War and served in Barry's Hotel and Hely's, Parnell Street.

She later resided at 77 Lower Drumcondra Road and was employed in the Capital Theatre, until her health declined.

May McLoughlin died on May 17th 1954 and was buried at Glasnevin Cemetery.

References:
RH; IMA, MSPC; IMA, BMH (WS 934); Charlie McGuire, *Seán McLoughlin, Ireland's Forgotten Revolutionary*, (2011); Brian Hughes, *Michael Mallin*, (16Lives series, 2012); *Irish Independent*, 18th May 1954, (dn).

Seán McLoughlin: (1895 – 1960)

Fianna Éireann. Lieutenant. D. Coy, 1st Batt, Dublin Brigade

Seán McLoughlin was born on June 2nd 1895 and resided at 4 North King Street. His father, Patrick "Ruggie" McLoughlin, was a coal porter and an acquaintance of Jim Larkin. Seán joined Fianna Éireann and the Gaelic League in 1910. He joined the Volunteers in 1913 and was appointed lieutenant in D. Company, 1st Battalion, Dublin Brigade. In 1915 he was sworn into the IRB by Tom Clarke.

On Easter Monday, D. Company occupied the Mendicity Institute, Usher's Quay, under the command of Seán Heuston, with orders to stop troop movements from the Royal Barracks on the opposite side of the quays for four hours. From Monday to Wednesday Seán McLoughlin made several trips to the GPO, carrying dispatches, supplies and reporting on the situation in the Mendicity Institute. On Wednesday as he returned from the GPO with Paddy Stephenson, the British troops made their final assault on the Mendicity Institute. He spent Wednesday night manning the barricades in Chancery Lane, and returned to the GPO the following morning. Throughout the week James Connolly had been impressed by McLoughlin, and on Thursday he sent him in charge of thirty Volunteers to hold positions in the Independent Newspaper Offices and the Lucas Lamp Building. They were ordered back to the GPO on Friday by P.H. Pearse and as the fire took hold he was engaged in removing ammunition and homemade bombs from the basement. In the ensuing chaos at the evacuation of the GPO, he took charge and ushered the garrison into Henry Place. He was an adviser at the last meeting of the Provisional Government in a Moore Street shop and James Connolly proposed that he should be given his command that of commandant general and this was agreed. He had already employed Volunteers in boring through the walls of the houses and he then organised a party to attack the enemy barricade at Parnell Street. The attack was postponed for an hour and it was decided to negotiate a surrender.

When an unconditional surrender was declared, McLoughlin organised the Volunteers in Moore Street, and insisted that they march in military formation and bearing arms, contrary to General Lowe's orders. After spending the night outside the Rotunda, he was detained in Richmond Barracks. He was deported to Knutsford Jail on May 1st and interned in Frongoch until Christmas 1916.

From 1917 to 1919 he was a Volunteer organiser in the Limerick and Tipperary areas, under the direction of Michael Collins. His health suffered and Collins sent him to Scotland to procure arms and ammunition. In October 1921 he was a founder member of the Communist Party of Ireland with Roddy Connolly. At the outbreak of the Civil War, he was invited back from Scotland, where he was politically active, by the Republican leaders. He operated in the Kilmallock area and was captured and detained in Limerick Jail.

After the Civil War, he was involved in the trade union movement and clashed with Jim Larkin during the Inchicore railway strike in 1924. Shortly afterwards, because of the constant harassment of his family, which included his elderly parents being beaten by members of the Free State Army, he left Ireland for good. He eventually settled in Sheffield and remarried. He continued his involvement in labour politics and served several jail terms during the General Strike of 1926. He found employment as a clerk in Sheffield City Council.

Seán McLoughlin died in Sheffield on February 13th 1960 and in accordance with his wishes, his ashes were scattered over Howth Head by his son, Jack, shortly afterwards.

References:

RH; IMA, MSPC; IMA, BMH (WS 290); NLI, *William O'Brien Papers: How Inchicore was lost, Seán McLoughlin*, (Ms 15,670) & (Ms 15,673); *The Camillian Post*, (Spring 1948); HI, *The Boy Commandant of 1916*, Charlie McGuire, (Mar/April 2006); Max Caulfield, *The Easter Rebellion*, (1963); John Heuston, OP, *Headquarters Battalion, Easter Week 1916*, (1966); Thomas Coffey, *Agony at* Faster, (1969); Donnca Ó'Dúlaing, *Voices of Ireland*, (1984); Peter DeRosa, *Rebels*, (1991); Joe Good, *Enchanted by Dreams*, (1996); Matthew O'Dwyer, *Biographical Dictionary of Tipperary*, (1999); Charlie McGuire, *Roddy Connolly & the Struggle for Socialism in Ireland*, (2008); Charlie McGuire, *Seán McLoughlin, Ireland's Forgotten Revoutionary*, (2011); Lorcan Collins, *James Connolly*, (16Lives series, 2012); Derek Molyneux & Darren Kelly, *When the Clock Struck in 1916: Close Quarter Combat in the Easter Rising*, (2015); *Irish Echo*, 19th April 2006, (na).

Charles (Charlie) McMahon: (1904 – 1987)
Fianna Éireann

Charlie McMahon was born in Ballina, County Mayo, in 1904 and was two years old when his family moved to Dublin. He joined Fianna Éireann while still attending school and on Easter Monday, at the age of eleven, he reported to the GPO. For three days he carried food parcels and dispatches to various locations, including the Vitriol Works, Ballybough and to Amiens Street. Because of his young age, he was sent home on Wednesday. In 1918 he joined B. Company, 2nd Battalion and carried out intelligence work. He took part in a number of operations, including an attack on a Black and Tan convoy at The Thatch, Whitehall, where he was injured. In May 1921 he was seriously wounded in the head during the attack on the Custom House. He spent a long time in hospital and when he was discharged in 1922, he joined the Free State Army. During the Civil War he took part in the attack on the Four Courts. Because of difficulties resulting from his head wound, he was declared medically unfit and discharged from the army in 1924. In December 1925 Dr. Sir William deCourcy Wheeler performed an operation and removed the bullet from behind his brain that had been lodged there for over four years.

He was a leading GAA player in his day, and played his club hurling with St Kevin's and Young Ireland's and football for St Laurence O'Toole's. He won an All-Ireland Senior Hurling medal with Dublin in 1938 and two National Hurling League medals in 1929 and 1939.

He resided at 96 Edenmore Avenue, Raheny and was a quantity surveyor by profession.

Charlie McMahon died on December 5th 1987 and was buried at Fingal Cemetery, Balgriffin, three days later.

References:
IMA, MSPC; *Irish Press*, 7th December 1987, (dn).

Daniel (Dan) McMahon

Irish Citizen Army. Roll of Honour

Dan McMahon, of 17 Newmarket, the Coombe, was a member of the Irish Citizen Army. On Easter Monday and Tuesday he was engaged in making grenades in the GPO, under the command of quartermaster, James O'Neill, who was in charge of munitions. On Wednesdsay, he was sent with fourteen other Volunteers to reinforce the garrison in the Metropole Hotel, under the command of lieutenant Oscar Traynor. For the next two days he manned a window on the top floor of the Metropole, where he came under constant sniper-fire. He returned to the GPO on Friday, when the occupants of the Metropole were forced to retreat because of the inferno. He spent Friday night in the houses in Moore Street, after the GPO was evacuated. He was deported to Stafford Jail on May 1st and interned in Frongoch until Christmas 1916.

Dan McMahon, of 20 Summerhill, in the north inner-city, died on July 15th 1940.

References:
RH; IMA, MSPC; NLI, *Lynch Papers*, (Ms 11,131) & *William O'Brien Papers*, (Ms 15,673); Ann Matthews, *The Irish Citizen Army*, (2014); *Irish Press*, 16th July 1940, (dn).

Patrick (Paddy) McMahon: (1893 – 1968)

C. Coy, 2nd Batt, Dublin Brigade. Roll of Honour

Paddy McMahon, a native of Milltown, County Kerry, was born in 1893. He went to England to work and gained experience in accountancy, before returning to Ireland. He became a member of C. Company, 2nd Battalion, Dublin Brigade and he reported to the GPO on Easter Monday. At midnight he went with a detachment, under the command of Sam O'Reilly, to the railway bridge at the North Circular Road and fought there until Tuesday evening when the position was abandoned, because of an artillery attack. With JK O'Reilly and others, he made his way to Finglas but failed to make contact with the Fingal Brigade. They returned to the city and joined a volunteer post at North King Steet. On Wednesday he was sent to Martin Conlon's house in Cabra Park, to retrieve a first aid outfit and was arrested, en route. He was detained until Friday evening and was then released. He tried in vain to rejoin a volunteer position and eventually made his way home.

In late 1916 he transferred to his brother's unit, B. Company, 2nd Battalion and took part in many operations. He was arrested in April 1920 and was released after a twelve day hunger strike. He was involved in attacks on British forces at Drumcondra and Ballybough and was in charge of the ambush at the Thatch, Whitehall, in 1921. During the Civil War he took the Republican side and in June 1922 he was sent to Germany to purchase arms. On his return he was garrisoned between Cassidy's Public House and Parnell Square and was later involved in an attack on Free State forces at the North Wall. He joined Clery's, in O'Connell Street and became chief accountant, Secretary and later a Director of the company.

Paddy McMahon, of 21 Seafield Avenue, Clontarf and formerly of St Mary's, Portmarnock, died on August 26th 1968.

References:
RH; IMA, MSPC; *Irish Press*, 27th August 1968, (obit).

210

Sarah (Sorcha) McMahon (Mrs. Sorcha Rogers): (1888 – 1970)

Secretary. Cumann na mBan, (Árd Craobh). Roll of Honour

Sorcha McMahon was born in 1888. She was secretary of the Cumann na mBan's Árd Croabh, and she arrived at the GPO on Easter Monday at 5.30 pm. During Easter Week, she carried over fifty dispatches from the GPO to various locations, including Mrs Clarke's home on Richmond Road. She also collected arms and ammunition on her return journeys. On Friday she was unable to get back to the GPO from Church Street, and on the following day she returned to Mrs Clarke's house.

After the Rising she took a prominent part in the Prisoners' Dependents Fund, acting as secretary, and in 1918 she went to work for Michael Collins. She was in charge of documents and funds, which she kept at her home.

She was married to Thomas Rogers and they resided at the Blue Lagoon Garage, Howth Road, Kilbarrack.

Sorcha Rogers died on December 13th 1970.

References:

RH; IMA, MSPC; NLI, *Lynch Papers*, (Ms 11,131); *Irish Press*, 14th December 1970, (dn).

Seán McMahon: (1896 - 1921)

Section Commander. C. Coy, 3rd Battalion, Dublin Brigade. Roll of Honour

Seán McMahon was born in 1896 and resided at 1 Lower Dominic Street. He was employed in Jameson's Distillary, Bow Street, and joined the Volunteers in 1913. He was a section commander in C. Company, 3rd Battalion, Dublin Brigade, when he reported to the GPO on Easter Monday. He fought in the Imperial Hotel and the GPO. After the surrender, he was deported to Wakefield Jail, but was released in June because of ill health.

He rejoined his unit in 1917 and served until November 1920 when he was diagnosed as suffering from tuberculosis.

Seán McMahon passed away in the Pigeon House Sanitorium on April 16th 1921.

References:

RH; IMA, MSPC; *Irish Independent*, 18th April 1921, (dn).

Patrick McManus: (1883 - 1938)

Liverpool Company, (Kimmage Garrison). Roll of Honour

Patrick McManus, a native of Omeath, County Louth, was born in 1883 and spent his early years in Liverpool. He was involved in the Irish Ireland movement, and later joined the Volunteers in Liverpool in 1914. He returned to Ireland in February 1916 to take part in the Rising, and joined the Volunteer Camp at Kimmage, where he was engaged in making munitions. He later transferred to 28 North Frederick Street, a house that was also used by members of the Kimmage Garrison. On Easter Monday morning he marched from Liberty Hall to the GPO, and was sent to Annesley Bridge, Fairview, where he served until Tuesday evening when the main body of men in the Fairview and Ballybough area withdrew to the GPO. On Thursday afternoon he was sent in a party, under the command of Lieutenant Paddy Shortis, to occupy a licensed premises at the corner of Liffey Street. They barricaded the building and came under heavy fire from a British armoured car. They returned to the GPO on Friday morning and he was part of the main evacuation of the burning building on Friday evening. He was deported to Knutsford Jail on May 1st and interned in Frongoch until Christmas, 1916.

He returned to Omeath after his release from internment and set up a Volunteer Company there in 1917. In October 1918 he returned to Liverpool and was engaged to sending arms to Dublin. He took no part in the Civil War.

In later years, he resided at 172 North King Street. He was employed in the Post Office Engineering Dept. in the GPO, and was member of the Association of Easter Week Men.

The body of Patrick McManus was taken from the River Liffey at Ringsend, on January 31st 1938 and he was buried two days later in his native Omeath, County Louth.

References:
RH; IMA, MSPC; John Heuston OP, *Headquarters Battalion, Easter Week 1916*, (1966); Ann Matthews, *The Kimmage Garrison 1916*, (2010); *Irish Independent*, 1st February 1938, (obit).

Bernard (Brian) McMullen: (1890 – 1958)

Glasgow Company, (Kimmage Garrison). Roll of Honour

Brian McMullen was born in 1890 and joined the IRB and the Volunteers in Glasgow in 1914. Prior to the Rising, he came to Dublin with a group of Volunteers from Glasgow, and joined the Volunteer Camp at Kimmage, under the assumed name of Joseph O'Brien. On Easter Monday he left 28 North Frederick Street with Charles Carrigan, and reported to Liberty Hall. He was sent to Hopkins & Hopkins, at the corner of Eden Quay and Sackville Street, and also fought at Kelly's Gun Shop. On returning to the GPO on Tuesday, he was sent to the Metropole Hotel where he fought until Friday. After the surrender he was deported to Stafford Jail and interned in Frongoch until August 1916. He found employment in Limerick after his release from internment, and joined the local Volunteer Company there. Between June and August 1922, he was interned in Dundalk Jail. On his release, he became a trade union organiser and took no further part in the War of Independence.

He later lived in 14 Pleasants Street, off Camden Street, and was an unemployed member of the executive of the Veterans Association. He highlighted the plight and grievances of the destitute and unemployed survivors of Easter Week in a letter to the Evening Mail on April 25th 1942.

Brian McMullen, of Marshalsea Barracks, Thomas Street, died in May 1958 and was buried at Glasnevin Cemetery.

References:

RH; IMA, MSPC; John Heuston OP, *Headquarters Battalion, Easter Week 1916*, (1966); Ann Matthews, *The Kimmage Garrison 1916*, (2010).

John McNally: (1896 – 1965)
Lusk Company, Fingal Brigade. Roll of Honour

John McNally was born in 1896 and resided at Chapel Green, Lusk. He was a member of Lusk Company, Fingal Brigade and on Easter Monday, he joined his fellow brigade members under the command of Thomas Ashe at Finglas. On the following day, he was part of the group that was sent to the GPO under the command of Lieutenant Richard Coleman and on his arrival he was put guarding the prisoners. He manned the top floor windows at the Princes Street corner on Wednesday and on Thursday he helped move explosives and ammunition to the ground floor. He spent Friday night in the houses in Moore Street and after the surrender he was deported to Knutsford Jail on May 1st and was later interned in Frongoch until July 1916.

On the reorganisation of the Volunteers in 1917 he rejoined the Lusk Company and served until the summer of 1920, when he had a breakdown in his health and was hospitalised until that Christmas. He resumed duty in July 1921 and served until the Truce, but took no part in the Civil War.

John McNally, a farmer from Chapel Green, Lusk, died on May 10th 1965 and was buried at St Macullin's Cemetery, Lusk, County Dublin.

References:

RH; IMA, MSPC; NLI, *Lynch Papers*, (Ms 11,131); *Irish Independent*, 11th May 1965, (dn).

Liam McNeive: (1895 – 1981)

Lieutenant. Liverpool Company, (Kimmage Garrison). C. Coy, 2nd Batt, Dublin Brigade. Roll of Honour

Liam McNeive was born in 1895. He was a shop assistant in Liverpool when he joined the local Volunteers. He later became a member of the IRB and was a lieutenant in the Liverpool Company when he arrived in Dublin with other Merseyside Volunteers before the Rising. After gaining employment in Dublin in March 1916, he left Kimmage and joined C. Company, 2nd Battalion, Dublin Brigade. Because of the countermanding order, he had decided to go the Fairyhouse Races on Easter Monday. When he reached town he realised that the Rising was about to begin and made his way to Liberty Hall. He spent the next few days in the GPO manning the ground floor windows at the Princes Street corner. On Thursday, he was posted to the roof and later was involved in the futile efforts to quell the fire there. He was in the advance party, led by The O'Rahilly that attempted to storm the British barricade at the far end of Moore Street. He spent Friday night in a house in Moore Street, under the command of Captain Leo Henderson and surrendered with the rest of the garrison the following afternoon. He was deported to Knutsford Jail on May 1st and interned in Frongoch, until August 3rd 1916. He rejoined C. Company, 2nd Battalion in 1917 and in 1918 he went to Mayo and organized Volunteers in Logboy and Ballyhaunis. He also organized Volunteers in Kingscourt, County Cavan. He took no part in the Civil War.

He had an address at 58 Parnell Street and in later life resided at 9 Eaton Rod, Terenure.

Liam McNeive died on May 30th 1981, at St Anthony's Nursing Home, Mount Merrion and was buried at Deansgrange Cemetery.

References:

RH; IMA, MSPC; NLI, *Lynch Papers*, (Ms 11,131); John Heuston OP, *Headquarters Battalion, Easter Week 1916*, (1966); Ann Matthews, *The Kimmage Garrison 1916*, (2010); *Evening Herald*, 30th May 1981, (dn).

Peter McPartlin: (1876 - 1949)

Hibernian Rifles. Roll of Honour

Peter McPartlin was born in Sligo, in 1876. He resided at 32 St Joseph's Place, Dorset Street, and was a plasterer by trade. He joined the Hibernian Rifles (American Alliance) in 1913 and fought in the GPO throughout Easter Week. He arrived with the other members of the Hibernian Rifles at midnight on Easter Monday, and was sent to Hopkins & Hopkins, at the corner of Eden Quay, on Tuesday morning. He fought there under the command of Seamus Robinson, until Thursday morning, when he returned to the GPO under heavy machine-gun fire. Later on

Thursday, he was posted to the Independent Newspaper Offices, in Middle Abbey Street, under the command of Seán McLoughlin. They were ordered to return to the GPO on Friday morning and he left the burning building that evening with the garrison. After the surrender he was deported to Stafford Jail on May 1st and interned in Frongoch.

In early 1917, he joined E. Company, 2nd Battalion, Dublin Brigade, and fought in the War of Independence. He was excused from duty in 1918 when his wife died, leaving nine children. His brother, Thomas, was Leas-Caothaoireach of the First Seanad.

Peter McPartlin died on June 6th 1949 and was buried at Glasnevin Cemetery.

References:
RH; IMA, MSPC; *Irish Press*, 9th June 1949, (obit).

John McQuaid
Sergeant. F. Coy, 2nd Batt, Dublin Brigade

John McQuaid, of 1 Rose Terrace, Wharf Road, East Wall, was a sergeant in F. Company, 2nd Company, Dublin Brigade. He acted as a "pivot" in F. Company's mobilisation scheme. On Easter Monday, he took up a position in Gilbey's shop, Ballybough Bridge. Frank Henderson, who was in command there, described him as "a splendid Volunteer". On Tuesday evening he moved into the GPO and fought there for the remainder of the week. He was deported to Knutsford Jail on May 3rd and interned in Frongoch, until July 18th 1916.

Owing to domestic difficulties, John McQuaid enlisted in the British Army after his release from internment, and later emigrated to New Zealand.

References:
Michael Hopkinson, *Frank Henderson's Easter Rising Recollections as a Dublin Volunteer*, (1998).

Patrick Meagher: (1877 - 1952)
B. Coy, 1st Batt, Dublin Brigade. Roll of Honour

Patrick Meagher was born in 1877 and resided at 138 Upper Dorset Street. He was a member of B. Company, 1st Battalion, Dublin Brigade, and fought at North Circular Road railway bridge, at Phibsborough and in the GPO during Easter Week. He was among the last to leave the GPO on Friday evening, and was a stretcher-bearer for James Connolly at the evacuation. After the Rising, he was deported to Stafford Jail on May 1st and later interned in Frongoch, until July 26th 1916.

He took part in the War of Independence and the Civil War, when he took the Republican side and fought in the Hamman Hotel in O'Connell Street in 1922.

He later resided at 98 Upper Dorset Street and was an executive member of the Irish House and Shop Painter's Union.

Patrick Meagher died on December 8th 1952 and was buried at Glasnevin Cemetery.

References:
RH; IMA, MSPC; *Sinn Féin Rebellion Handbook, Easter 1916*, Weekly Irish Times, (1917); *Irish Press*, 10th December 1952, (dn).

Thomas Meehan: (1898- 1954)
Fianna Éireann

Thomas Meehan, of 46 Hardwicke Street, Dublin, joined the Robert Emmet (North Wall) Sluagh of Fianna Éireann, at 10 Belvedere Place, in 1911. He took part in the Howth gun running with other members of his sluagh, including Paddy and Garry Holohan, under the command of Captain Michael Lonegan. He was a member of the GPO Garrison in Easter Week. After the Rising, he became a member of H. Company, 4th Battalion, Dublin Brigade and fought in the War of Independence. He worked in the Liffey Dockyard.

Thomas Meehan, of 24 Killane Road, East Wall, died on October 21st 1954 and was buried at Mount Jerome Cemetery, Harold's Cross.

References:
 IMA, BMH (WS 755, *Seán Prendergast*); *Irish Press*, 22nd October 1954, (obit).

Seán Milroy: (1877 – 1946)
D. Coy, 2nd Batt, Dublin Brigade & Staff Captain, G.H.Q. Roll of Honour

Seán Milroy was born to Irish parents in Maryport, Cumberland, in the north of England, and as a young man he went to Cork to work. He was an early member of Sinn Féin and was imprisoned in 1915, he was also a friend of Arthur Griffith. He joined D. Company, 2nd Battalion, Dublin Brigade, and was a staff captain with GHQ during the Rising. On Easter Tuesday, he was part of a group that occupied the Royal Exchange Hotel in Parliament Street. He returned to the GPO on Wednesday, and on Thursday, Seán MacDiarmada sent him in charge of a group of 11 Volunteers to occupy the Lucas Cycle Store, at the corner of Liffey Street. They were later ordered to return to the GPO and he was part of the main evacuation of the building on Friday evening. After the surrender, he was deported to Knutsford on June 7th, and interned in Frongoch, until Christmas 1916.

A confectioner with an address at 82 Talbot Street, he was elected to the standing committee of Sinn Féin in 1917. The following year, he was arrested in connection with the alleged German Plot. He was imprisoned in Lincoln Jail with Eamon DeValera and Seán McGarry, from where they escaped on January 3rd 1919. During the War of Independence he was interned in Ballykinlar Camp in 1921. He voted for the Treaty and was a supporter of the Cumann na nGaedheal Government. In 1923 he was elected TD for Cork, but the following year he resigned from the Dáil on the issue of the Army Mutiny. He then served as a member of the Seanad from 1928 to 1936.

Seán Milroy, of 25 Fitzwilliam Square, died on November 30th 1946 and was buried at Glasnevin Cemetery.

References:
 RH; Dorothy Macardle, *The Irish Republic*, (1937); C.S. Andrews, *Dublin Made Me*, (1979); Anthony J. Jordan, *W.J. Cosgrave 1880-1965, Founder of Modern Ireland*, (2006); *Sunday Independent*, 1st December 1946, (obit); *Irish Independent* & *Irish Press*, 2nd December 1946, (obits).

James Minahan: (1895 – 1960)
F. Coy, 1st Batt, Dublin Brigade

James Minahan was born in 1895 and resided at 12 Burgh Quay. He was a motor mechanic by trade and was a member of F. Company, 1st Battalion, Dublin Brigade. On Easter Monday, he was involved in the attempt to cause explosions at Liffey Junction and disrupt communications. He later reported to the GPO and served there until the evacuation. He was deported to Knutsford Jail on May 1st and was interned in Frongoch until Christmas 1916.

After his release from internment, he rejoined his unit and fought in the War of Independence. He was arrested in February 1918 and was released from Mountjoy Jail, after he had taken part in a hunger strike. He was arrested again in May 1918, and was interned in Usk Prison, in Monmouthshire, Wales. He was transferred to Gloucester Jail and was released in March 1919. On his release from internment, he served in the North Kildare area and took part in raids for arms, as well as the transportation of arms. He took no part in the Civil War and lived abroad for twenty years, before returning to Ireland in 1948.

James Minahan, of 42 York Street, died in Mercer's Hospital, on August 16th 1960 and was buried at Mount Jerome Cemetery, Harold's Cross.

References:

IMA, MSPC; *Sinn Féin Rebellion Handbook, Easter 1916*, Weekly Irish Times, (1917); *Evening Herald*, 16th August 1960, (dn).

Patrick (Paddy) Mitchell: (1891 - 1966)
E. Coy, 2nd Batt, Dublin Brigade

Paddy Mitchell was born in 1891 and was a native of Collentra, Co. Wicklow. He was a bricklayer by trade and resided at 82 Amiens Street, when he joined E. Company, 2nd Battalion, Dublin Brigade in 1914. On Easter Monday morning he was in the party sent to the Magazine Fort in the Phoenix Park. He then made his way to the GPO and acted as medical orderly there for the rest of the week. When James Connolly received his second wound in William's Lane, Paddy with assistance from George Plunkett, carried him back to the GPO and he attended to him in the Red Cross station. On Friday he accompanied the wounded to Jervis Street Hospital and was subsequently detained. He was deported to Knutsford on June 2nd and interned in Frongoch, until July 26th 1916.

After his release, he rejoined his old unit and fought in the War of Independence. He took part in a number of operations and was arrested and interned in February 1921. He was released just before the Truce and joined the Free State Army in March 1922. He served as a lieutenant in the Military Police, and resigned with the rank of captain in 1928.

In his younger days, he was a prominent member of the St Laurence O'Toole's GAA Club and was a popular boxing delegate and referee.

Paddy Mitchell, of 9 McMahon Street, South Circular Road, died on April, 7th 1966 and was buried at Rathdrum Cemetery, Co. Wicklow.

References:
IMA, MSPC; NLI, *Lynch Papers*, (Ms 11,131); Jimmy Wren, *Saint Laurence O'Toole GAC Centenary History, 1901-2001*, (2001); *Irish Independent*, 9th April 1966, (dn).

Charles (Charlie) Molphy: (1899 - 1975)
C. Coy, 1st Batt, Dublin Brigade. Roll of Honour

Charlie Molphy was born in 1899 and resided at 89 Ballybough Road. He attended O'Connell Schools, North Richmond Street, and was a member of C. Company, 1st Battalion, Dublin Brigade. He fought in the GPO throughout Easter Week, and after the surrender he was released because of his youth.

During the War of Independence he became quartermaster of C. Company, 1st Battalion and was interned in 1921. He joined the Free State Army after the War of Independence and resided at 118 Navan Road.

Charlie Molphy, of 19 Marguerite Road, Glasnevin, died on October 6th 1975 and was buried at Glasnevin Cemetery two days later.

References:
RH; IMA, BMH (WS 755, *Seán* Prendergast); *Evening Herald*, 7th October 1975, (dn).

James Mooney: (1895 - 1961)
G. Coy, 2nd Batt, Dublin Brigade

Jim Mooney was born at Seville Place, North Wall, in 1895. His family moved to Wales when he was seven years old and remained there for several years. He returned to Ireland and lived in Celbridge. He was working in Miltown Malbay, County Clare, when he joined the Volunteers. On returning to Dublin, he joined G. Company, 2nd Battalion, Dublin Brigade, under the command of Dick McKee. He was attending the Fairyhouse Races on Easter Monday, when he heard that the Rising had begun. He returned to Dublin and attempted to join his unit in St Stephen's Green, but when he found the gates locked, he made his way to the GPO. He fought on the roof of the GPO through the week, and when flames engulfed the building, he was engaged in fighting the fire. At the evacuation on Friday evening he was among the party led by The O'Rahilly into Moore Street. After the surrender he was deported to Knutsford Jail on May 1st and interned in Frongoch until Christmas 1916.

On his release from internment, he resided at 120 Capel Street and was employed as a draper's assistant. He joined E. Company, 2nd Battalion, Dublin Brigade, in 1917 and served until 1919, when he went to Manchester seeking employment.

Jim Mooney emigrated to the United States in 1920 and died in New York on December 10th 1961.

References:

IMA, MSPC; *Sinn Féin Rebellion Handbook, Easter 1916*, Weekly Irish Times, (1917); Seán Cronin, *Our Own Red Blood: the Story of the 1916 Rising*, (1966).

Patrick C. Mooney: (1895 - 1946)
B. Coy, 2nd Batt, Dublin Brigade. Roll of Honour

Patrick Mooney was born in 1895 and resided at 15 Fleet Street. He joined the National Guard Boy Scouts in 1912 and later became a member of B. Company, 2nd Battalion, Dublin Brigade. On Easter Monday he reported to the GPO and was sent to Ballybough. He was stationed at Lambe's Public House, until recalled to the GPO on Tuesday evening. He was sent to McDowell's Shop, Henry Street and also helped in boring the walls from the Coliseum Theatre back to the GPO. On Friday evening, he left the GPO in the advance party, led by The O'Rahilly, into Moore Street. He was deported to Knutsford on May 1st and later interned in Frongoch, until July 15th 1916.

In September 1917 he was one of the Sinn Féin prisoners who went on hunger strike with Thomas Ashe in Mountjoy Jail. He travelled to Glasgow in 1919, under the assumed name of Seán Watters, after his house was raided and his father was arrested. He joined the Scottish Brigade of the IRA and was active until the Truce.

When he returned to Ireland, he found employment at Baldonnel Aerodrome. During the emergency years, he joined the Engineer Corps of the 26th Infantry Battalion.

Patrick Mooney, of Tonguefield Road, Crumlin, died on October 16th 1946 and was buried at Mount Jerome Cemetery, Harold's Cross.

References:

RH; IMA, MSPC; *Sinn Féin Rebellion Handbook, Easter 1916*, Weekly Irish Times, (1917); *Irish Press*, 17th October 1946, (obit).

Patrick Moore (Ó Mórdha): (1891 - 1950)
B. Coy, 1st Batt, Dublin Brigade. Roll of Honour

Patrick Moore was born in 1891 and resided at 16 Joseph's Square, Vernon Avenue, Clontarf, when he joined the Volunteers in 1913. He was a member of B. Company, 1st Battalion, Dublin Brigade and was involved the Howth gun running, the following year.

On Easter Monday he was on guard outside the GPO and for the remainder of the week he manned the windows, there. He was also sent out to commandeer food and medical supplies. On Friday he accompanied a wounded Volunteer to the Coliseum Theatre, Henry Street, for first aid treatment. He remained there that night and was captured in Abbey St the next day. He was detained at Trinity College and was deported to Wakefield Prison on May 6th. He was interned in Frongoch, until July 17th 1916 and on his release he fought in the War of Independence. During the Civil War he fought on the anti-Treaty side and was part of the Four Courts Garrison, in 1922.

He was married to Cathleen Gillis and she, her brother and her brother-in-law, were interned at the British Military rifle range on Bull Island, during the Rising, when their house, Cluny, Clontarf Road, that had been used to manufacture bombs, was raided.

His brother, Seán, was a prominent Trade Union leader and a member of the Four Court Garrison in 1916.

Patrick Moore, of 52 East Wall Road, died on May 28th 1950 and was buried in Kilbarrack Cemetery.

References:
RH; IMA, MSPC; *Irish Press*, 30th May 1950, (obit).

Edward John Moore: (1892 – 1982)
C. Coy, 1st Batt, Dublin Brigade. Roll of Honour

John Moore was born in 1892 and became a member of C. Company, 1st Battalion, Dublin Brigade, in January 1916. He was late for his company's mobilisation at Columcille Hall on Easter Monday and made his own way to the GPO. He fought throughout the week in the GPO until Friday, when he was sent to the Coliseum Theatre, Henry Street. On Friday he was in the party that escorted the wounded to Jervis St Hospital and he returned to the occupied buildings in Henry Street and spent the night, there. On Saturday morning he was arrested in a lane, beside McBirney's Shop, near O'Connell Bridge and taken to Trinity College for interrogation. While there, he managed to join a group of civilians that were being escorted to the Mansion House and made his escape. He went to his employer, Henry O'Neill, who gave him food and money and arranged for him to work in Galway, in order to evade arrest. He rejoined his unit at the reorganisation of the Volunteers and served until October 1917, when he went to work in Belfast.

John Moore, of Beechview, Deansgrange Road, Blackrock, died in St Michael's Hospital, Dun Laoghaire, on December 12th 1982 and was buried at Deansgrange Cemetery.

References:
RH; IMA, MSPC; *Irish Independent*, 13th December 1982, (dn).

John Moore: (1896 – 1948)
Irish Citizen Army, (North Wall Section)

John Moore was born in 1896 and resided at 9 Newfoundland Street, Sheriff Street. He joined the Irish Citizen Army, North Wall Branch, after the 1913 Lockout in Dublin. On Easter Monday, he was sent to the Imperial Hotel above Clery's Department Store, across the street from the GPO. He fought there until forced to evacuate the premises on Thursday night because of the inferno. Following the evacuation, his party made its way into the north inner-city, and they were arrested on Friday morning in a tenement in North Cumberland Street. He was taken to the Custom House for interrogation, and was deported to Knutsford Jail on May 3rd. He was interned in Frongoch until August 1916 and on release worked as a docker on the North Wall. He was employed by Burns & Laird Shipping, and was engaged in collecting arms and ammunition from their cargo boats coming from Glasgow. He was also a member of the Workers Union of Ireland.

John Moore, of 318 Ballybough House, Poplar Row, died on January 14th 1948 and was buried at Glasnevin Cemetery.

References:
IMA, MSPC; NLI, *William O'Brien Papers*, (Ms 15,673); Ann Matthews, *The Irish Citizen Army*, (2014); *Evening Herald*, 16th January 1948, (dn).

Patrick (Paddy) Morrin: (- 1938)
Glasgow Company, (Kimmage Garrison)

Paddy Morrin was a steeplejack by trade and was a captain in the Glasgow Company Volunteers. He came to Dublin with other Volunteers from Scotland to take part in the Easter Rising, and was stationed at Larkfield, Kimmage. On Easter Monday he was posted to O'Connell Bridge and later Kelly's Gun Shop, at the corner of Bachelor's Walk. After the evacuation of the GPO, he was in the group that bored through the walls of the shops in Moore Street on Friday night and Saturday morning. He was one of the Volunteers, under the command of Seán McLoughlin, who were prepared and waiting to charge the British Army barricade at the top of Moore Street when the decision to surrender was made.

Paddy Morrin returned to Glasgow and was living at 10 Robson Street, when he died on 20th November, 1938, as the result of a roofing accident.

References:
IMA, BMH (WS 290, *Seán McLoughlin*); Joe Good, *Enchanted by Dreams*, (1996); Ann Matthews, *The Kimmage Garrison*, (2010); *Irish Press*, 23rd November 1938, (obit).

Henry Moughan: (1896 – 1965)

B. Coy, 2nd Batt, Dublin Brigade

Henry Moughan was born in 1896 and resided at 2 Heuston's Cottages, Newfoundland Street, North Wall. He was employed as a grocer's assistant, and joined B. Company, 2nd Battalion, Dublin Brigade, in 1915. He reported to the GPO on Easter Monday, and was sent to bill post the Proclamation on O'Connell Bridge. He was later engaged in boring through the walls from house to house in Henry Street, and was also stationed at McDowell's Jeweller's, Henry Street. When he returned to the GPO, he was posted to the ground floor windows and remained there until the evacuation on Friday evening. After the surrender he was deported to Wakefield Jail on May 6th, and was released after two months detention.

He enlisted in the Free State Army in February 1923, and was discharged in December 1923. He was later a civilian employee in the Army Corps of Engineers, at Collins Barracks, Dublin.

Henry Moughan, of 6 Shelmalier Road, East Wall, died on February 12th 1965 and was buried at Glasnevin Cemetery.

References:

IMA, MSPC; *Evening Herald*, 13th February 1965, (dn).

Andrew (Andy) Mulligan: (1877 - 1942)

Irish Citizen Army, (Gloucester Street Section)

Andy Mulligan was born in 1877 and lived at 4 Willet Place, Summerhill. He worked as a coal carter. A small, dapper man, he was known as "Dazzler" because his shoes were always highly polished. He was a member of the Irish Citizen Army and assisted Peter Ennis, the caretaker of Liberty Hall and replaced him for a time in 1915, when he was ill. He was the steward for the organised card games of "House" (Pongo), which were held in the backroom of Liberty Hall, to raise funds. When Peter Ennis returned to his post in Liberty Hall in early 1916, "Dazzler" took up a similar position at Croydon Park. He brought the type-set from West's Printers in Capel Street to Liberty Hall in a handcart for the printing of the Proclamation. On Easter Monday he ferried ammunition from Liberty Hall to the GPO in a cab, and then fought there for the remainder of the week. After the surrender he was deported to Knutsford on May 1st and interned in Frongoch until August 1916.

He was involved in the reorganisation of the Irish Citizen Army after the Rising, and served until March 31st 1917, after which he took no further part because of ill health.

Andy Mulligan was nine years an invalid before he died in St Kevin's Hospital, on September 5th 1942, and was buried at Glasnevin Cemetery.

References:

IMA, MSPC; NLI, *William O'Brien* Papers, (Ms 15,673); Ann Matthews, *The Irish Citizen Army*, (2014); *Evening Herald*, 7th September 1942, (dn); *Sunday Press*, 30th November 1952, (na, *Kathleen Mulligan interview*).

Dominic C. Mulvey: (1897 - 1950)
E. Coy, 4th Batt, Dublin Brigade. Roll of Honour

Dominic Mulvey was born in 1897 and lived at Fonthill Abbey, Rathfarnham. He was a member of E. Company, 4th Battalion, Dublin Brigade, and on Easter Monday he made his way with his unit, including his brother William, to the GPO. Initially he was posted to a ground floor window, and later in the week to the Dublin Bread Company Building and then to Hopkins & Hopkins at the corner of Eden Quay. While posted there, he received a machinegun wound, and was forced to return to the GPO under enemy fire. He was treated in the Red Cross hospital in the GPO, and remained there until the evacuation on Friday. He was deported to Knutsford Jail on 1st May. He rejoined E. Company, 4th Battalion, at its reorganisation in 1917, and served until 1920, after which time he gathered intelligence through his work as an insurance agent.

Dominic Mulvey, of 122 Leinster Road, Rathmines, died on January 22nd 1950 and was buried in Tallaght.

References:
RH; IMA, MSPC; NLI, *Lynch Papers*, (Ms 11,131); *Irish Independent*, 23rd January 1950, (dn).

Stephen (Steenie) Mulvey: (1878 – 1954)
Bray Company

Stephen "Steenie" Mulvey was born in 1878 and he joined the Bray Volunteer Company in 1913. On Easter Monday he cut the communication lines in the Bray area and then walked from Bray to Dublin, to join the GPO Garrison. He arrived there on Tuesday morning, and was sent across the street to Reis's Chambers. He also served in the Dublin Bread Company Building and in the Hibernian Bank. On Thursday he retreated to the GPO under heavy machine-gun fire and was slightly wounded. He went with the wounded to Jervis Street Hospital on Friday and after his wound was attended to, he returned to the Coliseum

Theatre where he spent the night. He evaded capture at the surrender and after three weeks he returned to Bray. He was arrested soon afterwards, but was later released.

During the War of Independence he became a member of E. Company, 6th Battalion, South Dublin Brigade. He was arrested after an attack on Bray RIC Barracks in April 1921, and was interned for eight months. He took the Republican side in the Civil War, and was involved in a number of attacks on Free State Forces in the Wicklow area.

He was a well known Gaelic footballer and won an All-Ireland medal in 1902 with Dublin (Bray Emmets Selection). He was employed the Bray Urban District Council for many years.

Steenie Mulvey, of 18 St Brigid's Terrace, Dargle Road, Bray, died on October 19th 1954, and was buried at St Peter's Cemetery, Bray, County Wicklow.

References:
IMA, MSPC; *Irish Press*, 22nd October 1954, (dn).

William R. Mulvey: (1895 - 1964)

E. Coy, 4th Batt, Dublin Brigade. Roll of Honour

William Mulvey was born in 1895 and resided at Fonthill Abbey, Rathfarnham. He was a member of E. Company, 4th Battalion, Dublin Brigade and with his brother, Dominic and other members of his unit, he reported to the GPO on Easter Monday. He was posted to the roof with other Rathfarnham men, while Dominic was sent to one of the ground floor windows. He remained at this post until Friday, when the position came under heavy artillery shelling and was abandoned. He and other Volunteers were wounded by shrapnel as they retreated from the roof. After the GPO was evacuated, he spent Friday night in the occupied houses in Moore Street. He was later deported with Dominic to Knutsford Jail on May 1st and was interned in Frongoch until July 21st 1916.

In 1917 he rejoined E. Company, 4th Battalion, and served until 1920. He took the Republican side in the Civil War and was active in the Rathfarnham and Templeogue area.

William Mulvey, of 28 St Enda's Road, Terenure, died on December 20th 1964 and was buried at Cruagh Cemetery, Rathfarnham.

References:
RH; IMA, MSPC; NLI, *Lynch Papers*, (Ms 11,131); *Evening Herald*, 21st December 1964, (dn).

Michael Mulvihill: (1880 – 1916). Killed in Action

London Company, (Kimmage Garrison). Roll of Honour

Michael Mulvihill was born in Ardroughter, Ballyduff, Co. Kerry, on April 2nd 1880. His father John was a schoolteacher. In 1898 he emigrated to London and within two years had secured a clerical post in the Civil Service. He joined the London Company of Volunteers with Michael Collins, Denis Daly and Austin Kennan. Having received his conscription notice, he left for Dublin with Austin Kennan, his brother-in-law, and Seán McGrath, on Good Friday and reported to the Volunteer Camp, at Larkfield, Kimmage. On Easter Monday he was posted to the front section of the centre of the roof of the GPO. He was moved to a different position on the ground floor on Friday and at the evacuation, joined the party led by The O'Rahilly into Moore Street. While crossing the junction of Henry Place and Moore Lane, the party came under heavy fire, and his body was later found at this spot.

Michael Mulvihill was buried in the 1916 Plot in Glasnevin Cemetery. In 1966 a plaque in memory of Michael Mulvihill was unveiled at his birthplace in Ardroughter, Ballyduff.

References:
RH; *Catholic Bulletin*, December 1917; Ray Bateson, *They Died by Pearse's Side*, (2010); Ann Matthews, *The Kimmage Garrison 1916*, (2010); Ray Bateson, *Memorials of the Easter Rising*, (2013).

Fintan Murphy: (1893 – 1960)

E. Coy, 4th Batt, Dublin Brigade. Roll of Honour

Fintan Murphy was born in Brixton, London, in 1893. He was the son of Frank Murphy, the founder of the Irish Self-Determination League of Great Britain. At an early age he came to Ireland and was educated at St Enda's in Rathfarnham, where he was taught by P.H. Pearse and Thomas McDonagh. In 1912 he went to London, and became a member of the South London Volunteer Company in 1914. When he returned to Dublin in January 1916, he transferred to E. Company, 4th Battalion, Dublin Brigade. On Easter Monday, he arrived late at the GPO with his Rathfarnham Company and they were forced to climb through a window in Prince's Street to gain entry. He was posted to the roof and remained there until Wednesday, when he was transferred to the barricades.

On Friday when the GPO was evacuated, he retreated with the main body of men into Moore Street under heavy machinegun fire from the direction of Parnell Street. After surrendering, he was interned in Frongoch and was released at Christmas, 1916.

An associate of Michael Collins, he was quartermaster general of the reorganised general staff of the Irish Volunteers. He assisted in the escape of Eamonn deValera from Lincoln Jail in 1919. His wife, Margaret McDonagh Murphy, whom he married in 1925, was the widow of Joseph McDonagh who died in 1922 after taking part in a hunger strike and was the brother of the executed Thomas McDonagh.

For a time, he was president of the Maritime Institute and was later associated with McDonagh & Boland Income Tax Experts.

Fintan Murphy, of Mountainview Road, Ranelagh, died on September 12th 1960 and was buried at Glasnevin Cemetery.

References:

RH; IMA, MSPC; NLI, *Lynch Papers*, (Ms 11,131); *Irish Independent*, 12th September 1960, (obit); *Irish Press*, 13th September 1960, (obit).

Kathleen Murphy (Mrs. Kathleen Patton):
(1897 – 1966)
Cumann na mBan, (Liverpool Branch). Roll of Honour

Kathleen Murphy was born in 1897, and became a school teacher in Liverpool. She was a member of Sinn Féin, Roger Casement Branch in Liverpool. In 1915 she joined Cumann na mBan and travelled to Dublin prior to the Rising. She served in the GPO throughout Easter Week and worked in the canteen. She delivered provisions to the small garrison in Kelly's Gunpowder Shop, while under heavy sniper fire. She was in the group that was ordered by P.H. Pearse to leave the GPO on Friday. She was captured shortly afterwards and was taken to the North Dublin Union, where she was interrogated and later released.

She returned to England and continued to serve with Cumann na mBan. In 1916 and 1917 she made regular visits to the Irish internees in Knutsford Jail, Dartmoor Jail and in Frongoch. She continued to serve with Cumann na mBan throughout the War of Independence, until the Truce.

Kathleen Patton, (nee Murphy), of 35 Central Park Avenue, Wallasey, Cheshire, died on September 6th 1966.

References:
  RH; IMA, MSPC; *Sinn Féin Rebellion Handbook, Easter 1916*, Weekly Irish Times, (1917).

Martin Murphy: (1881 – 1961)
B. Coy, 2nd Batt, Dublin Brigade

Martin Murphy was born in 1881 and was a native of Curry, County Sligo. He returned to Dublin from England two months before the Rising, and joined B. Company, 2nd Battalion, Dublin Brigade. He reported to the GPO on Easter Monday and was engaged in making bombs and grenades. On Tuesday and Wednesday he was stationed on the roof of the GPO, and on Thursday he was sent to the Metropole Hotel. Charles Saurin referred to him as "a little Sligo man, who had been sent into the Metropole, as a bomber". He returned to the GPO with the Metropole Hotel Garrison on Friday, and was part of the evacuation of the building on Friday evening. He was involved in boring through the walls of the houses in Moore Street on Friday night. After the surrender, he was deported and interned in Frongoch until Christmas 1916.

He returned to Sligo on his release from internment and rejoined the Volunteers. He organised the Cashel Company and was involved in anti-conscription work and assisted in establishing a Republican court in Curry. In 1920 he emigrated to the United States, but returned to Sligo from Chicago in 1950.

Martin Murphy died at Cashel, Tubbercurry, County Sligo, on April 4th 1961.

References:
  IMA, MSPC; IMA, BMH (WS 288, *Charles Saurin*).

Michael Murphy: (1895 - 1950)

A. Coy, 2nd Batt, Dublin Brigade. Roll of Honour

Michael Murphy was born in 1895 and lived at 2 Florence Villas, Botanic Avenue. A baker by trade, he joined A. Company, 2nd Battalion, Dublin Brigade in 1914. On Easter Monday and Tuesday he was stationed in the Fairview area. He marched into the GPO on Tuesday evening, under the command of Captain Frank Henderson. He was sent to the Imperial Hotel and remained there until the building was evacuated on Thursday night. He retreated into the north inner city, but was captured and taken to the Custom House for interrogation. On June 2nd he was deported to Wandsworth Jail, and was interned in Woking Jail, Wormwood Scrubs and Frongoch. He was a member of the prisoner's camp committee at Frongoch and took part in a hunger strike there, before he was released at Christmas 1916.

Upon his release from internment, he rejoined his unit and set up a munitions factory at his place of work. In April 1919 he married Martha Kelly, who he first met in the Imperial Hotel in Easter Week, and they moved to 1 Leinster Avenue, North Strand. When Frank Teeling escaped from Kilmainham Jail in February 1921, he hid at the Murphy's house for three months. His mother's house at Florence Villa's was also used to shelter members of the Dublin Brigade. He was arrested for his involvement in the attack on the Custom House in May 1921 and was imprisoned in Arbour Hill. He was transferred to Kilmainham Jail, where he temporarily lost his sight and was released on medical grounds in December, 1921. During the Civil War he took the Republican side with the rank of captain and was the O/C during the occupation of Barry's Hotel. He was arrested and interned in Portlaoise Jail, from where he was released in March 1923, on medical grounds. Michael and Martha Murphy reared sixteen children.

Michael Murphy died on November 6th 1950, seven years after Martha, and was buried at Glasnevin Cemetery.

References:
RH; IMA, MSPC; *Sinn Féin Rebellion Handbook, Easter 1916*, Weekly Irish Times, (1917); *Irish Press*, 8th November 1950, (obit).

Michael P. Murphy (Micheál Ó Murchú): (- 1953)

London Company, (Kimmage Garrison)

Michael Murphy was a native of Cappoquinn, County Waterford. He was an accountant by profession and was working in London, when he returned to fight in the Rising. He was part of the Kimmage Garrison and was stationed in the GPO during Easter Week. He was interned in Frongoch after the surrender and on his release from internment; he joined E. Company, 2nd Battalion, Dublin Brigade.

He fought in the War of Independence and was imprisoned in Lincoln Jail. During the Civil War he took the Republican side and was interned in the Curragh Camp. In later life, he was accountant to the National Greyhound Racing Company at Shelbourne Park.

Michael Murphy, of Lansdowne Road, Ballsbridge, died on February 18th, 1953 and was buried at Deansgrange Cemetery.

References:
  IMA, MSPC; Ann Matthews, *The Kimmage Garrison 1916*, (2010).

Peadar J. Murphy, (Peadar Ó Murchadha):
(1883 – 1968)

Liverpool Company, (Kimmage Garrison). Roll of Honour

Peadar Murphy was born in 1883. He joined the IRB in Drogheda in 1908 and later became a member of the Volunteers. He was a printer by trade, and went to work in Liverpool, where he joined the Liverpool Volunteers. He returned to Dublin in early 1916 and joined the Volunteer Camp at Kimmage, where he was engaged in munition and bomb making. On Easter Monday, he manned a window in the GPO. He was beside Seán Nunan when they fired at the advancing Lancers. On Easter Wednesday, the first of the shells exploded on the GPO, and shortly after he removed an unexploded shell from the building. At the evacuation, he was in a group of nine who came under heavy fire in Moore Street that resulted in five being wounded. They took refuge in a stable and remained there until the surrender the following day. He was deported to Stafford Jail on May 1st and then interned in Wormwoods Scrubbs and Frongoch until Christmas 1916.

After his release from internment he joined C. Company, 4th Battalion, Dublin Brigade and served until 1918 when he moved to Wexford. In 1920 he transferred to Drogheda and was appointed adjutant of B. Company, Drogheda Battalion in 1921. He served until the outbreak of the Civil War when he remained neutral.

He was employed as a bookbinder and was active in the Gaelic League.

Peadar Murphy, of 11 Ardbeg Grove, Blackrock, died on February 25th 1968 and was buried at Deansgrange Cemetery.

References:
  RH; IMA, MSPC; Ann Matthews, *The Kimmage Garrison 1916*, (2010); *Evening Herald*, 29th October 1964, (na, *a profile*); *Irish Press*, 26th February 1968, (obit).

Robert J. Murphy: (1901 -   )

Fianna Eireann. Roll of Honour

Robert Murphy was born in 1901 and resided at 31 Usher's Quay. He was a member of Fianna Éireann and reported to the GPO on Easter Monday. Initially he was posted to the roof of the GPO and was later sent to the Four Courts with a dispatch for Commandant Ned Daly. On Wednesday he was sent to the Metropole Hotel, but returned to the GPO when the hotel was evacuated on Friday. He then left the GPO at the evacuation on Friday evening. After the surrender, he was held in Richmond Barracks until May 12th and was released on May 12th, because of his young age.

Early in 1917 his older brother, Hubert, who was a member of the Four Courts Garrison during the Rising, brought him into A. Company, 1st Battalion, Dublin Brigade. He later transferred to the 5th Battalion, Engineers and was arrested in November 1920. He was interned in Ballykinlar Camp with Hubert, and was released in December 1921. In July 1922 he joined the Free State Army, with the rank of lieutenant, and served at the Four Courts and in Kilkenny. On his demobilization from the army, he emigrated to the United States. He returned to Ireland in 1932 and became secretary of the United Stationary Engine Drivers Trade Union. In May 1940 he was arrested for the robbery of the Royal Bank of Ireland, at Cornmarket and sentenced to five years penal servitude.

Robert Murphy unsuccessfully applied in the early 1950's for the restoration of his army pension, which had been forfeited from the time of his conviction.

References:
RH; IMA, MSPC.

Stephen Murphy: (1900 - 1979)

Irish Citizen Army, (Church St Section). Roll of Honour

Stephen Murphy was born in 1900 and resided at 34 Old Church Street. He was a member of the Irish Citizen Army and he reported to the GPO on Easter Monday from where he was sent out with other youths to post the Proclamation around the city centre. He was later sent to Jacob's Biscuit Factory, Bishop Street, with ammunition and returned to the GPO on Easter Monday night. He spent Tuesday in the GPO, and on Wednesday he was sent to North King Street. He was unable to return to the GPO and evaded capture.

After the Rising he joined the reorganized Irish Citizen Army and took part in a number of operations, including an attack on an American ship docked in Dublin port in search of arms. On Armistice night, November 18th 1918, he was one of the defenders of Liberty Hall. He took the Republican side in the Civil War and he was wounded in Moran's Hotel, on June 30th 1922. A bullet went through his shoulder, and he spent fourteen days in St Vincent's Hospital. On his discharge from hospital he was cared for by Dr Kathleen Lynn at Cullenswood House. He was arrested in late August 1922, and was interned at Newbridge Barracks for eleven months.

He was Pipe Major of the Fintan Lalor Pipe Band for many years and was also Treasurer of the Kilmainham Restoration Committee.

Stephen Murphy, of 17 Turlough Gardens, Philipsburgh Avenue, died on March 11th 1979 and was buried at Glasnevin Cemetery.

References:
RH; IMA, MSPC; NLI, *William O'Brien Papers*, (Ms 15,673); Ann Matthews, *The Irish Citizen Army*, (2014).

Eileen Murray: (1890 – 1942)

Cumann na mBan. Roll of Honour

Eileen Murray, who was deaf, was born in 1890 and resided at 6 Killarney Parade, North Circular Road. She joined Cumann na mBan in 1915. She was moblised on Easter Monday night and with her friend, Bridie Richards, reported to the Hibernian Bank on Tuesday. She was there on Wednesday when Captain Tom Weafer was shot and when the post came under heavy shelling she crossed the street to the GPO, where she attended to the wounded. She was anxious about the safety of her family and made her way home, but was unable to return to the GPO because of the military cordon. After the Rising, she continued her involvement in Cumann na mBan and collected for the Prisoners' Dependents Fund.

Eileen Murray, of 6 Killarney Parade, died in October 1942.

References:
RH; IMA, MSPC.

Joseph (Joe) Murray: (1872 - 1949)

B. Coy, 1st Batt, Dublin Brigade

Joe Murray was born in 1872 in Drogheda, County Louth. He was a member of Sinn Féin and joined the IRB in 1912. He became a member of B. Company, 1st Battalion, Dublin Brigade, in 1913. He also founded a rifle club in 1913 and many of the club's members were Volunteers and Irish Citizen Army men. A close friend of James Connolly, he was one of the last people to speak to him before the surrender.

He resided at Hamilton Row and was engaged in gathering intelligence information, in Easter Week. On Easter Monday he was sent to Father Mathew Park, Fairview and later to Cabra Bridge. On Tuesday he directed Captain Jim O'Sullivan and his unit into the GPO from Cabra. He later took part in the raid for arms on the AOH Hall, Parnell Square. On Wednesday he gathered information in the Fairview and Church Street areas. James Connolly sent him to the Four Courts on Thursday with a message for Captain Ned Daly, warning him of a possible attack by British Troops from the Capel Street direction. Because of the British Army positions, he could only get as far as Dominic Street on his attempted return to the GPO. He was detained in Dublin Castle on the following Monday, as he and Volunteer John O'Mahoney, passed by Trinity College. They were held in a guardroom with other Volunteers and after five days of interrogation, he was deported to Wakefield Prison on May 6th.

On his release from Frongoch at Christmas 1916, he continued his membership in Sinn Féin and was on its executive until the Truce in 1921. He took the Republican side in the Civil War and was involved in the occupation of Barry's Hotel, Great Denmark Street.

He later resided at 58 Lower Drumcondra Road and was a commercial traveller until his retirement.

Joe Murray died on November 10th 1949 and was buried at Glasnevin Cemetery.

References:

IMA, MSPC; *Sinn Féin Rebellion Handbook, Easter 1916*, Weekly *Irish Times*, (1917); *Irish Independent*, 11th November 1949, (obit); *Irish Press*, 12th November 1949, (obit).

Mae Murray: (1898 - 1959)

Cumann na mBan

Mae Murray was born in 1898 and was a member of Inghindhe na hÉireann, an organisation that merged with Cumann na mBan, in 1914. She was mobilised on Easter Monday and spent Monday and Tuesday with Margaret Walsh, delivering ammunition and dispatches to outposts in the vicinity of the GPO. By Wednesday the bombardment was so heavy that they were unable to leave the GPO. Her brother, Patrick, was also a member of the GPO Garrison. In the company of Louise Gavan Duffy and Peggy Downey, she went to the Jacob's Garrison on Saturday to notify Thomas McDonagh and John McBride of the surrender. She evaded capture and succeeded in getting home.

She took the Republican side during the Civil War. She was detained in Kilmainham Jail in 1923 and went on hunger strike for ten days.

Mae Murray, of 9 Montague Place, died on January 21st 1959 and was buried at Mount Jerome Cemetery, Harold's Cross.

References:
  IMA, MSPC; *Irish Press*, 23rd January 1959, (obit).

Patrick J. Murray: (1888 - 1952)

B. Coy, 1st Batt, Dublin Brigade. Roll of Honour

Patrick Murray was born 1888 and was a native of Dunmore, County Galway. He was a member of the IRB and was a founder member of the Volunteers, joining at the Rotunda, in November 1913. He was a member of B. Company, 1st Battalion, Dublin Brigade and took part in the Howth and Kilcoole gun running incidents. He resided at 23 Dolphin Barn Street and worked as grocers assistant, in 1916. Before the Rising he was engaged in the manufacture of munitions at Cluny House, Clontarf. On Easter Monday he was put in charge of the defence of two windows in the GPO and fought there for the remainder of the week. He in the advance party led by The O'Rahilly into Moore Street and received a bullet wound to his right knee. He was carried into a house in Moore Street, where he was treated by Dr James Ryan, who was then a medical student. He was later detained at the hospital at Dublin Castle until late July, when he was transferred to Frongoch. He was interned in Frongoch until Christmas 1916 and on his release he rejoined his unit. He was appointed Quartermaster of B. Company and was involved in the purchase and distribution of arms, during the War of Independence.

In later years he ran a grocery and hardware business at 32 North King Street.

Patrick Murray, of 14 Villa Bank, Phibsborough, died on the April 18th 1952 and was buried in Glasnevin Cemetery.

References:
  RH; IMA, MSPC; *Irish Press*, 21st April 1952, (obit).

Thomas (Tom) Murray: (1892 - 1962)

E. Coy, 2nd Batt, Dublin Brigade. Roll of Honour

Tom Murray was born in 1892 and resided at 102 Lower Gardiner Street. He was working in the printing trade with Cherry & Smallbridge's, North Wall, at the time of the Easter Rising. He became a member of E. Company, 2nd Battalion, Dublin Brigade, in 1915. On Easter Monday he reported to Father Mathew Park, Fairview and was posted to the Vitriol Works, Ballybough. He was later stationed at Annesley Bridge and moved into the GPO on Tuesday evening with the main body of Volunteers from the Fairview area. He was sent to the Metropole Hotel and was later stationed at Mansfield Shop, at the corner of Middle Abbey Street and Sackville Street. After the surrender he was deported to Stafford Jail on May 1st and interned in Frongoch until Christmas 1916.

When he returned to Dublin, he found that he had lost his job, like so many others, as a consequence of his part in the Rising. He rejoined his unit and took part in the War of Independence until August 1917, when owing to unemployment, he emigrated to England. He later returned to Dublin and worked in the Ormond Printing Works and was a founder member of the Irish Bookbinders Union.

Tom Murray, of 114 Newgrange Road, Cabra, died on October 2nd 1962 and was buried at Glasnevin Cemetery.

References:
RH; IMA, MSPC; *Irish Independent*, 3rd October 1962, (dn).

Francis D. (Frank) Murtagh: (1898 - 1969)

F. Coy, 2nd Batt, Dublin Brigade. Roll of Honour

Frank Murtagh was born in 1898 and lived at 196 Parnell Street. He joined the Volunteers in 1913, and was a member of F. Company, Dublin Brigade, in 1916. He was employed as a cinema operator at the Mary Street Picture House. After he arrived at the GPO on Easter Monday he was put on sentry duty at the main door. On Tuesday morning he was granted permission to attend the funeral of his brother's young son, and returned to the GPO immediately afterwards. For the remainder of the week he was stationed at Room No. 9, under the command of William McGinley. After the surrender he was deported to Stafford Jail on May 1st and interned in Frongoch until August 1916.

He assisted in the reorganisation of his unit in the early months of 1917 and was involved in a number of operations during the War of Independence, including an ambush at Newcomen Bridge, North Strand, armed patrols and raids for arms. He served until April 1922 and took no part in the Civil War. In later years he resided at 44 Mountpelier Hill, Parkgate Street and worked for the Dublin Gas Company, D'Olier Street.

Frank Murtagh died on May 28th 1969 and was buried at Deansgrange Cemetery.

References:
RH; IMA, MSPC; *Irish Independent*, 29th May 1969, (dn).

Joseph Murtagh (John O'Connor): (1900 - 1964)
Fianna Eireann

Joseph Murtagh, was born in 1900. He was christened John O'Connor and as an infant he was given to Mrs Murtagh, of 12 Byrnes Lane, Dollymount, to raise. He joined the Clontarf branch of Fianna Éireann in 1914. He served in the GPO during Easter Week, and after the surrender he was detained in Richmond Barracks, where he was handed a watch-chain by Seán MacDiarmada as a souvenir. He was released from detention on May 12th, because of his young age.

He transferred to F. Company, 2nd Battalion, Dublin Brigade, in 1917 and took part in an ambush on the Malahide Road and an attack on Raheny RIC Barracks. He joined the Active Service Unit in 1920. In July 1921 he was arrested, and was interned in Ballykinlar Camp until January 1922. He joined the Free State Army and was seriously wounded in Capel Street during the fighting around the Four Courts in June 1922. He was hospitalised until August 1922 and later transferred to the Kerry Command. He was discharged, medically unfit, with the rank of lieutenant in March 1924.

In 1929 he emigrated to the United States, using his birth name John O'Connor. He returned to Ireland and in 1939 was living at 83 North Strand Road. When his health broke down, he went to live with his married daughter in London.

Joseph Murtagh died in London on June 12th 1964.

References:
IMA, MSPC; *Sinn Féin Rebellion Handbook, Easter 1916*, Weekly Irish Times, (1917).

John P. Newman: (1896 - 1969)
E. Coy, 2nd Batt, Dublin Brigade

John Newman was born in 1896 and grew up in the Gate Lodge of Marino House, Fairview. He was the son of James Newman, a Fenian from Athboy, Co. Meath, and was educated at St Joseph's CBS, Marino. He played Gaelic football for Marino Gaels GFC and worked for the Dublin Bread Company and later in Eason's. He was a member of E. Company, 2nd Battalion and on Easter Monday he was in the party that moved into the GPO from the Fairview area. At various stages during the week, he served under Captain Thomas Weafer in the Hibernian Bank and in the Metropole Hotel. After the surrender he was deported to Wakefield Prison on May 6th and interned in Frongoch, until July 17th 1916.

At the reorganisation of the Volunteers in 1917, he re-joined his unit and fought in the War of Independence. He was arrested in January 1921 and was interned at Rath Camp, in the Curragh, until December 1921. In 1922 he joined the Free State Army and took part in the fighting in the O'Connell Street area during the Civil War. He was discharged from the army with the rank of sergeant in November 1923.

He married Anne Larkin and they emigrated to Boston in 1929. They later moved to Houston, Texas, where he was employed as a surveyor in the City of Houston Department of Public Works.

John Newman, of 1223 Coulson Circle, Hill Road, Houston, Texas, died on January 1st 1969 and was buried at Rosewood Memorial Park Cemetery.

References:

IMA, MSPC; *Scoil Íosaif, Marino, 1916-1966, (a 1916 Jubilee Publication)*, (1966).

Máire Ní Ainle (Moira Hanley): (1891 - 1954)
Adjutant. Cumann na mBan, (Ranelagh Branch). Roll of Honour

Moira Hanley was born in 1891 and was a noted Gaelic scholar. During her student days at UCD, she associated with Phyllis Ryan, who later married Seán T. O'Kelly. They were both members of the Ranelagh Branch of Cumann na mBan and were attached to the GPO Garrison during Easter Week, where Moira was engaged in carrying despatches.

During the War of Independence her home at 42 Sandford Road, Ranelagh, was used by E. Company, 3rd Battalion, Dublin Brigade. For many years she a member of the teaching staff at the Dominican Convert, Muckross Park, Donnybrook.

Máire Ní Ainle died on November 26th 1954 and was buried at Glasnevin Cemetery.

References:

RH; *Irish Press*, 29th November 1954, (dn); *Irish Independent*, 30th November 1954, (dn).

Áine Ní Riain (Anne Ryan): (- 1955)
Cumann na mBan, (Tullamore Branch). Roll of Honour

Anne Ryan was a native of Lenamore, County Longford and she joined the Cumann na mBan, Tullamore Branch, in 1915. She came to Dublin on Holy Saturday night in 1916. She reported to the GPO on Easter Monday, and early on Tuesday morning she posted to Reis's Chambers and from there she was sent to the Hibernian Bank. She volunteered with Máire English, also a member of Cumann na mBan, to return to Reis's on Tuesday night. She was in the Hibernian Bank again on Wednesday and after the death of Captain Tom Weafer, she accompanied the wounded Volunteers across the street to the GPO under heavy fire. On Thursday she worked in the kitchen in the GPO and she accompanied the wounded Volunteers to Jervis Street Hospital on Friday. Her group were not admitted to the over-crowded hospital and they attempted to reach the Dominican Convent in Eccles Street. They were arrested on the North Circular Road and taken to Broadstone Station, where they were released after interrogation.

In June 1916 she transferred to the Cumann na mBan, Árd Craobh and became a committee member of the National Aid and Prisoners Dependents Fund. She was appointed quartermaster of the Árd Craobh Branch in 1920, while her sister, Éilis, who served in the Four Courts in Easter Week, was captain in the Árd Craobh from 1921. She took the Republican side during the Civil War and served in Barry's Hotel, the Hamman Hotel and Scott's Building in Upper O'Connell Street. She became acting adjutant of 2nd Battalion, Dublin Brigade in early 1923, because so many Volunteers were imprisoned.

Áine Ní Riain, of 25 Upper Gardiner Street, Dublin, died on January 29th 1955 and was buried at Ardagh Cemetery, County Longford.

References:

RH; IMA, MSPC; IMA, BMH (WS 887); NLI, *Lynch Papers*, (Ms 11,131); *Sunday Press*, 30th January 1955, (obit).

Veronica Ní Riain (Mrs Veronica Ui Glasain):
(1889 – 1962)
Cumann na mBan, (Árd Craobh Branch). Roll of Honour

Veronica Ryan, the daughter of William P. Ryan, a noted Irish journalist and author, was born in Liverpool in 1889. She was a teacher by profession, and was devoted to the Irish language. She was a member of the Keating Branch of the Gaelic League and of Inghinidhe na hÉireann. She was also a founder member of Cumann na mBan and was attached to the Árd Craobh Branch. She was not mobilised on Easter Monday and on Tuesday morning she reported to the Hibernian Bank where she was engaged in first aid work and preparing food. She was there when Captain Weafer was fatally wounded and later on Wednesday she returned to the GPO., accompanying the wounded Volunteer across the street under heavy fire. On Wednesday night she was instructed by Tom Clarke to contact Volunteers in North County Dublin, who had not reported for duty and to mobilise them to proceed to Ashbourne. After carrying out her instructions she tried unsuccessfully to return to the GPO on Thursday and Friday. She was held for some time at a British Army barricade, before being released. During the War of Independence she was involved with the National Aid and Prisoners Dependents Fund and was in charge of collecting centres for IRA funds. She visited prisoners in Mountjoy Jail during the hunger strikes in 1920.

In 1926 she married James Gleeson, who was also a teacher by profession, and they resided at 32 North Frederick Street.

Veronica Gleeson died on February 2nd 1962 and was buried at Mount Jerome Cemetery, Harold's Cross.

References:

RH; IMA, MSPC; NLI, *Lynch Papers*, (Ms 11,131); *Evening Herald*, 5th February 1962, (obit).

Michael Nolan: (1866 - 1927)
Irish Citizen Army, (Baldoyle Section)

Michael Nolan was born in Carlow in 1866 and lived at Burrowfield Cottages, Baldoyle, prior to the Rising. He joined the Irish Citizen Army in 1914 and was a member of the Baldoyle Section, under the command of Captain James McCormack. On Easter Monday he reported to the GPO and fought there throughout the week. After the surrender he was deported to Stafford Jail on May 1st and was interned in Frongoch until Christmas 1916.

After his release from internment he transferred to the IRA and fought in the War of Independence. He was later employed as a branch secretary in the Workers' Union of Ireland.

On December 23rd 1927 his body was found by Isaac Delemere, a sheep farmer, in a field at Kilmacanogue, County Wicklow. An inquest jury later found that Michael Nolan's death was caused by a self-inflicted bullet wound.

References:

NLI, *William O'Brien*, (Ms 15,673); Ann Matthews, *The Irish Citizen Army*, (2014); *Irish Independent*, 26th December 1927, (dn); *Irish Independent*, 27th December 1927, (obit).

Ellen Noone (nee Hartnett): (1882 - 1947)
Irish Citizen Army. Roll of Honour

Ellen Hartnett was born in 1882. She joined the GPO on Easter Tuesday and spent the remainder of the week working in the kitchen. Her nieces, Bridget and Ellen Lambert from Milltown, were also in the GPO Garrison. On Friday she was among a group of women who were ordered to leave the GPO. They were later taken by the military to Broadstone Station and interrogated before being released shortly afterwards. They went to the night refuge in Henrietta Street and then proceeded home on the following day. She became a member of the Dundrum Branch of Cumann na mBan, and served during the War of Independence. During the Civil War she gave accommodation to several Republicans who were on the run.

She married James Noone and they lived at 21 Church Gardens, Rathmines.

Ellen Noone passed away on January 20th 1947 and was buried in Mount Jerome Cemetery, Harold's Cross.

References:

RH; IMA, MSPC; *Irish Press*, 23rd January 1947, (obit).

Frederick (Fred) Norgrove: (1903 - 1973)
Irish Citizen Army, (Boys Corps)

Fred Norgrove was born in 1903 and was the youngest of five members of the Norgrove family from 15 Strandville Avenue, North Strand, who took part in the Easter Rising. He was a member of the Irish Citizen Army's Boys Corps and served in the GPO during Easter Week. He later took part in the War of Independence. During the Civil War, he took the Republican side and was interned in the Curragh Camp in 1923.

He later resided at 50 St Aidan's Park Road, Marino and was a Church of Ireland warden in St Canice's Parish, Finglas and St Matthew's, Irishtown.

Fred Norgrove, of 5 Eden Road, Greystones, died on October 31st 1973, in Baggot Street Hospital and was buried at Redford Cemetery, Greystones, County Wicklow.

References:
John Heuston OP, *Headquarters Battalion, Easter Week 1916*, (1966); *Irish Times*, 31st October 1973, (dn).

James Norton: (1895 - 1945)
F. Coy, 1st Batt, Dublin Brigade. Roll of Honour

James Norton was born in 1895. A shop assistant by trade, he lived at 41 Parnell Square, and was a member of F. Company, 1st Battalion, Dublin Brigade and fought in the GPO during Easter Week. After the surrender he was deported to Knutsford Jail on May 1st and interned in Frongoch until Christmas 1916.

On his release from internment, he rejoined his unit and was appointed his company's armourer. He took part in a number of operations, including the raid for arms at Baldonnel Aerodrome, in 1919 and the destruction of the telephone exchange at Hollybank Road, Drumcondra. He also took part in the Custom House attack in May 1921. He transferred to the South County Dublin Battalion and took the Republican side in the Civil War. He was involved in the attack on Baltinglass Barracks and in the engagement with Free State Troops in the Blessington area. He spent most of the Civil War on the run and evaded capture.

In later years he was employed in Dublin Corporation's Waterworks Dept and was a member of the 26th Infantry Battalion, during the emergency years.

James Norton, of 99 Keeper Road, Drimnagh, died on October 27th 1945 and was buried in Mount Jerome Cemetery, Harold's Cross.

References:
RH; IMA, MSPC; *Irish Press*, 30th October 1945, (obit).

Michael Nugent: (1892 – 1971)

C. Coy, 3rd Batt, Dublin Brigade. Roll of Honour

Michael Nugent was born in 1892 and resided at 77 Aungier Street. He was a member of C. Company, 3rd Battalion, Dublin Brigade. He reported to the GPO on Easter Monday and was posted to the Abbey Street and Liffey Street area. On the following day, he was sent across the street from the GPO to the Imperial Hotel. He returned to the GPO on Wednesday, and manned the windows there until the next day. He was on the roof of the GPO on Thursday evening when the bombardment began. On Friday he assisted in bringing the wounded to the Coliseum Theatre in Henry Street and left the GPO at the evacuation on Friday evening. He was one of the stretcher party that carried James Connolly to Dublin Castle. He was deported to Wakefield Prison on May 6th and interned in Frongoch, until July 31st 1916.

After his release from internment he rejoined his unit, but ended his service in August 1917 due to ill health.

Michael Nugent, of 5 McDonagh House, Whitefriar Street, died on October 17th 1971 and was buried at Mount Jerome Cemetery, Harold's Cross.

References:
RH; IMA, MSPC; NLI, *Lynch Papers*, (Ms 11,131); *Irish Press*, 18th October 1971, (obit).

Patrick Nugent: (1894 - 1967)

C. Coy, 2nd Batt, Dublin Brigade. Roll of Honour

Patrick Nugent was born in 1894 and resided at 8 Charleville Avenue, North Strand. He was a coachbuilder by trade and was a member of C. Company, 2nd Battalion, Dublin Brigade. He reported to the GPO on Easter Monday and was posted to the roof, where he was stationed with London Volunteers; Austin Kennan and Michael Mulvihill. On Thursday evening when Volunteer Paddy McGrath Junior, was seriously wounded, he carried him from the roof to the ground floor. He was part of the main body at the evacuation of the GPO on Friday evening, and after the surrender he was deported to Knutsford Jail on May 1st. He was interned in Frongoch until Christmas 1916 and on his release hr rejoined his unit.

He served during the War of Independence and was involved in an attack on a military tender at Ballybough and in an ambush in Amiens Street in 1921. He joined the Free State Army in 1922 with the rank of private and was discharged in April 1924.

In 1926 he went to work in England and returned with his family to Dublin in 1932. They resided at 18 Berkeley Street, off Blessington Street, until 1951, when they emigrated to the United States.

Patrick Nugent died in New Jersey, on June 7th 1967.

References:
RH; IMA, MSPC; *Sinn Féin Rebellion Handbook, Easter 1916*, Weekly Irish Times, (1917).

Ernest (Ernie) Nunan: (1898 - 1973)

London Company, (Kimmage Garrison).

Ernie Nunan was born in London to Irish parents in 1898. His father was member of the IRB and Ernie joined the Gaelic League and later became a member of the Volunteers in London. With his brother, Seán, he came to Dublin and joined the Volunteer Camp at Kimmage before the Rising. On Easter Monday he received superficial wounds while stationed at a ground floor window. The following day he was in a group that bored through the walls into the Wax Museum in Henry Street. Effigies of King George V and Lord Kitchener that were found there were taken back to the GPO and placed on the barricades. After the surrender he was deported to Stafford Jail on May 1st and then interned in Frongoch. While there, he was court-martialled as "a conscript who did not report for service in the British Army" and was sent to Winchester Jail. He was transferred to Exeter Jail and released at the general amnesty in 1917.

He fought in the War of Independence and took the Republican side in the Civil War. He was interned in Mountjoy Jail and the Curragh Camp and took part in a hunger strike while in detention.

He later went to sea, working for the P&O Line, and spent thirteen years working on ships, becoming a ship's purser. In 1939 he joined the Irish Marine Service and later joined Irish Shipping Ltd.

Ernie Nunan died on December 28th 1973 and was buried at St Joseph's Cemetery, Bohernabreena, Tallaght.

References:

RH; Max Caulfield, *The Easter Rebellion*, (1963); Thomas Coffey, *Agony at Easter*, (1969); Ann Matthews, *The Kimmage Garrison 1916*, (2010); *Irish Press*, 29th October 1966, (na, *lecture on the Kimmage Garrison*); *Irish Independent*, 29th December 1973, (dn).

Seán Nunan: (1891 – 1981)

London Company, (Kimmage Garrison). Roll of Honour

Seán Nunan was born in London to Irish parents in 1891. He was a member of the London Volunteers and came to Dublin with his brother Ernie, and joined the Volunteer Camp at Kimmage. He spent Easter Week manning the ground floor windows in the GPO. He recalled that on Friday he and Ernie were ordered to target a British sniper, but they were unsuccessful in their attempts. He also recalled that after the evacuation of the GPO, he witnessed George Plunkett drag a wounded British soldier to safety while under heavy fire in Moore Street.

For his part in the Rising he was deported to Stafford Jail on May 1st and later interned in Frongoch. On his release in March 1917, he was appointed to the HQ staff of Sinn Féin.

He was one of four clerks who served the first meeting of the First Dáil in the Mansion House in 1919, and he travelled to the United States in the role of private secretary to Éamon deValera in that same year. In 1921 he played a major part in the acquisition of some Thompson machine guns. He fought on the Republican side in the Civil War and was imprisoned. On his release he went to New York and worked for a brokerage firm on Wall Street. When Fianna Fáil came to power, he joined the Irish Civil Service and worked in the diplomatic service in London, New York and Washington. He returned to Dublin as Assistant Secretary and then as Secretary of the Department of External Affairs, before retiring in 1955. He joined the Board of the *Irish Press* in 1965, and was an active member at the time of his death, aged ninety.

Seán Nunan, of Dun Mhuire, Vico Road, Dalkey, died on January 30th 1981 and was buried at Glasnevin Cemetery.

References:

RH; NLI, *Lynch Papers*, (Ms 11,131); Max Caulfield, *The Easter Rebellion*, (1963); Thomas Coffey, *Agony at Easter*, (1969); Eileen McGough, *Diarmuid Lynch, a Forgotten Irish Patriot*, (2013); *Irish Press*, 21st January 1969 (na, *Seán Nunan interview*); *Irish Press*, 1st February, 1981, (obit).

Séamus Ó Braonáin (Brennan): (1887 - 1968)

Offaly Company, Athlone Brigade, (Kimmage Garrison). Roll of Honour

Seamus Brennan was born in Tullamore, County Offaly. He was already a member of the Gaelic League and Sinn Féin, when he joined the local Volunteers in 1914. After the incident in the Sinn Féin rooms at William Street, Tullamore, on March 20th 1916, when Peadar Bracken fired at members of the RIC, he went on the run with Bracken. When Liam O'Brien delivered the countermanding order to the Athlone Brigade on Easter Sunday, he and Peadar Bracken took a lift to Dublin with O'Brien in his car. They reported to the Volunteer Camp at Larkfield, Kimmage and travelled to Liberty Hall the following morning with the garrison. On arriving there, James Connolly promoted him to captain. In the GPO, he took charge of some of the Kimmage Garrison and secured the Henry Street entrance to the building, and afterwards occupied outposts in Henry Street and Sackville Street area. He and Joe Gahan occupied the Royal Bank in Sackville Street until Thursday, when they retired to the GPO. After the evacuation of the GPO, he and Brian O'Higgins occupied Cogan's Confectionary Shop at the corner of Moore Street until the surrender. He was court-martialled in Richmond Barracks on a charge relating to the shooting incident in Tullamore and given a lengthy sentence, but was released following a petition to the British Prime Minister, Asquith, when he visited Dublin after the Rising.

He joined F. Company, 1st Battalion, Dublin Brigade and fought in the War of Independence. He was wounded in an escape bid from Ballykinlar Camp.

He later worked in Tullamore, before joining a firm of Dublin Building Contractors. In the 1930s he was appointed National Health Inspector, and after his retirement became president of the Polio Fellowship of Ireland.

Seamus Brennan, of 8 Leinster Road, Rathmines, died on February 20th 1968 and was buried at Glasnevin Cemetery.

References:

RH; IMA, MSPC; NLI, *Lynch Papers*, (Ms 11,131); Thomas Coffey, *Agony at Easter*, (1969); *Midland Tribune*, April 1966, (*1916 Jubilee Supplement*); *Evening Herald*, 21st February 1968, (dn); *Irish Press*, 21st February 1968, (obit).

Eoghan O'Brien: (1876 – 1964)

B. Coy, 4th Batt, Dublin Brigade. Roll of Honour

Eoghan O'Brien, a pioneer of the Gaelic League, was born in 1876 and resided at 7 Bessborough Parade, Rathmines. He joined the Volunteers at the inaugural meeting at the Rotunda in 1913, and became a member of B. Company, 4th Battalion, Dublin Brigade. On Easter Monday he was mobilised at Larkfield, Kimmage and travelled to the GPO with a party of twenty four Volunteers. He was a friend of P.H. Pearse and was promoted to second lieutenant. He was put in charge of twelve Volunteers on the roof of the building and fought there for the remainder of the week. After the surrender he was deported to Stafford Jail on May 1st and was interned in Frongoch until Christmas 1916.

He helped reorganise his unit and served until the end of 1917, when he resigned to concentrate on his work for the Gaelic League. His brother, Peadar, vice commandant of 4th Battalion, was part of the Marrowbone Lane Garrison in 1916.

He later lived in Howth, and was employed in the Dept of Education.

Eoghan O'Brien died on May 28th 1964 and was buried at Glasnevin Cemetery.

References:

RH; IMA, MSPC; *Sinn Féin Rebellion Handbook* 1916, Weekly Irish Times, (1917); *Irish Press*, 30th May 1964, (obit).

John O'Brien: (1897 - 1963)

F. Coy, 2nd Batt, Dublin Brigade. Roll of Honour

John O'Brien was born in 1897 and was a native of Slane, County Meath. In 1916 he resided at 487 North Circular Road and was a builder's apprentice. He was a member of F. Company, 2nd Battalion, Dublin Brigade and on Easter Monday he reported to Father Mathew Park, Fairview. He was stationed at Lambe's Public House, Ballybough Bridge and was later detailed to prevent troops advancing along the Great Northern Railway Line. On Tuesday evening he withdrew with Fairview Garrison to the GPO and fought at the Henry Street wing for the rest of the week. He spent Friday night in the houses in Moore Street after the GPO was evacuated. He was deported to Knutsford Jail on May 1st and interned in Frongoch until September 1916.

He rejoined his unit on after his release from Frongoch and served until October 1917 when he left Dublin to take up employment as a builder.

He later became a well known building contractor and resided at 8 Crannagh Grove, Rathfarnham.

John O'Brien died on May 16th 1963 and was buried at Mount Jerome Cemetery, Harold's Cross.

References:

RH; IMA, MSPC; NLI, *Lynch Papers*, (Ms 11,131); *Sinn Féin Rebellion Handbook 1916*, Weekly Irish Times, (1917); *Irish Independent*, 20th May 1963, (obit).

Matthew (Matt) O'Brien: (1898 – 1969)

A. Coy, 3rd Batt, Dublin Brigade. Roll of Honour

Matt O'Brien was born in 1898 and resided at 2 Walker's Cottages, Mountpleasant Avenue, Ranelagh. He was a member of A. Company, 3rd Battalion, Dublin Brigade and he spent Easter Weekend on armed duty at the arms dump at Coleman's Forge, Camden Place with Christopher Byrne, who was also a member of A. Company, 3rd Battalion. He reported to the GPO on Easter Monday and was engaged in sniping from the roof. He also fought at outposts in Abbey Street and Henry Street later in the week. After the surrender he was deported to Stafford Jail on May 1st and interned in Frongoch until July 20th 1916.

He rejoined his unit in 1917 and took part in many operations during the War of Independence. In March 1921 he was transferred to the East Wicklow Brigade by GHQ with the rank of captain. He was involved when an RIC member was shot dead in Rathdrum, and took part in an ambush of British Forces at Murragh, North County Dublin. He took the Republican side in the Civil War and was garrisoned at Craig Gardens and Harcourt Street Railway Station. He was arrested in August 1922 and interned until February 1924. He later was employed in the Dept of Social Welfare, at the Custom House.

Matt O'Brien, of Moyne Road, Ranelagh, died on January 21st 1969.

References:
RH; IMA, MSPC; *Sinn Féin Rebellion Handbook* 1916, Weekly Irish Times, (1917); *Irish Press*, 22nd January 1969, (dn).

Michael O'Brien: (1891 - 1954)

D. Coy, 4th Batt, Dublin Brigade. Roll of Honour

Michael O'Brien was born in 1891 and resided at 2 Tivoli Avenue, Harold's Cross. He was a painter by trade, and joined the Volunteers at the Rotunda, in 1913. He was a member of D. Company, 4th Battalion, Dublin Brigade with his brother, Stephen, who fought in the South Dublin Union in Easter Week. He wasn't mobilised on Easter Monday, so he made his way to Larkfield, Kimmage and from there, travelled to the GPO with a party of Volunteers. Initially he was involved in erecting barricades, but later was stationed on the GPO roof as a sniper for the remainder of Easter Week. He was deported to Knutsford Jail on May 1st. He was later transferred to Wormwood Scrubs and then interned in Frongoch, until Christmas 1916.

After his release from internment he rejoined his unit and took part in the funeral of Thomas Ashe in 1917. In March 1919 he was seriously injured in the course of his employment and was forced to retire from active service with the Volunteers. He later served with the 26th Infantry Battalion during the emergency years.

Michael O'Brien, of 6 Cherryfield Avenue, Walkinstown, died on April 25th 1954.

References:
RH; IMA, MSPC; *Sinn Féin Rebellion Handbook 1916*, Weekly Irish Times, (1917); *Irish Press*, 28th April 1954, (dn).

Thomas (Tom) O'Brien (Bryan): (1875 – 1956)

Irish Citizen Army, (North Wall Section)

Tom O'Brien was born in Prosperous, County Kildare, in 1875. He was also known as Tom Brien and Tom Bryan. He was working as a dock worker and lodging at 31 Guild Street, North Wall, when joined the Irish Citizen Army in 1915. He was one of the guard placed outside Liberty Hall by James Connolly a month before the Rising. On Easter Monday he was assigned to guard James Connolly as they left Liberty Hall, and proceeded to the GPO. Later that evening he was in the party, led by Captain Frank Thornton, who were sent to support the Volunteers in the City Hall area. They were prevented from occupying the Telephone Exchange at Fleet Street, by sniper fire from the rooftops in the area. They returned to the GPO on Tuesday, and from then until Thursday, he fought in the Imperial Hotel in Sackville Street, when fire forced the occupants to retreat to the GPO. On Friday he was engaged in fighting the fires in the GPO, until the evacuation. He was deported to Stafford Jail on May 1st and then interned in Frongoch until August 3rd 1916.

On his release from Frongoch, he continued to serve in the Irish Citizen Army, until he returned to live in Prosperous in 1919. His home in Kildare was used as a safe house by many men on the run during the War of Independence.

Tom Bryan, of Downings, Prosperous, died on January 2nd 1956 and was buried at Caragh Cemetery, County Kildare.

References:
RH; IMA, MSPC; NLI, *Lynch Papers*, (Ms 11,131) & *William O'Brien Papers*, (Ms 15,673); Ann Matthews, *The Irish Citizen* Army, (2014); *Irish Press*, 3rd January 1956, (obit).

William J. O'Brien: (1897 – 1972)

A. Coy, 1st Battalion, Dublin Brigade

William O'Brien was born in 1897 and resided at 50 Aranmore Terrace, North Circular Road. He was employed as a clerk and was a member of A. Company, 1st Battalion, Dublin Brigade. On Easter Monday he reported to the GPO and he was posted to the roof. He was one of the Volunteers who assisted Volunteer Paddy McGrath Junior, when he was seriously wounded in the head and chest, and helped him down from the roof on Thursday evening. At the evacuation on Friday evening he received a wound over his right eye. He was deported to Knutsford Jail on May 1st and interned in Frongoch until July 18th 1916.

He rejoined his unit at its reorganisation and served until 1920, when he emigrated to the United States.

William O'Brien, of 25th Avenue, Gulfport, Mississippi, died on December 14th 1972.

References:
IMA, MSPC; *Sinn Féin Rebellion Handbook 1916*, Weekly Irish Times, (1917).

James (Jimmy) O'Byrne: (1897 - 1981)

A. Coy, 3rd Batt, Dublin Brigade. Roll of Honour

Jimmy O'Byrne was born in 1897 and resided at 2 Camden Place. He was a member of Fianna Éireann and he joined A. Company, 3rd Battalion, Dublin Brigade in 1915. He reported to the GPO on Easter Monday and was posted to the Dublin Bread Company across the street. When the building came under an intense bombardment on Thursday he was forced to dash across the street to the GPO under heavy sniper fire. On Friday as he watched the Imperial Hotel and surrounding buildings ablaze, The O'Rahilly, who was standing beside him, turned to him and said that the reason for the hotel's destruction "was to show you and me what they think of poor old Ireland". After the surrender he was deported to Stafford Jail on May 1st and interned in Frongoch until July 18th 1916.

He rejoined his old unit in 1917 and served through the War of Independence. In 1922 he joined the Free State Army with the rank of corporal and was demobilised in 1924. He later worked as a hairdresser.

Jimmy O'Byrne of 56 Mary Street, died on July 12th 1981 and was buried at Glasnevin Cemetery.

References:
RH; IMA, MSPC; Max Caulfield, *The Easter Rebellion*, (1963); Thomas Coffey, *Agony at Easter*, (1969); *Evening Herald*, 12th July 1981, (dn).

James O'Byrne: (1894 - 1947)

Captain. F. Coy, 2nd Batt, Dublin Brigade. Roll of Honour

James O'Byrne was born in 1894 and resided at 44 Mayor Street, North Wall. He was employed as a library assistant in Charleville Mall Library, North Wall and was a member of F. Company, 2nd Battalion, Dublin Brigade. On Easter Monday and Tuesday he was stationed in the Fairview area. He entered the GPO on Tuesday evening and was posted to the Metropole Hotel. After the surrender he was deported to Knutsford Jail on May 1st, and interned in Frongoch until July 27th 1916.

On his release from internment, he helped reorganise his unit and took part in the armed patrols and raids for arms. He was mobilised in October 1921 to take part in an attempt to rescue Kevin Barry, which was later called off. He was arrested in November 1921 and interned in Ballykinlar Camp, until December 1921. He joined the Free State Army with the rank of captain and fought in Wexford, Waterford and Cork during the Civil War. He also served as Adjutant at Athlone Barracks and Tintown Camp, in the Curragh. He left the army in 1924 and returned to the library service.

He later resided at 91 Ballymun Road and was assistant librarian at Kevin Street Public Library.

James O'Byrne collapsed at Kevin Street Public Library and died on admission to Meath Street Hospital, on November 13th 1947. He was buried at Glasnevin Cemetery two days later.

References:

RH; IMA, MSPC; *Sinn Féin Rebellion Handbook* 1916, Weekly Irish Times, (1917); *Irish Press*, 14th November 1947, (dn).

Pádraig (Páidí) Ó Caoimh (O'Keeffe): (1881 - 1973)
D. Coy, 3rd Batt, Dublin Brigade. Roll of Honour

Páidí Ó Caoimh was born in Rathmore, County Kerry, in 1881. He joined the Postal Service and was transferred to London, where he joined the IRB. He returned to Dublin and again was involved in IRB activities. He was appointed Joint-Honorary Treasurer of Sinn Féin in 1908, and two years later he married Cáit dePaor. He was involved in landing guns at Kilcoole, County Wicklow, in 1914. He a member of D. Company, 3rd Battalion, Dublin Brigade and on Easter Monday he left his residence at 21 Lower Camden Street and reported to the GPO. He was sent to the Imperial Hotel and fought there until Thursday, when the building was evacuated. His party attempted to escape out of the city, but encountered barricades everywhere. He was eventually taken prisoner in Gloucester Street and detained in the Custom House, before being transferred to Richmond Barracks. He was deported and later interned in Frongoch until Christmas, 1916.

On his release in 1917 he became general secretary of Sinn Féin, and was responsible for organising the campaign for the 1918 General Election. He was arrested again for making a seditious speech in 1921 and was imprisoned in Mountjoy Jail. He went on hunger strike, and was released at the Truce in July of that year. He was a TD for two years and took the pro-Treaty side in the Civil War. He joined the Free State Army and became deputy governor of Mountjoy Jail. Of that time he said, "Those were the most miserable days of my life. I had to supervise executions and all the men being shot were my personal friends before the war." He later joined the staff of Seanad Éireann and was assistant clerk there, until his retirement in 1946.

Pádraig Ó Caoimh died at his residence at 3 Leinster Road, Rathmines, on September 21st 1973 and was buried at Deansgrange Cemetery.

References:

RH; IMA, MSPC; NLI, *Lynch Papers*, (Ms 11,131); Thomas Coffey, *Agony at Easter*, (1969); Ernie O'Malley, *The Singing Flame*, (1978); David Fitzpatrick, *Harry Boland's Irish Revolution*, (2003); Tim Cadogan & Jeremiah Falvey, *A Biographical Dictionary of Cork*, (2006); *Irish Press*, 21st January 1969, (na, *a profile*); *Irish Press*, 27th September 1973, (obit).

Kevin O'Carroll: (1899 - 1972)

E. Coy, 4th Batt, Dublin Brigade. Roll of Honour

Kevin O'Carroll was born in 1899 and lived at Washington Lodge, Grange Road, Rathfarnham in 1916. He left Rathfarnham with E. Company, 4th Battalion, Dublin Brigade on Easter Monday morning and arrived at the GPO at 2.00 pm and remained there throughout Easter Week. On Friday he was shot in the stomach while beside The O'Rahilly in Moore Street. He was taken to the military hospital in Dublin Castle and then interned in Frongoch until July 27th July 1916.

He rejoined his unit in 1917, and was involved in many operations, acting as section commander. In January 1921 he took part in an ambush at Kenilworth Square. Shortly afterwards, he was arrested and interned in Rath Camp, remaining there until December 1921. He took the Republican side in the Civil War. He was a compositor by trade and assisted in printing the Republican newspaper, *An t-Óglach*. In October 1922, he was arrested and was interned at Hare Park, where he took part in a hunger strike before his release in late 1923.

In later years he lived at 74 St Mobhi Road and was a member of the Kilmainham Jail Restoration Committee.

Kevin O'Carroll died on October 17th 1972 and was buried at Balgriffin Cemetery.

References:
RH; IMA, MSPC; *An Phoblacht*, April 1930; Max Caulfield, *The Easter Rebellion*, (1963); *Evening Herald*, 18th October 1972, (dn).

Mary O'Connell: (- 1933)

Cumann na mBan. Roll of Honour

Mary O'Connell was the daughter of Rickard O'Connell, B.L., Kent Lodge, Spa, Tralee and a relative of "The Liberator", Daniel O'Connell. A friend of the 1916 leaders, she served in the first aid section in the GPO during Easter Week. After the Rising she resided at 3 Sydney Terrace, Upper Leeson Street and was associated with Republican activities and the Republican prisoners.

Mary S. O'Connell died on January 20th 1933 and was buried at Glasnevin Cemetery.

References:
RH; *Irish Independent*, 21st January 1933, (obit).

James O'Connor: (1897 – 1957)
B. Coy, 1st Batt, Dublin Brigade. Roll of Honour

James O'Connor, of 10 Beresford Place, was born in 1897 and educated at Westland Row CBS. He entered All Hollows, but left the seminary and joined his friends in B. Company, 1st Battalion, Dublin Brigade, some time before the Rising. On Easter Monday, he reported to the GPO and was a sniper at a second floor window throughout the week. He was in the advance party led by The O'Rahilly into Moore Street, on Friday evening. He was wounded in the vicinity of Coles Lane and took cover as best he could until the surrender. He was deported to Stafford Jail and transferred to Wormwoods Scrubs, before he was eventually interned in Frongoch until Christmas 1916. While in Frongoch he became friends with Michael Collins.

He rejoined his unit in 1917 and continued fighting in the War of Independence, along with his brothers, Eddie and Stephen. Because he lost his job after the Rising he went to England to find work. He later married in England and on his return to Ireland, he lived at Clonliffe Road and was a civilian employee in the Army Corps of Engineers.

James O'Connor, of 5 St Declan's Road, Marino, died on October 3rd 1957 and was buried in Mount Jerome Cemetery, Harold's Cross.

References:
RH; IMA, MSPC; NLI, *Lynch Papers*, (Ms 11,131); *Sunday Press*, 6th October 1957, (dn).

John (Blimey) O'Connor: (1896 - 1979)
London Company, (Lieutenant. Kimmage Garrison). Roll of Honour

Johnny "Blimey" O'Connor was born in 1896 and resided at White Lion Street, Islington. He was a member of the IRB and the London Company Volunteers. He came to Dublin with Michael Collins, Joe Good, Frank Kelly and the Nunan brothers in early 1916 and joined the Kimmage Garrison. On Easter Monday he was sent to the Dublin School of Telegraphy in Sackville Steet with Marconi Operators Fergus O'Kelly and David Bourke and with great difficulty they succeeded in transmitting the news that the Rising had taken place. "Blimey" O'Connor, the

London electrician, who got his nickname because of his Cockney accent, made several dashes across the street to the GPO under heavy fire. After the evacuation of the GPO he spent the night in the houses in Moore St. He was deported to Stafford Jail on May 1st and interned in Frongoch until Christmas 1916.

Early in 1917 he returned to Dublin and rejoined E. Company, 2nd Battalion, Dublin Brigade. He was also appointed staff lieutenant, Fianna Éireann at the same time. He was involved in an attack on the Dublin Metropolitan Police in September 1917 at the time of the hunger strikes in Mountjoy Jail. He was employed as an electrician by Dockrell's Builder's Providers and when he was sent by his employers to work in the Mullingar area, he recruited and trained Volunteers there. When he was sent to work in Sligo, he helped reorganise the Tubbercurry Battalion. On his return to Dublin in April 1921, he was arrested and held until June 1921. In April 1922 he was attached to the 5th Battalion Engineers and was sent to Buttevant, County Cork, to establish a munitions factory. He took the Republican side in the Civil War and took part in engagements with Free State Forces at Macroom. When he returned to Dublin he was arrested and interned from April 1923 to April 1924, during which time he took part in a twenty three day hunger strike.

For many years he was employed as an ESB official.

Johnny "Blimey" O'Connor died at his daughter's residence, at 83 St Mobhi Road, Glasnevin, on April 22nd 1979 and was buried at Deansgrange Cemetery.

References:

RH; IMA, MSPC; Thomas Coffey, *Agony at Easter*, (1969); Joe Good, *Enchanted by Dreams*, (1996); *Irish Press*, 30th March 1959, (na, *interview*); *Irish Press*, 23rd April 1979, (dn).

Patrick O'Connor: (1882 - 1916). Killed in Action
Volunteer. Roll of Honour

Patrick O'Connor, a native of Rathmore, County Kerry, joined the Civil Service in London in 1900 and worked in the Post Office, there. After some years, he transferred to Dublin and became active in the Gaelic League. Having attended the funeral of his brother, Denis, in Kerry on Good Friday, he returned to Dublin and reported to the GPO on Easter Monday evening. P.H. Pearse sent him across to the Imperial Hotel, where he helped in boring through the walls into adjoining buildings. On Wednesday as the fire spread, he was engaged in fighting the flames. The building was evacuated the following day and during the retreat, he was shot dead in the vicinity of Cathedral Street.

Patrick O'Connor was buried in the 1916 Plot in Glasnevin Cemetery.

References:

RH; *Catholic Bulletin*, March 1919; *Kerry's Fighting Story*, (1947); Ray Bateson, *They Died by Pearse's Side*, (2010); Ray Bateson, *Memorials of the Easter Rising*, (2013).

Patrick O'Connor: (1883 - 1943)

E. Coy, 4th Batt, Dublin Brigade. Roll of Honour

Patrick O'Connor was born in 1883 and resided at Main Street, Rathfarnham. He was a cooper by trade and joined the local E. Company, 4th Battalion, Dublin Brigade, before the Rising. On Easter Monday he travelled to Liberty Hall with his unit and transferred ammunition from there to the GPO. He spent the early part of week on the roof of the GPO, and later he was involved in boring through the walls of buildings in Abbey Street. After the surrender he acted as stretcher bearer, carrying the wounded to the hospital in Dublin Castle. He was deported to Wakefield Jail on May 6th and interned in Frongoch until July 27th 1916.

On his release from internment, he lost his job at Guinness's Brewery as a result of his part in the Rising. He rejoined his E. Company, 4th Battalion and took part in armed patrols during the War of Independence. He played a prominent role in gathering intelligence in the course of his work as an insurance agent, until he moved to Cork in 1921 to work.

He later lived at 1 Charleville Mall, North Strand, but after the bombing there in 1941, he moved to Cabra, like many other people from the area who were rendered homeless.

Patrick O'Connor of 43 Dingle Road, Cabra, died on May 29th 1943 and was buried at Glasnevin Cemetery.

References:
RH; IMA, MSPC; *Irish Press*, 31st May 1943, (obit).

Peter O'Connor: (1899 – 1963)

B. Coy, 4th Batt, Dublin Brigade. Roll of Honour

Peter O'Connor was born in 1899 and was an apprentice plumber, residing at 58 Harold's Cross Road in 1916. He was a member of Fianna Éireann and B. Company, 4th Battalion, Dublin Brigade. On Easter Monday he went with unit to the South Dublin Union, and was posted to the South Circular Road Gate. The post was taken by British troops that afternoon, but he managed to escape and went to Larkfield, Kimmage. He then travelled on Easter Monday night with a party, under the command of Lieutenant Larry Murtagh, to the GPO. James

Connolly sent him to Parnell Square on Wednesday to collect two tins containing explosive powder for the use in making grenades. On his return, he was hailed from a window of the GPO by his father, Thomas, who was also a member of the GPO Garrison. After the surrender, he was detained in Richmond Barracks, but was released from detention on May 24th, because of his young age.

He continued to be active as member of the 4th Battalion through the War of Independence and in 1921 he transferred from B. Company to G. Company, becoming a section commander. During the Civil War he took the Republican side and was involved in actions against Free State forces at Terenure and Rathfarnham. In October 1922 he was made 4th Battalion Quartermaster, Republican Forces. He was arrested in November 1922 and interned in Hare Park, the Curragh Camp, until August 1923.

He became a well known builder and was Managing Director of O'Connor & Co., Kilmacud. He was also a director of the Irish Industrial Benefit Society and in 1960 he became a member of the Kilmainham Jail Restoration Committee, dedicating all his spare time to the project.

Peter O'Connor of 86 Lower Kilmacud Road, died on May 28th 1963 and was buried at Mount Jerome Cemetery, Harold's Cross.

References:
RH; IMA, MSPC; *Irish Press*, 28th May 1963, *(app)*.

Rory O'Connor: (1883 – 1922)
Volunteer. Headquarters Staff

Rory O'Connor was born in Dublin in 1883 and was educated at St Mary's College, Clongowes Wood College and UCD. He worked in Canada as a railway engineer from 1911 until his return to Ireland in 1915. He joined the Ancient Order of Hibernians and was a member of the IRB. He prepared for the Rising with P.H. Pearse and Joseph Plunkett at Larkfield, Kimmage; and worked tirelessly in the weeks leading up to the Rebellion. He was wounded in the GPO during Easter Week, and was brought to Mercer's Hospital, from where he escaped and evaded capture.

He was employed as an engineer with Dublin Corporation's Paving Dept, and in 1919 he was granted indefinite leave without salary at the request of Alderman William Cosgrave; to conduct army and local government work for the Republican Government. In 1920 he was arrested and tortured by the Auxillaries and later escaped from the Curragh Camp. He was made IRA Director of Engineering during the War of Independence. He took the anti-Treaty side during the Civil War, and became Chairman of the Military Council of the IRA in 1922. He led the anti-Treaty force that occupied the Four Courts in June 1922, and after the garrison's surrender he was arrested and detained in Mountjoy Jail. On December 7th 1922 Seán Hales TD was shot outside Dáil Éireann, and two days later Rory O'Connor was executed, along with Liam Mellows, Dick Barrett and Joe McKelvey, who had also been captured at the fall of the Four Courts. The execution orders were signed by Kevin O'Higgins, for whom Rory O'Connor had acted as best man at his wedding less than a year earlier.

References:

IMA, MSPC; Dorothy Macardle, *The Irish Republican*, (1937); Calton Younger, *Ireland's Civil War*, (1971); Tim Pat Coogan, *The IRA*, (1971); C.S. Andrews, *Dublin Made Me*, (1979); Michael Hopkinson, *Green against Green: the Irish Civil War*, (1992); Diarmaid Ferriter, *A Nation and not a Rabble, the Irish Revolution, 1913-1923*, (2015).

Thomas O'Connor: (1863 -   )
E. Coy, 4th Batt, Dublin Brigade

Thomas O'Connor, a native of Glencullen, County Dublin, was born in 1863. He resided at 58 Harold's Cross and was stone mason by trade in 1916. He was fifty three years old and a member of E. Company, 4th Battalion, Dublin Brigade, when he took part in the Rising. He was stationed at the barricaded windows of the GPO throughout Easter Week and it was from there that he hailed his sixteen year old son, Peter, as he returned, having been sent to Parnell Square on a mission by James Connolly.

Thomas O'Connor was deported to Stafford Jail on May 1st and then interned in Frongoch until Christmas 1916.

References:

Sinn Féin Rebellion Handbook 1916, Weekly Irish Times, (1917); *Irish Press*, 28th May 1963, (app, *of Peter O'Connor*).

Tomás Ó Donnachada (Thomas O'Donoghue):
(1889 - 1963)
London Company, (Kimmage Garrison). Roll of Honour

Thomas O'Donoghue was born in Cahirciveen, County Kerry, in 1889. He emigrated to London to find employment and he shared rooms with Michael Collins. He also became a member of the Gaelic League, the Volunteers and the GAA while in London. Prior to the Rising, he came to Dublin with the other London Volunteers, including his brother, Patrick and stayed at Larkfield, Kimmage. He entered the GPO on Easter Monday with the Kimmage Garrison and fought there throughout the week. After the surrender he was deported to Knutsford Jail on May 1st and interned in Frongoch until Christmas 1916. He was one of the Frongoch prisoners, who later became TDs at the time of the Treaty. He became a member of the Kerry County Council and took part in several operations against the Black & Tans. He was elected TD for North Kerry and Limerick West in the Second Dáil. During the Civil War, he took the Republican side and was interned in Newbridge Barracks, where he went on hunger-strike in 1923.

On his release he took a teaching post in Limerick, but later lost his position in the VEC because he refused to take the Oath of Allegiance. When Fianna Fáil came to power in 1932, he obtained a post in the Civil Service.

Thomas O'Donoghue, of 101 Cabra Road, Dublin, died on June 12th 1963 and was buried at Glasnevin Cemetery.

References:
RH; IMA, MSPC; Ann Matthews, *The Kimmage Garrison, 1916*, (2010); *Irish Independent*, 13th June 1963, (obit).

Patrick O'Donoghue: (1898 – 1986)
London Company, (Kimmage Garrison)

Patrick O'Donoghue was born in Cahirciveen, County Kerry, in 1898. After leaving school, he emigrated to London and found employment with the Western Union Company. He joined the Volunteers in London and returned to Dublin on Good Friday, and joined the Volunteers at the Larkfield, Kimmage. He fought with the men from the Kimmage Garrison, which included his brother, Tomás, in the GPO throughout Easter Week. At the surrender he evaded capture and went into hiding, before he made his way back to London a few weeks later.

In January 1917 he returned to Ireland and joined the Cahirciveen Company, Kerry Brigade. He served there until November 1917, when he was arrested and held in Cork Jail. While interned there, he went on hunger strike and was released in December 1917. On his release from Cork Jail he joined the 2nd Battalion, No.1 Cork Brigade, until he was arrested again in November 1921 and interned on Spike Island until December 1921. He joined the Free State Army in 1922 and served during the Civil War. In 1929 he retired from the army with the rank of captain and returned to England. He lived in England for over forty years, before he returned to live in Galway.

Patrick O'Donoghue, a retired shopkeeper, of Caheroyan, Athenry, County Galway, died on September 8th 1986.

References:
IMA, MSPC; Ann Matthews, *The Kimmage Garrison 1916*, (2010).

William P. O'Donoghue: (1893 – 1975)
Liverpool Company, (Kimmage Garrison)

William O'Donoghue, a native of Clonmore, Hacketstown, County Carlow, was born in 1893. He returned to Ireland with the Liverpool Volunteers to take part in the Rising and resided at 28 North Frederick Street with others associated with the Kimmage Garrison. He fought in the GPO throughout Easter Week, and after the surrender he was deported to Knutsford Jail on May 1st. He was interned in Frongoch until September 1916.

On his release from internment, he joined D. Company, 2nd Battalion, Dublin Brigade and later transferred to A. Company, 3rd Battalion, Carlow Brigade, with the rank of captain. He reorganised the 3rd Battalion and was appointed commandant. He was involved in numerous operations, including an attack at Tullow RIC Barracks, where two RIC constables were killed. In February 1921, he was arrested and interned at Rath Camp, where he made an unsuccessful bid to escape. As a result, he was sentenced to twelve months hard labour in Cork Jail, but escaped from there in November 1921. He joined the Free State Army in 1922 and served through the Civil War. In 1923 he transferred from the Army Supply Corps to the Coastal Marine Service and was demobilised in March 1924 with the rank of lieutenant. He rejoined the Army in 1940 and served until 1946 with the rank of lieutenant.

In later years he was employed by the ESB and resided at 2 Cross Avenue, Blackrock. William O'Donoghue died on October 7th 1975.

References:
IMA, MSPC; Donal O'Donovan, *Kevin Barry and his Time*, (1989); Ann Matthew, *The Kimmage Garrison 1916*, (2010).

Elizabeth O'Farrell: (1883 – 1957)
Cumann na mBan. Irish Citizen Army. Roll of Honour

Elizabeth O'Farrell, the daughter of a Dublin docker, was born at 33 City Quay, on August 5th 1883. She attended the Sisters of Mercy Convent School, Townsend Street and later became a member of the Gaelic League. In 1914 she joined Cumann na mBan with her neighbourhood friend, Julia Grenan.

She was a member of the Irish Citizen Army during Easter Week. On Easter Monday she was sent to Galway with a message that the Rising was to begin, and the Galway Volunteers, under Liam Mellowes, fought at Oranmore, Clarinbridge and Athenry. She returned to Dublin and after passing through a number of barricades, reported to the GPO. Having trained in first aid, she tended to the wounded. and later in the week, she was sent with dispatches to the Four Courts Garrison and the College of Surgeons. At the evacuation of the GPO on Friday evening, she, Julia Grenan and Winnie Carney, were the only women remaining. On Saturday she was sent by P.H. Pearse, under the protection of a white flag, to Brigadier General Lowe, with a request to enter into negotiations. It was agreed that Pearse should surrender to Lowe in person and she accompanied him to Parnell Street. She was detained overnight and on the following day she took the surrender order to the commandants of the garrisons. After the Rising, she was detained in Ship Street Barracks and Kilmainham Jail, before being released after a short period, due to the petitioning of General Lowe.

She later trained as a midwife in the National Maternity Hospital, Holles Street and worked as a district nurse. For many years she shared a house with Julia Grenan at 27 Lower Mount Street and remained active in Republican politics.

Elizabeth O'Farrell died on June 25th 1957 and was buried at Glasnevin Cemetery. In January 1967 a plaque in her honour was erected in the new unit in Holles Street Maternity Hospital and City Quay Park was renamed Elizabeth O'Farrell Park in her memory.

References:

RH; *Catholic Bulletin*, April 1917; *DIB*, Frances Clarke, (James Quinn, Ed, 2009); R.M. Fox, *Green Banners: the Story of the Irish Struggle*, (1938); Ruth Taillon, *Women of 1916*, (1999); Irish Mail on Sunday, 14th January 2007, (na); *Irish Independent* & *Irish Press*, 26th June 1957, (obits).

Liam O'Gorman
Volunteer. Roll of Honour

Liam O'Gorman of 4 Lombard Street West, served as a boy in the 1867 Fenian Uprising and later with the Land League. He joined the Volunteers at the Rotunda in 1913 and fought in the GPO in Easter Week. He evaded capture and although of an advanced age, he later fought in the War of Independence with the South Dublin Battalion of Irish Citizen Army from 1921 to 1923.

Liam O'Gorman was listed as a deceased member of the GPO Garrison when the Roll of Honour List was compiled.

References:

RH. *Pádraig Ó'Briain Papers*, *(private collection)*.

Mary O'Hanrahan: (1882 - 1957)

Cumann na mBan, (Fairview Branch). Roll of Honour

Mary O'Hanrahan was born in 1882 and resided at 149 North Strand Road. She was a member of the Fairview Branch of Cumann na mBan and a member of the Oliver Bond Hurling Club. She was part of the GPO Garrison during Easter Week and was engaged in cooking duties and she assisted in first aid duties. On Friday, she was arrested with other Cumann na mBan members at the North Circular Road and brought to Broadstone Station for interrogation, before being released. Her brothers, Joseph and Edward, who were members of E. Company, 2nd Battalion, fought in the Jacob's Garrison. She later took an active part in the War of Independence and assisted in the distribution of the Volunteers Prisoners Dependent Fund. Her home and shop at 149 North Strand Road was used as an arms depot and dispatch calling office. She also provided safe houses for men on the run. During the Civil War she took the Republican side and continued storing arms and ammunition up until the ceasefire in 1923.

Mary O'Hanrahan died on February 11th 1957 and was buried at Glasnevin Cemetery.

References:
RH; IMA, MSPC; *Irish Press*, 16th February 1957, (dn).

Annie O'Higgins: (- 1935)

Cumann na mBan. Roll of Honour

Dublin born Annie O'Higgins, was a music teacher in Carrickmacross, County Monaghan, and was home visiting her mother in Dublin for Easter when the Rising began. She was a member of Cumann na mBan and reported to the GPO on Easter Monday. She was sent to the Hibernian Bank on Tuesday and stayed there until midday on Wednesday, cooking for the garrison. She returned to the GPO and was sent on a mission the next day to Carrickmacross. Although she managed to make her way through the British lines to Monaghan, she was arrested there and brought to Armagh Jail.

After her release from jail, she lost her job and returned to Dublin. She was a fine musician and composer and had a keen interest in literature and art, also. She later taught at the School of Music in Dublin.

Annie O'Higgins tragically lost her life with her mother in a fire at her home at 16 Parnell Square, on August 18th 1935.

References:
RH; *Capuchin Annual*, 1936; *Irish Independent*, 21st April 1935, (obit).

Brian O'Higgins: (1882 – 1963)

B. Coy, 2nd Batt, Dublin Brigade.

Brian O'Higgins was born at Kilskyre, County Meath, on July 1st 1882. In 1901 he was working as a barman in Dublin and was a member of Saint Finian's Hurling Club. He joined the O'Growney Branch of the Gaelic League, becoming involved in the Irish language revival movement. His health declined in 1903 and he returned to live in his native Meath. In 1906 he became an Irish language teacher, and also composed many Irish ballads. He became a good friend of P.H. Pearse, after they first met in 1906. A member of B. Company, 2nd Battalion, Dublin Brigade, on Easter Monday he was in a group of Volunteers who were held at 41 Parnell Square as reservists, on account of their age, health or physical condition. This group was called to the GPO at six o'clock that evening. He was put on guard duty at the main entrance to the GPO and he later served under Quartermaster Michael Staines. He assisted in the evacuation of the wounded from the GPO on Friday evening and spent the night in a shed off Moore Street. He was deported to Stafford Jail on May 1st and interned in Frongoch until February 1917.

On his release he became secretary of O'Curry College, an Irish college, in Carrigaholt, County Clare. On May 18th 1918 he was arrested and deported to Birmingham Jail, and was elected Sinn Féin candidate for West Clare. He was elected to the First Dáil and during the Civil War he took the anti-Treaty side. During the Civil War, he was imprisoned in Oriel House, Mountjoy Jail and Tintown and went on hunger strike for twenty five days.

He published *"A Soldier's Story of Easter Week"* in 1925 and the first *"Wolfe Tone Annual"* in 1932. Earlier, in 1908, he published *"By a Hearth in Éireann"* and *"Hearts of Gold"* in 1918, under the pseudonym, Brian na Banban.

Brian O'Higgins died on March 10th 1963 and was buried at Glasnevin Cemetery.

References:

RH; *Capuchin Annual*, 1963; Max Caulfield, *The Easter Rebellion*, (1963); Brian O'Higgins, *The Soldiers Story of Easter Week*, (1966); W.J. Brennan-Whitmore, *Dublin Burning*, (1996); *Encyclopedia of Ireland*, (Brian Lalor, Ed, 2003); *Irish Independent* & *Irish Press*, 11th March 1963, (obits).

Doctor Eamon (Ted) O'Kelly: (1883 - 1941)

Lieutenant. G.H.Q. & Maynooth Company, Kildare Brigade. Roll of Honour

Ted O'Kelly a native of Maynooth, was born in 1883. He was educated at Castleknock College and was a medical student when he was appointed by P.H. Pearse to organise the Volunteers in Kildare in 1915. On Easter Monday, he left Maynooth from the back of Domhnall Ó Buachalla's shop with fifteen local Volunteers and travelled to Dublin along the Royal Canal bank. They arrived at the GPO the following morning, having spent the night in Glasnevin Cemetery. He was sent by James Connolly to Parliament Street with this group to support the Volunteers and Irish Citizen Army men in the City Hall area. They occupied the Royal Exchange Hotel in Parliament Street and when Volunteer Ned Walsh of the Hibernian Rifles was mortally wounded on the roof, Ted O'Kelly crawled up to where he lay and gave him what aid he could. With their position untenable and Parliament Street almost completely surrounded by British Troops, he and the remainder of the Maynooth men made a successful dash to the GPO without any casualties. He was wounded in the heel later in the week and was in the group of wounded Volunteers brought to Jervis Street Hospital on Friday. His aunt, Sr Assisium, was a nun in the hospital and with her aid and that of Josephine Stallard, his future sister-in-law, he hid from the British Troops who were rounding up all wounded Volunteers that were hospitalised. Later he was taken to Kingsbridge Station, disguised as a priest and travelled to Josephine Stallard's family home, Danville House, Kilkenny.

He rejoined the Volunteers in 1917 and was appointed Commanding Officer, 4th Battalion, Dublin Brigade. In 1918 he married Maisie Stallard, while in 1921 her sister Josephine, a qualified doctor, married Liam Clarke, who was seriously wounded in the GPO in Easter Week. He was arrested in 1919 and sentenced to two years imprisonment, but was released early after he took part in a hunger strike. In 1920 he was badly injured, while escaping from a Black and Tan raid and was hospitalised for four months. His injuries forced him from his position in the IRA and to cease active service.

He took the Republican side in the Civil War, but he took no active part.

He later had a medical practice at 30 Oakley Square, London.

Doctor Ted O'Kelly was killed in April 1941 when his residence was hit by a bomb during the London Blitz, and he was buried at St Pancras Cemetery, Finchley.

References:

RH; IMA, MSPC; NLI, *Lynch Papers*, (Ms 11,131); *Castleknock College Chronicle*, June 1902; *An t-Óglach*, May 1926; James Durney, *On the One Road*, (2001); *Leinster Leader*, 26th April 1941, (obit).

Fergus O'Kelly: (1895 – 1979)
Lieutenant. G.H.Q. & 2nd Batt.

Fergus O'Kelly was born in 1895 and living in Howth when he joined the Volunteers at the inaugural meeting in the Rotunda, in November 1913. He joined the 2nd Battalion, Dublin Brigade and was attached to the Signalling Company, where he received instruction in Morse code. He was in close touch with Joseph Plunkett and his brothers at Larkfield, Kimmage, where they attempted to construct a transmitter set and receiving apparatus. On Easter Monday afternoon, he was instructed by Joseph Plunkett to take some men and occupy the Dublin Wireless School of Telegraphy, across the street from the GPO, at Reis's Chambers. With great difficulty the disconnected wireless apparatus was assembled and an ariel was erected on the roof despite the heavy sniper fire. He and David Bourke were the wireless operators who transmitted the first message on Tuesday, while other Volunteers present in the wireless school included Arthur Shields, "Blimey" O'Connor and Luke Kennedy. The message, proclaiming the Irish Republic and that Dublin City had been taken by the Irish Republican Army, was picked up by ships at sea and the news appeared in the following days newspapers in the United States. On Wednesday he was ordered to abandon the post, but when he reached the GPO he was ordered by James Connolly to return and retrieve the wireless apparatus. Because of the heavy gunfire, only part of the dismantled equipment was retrieved, and two Volunteers were seriously wounded in the operation. He remained in the GPO and was engaged in fighting the fires that engulfed the building on Friday. After the surrender, he was deported and interned in Frongoch until August 1916.

After the reorganisation of the Volunteers in early 1917, he continued to serve as a staff lieutenant of GHQ under Rory O'Connor, Director of Engineering. He transferred to G. Company, 4th Battalion, in 1918 and took part in numerous operations, including the attack on British Forces in Terenure in January 1921. In February 1921 he was sent to organise a company in the Howth and Baldoyle area with the rank of captain. He took the Republican side during the Civil War and served in the garrison at Jameson's Distillery, Marrowbone Lane. He was involved in the unsuccessful attempt to tunnel into Mountjoy Jail and in two abortive attacks on Baldonnel Aerodrome. He was arrested in December 1922 and was interned in Newbridge and Hare Park until March 1924.

Fergus O'Kelly, of 35 Granville Avenue, Dun Laoghaire, died on June 26th 1979.

References:

RH; IMA, MSPC; IMA, BMH (WS 351); NLI, *Lynch Papers*, (Ms 11,131); Max Caulfield, *The Easter Rebellion*, (1963); Thomas Coffey, *Agony at Easter*, (1969); Peter De Rosa, *Rebels, the Irish Rising of 1916*, (1991); *Irish Press*, 27th June 1979, (dn).

Maura O'Kelly: (- 1959)
Cumann na mBan

Maura O'Kelly was a native of Carraroe, County Galway. She was a member of Cumann na mBan and served with the GPO Garrison in Easter Week.

She joined the New Ireland Assurance Co. as a clerk at its foundation in 1918.

Maura O'Kelly of 73 Royal Canal Terrace, Phibsboro, died on January 24th 1959 and was buried at Mount Jerome Cemetery.

References:
Irish Press, 27th January 1959, (dn).

Seán T. O'Kelly: (1882 – 1966)
Staff Captain. G.H.Q. Roll of Honour

Seán T. O'Kelly was born in Dublin on August 25th 1882 and resided at 55 Wellington Street in the north inner-city. He was educated at O'Connell Schools, North Richmond Street and joined the Gaelic League in 1898, and was also a member of the IRB, the Celtic Literary Society and the Confederate Hurling Club. In 1898 he was employed as a library assistant in the National Library of Ireland but left after four years to become manager of *An Claidheamh Solais,* the organ of the Gaelic League. A founder member of Sinn Féin in 1905, he was the youngest representative elected to the Dublin Corporation the following year. He was also a founder member of the Volunteers in 1913. In 1915 he was elected general secretary of the Gaelic League in which year he travelled to New York to update Clan na nGael on the preparations for the Rising. On Easter Monday he was a staff captain in the GPO and was sent to Martin Conlon's house in Cabra Park, to release Bulmer Hobson, who was being held prisoner. He was later sent with a party of men to disperse looters in the vicinity of the GPO. James Connolly sent him on various missions throughout the week and on Thursday he was sent to the home of Mrs Tom Clarke, at Richmond Road, Fairview. He found himself cut off on his return to the GPO, and received a leg wound attempting to climb over a barricade. He made his way to his home at Upper Rutland Street and was arrested there on the following Monday. He was deported to Stafford Jail on the next day, May 1st and was interned in Frongoch.

In 1918 he married Mary Kate Ryan, and in the general election of that year he was elected Sinn Féin MP for the College Green Division, Dublin. He was elected Ceann Comhairle to the First Dáil in 1919, and also attended the Paris Peace Conference as the Irish Envoy in the same year. He opposed the Treaty in 1921 and was a founder member of Fianna Fáil in 1926. He was Vice-President of the Executive Council, when Éamon deValera took office in 1932. His wife, Mary Kate, died in 1934 and he married her sister, Phyllis, in 1936. He was Minister for Local Government from 1932 to 1937 and Tánaiste from 1937 to 1945. He was also appointed Minister for Finance in 1941 and held that office until he was elected President of Ireland in 1945. He was elected President for a second term in 1952, and on St Patrick's Day, 1959, he addressed joint sessions of the United States Congress in Washington, DC.

Seán T. O'Kelly died on November 23rd 1966 and was buried at Glasnevin Cemetery.

References:

RH; Dorothy Macardle, *The Irish Republic*, (1937); Seán O'Kelly, *Seán T.*, (1972); W.J. Brennan-Whitmore, *Dublin Burning*, (1996); Diarmaid Ferriter, *A Nation and not a Rabble, the Irish Revolution, 1913-1923*, (2015); *Irish Independent, Irish Press* & *Irish Times*, 24th November 1966, (na, *obits, career & tributes*).

Jeremiah (Diarmuid) O'Leary: (1889 – 1960)
London Company, (Kimmage Garrison)

Diarmuid O'Leary was born of Irish parents in Colchester in 1889. At an early age, a schoolyard accident resulted in permanent damage to his hip, which left him lame for the rest of his life. In 1908 he joined the Clapham Branch of the Gaelic League in London and, with his brother David, he joined the IRB in 1910. He was involved in organising relief aid for those affected by the Lockout in Dublin in 1913. Both brothers later joined the London Company of Volunteers in 1914. Before the Rising, he was involved in organising the passage of arms through London for Volunteers in Ireland. He arrived in Dublin on Good Friday, 1916, accompanied by his brother and other Volunteers. On Easter Monday he went to an address in Seville Place with Seán McGrath and Liam O'Kelly and gathered ammunition there and brought it back to the GPO. Later that afternoon he was asked by P.H. Pearse to organise a group from the GPO to prevent looting in the vicinity of North Earl Street and Abbey Street. It was well after midnight before this task was completed, and they found it was impossible to gain entry to the GPO, so he sought refuge in digs in Gardiner Street. On his return to the GPO the following day, Michael Collins suggested that, because he was a stranger in the city, he should go to Amiens Street Station, pretend to be a tourist and mingle with the crowds in an effort to gather some intelligence information. He checked the morgue on Wednesday to see if any of his London Volunteers had been killed, and later that day was arrested by detectives from G Division. After being held in Richmond Barracks for nearly two weeks, he was deported to Wakefield Prison on June 2nd, and later interned in Frongoch.

On his release from Frongoch he joined E Company, 2nd Battalion. However, because of his lameness, he was confined to indoor duties including involvement in the National Aid and Volunteer Dependents' Fund. He was later an assistant to Michael Collins in the Bachelor's Walk offices. He was then sent as a Sinn Féin election organiser to Waterford in 1918.

He married Philomena, the eldest daughter of Count Plunkett, in August, 1918 and their new home on Morehampton Road was used throughout this time by Active Service Units, Cumann na mBan and *The Irish Bulletin* was printed there for a while.

He was involved in the reorganisation of the ITGWU and was employed at the head office from 1919 until 1927, when he secured as position as Industrial Inspector in the Dept of Industry and Commerce. He worked there for many years and was also a councillor for Dublin Corporation.

Diarmuid O'Leary, of 54 Morehampton Road, died on January 3rd 1960 and was buried at Deansgrange Cemetery.

References:

IMA, BMH (WS 1108); Ann Matthews, *The Kimmage Garrison 1916*, (2010); Geraldine Plunkett Dillon, *All in the Blood*, (2014); *Evening Herald*, 4th January 1960, (obit).

Eamon J. O'Mahony: (1897 - 1968)
B. Coy, 2nd Batt, Dublin Brigade. Roll of Honour

Eamon O'Mahony was born in 1897 and resided at 7 Richmond Avenue West, Drumcondra in 1916. He was educated at O'Connell Schools, North Richmond Street, and became a member of B. Company, 2nd Battalion, Dublin Brigade, in 1913. He was involved in the Howth gun running in July 1914 and shortly before the Rising, he brought explosives from Dolphin's Barn to Father Mathew Park, Fairview. On Easter Sunday night he stood guard at the 2nd Battalion arms dump at Father Mathew Park. Alongside his brother, Matt, he fought in the GPO throughout Easter Week. After the surrender he was held in Richmond Barracks and was released from there on May 12th, because of his youth.

After the Rising, he helped reorganise his unit and was involved in a number of operations, including the hold-up of a train, carrying arms at Newcomen Bridge and the planned attack on the B&I Stores, North Wall. He was promoted to lieutenant of 2nd Battalion in 1917, and on St Patrick's Day 1918 he was arrested and imprisoned for assaulting a police constable at Marino. In 1920 he was appointed lieutenant with GHQ and served as a Training Officer under JJ O'Connell, until the Truce. He took no part in the Civil War.

In later life he lived at Shelmartin Avenue, Marino and also 35 Celtic Park Avenue, Beaumont. He was employed in Irish Life Assurance and was a lifelong member of Bohemians FC.

Eamon O'Mahony died on May 5th 1968 and was buried in Glasnevin Cemetery.

References:

RH; IMA, MSPC; *Evening Herald*, 7th October 1968, (dn).

John O'Mahony: (- 1934)
Volunteer

"Big" John O'Mahony was a native of Thomastown, County Kilkenny. He came to Dublin at a young age and by 1916, he was the proprietor of Fleming's Hotel, 31-32 Gardiner Place. He was a prominent member of Sinn Féin and he fought in the GPO in Easter Week. After the surrender he was deported to Wakefield Prison on June 2nd and interned in Lincoln Jail and later Frongoch until July 27th 1916.

He was elected Sinn Féin MP for Fermanagh South in 1918 and for Fermanagh and Tyrone in 1921. O'Mahony voted against the Treaty. He also served on many Sinn Féin Executives.

John O'Mahony died on November 28th 1934 and two days later his funeral cortege stopped in silence outside the GPO en route to Glasnevin Cemetery.

References:

Sinn Féin Rebellion Handbook 1916, Weekly Irish Times, (1917); Seán O'Mahony, *Frongoch, University of Revolution*, (1987); *Irish Independent*, 30th November 1934, (obit). Jim Maher, *In the shade of Slievenamon, The Flying Column, West Kilkenny, 1916-1921* (Dublin 2015).

Matthew J. (Matt) O'Mahony: (1895 - 1981)
B. Coy, 2nd Batt, Dublin Brigade. Roll of Honour

Matt O'Mahony was born in 1895 and resided at 7 Richmond Avenue West, Drumcondra. In 1913 he joined the Volunteers and became a member of B. Company, 2nd Battalion, Dublin Brigade. He was mobilised on Easter Monday morning and reported to Father Mathew Park, Fairview. He was in a party, under the command of Captain Frank Henderson, who occupied Gilbey's Wine Shop, Ballybough Bridge. On Tuesday evening he left Gilbey's and proceeded to the GPO with the Fairview contingent. He was posted to the Imperial Hotel, across the street from the GPO and remained there until the building was evacuated on Thursday night because of the fire. He retreated in the direction of Gloucester Street with other Volunteers, and found refuge in a yard in Thomas Lane. On Friday morning they went to the vestry of the Pro-Cathedral in Marlborough Street and after fifteen minutes they were arrested and taken to the Custom House. He was detained and interrogated there, until May 7th when he was released. He took no part in the War of Independence. His brother, Eamon, was also a member of the GPO Garrison.

Matt O'Mahony, of 50 Church Street, Skerries, died on October 26th 1981 and was buried at Holmpatrick Cemetery, Skerries.

References:

RH; IMA, MSPC; *Irish Press*, 26th & 27th October 1981, (dn).

George Oman: (1896 - 1977)

Irish Citizen Army, (High St Section). Roll of Honour

George Oman was born in 1896 and lived at 48 High Street. A watchmaker by trade, he joined the Irish Citizen Army in 1914 with his brother, William. He was also a bugler and he sounded the Last Post at the burial of O'Donovan Rossa at Glasnevin Cemetery, on August 1st 1915. For several weeks before the Rising, he did guard duty at Liberty Hall. On Easter Monday evening he left the GPO in a party under the command of Captain Frank Thornton, which attempted to reach the besieged Volunteers in City Hall. They failed to get through and spent the night in Fleet Street, before they were recalled to the GPO. This party was then ordered to take over the Imperial Hotel and before they left the GPO, James Connolly promoted him to First Lieutenant. When the burning hotel was abandoned on Thursday, he unsuccessfully attempted to return to the GPO. He was captured on Friday and taken to the Custom House for interrogation. He was held until Sunday and was then released after he convinced his captors that he was under age.

He joined E. Company, 1st Battalion, in 1917 and served until 1919. He didn't take part in the Civil War. An Irish language enthusiast, he was a member of the Keating Branch of the Gaelic League and he founded the Liam Partridge Branch in Inchicore, when he lived at 16 Kickham Road.

George Oman, of 23 James's Street, died on October 17th 1977 and was buried in Mount Jerome Cemetery.

References:

RH; IMA, MSPC; NLI, *William O'Brien Papers*, (Ms 15,673); Ann Matthews, *The Irish Citizen Army*, (2014); *Evening Herald*, 18th October 1977, (dn).

Donough Ó Mórdha, (O'Moore): (1900 – 1967)
Fianna Éireann. Roll of Honour

Donough O'Moore, of 16 Lower St. Colomba's Road, Drumcondra, was born in 1900. He lost his leg at a young age, but this did not prevent him from becoming a member of Fianna Éireann. He was one of the youngest in the GPO during Easter Week. On Easter Monday he was stationed in the locker room in Henry Street with Volunteers from the 1st Battalion. He was detained in Richmond Barracks after the surrender. He had been reported dead and his family were preparing for his funeral when he returned home after his release on May 12th.

In 1917 he joined F. Company, 2nd Battalion, Dublin Brigade in 1917 and was appointed quartermaster. He fought in the War of Independence and was arrested in November 1920 and interned in Mountjoy Jail until February 1921. While in prison he concealed a couple of rounds of ammunition in his wooden leg. In the Civil War he took the anti-Treaty side with his brother Patrick, who was also a member of the GPO Garrison. He fought at 42 North Georges Street, Barry's Hotel and the Hamman Hotel and was later arrested and imprisoned in Mountjoy Jail in August 1922. In January 1923 he was transferred to Newbridge Barracks, where he took part in a hunger strike and was released from Tintown Camp in February 1923. His brothers, Patrick and Anthony and his sister, Eileen, who was a member of Cumann na mBan, were all imprisoned during the Civil War.

For many years he was employed in the Clerical Dept of CIE and was a member of the O'Donovan Rossa Cumann of Fianna Fáil. In the late 1940's and early 1950's he was Chairman of the Custom House Memorial Committee.

Donough O'Moore, of 137 Larkhill Road, Whitehall, died on January 4th 1967 and was buried at Glasnevin.

References:
RH; IMA, MSPC; *Irish Press*, 5th January 1967, (obit).

Patrick Ó Mórdha, (O'Moore): (1898 - 1958)
E. Coy, 2nd Batt, Dublin Brigade. Roll of Honour

Patrick O'Moore was born in 1898 and resided at 16 Lower St. Colomba's Road, Drumcondra. He was a founder member of Fianna Éireann and later a member of E. Company, 2nd Battalion, Dublin Brigade. He was employed as a clerk. On Easter Monday he reported to the GPO with his younger brother, Donough. He was mainly engaged in sniping in the early part of the week and he was later sent to an outpost in Henry Street by James Connolly. While in Henry Street, he was wounded in the hand and his party was later recalled to the GPO. He was in charge of a party that escorted the wounded to Jervis Street Hospital, where he was arrested. On May 6th he was deported to Wakefield Jail and interned in Frongoch until July 26th 1916.

After his release from internment, and in consultation with Brigade Officers, he joined the British Army to secure military training. He was drafted for active service in France and transferred to the Machine Gun Corps, also known as the Suicide Club. In 1920 he deserted the British Army, when he was due for promotion to lieutenant, and re-joined the IRA. He took part in an attack on the London and North Western Railway Hotel, North Wall and was arrested in March 1921. He was interned in Rath Camp, the Curragh, until December 1921, and in early 1922 he joined the National Army. He later left and joined the anti-Treaty Forces and fought in the Four Courts during the Civil War, before he was captured and interned until 1924. His brothers, Donough and Anthony, fought on the Republican side and were also imprisoned with him, while his sister, Eileen, also took the Republican side.

Patrick O'Moore emigrated to Australia in 1926 and died in Brisbane on My 11th 1958.

References:

RH; IMA, MSPC; *Sinn Féin Rebellion Handbook 1916*, Weekly Irish Times, (1917).

Colm Ó Murchadha (Murphy): (1889 – 1939)

F. Coy, 1st Batt, Dublin Brigade

Colm Ó'Murchadha, the son of a Dublin furniture merchant, was born in 1889 and educated at Westland Row CBS. He entered the Civil Service in 1909 and was appointed to a post in London before he was transferred to the Irish Land Commission. He became a member of F. Company, 1st Battalion, Dublin Brigade and resided at 9 St Brigid's Road, Drumcondra, in 1916. He fought in the GPO throughout Easter Week and after the surrender he was deported to Stafford Jail on May 1st.

On his release from internment in Frongoch, he became a teacher in Castleknock College. He also took over as editor of the Gaelic newspaper, *"An Claidheamh Soluis"*. He was appointed assistant secretary to the 1st Dáil, and when Dermot O'Hegarty went to London with the Treaty Delegation, he acted as secretary in his place. He was in favour of the Treaty and joined the Free State Army. After the Treaty he was appointed First Clerk of Dáil Éireann.

In later years he gave great service in the promotion of the Irish language with the Translation Dept in the Oireachtas.

Colm Ó'Murchadha died at his residence, "Lea Doire", 93 Pembroke Road, on December 14th 1939.

References:

IMA, MSPC; *Sinn Féin Rebellion Handbook* 1916, Weekly Irish Times, (1917); *Irish Press*, 15th December 1939, (obit & app).

Michael Ó Murchú (Murphy): (1886 - 1965)

B. Coy, 2nd Batt, Dublin Brigade. Roll of Honour

Michael Murphy was born in 1886 and was a stonemason by trade. He was an early member of the Gaelic League and Sinn Féin, and joined the Volunteers at its inception in 1913 as a member B. Company, 2nd Battalion, Dublin Brigade. He was not mobilised on Easter Monday and when he heard that his unit was posted to Jacob's Biscuit Factory, he set out to join them there. As he passed the GPO with his rifle in hand, he was called by The O'Rahilly to join the GPO Garrison. He was put in charge of the barricade on the ground floor at the Prince's Street side of the building and remained there throughout the week. As he crossed between Henry Place and Moore Lane, after the GPO was evacuated on Friday evening, he was hit in the foot by a machine gun bullet. After the surrender he was deported to Knutsford Jail on May 3rd and interned in Frongoch until Christmas 1916.

He took no further part in the War of Independence on his release from internment. He was employed as an ITWUI organiser, and was later Gaelic Editor of the *Irish Independent*. He was also an Irish Placenames Commision Officer.

Michael Ó' Murchú, of 112 North Circular Road, died on December 6th 1965 and was buried at Glasnevin Cemetery.

References:
RH; IMA, MSPC; *Sinn Féin Rebellion Handbook 1916*, Weekly Irish Times, (1917); *Irish Press*, 8th December 1965, (dn).

James O'Neill: (1890 – 1954)

A. Coy, 3rd Batt, Dublin Brigade. Roll of Honour

James O'Neill was born in 1890 and resided at 102 Lindsay Road, Glasnevin. He was an upholsterer by trade and joined A. Company, 3rd Battalion, Dublin Brigade, in 1914. On Easter Monday 1916, he manned the ground floor windows on the Prince's Street side of the GPO. He spent the remainder of the week fighting on the ground floor, and on Friday he left the GPO with the party led by The O'Rahilly. He fought his way up Moore Street as far as he could and witnessed The O'Rahilly fall. When a Volunteer beside him was wounded in the foot, he helped him into Samson's Lane. He was in the group of Volunteers who then attempted to get up Cole's Lane and when two more Volunteers were wounded, this group retreated to Samson's Lane, spending the night in a stable. After the surrender he was deported to Knutsford Jail on May 1st and interned in Frongoch until July 18th 1916.

He joined F. Company, 2nd Battalion, Dublin Brigade, in 1917 and was appointed assistant quartermaster. He was involved in a numerous operations, including the burning of Raheny RIC Barracks and the raid on the Rotunda Rink for the Dublin Castle mail.

He took part in the attack on the Custom House in May 1921, after which he was promoted to quartermaster of 2nd Battalion. In the Civil War he took the Republican side and fought at Hely's Public House, Marlborough Street and Findlater's, O'Connell Street. He was arrested in July 1922 and interned until June 1923.

He was secretary of the Amalgamated Union of Upholsterers, from 1923 to 1936. During the emergency years he was a member of the 26th Infantry Battalion.

James O'Neill, of 20 Dowth Road, Cabra, died on July 26th 1954, aged 63 years.

References:

RH; IMA, MSPC; NLI, *Lynch Papers*, (Ms 11,131); *Irish Press*, 27th July 1954, (obit).

James O'Neill: (1890 – 1952)

Quartermaster, Irish Citizen Army. Roll of Honour

James O'Neill, of St Catherine's, Lucan, was born in 1890. He was a building contractor and was associated with James Connolly in organising the Irish Citizen Army. He had a licence to carry explosives and was very active in manufacturing and supplying armaments, prior to the Rising. On the morning of Easter Monday he was appointed quartermaster of the Irish Citizen Army and he organised the transport of munitions and supplies from Liberty Hall to the GPO by cab, lorry and cart. In the GPO he was put in charge of the Armourer's Section in the Main Sorting Office at the back of the Main Hall. Later, he was put in charge of bomb making and engineering, while Michael Staines took charge of munitions. On Tuesday he was ordered to erect a barbwire barricade across Sackville Street. He continued making explosives through the week, and was wounded in the ankle during the evacuation of the GPO and was forced to spend the night with other wounded Volunteers in a mineral store, off Moore Street. After the surrender he was deported to Knutsford Jail and interned in Frongoch until Christmas, 1916.

On his release from internment, he was appointed commandant of the Irish Citizen Army in 1917. While in Mountjoy Jail, he took part in a hunger strike, in 1920. He held the command in the Irish Citizen Army until 1921, when he was dismissed. Frank Robbins in his book *"Under the Starry Plough"* cited his lack of ability to pursue the Connolly philosophy as the reason for his dismissal. He did not take part in the Civil War, but was arrested in July 1922 and interned until June 1924. He worked for many years as a building contractor in Dublin, and lived in Donnycarney and later in Sutton. He emigrated to South Africa for health reasons in 1947.

James O'Neill died on June 18th 1952 in Pietermaritzburg, Natal, South Africa.

References:

RH; IMA, MSPC; NLI, *Lynch Papers*, (Ms 11,131) & *William O'Brien Papers*, (Ms 15,673); R.M. Fox, *The History of the Irish Citizen Army*, (1943); Frank Robbins, *Under the Starry Plough: Recollections of the Irish Citizen Army*, (1977); Ann Matthews, *The Irish Citizen Army*, (2014); *Irish Independent* & *Irish Press*, 2nd July 1952, (obits).

John O'Neill: (1876 - 1924)
Irish Citizen Army. Roll of Honour

John O'Neill resided at 28 East Arran Street and was one of two Irish Citizen Army men named, John O'Neill, who fought in the GPO during Easter Week. He was sent to Imperial Hotel, under the command of Captain Brennan-Whitmore and retreated with the garrison when they were forced to abandon the blazing building on Thursday. He made his into the north inner-city and evaded capture before going on the run as a consequence of which, his health failed.

John O'Neill, who suffered with a heart condition and bronchitis, died on March 6th 1924 and was buried at Glasnevin Cemetery.

References:

RH; IMA, MSPC; NLI, *William O'Brien*, (Ms 15,673); Ann Matthews, *The Irish Citizen Army*, (2014); *Evening Herald*, 7th March 1924, (dn).

John O'Neill: (- 1958)
Irish Citizen Army, (Gloucester St Section). Roll of Honour

John O'Neill resided at 61 Ballybough Road and became Secretary of the ITGWU No. 1 Branch, in 1911. He joined the Irish Citizen Army at its foundation, and contested the municipal elections for Labour in 1915. He was one of two Irish Citizen Army men named John O'Neill that fought in the GPO during Easter Week. After the surrender, he was deported to Wandsworth Jail on May 8th and interned in Frongoch until Christmas 1916.

He rejoined the Irish Citizen Army at its reorganisation in 1917 and became a Justice of the Republican Courts between 1919 and 1921 and ceased activity in January 1922.

John O'Neill, of 6 Inver Road, Cabra West, died on January, 30th 1958 and was buried at St Fintan's Cemetery, Sutton.

References:

RH; IMA, MSPC; NLI, *William O'Brien Papers*, (Ms 15,673); Frank Robbins, *Under the Starry Plough: Recollections of the Irish Citizen Army*, (1977); Francis Devine, *Organising History: a Centenary of SIPTU, 1909-2009*, (2009); Ann Matthews, *The Irish Citizen Army*, (2014); *Irish Independent*, 31st January 1958, (dn).

William (Billy) O'Neill: (1877 - 1952)

B. Coy, 1st Batt, Dublin Brigade

Billy O'Neill was born in 1877 and resided at 7 North Great Georges Street. He was a printer by trade, and was a member of the IRB. He later joined B. Company, 1st Battalion, Dublin Brigade, at its inception. On Easter Monday, he was mobilised at 41 Parnell Square and later reported to the GPO. He was sent to North Earl Street that evening, and was posted to Tyler's Boot Shop. On Wednesday, he crossed the street to Noblett's Confectioners and served there until Thursday evening. When the block of buildings was evacuated, he helped the Imperial Hotel Garrison through the hole that had been bored in the wall. Because of his knowledge of the north inner city, he volunteered to lead the party, under the command of Captain Brennan-Whitmore, to Fairview. They came under fire when they reached Gloucester Street and they dispersed and entered different tenement houses. He was arrested in North Cumberland Street, with Patrick Touhy, who was a member of the Irish Citizen Army. He was deported to Stafford Jail on May 1st and interned in Frongoch until Christmas 1916.

He rejoined his unit in 1917, but suffered poor health following his internment in Frongoch. He was instructed to reform the IRB and was an active member until the Truce.

He lived at 15 Faulkner's Cottages, Old Kilmainham and was employed in the Stamp Dept, Dublin Castle. He later refused to sign the Roll of Honour.

Billy O'Neill died on May 10th 1952 and was buried at Glasnevin Cemetery.

References:

IMA, MSPC; *Sinn Féin Rebellion Handbook 1916*, Weekly Irish Times, (1917); *Sunday Press*, 11th May 1952, (dn).

Michael J. O'Rahilly (The O'Rahilly):
(1875 – 1916) Killed in Action.
G.H.Q. Staff. Roll of Honour

Michael O'Rahilly, The O'Rahilly, was born in Ballylongford, County Kerry on April 22nd 1875. He was educated at Clongowes and emigrated to the United States, in 1898. In 1909, he returned to Ireland, and in 1912 became a member of the Executive of the Gaelic League. A founder member of the Volunteers in 1913, he was involved in directing the landing of weapons at Howth, in July 1914. Because he was not a member of the IRB he was excluded from planning the Rising. He agreed with Eoin MacNeill in his efforts to stop the Rising and he travelled to Limerick with the countermanding order. When he returned to Dublin he found the fighting had started and he joined the GPO Garrison. He fought throughout the week from the upstairs floor and took charge of the fire fighting efforts when flames spread through the building. On Friday evening, he led an advance party of Volunteers from the GPO into Moore Street, where they came under heavy enemy fire. As he led a charge on the barricade at the top of the street he was wounded. Bleeding profusely, he made it to Sackville Lane, where he propped himself against a wall and wrote a note to his wife before he died. That note was reproduced on a memorial plaque erected where he died that was unveiled by his daughter-in-law, Bláthnaid Úi Rathaille, on April 29th 2005.

The O'Rahilly, who was forty one years old, left a wife and five children when he was killed.

References:

RH; Dorothy Macardle, *The Irish Republic*, (1937); Diarmaid Lynch, *The IRB and the 1916 Insurrection*, (1950); Max Caulfield, *The Easter Rebellion*, (1963); Marcus Bourke, *The O'Rahilly*, (1967); Aodhagán O'Rahilly, *Winding the Clock: The O'Rahilly and the 1916 Rising*, (1991); Desmond Fitzgerald, *Desmond's Rising*, (2006); Charles Townshend, *Easter 1916, the Irish Rebellion*, (2006); Ray Bateson, *They Died by Pearse's Side*, (2010); Charlie McGuire, *Seán McLoughlin: Ireland's Forgotten Revolutionary*, (2011).

Liam Ó Raogáin (Regan): (1888 – 1965)

Maynooth Company, Kildare Brigade. Roll of Honour

Liam O'Raogain was born in 1888 and was an Irish speaker from the Ring Gaeltacht, Co. Waterford. He was employed as a foreman in Ua Buachalla's shop in Maynooth, when he joined the local Volunteers. He left with the Maynooth Volunteers on Easter Monday and arrived at the GPO early the following morning. The Maynooth party were sent to Parliament Street, and he fought on the roof of the Royal Exchange Hotel. They were later recalled to the GPO, where he fought for the remainder of the week. He was deported to Knutsford Jail on May 1st, and then interned in Frongoch.

On his release he rejoined the reorganised local Volunteers and fought in the War of Independence. In 1920 he took part in the burning of the Maynooth Courthouse and the destruction of Maynooth RIC barracks. He was also involved in attacks on the RIC barracks in Kilcock, Celbridge and Salmon Leap. He was arrested by the military, but managed to escape and go on the run. Although he was a member of a flying column during the Truce, he did not take part in the fighting during the Civil War.

He moved to Kells and was manager of a grocery store there, until 1939. He then moved to Wexford, where he remained for the rest of his life.

Liam O'Raogain, of Bishop's Water, Wexford, died in St Anne's Hospital, Northbrook Road, Ranelagh, on May 16th 1965 and was buried at St Ibar's Cemetery, Crosstown, County Wexford, two days later.

References:

RH; IMA, MSPC; *Sinn Féin Rebellion Handbook 1916*, Weekly Irish Times, (1917); *Sunday Press*, 24th & 31st April 1960, (na); *Irish Independent* & *Irish Press*, 18th May 1965, (obits).

Aileen Mary O'Reilly (Mrs. Aileen O'Connor):
(1894 – 1973)

Cumann na mBan (Árd Craobh)

Aileen O'Reilly, from Drumcondra, was born in 1894. She was a member of Cumann na mBan, Árd Branch and she reported to the GPO on Easter Monday. She was sent across to the Hibernian Bank and helped with the cooking and first aid duties. On Tuesday she returned to the GPO and was sent home on Wednesday with Miss Foley to get some rest. On her return to the GPO on Thursday, she was stopped by British Troops at a cordon at Drumcondra Bridge, and was not allowed proceed to the city. Later that day she was visited by Annie O'Higgins, who was on a mission to Monaghan and instructed to remove arms and ammunition from the homes of local Volunteers who were fighting in the Rising. She travelled to a quarry in North County Dublin and burned some knapsacks and buried arms and ammunition. She then returned home and evaded capture.

In 1917 she did secretarial work at the Sinn Féin Offices in Dawson Street and was engaged in bringing parcels to Republican prisoners.

Aileen O'Connor, of 15 St Anne's, Merrion Road, died on September 10th 1973 and was buried at Deansgrange Cemetery.

References:
IMA, MSPC; *Irish Independent*, 11th September 1973, (dn).

Desmond O'Reilly: (1898 - 1969)
B. Coy, 1st Batt, Dublin Brigade

Desmond O'Reilly, of 181 North Circular Road, was one of five brothers who, along with their father, J.K. O'Reilly, took part in the Easter Rising. He joined B. Company, 1st Battalion, Dublin Brigade, in 1914 and took part in the Kilcoole and Howth gun running. He also took part in a raid for arms from the Redmond Volunteers at the North Wall, in 1915. On Easter Monday he reported to Cabra Bridge, North Circular Road and served there until Tuesday afternoon, when he withdrew to Glasnevin Cemetery and from there, to the GPO that evening. He fought on the roof of the GPO for most of the week, and left with the Garrison when the building was evacuated on Friday evening. After the surrender he was deported to Stafford Jail on May 1st and interned in Frongoch until July 26th 1916.

On his release from internment, he rejoined his unit and took part in many engagements during the War of Independence. He was attached to the 1st Brigade's Intellegence Staff, in 1919 and was involved in the arrest and execution of a spy known as "Hoppy" Byrne in May 1921. He took the Republican side in the Civil War, and was appointed captain by Oscar Traynor, during the fighting in O'Connell Street, in June 1922, where he took over the Hamman Hotel and later Findlater's in O'Connell Street. He was later in charge of the attack on the Free State Garrison at Bridgeman's Corner, when prisoners were taken. He was captured in July 1922 and interned at Mountjoy Jail and later in Newbridge, where he took part in a number of hunger strikes and was released in December 1923.

He later refused to sign the Roll of Honour. He lived at Balkhill Road, Howth Summit and employed as a buyer for Switzer's & Co., Grafton Street, for many years.

Desmond O'Reilly died suddenly near his home in Howth, on August 4th 1969 and was buried at St Fintan's Cemetery, Sutton.

References:

IMA, MSPC; *Sinn Féin Rebellion Handbook* 1916, Weekly Irish Times, (1917); *Irish Press*, 5th August 1969, (obit).

Donal O'Reilly: (1902 – 1968)

Fianna Éireann

Donal O'Reilly was born in 1902 and resided at 181 North Circular Road. He was a member of Fianna Éireann and he reported to the GPO on Easter Monday. Because of his youth, he was not allowed in and on his way home, witnessed the looting in the streets. He returned to the following day and distributed copies of the *"War News"*. Having gained entry, he was then sent out with dispatches. On Thursday he made his way across Sackville Street, through Marlborough Street, up Hutton's Place and eventually to derelict buildings in Berekley Road, where he hid until Sunday morning. His father, J.K. and his four brothers, Desmond, Kevin, Sam and Thomas, fought at Cabra and later in the GPO during Easter Week.

He fought in the War of Independence and served with the 5th Battalion, Engineers. In the Civil War he took the Republican side, and was in the Four Courts, in 1922. He was imprisoned in Newbridge Barracks and Mountjoy Jail and went on hunger strike.

During the Spanish Civil War he fought with Frank Ryan and the Irish Unit of the International Brigade, and was wounded at the Battle of Cordova, in December 1936.

When he returned to Ireland, he became a trade union activist and was on the Executive Committee of the Plasterers' Union. He was also a delegate to the Dublin Trades Council and the Irish Congress of Trade Unions.

Donal O'Reilly of 31 Cabra Park, Phibsboro, died suddenly on April 7th 1968 and was buried at Glasnevin Cemetery.

References:

Michael O'Riordan, *The Connolly Column: the Story of the Irishmen who fought in the Ranks of the International Brigades*, (1979); *Irish Press*, 9th April 1968, (obit).

John O'Reilly: (1896 - 1946)

F. Coy, 2nd Batt, Dublin Brigade. Roll of Honour

John O'Reilly was born in 1896 and resided at 3 Ballybough Lane. He was a member of F. Company, 2nd Battalion, Dublin Brigade and reported to Father Mathew Park on Easter Monday. He was in the party, led by Captain Frank Henderson that held Ballybough Bridge until Tuesday evening, when they were ordered into the GPO. During the week he was engaged in erecting barricades, clearing looters and manning the windows. On Friday he helped to fight the fire and recalled being addressed by Seán MacDiarmada and P.H. Pearse before the evacuation into Henry Place. He spent Friday night boring holes through the walls of the Moore Street houses. After the surrender he was deported to Stafford Jail on May 1st and interned in Frongoch until July 18th 1916.

After his release from internment, he rejoined his unit and fought in the War of Independence. In 1920 he was involved in the ambush of British Forces at Malahide Road, and took part in the attack on the London North Western Railway Hotel, North Wall, in 1921. In May 1922 he joined the Criminal Investigation Dept and served through the Civil War. He joined An Garda Síochana in 1924, and served until his death.

John O'Reilly, of 23 Croydon Green, died as the result of an accident on January 23rd 1946 and was buried at Mount Jerome Cemetery, Harold's Cross.

References:
RH; IMA, MSPC; NLI, *Lynch Papers*, (Ms 11,131); *Irish Press*, 24th January 1946, (obit).

John Kevin (J.K.) O'Reilly: (1860 – 1929)

B. Coy, 1st Batt, Dublin Brigade. Roll of Honour

J.K. O'Reilly was born in Virginia, Co. Cavan in 1860. He was educated locally and later moved to Belfast, where he worked as a newspaper reporter. In 1890, he opened a public house in Little Bray, Co. Wicklow, called the Coach & Horses and later married Kathleen Curran, a relative of Sarah Curran.

He went to the United States in 1900 to raise funds for the Irish Brigade fighting in the Boer War. He also wrote the popular ballad, *"Wrap the Green Flag Around Me Boys"* and was a friend of Arthur Griffith and Willie Rooney, a founder of the Celtic Literary Society. He was a member of the IRB, and was a steward at the inaugural meeting of the Irish Volunteers at the Rotunda in 1913. Along with his five sons, Kevin, Sam, Desmond, Thomas and Donal, he was a member of B. Company, 2nd Battalion, Dublin Brigade. On Easter Monday they all mobilised and reported to the 1st Battalion HQ at Columcille Hall, Blackhall Street, with the exception of fourteen year old Donal. They then proceeded to Cabra Bridge, on the North Circular Road and served there until the outpost came under heavy artillery fire. He and his sixteen year old son, Tommy, retreated to the Father Mathew Hall, in Church Street and on Wednesday they went to the GPO, where they remained until the evacuation on Friday evening. He was deported to Wandsworth Jail on May 9th and interned in Frongoch until Christmas 1916.

After his release from internment , he returned to work in accounting. He became a friend of Michael Collins and was appointed Head of the Financial Dept. in the 1st Dail.

J.K. O'Reilly, of 181 North Circular Road, died on April 26th 1929 and was buried at Glasnevin Cemetery.

References:

RH; Cavan County Council, *Official Guide to County Cavan, a profile*, (1984); Seán Cronin, *Our Own Red Blood*, (1976); *Irish Independent*, 29th April 1929, (dn).

Joseph O'Reilly: (- 1970)

Irish Citizen Army, (North Wall Section). Roll of Honour

Joseph O'Reilly resided at 38 Commons Street, off Sheriff Street, and was a dock worker. He was a member of the Irish Citizen Army and on Easter Monday he commandeered a funeral carriage to convey guns and ammunition from Liberty Hall to the GPO. He manned the window above the main entrance of the GPO during the week, and on Friday he helped with the removal of grenades and explosives. He was manning a barricade in Henry Place when the surrender was announced. On May 1st he was deported to Stafford Jail and interned in Frongoch until Christmas 1916.

He rejoined his unit on his release from internment and fought in the War of Independence. He took part in the fight with the police in Dawson Street, in May 1919, and was involved in the protection of Liberty Hall in November of that year. He served until 1920 when, owing to his wife's illness, he took no further part.

He was a civilian employee of the Army Corps of Engineers and lived for many years at 2 Cards Lane, Spring Garden Street, and later at 3 Croke Villas, Ballybough.

Joseph O'Reilly died on January 11th 1970 and was buried at Kilbarrack Cemetery.

References:

RH; IMA, MSPC; NLI, *Lynch Papers*, (Ms 11,131) & *William O'Brien Papers*, (Ms 15,673); Ann Matthews, *The Irish Citizen Army*, (2014); *Evening Herald*, 12th January 1970, (dn).

Joseph (Joe) O'Reilly: (1893 – 1943)

London Company, (Kimmage Garrison). Roll of Honour

Joe O'Reilly was born in 1893 and left his native Bantry for London, in 1911. He joined the Postal Service there, where he met Michael Collins and joined the London Volunteers. With other members of the London Volunteers, he returned to Dublin early in 1916 and joined the Kimmage Volunteer Camp. He fought in the GPO throughout Easter Week, and after the surrender he gave his old family address at Chapel Lane, Bantry, to the authorities. He was deported to Stafford Jail on May 1st and was interned in Frongoch until Christmas 1916.

He became assistant to Michael Collins when he was appointed secretary of the National Aid Association. On the establishment of the Free State Army, he was raised to the rank of colonel and become Michael Collins' Aide-de-Camp and the close association between the two men lasted until Michael Collins' death. He later served as Aide-de-Camp to WT Cosgrave in his capacity as first President of the Executive Council, and was later appointed Director of Purchases under the Commissioners of Public Works.

Joe O'Reilly resided at 134 South Circular Road and passed away at a private nursing home on August 8th 1943.

References:

RH; IMA, MSPC; Margery Forster, *Michael Collins, the Lost Leader*, (1972); Tim Pat Coogan, *Michael Collins, a biography*, (1990); *Irish Independent*, 9th August 1943, (obit & *W.T. Cosgrave tribute*); *Irish Press*, 9th August 1943, (obit).

Mary (Molly) O'Reilly: (1899 – 1950)

Irish Citizen Army. Roll of Honour

Molly O'Reilly was born in 1899 and was chosen by James Connolly to hoist the green flag with the gold embossed Starry Plough above Liberty Hall, during a ceremonial parade on Palm Sunday, a week before the Rising. It was the first time James Connolly appeared in public in uniform. Because she was so small, she was lifted onto a chair to hoist the flag. She spent Easter Week as a despatch courier between the GPO and City Hall and others outposts.

After the Rising, she went to Yorkshire to study

nursing, but returned to Ireland during War of Independence and joined Cumann na mBan, becoming active with the IRA as a safe house organiser. She was instructed to take employment in the United Services Club, where she gathered intelligence on the English Officer membership and she also worked at the Bonne Bouche Club, where she was able to identify thirty to thirty five Officers there. She took the Republican side in the Civil War and reported to Commandant Paddy O'Doherty in Moran's Hotel. She remained there for a week and was later arrested on the orders of the Minister for Defence, Richard Mulcahy. After eight months imprisonment, she went on hunger strike for sixteen days, before her release in 1923.

In 1926, she married Edward Corcoran, who was a native of Clonmel, County Tipperary. He was a member of the IRA, who had taken part in the Custom House raid in 1921, with the Dublin Brigade. They resided at 45 Leix Road, Cabra, where they set up the Roger Casement Cumann of Fianna Fail.

Molly Corcoran died on October 4th 1950 and was buried in Glasnevin Cemetery.

References:

RH; IMA, MSPC; NLI, *William O'Brien Papers*, (Ms 15,673); Max Caulfield, *The Easter Rebellion*, (1963); Ann Matthews, *The Irish Citizen Army*, (2014); *Irish Press*, 6th October 1950, (obit); *Irish Daily Mail*, 10th April 2009, (na).

Michael W. O'Reilly: (1889 – 1971)

F. Coy, 2nd Batt, Dublin Brigade. Roll of Honour

Michael O'Reilly was born in Stillorgan on December 11th 1889. He was educated at Stillorgan National School and the CBS, Dun Laoghaire. On leaving school, he was apprenticed to Bewley's and worked in their Blackrock and Henry Street branches. In 1910 he joined the Prudential Insurance Company as an agent for the Dalkey area, and he joined the IRB the following year. He married Cathleen Cooney on January 25th 1911 and they resided at Maryville Terrace, Dalkey. They moved to 30 O'Connell Villas, Fairview, in September 1913 after he was promoted to Assistant Superintendent for the Prudential Insurance Company for the Clontarf district. He joined the Volunteers in November, 1913 and was elected Captain of F. Company, 2nd Battalion. He was also involved in the Howth gun-running. Early in 1916 he was transferred to GHQ as assistant adjutant of the Dublin Brigade. He was appointed Aide de Camp to Commandant Joseph Plunkett on Easter Monday and on entering the GPO he organised the barricading of the windows and the erection of barricades at Abbey Street. He went with Paddy McGrath to 46 Parnell Square on Tuesday and brought back the National Volunteers arms and ammunition to the GPO. On Wednesday and Thursday he was in charge of the Volunteers at the ground floor windows, and on Friday he supervised efforts to control the fire. He was among the last to evacuate the GPO, and he helped bring the wounded from Henry Street to a cottage at the corner of Moore Street, where Dr. Ryan had set up his quarters. While in Moore Street, he offered his handkerchief, used by Elizabeth O'Farrell, as the white flag for the initial surrender. After the surrender he was deported to Knutsford Jail on May 1st and interned in Reading Jail and Frongoch until Christmas 1916. He was elected Camp Commandant in the North Camp in Frongoch.

He went to Wexford when he was released from internment, where he worked for the Royal Liver Friendly Society, in charge of the Enniscorthy district. He also joined the local Volunteers and became Brigade Commandant. In October 1917 he was elected to the Executive Council of the Volunteers. He chaired the first meeting in January 1918, when the formation of the New Ireland Assurance Society was proposed and he was instrumental in drawing up the rules of the society.

He was also served as a director on the boards of the Irish National Insurance Company, Solus Teo and was president of the Federation of Irish Manufacturers in 1941 & 1942. The National University of Ireland conferred him with a Degree of Doctor of Laws, Honoris Causa, for his role in economic development of Ireland, in April 1964.

Michael W. O'Reilly, L.L.D., F.C.I.I., P.C, of 59 Ailesbury Road, Ballsbridge, died on November 21st 1971 and was interred in the family vault at St Andrew's Church, Westland Row.

References:

RH; IMA, MSPC; IMA, BMH (WS 806); NLI, *Lynch Papers*, (Ms 11,131); *Capuchin Annual*, 1967; Max Caulfield, *The Easter Rebellion*, (1963); Thomas Coffey, *Agony at Easter*, (1969); Peter De Rosa, *Rebels: the Irish Rising of 1916*, (1991); *Irish Independent*, 21st February 1964, (na, *interview*); *Irish Press*, 22nd November 1971, (obit); *Irish Press*, 3rd December 1971 (app).

Samuel (Sam) O'Reilly: (1896 – 1988)

B. Coy, 1st Batt, Dublin Brigade

Sam O'Reilly was born in 1896 and resided at 181 North Circular Road. Like his father, J.K., he was a member of the IRB and was present at the formation of the Volunteers at the Rotunda in November 1913. He was a member of B. Company, 1st Battalion and took part in the Howth gun running. He fought in the Rising with his father and four brothers. On Easter Monday he was in charge of a party that was sent to cut the railway lines near Broadstone, to prevent trains carrying troops from entering the city. When the barricade they manned in Phibsboro was destroyed by artillery fire, they retreated to the GPO. At the evacuation of the GPO on Friday evening, P.H. Pearse ordered him the carry out a final search and he was the last Volunteer to leave the building. He was deported to Knutsford Jail on May 1st and interned in Frongoch.

During the conscription crisis he was one of the IRB men in the House of Commons gallery with orders to shoot British Ministers, if the order for conscription in Ireland was passed. He spent time during the War of Independence, as a gun runner and courier for the IRB, travelling around the world as a seaman. He was arrested in 1920 and interned in Mountjoy Jail, where he went on hunger strike.

In 1922 he emigrated to the United States and lived in New York.

Sam O'Reilly died in Ronkonkomo, New York, on June 30th 1988.

References:

Sinn Féin Rebellion Handbook 1916, Weekly Irish Times, (1917); Seán Cronin, *Our Own Red Blood*, (1976); *Irish Press*, 26th April 1977, (*Proclamation to Sam O'Reilly in New York City Hall*); *Irish Times*, 2nd August 1988, (obit*).

Thomas (Tommy) O'Reilly: (1900 - 1985)
Fianna Éireann

Tommy O'Reilly was born in 1900 and resided at 181 North Circular Road. He joined Fianna Éireann in 1913, and on Easter Monday he accompanied his father and three brothers to the 1st Battalion HQ at the Columcille Hall, Blackhall Street. From there they went to the outpost at Cabra Bridge and he helped erect the barricade. On Tuesday, when the position came under heavy artillery fire, he and his father retreated to Father Mathew Hall, Church Street, which was part of the Four Courts Garrison. On Wednesday evening, they both went to the GPO, where he spent the night. He was sent home on Thursday evening, and on Friday he was prevented from returning to the GPO by the military cordon.

In 1917 he joined to B. Company, 1st Battalion, Dublin Brigade, and was involved in many operations. He transferred to GHQ as part of Michael Collins's staff in March 1921 and took part in the arrest and execution of a spy, known as "Hoppy" Byrne, in May 1921. He was later arrested and interned until December 1921. In the Civil War he fought on the Republican side, and was involved in the occupation of the Four Courts. He was arrested at the fall of the Four Courts and interned until December 1923, along with his brothers, Desmond and Donal.

He was an employed at Lower Gardiner Street Employment Exchange for many years and lived at 81 Mobhi Road.

Tommy O'Reilly was residing at 79 Gracepark Road, Drumcondra, when he died on August 27th 1985 and was buried in Glasnevin Cemetery.

References:

IMA, MSPC; *Irish Press*, 27th August 1985, (obit).

Thomas O'Reilly: (- 1916). Killed in Action
Irish Citizen Army, (Dorset St Section). Roll of Honour

Thomas O'Reilly, an electrician from 43 Geraldine Street, was a member of the St James's Brass and Reed Band and the Emeralds GFC. He joined the Irish Citizen Army, in 1915 and was attached to the Dorset Street Section. He left Liberty Hall on Easter Monday for the GPO, and fought there throughout the week. His brother, John, fought in the City Hall area, while another brother, Patrick, fought with the St Stephen's Green Garrison. On Thursday he was badly wounded in the abdomen. He was taken to Jervis Street Hospital, where he later died.

Thomas O'Reilly was buried in the St Paul's Section in Glasnevin Cemetery on May 1st 1916.

References:
RH; *Catholic Bulletin*, July 1916; Ray Bateson, *They Died by Pearse's Side*, (2010).

William O'Reilly: (1896 - 1951)
E. Coy, 4th Batt, Dublin Brigade. Roll of Honour

William O'Reilly, of Rathfarnham Castle, was born in 1896. He joined E. Company, 4th Battalion, Dublin Brigade at its formation in 1913. He reported to the GPO on Easter Monday and was stationed on the roof. He fought there for the rest of the week, until the evacuation on Friday evening. He was deported to Stafford Jail and interned in Frongoch until Christmas 1916.

On his release from internment he continued to play a part in the War of Independence. He transferred to A. Company, 4th Battalion, in 1917 and took part in armed patrols and raids for arms. He was arrested in November 1920 and interned until December 1921. In 1922 he joined the Free State Army with the rank of Colonel and was ADC to Governor General Healy. He left the army in 1926 to join the ESB. After World War Two he resided at St Bernard's, Carrickmines and he became a sales agent for an English firm of textile manufacturers.

Col. William J. O'Reilly died in St Michael's Hospital, Dun Laoghaire, following an accident, when the car he was in crashed into a wall at Shankill, on January 28th 1951 and he was buried in Deansgrange Cemetery.

References:
RH; IMA, MSPC; *Sinn Féin Rebellion Handbook* 1916, Weekly Irish Times, (1917); *Irish Independent*, 29th January 1951, (obit).

Joseph O'Rorke: (1893 – 1980)
B. Coy, 2nd Batt, Dublin Brigade

Joe O'Rorke was born in Dublin in 1893 and was educated at Westland Row CBS and later O'Connell Schools, North Richmond Street. He was sworn into the Clarence Mangan Branch of the IRB in 1911 and joined the Volunteers, in 1913. In 1916 he resided at 14 Carlingford Terrace, Drumcondra and was a member of B. Company, 2nd Battalion, Dublin Brigade. On Easter Monday he reported to the 2nd Battalion Headquarters at Father Mathew Park, and took part in the action in the Fairview and Ballybough area. He moved with his unit into GPO on Tuesday evening and fought there for the rest of the week. After the surrender he was deported to Stafford Jail on May 1st and interned in Frongoch until Christmas 1916.

He fought in the War of Independence and took the Republican side in the Civil War. At the fall of the Four Courts in July 1922, he appears in the well known photograph of the wounded Republican being helped into an ambulance by Free State soldiers. He was taken to the Mater Hospital, from where he escaped.

He emigrated to South Africa in 1925, before returning to Dublin seven years later. He was an invalid for twenty three years. He refused to sign the Roll of Honour.

Joe O'Rorke, of 29 Newbridge Avenue, Sandymount, died on July 16th 1980.

References:
IMA, MSPC; *DHR*, December 1980; *Sinn Féin Rebellion Handbook* 1916, Weekly Irish Times, (1917).

Michael O'Shea: (1881 - 1939)
Liverpool Company, (Kimmage Garrison)

Michael O'Shea was born in Tipperary Town, in 1881 and went to work in England in the years before the Rising. He joined the IRB and the Volunteers in Liverpool and returned to Dublin, in January 1916. He joined the Volunteer Camp at Larkfield, Kimmage and was engaged in munition making. While at Kimmage, he fell twenty feet from a ladder and was injured. He fought in the GPO throughout Easter Week. After the surrender, he was deported Knutsford Prison on May 1st and interned in Frongoch, until Christmas 1916.

In 1917 he re-joined the Volunteers, and returned to Tipperary in December 1918. He transferred to the Tipperary 2nd Brigade and was involved in a number of operations, including the raid on the Military Stores at Limerick Junction. He was later elected lieutenant and sent to Dublin to purchase arms from Phil Shanahan. During the Truce, he took part in the occupation of the Military Barracks in Tipperary Town. At the outbreak of the Civil War he took the Republican side and joined Ryan's Flying Column. He was captured in Aherlow, and interned in Tintown Camp. He went on hunger strike for twenty five days, before he was released in November 1923.

His suffered poor health for many years, which was attributed to the head injury he received at Kimmage before the Rising, and to the effects of the hunger strike.

Michael O'Shea, of 52 O'Connell Road, Tipperary Town, died on December 30th 1939 and was buried in St Mary's, the old cemetery in Tipperary Town.

References:

IMA, MSPC; Ann Matthews, *The Kimmage Garrison 1916*, (2010); *Irish Press*, 1st January 1940, (obit).

Gearóid O'Sullivan: (1891 – 1948)
Volunteer, G.H.Q. Staff. Roll of Honour

Gearóid O'Sullivan was born in Skibbereen, County Cork, in 1891. He came to Dublin and was educated at St Patrick's College, Drumcondra and UCD, where he graduated with a MA in Celtic Studies. In 1913 he resided at 44 Mountjoy Street when he joined the Volunteers. He was a fluent Irish speaker and taught at the Keating Branch of the Gaelic League. On Easter Monday he entered the GPO as Aide de Camp to Seán MacDiarmada. Early that afternoon, between one and two o'clock, he hoisted the Tricolour over the GPO and he fought from there the remainder of the week. After the surrender, he was deported and then interned in Frongoch, until Christmas 1916.

He took part in the War of Independence and in 1920 he became Adjutant General of the IRA. He joined the Free State Army after the Treaty and held the same rank. In 1924 he resigned his position as a result of the Army Mutiny and studied Law. He was elected Cumann na nGael TD for Carlow/Kilkenny, (1921-23) and Dublin County, (1927-1937). In 1927 he was called to the Bar and was appointed Judge Advocate General, until 1932. He also taught for many years both in Dublin and at Knockbeg College, Carlow.

Gearóid O'Sullivan died at his residence at St Kevin's Park, Dartry, on March 26th 1948 and was buried at Glasnevin Cemetery.

References:

RH; IMA, MSPC; Seán O'Mahony, *Frongoch: University of Revolution*, (1987); John P. Duggan, *A History of the Irish Army*, (1991); Gerard MacAtasney, *Seán MacDiarmada: the Mind of a Revolution*, (2004); Tim Cadogan & Jeremiah Falvey, *A Biographical Dictionary of Cork*, (2006); Ray Bateson, *Memorials of the Easter Rising*, (2013); *Irish Press*, 26th March 1948, (dn); *Irish Independent*, 27th March 1948, (obit).

James O'Sullivan: (1865 - 1920)

Volunteer. G.H.Q. Publicity Staff. Roll of Honour

James O'Sullivan resided at 8 Little Denmark Street, and was an old member of the printer's union, the Dublin Typographical Provident Society. He was one of the printers of the *Irish War News* issued from the GPO during Easter Week. He was part of a four man team, under the command of Joe Stanley, who commandeered O'Keefe's Printing Works, Halston Street, for this purpose. 12,000 copies were printed on Tuesday from a manuscript written by P.H. Pearse, while a second, *War Bulletin*, appeared on Thursday of Easter Week.

James O'Sullivan died in Harold's Cross Hospice on July 6th 1920.

References:

RH; John O'Connor, *The 1916 Proclamation*, (1999); Tom Reilly, *Joe Stanley: Printer to the Rising*, (2005); *Evening Herald*, 7th July 1920, (dn).

Seamus (Jim) O'Sullivan: (1891 - 1974)

Captain. B. Coy, 1st Batt, Dublin Brigade. Roll of Honour

Jim O'Sullivan was born in Cork City, in 1891 and resided at 23 Arranmore Avenue, Phibsboro, in 1916. He was a member of the McHale Branch of the Gaelic League and he joined the Volunteers in November 1913, at the Rotunda. He took part in the Howth gun-running in 1914, and became one of Commandant Edward Daly's closest friends. Some weeks before the Rising, he was sent to organise the Wexford Brigade and did similar work in County Dublin and Cavan. On Easter Monday members of B. Company, 1st Battalion, under his command, erected barricades at Cabra Road and at the North Circular Road. The following day a battery of four eighteen-pounder guns let loose on the Volunteer positions, and the barricades were destroyed under the heavy artillery barrage. He withdrew his men, sending some to join Thomas Ashe in Ashbourne, while he and others joined the GPO Garrison and some were also captured. After arriving in the GPO on Tuesday, he was put in charge of the roof and top floor of the building by P.H. Pearse. He was among the group that followed The O'Rahilly into Moore Street on Friday evening. After the surrender, he was sentenced to death, which was commuted to eight years penal servitude. He served time in Pentonville, Lewes, Portland and Dartmoor Jails and was released as part of the general amnesty on June 16th 1917.

He continued his part in the War of Independence and was again arrested, serving time in Belfast Jail. While on the run in 1918, he went to Limerick, where he married

Laura Daly, the sister Commandant Edward Daly, and he lived for a time in the attic of the Daly's home to evade the authorities. Laura Daly also served in the GPO in Easter Week. They raised two boys and two girls, and Michael Collins was godfather to their son, John.

He managed the Daly's bakehouse and later opened a restaurant with Laura at 3 O'Connell Street and made a great contribution to the commercial life of the city. In the 1930's he was employed by the Hospitals Trust in Dublin, before returning to manage their Limerick office. He took up an administrative position, when his son Ned opened O'Sullivan's Shoes, at 114 O'Connell Street, Limerick.

Jim O'Sullivan died on February 26th 1974 and was buried in Mount Saint Lawrence Cemetery, Limerick.

References:

RH; IMA, MSPC; *Catholic Bulletin*, July 1917; Kathleen Clarke, *Revolutionary Woman*, (1991); Helen Litton, *Ned Daly*, (16Lives series, 2013); *Evening Herald*, 26th February 1974, (dn); *Limerick Leader*, 2nd March 1974, (obit).

William O'Toole: (1887 – 1966)

Irish Citizen Army. Roll of Honour

William O'Toole was born in Wicklow, in 1891 and resided at 31 Lower Erne Street, in 1916. He was employed as a dock worker and was a corporal in the Irish Citizen Army. On Easter Monday he left Liberty Hall in the afternoon and reported to the GPO. He served there until Tuesday night when he was sent to the Metropole Hotel, under the command of Oscar Traynor and he fought there until the garrison returned to the GPO on Friday. After the evacuation of the GPO on Friday evening, he was wounded in the leg in Moore Lane, and was taken to the hospital at Dublin Castle on Saturday. He was deported to Wakefield Prison on May 6th and was interned in Frongoch until July 18th 1916.

On his release from internment, he re-joined the Irish Citizen Army and served until the Truce, in 1921.

William O'Toole, of 237 St Teresa's Gardens, Donore Avenue, took part in the 1916 Jubilee Celebrations in Dublin, shortly before his death on July 23rd 1966.

References:

RH; IMA, MSPC; NLI, *William O'Brien Papers*, (Ms 15,673); Ann Matthews, *The Irish Citizen Army*, (2014); *Sunday Press*, 24th July 1966, (dn).

Matthew (Matt) Parnell: (1899 – 1918)

F. Coy, 2nd Batt, Dublin Brigade. Roll of Honour

Matt Parnell was born in Dublin in 1899, and was educated at Little Strand Street School. In 1916 he was living at 38 Susanville Road, Drumcondra, and was a member of F. Company, 2nd Battalion, Dublin Brigade. On Easter Monday he joined his company in the Fairview area and proceeded to the GPO with them on Tuesday evening. He was sent to the Imperial Hotel, and fought there until the garrison was forced out when the building was engulfed by the fire on Thursday. During the evacuation of the Imperial Hotel, he fell twenty feet from a window and later made his way to North Cumberland Street, where he was captured. He was deported to Wandsworth Jail on May 9th, but was released soon after because of his youth.

Matt Parnell was just twenty two years of age when he passed away on July 12th 1918 and was buried at Glasnevin Cemetery. It was believed that his early death was caused by his fall evacuating the Imperial Hotel and as a result of his imprisonment.

References:

RH; IMA, MSPC; *Catholic Bulletin*, December 1918; Ray Bateson, *They Died by Pearse's Side*, (2010); *Irish Independent*, 13th July 1918, (dn).

William (Liam) Parr (alias, Power): (1892 - 1934)

Manchester Company, (Kimmage Garrison)

Liam, the eldest son of Christopher and Stella Parr, was born in 1892 and resided at 11 Herberton Lane, Rialto. As a youth, he learned to play the war pipes and to speak the Irish language. In 1911 at the age of nineteen, he moved to Stockport and worked as a shop porter for an aunt. While in the Manchester region, he joined the Gaelic League and helped form a company of Volunteers. A few months before the Rising, he returned to Dublin and joined the Volunteers at Larkfield, Kimmage. He used the alias Liam Power, and before Easter Week he stayed at 28 North Frederick Street, with a small group of Kimmage Garrison men. He attended a céilidhe at the Fowler's Hall, Parnell Square on Easter Sunday with Gilbert Lynch, another Manchester Volunteer and he reported to the GPO on the following day and fought there, throughout Easter Week. There was a report of him fighting with Eamonn Ceannt in the South Dublin Union, but this seems to be inaccurate. There was another Liam Power, one of three brothers from Bluebell, who fought with the Marrowbone Garrison. After the surrender he was deported to Knutsford Jail on May 1st and interned in Frongoch until Christmas, 1916. He was also sent to Wandsworth Jail for interrogation. While in Frongoch he was listed as singing, the *"Vales of Arklow"* in a concert held on August 8th.

On his release from internment, he resumed his activities with the Volunteers in Dublin. In 1917 he accompanied Eamonn deValera and Larry Ginnell on the election campaign in East Clare. He continued to play the war pipes and became a member of the James Connolly Pipe Band, which later was absorbed into the Fintan Lalor Pipe Band. In 1918, while still serving with the Dublin Brigade, he became associated with the Irish National Insurance Company, College Green. He was active on Bloody Sunday and soon afterwards he returned to Stockport. He later married and raised three children in Stockport and was employed as a plumber.

Liam Parr's health deteriorated and he died in 1934.

References:

Liam Parr private papers, (ref, *Robin Stocks*); *Sinn Féin Rebellion Handbook 1916*, Weekly Irish Times, (1917); John Heuston OP, *Headquarters Battalion Handbook 1916*, (1966).

P.H. Pearse: (1879 – 1916). Executed Leader

Commandant General, Commander in Chief, Army of the Irish Republic. Director of Organisation of the Irish Volunteers.

P.H. Pearse was born on November 10th 1879, at 27 Great Brunswick Street, the son of an English father and an Irish mother. His London born father was a monumental sculptor and his mother was a native of Nobber, County Meath. He was educated at Westland Row CBS, the Royal University of Ireland and King's Inns. In 1895 he joined the Gaelic League, reflecting a deep interest in the Irish language and its revival. He was called to the bar, but never practised. He became editor of *An Claidheamh Solus*, the official journal of the Gaelic League and lectured in Irish at UCD. To improve his Irish, he made frequent trips to the Gaeltacht. He supported Sinn Féin and contributed to the *United Irishman*, edited by Arthur Griffith. In 1908 he founded St Enda's, a bi-lingual school for boys, at Cullenwood House, Ranelagh. Two years later the school moved to the Hermitage, Rathfarnham, where the teaching staff included Thomas McDonagh. In December 1913 Bulmer Hobson swore him into the IRB and he was co-opted on to the Supreme Council and was elected to the Provisional Committee of the Irish Volunteers. During the Lockout in 1913, he spoke out publicly in favour of the workers. In February 1914, he went to the United States to raise funds for St Enda's and, with the support of John Devoy and Joseph McGarrity, gave lectures in New York and Philadelphia. He delivered the oration at the grave of the Fenian, Jeremiah O'Donovan Rossa, at Glasnevin, in August 1915.

On Easter Monday, as Commandant General and Commander in Chief of the Army of the Irish Republic, he read the Proclamation to the public outside the GPO. During the occupation of the GPO he left military decisions to James Connolly, a former soldier. Throughout the week he rallied and encouraged the members of the garrison. On Easter Tuesday evening, when sixty five men from the Fairview area arrived, he stood on a table and addressed them with a stirring oration. He drafted and issued the *Irish War News* from the GPO on Tuesday and *the War Bulletin* on Thursday. After the evacuation of the GPO on Friday evening, and having spent that night in the Moore Street houses, he decided to surrender on Saturday afternoon to prevent the further loss of life.

P.H. Pearse was executed by firing squad on May 3rd in Kilmainham Jail and buried in a quicklime grave in Arbour Hill.

References:

RH; Louis Le Roux, *Patrick H. Pearse*, (*translated by Desmond Ryan*, 1932); Dorothy Macardle, *The Irish Republic*, (1937); *Dublin's Fighting Story*, (1948); Desmond Ryan, *The Rising: the Complete Story of the Rising*, (1949); Max Caulfield, *The Easter Rebellion*, (1963); Thomas Coffey, *Agony at Easter*, (1969); Xavier Carty, *In Bloody Protest: the Tragedy of Pearse*, (1978); Ruth Dudley Edwards, *Patrick Pearse: the Triumph of Failure*, (1990); Michael Foy & Brian Barton, *The Easter Rising*, (1999); Charles Townshend, *Easter 1916, the Irish Rebellion*, (2005); Clair Willis, *Dublin 1916, the Siege of the GPO*, (2009); Ray Bateson, *They Died by Pearse's Side*, (2010); Brian Crowley, *Patrick Pearse: a Life in Pictures*, (2013).

William (Willie) Pearse: (1881 – 1916). Executed Leader

Staff Captain, G.H.Q. & E. Company, 4th Batt, Dublin Brigade.
Roll of Honour

Willie Pearse was born on April 15th 1881, at 27 Great Brunswick Street. He was the younger brother of P.H. Pearse, and was educated at Westland Row CBS. He studied sculpture and art at the Metropolitan School of Art in Dublin and also in Paris. When his father died in 1900, he took over the running of the family monumental sculpture business for several years. He became an art teacher, when P.H. Pearse founded St Enda's College, Rathfarnham. He was a member of the Gaelic League and the IRB. In 1913 he joined the Volunteers, becoming a captain in E. Company, 4th Battalion, Dublin Brigade.

On Easter Monday he entered the GPO by his brother's side, as his Aide de Camp. After the surrender he was detained in Richmond Barracks, where he was court marshalled and sentenced to death.

Willie Pearse was executed by firing squad in Kilmainham Jail on May 4th 1916.

References:

RH; Max Caulfield, *The Easter Rebellion*, (1963); Thomas Coffey, *Agony at Easter*, (1969); Xavier Carty, *In Bloody Protest: the Tragedy of Patrick Pearse*, (1978); Ruth Dudley Edwards, *Patrick Pearse: the Triumph of Failure*, (1990); Charles Townshend, *Easter 1916, the Irish Rebellion*, (2005); Ray Bateson, *They Died by Pearse's Side*, (2010).

Liam Pedlar: (1886 - 1963)

Volunteer, (Philadelphia). Roll of Honour

Liam Pedlar was born in Downpatrick, County Down, in 1886 and went to work in Glasgow at a young age. While in Glasgow he joined the IRB and in 1910 he emigrated to the United States. He joined Clan na nGael in Philadelphia and became an American citizen. He returned to Glasgow and came to Dublin on Good Friday 1916, to take part in the Rising. On Easter Monday he reported to the GPO, and was stationed at the Henry Street side of the building. He was sent to the wireless station at Reis's Chambers on Tuesday, and later served in the Dublin Bread Company Building until Thursday, when he returned to the GPO. After the surrender he was deported to Wandsworth Jail on May 9th and interned in Frongoch until Christmas 1916.

He joined G. Company, 3rd Battalion, in 1917 and was later arrested and interned in Oxford Jail before his release in June of that year. In 1918 he was deported to the United States, but returned to Ireland shortly afterwards. He was arrested and sentenced to four months imprisonment and again deported to America. Before his deportation, he took legal action against the Head of the Dublin Metropolitan Police for money taken from him on his arrest, and won his case after it been heard by the House of Lords. He worked with Éamon deValera on the Dáil Loan Campaign in America, in 1919. He also assisted Harry Boland and Seán Nunan in the gathering of arms in America, and was in charge of the transportation of Thompson submachine guns to Ireland. In December 1921 he returned to Dublin to take part in the final Treaty discussions. He took the anti-Treaty side in the Civil War and fought in Barry's Hotel and the Hamman Hotel.

He was appointed the first general secretary of Fianna Fáil, a position he held until he joined the *Irish Press*, in 1931. He was circulation manager of the *Irish Press* and held the position until his death.

Liam Pedlar died on December 29th 1963 and was buried at Glasnevin Cemetery.

References:

RH; IMA, MSPC; Gerard MacAtasney, *Seán MacDiarmada: the Mind of a Revolution*, (2004); Eileen McGough, *Diarmuid Lynch: a Forgotten Patriot*, (2013); *Evening Herald*, 3rd July 1919, (*action against the DMP Commissioner*); *Irish Independent* & *Irish Press*, 30th December 1963, (obits).

George Plunkett: (1894 - 1944)

Captain. Volunteer, (Kimmage Garrison)

George Plunkett, the brother of Joseph and Jack, was born in 1894 and educated at Stoneyhurst College, Lancashire, England. Prior to the Rising he was an architectural student, and was also in charge of the Volunteers who had returned from England and were staying at Larkfield, Kimmage. On Easter Monday he led a party of over forty men to the GPO and fought there throughout the week. On Thursday he was one of the first to come to James Connolly's aid after his ankle was shattered near Abbey Street, and helped carry him back to the GPO. After the surrender, he was sentenced to death, which was commuted to penal servitude.

Following his release from jail in 1917, he rejoined the Volunteers and fought throughout the War of Independence. He fought on the Republican side during the Civil War and was a member of the Four Courts Garrison. He was a fluent Irish speaker and scholar and was a life-long friend of Rory O'Connor, who led the occupation of the Four Courts and was executed in December 1923. In 1923 he was imprisoned with his brother, Jack and took part in a forty day hunger strike.

He moved his family from Stillorgan to Ballymascanlon House, Dundalk, in 1943.

George Plunkett died on January 21st 1944, from head injuries received when thrown from a pony and trap, at the Crescent, Dundalk and was buried at Ravensdale Cemetery, Dundalk.

References:

Desmond Ryan, *The Rising: the Complete Story of Easter Week*, (1949); John Heuston OP, *Headquarters Battalion, Easter Week 1916*, (1966); Max Caulfield, *The Easter Rebellion*, (1963); Thomas Coffey, *Agony at Easter*, (1969); Peter DeRosa, *Rebels: the Irish Rising 1916*, (1991); Ann Matthews, *The Kimmage Garrison, 1916*, (2010); Geraldine Plunkett Dillon, *All in the Blood*, (2012); *Irish Press*, 22nd January 1944, (obit); *Irish Independent*, 24th January 1944, (obit).

John (Jack) Plunkett: (1897 - 1960)
Lieutenant. Volunteer, (Kimmage Garrison)

Jack Plunkett, the younger brother of Joseph and George, was born in 1897 and joined the Volunteers in 1913, when a student at Clongowes Wood College. He joined his brother Joseph's staff in 1915, and was made a lieutenant, prior to the Rising in 1916. On entering the GPO on Easter Monday, he was put in charge of a section of the ground floor, near the Princes Street side. He then went with a group to the National Volunteers HQ in Parnell Square and returned to the GPO with arms and ammunition. Later in the week he took out a sniper on the burnt out roof of the Imperial Hotel, who had been firing on Volunteers engaged in fighting the fires in the GPO. He was one of the last Volunteers to leave the GPO at the evacuation on Friday evening. After the surrender he was sentenced to death, which was commuted to ten years penal servitude. He was imprisoned in several jails in Britain and was released in 1917.

During the War of Independence he was on the staff of Rory O'Connor, the IRA Director of Engineers. He took the Republican side in the Civil War. He was a member of the Four Courts Garrison in 1922 and was later imprisoned.

He later resided at 51 Eglinton Road, Donnybrook and was an electrical engineer in the ESB for many years.

Jack Plunkett died on August 27th 1960 and was buried at Glasnevin Cemetery.

References:
IMA, BMH (WS 488); Max Caulfield, *The Easter Rebellion*, (1963); Seán MacEntee, *Episode at Easter*, (1966); John Heuston OP, *Headquarters Battalion, Easter Week 1916*, (1966); Michael Foy & Brian Barton, *The Easter Rising*, (2000); Ann Matthews, *The Kimmage Garrison, 1916*, (2010); Geraldine Plunkett Dillon, *All in the Blood*, (2012); *Sunday Press*, 28th August 1960, (obit); *Evening Herald*, 29th August 1960, (obit).

Joseph Mary Plunkett: (1887 – 1916). Executed Leader
Commandant. Director of Operations, G.H.Q. Roll of Honour

Joseph Mary Plunkett, the son of George Noble Count Plunkett, was born in Dublin in 1887. He was educated at Belvedere College, Stoneyhurst College, Lanchashire and UCD. He suffered from poor health and after his graduation he spent time in Italy, Egypt and Algeria. When he returned to Dublin, he became a member of the Gaelic League and also published his first collection of poetry, "*The Circle and the Sword*". With his friends, Thomas McDonagh and Edward Martyn, he was a founder member of the Irish Theatre, in Hardwick Street. He joined the Volunteers at the inaugural meeting in 1913 and also became a member of the IRB. In 1915 he travelled to Berlin to assist Roger Casement in his efforts to procure arms and support for the rebellion in Ireland, and he later went to New York to report to the leaders of Clan na nGael on the preparations for the Rising. On his return to Dublin, he was appointed a member of the Military Council of the IRB, and he worked on strategic plans for the Rising, which were approved by James Connolly. Early in 1916 he became ill and had to undergo surgery for glandular tuberculosis. When he took his place in the GPO with his aide-de-camp, Michael Collins, on Easter Monday, he was a dying man. He was incapacitated for the first few days, but rallied towards the end of the week and he took command for a while when P.H. Pearse was overcome with exhaustion. He took an active part in the evacuation of the GPO on Friday evening. After the surrender he was court-marshalled and sentenced to death in Richmond Barracks. Joseph Plunkett married his fiancée, Grace Gifford, in the prison chapel in Kilmainham Jail, a few hours before his execution by firing squad, on May 4th 1916. He was buried in Arbour Hill with the other executed leaders of the Rising.

References:

RH; Dorothy Macardle, *The Irish Republic*, (1937); Max Caulfield, *The Easter Rebellion*, (1963); Thomas Coffey, *Agony at Easter*, (1969); Ruth Dudley Edwards, *Patrick Pearse: the Triumph of* Failure, (1990); W.J. Brennan-Whitmore, *Dublin Burning*, (1996); Michael Foy & Brian Barton, *The Easter Rising*, (2000); Charles Townshend, *Easter Rising, the Irish Rebellion*, (2005); Clair Willis, *Dublin 1916, the Siege of the* GPO, (2009); Ann Matthews, *The Kimmage Garrison, 1916*, (2010); Ray Bateson, *They Died by Pearse's Side*, (2010); Geraldine Plunkett Dillon, *All in the Blood*, (2012).

Vincent Poole: (1880 – 1955)
Captain. Irish Citizen Army, (Gloucester St Section)

Vincent Poole, a member of a large Dublin family, was born in 1880. He was the younger brother of Joseph Poole, one of the Invincibles, who was executed in 1883. In his younger days, he joined the British Army and fought in the Boer War. When he returned to Ireland, he joined the ITGWU and, after the 1913 Lockout, he became a member of the Irish Citizen Army. In 1916 he was living at 6 Lower Marlboro Street, and was a Dublin Corporation employee. On Easter Monday he was one of a party that occupied the Vitriol Works, Ballybough and later operated on the railway line at Fairview. After his party was ordered back to the GPO on Tuesday evening, he was sent to the Metropole Hotel. Volunteer Tom Leahy, recalled that Vincent Poole told tales of his experiences in the Boer War and that his advice was very useful when they came under sniper fire. He also recalled that several snipers fell to Vincent Poole's shooting. He returned to the GPO when the Metropole Hotel was abandoned, and left with the evacuation on Friday evening. After the surrender, he was court-martialled and sentenced to death, which was commuted to five years penal servitude. He was interned in Portland, Lewes, Parkhurst and Pentonville Jails, and was one of the instigators of a hunger strike at Lewes Jail.

After his release from prison on June 16th 1917, he suffered ill health for a period and in 1920 he joined the 5th Battalion Engineers, IRA. He took the anti-Treaty side in the Civil War and fought in the defence of the Four Courts and the Hamman Hotel. After the surrender at the Four Courts in July 1922, he was imprisoned in Mountjoy Jail.

Vincent Poole, of 22 Lower Dominic Street, died on June 25th 1955 and was buried at Mount Jerome Cemetery, Harold's Cross.

References:

IMA, MSPC; IMA, BMH (WS 660, *Tom Leahy*); NLI, *William O'Brien Papers*, (Ms 15,673); Frank Robbins, *Under the Starry Plough: Recollections of the Irish Citizen Army*, (1977); Michael Hopkinson, *Frank Henderson's Easter Rising Recollections of a Dublin Volunteer*, (1998); Ann Matthews, *The Irish Citizen Army*, (2014); *Evening Herald*, 7th April 2008, (na, *the Poole brothers*); *Irish Press*, 27th June 1955, (obit); *Irish Independent*, 28th June 1955, (obit).

Seán Price: (1895 – 1978)

Section Commander. B. Coy, 1st Batt, Dublin Brigade. Roll of Honour

Seán Price was born in 1895 and resided at 15 Killarney Parade, North Circular Road. He was educated at O'Connell Schools, North Richmond Street, and joined B. Company, 1ˢᵗ Battalion, Dublin Brigade, in 1914. His sister, Leslie (Mrs Tom Barry), was also a member of the GPO Garrison, while his brother, Eamon, fought with the Jacob's Garrison. On Easter Monday, he and other members of B. Company took up positions at the Cabra Bridge barricade. They were forced to withdraw because of the British shelling on Wednesday, and after spending the night in a hayshed in Finglas, he made his way to the GPO, where he fought for the remainder of the week. He was one of James Connolly's stretcher-bearers at the evacuation of the GPO. After the surrender he was deported to Stafford Jail on May 1ˢᵗ and interned in Frongoch until Christmas 1916.

On his release from Frongoch, he rejoined his old unit and fought in the War of Independence. He was promoted to lieutenant and took part in a number of operations, including the raid on the Independent Newspaper Offices and the attempted attack on train carrying troops at Ashtown. In May 1921, he was involved in the arrest and execution of a spy named "Hoppy" Byrne at Smithfield, and the attack of British troops at Findlater Place. During the Truce he took part in the occupation of the Fowler Hall and was later briefly interned. He took the Republican side in the Civil War and was involved in the occupation of the Hamman Hotel. He was arrested in August 1922 and was interned until December 1924.

He was a blacksmith by trade and later resided at 12 Church Avenue, Drumcondra.

Seán Price died on December 1ˢᵗ 1978 and was buried at Glasnevin Cemetery.

References:

RH; IMA, MSPC; IMA, BMH (WS 769); *Sinn Féin Rebellion Handbook 1916*, Weekly Irish Times, (1917).

Charles M. Purcell: (1893 - 1970)

C. Coy, 1st Batt, Dublin Brigade. Roll of Honour

Charles Purcell was born in 1893 and resided at 35 St James Avenue, Clonliffe Road. He was employed as a draper's assistant, and was a member of C. Company, 1st Battalion, Dublin Brigade. On Easter Monday reported to the GPO and was stationed in the instruments room, under the command of Captain Michael Collins. After the surrender he was deported to Knutsford Jail on May 1st and interned in Frongoch until Christmas, 1916.

On his release from internment, he fought in War of Independence. He joined the Free State Army in May 1922, and at the outbreak of the Civil War he was engaged as a machine-gunner at the entrance gates to the Four Courts. He was discharged from the army with the rank of corporal in March 1925, at his own request.

He was later employed in the Public Record Office in the Four Courts and resided at 38 Shelmartin Avenue, Marino.

Charles Purcell died on May 16th 1970 and was buried at Glasnevin Cemetery.

References:
RH; IMA, MSPC; *Evening Herald*, 18th May 1970, (dn).

James Quinn: (1881 - 1944)

Hibernian Rifles

James Quinn was born in 1881 and was originally from Kingscourt, County Cavan. He worked in Dublin as a springsmith and joined the Volunteers in 1913. He transferred to the Hibernian Rifles, which was attached to the AOH (Irish American Alliance), in 1914. He mobilised at 28 North Frederick Street on Easter Monday and marched with twenty other Hibernian Rifle Volunteers, from there, to the GPO at midnight. He was then put on sentry duty at Prince's Street and at two o'clock on Tuesday afternoon, he was sent by P.H. Pearse with a message for Father Graham in Drumcondra. He then carried several despatches between them, before delivering a final one on Wednesday evening. He was unable to return to the GPO because a military cordon surrounded the inner city area.

He later lived at 9 Rutland Place, Parnell Square and manufactured springs for motorcars.

James Quinn died on September 25th 1944 and was buried at Glasnevin Cemetery.

References:
IMA, MSPC; *Irish Independent,* 26th September 1944, (dn).

Margaret Quinn: (1869 – 1942)

Cumann na mBan. Roll of Honour

Margaret Quinn was born in 1869 and resided at 35 Lower Dorset Street. She was a widow, and in 1915 she joined Árd Craobh, Cumann na mBan. On Easter Monday she reported to the Cumann na mBan Headquarters and was told to await orders. She was sent to the GPO on Tuesday, and then she went to the Hibernian Bank, at the corner of Abbey Street. She set up a first aid centre with other women in the building next to the bank on the orders of Captain Thomas Weafer. She attended to the wounded there until six o'clock on Wednesday, when she was sent home to rest with orders to return on Thursday morning. The following morning she was unable to return to the GPO because of the military cordon that surrounded the city.

Her son, Thomas, was a member of the IRA, and fought in the War of Independence. Margaret Quinn died on June 25th 1942 and was buried at Glasnevin Cemetery.

References:

RH; IMA, MSPC; NLI, *Lynch Papers*, (Ms 11,131); *Irish Press*, 26th June 1942, (dn).

Patrick Rankin: (1887 - 1964)

B. Coy, 2nd Batt, Dublin Brigade. Roll of Honour

Patrick Rankin was born in 1887 and resided at 24 Queen Street, Newry, County Down. In 1907 he became a member of the IRB, and he emigrated to Canada in 1913. A year later he moved to Philadelphia, where he joined the National Guard. He returned to Ireland in January 1915 and joined the Dundalk Battalion, Louth Brigade. On Easter Monday he delivered arms from Newry to Paddy Hughes in Dundalk. On Tuesday, he cycled from Newry to Dublin to take part in the Rising. When he reported to the GPO Tom Clarke enquired about the situation in the North. He was then given a rifle and posted to the roof of the GPO. He was also engaged in boring through the walls of the GPO into the buildings in Henry Street. After the surrender he was deported to Stafford Jail on May 1st and was interned in Frongoch until July 21st 1916. On his release from internment, he joined B. Company, 2nd Battalion, Dublin Brigade and later transferred to the Newry Company. He was imprisoned in Belfast Jail in 1920 and later Wormwood Scrubs, where he went on hunger strike.

He was a civilian employee of the Army Corps of Engineers for many years.

Patrick Rankin died at his residence at Nicholstown, Kilcullen, on September 17th 1964 and was buried in the Old Cemetery, Newry.

References:

RH; IMA, MSPC; NLI, *Lynch* Papers, (Ms 11,131); Sinn *Féin Rebellion Handbook 1916*, Weekly Irish Times, (1917); *Irish Independent, Irish Press* & *Evening Herald*, (obits).

Thomas Rath: (1889 - 1984)

C. Coy, 2nd Batt, Dublin Brigade. Roll of Honour

Thomas Rath was born in 1889 and resided at 12 Grand Canal Harbour, off James's Street. He joined the Volunteers in 1913 and became a member of C. Company, 2nd Battalion, Dublin Brigade. On Easter Monday he reported to Father Mathew Park, Fairview, and was stationed at the Vitriol Works, Ballybough. On Monday evening he was sent to the GPO, where he was given a rifle and was later sent across to Reis's Chambers to assist in the erecting of wireless apparatus. He returned to the GPO and was posted to the second floor. He was then sent back to Reis's Chambers and he witnessed the fatal shooting of Captain Thomas Weafer in the Hibernian Bank on Wednesday. He crossed under heavy fire to the GPO, and on Thursday he manned the ground floor windows. On Friday evening, after the evacuation of the GPO, he spent the night in the houses in Moore Street. Following the surrender he was deported to Stafford Jail on May 1st and interned in Frongoch until Christmas, 1916.

He rejoined his unit on his release from internment and served until 1918, when ill health prevented him from taking part in military activities.

After the Rising he was employed as a clerk at Boland's Mill, Grand Canal Place and when he retired he became a resident at Nazareth House, Malahide Road.

Thomas Rath died at Nazareth House on May 10th 1984 and was buried at Glasnevin Cemetery.

References:
RH; IMA, MSPC; NLI, *Lynch Papers*, (Ms 11,131); *Irish Independent*, 11th May 1984, (dn).

Andrew (Andy) Redmond: (1890 – 1951)

Irish Citizen Army, (High St Section). Roll of Honour

Andy Redmond was born in 1890 and resided at 9 Curzon Street, South Circular Road. He was employed as a grocer's porter and joined the Irish Citizen Army, in 1913. On Easter Monday, he was sent to take up positions in the Ballybough and Fairview area. He served there until his party was withdrawn to the GPO on Tuesday evening. He was then sent to the Metropole Hotel, under the command of Oscar Traynor and fought there until Friday, when the party there returned to the GPO. After the evacuation of the GPO on Friday evening, he spent the night in Moore Street and remained there until the surrender on the following afternoon. He was deported to Stafford Jail on May 1st and then interned in Frongoch until Christmas, 1916.

On his return to Dublin after his release from internment, he joined D. Company, 2nd Battalion, Dublin Brigade and took part in the War of Independence. He took part in a number of operations, including the attack on British Forces in Dorset Street in March 1921. His brother, John, also fought in the GPO in Easter Week.

Andy Redmond of 63 Dolphin Road and late of Belmont Terrace, Terenure, died on March 9th 1951 and was buried at Templeogue Cemetery.

References:
RH; IMA, MSPC; NLI, *William O'Brien Papers*, (Ms 15,673); Ann Matthews, *The Irish Citizen Army*, (2014); *Irish Independent*, 10th March 1951, (dn).

Annie Redmond: (1885 - 1933)

Cumann na mBan. Roll of Honour

Annie Redmond's husband, Patrick, was the caretaker of Father Mathew Park, Fairview, which was used as H/Q of 2nd Battalion, Dublin Brigade, in 1916. She was a member of Cumann na mBan, while her husband was a member of F. Company, 2nd Battalion, Dublin Brigade. During Easter Week she was member of the GPO Garrison, and served as a courier, while Patrick was part of the Jacob's Garrison. Harry Colley recalled that when the Imperial Hotel was under heavy fire, she managed to get out with dispatches and then succeeded in getting back.

During the War of Independence her residence at 24 Charleville Avenue, North Strand, was used as a refuge for men on the run. She was associated with the Republican side during the Civil War and in later life, she was a member of Fianna Fáil.

Annie Redmond passed away on April 10th 1933.

References:
RH; IMA, BMH (WS 1687, *Harry Colley*); *Irish Press*, 12th April 1933, (obit).

John Timothy Redmond: (1892 – 1952)

Irish Citizen Army, (S. C. R. Section). Roll of Honour

John Redmond was born in 1892 and resided at 9 Curzon Street. He was employed as a grocer's assistant and joined the Irish Citizen Army, South Circular Road Section, in 1913. On Easter Monday he was in a group, led by Captain Frank Thornton, which was sent to the Telephone Exchange Building in Crown Alley. They returned to the GPO on Tuesday, and he was sent to the Imperial Hotel with six other men. When flames engulfed the Imperial Hotel on Thursday, he retreated with the garrison into the north inner city. Because he was dressed in civilian clothes, he attempted to mingle with the churchgoers in the Pro-Cathedral, Marlborough Street, but he was identified and arrested. He was taken to the Custom House for interrogation and was eventually released on the following Wednesday.

He rejoined the Irish Citizen Army, in 1917 and transferred to D. Company, 2nd Battalion, Dublin Brigade, in 1919. He served through the War of Independence up to the Truce, and joined the Free State Army in May 1922. He held the rank of sergeant major and was discharged from the army in January 1924. His brother, Andy, was also a member of the Irish Citizen Army and of the GPO Garrison.

John Redmond, of 16c Iveagh Buildings, Kevin Street, died on July 20th 1952.

References:
RH; IMA, MSPC; NLI, *Lynch Papers*, (Ms 11,131) & *William O'Brien Papers*, (Ms 15,673); *Pádraig Ó'Broin Papers*, (*private collection*); Ann Matthews, *The Irish Citizen Army*, (2014).

John Reid: (- 1979)

B. Coy, 2nd Batt, Dublin Brigade. Roll of Honour

John Reid, a porter from 41 St Mary's Terrace, Ballybough, was a member of B. Company, 2nd Battalion, Dublin Brigade. He reported to the 2nd Battalion Headquarters at Father Mathew Park, Fairview, on Easter Monday and then marched to the GPO with the Volunteers, under the command of Captain Thomas Weafer. He helped erect a barricade in Abbey Street, and took up a position at a window in Reis's Chambers. On Tuesday he manned a window on the first floor of the Hibernian Bank with the actor, Arthur Shields. The following day, while positioned on the roof of the Hibernian Bank, he picked off several troops with his Howth rifle, but as the fight wore on he and his comrades were forced from the roof by the tremendous volume of the enemy fire. On Thursday he was sent from the GPO with a group to occupy houses in the Abbey Street and Liffey Street area and he fired on an armoured car from a position on the roof of a Henry Street warehouse. He was ordered back to the GPO on Friday, and helped to remove bombs and gelignite from the basement when the fire became uncontrollable. After the evacuation of the GPO he spent the night in Moore Street. He was deported to Knutsford Jail on May 1st and interned in Frongoch until Christmas 1916.

He rejoined his unit with the rank of section commander and stood under arms during the conscription threat in 1918. He was involved in the attack on British Forces at the Thatch, Whitehall, in May 1921. He took the Republican side in the Civil War and fought in the Gardiner Street area.

John Reid lived at 71 Amiens Street for many years, but was residing at 3 Harbour Road, Skerries, when he died on June 30th 1979.

References:
    RH; IMA, MSPC; NLI, *Lynch Papers*, (Ms 11,131); *Sinn Féin Rebellion Handbook, 1916*, Weekly Irish Times, (1917); Max Caulfield, *The Easter Rebellion*, (1963).

Matthew Reilly: (1884 – 1974)

Unattached. Roll of Honour

Matthew Reilly was born in 1884. He employed as a chauffeur and resided at 22 Ailesbury Road, Ballsbridge. He was not attached to the Volunteers, but was asked by Seán McDermott, who he knew, to take part in the Rising. From Easter Monday to Wednesday, he drove around the city collecting arms, ammunition and provisions for the GPO Garrison. On one occasion his car was ambushed at St Stephen's Green, but he managed to evade capture. He was in the group that was sent by P.H. Pearse to occupy the Freeman's Journal's offices on Wednesday evening and he fought there until the position was abandoned. On Friday he carried bombs to the basement in the GPO and as the fire engulfed the roof, he was involved in removing the bombs and ammunition from the basement to safety. He was deported to Knutsford Jail on May 1st and released from there on June 16th 1916.

He joined A. Company, Dublin Brigade, in 1917 and ceased activities in 1920, when he accompanied his employer, Judge Smith, to England.

Matthew Reilly, of 40 Portmahon Drive, Rialto, died on November 7th 1974.

References:

RH; IMA, MSPC; *Sinn Féin Rebellion Handbook 1916*, Weekly Irish Times, (1917); *Irish Press*, 9th November 1974, (dn).

John R. Reynolds: (1868 - 1946)
B. Coy, 2nd Batt, Dublin Brigade. Roll of Honour

John R. Reynolds was born in Tipperary, in 1868 was living at 16 Clonmore Road, Ballybough in 1916. He was a member of the IRB and joined B. Company, 2nd Battalion, Dublin Brigade in 1913. He was also a member of the John O'Mahony Hurling Club. An accountant by profession, he was appointed auditor to the Volunteers, and was also friends to many of the leaders. In the week before the Rising, P.H. Pearse appointed him acting captain of a company of civil servants and others who could not openly identify with the Volunteers. On Easter Monday this company was kept in reserve at 41 Parnell Square, until he led them into the GPO later that evening, under orders from Pearse. He served in the GPO throughout the week, beside his daughter Molly, who was a member of Cumann na mBan. At the evacuation on Friday evening he took charge of a group that took cover in stables in Samson's Lane, at the rear of William's Store, Henry Street. He was court-martialled in Kilmainham Jail after the surrender, but was acquitted and released. His three sons also took part in the Rising. He was among a small group that was permitted to visit Seán MacDiarmada in Kilmainham Jail shortly before his execution, and during this visit Seán MacDiarmada made him sole executor of his will.

He was a founder of the Prisoners Dependents Fund and was also involved in the distribution of funds. In June 1916 he was arrested and deported to Worcester, England and he returned to Ireland on his release in March 1917. He rejoined the Volunteers and assisted in the reorganisation. He also acted as a Republican court judge in North Great Georges Street. He later formed his own accountancy firm, Messrs John R. Reynolds & Co. and resided at An Cuan, Sutton.

John R. Reynolds died on March 21st 1946 and was buried in St Fintan's Cemetery, Sutton.

References:

RH; IMA, MSPC; IMA, BMH (WS 156, *Molly Reynolds*) & BMH (WS 399, *Richard Mulcahy*); Gerard MacAtasney, *Seán MacDiarmada: the Mind of a Revolution*, (2004); Eileen McGough, *Diarmuid Lynch: a Forgotten Irish Patriot*, (2013); *Irish Press*, 7th March 1939, (*interview*); *Irish Press*, 23rd March 1946, (obit).

Mary (Molly) Reynolds: (1896 – 1979)

Commandant. Cumann na mBan. Roll of Honour

Molly Reynolds, the daughter of John R. Reynolds, was born in 1896 and was reared at 16 Clonmore Road, Ballybough. She joined Cumann na mBan in 1913 and two years later formed the Fairview Branch of Cumann na mBan that met at Father Mathew Park, Philipsbourgh Avenue.

On Easter Monday she reported to the St. Stephen's Green Garrison with other women from the Fairview Branch. She was then sent to the GPO with Stasia Toomey and they served at the first aid casualty station at the back of the main hall, treating the wounded.

On Friday she accompanied the wounded to Jervis Street Hospital. They left the GPO and moved through the bored walls of the buildings in Henry Street, making their way to Abbey Street, where Fr. Flanagan from the Pro-Cathedral and Captain Mahony, a British Medical Officer who had been held captive in the GPO, arranged a military escort to the hospital. She and the other women attendants spent the night in Jervis Street Hospital and the next morning were told to go home. As she passed the Rotunda Hospital on her way home, Molly saw her father among the Volunteers prisoners there.

Molly Reynolds was prominent in the anti-conscription campaign in 1918 and assisted Liam Mellowes in the importation of arms from 1919 to 1921.

Molly Reynolds, of 156 Dunluce Road, Clontarf, died on April 21st 1979 and was buried at Glasnevin Cemetery.

References:

RH; IMA, MSPC; IMA, BMH (WS 156); NLI, *Lynch Papers*, (Ms 11,131); Ruth Taillon, *Women of 1916*, (1996); Ann Matthews, *Renegades: Irish Republican Women, 1900-1922*, (2010); *Irish Press*, 22nd April 1979, (dn).

Peter J. Reynolds: (1888 - 1979)

Coy, 1st Batt, Dublin Brigade. Roll of Honour

Peter Reynolds was born in 1888 and was proprietor of bicycle and motorcycle shop at 64 North King Street. He joined the Volunteers at the inaugural meeting at the Rotunda, Dublin, on the November 25th 1913, and was involved in the Howth gun running in 1914, where he helped unload rifles and ammunition to a motor van. On Easter Monday he delivered arms and gelignite in his motorcycle side-car to the GPO. He helped to overturn a tram in Sackville Street in order to make a barricade. Throughout the week he delivered despatches by motorcycle to various garrisons, under constant sniper fire. On Thursday he made his last dash under heavy fire to the South Dublin Union and returned unscathed. That night, as flames spread in the GPO, he decided he wasn't going to surrender and he made his way to a lane off Moore Street, where he was joined by three other Volunteers. After a narrow escape from British soldiers, they went westward through houses and over roofs. He met his brother, who was a British soldier home on leave and who had been out looking for him, in Capel Street. His brother gave him an army pass that enabled him to pass through the military cordon and escape with his wife and two children out of the city, on his motorcycle and side-car. They remained with friends in the country until it was safe to return to the city.

He rejoined his old unit in 1917 and fought in the War of Independence. He was suspected of being involved in the shooting dead of two British soldiers when an armoured car was captured during an attempted rescue of Seán MacEoin from Mountjoy Jail. He was subsequently arrested and held without charge until December 21st 1921.

When his motorcycle shop burned down in 1926, he moved to England and was employed by the London Fire Brigade for many years. During the emergency years he joined 26th Battalion Infantry Brigade.

Peter Reynolds died in Hemel Hampstead, Hertfordshire, on December 27th 1979.

References:
RH; IMA, MSPC; IMA, BMH (WS 350); *Irish Press*, 30th October 1965, (*letter from Peter Reynolds, Watford, England, re the proposed 1966 celebrations*); *Irish Independent*, 28 December 1979, (dn).

Bridie Richards: (1891 – 1970)
Cumann na mBan, (Árd Craobh). Roll of Honour

Bridie Richards was born in 1891. She was schoolteacher and resided at 17 Kenmare Parade, North Circular Road. She was a member of the Gaelic League and joined Cumann na mBan in 1915. On Easter Monday she was mobilised to go to Dominic Street Priory and to wait for further orders. She was instructed to go to the Hibernian Bank on Tuesday, and was engaged in cooking and first aid duties there. After Captain Weafer was killed, she crossed the street under heavy fire to the GPO with others on Wednesday evening. She became ill on Thursday, and James Connolly sent her home. After the Rising she became involved in collections and distribution for the Prisoner Dependents Fund. In 1917 she joined the Colmcille Branch of Cumann na mBan, and remained a member until the Truce.

Bridie Richards, a retired schoolteacher at Gardiner Street Convent School, died on January 3rd 1970 and was buried at Glasnevin Cemetery.

References:
RH; IMA, MSPC; *Irish Press*, 4th January 1970, (dn).

Henry (Harry) Ridgeway: (1894 – 1979)

Lieutenant. C. Coy, 2nd Batt, Dublin Brigade. Roll of Honour

Harry Ridgeway was born in 1894 and resided at 163 Parnell Street. He was educated at O'Connell Schools, North Richmond Street and he was a hairdresser by trade. He joined the Volunteers in 1913 and became first aid officer with the 2nd Battalion. He was involved in the Howth gun running in 1914.

On Easter Monday he served in the Fairview and Ballybough area, before joining the GPO Garrison on Tuesday evening. He was sent to the Metropole Hotel, where he remained until garrison returned to the GPO on Friday. At the evacuation of the GPO on Friday evening, he and Oscar Traynor attended to Arthur Wicks who had been fatally wounded, and he and Christopher Tallon then carried the English socialist into the houses in Moore Street. After the surrender, a British Army Officer tore the Red Cross amulet from his uniform with his bayonet. However, another British Officer, who was a former neighbour of Harry's, intervened and prevented any further ill-treatment. He was among the first group of Volunteers deported to Knutsford Jail on May 1st and was interned in Frongoch, until July 18th 1916.

During the War of Independence his home at Parnell Street, was raided on a number of occasions by the British Military. His brothers, Thomas and Charles, took the anti-Treaty side during the Civil War and both were imprisoned.

For many years he was proprietor of a barber's shop on Westmoreland Street at the D'Olier Street junction and he resided at 15 Seaview Avenue, Clontarf.

Harry Ridgeway died on August 22nd 1979 and was buried in St Fintan's Cemetery, Sutton.

References:
RH; IMA, MSPC; IMA, BMH (WS 7, *Liam Ó'Briain*) & BMH (WS 1,765, *Seán T. O'Kelly*); Michael Hopkinson, *Frank Henderson's Easter Rising: Recollection of a Dublin Volunteer*, (1998); Jim Corr, *Believed to be in Ireland*, (unpubished); *Irish Press*, 24 April 1979, (obit).

Christopher Ring: (1881 – 1941)

C. Coy, 2nd Batt, Dublin Brigade. Roll of Honour

Christopher Ring was born in 1881 and resided at 5 Sackville Gardens, Ballybough. He was educated at St Joseph's CBS, Fairview and was one of five brothers, who were part of the GPO Garrison. Like three of his brothers, he was a carpenter by trade and he became a member of C. Company, 2nd Battalion, Dublin Brigade, in 1915. On Easter Monday he reported to the GPO with his brothers and was sent back to Ballybough. He went to Father Mathew Park and returned to the GPO on Monday evening. He served in Reis's Chambers and in the Dublin Bread Company with his brother, Patrick, until the buildings were evacuated on Wednesday. He made his way back across the street to the GPO under heavy sniper fire and joined his brothers, Joe, Leo and Patrick, who were engaged in boring through the walls of the buildings in Henry Steet. They managed to get up as far as Arnott's and Frank Henderson later recalled how invaluable the Ring brothers in this undertaking. He was deported to Stafford Jail on May 1st, and interned in Frongoch, until July 18th 1916.

He rejoined his old unit in 1917 and was attached to the Medical Corps, under the command of Captain John Doyle. In 1919 he was mobilised for a raid for arms at the North Wall. He was arrested in December 1920 and was interned in Ballykinlar Camp until March 1921. He didn't take an active part in the Civil War.

He was employed as a carpenter in the Board of Works and was No.4 Branch Secretary of the Amalgamated Woodworkers' Union.

Christopher Ring died on October 15th 1941 and was buried at Glasnevin Cemetery.

References:
RH; IMA, MSPC; *Scoil Iósaif, Marino, 1916-1966, (a 1966 Jubilee Publication)*, (1966); Michael Hopkinson, *Frank Henderson's Easter Rising: Recollections of a Dublin Volunteer*, (1998); *Irish Independent* & *Irish Press*, 16th October 1941, (obits).

Joseph (Joe) Ring: (1890 – 1953)

C. Coy, 2nd Batt, Dublin Brigade. Roll of Honour

Joe Ring was born in 1890 and resided at 17 Clonmore Terrace, Ballybough, in 1916. He was a carpenter by trade and became a member of C. Company, 2nd Battalion in 1914. He reported to the GPO on Easter Monday with his four brothers and was sent back to the Summerhill area. Later on Monday he was involved in the attack on British Troops at East Wall Road. He was stationed at Lambe's Public House, Ballybough Bridge throughout Monday night and returned to the GPO on Tuesday evening. He was engaged in boring through the walls between the Coliseum Theatre and Arnott's, Henry Street on Wednesday and Thursday with his brothers; Leo, Christopher and Patrick. After the surrender he was deported to Stafford Jail on May, 1st and interned in Frongoch, until July 26th 1916.

On his release from internment he rejoined his old unit and was attached to the Engineer Corps. His house was used as an arms dump and a refuge for men on the run and was raided several times. He served up until 1920.

In his younger days, he was a very good soccer player and played for Richmond Utd. He was trainer to Drumcondra FC from the late 1920s to the early 1930s. During the emergency years he served with the 26th Infantry Battalion and, like his older brother, Christopher, he was employed as a carpenter in the Board of Works.

Joe Ring died on Christmas Day, 1953 and was buried in Glasnevin Cemetery.

References:

RH; IMA, MSPC; *Scoil Iósaif, Marino, 1916-1966, (a 1916 Jubilee Publication),*, (1966); Michael Hopkinson, *Frank Henderson's Easter Rising: Recollections of a Dublin Volunteeer,* (1998); *Evening Herald,* 12 April 2006, (na); *Irish Independent,* 29 December 1953, (obit).

Leon (Leo) Ring: (1892 – 1962)

C. Company, 2nd Batt, Dublin Brigade. Roll of Honour

Leo Ring was born in 1892 and resided at 4 Sackville Gardens, Ballybough in 1916. He was educated at St Joseph's CBS, Fairview and was a carpenter by trade. He joined C. Company, 2nd Battalion, Dublin Brigade, in 1915. On Easter Monday he reported to the GPO with his brothers, Christopher, Joe, Patrick and Liam, and he was sent to the Fairview area. Later that afternoon he was in the group that engaged British Troops at East Wall Road. He was stationed at Lambe's Public House, Ballybough, from Monday night until Tuesday evening, when he went to the GPO. He was posted to McDowell's Jewellers, Henry Street and was engaged in boring through the walls of buildings in Henry Street on Wednesday and Thursday. Before the surrender on Saturday he was wounded in the arm in Moore Lane, and was later taken to the hospital at Dublin Castle. After the surrender he was deported and later interned in Frongoch with his four brothers.

On his release from internment at Christmas 1916, he rejoined C. Company, 2nd Battalion and served until November 1920, when he married and moved to Mountmellick. Late in 1921 he was arrested in Portarlington and detained until the Truce. He remained in Portarlington and took up farming.

Leo Ring, of Sallypark House, Ballybrittas, County Laois, died on February 3rd 1962 and was buried at Killenard Cemetery, Portarlington.

References:

RH; IMA, MSPC; *Scoil Iósaif, Marino, 1916-1966, (a 1916 Jubilee Publications),* (1966); Michael Hopkinson, *Frank Henderson's Easter Rising: Recollections of a Dublin Volunteer,* (1998); *Nationalist & Leinster Times,* 8th February 1962, (obit).

Liam Ring (Ó Rinn): (1886 - 1943)
Lieutenant. C. Coy, 2nd Batt. Dublin Brigade. Roll of Honour

Liam Ring was born in 1886 and resided at 4 Sackville Gardens. He was one of five brothers from Ballybough who fought in the Easter Rising. He was educated at St Joseph's CBS, Fairview, and on leaving school he joined the Gaelic League in the Clann na hÉireann Hall, Richmond Road. He made an intensive study of the Irish language and after working in a law office, became a member of staff in the Gaelic League Headquarters. In 1913 he was also a member of the IRB when he joined C. Company, 2nd Battalion, Dublin Brigade, with his brothers. On Easter Monday he reported to the GPO with his brothers and was sent back to Ballybough. Later that afternoon he took part in the attack on British Troops at East Wall Road and that night he was promoted to the rank of second lieutenant in Lambe's Public House, Ballybough Bridge. He reported to the GPO on Tuesday evening with the Fairview contingent and was sent to Henry Street to commandeer food and supplies. On his return to the GPO he was put in charge of Volunteers manning several windows. After the surrender he was deported to Stafford Jail on May 1st and interned in Frongoch until Christmas 1916.

On his release from internment, he fought in the War of Independence and was interned in Ballykinlar Camp. While in prison he translated the *"Soldier's Song"* into Irish and *Amhrán na bhFiann* later became the official Irish National Anthem. He wrote an Irish column in the *Freeman's Journal* for many years. On the establishment of the Irish Free State, he was appointed a senior translator in the Translations Office, in Dáil Éireann, and later became Chief Translator.

He had a keen interest in languages and studied Russian, French, Italian, German, Dutch and Afrikaans. He also studied painting at the Dublin School of Art and in Paris and had his work accepted in the RHA. He was the author of original works in Irish and of many translations. His book *"Mo Chara Stiofán"*, about his friend Stephen McKenna, was awarded the President's Prize for the best book in 1941.

Liam Ring, of 32 Seafield Road, Clontarf, died in October 1943 and was buried at Glasnevin Cemetery.

References:

RH; IMA, MSPC; IMA, BMH (WS 264, Anne *Ceannt*) & BMH (WS 850, *Patrick Colgan*); *Irish Independent*, 4th October 1943, (obit).

Patrick Ring: (1884 – 1927)

C. Coy, 2nd Batt, Dublin Brigade. Roll of Honour

Patrick Ring was born on May 30th 1884 and resided at 4 Sackville Gardens, Ballybough. His father, Patrick, was a native of County Kilkenny and his mother, Eilís, came from County Louth. He was a carpenter by trade and was residing at 6 Sackville Gardens, in 1916. He reported to the GPO on Easter Monday with his brothers; Christopher, Liam, Joe and Leo, and they were sent back to Fairview. They returned to the GPO later on Monday evening and he and Christopher were sent across the street to Reis's Chambers to assist in erecting the wireless apparatus there. He remained there until Wednesday and he was then posted to Henry Street. After the surrender he was deported to Stafford Jail and later interned with his four brothers in Frongoch. He was released from internment on July 26th 1916 and rejoined his unit.

He fought in the War of Independence and was interned in Ballykinlar Camp with two of his brothers.

Patrick Ring died at his residence at 6 Sackville Gardens, Ballybough, on January 30th 1927 and was buried three days later at Glasnevin Cemetery.

References:
RH; *Scoil Iósaif, Marino, 1916-1966, (a 1916 Jubilee Publication)*, (1966); Michael Hopkinson, *Frank Henderson's Ester Rising: Recollections of a Dublin Volunteer*, (1998); *Irish Independent*, 17th Februrary 1927, (dn).

Seamus Robinson: (1890 - 1961)

Glasgow Volunteers, (Kimmage Garrison). Roll of Honour

Seamus Robinson was born in Belfast in 1890, and was educated there by the Christian Brothers. He was a member of the Oscars Hurling Club that was set up in Belfast by Bulmer Hobson. He emigrated to Scotland and was residing at 10 Robson Street, Glasgow, when he joined the Volunteers and the Gaelic League. Before the Rising he returned to Ireland and joined the Volunteer Camp at Kimmage. On Easter Monday he was in charge of a small group of Volunteers that occupied Hopkins & Hopkins Jewellers at the corner of Eden Quay. They came under constant sniper fire from the roof of Trinity College, but held this position until they were forced to retreat on Thursday when the building was engulfed by fire. He made his escape to the Metropole Hotel and fought there until the garrison retreated to the GPO on Friday. He left the GPO on Friday evening at the evacuation. He was in the group, under the command of Seán McLoughlin, which was in Sackville Lane waiting to attack the barricade at the top of Moore Street, when the decision to negotiate a surrender was made on Saturday afternoon. He was deported to Stafford Jail on May 8th and interned in Reading Jail, before being transferred to Frongoch and released at Christmas 1916.

In 1917 he went to work in Ballagh, County Tipperary and was elected O/C of the Tipperary 3rd Brigade. With Dan Breen, Seán Treacy and Seán Hogan, he led the Soloheadbeg Ambush on January 21st 1919. He took part in the rescue of Seán Hogan at Knocklong Railway Station in May 1919. Soon after he was arrested for drilling and was imprisoned in Belfast Jail until October 1919. He was involved in the assassination attempt on the Lord Lieutentant, Lord French, at Ashbourne, County Dublin, in December 1919. In 1921 he was elected to Dáil Éireann, as a TD for East Tipperary. He took the anti-Treaty side in the Civil War, and men from the 3rd Tipperary Brigade, under his command reinforced the Four Courts Garrison. After the Civil War he joined Fianna Fáil and became a senator in 1928. He was appointed to advisory committee of the Military Service Board in November 1935 and he was a member of the Bureau of Military History in 1949. He was appointed to the Military Registrations Board in 1953.

Seamus Robinson, of 18 Highfield Road, Rathgar, died on December 8th 1961 and was buried at Glasnevin Cemetery.

References:

RH; IMA, MSPC; IMA, BMH (WS156); Desmond Ryan, *Seán Treacy and the 3rd Tipperary Brigade*, (1945); Thomas Coffey, *Agony at Easter*, (1969); Frank Robbins, *Under the Starry Plough: Recollections of the Irish Citizen Army*, (1977); Michael Hopkinson, *Green against Green: the Irish Civil War*, (1988); John P. Duggan, *History of the Irish Army*, (1991); Joe Good, *Enchanted by Dreams*, (1996); Ann Matthews, *The Kimmage Garrison* 1916, (2010); Charlie MsGuire, *Seán McLoughlin, Ireland's Forgotten Revolutionary*, (2011); *Irish Press* & *Evening Herald*, 9th December 1961, (obits).

Thomas J. Roche: (1891 - 1969)
E. Coy, 2nd Batt, Dublin Brigade. Roll of Honour

Thomas Roche was born in 1891 and resided at Seville Place. He was a market worker and was a member St Laurence O'Toole's GAA Club. In 1915 he joined E. Company, 2nd Battalion, Dublin Brigade. On Easter Monday he was mobilised by Michael Colgan and reported to St Stephen's Green. He was sent from there to the GPO, and was engaged in erecting barricades and manning windows on the first floor. On Wednesday he got permission to escort a friend down Mary Street, but his return route was blocked. He made his way to the Four Courts Garrison and was stationed at the Church Street barricades. He also guarded prisoners in the Father Mathew Hall. At the surrender on Saturday, he took refuge in a room in the Capuchin Church and evaded capture by mingling with the churchgoers as they left Mass on Sunday morning. He was arrested two weeks later and taken to Dublin Castle for questioning, but was later released.

He rejoined his unit and fought in the War of Independence. He joined the Free State Army in 1922 and during the Civil War he took part in the attack on the Four Courts, where he was badly injured in a mine explosion. He spent six weeks in the Richmond Hospital and, on his return to duty, took part in engagements in Tipperary, Limerick and Clare. He was hospitalised again in December 1922 and was discharged from the army in April 1923, medically unfit.

In later years he lived at 72 Monasterboice Road, Crumlin and was employed in the Stationary Office, Beggar's Bush.

Thomas Roche died on March 15th 1969 and was buried at Glasnevin Cemetery.

References:
RH; IMA, MSPC; *Sunday Independent*, 16th March 1969, (dn).

William (Liam) Roche: (1892 - 1953)
Liverpool Company, (Kimmage Garrison). Roll of Honour

Liam Roche was born in Liverpool in 1892, of Wexford parents. He was member of the Gaelic League and Liverpool Volunteers. He came to Dublin before the Rising, and joined the Volunteers at Larkfield, Kimmage. On Easter Monday he assisted in clearing the staff and the public, including some British army officers, from the GPO and then stood guard at the main door. He was later posted to the barricaded ground floor windows, where he was wounded in the right arm by the accidental discharge of a shotgun. The following day he was sent with a despatch to Camden Street and after seeking further treatment for his wounds in Jervis Street Hospital after his stitches burst, he was ordered home at 3.00 am.

At the reorganisation of the Volunteers, he joined the 5th Battalions Engineers and fought in the War of Independence. He was involved in purchasing arms and ammunition and took part in raids for arms. In 1921, he laid landmines at Palmerstown and took part in armed street patrols. At the time of the Truce, he was in the battalion training camp at Pine Forest and was Acting Company Adjutant of 3rd Coy, 5th Batt. He later served in the Free State Army in 1923.

Liam Roche, of 2 Collins Avenue West, Donnycarney, passed away, after a long illness, on April 6th 1953.

References:
RH; IMA, MSPC; NLI, *Lynch Papers*, (Ms 11,131); *Irish Press*, 7th April 1953, (dn); *Irish Press*, 8th April 1953, (obit).

William Ross: (1875 - 1968)
B. Coy, 1st Battation, Dublin Brigade

William Ross was born in 1875 and resided at 11 Lower Sherrard Street. He was a tailor by trade and a member of the IRB. He joined the Volunteers in 1913 and was a member of B. Company, 1st Battalion, Dublin Brigade. Initially, he fought at the barricade at Cabra Bridge and later withdrew to the GPO when the position was abandoned. When he arrived at the GPO on Wednesday morning, he was sent to Lucas's Cycle Shop in Middle Abbey Street, under the command of Seán Milroy, and remained there until Friday. He took part in the evacuation of the GPO on Friday evening, and after the surrender he was deported to Stafford Jail on May 1st. He was released from internment in Frongoch at Christmas 1916 and rejoined his unit.

He fought in the War of Independence and was involved in numerous ambushes in the north inner city area, most notably the attack at Cross Guns Bridge, Phibsboro, on the King's Messenger escorted by armoured cars. He was wounded in a later ambush in Parnell Street. He took the Republican side in the Civil War and fought in the Fowler's Hall, Barry's Hotel, the Hamman Hotel, the Gresham Hotel and the CYMS Building in O'Connell Street. He also took part in the attack on Broadstone Station and in the destruction of a number of bridges.

He suffered with asthma and rheumatism for many years as a result of his time on active service, and in particular his hunger strike and ill treatment in Frongoch.

William Ross, of 90 Lower Drumcondra Road, died on June 23rd 1968 and was buried at Glasnevin Cemetery.

References:
  IMA, MSPC; *Sinn Féin Rebellion Handbook 1916*, Weekly Irish Times, (1917); *Irish Press*, 24th June 1968, (obit).

Charles (Charlie) Rossiter: (1892 – 1969)
F. Coy, 2nd Batt, Dublin Brigade. Roll of Honour

Charlie Rossiter was born in 1892 and resided at 2 Sallypark Cottages, Philipsburgh Avenue. He was a painter by trade, and joined the Volunteers at the inaugural meeting at the Rotunda in 1913. He was a member of F. Company, 2nd Battalion, Dublin Brigade and on Easter Monday he reported to the Clann na hÉireann Hall on Richmond Road and from there he was sent to mobilise other Volunteers in the Fairview area. Afterwards, he was in the group that occupied Gilbey's Wine Stores, Ballybough Bridge and that remained there until they were ordered into the GPO on Tuesday evening. He manned the barricaded windows in the GPO for the rest of the week. At the evacuation of the GPO on Friday evening, he was the last person to speak to Harry Coyle, a comrade from the same company, before he was killed. After the surrender he was deported to Knutsford Jail on May 1ˢᵗ and interned in Frongoch until July 18ᵗʰ 1916.

On his release from Frongoch, he rejoined his unit and fought in the War of Independence. He took part in armed patrols and was involved in the raid for arms at the B&I Stores, North Wall. He was mobilised for an attack on a troop train at Killester, which was called off.

He was employed for some time in the Dept of Social Welfare and resided at Sackville Avenue, Ballybough.

Charlie Rossiter resided at Clonmellon, County Westmeath in later years, and died there on September 3ʳᵈ 1969.

References:

RH; IMA, MSPC; *Scoil Iósaif, Marino, 1916-1966, (a 1916 Jubilee Publication)*, (1966); *Irish Press*, 4ᵗʰ September 1969, (obit).

Seán Russell: (1893 – 1940)

Section Commander. E. Coy, 2nd Batt, Dublin Brigade

Seán Russell was born in 1893 and resided at 68 North Strand Road. He was a carpenter by trade and joined the Volunteers at the Rotunda in 1913. He was Section Commander of E. Company, 2ⁿᵈ Battalion, Dublin Brigade, and on Easter Monday he fought at Annesley Bridge. He was in charge of twelve Volunteers that prevented the British Troops from North Bull Island from reaching the city for two days. They were ordered into the GPO on Tuesday evening and he was then sent to the Metropole Hotel, under the command of Lieutenant Oscar Traynor. He remained there until Friday, when the garrison retreated to the GPO. After the surrender he was deported to Knutsford Jail on May 1ˢᵗ and interned in Frongoch until July 31ˢᵗ 1916.

He rejoined his old unit on his release from internment and fought in the War of Independence. He was appointed Director of Munitions in the Headquarters Staff of the IRA. He played a major part in the events of Bloody Sunday, November 21ˢᵗ 1920, when fourteen British Agents were shot. He fought on the Republican side in the Civil War and was interned after the fall of the Four Courts Garrison.

He remained active in the IRA and visited Russia in 1926 with Gerry Boland, in an attempt to secure arms. When Éamon deValera outlawed the IRA, Russell, who was quartermaster general, travelled to the Untied States to seek support from Joe McGarrity and Clan na Gael. On his return he was made chief of staff at an IRA Convention held in April 1938. The IRA declared war on Britain in 1939, and carried out a series of bombings there, including one that August at Broadgate, Coventry that killed five people and injured seventy. He then went to the United States and from there to Germany, where he sought aid for the IRA. In Germany, he met the Socialist Republican Frank Ryan, and both returned to Ireland by U Boat. However before they reached their destination, Russell became ill, complaining of stomach pains.

Seán Russell died on board the U Boat on August 14th 1940, and was buried at sea, one hundred miles west of the Galway coast. A statue was erected in his memory in Fairview Park in 1951. Over the years it was vandalised on numerous occasions and was replaced with a bronze version in 2009.

References:

DIB, James McGuire, (James Quinn, Ed, 2009); HI, May/June 2005, (*Brian Hanley article*); Seán Cronin, *The McGarrity Papers,* (1972); Conor Foley, *Legion of the Rearguard: the IRA and the Modern Irish State,* (1992); Tim Pat Coogan, *The IRA,* (1995); Uinseann MacEoin, *The IRA in the Twilight Years,* (1997); J. Bowyer Bell, *The Secret Army,* (1998); Brian Hanley, *The IRA, 1926-1936,* (2002).

Catherine Ryan (Mrs. Catherine Treston):
(1890-1928)
Nurse, First Aid Station, GPO. Roll of Honour

Catherine Ryan served as a nurse in the first aid station in the GPO throughout Easter Week. She was detained in Kilmainham Jail after the surrender and was released on May 22nd 1916.

She was married to William Treston, who was dentist by profession and they resided at 7 Ballybough Road.

Catherine Treston died on April 18th 1928.

References:
RH; IMA, BMH (WS 359, *Eva Burke*) & BMH (WS 909, *Michael Flanagan*); *Sinn Féin Rebellion Handbook 1916,* Weekly Irish Times, (1917); *Irish Independent,* 20th April 1928, (dn).

Desmond Ryan: (1893 – 1964)

E. Coy, 4th Batt, Dublin Brigade

Desmond Ryan was born in Dulwich, London, in 1893, the son of journalist William P. Ryan. His family returned to Dublin in 1905 and he continued his education at Westland Row CBS and then at St Enda's College, Rathfarnham. Later, while studying in UCD, he lived at St Enda's and was secretary to P.H. Pearse. He was a member of E. Company, 4th Battalion, Dublin Brigade, which was the local Rathfarnham Company. On Easter Monday to Wednesday he fought on the roof of the GPO, and on Thursday he manned the entrance at Prince's Street. He was stationed at the ground floor windows on Friday until the building was evacuated. After the surrender, he was deported to Stafford Jail on May 1st and interned in Frongoch, until July 27th 1916.

Following his release from internment, he worked as a journalist with the *Freeman's Journal*. He supported the Treaty, but became disillusioned with the Civil War and moved to London where he worked as a journalist, before returning to Ireland in 1939.

Author and historian, he wrote biographies on P.H. Pearse, James Connolly, Éamon deValera, John Devoy and Seán Treacy, as well as an autobiography, *Remembering Sion* (1935), *The Rising* (1949) and *The Workers' Republic"* (1951).

Desmond Ryan resided at 3 Charleston Road, Rathmines and died in a Dublin hospital on December, 23rd 1964.

References:

RH; IMA, MSPC; IMA, BMH (WS 724 & 725); Desmond Ryan, *Remembering Sion: a Chronicle of Storm and Quiet*, (1935); Max Caulfield, *The Easter Rebellion*, (1963); John Heuston OP, *Headquarters Battalion, Easter Week 1916*, (1966); Ruth Dudley Edwards, *Patrick Pearse: the Triumph of Failure*, (1977); Seán O'Mahony, *Frongoch: University of Revolution*, (1987); Charles Townshend, *Easter 1916, the Irish Rebellion*, (2006); *Irish Independent, Irish Press* & Irish Times, 24th December 1964, (obits).

Doctor James Ryan: (1891 – 1970)

Medical Officer. B. Coy, 1st Batt, Dublin Brigade. Roll of Honour

James Ryan was born near Taghmon, County Wexford, on December 6th 1891. He was educated at St Peter's College, Wexford, and Ring College, County Waterford. He later lived at 19 Ranelagh, while studying medicine in UCD. He joined B. Company, 1st Battalion, Dublin Brigade, in 1913, and the IRB the following year. He was a final year student, when he was placed in charge of the hospital in the GPO during Easter Week. His sisters, Phyllis (Mrs Seán T. O'Kelly) and Mary Josephine (Mrs Richard Mulcahy) were also members of the GPO Garrison. He tended to James Connolly when his ankle was shattered by shrapnel on Thursday, and at one stage discussed with Connolly the need for a possible amputation. At the evacuation the medical supplies he was carrying got caught in a gateway, and he was forced to disentangle it while under fire before hiding in a doorway until nightfall. He was deported to Stafford Jail on May 1st and interned in Frongoch, until July 29th 1916.

On his release from internment, he returned to Wexford and set up a medical practice. He also became O/C of the Wexford Brigade of the IRA and was interned on Spike Island. After fours years in Wexford, he returned to Dublin and set up his medical practice in Harcourt Street. He opposed the Treaty, and fought with Republican side in the Civil War. He was a member of the Four Courts Garrison in 1922 and was later imprisoned.

He gave up his medical practice in 1925 and bought a farm in Kendelstown, near Delgany, County Wicklow. In 1926 he was a founding member of Fianna Fáil and served as TD for Wexford from 1927 to 1965. During his political career he was Minister for Agriculture from 1932 to 1947, Minister for Health and Social Welfare from 1947 to 1948, and Minister for Finance on two occasions, from 1951 to 1954 and from 1957 to 1965. On retiring as a TD, he was elected to the Seanad and he served there until 1969. His son and grandson, both named Eoin, also served as TD's.

Doctor James Ryan died at his home at Kendlestown, Delgany, on September 25th 1970 and was buried at the Redford Cemetery, Greystones, County Wicklow.

References:

RH; *Capuchin Annual*, 1942; *DIB*, Patrick Maume, (James Quinn, Ed, 2009); Max Caulfield, *The Easter Rebellion*, (1963); Thomas Coffey, *Agony at Easter*, (1969); Risteárd Mulcahy, *Richard Mulcahy: a family memoir*, (1999); Michael Foy & Brian Barton, *The Easterr Rising*, (2000); *Irish Times*, 15th -17th March 1967, (na, *by Michael McInerney, 3 parts*); *Irish Press*, 26th September 1970, (obit); *Sunday Press*, 27th September 1970, (obit).

Laurence (Larry) Ryan: (1892 - 1924)
Manchester Company, (Kimmage Garrison)

Larry Ryan was born in Salford in 1892 and was employed as a clerk in J. Roscoe & Co., a canal coal haulage firm, on the Ashton canal in Manchester. He was one of fourteen Volunteers from Manchester that crossed over to Dublin before the Rising and joined the Volunteer Camp at Larkfield, Kimmage. He fought with the Kimmage Garrison in the GPO during Easter Week and after the surrender he was deported to Stafford Jail on May 1st.

On his release from Frongoch, he worked as a merchant seaman on boats travelling between Liverpool and New York. This enabled him to smuggle guns into Ireland, and he was arrested and imprisoned in the Tombs prison in New York for a period for the possession of guns. His health broke down while in prison after he developed kidney problems. He joined the Free State Army in May 1922 and was attached to the Supply Dept, as a clerk. He was sent to St Bricin's Military Hospital to have some teeth extracted and while waiting to be attended to, he fell unconscious and never recovered.

Larry Ryan died of kidney failure in St Bricin's Military Hospital, Arbour Hill, on August 7th 1924 and was buried in Glasnevin Cemetery.

When his mother, Mary, applied for his pension on the grounds that he died from the effects of the hardship he endured as a Volunteer, her application was turned down on the basis that there was no evidence that his death was connected to his service.

References:
IMA, MSPC; *Evening Herald*, 9th August 1924, (dn)

Mary Josephine Ryan (Mrs. Mary Josephine Mulcahy): (1884 – 1977)

Secretary. Cumann na mBan Executive. Roll of Honour

Mary Josephine Ryan was born at Tomcoole, near Taghmon, in County Wexford, on the December 29th 1884. She was educated at the Loreto Abbey in Gorey, Loreto College in Dublin and the old Royal University in Dublin. She trained to be a teacher in London, and established a branch of Cumann na mBan while there. She then spent two years teaching in Germany, a further four years back in London, before returning to Dublin in 1915 to teach in the newly established Rathmines Technical School. In 1916 she was secretary of the Cumann na mBan Executive, and on Easter Monday she was mobilised along with her sister Phyllis, who later married Seán T. O'Kelly, to the Broadstone Railway Station. They reported to the GPO on Tuesday and served as dispatch couriers during Easter Week. At the time of the surrender she was in Jacob's with Phyllis. Her brother, Dr James Ryan, also served in the GPO. She was engaged to be married to Seán MacDiarmada at the time of his execution. Immediately after the Rising, she was sent to the United States with a message for John Devoy and to report on the Rising. In 1919 she married General Richard Mulcahy, Chief of Staff of the IRA, and together they had six children. Their son, Dr Risteárd Mulcahy, the well known cardiologist, was a former president of the Irish Heart Foundation; while their daughter, Neilí, designed the uniforms for Aer Lingus in 1962.

Mary Josephine Mulcahy died on April 11th 1977, aged 91 and was buried at Ballymoneen Cemetery, County Tipperary.

References:

RH; IMA, MSPC; Risteárd Mulcahy, *Richard Mulcahy: a family memoir*, (1999); Gerard MacAtasney, *Seán Mac Diarmada: the Mind of a Revolution*, (2004); *Irish Press*, 12th April 1977, (obit).

Oliver Ryan: (1885 – 1938)

Maynooth Company, Kildare Brigade. Roll of Honour

Oliver Ryan, who worked at Maynooth College, joined the Maynooth Company when they left the college on their way to Dublin by the Royal Canal on Easter Monday evening. They reached the GPO on Tuesday morning, after spending the previous night in Glasnevin Cemetery. He was in the group that was sent to Parliament Street by James Connolly, to reinforce the Irish Citizen Army men in the area. They defended positions in the Royal Exchange Hotel, Parliament Street and later Shortall's Shop, before retreating to the GPO. He fought on the roof of the GPO for the rest of the week. He was deported to Knutsford Jail and interned in Frongoch. After his release he rejoined his unit and served until 1918.

Oliver Ryan died on July 22nd 1938.

References:

RH; IMA, MSPC.

Phyllis Ryan (Mrs. Phyllis O'Kelly): (1895 - 1983)
Unattached. Roll of Honour

Phyllis Ryan was born in Tomcoole, County Wexford in 1895. Her family were from a farming background and she was the youngest of twelve children. She was educated at the Convent of Mercy, Gorey and later graduated with a M.Sc. from the National University. Before the Rising, she and her sister, Mary Josephine, were sent to Wexford with despatches by Seán McDermott. She accompanied Mary Josephine, who mobilised at Broadstone Railway Station, on Easter Monday and they reported to the GPO on Tuesday. She was engaged in cooking duties and on Wednesday she was sent with Mary Josephine to Drumcondra by P.H. Pearse, with messages for the families of two military prisoners held captive in the GPO. They also delivered a message to Father Conan, at the Archbishop's Palace. They could not get back to the GPO until the following morning, because of the military cordon. They were sent out again with dispatches on Thursday and on this occasion, they were unable to get back to the GPO.

She was not a member of Cumann na mBan during Easter Week, but she joined the Ranelagh Branch in 1917, and was appointed captain. She was later appointed to the Cumann na mBan Executive and organised branches in Ennis, Fermoy, Limerick, South Wexford and Tullamore, She took the Republican side during the Civil War and remained in charge of the Cumann na mBan Headquarters, at Dawson Street.

Her sister, Mary Kate, married Seán T. O'Kelly in 1916 and she passed away in 1934. Phyllis became his second wife in 1936 and became First Lady, when he became President of Ireland, in 1945.

Phyllis O'Kelly died on November 19th 1983 and was buried at Glasnevin Cemetery.

References:
RH; IMA, MSPC; Risteárd Mulcahy, *Richard Mulcahy: a family memoir*, (1999); Sinéad McCoole, *No Ordinary Women: Irish Female Activists in the Revolutionary years, 1900-1923*, (2004); Clair Willis, *Dublin 1916, the Siege of the* GPO, (2009); Ann Matthews, *Renegades: Irish Republican Women 1900-1922*, (2010); *Irish Press*, 25th June 1945, (na); *Sunday Independent*, 2nd March 1980, (na); *Sunday Independent*, 20th November 1983, (obit).

Thomas Ryan
Volunteer, G.H.Q. Publicity Staff. Roll of Honour

Thomas Ryan resided at Iveagh House, Bride Street and was a printer by trade. He was a member of the special printing team, under the command of Joe Stanley, who left the GPO and commandeered O'Keefe's Printing Works, Halston Street, for the purpose of printing the *Irish War News*.

Thomas Ryan emigrated to England and was living in Birmingham in 1936.

References:
RH; NLI, *Lynch Papers*, (Ms 11,131); Tom Reilly, *Joe Stanley: Printer to the Rising*, (2005).

William (Dan) Ryan: (1892 – 1958)

C. Coy, 2nd Batt, Dublin Brigade

Dan Ryan was born in 1892 and was a native of Rossmore, Thurles, County Tipperary. He worked as a barman in O'Meara's Public House, 70 North Strand Road. In 1916, along with his work colleague Dan Canny, he was a member of C. Company, 2nd Battalion, Dublin Brigade. He fought in the GPO during Easter Week and was wounded there. After the surrender, he was deported to Knutsford Jail and then transferred to Wormwoods Scrubs.

He took part in the War of Independence and was forced to go on the run. Later he continued to work as a barman in Dublin and played hurling for Faugh's GAA Club.

He emigrated to Australia in 1928 where he built up an extensive bar business.

Dan Ryan died in December 1958 in Brisbane, Australia.

References:
> *Irish Press*, 31st December 1958, (obit); *Irish Independent*, 1st January 1959, (obit).

Charles Saurin: (1894 - 1964)

F. Coy, 2nd Batt, Dublin Brigade. Roll of Honour

Charles Saurin was born in 1894 and resided at The Cottage, Vernon Avenue, Clontarf. He was educated at St Joseph's CBS, Fairview and later was employed as a clerk. He joined F. Company, 2nd Battalion, Dublin Brigade in July 1914. On Easter Monday he was in a party, under the command of Lieutenant Leo Henderson, who were detailed to intercept British Troops coming from the Musketry School on Bull Island. They engaged the troops on the railway line in Fairview, and forced them to move down to the docks area. He then proceeded with a group of Volunteers to the GPO, arriving there at 7 o'clock in the evening. He was sent back to Fairview and was in the group that occupied Lambe's Public House, Ballybough Bridge. On Tuesday evening at 8 o'clock he was one of 63 Volunteers and three prisoners, who marched from Fairview to the GPO. When attempting to enter the GPO he received a deep cut to his right hand. He was sent to the Metropole Hotel, under the command of Lieutenant Oscar Traynor, and held out with the garrison there until the bombardment forced them to retreat to the GPO on Friday. During the evacuation of the GPO he was wounded in the same hand while in Henry Place. He was deported to Knutsford Jail on May 1st and interned in Frongoch until July 13th 1916.

During the War of Independence he was adjutant of the Dublin Brigade, under the command of Dick McKee and Oscar Traynor. He joined the Free State Army in 1922 and became brigade adjutant in the Transport Corps. In 1927 he was transferred to the Army Records Office and became head of the department in 1935. He became staff officer to the Director of the FCA in 1947 and became a member of staff of the Bureau of Military History from 1950, until his retirement in 1953 with the rank of lieutenant colonel.

His brother, Thomas, fought in the British Army in France in 1916, while another brother, Frank, was intelligence officer under the command of Michael Collins during the War of Independence.

Lieutenant Colonel Charles Saurin, of Courtmacsherry, County Cork, died on November 7th 1964 and was buried at Clontarf Cemetery.

References:

RH; IMA, MSPC; IMA, BMH (WS 288); NLI, *Lynch Papers,* (Ms 11,131); *An t-Óglach,* March 1926; *Scoil Iósaif, Marino, 1916-1966, (a 1916 Jubilee Publication),* (1966); Max Caulfield, *The Easter Rebellion,* (1963); Michael Foy & Brian Barton, *The Easter Rising,* (2000); *Irish Independent* & *Irish Press,* 9th November 1964, (obits).

John J. Scollan: (1876 – 1962)

Captain. Hibernian Rifles. Roll of Honour

John J. Scollan was born in Derry, in 1876. He came to Dublin in 1911 and resided at 18 Saint Joseph's Avenue, Drumcondra. He was a journalist and secretary of the AOH (American Alliance) and he was founder of the Hibernian Rifles. During the Lockout in 1913, he organised for funds of over £1,000 to be sent from the AOH (American Alliance) in the United States to assist members of the Hibernian Rifles who were on strike. He was the editor and publisher of the journal *the Hibernian,* which had been suppressed on numerous occasions by the authorities. He arranged the purchase of 100 rifles from the Enniskillen Fusiliers

that were stationed in Dollymount, in 1914. In 1915 he paid for Nora Connolly's passage to the United States, she had despatches for the German Ambassador. On Easter Monday he was captain of about 30 members of the Hibernian Rifles, who mobilised at their headquarters at 28 North Frederick Street. After waiting in reserve all day, he received orders from James Connolly to proceed to the GPO at midnight, and on entering the building his men were ordered to break and barricade the upper windows.

He and ten other Hibernian Rifle men accompanied a party of Maynooth Volunteers that were sent to relieve the Irish Citizen Army men surrounded in the Evening Mail Offices early on Tuesday morning. When they reached Parliament Street, they occupied the roof of the Royal Exchange Hotel and fought from there throughout the day. He was beside Edward Walsh, a member of the Hibernian Rifles, when he was mortally wounded in action. That evening the position was evacuated and, led by Captain Tom Byrne, the party returned to the GPO. James Connolly asked him to go to the Broadstone Railway Station on Friday morning to assess the situation in the area, and on his way there he was arrested by a British sentry. He was deported to Wandsworth Jail on June 2nd and interned in Frongoch. He was later transferred to Reading Jail and then to Wormwood Scrubs, before his release at Christmas 1916.

He was employed as a proof reader in the *Irish Press*, from 1932 until his retirement in 1953.

John J. Scollan died on September 9th 1962 and was buried at Mount Jerome Cemetery, Harold's Cross.

References:

RH; IMA, MSPC; IMA, BMH (WS 318 & 341); NLI, *Lynch Papers*, (Ms 11,131); Diarmaid Ferriter, *A Nation and not a Rabble: the Irish Revolution, 1913-1923*, (2015); *Irish Press*, 10th September 1962, (obit); *Irish Independent*, 11th November 1962, (obit).

Francis (Frank) Scullin: (1894 - 1961)

Glasgow Company, (Lieutenant. Kimmage Garrison). Roll of Honour

Frank Scullin was born in Dublin, in 1894. He moved to Scotland and joined the Glasgow Volunteers with his brother, Patrick, before the Easter Rising. He was a lieutenant with the Kimmage Garrison and he reported to the GPO on Easter Monday. With directions given by Seán McLoughlin, he guided a group of Volunteers from North County Dublin, under the command of Richard Coleman, to the Mendicity Institute on Tuesday, and then returned to the GPO. He was wounded in the back on Wednesday as he brought reinforcements to Reis's Chambers and was taken to Sir Patrick Duns Hospital. He was later deported and interned in Frongoch, until Christmas 1916.

He returned to Dublin and resided at 409 North Circular Road. He joined F. Company, 1st Battalion, Dublin Brigade and fought through the War of Independence. He took the Republican side in the Civil War and took part in the occupation of the Fowler Hall, Barry's Hotel, the Hamman Hotel. He was involved in the attack on Broadstone Railway Station, in the Blessington Street ambush, and in the destruction of the railway line at Liffey Junction. He was arrested in March 1923 and imprisoned in Tintown and Hare Park. He was released in May 1924, after a thirty five day hunger strike.

He later lived at 26 Annamoe Drive, Cabra and was employed by the ESB.

Frank Scullin died on May 14th 1961 and was buried at Glasnevin Cemetery.

References:

RH; IMA, MSPC; Ann Matthews, *The Kimmage Garrison 1916*, (2010); *Irish Press*, 15th May 1961, (obit).

Leo (Paddy) Scullin: (1889 - 1938)

Glasgow Company, (Kimmage Garrison). Roll of Honour

Paddy Scullin was born in 1889 and educated at O'Connell Schools, North Richmond Street. He joined the Volunteers in Glasgow with his brother, Frank. Both returned to Dublin before the Rising, and joined the Volunteer Camp at Larkfield, Kimmage. On Easter Monday he served at the North Circular Road Bridge and remained there until Tuesday when the post was abandoned. He made his way to Finglas Bridge and then to Glasnevin Cemetery, where he slept the night, before he reached the GPO on Wednesday morning. He and Liverpool Volunteer, Liam Dickenson, were sent to retrieve some arms at a house near Finglas Bridge, on Wednesday night. They failed to retrieve the arms and on Thursday morning they were unable to return to the GPO because of the military cordon. They were arrested after the surrender in Tyrrelspass, County Westmeath, as they attempted to reach Athenry, County Galway. He was deported to Wakefield Jail on June 2nd and interned in Frongoch until Christmas 1916.

On his release from internment, he took part in the War of Independence and was appointed lieutenant in F. Company, 1st Battalion, Dublin Brigade. He was arrested and imprisoned for eighteen months in 1919, and on several occasions he was used as a hostage by Black and Tans during night raids. He took the Republican side in the Civil War and took part in a hunger strike while interned in the Curragh Camp.

For many years he was employed by the ESB.

Leo (Paddy) Scullin, late of 409 North Circular Road, died on October 30th 1938 and was buried in the Republican Plot at Glasnevin Cemetery.

References:

RH; IMA, MSPC; Ann Matthews, *The Kimmage Garrison 1916*, (2010); *Irish Independent*, 30th October 1938, (obit).

Patrick J. Seely (Sealy): (1894 – 1972)

D. Coy, 4th Batt, Dublin Brigade

Patrick Seely was born in 1894 and resided at 4 Strand Cottages, Rathfarnham. He joined D. Company, 4th Battalion, Dublin Brigade, in 1914. On Easter Monday he reported to Larkfield, Kimmage and remained there until midnight, when he proceeded to the GPO. He served there until Wednesday evening, when he became ill and was sent home by James Connolly.

He rejoined his unit in 1918, while he was working as a railway porter at Kingsbridge Railway Station. He operated under intelligence officer, Mollie Gleeson, in transporting ammunition and dispatches to Limerick Junction. During the Civil War he assisted members of the Tipperary Flying Column, who were temporarily attached to the South Dublin Brigade, to escape when they evacuated Blessington.

Patrick Seely, of 54 Sperrin Road, Drimnagh, died on February 27th 1972 and was buried at Glasnevin Cemetery.

References:

IMA, MSPC; *Evening Herald*, 28th February 1972, (dn).

James Seville: (1896 - 1961)
Fianna Éireann. Roll of Honour

James Seville was born in 1896 and was a member of Fianna Éireann. He reported to the GPO on Easter Monday and was sent to the Vitriol Works, Ballybough on Tuesday morning. He captured the British Medical Officer, Captain John Mahony, at North Strand and brought him as a prisoner to the GPO on Tuesday evening. He fought in the GPO during Easter Week and at the evacuation he was in the advance party that was led by The O'Rahilly into Moore Street, where he found refuge in the cellar of a shop, allowing him to evade capture after the surrender.

After the Rising he joined F. Company, 1st Battalion, Dublin Brigade and fought in the War of Independence. He was arrested in February 1921 and was interned in Arbour Hill and Rath Camp.

James Seville, of 17 Ferns Road, Kimmage and formerly of Findlater's Place, died on December 17th 1961 and was buried at Glasnevin Cemetery.

References:
RH; IMA, MSPC; *Evening Herald*, 19th December 1961, (dn).

James Sexton: (1893 – 1984)
C. Coy, 2nd Batt, Dublin Brigade. Roll of Honour

James Sexton was born in 1893 and resided at 27 Summerhill. He was educated at O'Connell Schools, North Richmond Street and later secured employment as a parcel's clerk in the Dublin United Tramways Co. After the 1913 Lockout, when the trade union workers returned to work, he lost his job for refusing to resign from the Transport and General Workers Union. He then took casual work as a docker and in 1914 joined the Volunteers. In 1916 resided at 11 Upper Gloucester Place and on Easter Monday he reported to Father Mathew Park, Fairview and escorted a horse-drawn lorry loaded with arms and first aid supplies to the GPO. He posted to the Princes Street side of the building after his arrival, there. The following day he was posted to the Henry Street side of the roof with ten other Volunteers, under the command of Lieutenant Joe Twamley. On Thursday they came under artillery shelling, and they were forced down on Friday when fire engulfed the roof. After the evacuation, he was beside Harry Coyle when he was killed in Moore Street, at the corner with Henry Place. He was deported to Knutsford Prison on May 1st and interned in Frongoch until July 31st 1916.

He took part in the War of Independence and was interned in Ballykinlar and the Curragh Camp. During the Civil War he fought on the Republican side. He went to live with his family at 2 Tolka Road, Ballybough, in 1933 and devoted a great deal of time to youth activities in the area. After its formation in 1943, he was involved with Stella Maris Boys FC for over thirty years.

James Sexton, who was a Dublin Corporation employee for many years, died on December 5th 1984, aged 91, and was buried at Glasnevin Cemetery.

References:
RH; IMA, MSPC; NLI, *Lynch Papers*, (Ms 11,131); *Irish Press*, 6th December 1984, (obit).

Francis (Frank) Sheridan: (1863 – 1916)
E. Coy, 4th Batt, Dublin Brigade. Roll of Honour

Frank Sheridan was born in Rathfarnham, in 1863 and was a house painter by trade. He was active in the Gaelic League and was a member of the Michael Dwyer's GAA Club. He joined the Volunteers at the inaugural meeting in the Rotunda, in 1913. On Easter Monday he was mobilised and reported to the GPO. He was sent the following day on Volunteer business to a hospital to see a wounded comrade, when he suddenly collapsed. He didn't make it back to the GPO until Wednesday, and although he was advised by his O/C to return home, he insisted on remaining and helped tend to the wounded. After conveying the wounded to Jervis Street Hospital on Friday, he was taken into custody. While in Richmond Barracks his health deteriorated and he was released. Frank Sheridan of 5 Castleview, Rathfarnham, died suddenly on November 20 1916, leaving an only daughter, and was buried at Glasnevin Cemetery.

References:
RH; *Catholic Bulletin*, February 1918.

James Sheridan: (1888 - 1947)

B. Coy, 4th Batt, Dublin Brigade. Roll of Honour

James Sheridan was born in 1888. He was a house painter by trade and lived at 16 Mountainview Avenue, Harold's Cross. On Easter Monday he went to Larkfield, Kimmage, with a party of Volunteers under the command of Lieutenant Larry Murtagh. They arrived in the GPO the following morning, and they then divided into two groups; one moving on to the Four Courts and the other remaining in the GPO. He manned the ground floor windows and on Thursday he was posted to a position on the roof of the GPO. He was back manning the ground floor windows when the building was evacuated on Friday, and spent the night in occupied houses in Moore Street. After the surrender he was deported to Knutsford Jail on May 1ˢᵗ and was interned in Frongoch until August 1916.

He rejoined the Volunteers and fought in the War of Independence. He fought on the Republican side during the Civil War and was took part in armed patrols. He was involved in attacks on Free State Forces at Terenure and Rathfarnham Barracks. He was arrested and interned in Hare Camp, the Curragh, in August 1923.

James Sheridan, of 169 Harold's Cross Road, died on June 25ᵗʰ 1947 and was buried at Mount Jerome Cemetery, Harold's Cross.

References:
RH; IMA, MSPC; NLI, *Lynch Papers*, (Ms 11,131); *Irish Press*, 27ᵗʰ June 1947, (obit).

Arthur Shields: (1896 – 1970)

F. Coy, 2nd Batt, Dublin Brigade. Roll of Honour

Arthur Shields was born in Dublin on February 15ᵗʰ 1896 and was educated at Greenlanes National School, Clontarf (Seafield Road) and the Merchant Taylors School. His father, Adolphus Shields, was a journalist and Parnellite who was descended on his mother's side from the patriot, William Orr. His older brother, William, became famous as the Abbey actor and film star, Barry Fitzgerald. At the age of fourteen, he began work at the *Evening Telegraph* Newspaper and later worked for the publishers, Maunsel & Co. Because of his interest in acting, he joined the Abbey Theatre in 1914. After the Bachelor's Walk massacre on July 26ᵗʰ of the same year, he joined the Volunteers. He resided at 3 Seafield Road, Clontarf and was a member of F. Company, 2ⁿᵈ Battalion, Dublin Brigade in 1916. On Easter Monday he reported to the 2ⁿᵈ Battalion Headquarters, at Father Mathew Park and was given permission to go to the Abbey Theatre and deliver the manuscript of a play that was to be premiered there the following day. He then proceeded to the GPO and met James Connolly, who referred to Adolphus, his father, as a pioneer in the cause of Irish labour. He was then sent with a party to Reis's Chambers, across the street at the corner of Abbey

Street, with orders to set up a radio transmitter. Later that day he was posted to the Hibernian Bank, under the command of Captain Tom Weafer, and he spent the next two days carrying despatches to and from the GPO under heavy sniper fire. When the Hibernian Bank was evacuated on Thursday, he withdrew to the GPO. After the surrender he was deported to Knutsford Jail on May 1st and interned in Frongoch until August 1916.

On his release he returned to the Abbey, where he was a leading actor for twenty two years and appeared in first productions of the O'Casey plays. In 1936 he went to the United States to appear in John Ford's film production of *"The Plough and the Stars"*. He remained in America and became one of Hollywood's leading support actors, appearing in, among other films, *"She Wore A Yellow Ribbon"*, *"Long Voyage Home"*, *"Drums Along The Mohawk"*, *"National Velvet"* and *"The Quiet Man"*.

Arthur Shields died at his residence in Santa Barbara, California, on April 27th 1970 and he was buried in Deansgrange Cemetery.

References:

RH; IMA, MSPC; IMA, BMH (WS 288, *Charles Saurin*); NLI, *Lynch* Papers, (Ms 11,131); *An t-Óglach*, March 1926, (*Charles Saurin*); *DHR*, September 1988; Max Caulfield, *The Easter Rebellion*, (1963); *Evening Herald*, 1st May 1970, (dn).

Patrick Shortis: (1890 – 1916). Killed in Action
Lieutenant. F. Coy, 2nd Batt, Dublin Brigade. Roll of Honour

Patrick Shortis was born in Ballybunion, County Kerry, in 1890 and was educated locally and later at St Brendan's Seminary, Killarney. After four years there, he transferred to All Hollows College, Drumcondra, but he left before his Ordination. He received a BA Degree in the National University, and then attended the Wireless College in Cahirciveen, County Kerry. His next few years were spent in London, where he became active in the Volunteer movement. In January 1916 he returned to Dublin and became a lieutenant with F. Company, 2nd Battalion, Dublin Brigade. During Easter Week he was active in the GPO and in the area around Henry Street and Jervis Street. He led a party that occupied a warehouse in Henry Street and O'Neill's Public House, at the corner of Henry Street and Liffey Street, where they came under intense fire from a British armoured car until it withdrew on Thursday. His group were recalled to the GPO on Friday morning. At the evacuation of the burning building that evening, he fell under a hail of machine gun fire at the junction of Moore Street and Henry Place.

Patrick Shortis was buried in the 1916 Plot at Glasnevin Cememtery.

References:

RH; *Catholic Bulletin*, August 1916; Ray Bateson, *They Died by Pearse's Side*, (2010).

Matilda (Tilly) Simpson: (1895 - 1967)

Cumann na mBan (Fairview Branch). Roll of Honour

Tilly Simpson was born in 1895 and resided at Upton Cottage, Grace Park Terrace, Marino. She was a founder member of the Fairview Branch of Cumann na mBan and in her younger days she played camogie in Dublin. She reported to the GPO on Easter Monday and served in the first aid section through the week. On Friday she was in the party that accompanied the wounded Volunteers to Jervis Street Hospital. Led by Father Flanagan and the Indian Medical Service prisoner, Captain Mahony, they made their way to the hospital through the tunnelled walls of the Coliseum Theatre, Henry Street. Her brother, Terry, was a member of the Jacob's Garrison in Easter Week.

She transferred to the Árd Craobh Branch of Cumann na mBan in 1917 and took part in collecting for the Prisoners Dependents Fund. She was also involved in the anti-conscription campaign and in general elections work. She took the anti-Treaty side in the Civil War and served at Barry's Hotel and the Hamman Hotel. Her home at Upton Cottage was used as the Republican GHQ and was regularly raided by Free State Forces. She was arrested in February 1923 and interned in Kilmainham Jail and in the North Dublin Union.

Tilly Simpson died on June 5th 1967 and was buried in Drumcondra Graveyard.

References:
RH; IMA, MSPC; NLI, *Lynch Papers*, (Ms 11,131); Liz Gillis, *Women of the Irish Revolution, 1913-1923*, (2014); *Evening Herald*, 6th June 1967, (dn).

Doctor Peter Slattery: (1884 - 1954)

E. Coy, 4th Batt, Dublin Brigade. Roll of Honour

Peter Slattery, of 52 Thomas Street, Limerick, was born in 1884. He was a civil engineer by profession and prior to the Rising, he was teaching chemistry in St Enda's College, Rathfarnham. He was a member of E. Company, 4th Battalion, Dublin Brigade, and on Good Friday 1916 he was appointed Director of Engineers to the GHQ. On entering the GPO on Easter Monday, he was accidentally wounded, but remained active throughout the week. He was among the wounded Volunteers taken to Jervis Street Hospital on Friday. After the surrender he was sentenced to eight years penal servitude.

He was imprisoned at Dartmoor and other prisons, before he was released in June 1917. On Cathal Brugha's instructions, he gained employment in the Air Ministry in London for intelligence purposes. He brought the plans of Dublin's Custom House from the Office of Public Works in London, back to Dublin. He also purchased Thompson guns in America and brought them back to Ireland. He later become an instructor in munitions with the IRA and manufactured explosives during the War of Independence. He held degrees in medicine and engineering and when St Enda's re-opened, he was headmaster for a period. He supported the Treaty and joined the Free State Army with the rank of commandant in the Corps of Engineers. He later served in the Reserves and took up farming in Brittas, County Dublin.

Doctor Peter Slattery, of Timode House, Timode, County Dublin, died on June 11th 1954 and was buried at Glasnevin Cemetery.

References:

RH; IMA, MSPC; IMA, BMH (WS 176); *Irish Independent*, 14th June 1954, (obit); *Irish Press*, 15th June 1954, (obit).

Charles (Charlie) Smith: (1878 – 1942)

Lieutentant. Irish Citizen Army, (Gloucester St Section). Roll of Honour

Charlie Smith was born in 1878 and resided at 43 Foley Street, in 1916. He was a member of the Irish Citizen Army, Gloucester Street Section, and on Easter Monday he was one of a group, commanded by Captain Frank Thornton, that remained in Liberty Hall after the main body left for the GPO. That afternoon he brought the supplies from Liberty Hall to the GPO and was in a party that was sent to link up with Captain Seán Connolly in City Hall. They came under heavy fire from British Troops in the Crown Alley Telephone Exchange, and withdrew to a position in Daly's Public House on Fleet Street. On Tuesday morning they were recalled to the GPO and he was sent to the Imperial Hotel. He received a sledgehammer blow to his left knee, while engaged in boring through the wall to an adjacent building. When the Imperial Hotel was evacuated because of the intense fire on Thursday, he made his way to Waterford Street and evaded capture.

Because of his knee injury, he was unable to continue on active service, and in 1933 had his leg amputated from the knee down.

Charlie Smith, of 16 North Clarence Street, died on November 14th 1942 and was buried at Glasnevin Cemetery.

References:

RH; IMA, MSPC; NLI, *Lynch Papers*, (Ms 11,131) & *William O'Brien Papers*, (Ms 15,673); Ann Matthews, *The Irish Citizen Army*, (2014).

Lucy Smyth (Mrs. Lucy Byrne): (1882 – 1972)

Cumann na mBan, (Central Branch). Roll of Honour

Lucy Smyth was born in 1882. She was a member of the Central Branch of Cumann na mBan and on Easter Monday she was ordered to standby in the Blessington Street area, with other members of Cumann na mBan. They reported to the GPO on Tuesday, and on Wednesday morning she was sent to the Hibernian Bank. Later that night when the bank was evacuated, she returned to the GPO and tended to the wounded, including James Connolly. She accompanied the wounded to Jervis Street Hospital on Friday.

After the Rising she was involved in collection and distribution of funds for the Prisoners Dependents Fund. She married Tom Byrne, who also fought in the GPO in Easter Week and who became O/C of the 1st Battalion, IRA from 1917 to 1921. She was appointed first lieutenant of the Cumann na mBan, Árd Craobh Branch, in 1918. Her husband was arrested during a raid on their home late in 1919, and he was interned in Brixton Prison.

Mrs Lucy Byrne, of 71 Old Cabra Road, died on November 16th 1972.

References:
RH; IMA, MSPC; Liz Gillis, *Women of the Irish Revolution, 1913-1923*, (2014); *Irish Press*, 17th November 1972, (obit).

Christine Stafford Brooks: (1881 - 1950)

Cumann na mBan, (Central Branch). Roll of Honour

Christine Stafford was born in 1881 and was the daughter of the veteran Fenian, Matt Stafford. She resided at 23 Drumcondra Road and was a member of Cumann na mBan, Árd Craobh. She reported to the GPO on Easter Monday, and was sent to the wireless station at Reis's Chambers. On Wednesday she attended to the wounded and dying in the Hibernian Bank, including Captain Tom Weafer. When the bank was evacuated on Thursday, she was sent to mobilise men in the Drumcondra area to serve under Tom Ashe, in Ashbourne. She was unable to return to the GPO on Friday, because of the military cordon.

Later in 1916 she married Fred Brooks, who was a member of the Mendicity Institute Garrison. She was involved in National Aid work and in collecting money for arms. She took the Republican side in the Civil War and was imprisoned in Kilmainham Jail. She was ill-treated in prison and contracted sciatica and lost the sight in one eye. A letter smuggled out of prison was published, describing her condition, and as a result she was released.

Christine Stafford Brooks, of 17 Bantry Road, Drumcondra, died on April 27th 1950 and was buried at Glasnevin Cemetery.

References:
RH; IMA, MSPC; *Irish Independent*, 28th April 1950, (obit).

John (Jack) Stafford: (1886 – 1966)

Section Commander. B. Coy, 2nd Batt, Dublin Brigade

Jack Stafford, the son of the Fenian, Matt Stafford, was born in 1886 and joined the IRB in 1910. He joined the Volunteers at the inaugural meeting at the Rotunda in 1913, and became a member of B. Company, 2nd Battalion, Dublin Brigade. In 1914 he took part in the Howth gun running. He was not mobilised on Easter Monday, so he made his way to St Stephen's Green, where his O/C, Tom Hunter, told him to return home and get his rifle. On his return he fell in with a group of Volunteers, under the command of Seamus Devoy and reported to the GPO. This group was then sent across the street to the Hibernian Bank, where Captain Tom Weafer was in command. After the fatal shooting of Captain Weafer, he got on to a small balcony, from where he had a good view up Westmoreland Street. From here he engaged the enemy, but came under heavy fire. He was forced to withdraw indoors, when a bullet shattered the butt of his rifle, cutting his hand. When the Hibernian Bank was evacuated, he made his way out through the bored walls and over roofs. During the withdrawal his group was scattered and he managed to evade capture. He eventually made his way to his residence at 23 Drumcondra Road.

He rejoined the Volunteers in 1917 and became a member of the Active Service Unit. He was involved in an operation when a number of British agents were killed in the Mount Street area. The following day his house at Wellpark Avenue, Drumcondra, was raided by the Black and Tans, who were looking for his brother-in-law, Sam Ellis. He was interrogated for over an hour and was threatened with shooting.

He joined the Free State Army in 1922 with the rank of captain and served until 1929, when he transferred to the Reserve. He was called up for duty during the Emergency years and was later an official in the Dublin County Council Health Authority.

Jack Stafford, of Grace Dieu, Donabate, died on April 6th 1966 and was buried at Swords.

References:
IMA, MSPC; IMA, BMH (WS 818); *Evening Herald*, 7th April 1966, (obit).

Matthew (Matt) Stafford: (1853 – 1950)
Quartermaster. B. Coy, 2nd Batt, Dublin Brigade

Matt Stafford was born in Sutton, County Dublin, in 1853 and was educated at Baldoyle CBS. He began his working life in the victualling business. He witnessed the Fenian Rising of 1867, and joined the Fenian Brotherhood in 1870. He later joined the Gaelic League and Sinn Féin at both groups' foundation. He resided at 23 Drumcondra Road, Drumcondra and was Quartermaster of B. Company, 2nd Battalion, Dublin Brigade. He was not mobilised on Easter Monday and spent the week, at the age of sixty four, engaged in sniping in the Drumcondra area. He was arrested on May 3rd and court-martialled at Trinity College, but was released due to a lack of evidence. His son, Jack and daughter, Christina were part of the GPO Garrison, during Easter Week. In his pension application he refused to give details of his activities during Easter Week but Oscar Traynor stated that he was engaged in sniping in the 2nd Batallion area.

He took part in the War of Independence and took the Republican side in the Civil War. Seán O'Casey once described him, as "a fine old skin and a brave, honest man".

He was a founder member of Fianna Fáil in 1926, and served on the National Executive, from 1926 to 1947. He was a Senator from 1937 to 1948 and was a member of Dublin Corporation for many years. He was also a member of the Central Midwives Board and the Grangegorman Mental Hospital Committee.

Matt Stafford died on June 12th 1950 at his daughter's residence at 55 St Patrick's Road, Drumcondra, aged ninety eight.

References:
IMA, MSPC; *Irish Press*, 16th June 1947, (na, *presentation to Matt Stafford*); *Irish Press*, 13th June 1950, (obit).

Michael Staines: (1885 – 1955)
Quartermaster General. Irish Volunteers

Michael Staines was born on September 15th 1885 and raised in Newport, County Mayo. He moved to Dublin in 1902 and was employed in the manufacturing business. He was a member of the Gaelic League and joined the Volunteers at the inaugural meeting at the Rotunda, in 1913. He was appointed Quartermaster of A., B. and C. Companies, 1st Battalion, Dublin Brigade, which drilled at the Colmcille Hall, Blackhorse Street and later in 1915 he was promoted Dublin Brigade Quartermaster. He was appointed to P.H. Pearse's Staff and a few months before the Rising he replaced The O'Rahilly as Quartermaster General. In 1916 he resided at 63 Murtagh Road, Stoneybatter. On Easter Monday he was in charge of transferring munitions from Liberty Hall to the GPO and when The O'Rahilly arrived, his car was used for this purpose. On Thursday he was one of the first to find the wounded James Connolly, and with the help of George Plunkett and others, carried him back to the GPO. After the GPO was evacuated, he spent Friday night in the houses in Moore Street. He was deported to Wakefield Jail on May 6th and interned in Frongoch. His brother, Liam, was seriously wounded in the Mendicity Institute, during Easter Week.

On his release from internment, he was involved in the Irish National Aid Association and was a founder of New Ireland Assurance. He was elected a Sinn Féin MP for the St Michan's Constituency, Dublin, in 1918 and was an alderman with Dublin Corporation. He was a leading organiser of the Sinn Féin Courts and was interned, from December 1920 to August 1921. He also directed the Belfast Boycott in response to the anti-Catholic rioting in Belfast in 1920. He was elected Sinn Féin MP in 1921 for Dublin North West and helped organise An Garda Síochána in 1922, and was appointed its first Commissioner. He later clashed with the Republican element in the new force, in what became known as the Kildare Mutiny, and resigned his position. He remained an alderman with Dublin Corporation until 1925, and was a Senator from 1930 to 1936.

Michael Staines, of 8 Castle Avenue, Clontarf, died on October 25th 1955 and was buried at Clontarf Cemetery.

References:
IMA, BMH (WS 284); Thomas Coffey, *Agony at Easter*, (1969); Seán O'Mahony, *Frongoch: University of Revolution*, (1987); Peter DeRosa, *Rebels, the Irish Rising of 1916*, (1991); John P. Duggan, *A History of the Irish Army*, (1991); Michael Foy & Brian Barton, *The Easter Rising*, (2000); Charles Townshend, *Easter 1916, the Irish Rebellion*, (2006); Charlie McGuire, *Seán McLoughlin: Ireland's Forgotten Revolutionary*, (2011); *Irish Independent & Irish Press*, 27th October 1955, (obits).

Joseph (Joe) Stanley: (1890 – 1950)

Captain. G.H.Q. Publicity Staff. Roll of Honour

Joe Stanley was born in 1890 and resided at 36 Parnell Street, where his father had a drapery shop. He was educated at O'Connell Schools and was a school friend of Seán Heuston. He first worked as a clerk with the Great Southern and Western Railway, and in 1913 established his own printing and publishing business, Gaelic Press, at 30 Upper Liffey Street, when he bought the struggling printing business of his future father-in-law, Matt Walker. He became a member of the IRB and published material in support of the Republican Movement, including *The Gael*, *The Gaelic Athletic*, *The Hibernian*, *Honesty* and *The Spark*.

In June 1915 he married Annie Walker, who was an Abbey actress and was also known by the stage name, Eileen O'Doherty. Her sister Mary Elizabeth, was better known as the Abbey actress, Máire Nic Shiulbhaigh.

His publications were regularly suppressed, and his premises were raided and printing machinery confiscated. During Easter Week he was in charge of printing the bulletins issued by P.H. Pearse in the *Irish War News* from the GPO. Because his own printing works were closed by the authorities, he commandeered O'Keefe's Printing Works, Halston Street, for this purpose with a team of four printers that comprised of his father-in-law, Matt Walker and his brother-in-law, Charlie Walker, James O'Sullivan and Thomas Ryan. He spent the week travelling between Halston Street and the GPO, and spent between two and three hours there on each occasion. On Thursday, P.H. Pearse gave him a letter to deliver to Pearse's mother. For fear of being arrested and caught in possession of the letter, he passed it on to Matt Walker, who hand-delivered it to the Pearse family some weeks after the Rising. On May 12th he was escorted from Upper Liffey Street by British soldiers and detained in Richmond Barracks. He was deported to Knutsford Jail on June 2nd and interned in Frongoch until Christmas 1916. Before the Rising he was an active member of the Geraldine's GAA Club and while in Frongoch, he organised Gaelic football matches among the prisoners.

On his release from internment, he continued to be active in the national movement until the Truce. When the premises were again destroyed by the authorities, he moved his family to Drogheda, where he opened a cinema. In 1929 he took up a position as sub-editor of the *Daily Mail* newspaper in London and remained there for six years. He returned to Drogheda and became managing director of the *Drogheda Argus* newspaper. He was at one time a senior alderman on Drogheda Corporation and president of the Drogheda Rotary Club. He was also a keen golfer and set up a pitch and putt course at Hackett's Cross.

Joe Stanley died in the Lourdes Hospital, Drogheda, on June 2nd 1950 and was buried at St Peter's New Cemetery, Drogheda.

References:

RH; IMA, MSPC; John O'Connor, *The 1916 Proclamation*, (1999); Tom Reilly, *Joe Stanley: Printer to the Rising*, (2005); *Irish Press*, 3rd June 1950, (obit).

Mary Jane Stapleton (Mrs. Mary Slevin)
Clan na nGael Girls Scouts. Roll of Honour

Mary Stapleton was a member of Clan na nGael Girls Scouts and along with another member, Annie Tobin, served in the GPO during Easter Week.

Mrs Mary Slevin later resided at 23 Hardiman Road, Glasnevin.

References:
RH.

Charles Steinmayer: (1896 – 1965)
A. Coy, 3rd Batt, Dublin Brigade. Roll of Honour

Charles Steinmayer was born in 1896 and resided at 70 Lombard Street West, South Circular Road. He was employed as a clerk and was a member of A. Company, 3rd Battalion, Dublin Brigade. He wasn't mobilised on Easter Monday morning and arrived in the GPO late that night, having made his way first to Liberty Hall. He spent that night posted at the windows on the ground floor of the GPO. On Tuesday he was sent to disperse looters nearby, and on Wednesday he took up a position on the roof of the GPO. He joined the party defending the Metropole Hotel until they were forced out by the fire engulfing the building on Friday. He was in the group led by The O'Rahilly into Moore Street on Friday evening and he witnessed O'Rahilly fall and was forced to dive into a laneway to escape the gunfire. He took refuge in a tenement with Tony Swan, and later that night he was engaged in boring through the walls of the houses in Moore Street. After the surrender he was deported to Stafford Jail on May 1st and interned in Frongoch until Christmas 1916.

While in Frongoch he suffered with bronchitis and his release from internment he fell seriously ill. He went to Belleek, County Fermanagh, to improve his health and was engaged in training the local Volunteers there. When he returned to Dublin, he was arrested and interned at Ballykinlar Camp from September 1920 to December 1921. He joined the Free State Army in September 1922 and was discharged in January 1929, as medically unfit, with the rank of lieutenant.

Charles Steinmayer, of 117 Seafield Road, Clontarf, died on July 14th 1965.

References:
RH; IMA, MSPC; NLI, *Lynch Papers*, (Ms 11,131); *An t-Óglach*, 27th February 1926; Max Caulfield, *The Easter Rebellion*, (1963).

Patrick J. Stephenson: (1895 – 1960)

D. Coy, 1st Batt, Dublin Brigade & Fianna Éireann. Roll of Honour

Paddy Stephenson was born in 1895 and educated at O'Connell Schools, North Richmond Street. He was employed as an apprentice with the brush-making firm, Varians in Talbot Street and later as a stationer's assistant. He joined D. Company, 1st Battalion, in December 1913 and on Easter Sunday night he was in a party of Volunteers, which included his future brother-in-law, Paddy Kilmartin that stood guard at the D. Company's headquarters, at the Colmcille Hall, Blackhall Street. On Easter Monday he in the group, under the command of Seán Heuston, that occupied the Mendicity Institute building at Usher's Island. He went with Seán McLoughlin to the GPO on Wednesday, to report to James Connolly and to bring back munitions and supplies. On their return they found the Mendicity Institute under attack and as they watched from the other side of the Liffey, they were forced to flee to the Four Courts when their identity were revealed by on-lookers. They spent Wednesday night manning a barricade at Chancery Lane and they went to the GPO on Thursday. Paddy remained in the GPO until it was evacuated on Friday evening. He was deported to Knutsford Jail on May 1st and interned in Frongoch until August 1916. His father, Patrick Stephenson, of 76 Lower Gloucester Street, was a civilian casualty of the Rising when he was shot dead by a British army sniper.

In 1917 he was transferred to Fianna Éireann and was involved in its reorganisation. He also married Mary Kilmartin, of Stoneybatter, in the same year. She was a Cumann na mBan member and was attached to the Four Courts Garrison in Easter Week. He was appointed Adjutant General of the Fianna in Dublin and was involved in attacks on police and raids for arms and other operations. He rejoined D. Company, 1st Battalion in 1919 and served up to the Truce. He was a founder member of the Communist Party of Ireland in October 1921. He entered the library service in Dublin soon afterwards and in 1949 he was appointed Dublin City Librarian. He was a founder member of the Old Dublin Society and was its president, from 1957 to 1959. He was a president of the Literary Association of Ireland and was a member and treasurer of the PEN Club. He was keenly interested in Dublin history and published a number of papers in the Dublin Historical Record. One of his sons, Sam, was the well known architect, who designed the Central Bank and the Civic Buildings at Wood Quay.

Paddy Stephenson, of 3 Woodlands Avenue, Stillorgan, died on April 6th 1960 and was buried at Glasnevin Cemetery.

References:
RH; IMA, MSPC; IMA, BMH (WS 191, *Joe Reynolds*), BMH (WS 251, *Dick Balfe*), BMH (WS 328, *Garry Holohan*) & BMH (WS 569, *John A. Caffrey*); *DHR*, May 1960, (obit & photograph); Desmond Ryan, *The Rising*, (1949); Charlie McGuire, *Seán McLoughlin: Ireland's Forgotten Revolutionary*, (2011); *Irish Independent* & *Evening Herald*, 7th April 1960, (obits).

James (Jim) Stritch: (1853 - 1933)
I.R.B. Roll of Honour

As a boy, Jim Stritch, helped in the rescue of the Fenians, Colonel Kelly and Captain Deasy in Manchester on September 18th 1867, by taking hold of the prison van horses' reins. He was a prominent member of the Brothers Sheares Circle of the IRB and took part in the Land Wars. He was a branch president of the Irish National Foresters, 41 Parnell Square, which was a front for the IRB. Before the formation of the Volunteers, he was involved in the building of a hall built at the rear of the premises in Parnell Square, where IRB men drilled. He was a member of the O'Donovan Rossa Funeral Committee in 1915. In 1916, he resided at 51 Mountjoy Street and fought with the GPO Garrison during Easter Week. After the surrender he was detained in Kilmainham Jail and interned in Frongoch until July 27th 1916.

He continued to take part in the national cause and took the Republican side in the Civil War. Later, he was treasurer of the Wolfe Tone Memorial Association and a member of the National Graves Association. He was responsible for the formation of the Republican Brass and Reed Band, of which he was president. For many years he was an inspector in the Paving Department of Dublin Corporation.

Jim Stritch, the veteran Fenian, died on February 24th 1933 and was buried at Glasnevin Cemetery.

References:

RH; IMA, BMH (WS 234, *James Smyth*), BMH (WS 280, *Robert Holland*), BMH (WS 409, *Valentine Jackson*), BMH (WS 908, *Michael O'Flanagan*), BMH (WS 1,244, *Joseph O'Rourke*) & BMH (WS 1,765, *Seán T. O'Kelly*); Gerard MacAtasney, *Seán MacDiarmada: the Mind of a* Revolution, (2004); Seán O'Mahony, *Frongoch: University of Revolution*, (2005); *Irish Press*, 27 February 1933, (obit).

Pádraig Supple: (1897 - 1945)
Liverpool Company, (Kimmage Garrison). Roll of Honour

Pádraig Supple was born in Liverpool in 1897. Before the Rising, he came to Dublin with a group of Volunteers from Liverpool, and went to Larkfield, Kimmage. On entering the GPO on Easter Monday, he was in the squad that encountered seven British soldiers emerging from their guardroom. The sergeant in charge was felled by a Volunteer bullet, before it was discovered that the soldiers had no ammunition for their rifles and they were taken prisoner. He spent Tuesday and Wednesday manning the ground floor windows in the GPO. On Thursday he was sent by The O'Rahilly to help in breaking through the walls of the buildings in Henry Street. He was wounded on Friday and was taken to Jervis Street Hospital with other wounded men later that day. On Sunday he was removed from Jervis Street under armed guard, and taken to the hospital at Dublin Castle. He was deported to Knutsford Jail on June 7th and interned in Frongoch until Christmas 1916.

At the end of 1919, he returned to Liverpool and rejoined the Liverpool Company. He was involved in transporting arms to Ireland, and in June 1921 he was appointed battalion quartermaster. He was also involved in burning the homes of known Black and Tans in Liverpool, who were garrisoned in Ireland. He served until March 1922 and took no part in the Civil War. In later years he joined the Irish Civil Service and was attached to the Dept of Supplies.

Pádraig Supple, of 19 Auburn Avenue, Donnybrook, died on August 4th 1945 and was buried at Deansgrange Cemetery.

References:
RH; IMA, MSPC; NLI, *Lynch Papers*, (Ms 11,131); Ann Matthews, *The Kimmage Garrison 1916*, (2010); *Irish Press*, 7th August 1945, (obit).

Anthony (Tony) Swan: (1902 – 1973)

Fianna Éireann. Roll of Honour

Tony Swan was born in 1902 and resided at 13 Belvedere Avenue, North Circular Road. He was a member of Fianna Éireann and he reported to the GPO on Easter Monday. He was put on sentry duty on the ground floor and was one of those photographed by Volunteer Joe Cripps in the GPO during Easter Week. On Friday evening he was in the party led by The O'Rahilly into Moore Street. When the group came under heavy fire, he and Charles Steinmayer took cover in a deserted building before moving into a Mineral Water Works. On Saturday morning he joined the Volunteers at the barricade at the corner of Henry Place and Moore Street. He was detained in Richmond Barracks after the surrender, and was released from there on May 12th, because of his young age. His brother, Patrick, was a member of the Four Courts Garrison, during Easter Week.

He joined D. Company, 2nd Battalion, Dublin Brigade, in 1917 and was involved in armed patrols. Two years later, he transferred to A. Company, 2nd Battalion and was arrested and interned in Ballykinlar Camp from November 1920 to December 1921. After the Truce he joined the Free State Army and served for many years, retiring with the rank of commandant in the 1950's.

Commandant Anthony Swan, of Auburn, Newbridge, County Kildare, died on November 9th 1973 and was buried at St Conleth's Cemetery, Newbridge.

References:
RH; IMA, MSPC; NLI, *Lynch Papers*, (Ms 11,131); *Evening Herald*, 10th November 1973, (dn).

Patrick Swanzy: (1892 - 1974)

D. Coy, 2nd Batt, Dublin Brigade

Patrick Swanzy was born in 1892 and resided at 57 Lower Gloucester Street. He was a baker by trade and he played football for the Emeralds GAA Club. He was member of the Gaelic League and of D. Company, 2nd Battalion, Dublin Brigade. On Easter Monday morning he reported to Father Mathew Park, Fairview and was posted to Gilbey's, Ballybough Bridge. He remained there until Tuesday evening, when his party reported to the GPO. He was then sent to the Imperial Hotel, under the command of Captain Brennan-Whitmore. After the surrender he was deported to Knutsford Jail on May 3rd and interned in Frongoch until July 31st 1916.

He took part in many operations during the War of Independence and was a member of the Active Service Unit. In May 1921 he was captured at the burning of the Custom

House and was held prisoner in Mountjoy Jail and Kilmainham Jail until the Truce. He took the pro-Treaty side in the Civil War, and was one of Arthur Griffith's bodyguards. He fought against Republican forces at Jacob's Biscuit Factory on June 28th 1922, and acted as an intelligence officer, under the command of Captain Moynihan, in Oriel House. He joined the British Merchant Navy and served throughout World War Two, from 1942 to 1946.

Patrick Swanzy, of 5 Sitric Place, Stoneybatter, died on October 30th 1974.

References:
IMA, MSPC; *Sinn Féin Rebellion Handbook* 1916, Weekly Irish Times, (1917); W.J. Brennan-Whitmore, *Dublin Burning*, (1996); *Irish Press*, 31st October 1974, (obit).

Swedish Seaman (Name Unknown)
Volunteer, (Unattached)

On Easter Monday, 1916, two foreign seamen, a Swede and a Finn, arrived at the GPO and offered their services until their ship was due to depart on Thursday. They gained entry and were provided with a shotgun and a rifle by Captain Liam Tannam. When the shotgun, which was in the hands of the Finnish seaman, Antti Makapaltis, accidently went off slightly wounding Volunteer James Kenny, both men were transferred to the bomb making section. They were later posted to the roof, where they remained until the building was evacuated. After the surrender on Saturday, the Swedish seaman, whose name was unknown, was released from detention in Richmond Barracks, after the intervention of the Swedish Consul.

References:
IMA, BMH (WS 232, *Liam Tannam*); *An t-Óglach*, 23rd January 1926, (*Michael Staines*).

James Sweeney: (1889 - 1957)
E. Coy, 4th Batt, Dublin Brigade. Roll of Honour

James Sweeney was born in 1889 and resided at Butterfield Avenue, Rathfarnham. He was employed as a van driver and was a member of the E. Company, 4th Battalion, with his brother, Patrick. He also was a member of the Michael Dwyer's GAA Club. On Easter Monday morning he assembled with the rest of his company at Rathfarnham Church and arrived at the GPO at around two o'clock that afternoon. They were then divided into two groups, with some manning the ground floor windows, while the majority took up positions on the roof, under the command of Lieutenant Michael Boland. Before the surrender on Saturday afternoon, he volunteered for the bayonet charge on the British barricade at Parnell Street under the command of Seán McLoughlin, which was cancelled by P.H.

Pearse. He was deported with his brother, Patrick, to Stafford Jail on May 1st and they were both then interned in Frongoch until Christmas 1916.

In 1917 he was involved in reorganising his local Rathfarnham Volunteers and was appointed adjutant. He took part in the burning of Rockbrook RIC Barracks and in a number of armed raids. He was made company police sergeant and brought a number of robbers before the Republican Courts. He was arrested in September 1920, and sentenced to two years penal servitude. He was imprisoned in Mountjoy, Belfast, Liverpool and Nottingham Jails and was released at the Truce. He took no part in the Civil War.

James Sweeney, of 1 Butterfield Avenue, Rathfarnham, died on January 30th 1957 and was buried at Cruagh Cemetery, Rathfarnham.

References:
RH; IMA, MSPC; *Sinn Féin Rebellion Handbook 1916*, Weekly Irish Times, (1917); *Irish Press*, 31st January 1957, (dn).

Joseph (Joe) Sweeney: (1897 – 1980)
E. Coy, 4th Batt, Dublin Brigade. Roll of Honour

Joe Sweeney was born in Burtonport, County Donegal, in 1897. He was educated in Burtonport National School, St Enda's College, Rathfarnham and UCD. He joined the Volunteers in Burtonport and transferred to E. Company, 4th Battalion, Dublin Brigade, in Rathfarnham in September 1914. On Easter Monday 1916, he was studying in UCD and lodging in St Enda's, Rathfarnham, when he left Rathfarnham with his company and marched to the GPO. He fought on the roof and the ground floor of the GPO during Easter Week. After the surrender he was deported to Stafford Jail on May 1st and interned in Frongoch until July 31st 1916.

He was elected Sinn Féin MP for West Donegal in 1918. During the War of Independence he played a prominent part in the struggle in the north, and became commandant of the 1st Northern Division in 1921. He supported the Treaty and was appointed O/C of the Donegal Command in 1923. He was also TD for the West Donegal Constituency in 1922 and 1923. During the Army Mutiny in March 1924, he was acting Chief of Staff of the Free State Army and he was appointed adjutant general in 1928. He was appointed quartermaster general in February 1929 and later the same year, Chief of Staff of the Free State Army. In 1931 he was appointed GOC, Curragh Command and he retired from the army in 1940. He held the post of Insurance Inspector for Canada Life Assurance from 1940 to 1950. He was area officer of the Irish Red Cross Society for the 26 Counties, from 1950 to 1956 and general secretary, from 1956 to 1962.

Major General Joe Sweeney, of 26 Orchardstown Park, Templogue, died on November 25th 1980 and was buried at Dungloe Cemetery, County Donegal.

References:
RH; IMA, MSPC; *Capuchin Annual*, 1970; Max Caulfield, *The Easter Rebellion*, (1963); Seán O'Mahony, *Frongoch: University of Revolution*, (1987); Uinseann MacEoin, *Survivors*, (1987); John P. Duggan, *A History of the Irish Army*, (1991); *Evening Herald*, 26th November 1980, (dn).

Patrick Sweeney: (1879 - 1958)

E. Coy, 4th Batt, Dublin Brigade. Roll of Honour

Patrick Sweeney was born in 1879 and resided at Butterfield Avenue, Rathfarnham. He was a member of E. Company, 4th Battalion, Dublin Brigade and of the Michael Dwyer's GAA Club. When he arrived with the Rathfarnham Volunteers at the GPO on Monday afternoon, he was posted to the roof. He fought there until the position was abandoned on Thursday, when the roof became engulfed in fire. After the surrender, while in Richmond Barracks he was struck on the head by a British sergeant using the butt of a rifle, and he suffered from the effects of the injury for the rest of his life. He was deported to Stafford Jail on May 1st, with his younger brother, James and both were interned in Frongoch, until Christmas 1916.

After his release from internment, he was involved in reorganising E. Company, 4th Battalion and was involved in a number of raids for arms in the Rathfarnham area. He also took part in the attack on Rockbrook RIC Barracks, with his brother, James. He was arrested in September 1920 and was sentenced to two years penal servitude. He was released from Usk Prison in July 1921, at the time of the Truce. He took no part in the Civil War.

Patrick Sweeney, of 1 Butterfield Avenue, Rathfarnham, died on March 25th 1958 and was buried at Cruagh Cemetery, Rathfarnham.

References:

RH; IMA, MSPC; *Sinn Féin Rebellion Handbook 1916*, Weekly Irish Times, (1917); *Irish Press*, 27th March 1958, (dn).

Aoife Taaffe: (1890 -)

Cumann na mBan (Ard Craobh, Central Branch)

Aoife Taaffe was born in 1890, and resided at 36 Upper Buckingham Street in 1911. She was employed as a book-keeper and was a member of Cumann na mBan. During Easter Week, she was a member of the GPO Garrison.

She served through the War of Independence and took the Republican side in the Civil War. In 1923, she was arrested and interned in Kilmainham Jail.

Aoife Taafe did not sign the Roll of Honour, or apply for a Military Service Pension.

References:

IMA, BMH (WS 679, *Jack Shouldice*); Sinéad McCoole, *No Ordinary Women: Irish Female Activists in the Revolutionary years, 1900-1923*, (2004); Clair Willis, *Dublin 1916, the Siege of the GPO*, (2009).

Christopher Tallon: (1888 - 1979)
C. Coy, 2nd Batt, Dublin Brigade. Roll of Honour

Christopher Tallon was born in 1888 and resided at 2 Branvilla, North Richmond Street. He was employed as a night watchman at Artane Boys School and was a member of C. Company, 2nd Battalion, Dublin Brigade. On Easter Monday he was in the party that took over Lambe's Public House, Ballybough Bridge. After moving into the GPO on Tuesday evening, he was sent to the Metropole Hotel where he joined his brother Joseph, and he remained there for the rest of the week. As the GPO was about to be evacuated on Friday evening, he was near Arthur Wicks when he was seriously wounded. He and Harry Ridgeway then carried Arthur Wicks to the first aid section in Moore Street, after the evacuation, and he continued attending to the wounded there until the surrender. He was later deported to Knutsford Jail on May 1st and was interned in Frongoch with his two brothers, Joseph and James. All three brothers were released from Frongoch at Christmas 1916.

On his release from internment, he rejoined his unit and served until 1919, when he went to work in London. During the Emergency years, he served in the Dept of Defence.

Christopher Tallon, of 24 Anne Devlin Road, Rathfarnham, died on December 9th 1979 and was buried at Bohernabreena Cemetery.

References:
RH; IMA, MSPC; NLI, *Lynch Papers*, (Ms 11,131); Jim Corr, *Believed to be in Ireland*, (as yet, unpublished); *Irish Press*, 10th December 1979, (obit).

Seamus Ó Tallamháin (James Tallon): (1891 – 1969)
B. Coy, 1st Batt, Dublin Brigade. Roll of Honour

James Tallon was born in 1891 and resided at 2 Branvilla, North Richmond Street. He was educated at O'Connell Schools and TCD. He joined the Gaelic League in 1910. In 1916 he was a member of B. Company, 1st Battalion, Dublin Brigade and was employed as a clerk. He fought in the Easter Rising with his two brothers, Christopher and Joseph. On Easter Monday he was one of the Volunteers who manned the barricades at the North Circular Road and Cabra Bridge, under Captain Seamus O'Sullivan. They withstood a heavy artillery barrage until Captain

O'Sullivan decided to withdraw to the GPO. On their retreat, he was shot in the leg and received treatment in a doctor's house on the North Circular Road. He then took up a position with eight other Volunteers in Henry Dixon's house on the North Circular Road, but they soon were surrounded and were forced to surrender. He was deported to Wakefield Jail on May 6th and interned in Frongoch until Christmas 1916.

He was president of the Árd Craobh Branch of the Gaelic League for many years, and was founder of Coiste na bPáiste in 1934. He was a vocational teacher and taught Irish and other subjects until his retirement in 1959.

James Tallon, of 36 Grace Park Terrace, Drumcondra, died on March 21st 1969 and was buried at Glasnevin Cemetery.

References:

RH; IMA, MSPC; NLI, *Lynch Papers*, (Ms 11,131); *Irish Independent* & *Irish Press*, 22nd March 1969, (obits).

Seosamh Ó Tallamháin: (1889 – 1963)

C. Coy, 2nd Batt, Dublin Brigade

Joseph Tallon was born in 1889 and resided at 2 Branvilla, North Richmond Street. He was educated at Strand Street National School and O'Connell Schools, where he would teach in later years. On Easter Monday he served at Ballybough Bridge, and later in the week in the Metropole Hotel with his brother, Christopher. He was one of the stretcher-bearers who carried James Connolly to the military hospital in Dublin Castle. He was deported to Wakefield Prison with his brother James on May 6th, and interned in Frongoch, where they joined their brother, Christopher. All three brothers were released from Frongoch at Christmas 1916.

He was a well-known Irish scholar and Professor of Mathematics. He taught in Dungarvan, Omagh and Dundalk, before returning to Dublin to teach in O'Connell's in 1953. He resided at 118 Leinster Road, Rathmines and retired from teaching in 1961.

Joseph Tallon died on August 25th 1963 and was buried at Mount Jerome Cemetery, Harold's Cross.

References:

IMA, MSPC; Max Caulfield, *The Easter Rebellion*, (1963); *Irish Independent* & *Irish Press*, 27th August 1963, (obits).

Liam Tannam: (1895 - 1964)

Captain. E. Coy, 3rd Batt, Dublin Brigade & G.H.Q. Roll of Honour

Liam Tannam was born in 1895 and resided at 3 Wilton Terrace, Leeson Street. He joined the Volunteers in 1914, and became a member of the IRB in 1915. At twenty years of age, he was appointed captain of E. Company, 3rd Battalion and in 1916 he was the youngest company commander in the Dublin Brigade. On Easter Monday he was ordered to assemble his men at Cullenswood House, Ranelagh and from there proceed to the GPO. He was sent out to organise sentry groups at various points in the GPO area, and he then organised the removal of foodstuffs from the Metropole Hotel to the GPO. He was sent to the Imperial Hotel and Reis's Chambers to replace Captain Tom Weafer after he had been mortally wounded. He took up a position on the top of the Dublin Bread Company's tower and with the help of a young Volunteer, he put a machinegun on the roof of Trinity College out of action. He returned to the GPO where he remained until the evacuation. At the evacuation on Friday evening, he was detailed by P.H. Pearse to command a rearguard party. After the surrender he was one of three officers that accompanied the wounded James Connolly to Dublin Castle. He was deported and then interned in Frongoch with his brother, Michael, who fought in Boland's Mills.

He was released at Christmas 1916 and fought through the War of Independence. He took the Republican side in the Civil War and was interned from December 1922 to November 1923.

During the emergency years, he served with the 26th Infantry Battalion and in the Construction Corps, in Galway. In his younger days he was a member of the Clonliffe Harriers Athletic Club. He resided at 22 Nutley Avenue, Ballsbridge and was a former manager in the Rates Dept, in Dublin Corporation.

Captain Liam Tannam died on July 26th 1964 and was buried at Mount Jerome Cemetery, Harold's Cross.

References:
RH; IMA, MSPC; IMA, BMH (WS 242); John Heuston OP, *Headquarters Battalion, Easter Week 1916*, (1966); Charles Townshend, *Easter 1916, the Irish Rebellion*, (2006); *Irish Independent & Irish Press*, 37th July 1964, (obits).

Francis (Frank) Thornton (alias Frank Drennan):

(1891 - 1965)

Liverpool Company, (Kimmage Garrison). Roll of Honour

Frank Thornton was born in Drogheda in 1891 and educated at the CBS, Sunday's Gate, Drogheda. In 1912 he went work in Liverpool, where he joined the Gaelic League. He was also involved in the GAA in Liverpool, and he became a member of the IRB in February 1913. When the Volunteers were inaugurated in Liverpool later that year, he became a member and was in charge of the guard of honour when O'Donovan Rossa's remains arrived in Liverpool. He then escorted the coffin to Dublin and participated in the funeral procession to Glasnevin Cemetery. He returned to Dublin with members of the Liverpool Company, including his brothers Hugh and Paddy and his sister, Cumann na mBan member, Nora, prior to the Rising.

He was left in charge of Liberty Hall on Easter Monday, until he withdrew with his party to the GPO at 6.00 pm. He was then ordered to take twelve men and reinforce the Volunteers at City Hall, under the command of Captain Seán Connolly. They came under fire as they approached Crown Alley Telephone Exchange and were forced to take cover in houses in Fleet Street. On Tuesday morning they were instructed to return to the GPO, and from there he was sent with a group to occupy the Imperial Hotel. He was wounded twice during the fighting in Easter Week. After the surrender he was sentenced to death under the alias, Frank Drennan, but his sentence was reduced to ten years penal servitude.

He was re-arrested on his release from jail in 1917 and survived two hunger strikes in Dundalk and Belfast Jails. He was deported to Reading Jail, and on his release he was appointed to GHQ Intelligence by Michael Collins. In 1922 he joined the Free State Army with the rank of Colonel and during the Civil War he was seriously wounded in Kilkenny.

In 1918 he helped form the New Ireland Assurance Company and was appointed manager of the Head Office in 1928. He has a lifelong interest in the GAA and member of St Laurence O'Toole's. He later founded the New Ireland Hurling Club in 1928. He was adjutant of the 26th Infantry Battalion during the emergency years. In 1959 he was appointed General Manager of New Ireland Assurance Co.

Frank Thornton, of St Helen's Road, Booterstown, died suddenly on holiday in Spain on September 22nd 1965 and was buried in Glasnevin Cemetery.

References:
RH; IMA, MSPC; IMA, BMH (WS 510 & 615); Desmond Ryan, *The Rising: the Complete Story of Easter Week*, (1949); Michael Hopkinson, *Green against Green: the Irish Civil* War, (1992); W.J. Brennan-Whitmore, *Dublin Burning*, (1996); Michael Foy & Brian Barton, *The Easter Rising*, (2000); Jimmy Wren, *Saint Laurence O'Toole GAC Centenary History, 1901-2001*, (2001); Eileen McGough, *Diarmuid Lynch: a Forgotten Irish Patriot*, (2013); *Irish Press*, 24th September 1965, (obit).

Hugh Thornton: (1898 - 1922)

Liverpool Company, (Kimmage Garrison). Roll of Honour

Hugh Thornton, a native of Drogheda, was born in 1898. He returned to Ireland with the Liverpool Company of Volunteers that included his brothers, Frank and Paddy and his sister, Nora, before the Rising. He joined the Volunteer Camp at Larkfield, Kimmage and fought in the GPO throughout Easter Week. He was in the group of Volunteers photographed inside the GPO by Joseph Cripps. After the surrender he was deported to Stafford Jail on May 1st. and was interned in Frongoch, where, with others, he was forcibly conscripted. He was taken to Salisbury Plain and forcibly dressed in a khaki uniform which he cut to shreds, and as a result he spent six weeks in only his shirt. The British authorities failed to conscript him, and he was eventually released.

After his release from internment, he went to work in Bandon as a grocer's assistant and he was appointed vice commandant of the West Cork Brigade, IRA in 1919. He later returned to Dublin and was made intelligence officer of the 2nd Battalion, Dublin Brigade. In 1922 he joined the Free State Army with the rank of Captain.

Hugh Thornton was killed in a landmine explosion at Clonakilty, County Cork, on August 27th 1922 and was buried at Glasnevin Cemetery.

References:
RH; IMA, MSPC; IMA, BMH (WS 510, *Frank Thornton*); Seán O'Mahony, *Frongoch: University of Revolution*, (19870; *Freeman's Journal*, 1st September 1922, (obit); *Irish Independent*, 2nd September 1922, (obit).

Nora Thornton: (1895 – 1978)

Cumann na mBan, Liverpool. G.H.Q. Despatch Messenger

Nora Thornton was born in Drogheda, in 1895. She was the leader of the Cumann na mBan women in Liverpool and she came to Dublin with her brothers, Frank, Hugh and Paddy, prior to the Rising. On Easter Monday morning, she received instructions from Seán McDermott to travel to Tralee on the mail train with a despatch. When it was learned that she was being sought by the police, she went into hiding in Castlemaine, under the instructions of the Volunteer Executive in Kerry. She did not get back to Dublin until the week after the surrender.

She joined the Fairview Branch of Cumann na mBan, after the Rising and was involved in collecting and distributing money for the Prisoners Dependents Fund. She served with Cumann na mBan until the Truce.

Nora Thornton, of 38 Belgrave Square, Rathmines, died on June 28th 1978.

References:
IMA, MSPC; IMA, BMH (WS 510, *Frank Thornton*); *Evening Herald*, 30th June 1978, (dn).

Patrick (Paddy) Thornton: (1900 – 1921)

Liverpool Company, (Kimmage Garrison). Roll of Honour

Paddy Thornton was sixteen years old when he came to Dublin from Liverpool, prior to the Rising, with his brothers, Frank and Hugh, and his sister, Nora. He was part of the Kimmage Garrison that reported to Liberty Hall on Easter Monday. Later that evening he went to the GPO and was sent with a group to re-enforce the Volunteers in the Fairview area. He was slightly wounded at Fairview, and returned to the GPO on Tuesday evening, remaining there until the evacuation. He was detained in Richmond Barracks, but was released on May 12th because of his youth.

His health deteriorated, and he spent time in several sanatoria before he was discharged in 1919. He went to Drogheda and resumed activities.

In 1920 he was working as a manager in the Boyne cinema in Drogheda. He was removed from the cinema by a party of Black and Tans and brutally beaten.

Paddy Thornton succumbed to his injuries and died on February 6th 1921 and was buried at St Peter's Cemetery, Drogheda.

References:
RH; IMA, BMH (WS 510, *Frank Thornton*); *Irish Independent*, 7th February 1921, (dn); *Irish Independent*, 8th February 1921, (obit).

Annie Tobin (Mrs. Annie Soalfield): (– 1931)

Clan na nGael Girl Scouts. Roll of Honour

Annie Tobin was a member of the Clan na nGael Girl Scouts and served in the GPO during Easter Week. On Friday she was among those who were ordered to leave the GPO under the protection of a Red Cross flag.

She served through the War of Independence and took the anti-Treaty side in the Civil War. In June 1922 she was among four women in a party of Irregulars, under the command of Captain Seán Prendergast, who occupied Hughes's Hotel, opposite Moran's Hotel, Lower Gardiner Street. She acted as cook and messenger there. When Seán Prendergast arrived at Mountjoy Jail as a prisoner after the surrender of the Hughes's Garrison, he passed his Sam Brown belt to Annie as a souvenir.

Annie Soalfield, neeTobin, died on August 7th 1931.

References:
RH; IMA, BMH (WS 755, *Seán Prendergast*); Liz Gillis, *The Fall of Dublin*, (2011).

Maurice Tobin: (1898 – 1923)
Volunteer

Maurice Tobin was born in 1898 and resided at 28 Castlewood Avenue, Rathmines in 1916. He served in the GPO throughout Easter Week. After the surrender he was deported to Stafford Jail on May 1st and was released on May 29th 1916. His health broke down after his release from internment.

Maurice Tobin, of 16 Upper Fitzwilliam Street, died after a long illness on October 8th 1923 and was buried in the Republican Plot at Glasnevin Cemetery.

References:
Irish Independent, 11th October 1923, (obit).

Joseph (Joe) Toomey: (1884 – 1960)
B. Coy, 2nd Batt, Dublin Brigade. Roll of Honour

Joe Toomey was born in Wexford in 1884. He moved to Dublin at an early age and was educated at O'Connell Schools, North Richmond Street. He resided at 30 Clonliffe Avenue and was a fitter by trade. He played hurling for the Fianna HC. He was a member of the IRB and also of B. Company, 2nd Battalion, Dublin Brigade. He served with his sister, Statia, in the GPO during Easter Week, while his brother Jack fought in St Stephen's Green and Jacob's during the Rising. After the surrender he was deported to Knutsford Jail on May 1st and interned in Frongoch until Christmas 1916.

On his release from internment he rejoined his old unit at its reorganisation. He was engaged in making hand grenades from 1918, and in late 1919 he was attached to GHQ Intelligence, under the command of Martin Conlon. His unit was known as the "Labour Board" and its purpose was to infiltrate and control the trade union movement in Ireland. He was arrested in July 1920 and was released from Leicester Jail on June 6th 1921. After his release from prison he continued to serve with his unit up to the Truce. He took no part in the Civil War.

He was later employed as an engineer in the Board of Works and was a founder member of the Irish Engineering Union.

Joe Toomey, of 18 Kincora Avenue, Clontarf, died on September 12th 1960 and was buried at Mount Jerome Cemetery, Harold's Cross.

References:
RH; IMA, MSPPC; IMA, BMH (WS 336, *Garry Holohan*) & BMH (WS 821, *Frank Henderson*); *Irish Independent*, 14th September 1960, (dn); *Irish Press*, 14th September 1960, (obit).

Stasia Toomey (Mrs. Stasia Byrne): (1891 - 1966)

Cumann na mBan (Fairview Branch). Roll of Honour

Stasia Toomey was born in Wexford in 1891 before her family settled in Dublin when she was very young. Her mother Mary (nee Hayes) had been a member of the Ladies Land League in Wexford. Stasia was a member of Cumann na mBan, Fairview Branch and on Easter Monday, she and Molly Reynolds were sent from St Stephen's Green to the GPO. She was assigned to the first aid station on the first floor and spent the week attending to the wounded there. Her brother, Joe, was also in the GPO and her brother, Jack, was in the Jacob's Garrison. She helped escort the wounded to Jervis Street Hospital on Friday and the following day she was ordered by the military to leave the hospital and she arrived home that evening.

She was appointed secretary of the Fairview Branch of Cumann na mBan, in 1917 and also secretary of the National Aid Association's, No. 2 Area. She was involved in collecting and distributing for the Prisoners Dependents Fund. Her mother's house, at 88 Phibsboro Road, was a refuge for men on the run and the wounded Dan Breen was taken there after the ambush at Ashbourne. She served throughout the War of Independence until the Truce.

She was married to Seán Byrne, who had fought in the Four Courts and in the North King Street area during Easter Week.

Stasia Byrne, of 131 Larkfield Grove, Kimmage, died on August 4th 1966 and was buried at Mount Jerome Cemetery.

References:
RH; IMA, MSPC; NLI, *Lynch Papers*, (Ms 11,131); *Irish Independent* & *Irish Press*, 5th August 1966, (dn).

Oscar Traynor: (1886 – 1963)

Lieutenant. F. Coy, 2nd Batt, Dublin Brigade. Roll of Honour

Oscar Traynor, the son of a Fenian and Parnellite, was born in Abbey Street, Dublin, in 1886. He was educated at St Mary's CBS and on leaving school served his time in the printing trade. He was a keen athlete and played in goal for Belfast Celtic FC. After the shooting of civilians on Bachelor's Walk in 1914, he joined the Volunteers. He resided at 55 Jones's Road and was a member of F. Company, 2nd Battalion, Dublin Brigade, in 1916. On Easter Monday he served at Ballybough Bridge, where his party occupied buildings overlooking the bridge and its approaches,

until they were ordered to withdrew to the GPO on Tuesday evening. He was then ordered to take twenty men and occupy the Metropole Hotel and bore through the walls to Mansfield's corner, middle Abbey Street. They came under constant sniper and machine-gun fire, and from Thursday endured heavy shelling. They retreated, exhausted, on Friday, shortly before the main evacuation. At the evacuation of the GPO, he and Harry Ridgeway attended to the English socialist, Arthur Wicks, who received multiple wounds when Andy Furlong's ammunition pouch exploded. Christopher Tallon and Harry Ridgeway later carried Arthur Wicks into the houses in Moore Street. Traynor spent Friday night in Moore Street, and on Saturday afternoon he was in the party under the command of Seán McLoughlin, ready to attack the British Army barricade at Parnell Street, when it was decided to surrender. He was deported to Knutsford Jail on May 1st and interned in Frongoch until Christmas 1916.

He rejoined his old unit on his release from internment, and in March 1917 he was arrested and sentenced to three months for illegal drilling. When he was released he was promoted to captain of F. Company. He succeeded Dick McKee as commandant of the Dublin Brigade, after McKee's murder in November 1920. He directed and took part in many major operations in the Dublin area. On May 25th 1921, he was in charge of the burning of the Custom House, the greatest single action against the British during the War of Independence.

He took the Republican side in the Civil War and set up headquarters at Barry's Hotel and later at the Hamman Hotel. He was arrested and interned in Gormanstown Camp until 1924. He was elected as a Sinn Féin member of Dáil Éireann in 1925, and joined Fianna Fáil in 1927. He was TD for Dublin North in 1932, and was appointed Minister for Posts and Telegraphs in 1936. On the outbreak of WW2 in 1939, he was appointed Minister of Defence and he later became Minister of Justice in 1957 and held this position until his retirement in 1961. He succeeded Dr. William Hooper, as president of the FAI in 1953, and welcomed many visiting soccer teams to Ireland. The Oscar Traynor Cup, a prestigious cup competition in FAI junior football, was named in his honour.

Oscar Traynor died at his residence, 14 Dollymount Avenue, on December 14th 1963 and was buried in the Republican Plot at Glasnevin Cemetery.

References:

RH; IMA, MSPC; IMA, BMH (WS 340); NLI, *Lynch Papers*, (Ms 11,131); *DIB*, Marie Coleman, (James Quinn, Ed, 2009); *HI*, March/April 2010, (*Martin Flynn*); Max Caulfield, *The Easter Rebellion*, (1963); Kathleen Clarke, *Revolutionary Woman*, (1997); Tom Reilly, *Joe Stanley: Printer to the Rising*, (2005); Charles Townshend, *Easter 1916, the Irish Rebellion*, (2005); Charlie McGuire, *Seán McLoughlin; Ireland's Forgotten Revolutionary*, (2011); Diarmaid Ferriter, *A Nation and not a Rabble: Irish Revolution, 1913-1923*, (2015); Jim Corr, *Believed to be in Ireland*, (as yet, unpublished); *Sunday Press*, 15th December 1963, (obit); *Irish Press*, 16th December 1963, (obit).

Joseph Trimble: (1884 – 1956)

F. Coy, 1st Batt, Dublin Brigade. Roll of Honour

Joseph Trimble was born in 1884 and resided at 155 North Strand Road. He was a plumber by trade and a member of F. Company, 1st Battalion, Dublin Brigade. He was also a member of the IRB, and on Good Friday 1916 he stood armed guard at 41 Parnell Square, while P.H. Pearse attended a meeting inside. On Easter Monday he went from 41 Parnell Square to the GPO, and was posted to the roof at the Prince's Street side of the building. He served there for three days and was then stationed at various locations within the building. After the evacuation, he spent Friday night at the rear of William's Stores, Henry Street and surrendered there on Saturday. He was deported to Lewes on May 20th and detained in other English Jails. He was then interned in Frongoch until Christmas 1916.

According to his pension application, he took no active part in the Volunteers after his release from Frongoch, although his obituary stated that he was on active service during the War of Independence and a member of the Four Court Garrison, during the Civil War.

Joseph Trimble, of 48 Clogher Road, Crumlin, died on April 22nd 1956 and was buried at Glasnevin Cemetery.

References:
RH; IMA, MSPC; IMA, BMH (WS 638, *Patrick Caldwell*); Tom Reilly, *Joe Stanley: Printer to the Rising*, (2005); *Sunday Press*, 22nd April 1956, (obit); *Irish Independent*, 23rd April 1956, (obit).

George Tully: (1899 – 1985)

Irish Citizen Army, (Boys Corps)

George Tully was born in 1899 and resided at 18 Upper Gloucester Street. When he arrived at the GPO on Easter Monday, James Connolly ordered him to assist in breaking the glass in the windows and building barricades with ledgers and books. He was then sent out on scouting duties and he reported the presence of the Lancers at the Parnell Monument to the GPO Garrison. Later in the day he was sent with despatches to St Stephen's Green and Jacob's, and slept that night in the GPO. On Tuesday, he brought messages to and from the Imperial Hotel and later that night he was sent home by Captain Frank Thornton, because of his young age. He was arrested on Friday at his home, and taken to the Custom House for interrogation. He was then moved to Richmond Barracks and was deported to Wakefield Prison on May 6th, but was released from there six weeks later.

He rejoined the Irish Citizen Army at its reorganisation and he fired at the RIC as they attempted to arrest Captain O'Shea of the ICA. He moved around the country while engaged in his work as a tiler, and circulated copies of *An t-Óglach* on his travels. He also organised a company of the Irish Citizen Army at Gort, County Galway. During the Civil War, he took the Republican side and fought in Barry's Hotel and the Hamman Hotel. He was also involved in the blowing up of a bridge at Raheny.

He was a member of 26th Infantry Battalion during the emergency years.

He was a director of George Tully & Sons, Haymarket and resided at 30 Annamoe Road, Cabra,

George Tully died on February 14th 1985 and was buried at Glasnevin Cemetery.

References:

IMA, MSPC; IMA, BMH (WS 96, *John Hanratty*); John Heuston OP, *Headquarters Battalion 1916*, (1966); *Evening Herald*, 8th & 9th April 1966, (na, *interview*); *Irish Independent*, 15th February 1985, (dn).

Doctor John J. Tuohy: (- 1936)
Volunteer, Red Cross Section. Roll of Honour

Doctor John J. Tuohy was born in Ballaghaderreen, County Roscommon. He qualified in the mid 1880s in the College of Surgeon's, St Stephen's Green and later gained several distinctions at Edinburgh College of Surgeons. He practiced for seven years at St Just, Cornwall, before he returned to Dublin, and became Medical Officer at St Enda's College, Rathfarnham. He was a founder of the McHale Branch of the Gaelic League and was an early member of Sinn Féin. In 1916 he resided at 18 North Frederick Street, and during Easter Week he was attached to the Volunteer Red Cross Unit in Sackville Street, rendering valuable assistance to the wounded insurgents. His son, the famous artist, Patrick Tuohy RHA, who attended St Enda's College, did not take part in the Rising, but is sometimes confused with Patrick Tuohy of the Irish Citizen Army, who was part of the GPO Garrison.

Doctor John J. Tuohy died on August 16th 1936 and was buried at Glasnevin Cemetery. He was the oldest medical practitioner in Dublin at the time of his death.

References:

RH; IMA, BMH (WS 359, *Eva Burke*), BMH (WS 398, *Bridget Martin, nee Foley*) & BMH (WS 568, *Éilis Ní Chonaill*); *Irish Independent*, 17th August 1936, (obit).

Patrick C. Tuohy: (1861 – 1940)

Irish Citizen Army, (Aungier St Section). Roll of Honour

Patrick Tuohy was born in 1861 and resided at 73 Bride Street. He was a bricklayer by trade and was a member of the Irish Citizen Army. On Easter Monday he pushed a cart containing guns and ammunitions from Liberty Hall to the GPO. He also had in his possession the "Irish Republic" flag that was later hoisted on the roof of the GPO. Later that day, he was in the group, under the command of Captain Frank Thornton, which was sent to reinforce the City Hall Garrison. They came under fire from British troops in the Crown Alley Telephone Exchange and he spent Monday night occupying Delahunty's Public House, Fleet Street, before returning to the GPO on Tuesday. He was then posted across the street to the Imperial Hotel, and remained there until the building became engulfed in flames. After the hotel was evacuated he was captured by British troops as he made his escape. He was deported to Stafford Jail on May 1st and interned in Frongoch until July 31st 1916.

During the War of Independence he joined 5th Battalion, Engineers and was active up to the Truce. He took the Republican side in the Civil War. He fought in Moran's Hotel, with his former Irish Citizen Army comrade from Easter Week, Christy Poole, and both evaded capture.

Patrick Tuohy died on January 1st 1940 and was buried in Glasnevin Cemetery.

References:
RH; IMA, MSPC; NLI, *Lynch Papers*, (Ms 11,131) & *William O'Brien Papers*, (Ms 15,673); Ann Matthews, *The Irish Citizen Army*, (2014); *Irish Independent*, 2nd January 1940, (dn).

Cormac Turner: (1896 - 1968)

Glasgow Company, (Kimmage Garrison). Roll of Honour

Cormac Turner was born in 1896 and joined B. Company, 3rd Battalion, Dublin Brigade, in November 1913. He transferred to the Glasgow and West of Scotland Volunteers in November 1914 and procured ammunition and explosives, which were shipped to Ireland. He came back to Dublin in January 1916 and stayed at Larkfield, Kimmage. When the Kimmage Volunteers arrived in the GPO on Easter Monday, he was sent with Seamus Robinson and Seamus Landy to Hopkins & Hopkins Jewellery Shop, at the corner of Eden Quay. They came under fire from a British Army sniper, who was located in McBirney's Store on other side of the River Liffey, who had fatally shot several civilians. The sniper was silenced by Irish Citizen Army marksman, Andy Conroy, who was sent from the GPO. On Wednesday, Hopkins & Hopkins came under heavy machine gun fire from the roof of Trinity College and from Tara Street, and they were ordered to evacuate the building. He made his way to the Imperial Hotel and then into Noblett's at North Earl Street, where he remained until the building was abandoned on Thursday because of the intense fire engulfing the area. He was wounded while evading capture and was taken prisoner early on Friday morning in Marlborough Street. He was taken to Jervis Street Hospital and later made his escape from there, evading arrest.

After spending from October to December 1916 in the Richmond Hospital, suffering from pneumonia, he rejoined B. Company, 3rd Battalion, in 1917 and transferred to A. Company, 4th Battalion, months later. He married Cathleen Flanagan in Buncrana in 1918, with Éamon deValera in attendance, and for a time they lived at Glenlion, Bailey, Howth. She was a member of Inghinidhe na hÉireann in Derry and was a teacher in the Irish College in Cloughaneely, County Donegal.

He fought in the War of Independence and took the pro-Treaty side in the Civil War. He joined the Free State Army with the rank of adjutant in the Salvage Corps and later as captain in the Army Corps of Engineers. On retirement from the army, he was prominent in Fianna Fáil circles in the Harold's Cross area and in Old IRA Associations, while lobbying the Government on behalf of the employment and pensions of War of Independence veterans. He recorded his 1916 exploits in a series of articles in *An t-Óglach* in 1926 and took part in numerous radio broadcasts, relating to the events of 1916.

Cormac Turner, of 17 Richmond Hill, Rathmines, died on February 12th 1968 and was buried at Mount Jerome Cemetery, Harold's Cross.

References:

RH; IMA, MSPC; IMA, BMH (WS 156, *Seamus Robinson*), BMH (WS 244, *John Gallogley*), BMH (WS 353, *Kitty O'Doherty*) & BMH (WS 1,767, *Seamus Reader*); NLI, *Lynch Papers*, (Ms 11,131); Thomas Coffey, *Agony at Easter*, (1969); Michael Foy & Brian Barton, *The Easter Rising*, (1999); Paul O'Brien, *Blood on the Streets: 1916 and the Battle for Mount Street Bridge*, (2015); *Evening Herald*, 13th February 1968, (dn).

Francis (Frank) Turner: (1898- 1953)

C. Coy, 1st Batt, Dublin Brigade. Roll of Honour

Frank Turner was born in 1898 and resided at 10 Summerhill. He was employed a machinist and became a member of C. Company, 1st Battalion, Dublin Brigade in 1915. He fought throughout Easter Week in the GPO along with his father, Joseph and two brothers, Henry and Joseph. On Easter Monday he was engaged in erecting barricades and then manned the windows in the GPO until Tuesday. He was sent across the street to Reis's Chambers and the Dublin Bread Company Building on Wednesday. He was in a party of Volunteers, who occupied the Lucas Cycle Shop in middle Abbey Street, until they were ordered back to the GPO. On Friday he was wounded and taken to Jervis Street Hospital, where he was then arrested and taken to Ship Street Barracks. He was transferred to Richmond Barracks and then deported to Wakefield Prison on May 6th with his father, Joseph and his brother, Joseph (Junior). After his release from internment in September 1916, he lost his job and sought employment in England.

He returned to Ireland in 1920 and joined 5th Battalion, Engineers, IRA. In July 1922 he joined the Free State Army as a private, and served until February 1924, when he was discharged.

Frank Turner, of 97 Annamoe Drive, Cabra, died on March 23rd 1953.

References:

RH; IMA, MSPC; NLI. *Lynch Papers*, (Ms 11,131); *Evening Herald*, 24th March 1953, (dn).

Henry Turner: (1896 - 1970)
B. Coy, 2nd Batt, Dublin Brigade

Henry Turner was born in 1896 and resided at 10 Summerhill. He was a member of B. Company, 2nd Battalion, Dublin Brigade and he reported to the GPO on Easter Monday with his father, Joseph, and his brothers, Frank and Joseph. He fought in the GPO throughout Easter Week until the building was evacuated on Friday evening. He spent Friday night in the houses in Moore Street and surrendered on Saturday at Kelly's poultry shop. He was deported to Stafford Jail on May 1st and interned in Frongoch until July 26th 1916.

On his release from internment he worked as a seaman and took no further active part in the Volunteers.

Henry Turner, of 6 Scville Place, North Strand, died on January 6th 1970 and was buried at Deansgrange Cemetery.

References:

IMA, MSPC; *Sinn Féin Rebellion Handbook 1916*, Weekly Irish Times, (1917); *Evening Herald*, 7th January 1970, (dn).

Joseph Turner (Junior): (1899 -)
G. Coy, 1st Batt, Dublin Brigade

Joseph Turner was born in 1899 and resided at 10 Summerhill. He was a member of G. Company, 1st Battalion, Dublin Brigade and reported to the GPO Garrison on Easter Monday, with his father, Joseph and brothers, Frank and Henry. On Easter Monday and Tuesday he was stationed at the windows in the GPO, and the following day he was sent to the Metropole Hotel. He was wounded on Thursday, and was transferred with other wounded Volunteers to Jervis Street Hospital on Friday. He was transferred to Richmond Barracks and was deported to Wakefield Prison on May 6th with his father, Joseph and his brother, Frank, and was interned in Frongoch.

Joseph Turner later emigrated to England in search of employment and passed away there.

References:

NLI, *Lynch Papers*, (Ms 11,131); *Sinn Féin Rebellion Handbook 1916*, Weekly Irish Times, (1917).

Joseph Turner (Senior): (1861 - 1945)
G. Coy, 1st Batt, Dublin Brigade. Roll of Honour

Joseph Turner was born in 1861 and resided at 10 Summerhill. He joined the Volunteers at the inaugural meeting at the Rotunda, in 1913 and became a member of G. Company, 1st Battalion, Dublin Brigade. He had previously served with a militia unit of the British Army. He reported to the GPO on Easter Monday with his sons, Henry, Frank and Joseph. On Tuesday he was posted to the corner of Liffey Street, and when he returned to the GPO he was sent to the Metropole Hotel with seven other Volunteers. They then broke into the offices of the *Freeman's Journal* in Prince's Street. He received an injury to his back on Friday, and was taken to the first aid station in the GPO. He was deported to Wakefield Jail on May 6th with his sons, Frank and Joseph (Junior) and he was released from there at the end of July 1916.

After his release from internment, he was engaged in the reorganisation of his old unit and in drilling its members. He was involved in the moving of arms and took part in the Armagh election campaign. He served up to the Truce.

Joseph Turner, of 97 Annamoe Drive, Cabra, died on October 1st 1945 and was buried at Glasnevin Cemetery.

References:
RH; IMA, MSPC; *Sinn Féin Rebellion Handbook 1916*, Weekly Irish Times, (1917); *Irish Press*, 2nd October 1945, (obit).

John J. (Joe) Twamley: (1889 - 1965)
Lieutenant. A. Coy, 1st Batt, Dublin Brigade. Roll of Honour

Joe Twamley was born in 1889 and resided at 17 Garden Lane, Francis Street. He attended the inaugural meeting of the Irish Volunteers at the Rotunda, on November 25th 1913, and became a member of A. Company, 1st Battalion, Dublin Brigade. In 1916 he was employed as a linesman in the Engineering Dept of the Post Office and was stationed at Bray. He was one of a party of Volunteers and Irish Citizen Army men that gathered details of telegraph and telephone manholes throughout the city prior to the Rising. On Easter Monday, he cut all the telegraph, telephone and railway signal lines at Bray, and then made his way to the GPO. On Tuesday he led a party that erected a large barricade across lower Abbey Street, near the Hibernian Bank. When he returned to the GPO, he was stationed on the roof and when this position became engulfed in flames, he helped move explosives to the strong room in the basement. During the evacuation he pulled a wounded Volunteer to safety after they came under machinegun fire at the corner of Moore Lane and Henry Place. He spent the Friday night in the houses in Moore Street.

After the surrender he was deported to Stafford Jail on May 1st and interned in Frongoch until Christmas 1916.

He rejoined his unit at its reorganisation, and was involved in armed street patrols. He was mobilised for an attempt to rescue Kevin Barry that was called off. He served up to the Truce and took no part in the Civil War.

He later resided at 6 St Thomas Road, South Circular Road and was employed in the Engineering Section of the Dept of Post and Telegraphs.

Joe Twamley died on May 21st 1965 and was buried at Glasnevin Cemetery.

References:

RH; IMA, MSPC; Keith Jeffery, *The GPO and the Easter Rising*, (2006); Stephen Ferguson, *The GPO Staff in 1916: Business as Usual*, (2012); Eileen McGough, *Diarmuid Lynch: a Forgotten Irish Patriot*, (2013); Stephen Ferguson, *The GPO: Two Hundred Years of History*, (2014); *Evening Herald*, 21st May 1965, (dn).

Timothy (Tim) Tyrrell: (1887 – 1970)
Maynooth Company, Kildare Brigade. Roll of Honour

Tim Tyrrell was born in 1887 and joined the Maynooth Company of the Volunteers at its foundation in Kildare. He played for and captained Maynooth Gaelic football team, as well as the Kildare county team. On Easter Monday he left Maynooth with fifteen local Volunteers and travelled by the Royal Canal on foot to Dublin. They spent Monday night in Glasnevin Cemetery and arrived at the GPO on Tuesday morning. He was sent to Parliament Street and engaged with British troops that were attacking the Evening Mail Office. He received shrapnel wounds before returning to the GPO with his party on Tuesday night. On Thursday he was sent to an outpost in middle Abbey Street and remained there until his group was withdrawn to the GPO on Friday morning. He spent Friday night in the occupied houses in Moore Street. He was deported to Stafford Jail on May 1st and interned in Frongoch until Christmas 1916.

He fought during the War of Independence and took part in raids for arms. He was involved in the destruction of Maynooth RIC Barracks and of the railway lines in Maynooth and the wider Kildare area. During the Truce period he was appointed captain of his company. He took the Republican side in the Civil War and was involved in the attack on the Free State barracks at Lucan, and an attack on Free State officers. He was arrested following the fighting at Grangewilliam, County Kildare, in December 1922. He was sentenced to death, which was commuted to seven years imprisonment, and he was released in May 1924.

Tim Tyrrell, of Crewhill, Maynooth, died on November 8th 1970 and was buried at Larraghbryan Cemetery, Maynooth, County Kildare.

References:

RH; IMA, MSPC; NLI, *Lynch Papers*, (Ms 11,131); James Durney, *On the One Road*, (2001); *Irish Press*, 9th November 1970, (dn).

Domhnall Ua Buachalla (Daniel Buckley):
(1866 – 1963)

Lieutenant. Maynooth Company, Kildare Brigade. Roll of Honour

Domhnall Ua Buachalla was born in Maynooth in 1866. The son of a Kerry father and a Dublin mother, he worked in the family's grocery and drapery shop in Maynooth and was a member of the Gaelic League and Sinn Féin. An enthusiastic member of the GAA, he captained Maynooth and Kildare in football. He was prosecuted in 1909 for displaying his name in Irish above his shop and was defended in court by the newly qualified barrister, P.H. Pearse. He later joined the IRB and set up the Maynooth Company of Volunteers in 1914.

He mobilised the Maynooth Volunteers on Easter Sunday, but any movement was cancelled when he received Eoin Mac Neill's countermanding order. Later in the day he received a message from P.H. Pearse informing him not to leave the district, but to wait for further orders. On Easter Monday he was notified that the Rising had commenced by a passing van driver and in the absence of any dispatches or orders, he cycled to Dublin to assess the situation himself. He returned immediately to Maynooth and found Pat Colgan had mobilised the local Volunteers in his absence.

On Holy Thursday, Captain Tom Byrne, of B. Company, 1st Battalion, Dublin Brigade, was sent to organise the Maynooth Volunteers and at seven o'clock on Easter Monday he led the fifteen local men from the back of Ua Buachalla's shop in Main Street, by the Royal Canal towpath, to the GPO. When they arrived there early on Tuesday morning, having spent the previous night in Glasnevin Cemetery, he was in the group sent to the Royal Exchange Hotel, Parliament Street where British troops suffered heavy losses. He was recalled to the GPO, and took up a sniping position in Arnott's, Henry Street. He was then sent to the Dublin Bread Company, across the street from the GPO and remained there until he was recalled on Thursday. He was posted at the ground floor windows in the GPO until the building was evacuated on Friday evening. He evaded capture after the surrender in Moore Street, but was arrested near Broadstone Station later on Saturday. He was taken to Kilmainham Jail for interrogation and deported to Knutsford Jail on May 3rd. He was interned in Frongoch until Christmas 1916 and in early 1918 he became active in the anti-conscription campaign.

He was elected MP for Sinn Féin in December 1918. He opposed the Treaty and during the Civil War he was interned in the Curragh. He was a founder member of Fianna Fáil and was a TD from 1927 to 1932. At the request of Éamon deValera in 1932, he took the nominal post of Governor General in preparation for the final abolition of the Office in 1937.

Domhnall Ua Buachalla died on October 30th 1963 and after a state funeral, was buried in the family burial plot, at Laraghbryan Cemetery, Maynooth, County Kildare.

References:

RH; IMA, BMH (WS 194); NLI, *Lynch Papers*, (Ms 11,131); Eoghan Corry, *Kildare GAA, a Centenary History*, (1984); James Durney, *On the One Road*, (2001); Adhamhnán Ó'Súilleabháin, *Domhnall Ua Buachalla: Rebellious Nationalist, Relunctant Governor*, (2015); *Irish Press*, 28th November 1932, (na, *Governor General appointment, a profile*); *Irish Press*, 3rd February 1961, (na, *a profile*); *Irish Press*, 31st October 1963, (obit).

Michael Wade: (1863 - 1945)

Irish Citizen Army. Roll of Honour

Michael Wade was born in 1863 and resided at 24 North Great Charles Street. He was a member of the Irish Citizen Army, and on Easter Monday he manned the ground floor windows in the GPO. On Tuesday and Wednesday, he was attached to the arms and munitions section, under the command of Captain Seamus McGowan of the Irish Citizen Army. He was captured on Thursday in the Abbey Street area, and brought to Wellington Barracks, where he was held for three weeks. He was deported to Lewes Jail on May 20th and was released in August 1916.

On his release, he rejoined the Irish Citizen Army and later joined the 5th Battalion Engineers and fought in the War of Independence. He fought on the Republican side in the Civil War and was wounded in the Four Courts in July 1922. He was brought to the hospital at Mountjoy Jail and transferred to the hospital at the Curragh Camp. He was released from Tintown in March 1923.

Michael Wade, of 19 Northumberland Avenue, Dun Laoghaire, died on January 23rd 1945 and was buried at Glasnevin Cemetery.

References:

RH; IMA, MSPC; NLI, *Lynch Papers*, (Ms 11,131) & *William O'Brien Papers*, (Ms 15,673); Ann Matthews, *The Irish Citizen Army*, (2014).

Charles (Charlie) Walker: (1890 - 1954)

G. Coy, 1st Batt, Dublin Brigade. G.H.Q. Publicity Staff. Roll of Honour

Charlie Walker was born in 1890 and was the son of Matt and brother-in-law of Joe Stanley, who was the proprietor of the *Gaelic Press*. He was a member of G. Company, 1st Battalion, Dublin Brigade. He was part of the special printing team, under the command of Joe Stanley, which left the GPO and occupied O'Keefe's Printing Works in Halston Street and printed the *Irish War News* during Easter Week. He evaded capture after the Rising. His two brothers, Michael and John, were members of the Jacob's Garrison, and his sister was the distinguished actress, Máire Nic Siubhlaigh, who was a member of Cumann na mBan and also served with the Jacob's Garrison.

During the War of Independence he took part in armed patrols and was involved in the attack on British troops at North Frederick Street. He transferred to 5th Battalion, Engineers and operated the machine for printing *An t-Óglach*.

He later resided at 28 Joyce Road, Drumcondra and was employed as a printer in the Dept of Defence, for many years.

Charlie Walker died on April 9th 1954 and was buried at Glasnevin Cemetery.

References:

RH; IMA, MSPC; IMA, BMH (WS 266); John O'Connor, *The 1916 Proclamation*, (1999); Tom Reilly, *Joe Stanley: Printer to the Rising*, (2005); *Irish Press*, 10th April 1954, (dn).

Robert Henry (Harry) Walpole: (1895 - 1964)

Fianna Éireann. Lieutenant, F. Coy, 4th Batt, Dublin Brigade. Roll of Honour

Harry Walpole was born in 1895 and resided at 3 Ranelagh Road. He joined Fianna Éireann at its inception in 1909. He became a member of F.Company, 4th Battalion, Dublin Brigade and was later made a lieutenant. On Easter Monday he left Liberty Hall with the column that was led by Commandant General James Connolly. When they reached the GPO, Connolly handed him a green flag and told him to hoist it. With assistance from Seán Hegarty, he hoisted the green flag with the letters Irish Republic on it, on the Prince's Street side of the roof. Later the same day he took charge of a party of Volunteers and commandeered supplies from Findlater's Shop. He was engaged in sniping from the instrument room in the GPO on Tuesday, under the command of Michael Collins. He was also on sniping duty on Wednesday and Thursday. On Friday morning he helped transfer bombs to the basement. At the evacuation of the GPO he helped carry the wounded James Connolly into Moore Street and he spent the Friday night in the buildings there. On Saturday afternoon he was in the party ready to storm the British Army barricades at Parnell Street, when the decision to surrender was made. He was deported to Stafford Jail on May 1st and interned in Frongoch, where he joined his brother, Leo, who was in the Boland's Mills Garrison.

On his release from internment on July 26th 1916, he rejoined his old unit and fought in the War of Independence. He was captured and interned at Arbour Hill and Ballykinlar, from November 1920 to April 1921. He joined the Free State Army in 1922 with the rank of captain, and retired in 1925.

He took up a position as a laboratory technician in UCD and was later a sales representative for a flour milling firm. He rejoined the army and served through the emergency years.

Harry Walpole died suddenly at his residence at 26 Lower Stephen Street, on April 26th 1964 and was buried at Glasnevin Cemetery.

References:

RH; IMA, MSPC; IMA, BMH (218, *Harry Walpole & Theo Fitzgerald*); NLI, *Lynch Papers*, (Ms 11,131); Max Caulfield, *The Easter Rebellion*, (1963); Thomas Coffey, *Agony at Easter*, (1969); *Irish Independent* & *Evening Herald*, 27th April 1964, (obits).

Christopher (Christy) Walsh: (1895 - 1947)
Hibernian Rifles. Roll of Honour

Christy Walsh was born in 1895 and resided at 8 Lower Dominic Street. He was one of twenty Hibernian Rifle Volunteers, led by Captain J.J. Scollan, who set out from their headquarters at 28 North Frederick Street for the GPO on Easter Monday night. On Tuesday he was among a group of Volunteers, which included his father Edward, that were sent to relieve the party of Irish Citizen Army men surrounded in the Evening Mail Offices. He witnessed his father being mortally wounded in the Royal Exchange Hotel, and Captain Tom Byrne later sent him home. He returned to the GPO and was ordered to leave on Friday, before the evacuation that evening. He evaded capture after the Rising.

He continued to serve with the Hibernian Rifles until 1918, when he joined G. Company, 1st Battalion, Dublin Brigade. He fought in the War of Independence and joined the Free State Army in 1922. He was attached to the military police and in September 1922 he transferred as a guard to Leinster House.

He later resided at 50 Oliver Plunkett Avenue, Dun Laoghaire and was employed as an usher in Dáil Éireann, for many years.

Christy Walsh died on November 22nd 1947 and was buried at Deansgrange Cemetery.

References:
RH; IMA, MSPC; *Irish Press*, 24th November 1947, (dn).

Edward J. (Ned) Walsh: (1873 – 1916). Killed in Action
Sergeant. Hibernian Rifles. Roll of Honour

Ned Walsh was born in 1873 and resided at 8 Lower Dominic Street. He was employed as a carter and was a sergeant in the Hibernian Rifles. He reported to the GPO on Easter Monday night with the main group of Hibernian Rifles. He was in the party that was sent to relieve the Irish Citizen Army men in the Evening Mail Offices on Tuesday. According to his O/C, Captain John J. Scollan, he took up a position on the roof of the Royal Exchange Hotel, Parliament Street, where he was shot and was mortally wounded. His son, Christy, was with him at the time and was sent home by Captain Tom Byrne. Another account, however, gives Shortall's Shop, on the same block of buildings in Parliament Street, as the location of the shooting.

Ned Walsh died the next day in Jervis Street Hospital and was buried in St Paul's Section, at Glasnevin Cemetery, on May 2nd 1916. He was survived by his wife, Ellen, his daughter, Helena, his son, Christy and another son, Edward, who was born seven months after his death.

References:
RH; IMA, MSPC; IMA, BMH (WS 96, *John Hanratty*), BMH (WS 318, *John J. Scollan*) & BMH, (WS 564, *Tom Byrne*); Catholic Bulletin, October 1916; An t-Óglach, May 1926; Ray Bateson, *They Died by Pearse's Side*, (2010); Adhamhán Ó'Súilleabháin, *Domhnall Ua Buachalla: Rebellious Nationalist, Reluctant Governor*, (2015).

Helena (Eileen) Walsh: (- 1945)

Cumann na mBan

Eileen Walsh, of 102 Leeson Street, was member of Cumann na mBan. She reported to the GPO on Easter Tuesday and was sent to the Hibernian Bank, where she helped nurse Aoife deBúrca attend to the wounded. When the Red Cross unit was set up in an empty shop beside the Imperial Hotel, she assisted Doctor J.J. Tuohy. She crossed the street to the GPO under fire on Wednesday, and was assigned to cooking duties under Louise Gavan Duffy. On Friday at noon, P.H. Pearse ordered all women, except those nursing the wounded, to leave the building under a Red Cross flag. She was in the group arrested by British troops in Summerhill, at the North Circular Road and Portland Row junction. They were marched under escort to Broadstone Railway Station, where they were interrogated and later released.

She moved to Clonmel in 1917 and took no further part in Cumann na mBan.

Eileen Walsh, of 7 Russell Street, North Circular Road, died on December 27th 1945.

References:
IMA, MSPC.

James J. Walsh: (1880 – 1948)

Hibernian Rifles. Roll of Honour

J.J. Walsh was born in Rathroon, Bandon, County Cork, in 1880. He was educated locally and obtained a position in the Cork GPO. He was very active in the GAA in Cork. He became County Chairman in 1907 and was responsible for reforming and modernising the GAA in Cork. At a meeting in City Hall in December 1914 to establish the Volunteers in Cork, he was injured and hospitalised, following clashes with Redmondites. Shortly afterwards at a parade of Volunteers in Cork Cornmarket, he was identified as a leader, and the following day was ordered to leave Cork by "G. men" from Dublin Castle, and given the option of taking up a position in the GPO in Bradford, Yorkshire. He was later dismissed from his post, and on his return to Ireland he was arrested in Mallow and not allowed remain in Cork. He moved to Dublin and opened a tobacconist shop in Blessington Street. He joined the AOH (American Alliance) and became a member of the Hibernian Rifles.

On Easter Monday, he initially went to Fairview, before returning the North Frederick Street. He then reported to the GPO with twenty members of the Hibernian Rifles at midnight on Easter Monday, on orders from James Connolly. On Tuesday he sent Morse code messages, under a false identity, from the GPO to centres around the county and intercepted messages from the British Admiralty, at Cobh, County Cork. James Connolly sent him with a dispatch to the College of Surgeons in car driven by Volunteer Luke Kennedy. They came under heavy fire as they passed by Trinity College and on their return they broke into a shop in Bride Street and confiscated wire and detonators. They came under heavy fire again before reaching the GPO. After the surrender he was sentenced to death in Richmond Barracks, which was commuted to ten years penal servitude. He was imprisoned in Portland Jail and later Lewes Jail until 1917.

Although he was still banned from living in Cork, he was elected Sinn Féin MP for Cork City in 1918. He was a member of the First Dáil and voted for the Treaty. He served as a Cumann na nGaedhael TD for Cork Borough, from 1923 to 1927 and during this time he was Postmaster General and Minister for Posts and Telegraphs. He was also the chief organiser of the Táiltean Games in 1924, which was a great success, attracting participants of Irish descent from Australia, South Africa, South America, Canada, Great Britain and the United States.

He retired from politics in 1927 and set up a bus company in 1929. He became a leading industrialist in Dublin, and was a founder member of the Federation of Irish Industries in 1932 and served as its president from 1939 to 1941. He was also president of the Federation of Irish Manufacturers, but was forced to retire due to his failing health in 1946.

J.J. Walsh died at his residence at Ailesbury House, Ailesbury Road, Ballsbridge, on February 3rd 1948 and was buried at St Finbarr's Cemetery, Cork.

References:

RH; *DIB*, Patrick Maume, (James Quinn, Ed, 2009); *Bandon Historical Record*, No. 30, (2014); Seán O'Mahony, *Frongoch: University of Revolutionary*, (1987); Stephen Ferguson, *The GPO: 200 Years of History*, (2014); *Irish Independent*, 4th February 1948, (obit).

Margaret Walsh (Mrs. Margaret Jenkinson):
(- 1969)
Cumann na mBan, (Árd Craobh). Roll of Honour

Margaret Walsh joined of Cumann na mBan in 1915. She reported to the GPO on Easter Monday with her sisters, Martha and Mary Jo. She carried dispatches to the College of Surgeons on Tuesday and Wednesday, but could not get through the military cordon after that. On Thursday and Friday she tended to the wounded as a member of the Red Cross staff. She accompanied the wounded from the Coliseum Theatre in Henry Street to Jervis Street Hospital on Friday. Along with her sisters, Martha and Mary Jo, she succeeded in a second attempt to get through the military cordon and reach home.

After the Rising she transferred to the Fairview Branch of Cumann na mBan and was active with the National Aid and Prisoner's Dependents Fund. With her sister, Martha, she assisted prisoners who escaped from Mountjoy Jail in March 1919. She served through the War of Independence until the Truce in 1921.

Margaret Jenkinson (nee Walsh), of Church Road and later, of 12 Strangford Gardens, East Wall, died on December 28th 1969.

References:
RH; IMA, MSPC; *Irish Press*, 2nd January 1970, (dn).

Mark W. Walsh: (1896 - 1972)
F. Coy, 2nd Batt, Dublin Brigade. Roll of Honour

Mark Walsh was born in 1896 and resided at 25 Richmond Cottages. He was a member of F. Company, 2nd Battalion and reported to Father Mathew Park on Easter Monday. He remained in the Fairview area and moved back to the GPO with this group on Tuesday evening. He was assigned to guarding the British prisoners that were captured in Fairview and brought to the GPO. He was then stationed on the roof of the GPO and was later sent to Abbey Street. After the surrender, he was detained in Richmond Barracks and released after ten days. His sisters, Martha, Margaret and Mary Jo, were also members of the GPO Garrison.

He rejoined his unit and fought in the War of Independence until the Truce.

Mark Walsh later emigrated to England, where he died in Peckham, London, on April 28th 1972 and was buried at St Thomas's Cemetery in London.

References:
RH; IMA, MSPC;*Evening Herald*, 29th April 1972, (dn).

Martha (Birdie) Walsh (Mrs. Martha Slater): (1891 - 1960)
Inghnidhe na hÉireann. Roll of Honour

Martha Walsh, who was also known as "Birdie", was born in 1891. She was a member of Inghnidhe na hÉireann and on Easter Monday she reported to St Stephen's Green. She was sent to the GPO and served there throughout the week with her sisters, Margaret and Mary Jo, and her brother, Mark. She attended to the wounded and on Friday accompanied them to Jervis Street Hospital.

She later married Captain Tom Slater, Quartermaster of the Jacob's Garrison in 1916. During the War of

Independence she served with 2nd Battalion, Dublin Brigade and was involved in collecting for the National Aid and the Prisoners Dependent Fund. She was a courier with the Dept of Domestic Affairs and also took part in anti-conscription work. In March 1919 she assisted in the escape of Republican prisoners from Mountjoy Jail.

Martha Slater, of 38 Offaly Road, Cabra, died on January 1st 1960 and was buried at Glasnevin Cemetery.

References:

RH; IMA, MSPC; *Irish Press*, 4th January 1960, (obit).

Mary Josephine (Mary Jo) Walsh (Mrs. Mary Jo Rafferty): (1886- 1975)

Cumann na mBan, (Árd Croabh, Central Branch). Roll of Honour

Mary Jo Walsh was a member of the Árd Croabh (Central Branch) of Cumann na mBan and with her sisters, Margaret and Martha and brother, Mark, was part of the GPO Garrison during Easter Week.

Mary Jo Walsh was attached to the first aid section in the G.P.O. and attended the wounded. She assisted with carrying the wounded from the Coliseum Theatre through the bored walls in Henry Street to Jervis Street Hospital on Friday evening. On leaving Jervis Street Hospital on Saturday evening she was stopped by the military and returned to the hospital. In a second attempt to get away with Molly Reynolds they arrived at the latter's home at Clonmore Road, Ballybough where they spent Saturday night. In 1917-18 she organised a Cumann na mBan Branch in Ardee, Co. Louth and was appointed joint treasurer to the Cumann na mBan Executive. She was involved in anti-conscription work and the National Aid Fund. Her husband, Patrick Rafferty, took part in the War of Independence.

Mary Jo Rafferty, nee Walsh, of 1 St Eithne Road, Cabra, died on January 3rd 1975 and was buried at Mount Jerome Cemetery, Harold's Cross.

References:

RH; IMA, MSPC; *Irish Press*, 6th January 1975, (dn).

James Wardick (1887 -)
E. Coy, 4th Batt, Dublin Brigade. Roll of Honour

On Easter Monday, 1916, James Wardick, of Lower Rathfarnham, was one of thirty members of E. Company, 4th Battalion, who left from Rathfarnham Church and travelled to the GPO and fought there during Easter Week.

James Wardick was deported after the surrender and later interned in Frongoch, until July 21st 1916. He later resided at 23 Russell Avenue, Drumcondra, Dublin.

References:
RH; IMA, BMH (WS 141, *James Kenny*).

Patrick (Paddy) Weafer: (1896 - 1946)
E. Coy, 2nd Batt, Dublin Brigade. Roll of Honour

Paddy Weafer was born in 1896 and was a native of Ennicorthy. When he first moved to Dublin, he resided at 34 Richmond Place, North Circular Road. He played with Emeralds GFC and Saint Laurence O'Toole GAA Club and he became a member of E. Company, 2nd Battalion, in 1914. On Easter Monday, he was mobilised at Father Mathew Park, Fairview and was among those who occupied Lambe's Public House, Ballybough Bridge. On Tuesday he took part in the attack from Leinster Avenue on British Troops on the railway line at East Wall Road,. Later that evening he was in the Fairview contingent, under the command of Captain Frank Henderson that left for the GPO. While in the GPO he helped in the boring of holes in walls of buildings in Henry Street. After the surrender he was sentenced to six months hard labour and deported to Stafford Jail and then interned in Frongoch. His brother, Captain Thomas Weafer, was killed in the Hibernian Bank, during Easter Week, while his father, Patrick, and his brother, John, took part in the Rising in Enniscorthy, in 1916.

During the War of Independence he was employed as a merchant seaman and smuggled guns and ammunition into Ireland from the United States. Because of his IRB connections, he was closely associated with many leading Irish in America, including Liam Mellowes. Between trips to the United States, he was involved in a number of operations in Dublin, including the attempted rescue of Larry Ginnell MP from a prison van at Mountjoy Jail. He took part in raids for arms and in the burning of the Income Tax Office, Bachelor's Walk. He was arrested late in 1920 and interned for four months. He served until the Truce, and took no part in the Civil War. He later resided at Stanton Row, Clonmel and was employed in the Clonmel Shoe Factory.

Paddy Weafer died on June 16th 1946 and was buried in St Mary's Cemetery, Enniscorthy.

References:
IMA, MSPC; IMA, BMH (WS 150, *Seamus O'Meara*); NLI, *Lynch Papers*, (Ms 11,131).

Patrick (Pat) Weafer: (1890 -   )
Maynooth Company Volunteers, Kildare Brigade

Pat Weafer was born in Maynooth in 1890, and was a joiner by trade. At seven o'clock on Easter Monday evening he moved off from the back of Dómhnall Ó Buachalla's shop in Main Street, with fifteen Volunteers from Maynooth Company, in the direction of Dublin. They travelled cross country by the Royal Canal, and slept in Glasnevin Cemetery before reaching the GPO early on Tuesday morning. He was sent to relieve the Irish Citizen Army men in the City Hall area and fought in Parliament Street, until he was recalled to the GPO. He fought in the GPO and the Henry Street area until the evacuation on Friday evening. With fellow Maynooth Volunteers, Joe Ledwith and Pat Colgan, he evaded capture and made his way back to Maynooth, where he was later arrested. He was court-martialled on May 15th and sentenced to two years penal servitude, which was reduced to six months.

Pat Weafer served his sentence in Hare Park Prison, at the Curragh.

References:
    RH; IMA, BMH (WS 850, *Pat Colgan*); James Durney, *On the One Road*, (2001).

Thomas Weafer: (1890 – 1916). Killed In Action
Captain. E. Coy, 2nd Batt, Dublin Brigade. Roll of Honour

Thomas Weafer was born in Enniscorthy in 1890. He worked as a cabinet maker, before moving to Dublin, where he opened a shop at 582 North Circular Road, at the corner with Summer Street. He was appointed captain of E. Company, 2nd Battalion and was in charge of a raid on the London North Western Railway at North Wall in 1915, where arms and explosives were seized. On Easter Monday afternoon at 3 o'clock, he led the 2nd Battalion from Fairview towards the city. At Clarke's Bridge, he received a report that British troops were advancing from Dollymount, and he sent Captain

Frank Henderson with a party of men, including his brother, Paddy, back to take up positions at Ballybough Bridge. He the proceeded to the GPO and was sent across the street to occupy the entire block, from lower Abbey Street to Eden Quay. On Tuesday James Connolly sent Captain Liam Tannam to take over from him, as he was being attended to in the first aid treatment room by Doctor John Tuohy and some Cumann na mBan women. Captain Tannam returned to the GPO on Wednesday afternoon and shortly after, as Captain Weafer was descending the stairs, he was shot through a landing window in the Hibernian Bank and received a serious stomach wound. The shot came from a sniper in the vicinity of McBirney's on Aston's Quay, and Leslie Price, who narrowly missed being hit by the same bullet, said an Act of Contrition in his ear before he passed away minutes later. The Hibernian Bank was destroyed in the subsequent inferno and his body was consumed in the flames. His father, Patrick and his brother, John, took part in the Rising in Enniscorthy in 1916.

A memorial plaque to Captain Thomas Weafer was erected on the rebuilt bank building on Easter Sunday 1937, and the unveiling ceremony was attended by his widow and daughter.

References:

RH; IMA, BMH (WS 291, *Liam Daly*), BMH (WS 359, *Eva Burke*) & BMH (WS 1,754, *Leslie Barry, nee Price*); *Catholic Bulletin*, May 1917; Max Caulfield, *The Easter Rebellion*, (1963); Richard Roche, *Here's Their Memory*, (1966); Thomas Coffey, *Agony at Easter*, (1969); Michael Hopkinson, *Frank Henderson's Easter Rising; Recollections of a Dublin Volunteer*, (1998); Ray Bateson, *They Died by Pearse's Side*, (2010); *Irish Independent*, 26th March 1937, (*unveiling of plaque*). BMH (WS 242, Liam Tannam).

Thomas (Tom) Wheatley: (1879 - 1941)
B. Coy, 2nd Batt, Dublin Brigade. Roll of Honour

Tom Wheatley was born in 1879 and resided at 251 Richmond Road. He was educated at St Joseph's CBS, Marino and worked as a solicitor's clerk. He joined Sinn Féin in the Clann na hEireann Hall in Richmond Road, and was an early member of St Laurence O'Toole's GAA Club. He later became a member of B. Company, 2nd Battalion, Dublin Brigade. On Easter Monday he reported to Fr Mathew Park, Fairview and was sent to occupy a house at Clarke's Bridge on Summerhill Parade. He later proceeded to the GPO, where he manned the windows on the Prince's Street

side, until the evacuation on Friday evening. He was deported to Knutsford Jail on May 1st and was interned in Frongoch, until Christmas 1916.

On his release from internment, he rejoined his unit and was engaged as a drill instructor. He was involved in intelligence work in 1919 and he and other Volunteers tracked the movements of Lord French and members of the British GHQ staff for three weeks. In 1920 he went to work in Wicklow and ceased active service. He was employed as a civil servant for many years with the Dept of Finance.

Tom Wheatley died suddenly at his home at 8 North William Street, on December 3rd 1941 and was buried in Glasnevin Cemetery.

References:

RH; IMA, MSPC; NLI, *Lynch Papers*, (Ms 11,131); *Scoil Iósaif, Marino, 1916-1966, (a 1919 Jubilee Publication)*, (1966); Jimmy Wren, *Saint Laurence O'Toole GAC Centenary History, 1901-2001*, (2001); *Irish Independent*, 4th December 1941, (dn).

Joseph Whelan: (1886 - 1968)

Irish Citizen Army, (Gloucester St Section). Roll of Honour

Joseph Whelan was born in 1886 and resided at 92 Lower Gardiner Street. He was a member of the Irish Citizen Army and on Easter Monday he occupied the Vitriol Works, Ballybough Bridge, under the command of Captain Vincent Poole. He remained there until Tuesday evening and withdrew with the main Volunteer force from Fairview to the GPO. He was stationed in the Metropole Hotel, until the evacuation on Friday. After the surrender he was detained in Richmond Barracks and deported to Stafford Jail on May 1st.

After his release from Stafford Jail on June 7th, he transferred to A. Company, 1st Battalion, Dublin Brigade, and fought in the War of Independence. He was arrested in November 1920 and interned in Ballykinlar until December 1921. He took no part in the Civil War.

He was a former employee of W & R Jacobs and resided at 2 All Saints Drive, St Anne's, Raheny.

Joseph Whelan died on July 30th 1968 and was buried in Mount Jerome Cemetery, Harold's Cross.

References:
 RH; IMA, MSPC; *Evening Herald*, 1st August 1968, (dn).

Laurence Whelan: (1895 - 1960)

F. Coy, 2nd Batt, Dublin Brigade

Laurence Whelan was born in 1895 and resided at 13 North William Street. He was a cabinet maker by trade and was a member of F. Company, 2nd Battalion, Dublin Brigade. He reported to the GPO on Easter Monday and was sent across the street to Reis's Chambers. He then went to the Dublin Bread Company Building and was engaged in boring through the walls to the Hopkins & Hopkins building, at the corner of Eden Quay. He was wounded in the arm while entering the Hibernian Bank, and returned to the GPO. He was taken to Jervis Street Hospital on Wednesday, with other wounded Volunteers and with the aid of a hospital porter, he later made his way out through the rear of the hospital and evaded capture. His brother, William, was also a member of the GPO Garrison.

He rejoined his unit at its reorganisation in 1917 and transferred to 5th Battalion, Engineers, in 1919. He took part in a number of operations, including the raid on the Independent Newspaper Offices, the destruction of the Coast Guard Station at

Dollymount and the burning of the Custom House. During the Civil War, he fought on the Republican side in the Four Courts in June 1922. He was also involved in the destruction of the railway tracks at Liffey Junction, and was on the run until May 1923.

He served with the 26th Infantry Battalion during the emergency years. He was a director of O'Farrell & Whelan Furniture Manufacturers, Davitt Road. Inchicore and a former assistant secretary and treasurer of the Irish Society of Woodcutting Machinists.

Laurence Whelan, of 20 Carleton Road, Marino, died on January 30th 1960 and was buried at Glasnevin Cemetery three days later.

References:

IMA, MSPC; *Sunday Independent*, 31st January 1960, (dn).

William Whelan: (1892 – 1969)

E. Coy, 2nd Batt, Dublin Brigade

William Whelan was born in 1892 and resided at 31 Ballybough Road. He joined D. Company, 2nd Battalion, Dublin Brigade in 1914 and he mobilised at Father Mathew Park on Easter Monday. He was posted to the Vitriol Works, Ballybough, under the command of Captain Tom Craven and Vincent Poole of the Irish Citizen Army. He later went to Gilbey's Store, Ballybough Bridge and he withdrew to the GPO on Tuesday evening. He was posted to the Imperial Hotel and remained there until Thursday night. When the Imperial Hotel was evacuated because of the intense fire, he was captured in the Marlborough Street area. He was deported to Stafford Jail on May 1st and interned in Frongoch until Christmas 1916. His brother, Laurence, was also part of the GPO Garrison.

He rejoined his unit in 1917, and he was one of ten Volunteers that were sent to London in 1918, with orders to assassinate members of the British War Cabinet if conscription was introduced in Ireland. He returned to England in 1919 and formed a Volunteer Company in Middlesboro and was engaged in transporting arms and ammunition to Ireland. He was arrested and sentenced to five years penal servitude and was released from Dartmoor Prison after the Truce in 1921. On his return to Ireland he took up a commission in the Free State Army and was attached to the Army Corps of Engineers. He resigned from the army in 1927 with the rank of commandant.

William Whelan, of St Jude's, Newcourt Road, Bray, County Wicklow, died in Toronto, Canada, on September 15th 1969 and was buried there.

References:

IMA, MSPC; *Sinn Féin Rebellion Handbook 1916*, Weekly Irish Times, (1917); *Irish Press*, 17th September 1969, (obit).

Jack (Blanco) White: (1876 -   )
Irish Citizen Army, (Townsend St Section)

Blanco White was born in 1876 and resided at 6 Mark Street with his wife and two children in 1911. He was a merchant seaman and a member of the Irish Citizen Army, Townsend Street Section. He resided at 21 Luke Street in 1916, and fought in the GPO during Easter Week. In periods of inactivity, he amused his comrades with tales of his adventures at sea. On Wednesday he appeared on the roof of the GPO, and proceeded to instruct those around him in the use of homemade bombs, using the most colourful language. He evaded capture after the evacuation of the GPO on Friday evening.

After the Rising he went to Liverpool and was engaged in helping IRA men to get away to the United States and other parts of the world by sea. He was arrested in Liverpool in February 1919 and was imprisoned until June 1919. In 1936 the superintendent of the Catholic Seamen's Hostel, Southampton, stated in a letter to the Military Services Pension Board that he was discharged from hospital with stomach cancer, which was diagnosed as incurable.

Blanco White, with an address at Hampstead Way, London, was a patient at St Pancras Hospital in 1937.

References:
IMA, MSPC; IMA, BMH (WS 370, *Fintan Murphy*) & BMH (WS 724, *Desmond Ryan*); NLI, *William O'Brien Papers*, (Ms 15,673); Max Caulfield, *The Easter Rebellion*, (1963); Ann Matthews, *The Irish Citizen Army*, (2014).

John J. White: (1885-   )
E. Coy, 2nd Batt, Dublin Brigade. Roll of Honour

John White, of 10 Summer Street, was a member of E. Company, 2nd Battalion, Dublin Brigade. He fought in the GPO during Easter Week. After the surrender he was deported to Stafford Jail on May 1st and interned in Frongoch until July 26th 1916.

John White later resided at 2 St Aidan's Park Avenue, Marino.

References:
RH; *Sinn Féin Rebellion Handbook 1916*, Weekly Irish Times, (1917).

Michael White: (1884 - 1968)
C. Coy, 1st Batt, Dublin Brigade. Roll of Honour

Michael White was born in 1884 and educated at O'Connell Schools, North Richmond Street. He joined the Volunteers in 1913 and was one of eleven members of C. Company, 1st Battalion, Dublin Brigade, who fought in the GPO in Easter Week. On Easter Monday he was posted to man the windows and the following day he was sent to commandeer food and provisions from William's Store, Henry Street. He was sent by Seán McDermott to Wynn's Hotel in Abbey Street. He came under heavy sniper fire in Sackville Street and later in Marlborough Street and took refuge in a stable overnight. On Friday he mingled with civilians in the area and evaded capture. He left the city and stayed in Skerries for a period to avoid arrest. He had no further connection with the Volunteers after that.

He later lived at 55 Croydon Green, Marino and was employed for many years as a baker in Peter Kennedy Bakery Ltd, Parnell Street.

Michael White died on July 18th 1968 and was buried at Glasnevin Cemetery.

References:
RH; IMA, MSPC; NLI, *Lynch Papers*, (11,131); *Irish Press*, 20th July 1968, (obit).

W.J. Brennan-Whitmore: (1886 – 1977)
Adjutant, North Wexford Volunteers. Staff Officer, G.H.Q

W.J. Brennan-Whitmore was born in County Wexford in 1886. His parents died when he was young and he was reared by his uncle, James Brennan and his wife on their farm at Clonee, Ferns. After he was left Ferns National School, he worked as a grocer's assistant in Dublin for a short time. He then joined the British Army and served as sergeant with the Royal Irish Regiment in India. On his return to Ireland he found employment as a freelance journalist and in 1910 he joined Sinn Féin and the Gaelic League. He joined the Volunteers in 1913 and became O/C of the Ferns Company. He was appointed Adjutant of the North Wexford Brigade in 1914. He received his mobilisation orders from Thomas McDonagh on the Wednesday before Easter, and he travelled to Dublin on Good Friday. While in the GPO on Easter Monday, he was ordered by James Connolly to take a number of men and occupy the block of buildings between North Earl Street and the Imperial Hotel, across the street from the GPO. They held this position until Thursday night when heavy artillery fire forced them out of the burning buildings. He and other Volunteers were captured by British Troops as they attempted to reach the northern suburbs. They were surrounded in a tenement in the vicinity of Marlborough Street and North Cumberland Street and brought to the Custom House for interrogation. They were transferred to Richmond Barracks and he was deported to Knutsford Jail on May 3rd. He was interned in Frongoch until Christmas 1916 and, while there, he was made Camp Adjutant.

He returned to Wexford from Frongoch and worked as a journalist. He was arrested and deported in 1918 for his alleged part in the 'German Plot'. On his release he worked as an Intelligence Officer on Michael Collins's staff and married Anna Murphy in 1920. He took the pro-Treaty side in the Civil War and joined the Free State Army in 1922 with the rank of Commandant. He was editor of An tÓglach for a time, before retiring from the army in 1927. He took up farming in County Wexford and also founded a local newspaper in Gorey entitled 'The Record'. He was the author of "With the Irish in Frongoch", published in 1917 and "Dublin Burning", which was published posthumously in 1996.

William James Brennan-Whitmore died in December 1977.

References:

IMA, MSPC; *An t-Óglach,* January 1926; W.J. Brennan-Whitmore, *With the Irish in Frongoch,* (1917); Max Caulfield, *The Easter Rebellion,* (1963); Thomas Coffey, *Agony at Easter,* (1969); Seán O'Mahony, *Frongoch: University of Revolution,* (1987); W.J. Brennan-Whitmore, *Dublin Burning,* (1996); *Irish Press* & *Evening Herald,* 28th December 1977, (obits).

Arthur Wicks (alias John Neal): (1893 - 1916).
Killed in Action
Irish Citizen Army Volunteer, (Industrial Workers of the World)

Arthur Wicks was born in Norwich, on May 11th 1893 and was the son of a boot maker. He was associated with the IWW from 1911 to 1915 and played a prominent role in the London hotel strike in 1913, for which he was imprisoned. He came to Dublin in late 1915 because of the victimisation he encountered as a result of his part in the London hotel strike, and found employment as a waiter in the Shelbourne Hotel, using the alias John Neal. He was dismissed from the Shelbourne Hotel because of his trade union activities, and later worked at the Hotel Allen, Harcourt Street. In the months preceding the Rising, he was involved in running guns and ammunition by sea on behalf of the Irish Citizen Army. He was known to his comrades as John Neal and during Easter Week he was described as having a modern German service rifle, but not wearing any uniform. He was not in uniform because on Easter Monday he planned a trip to the Dublin mountains, when he discovered the Rising was going ahead. He was posted to the Vitriol Works, Ballybough and he was involved in blowing up the Great Northern Railway line at the viaduct at Fairview. He remained there until Tuesday night when his party left for the GPO. While in the GPO he used Nelson's nose as target practice, until ordered to stop by James Connolly. He was sent to the Metropole Hotel and in his account of the fighting there, Charles Saurin recalled a Jewish looking youth, who he described as one of the calmest and bravest individuals he had ever encountered, sitting out on a parapet of the hotel and scanning the surrounding area with field glasses during the bombardments of Wednesday and Thursday. On Friday, to keep morale up, he and a couple of other Volunteers donned chef's uniforms and cooked dinner in the hotel kitchen for members of the garrison, before they returned to the GPO. As members of the Metropole Garrison waited in the sorting room of the GPO for orders to evacuate,

Andy Furlong's ammunition pouch exploded, and Arthur Wicks suffered multiple wounds to his thigh. Harry Ridgeway and Oscar Traynor attended to him and he was later carried to the houses in Moore Street by Harry Ridgeway and Christopher Tallon. On Saturday, as he lay on the pavement, a British soldier loosened the binding that was restricting the flow of blood and he was taken by stretcher to Dublin Castle. He died that night in the Castle Yard as he was being taken to the emergency hospital.

Arthur Wicks was buried in Glasnevin Cemetery, but there is no recognition of him on the Roll of Honour List.

References:

The Irish Worker's Voice, 19th April 1930; *An t-Óglach*, 13th & 20th March 1926, (*Charles Saurin*); Max Caulfield, *The Easter Rebellion*, (1963); Joe Good, *Enchanted by Dreams*, (1996); Jim Corr, *Believed to be in Ireland* (as yet, unpublished).

Henry Willis: (1898 - 1951)
F. Coy, 1st Batt, Dublin Brigade. Roll of Honour

Henry Willis was born in 1898 and he joined the Volunteers, in 1913. He was a member of F. Company, 1st Battalion, Dublin Brigade. On Easter Monday he reported to Father Mathew Park and went with the column to the GPO led by Captain Thomas Weafer. He fought in the GPO throughout Easter Week and he was in the advance party, led by The O'Rahilly into Moore Street at the evacuation on Friday evening. He was detained in Richmond Barracks after the surrender and he was released after a week, because of his young age.

He was employed in the Engineering Dept of the Post Office, and late in 1916 was drafted as a civilian worker with the Royal Engineers to France, and remained there until the Armistice. On his return to Ireland in 1918, he rejoined F. Company and fought in the War of Independence until the Truce in 1921. He took no part in the Civil War.

In 1927 he joined Fianna Fáil and was an active member for many years.

Henry Willis, of 1 Waverley Avenue, Fairview, died on April 10th 1951 and was buried at Glasnevin Cemetery.

References:

RH; IMA, MSPC; *Irish Press*, 12th April 1951, (obit).

Esther Wisley (Mrs. Esther O'Moore): (1898 - 1953)

Cumann na mBan, (Fairview Branch). Roll of Honour

Esther Wisley was born in 1898 and resided at 30 Strandville Avenue, North Strand. She became a member of the Cumann na mBan, Clontarf Branch in 1915. She reported to St Stephen's Green on Easter Monday, but could not find her unit and went to Fairview. She then went to the GPO and served in the first aid section under the command of Louise Gavan Duffy. During the week she was sent by medical officer, Captain Doyle, to collect medical supplies from his home in Ballybough. On her return to the GPO she was accosted by a group of British Army separation women and was in danger of being attacked, when she produced an automatic pistol and proceeded on her way. She left the GPO with the first group of women on Friday morning, and was stopped by British troops in Summerhill. They were detained at Broadstone Railway Station for questioning, before being eventually released.

During the War of Independence she collected and distributed money for the Prisoners Dependents Fund. She was also involved in anti-conscription work and election duties. She took the Republican side during the Civil War and stored arms and assisted men on the run. She also served in Barry's Hotel. She later married Seán O'Moore, who fought in the Four Courts in 1916 and who was O/C of the 1st Battalion during the Civil War.

Esther O'Moore, of 151 Griffith Avenue, died on February 26th 1963 and was buried at Clontarf Cemetery.

References:
RH; IMA, MSPC; *Irish Press*, 28th February 1963, (obit).

James Wren: (1898 - 1953)

Volunteer, (Unattached). Roll of Honour

James Wren was born in 1898 and resided at 44 Portland Row, North Strand. He was educated at O'Connell Schools, North Richmond Street. His father, John Wren, who was a member of the United Irish League, took part in the Howth gun running. On Easter Monday, at the age of seventeen and a half, he accompanied his first cousin, Tommy Mahon, and friend, Paddy Halpin, to the GPO and offered his services. He was given a shotgun and put on sentry duty. He was later sent out with dispatches and was

attacked in the street by a pro-British crowd. He was badly beaten and he received a back injury. He made his way back to the GPO and was ordered home due to illness.

In May 1917 he joined F. Company, 2nd Battalion, Dublin Brigade and served in the War of Independence, taking part in many operations carried out by his unit. For a period he assisted his battalion quartermaster in collecting and transporting arms. He was on active service until the Truce, but took no part in the Civil War.

He served with the 26th Infantry Battalion, in the emergency years and was later on the Custom House Memorial Committee. He later resided at 163 Malahide Road, Donnycarney and he was employed as a rent collector for the Dublin Corporation, for many years.

James Wren died on December 30th 1953 and was buried at Glasnevin Cemetery.

References:

RH; IMA, MSPC; *Irish Press*, 31st December 1953, (dn & obit).

Nancy de Paor (Wyse Power): (1889 – 1963)

Cumann na mBan

Nancy de Paor was born in Dublin in 1889. Her mother, Jennie, nee O'Toole, was a founder of the Ladies Land League and later vice-president of Cumann na mBan and a prominent member of Sinn Féin. John Wyse Power, her father, was a founder of the GAA in Thurles in 1884 and a founder GAA Dublin County Board in 1886. Nancy joined Cumann na mBan, Ard Craobh branch in 1915 and on Easter Monday, P.H. Pearse sent her with a despatch for Dr Dundon, the Volunteer commander in Borris, County Carlow. From there, she proceeded to Kilkenny and returned by train

to Dublin on Tuesday evening. She reported to P.H. Pearse and later she accompanied her parents from their home in Henry Street to Walter Cole's house, in Mountjoy Square. On Wednesday she returned to her home with her mother, Jennie and organised food supplies that were taken to the GPO. She then accompanied Hannah Sheehy Skeffington from the GPO to the College of Surgeons with provisions. On her return to the GPO she was engaged in cooking duties. She was unable to reach the GPO from Mountjoy Square on Thursday, because the area was by then sealed off.

After the Rising she was one of two honorary secretaries of Cumann na mBan, under Countess Markievicz's presidency. Previously, she had studied at Bonn University and in 1921 she was sent to Berlin to set up a propaganda centre by Dáil Éireann. When the Free State was established, she returned to Dublin and joined the Civil Service. She retired with position of Principal Officer in 1954.

Dr. Nancy Wyse Power died on December 27th 1963.

References:

IMA, MSPC; IMA, BMH (WS 587); Marie O'Neill, *From Parnell to De Valera: a biography of Jennie Wyse Power*, (1991); Ruth Taillon, *Women of 1916*, (1996); *Modern Irish Lives*, (Louis McRedmond, Ed, 1996); Sinéad McCoole, *No Ordinary Women: Irish Female Activists in the Revolutionary Years, 1900-1923*, (2004); Ann Matthews, *Renegades: Irish Republican Women, 1900-1922*, (2010).

Epilogue

1. The Dublin Garrisons in 1916

GPO, General Headquarters

Commandant General Pádraig Pearse, Commander-in-Chief; Commandant General James Connolly, Commandant General of the Dublin Division; Commander Thomas Clarke, Military Committee, Provisional Government; Commander Sean McDermott, Military Committee, Provisional Government; Commander Joseph Plunkett, Military Committee, Provisional Government; the number of the garrison force was approximately 572 and was comprised of Irish Volunteers, mainly from 1st, 2nd & 4th Battalions, Irish Citizen Army, Hibernian Rifles & Cumann na mBan.

The General Post Office was the key building in the main street of the capital city. It was constructed between 1814 and 1818 at a cost of £50,000 from the designs of Francis Johnston. The building occupied a city block, with a 220 feet wide fifteen bay facade to Sackville Street, and return elevations to Prince's Street and Henry Street all faced in granite ashlar. The portico was in Portland stone surmounted by three statues representing Mercury, Hibernia and Fidelity. It was ironic that the new public office, through which the Irish Volunteers and associates stormed the building, was only completed in 1915. Its central feature, a curved compartmented ceiling spanning 40 feet, was destroyed as was the interior of the building in the ensuing military engagements. The facade and portico of the GPO survived and the building was gradually reconstructed during the 1920s and early 1930s. See Frederick O'Dwyer, 'The General Post Office (GPO)-a case study', in *Architecture 1600-2000, vol. iv, Art and architecture in Ireland* (Dublin, 2014), pp 194-5.

The Four Courts

Commandant Edward Daly, Officer-in-Command; the number of the garrison force was approximately 320 and was comprised of Irish Volunteers, mainly from 1st Battalion & Cumann na mBan.

St Stephen's Green / College of Surgeons

Commandant Michael Mallin, Officer-in-Command; Countess Markievicz, Second-in-Command; the number of the garrison force was approximately 137 and was comprised mainly of the Irish Citizen Army.

Jacob's Biscuit Factory
Commandant Thomas MacDonagh, Officer-in-Command; Captain Tom Hunter, Second-in-Command; Major John McBride, Military Advisor; the number of the garrison force was approximately 170 and was comprised mainly of Irish Volunteers, mainly from 2nd Battalion & Cumann na mBan.

Boland's Mills & Bakery
Commandant Éamon de Valera, Officer-in-Command; the number of the garrison force was approximately 170 and was comprised of Irish Volunteers, mainly from 3rd Battalion.

South Dublin Union
Commandant Eamon Ceannt, Officer-in-Command; Commandant Cathal Brugha, Second-in-Command; the number of the garrison force was approximately 200 and was comprised of Irish Volunteers, mainly from 4th Battalion & Cumann na mBan.

North County Dublin
Commandant Thomas Ashe, Officer-in-Command; Lieutenant Richard Mulcahy, Second-in-Command; the strength of the force was approximately 65 and was comprised of Irish Volunteers, mainly from 5th Battalion & Cumann na mBan.

City Hall area
Captain Seán Connolly, Officer-in-Command; the strength of the force was approximately 45 and was comprised of Irish Citizen Army & Cumann na mBan.

Dublin Battalions
At the time of the 1916 Rising there were five battalions in Dublin City & County: 1st Battalion covered the north city area; 2nd Battalion covered the north east area; 3rd Battalion covered the south east area; 4th Battalion covered the south west city & county area; 5th Battalion covered the north county area. After 1916 the 5th Battalion operated as the Fingal Brigade, while a new 5th Battalion was formed as the Engineers Battalion and a 6th Battalion was formed in the south Dublin area.

2. Where did the GPO Garrison come from?

According to the 1911 census, the last record of population prior to 1916 the population of Dublin City was 361,219. The city's official limits had been extended beyond the canals in 1900 to incorporate the townships of Clontarf, Drumcondra, Clonliffe, Glasnevin and New Kilmainham.   Until the biographical dictionaries of all the Dublin Garrisons are completed it is not possible to provide a definitive geography of the distribution of the physical force men and women in the city and county and beyond. It appears that the garrisons in specific locations were mainly peopled from the districts in which they were located. Table 1 indicates that the great majority of the GPO Garrison belonged to Dublin city and specifically the inner city as defined by the fifteen inner city wards. One suspects that because of its location and primacy as the Headquarter Garrison the GPO would have a wider geographical range of members than the others.

Dublin's inner city had a long tradition of physical force nationalism. Robert Emmet's insurrection, though risible in a military sense, inspired revolutionaries long beyond his defiant speech from the dock and his scaffold in Thomas Street. Most of the revolutionary clubs associated with the Irish Confederation in 1848 were found within the canals, and the Fenians in 1867 had their greatest strength here. Neither the Irish Confederation in 1848 nor the Fenians in 1867 struck a blow in the centre of the highly militarised capital. Who then were the men and women who took up arms in Easter Week 1916 and forged the title deeds of a nation in the furnace which destroyed many of the great buildings in the heart of Ireland's first city? What drove the 498 men and 74 women of the GPO Garrison to take such an extreme step?

One of the more striking features of the analysis of the addresses, when these can be ascertained, is that the majority of the combatants lived in the north inner city (287), the domain of the working and lower middle classes- labourers and skilled artisans. There were concentrations in Ballybough (24), Drumcondra (25), Fairview (13), Gardiner Street (10), North Circular Road (48), North Strand (23) and Summerhill (21). In County Dublin there was a significant concentration in what was then rural Rathfarnham, home to P.H. Pearse's school, St. Enda's (Scoil Éanna) (see appendix 3). More than a quarter of the garrison came from counties outside of Dublin, an indication of high in -migration to the city. Thirty of the thirty-two counties were represented; the exceptions were Armagh and Laois. Kildare had the greatest number (17) after Dublin with the counties of Kerry (11), Cork (10), Wexford (9) and Louth (9) next in importance. Those from outside Ireland were dominated by a relatively large contingent from England, who had been based at Kimmage before the Rising.

Table 1: Known addresses of GPO Garrison Members, 1916

North Inner City	South Inner City	North suburbs and Co. Dublin	South suburbs and Co. Dublin	Other counties outside Dublin	Outside Ireland
287	68	13	39	133	43

We do not know how many of these men and women were involved in the great lock out in 1913 when the employers, led by William Martin Murphy, and the trade unions, commanded by James Larkin, fought a bitter and protracted conflict. Some marched to Howth on 26 July 1914 to take delivery of the rifles and ammunition brought on board the *Asgard* from Hamburg. Others, especially those enrolled in the Irish Volunteers, must have heard Pádraig Pearse's oration at the graveside of the old Fenian Jeremiah O'Donovan Rossa in Glasnevin Cemetery in June 1915. Perhaps they had been politicised by the writings of Arthur Griffith and Pearse, who preached Mitchel's message that England's difficulty was Ireland's opportunity, and England had difficulties in 1916 as the Great War in Europe's mainland persisted. The outbreak of war led to the suspension of promised Home Rule, the consequent decline of the Home Rule Party and the split in the Irish Volunteers. The political vacuum was soon to be filled at first with gunfire and later with a new dynamic political movement.

3. Military and Cultural Organisations to which the GPO Garrison were affiliated

We get some answers as to the affiliations of the 572 men and women, listed in the *Biographical dictionary* above, from table 2, which divides the Garrison according to the military and cultural organisations to which they belonged.

Table 2: Military and Cultural Organisations Represented in the GPO

Organisation	Number present in the GPO
Irish Volunteers	401
Irish Republican Brotherhood	79
GAA	69
Gaelic League	66
Irish Citizen Army	63
Cumann na mBan	57
Fianna Eireann	20
Hibernian Rifles	20
Sinn Féin	17
Unattached	16
Clann na nGael Girl Scouts	4

Note: The discrepancy between total numbers in GPO and the numbers in table 2 is explained by the fact that many were members of more than one organisation.

The Irish Volunteers, the largest group in the GPO, were formed at a meeting in the Rotunda on 25 November 1913 in response to the formation of an armed Ulster Volunteer Force in 1912 that was pledged to resist the implementation of the Third Home Rule Bill. John Redmond, the leader of the Irish Parliamentary Party, caused a split in the Volunteers after the outbreak of the First World War in September 1914, by encouraging the 170,000 members to enlist in the British forces. A minority of 12,000 members, influenced by the IRB, who had infiltrated the organisation, prepared for an armed insurrection in Ireland. Initially the Rising was planned by the IRB to take place on Easter Sunday under the cover of manoeuvres but Eoin MacNeill, on discovering the subterfuge, countermanded the manoeuvre order. His action had greater repercussions outside Dublin but the leadership in the city, with its better communication network, decided to proceed, take to arms, seize the major buildings and proclaim an Irish Republic on Easter Monday 1916. Cumann na mBan, a women's auxiliary of the Irish Volunteers, was founded in 1914. It had 57 members in the GPO.

The Irish Republican Brotherhood, a secret oath –bound separatist organisation, was founded in Lombard Street Dublin in March 1858 by James Stephens and a number of associates who had been involved in the Irish Confederation and the James Fintan Lalor inspired Waterford Risings of 1849. A parallel organisation known as the Fenians was established in New York by John O'Mahony and Michael Doheny, who had been forced to flee from Ireland as a result of their activities in 1848. The IRB had survived the catastrophe of the 1867 Rising and though ostensibly underground it had assiduously infiltrated and influenced all other Nationalist bodies. Tom Clarke was the closest link between the hillside men of 1867 and the revolutionaries of 1916. Most of his co-leaders in the GPO Garrison were members of the IRB's Military Council.

The Gaelic Athletic Association founded by Michael Cusack in 1884 and the Gaelic League founded by Douglas Hyde in 1893 were twin organisations devoted to the ideal of an Irish Ireland through the resurrection of its hereditary games and language. Both had their headquarters in Dublin and in many instances combatants in the GPO were members of both groups. Sixty-nine of those who fought in the GPO in 1916 were members of the GAA, the best known been Harry Boland and Michael Collins. In contrast, only four known members of soccer clubs, including Oscar Traynor, a future Cabinet Minister, were members of soccer clubs, while rugby, cricket and hockey clubs had no known representatives (see appendix 7). These findings are tentative and further research is required. We do know, however, that some 300 members of GAA clubs participated in the Rising and the role of Dublin's GAA in it has been discussed in *The Gaelic Athletic Association in Dublin 1884-2000* (vol. 1, 1884-1959). The conclusion reached in this work stated:

Significantly, it was not Dublin's most successful and long-established clubs…who dominate the list, but the newer clubs such as O'Tooles, Crokes, Colmcilles and Bulfins. The common thread, which bound these newcomers, was a direct link with the Gaelic League. It was not so much membership of the GAA that motivated men and women to take up arms but rather membership of the Gaelic League (Nolan, 2005, vol. 1, p.126).

Seamus Ó Buachalla described the role of the Gaelic League as follows:

It offered Irish cultural separatism a rational intellectual basis and was a most potent factor in the creation of the new and urgent nationalism which paved the way for political independence (Séamus Ó Buachalla (ed.), *The letters of P.H. Pearse* (Gerrard's Cross, 1980), p.467).

The connection between the GAA and Gaelic League is best exemplified by St. Laurence O'Toole's Club. Located in the north inner city it developed initially from a Gaelic League branch. Twenty-one of its 82 members participated in the Rising. Tom Clarke and Seán Mac Diarmada, two signatories of the Proclamation and members of the Provisional Government, had associations with the club. Tom Clarke was president of O'Toole's Piper's Band and MacDiarmada was a non–playing member attached to the club's Gaelic League Branch.

The Irish Citizen Army was formed in Dublin in 1913, as a worker's defence force during the great labour troubles of that year. James Connolly organised and trained this worker's army and led them openly through the streets on route marches over a two-year period. The Citizen's Army also had a women's section.

Na Fianna Éireann, the republican youth movement, was founded in Dublin in 1909 by Countess Markievicz and Bulmer Hobson, with Con Colbert as chief instructor. Modelled on the 'boy scout' movement, it participated in the Howth gun running operation in 1914. The Hibernian Rifles was founded in 1912 as the military arm of the Ancient Order of Hibernians (Irish-American Alliance).

Sinn Féin was a political party founded by Arthur Griffith and Bulmer Hobson in 1905. Its primary role was to educate Nationalist opinion through newspapers and literature and prepare the people for self-government. Though the British authorities and the press labelled the Rising as a 'Sinn Féin rebellion', it had a minority role as table 2 shows. It was after the sequence of executions, imprisonment and internment of the men and women of 1916 that Sinn Féin became the leading Nationalist political party in the first Dáil. Clann na nGael Girl Scouts was founded in 1911 as the junior auxiliary of Cumann na mBan.

At least ten of the GPO Garrison had served in the British army prior to the Rising (appendix 6) and three of these had fought in the Boer War. The best known of these was James Connolly.

4. Age of GPO Garrison members

Revolutionaries are generally young and the majority of those who fought in 1916 were under 30 years of age (table 3). Charles Townshend quoted a St John's Ambulance volunteer, WG Smith, who noted 'Many of them were mere boys, in fact only about one in ten was a man…they had a great many young girls, ranging (in age) from about 13 to 20' (Charles Townshend, p. 165). The average age of a combatant in the GPO was 26 years. If the numbers are broken down into age cohorts the results are revealing. 72% of those present in the GPO, for whom we have a date of birth, were aged between 15 and 30. The equivalent figure for Dublin city in 1911 was 29.58%. 29% of the garrison were under 20, with 25 members under the age of 16. The youngest combatant was Charlie McMahon who was twelve, a full 51 years younger than Matt Stafford, who was the oldest combatant at 63.

Table 3: GPO Garrison divided according to age and compared with the average in Dublin city, census 1911

Age	15-20	Under 20	20-30	Total Under 30	30-40	40-60	60+	Total
GPO (1916)	140	145	217	362	96	35	1	494
%	28%	29.35%	43.93%	73.28%	19.43%	7.09%	0.20%	
Dublin City (1911)	29,461	118,490	60,887	179,377	47,305	54,161	23,959	304,802
%	9.6%	38.87%	19.98%	58.85%	15.52%	17.77%	7.86%	

Source: 1911 Census

5. Occupational Status

Analysis of the social classes of those who participated in the 1916 Rising, has led to the conclusion that 'the revolution of 1916 was to some extent a workingmen's revolution with strong assistance from the middle group of commercial classes' (Larsen and Snoddy, p.384). This conclusion is basically confirmed by table 4 which is an analysis of the occupations of 390 members (appendix 4) of the GPO Garrison (Social classes are based on the Classification of Occupations used by the 1851 Census

Commissioners, which formed the basis of Mary Daly's social and economic analysis in her 1984 study, *Dublin: the deposed capital*).

There were a relatively high number of professionals in the garrison but one has to remember that it was the headquarters of the newly declared Provisional Government of the Irish Republic and therefore differed in this important respect from the other Dublin garrisons. Almost nine percent (8.7%) can be defined as class 1 compared with the average for Dublin City of 5.5%. Dickson has calculated that of the 872 arrested and interned after the Rising only a mere 2 per cent came from professional and business families (Dickson, p. 449), which confirms the special status of the GPO. However, it must be remembered that the executions removed a significant proportion of the professional class. Social class 2 (employers, managers and senior clerical employees such as civil servants), was underrepresented in the GPO, primarily one suspects because these upwardly mobile classes were unlikely to be revolutionaries.

Analysis of the GPO Garrison demonstrates that it is the third social class (skilled workers, shop assistants, clerks) that is by far the largest group, forming 56.4% of the total. This class was also dominant in Dublin City but its proportion at 34.2% shows that it was greatly overrepresented in the GPO. Among this class were clerks (30), printers (22), grocer's assistants/barmen (19) and carpenters (17), occupations associated with the Catholic lower middle class. Some may have been migrants to the city, but all were literate and therefore receptive to the advanced nationalism of the capital city at a time of political and cultural ferment. Educated by the Irish Christian Brothers, who preached Ireland Catholic and Gaelic, a large number had gained confidence from participation in the Gaelic League and the GAA, and were politicised through membership of the Irish Volunteers, the IRB or Sinn Fein.

Table 4: Professions with ten or more participants in the GPO, 1916

Profession	Number	Social Rank
Clerk	30	3
Printer	22	3
Labourer	20	5
Grocers Assistant/Barman	19	3
Carpenter/Cabinet Maker	17	3
Teacher	17	1
Student	16	6
Painter/Decorator	12	3
Dock Worker	11	4
Shop Assistant	11	3
Civil Servant	10	1

Social class 4 (semi-skilled workers, domestic servants, carters and many engaged in transport) provided 17.9% of the Garrison, which is higher than the percentage (13.5%) of this class for the city population. The Irish Citizen Army cohort led by James Connolly obviously influenced this figure and 61.76% of the 34 for whom we have data belonged to class 4. What is perhaps most interesting is those who were absent. The two lowest social categories, class 5 (unskilled workers, hawkers etc.) with 5.6% and class 7 (workhouse inmates, those of unspecified but limited means) with no representation, constituted 5.6% of the GPO garrison as compared to their combined 35.7 per cent of the city population.

Table 5: Social class of population of Dublin City (1911), the GPO Garrison, executed leaders of 1916 and the Irish Citizen Army

Social Class	As % of Dublin City Population, 1911	As % of GPO Garrison	As % Executed Leaders	As % Irish Citizen Army
1. Professionals	5.5	8.7	40	0
2. Employers, managers and senior clerical such as civil servants	8.9	7.4	20	8.82
3. Skilled workers, shop assistants, clerks	34.2	56.4	40	29.41
4. Semi-skilled workers, domestic servants, carters and many engaged in transport	13.5	17.9	0	61.76

Source for Dublin figures: Daly, 1984

Note: The occupations of the six executed leaders who served in the GPO were: James Connolly (Trade Union Official), Joseph Plunkett (Journalist/Poet), Padraig Pearse (Teacher/Barrister), Sean MacDiarmada (Journalist), Thomas Clarke (Shop proprietor) and William Pearse (Monumental Sculptor).

6. Educational status

There is limited information relating to the educational status of the great majority of the GPO Garrison in 1916. Of the 93 for whom we have some details it is unclear whether references to Irish Christian Brothers Schools in various sources refer to primary or secondary education. The 1911 census recorded that 42,078 under the age of 14 in Dublin city were receiving education; the comparable figure for those over 14 was 4,858, so it is probable that the greater number in the GPO had received a primary education only. Table 6 shows that 67 of the 93 had attended an Irish Christian Brothers School. For those for whom information is known, the majority were educated at Christian Brother's Schools, particularly those located in the north city. It is rather paradoxical that the greatest number (29) was associated with O'Connell's CBS, whose foundation stone was laid in 1828 by Daniel O'Connell, Ireland's greatest constitutional politician of the modern age. St. Joseph's Fairview (11) was a much younger school, founded in 1888 to cater for the developing northern suburbs beyond the Royal Canal. St. Enda's (Scoil Éanna) had been relocated to Rathfarnham from Ranelagh in 1910 by P. H. Pearse, the school's founder, a member of the Provisional Government and joint military commander with James Connolly of the GPO Garrison. Only 12 of the 572 in the GPO Garrison had attended university.

Table 6: Schools attended by members of the GPO Garrison

School	Number	School	Number
O'Connell's CBS, North Richmond St	29	St. Malachy's Belfast	1
St. Joseph's CBS, Fairview	11	Belfast Municipal College	1
St. Enda's, Rathfarnham	10	St. Columba's, Derry	1
Westland Row CBS	6	Sisters of Mercy, Townsend Street	1
Synge Street CBS	4	Castleknock College	1
Clongowes	3	Belvedere College	1
St. Mary's College, Rathmines	2	CBS Belfast (Unidentified)	1
Dun Laoghaire CBS	2	St. Peter's , Wexford	1
Stoneyhurst College	2	Ring College, Waterford	1
Loretto, Balbriggan	1	Loreto, Gorey	1
St, Mary's Dominican College, Belfast	1	Loreto, Dublin	1
St. Patrick's, Dungannon	1	Mercy Convent, Gorey	1
Rockwell College	1	St. Brendan's, Killarney	1
St. Patrick's, Cavan	1	Baldoyle CBS	1
St. Laurence O'Toole CBS	1	CBS, Sunday's Gate, Drogheda	1
Lombard Street Convent	1	Plás Mhuire, St. Mary's Place CBS, Dublin	1
Francis Street CBS	1		

7. Family Networks

A striking aspect of the GPO Garrison is the number of people who had relations fighting alongside them, or in other garrisons across the city (see appendix 5). Families rather than communities had nurtured the separatist tradition. One hundred and six families had more than one sibling participating in the GPO Rising. There were some exceptional cases. Six members of the O'Reilly family - J.K. O'Reilly a Cavan- born publican, and his four sons, Desmond, Donal, Sam and Thomas were in the GPO, and a fifth son, who was in the Four Courts Garrison - participated in the Rising.

Six other families had five members out in the Rising:

> the Byrne brothers and sisters: (Alice (Coogan), Catherine (Rooney), Jack, Patrick & Peter, all *GPO*); the Foleys: (Brigid (Martin), Kate, Nora, Vera (*GPO*) and Michael (*Four Courts*; the Kavanagh brothers: (Michael & Seamus (*GPO*); Patrick & Peter (*both Boland's*) & Sean (*Marrowbone Lane*); the Kearns brothers: (Hugh (*GPO*); Frank, John, Joseph & Tom (*all Jacob's*); the Norgroves: Fred (*GPO*-son); George (father), Annie (mother), Emily (daughter) (*all City Hall*) & Maria (*St Stephen's Green*- daughter); the Ring brothers: Christopher, Joe, Leo, Liam and Patrick (all *GPO*).

8. Casualties and Prisoners

Fifteen members of the GPO Garrison died during Easter Week; all were men (appendix 1). Sixty-nine were injured, again all were men (appendix 2). Most were treated in Jervis Street Hospital. P. H. Pearse, James Connolly, Joseph Plunkett, Thomas J. Clarke, Seán Mac Diarmada and Willie Pearse were among those executed by firing squad after been found guilty by a secret courts-martial.

It is estimated that 2,491 men and women were deported for being complicit in the Easter Rising. After their detention members of the GPO Garrison were sent initially to prisons throughout Britain at Aylesbury (1), Knutsford (119), Stafford (123), Wakefield (36) and Wandsworth (16). Once members of the Garrison had been processed at these various prisons, most (308) were interned at Frongoch, an abandoned distillery in Merionethshire, Wales, that had housed German prisoners of war until 1916.Those whose death sentences or sentences to penal servitude were commuted, were sent to Dartmoor, before being dispersed to jails throughout Britain, including Lewes, Lincoln, Parkhurst, Pentonville, Portland, Reading, Woking, Worcester and Wormwoods Scrubs. A number of the seriously wounded were hospitalised and on recovery sent directly to Frongoch from Dublin Castle in the weeks and months after the Rising.

The majority of Cumann na mBan members evaded capture, or were released shortly after interrogation in Broadstone, or after arrest and detention in Kilmainham. Most of those under twenty were released from Richmond Barracks, or at the surrender. Some deportees to Britain were released from prison and subsequently interned in Frongoch. A number, especially those familiar with the inner-city, evaded capture after the surrender. Some of the Kimmage Garrison gave false names at the surrender, for fear of reprisals for evading conscription in Britain.

(**Note**: See 'Prisoners deported and released-official lists ', in *1916 Rebellion handbook,* first published by *Weekly Irish Times,* Dublin, 1916, reprinted with introduction and index (Dublin, 1998), pp 67-96).

9. Civil War

The most noteworthy fact about the GPO Garrison was that the majority, almost 41%, remained neutral during the Civil War. Of those who participated in the Civil War, 35.4% took the Anti-Treaty side (see appendix 8). This is almost 10% greater than the percentage who cast first preference votes in favour of Anti-Treaty candidates in 1922. Support for the Republicans or Irregulars is to be expected of a group that had adopted a radical position in 1916, and fought the War of Independence.   One suspects that the 24% of the GPO Garrison who supported the Pro-Treaty side in the Civil War were influenced by key leaders such as Michael Collins and Arthur Griffith.

The figures for female members of the Garrison show a distinct bias against the Treaty. Of those women whose position in the Civil War is known, 10 remained neutral, 33 took the anti-Treaty side and none supported the Treaty. All six female TDs, Kathleen Clarke, Ada English, Mary McSwiney, Constance Markievicz, Kathleen O'Callaghan and Margaret Pearse, voted against the Treaty in January 1922.

Table 7: Positions taken in the Civil War

GPO Garrison- Civil War				
	Total whose position in the civil war is known	Pro- Treaty	Neutral	Anti- Treaty
Number	442	105	180	156
As % of those known	100%	23.81%	40.82%	35.37%
June 1922 General Election				
Parties	Total	Pro-Treaty	Labour and others	Anti-Treaty
First Preference Votes	520,283	239,193	147,226	
	133,864			
% of First Preference Votes	100%	45.9%	28.3%	25.7%

10. The GPO Garrison after the wars were over

The executions in the immediate aftermath of the Rising and deaths in the Civil War removed a potential leadership cadre from Irish political life. Table 8 shows that some survivors of the cataclysms had central roles in government up until the 1960s. It also appears that a disproportionate number of those who fought in the GPO worked in the public service (see appendix 10). In rural Ireland the reward for freedom fighters was land allocated through the agency of the Irish Land Commission; in urban centres, such as Dublin, it was permanent and pensionable positions in the civil service or semi-state bodies.

Table 8: Prominent political positions held by members of the GPO Garrison

Position	Number	Name
President of Ireland	1	Seán T. O'Kelly
Governor General	1	Domhnall Ua Buachalla
Chairman of Provisional Government/Taoiseach	2	Michael Collins Seán Lemass
Tánaiste	3	Seán T. O'Kelly, Seán Lemass, Sean MacEntee
Cabinet Minister	8	Michael Collins, Desmond Fitzgerald, Seán Lemass, Sean MacEntee, Seán T. O'Kelly, Dr. James Ryan, Oscar Traynor, JJ Walsh
TD/MP	25	Harry Colley, Michael Collins, Roddy Connolly, Denis Daly, Desmond Fitzgerald, Paul Galligan, Richard Gogan, Tom Harris, Sean Hayes, Seán Lemass, Diarmuid Lynch, Sean MacEntee Sean McGarry, Sean Milroy, Páidí O'Caoimh, Tomás O'Donnachada, Brian O'Higgins, Seán T. O'Kelly, John O'Mahony, Gearóid O'Sullivan, Seamus Robinson, Dr. James Ryan, Oscar Traynor, Domhnall Ua Buachalla, JJ Walsh
Senator	9	Harry Colley, Roddy Connolly, Nora Connolly-O'Brien, Desmond Fitzgerald, Linda Kearns, Sean Milroy, Dr. James Ryan, Matt Stafford, Michael Staines

Note: Two other Taoisigh fought elsewhere in 1916, Eamon de Valera (Boland's Mills) and WT Cosgrave (South Dublin Union).

Twenty-seven of those in the GPO held positions in Dublin Corporation at some stage in their lives, with a further five working for county councils outside the corporation area. Many more had positions with the Board of Works/Office of Public

Works, with semi-state bodies, such as ESB, and as teachers, gardai and especially in the Civil Service (appendix 10). Included in this number was J. J. McElligott, who served as secretary of the Department of Finance from 1927 to 1953.

Table 9: GPO veterans employed by the state

Area	Number
Civil Service	64
Dublin Corporation	27
Semi-State Bodies	12
Schoolteachers	12
An Garda Siochana	10
Board of Works/OPW	9
Other County Council's	5
Prison Service	1

Reflecting the role of Connolly's Citizen Army, a significant number of the GPO Garrison (24), acted as officials within various trade unions, before, during and after the Rising (see appendix 11).

Emigration post-1916

'A large part of the emigration in 1911-26', stated the Commission on emigration in 1954,'may be attributed to the political changes which occurred in that period '(*Commission on emigration and other population problems 1948-1954, reports* (Dublin, 1954), p. 116). The Commission estimated that the net annual emigration rate for the period 1911-1926 was 27,002 per annum. Many of these, the young males in particular, may have left Ireland in the 1920s because of the 'political changes', brought about by the Civil War in particular. Appendix 12 lists the 54 known members of the GPO Garrison who subsequently immigrated. Twenty-four moved to England and the same number immigrated to the United States. Much smaller numbers immigrated to Scotland (3), Australia (3), South Africa (2), Canada (1) and New Zealand (1). At least four of these immigrated to both England and the United States, in a step-migration process which was a feature of Irish immigration in general. This explains the discrepancy between the total number and the numbers going to various destinations. Sixteen of the 54 returned to live in Ireland, mainly after retirement.

The final appendix identifies the 43 members of the GPO Garrison who are listed in the nine volumes *Dictionary of Irish Biography* published in 2009. Their participation in the Easter Rising 1916 as members of the GPO Garrison is by no means the only reason why they are given this posthumous accolade, if we note that 529 members of the Garrison are not in this latter-day roll of honour. Hopefully, *The GPO Garrison Easter Week 1916 a Biographical dictionary* will bring them all out of the smoke which engulfed the GPO and their young lives in that fateful week of Easter 1916.

REFERENCES

Joost Augusteijn, *Patrick Pearse. The making of a revolutionary* (Chippenham and Eastbourne, 2010).

Mike Cronin, William Murphy and Paul Rouse (eds), *The Gaelic Athletic Association, 1884-2009* (Dublin, 2009: Irish Academic Press).

Mary E. Daly, *Dublin: the deposed capital. A social and economic history, 1860-1914* (Cork, 1984).

David Dickson, *Dublin. The making of a capital city* (London, 2014).

David Fitzpatrick, *Harry Boland's Irish Revolution* (Cork, 2003).

R.M. Fox, *The history of the Irish Citizen Army* (Dublin, 1944).

Keith Jeffery, *The GPO and the Easter Rising* (Dublin, 2006).

Michael Laffan, *The resurrection of Ireland: the Sinn Féin Party, 1916-1923* (Cambridge, 1999).

Stein Larsen and Oliver Snoddy, '1916- A Workingmen's Revolution?' in *Social Studies*, 2 (1973), pp 377-98.

John McCann, *War by the Irish* (Tralee, 1945).

Roger McHugh (ed.), *Dublin 1916* (London, 1966).

Ruth McManus, *Dublin 1910-1940: shaping the city and suburbs* (Dublin, 2002).

William Nolan (ed.), *The Gaelic Athletic Association in Dublin, 1884-2000* (Dublin, 2005).

Séamus Ó Buachalla (ed.), *The letters of P.H. Pearse with a foreword by F.S. L. Lyons* (Gerrard's Cross, 1980)

Jacinta Prunty, *Dublin slums 1800-1925: a study in urban geography* (Dublin, 1999).

Charles Townshend, *Easter 1916: the Irish Rebellion* (London, 2006).

Weekly Irish Times, Rebellion handbook (Dublin, 1916, reprinted with introduction and index Dublin, 1988)

Padraig Yeates, *A city in wartime: Dublin 1914-1918* (Dublin, 2011).

List of Appendices

11. Members of GPO Garrison killed in action.

12. Members of GPO Garrison wounded in action.

13. Known addresses of members of GPO Garrison.

14. Known occupations of members of GPO Garrison.

15. Members of GPO Garrison who were related to other combatants in 1916.

16. Members of GPO Garrison who served in armies outside Ireland.

17. Sporting organisations to which members of the GPO Garrison belonged.

18. The GPO Garrison in the Civil War.

19. Political involvement of members of GPO Garrison post-1916.

10. Members of GPO Garrison who were subsequently employed in the Public Sector.

11. Members of GPO Garrison who were subsequently Trade Union Officials.

12. Members of GPO Garrison who emigrated after the Rising.

13. People whose obituaries state they were in the GPO Garrison but do not appear in official sources.

14. Members of GPO Garrison whose biographies are in the *Dictionary of Irish Biography*.

Appendices

Appendix 1: Members of GPO Garrison killed in action

Charles Carrigan, Edward Cosgrave, Harry Coyle, Jack Kealy, Gerald Keogh, Francis Macken, James McCormack, Michael Mulvihill, Patrick O'Connor, The O'Rahilly, Thomas O'Reilly, Patrick Shortis, Ned Walsh, Thomas Weafer, Arthur Wicks (John Neal).

Appendix 2: Members of GPO Garrison wounded in action

Michael Boland: wounded on the roof of GPO.

John Caffrey: shot in the lung in the vicinity of Liberty Hall and died in 1933 from the wound.

Liam Clarke: lost his left eye and received serious head injuries and a broken kneecap, when a homemade bomb accidentally exploded in his face in the GPO.

Harry Colley: severely wounded, when charging a British Army barricade in the Gloucester Street area.

James Connolly: ankle shattered by shrapnel in Abbey Street.

Thomas Corbally: cut by broken glass, entering the GPO.

Andy Conroy: shot in the abdomen, retreating from Hopkins & Hopkins to the GPO.

Tom Crimmins: wounded in the ankle in Moore Street with The O'Rahilly.

Liam Cullen: wounded in the GPO and wounded again in the knee and neck, evacuating the GPO.

Michael Dowling: shot in the foot in Moore Street and had his big toe amputated in Dublin Castle hospital.

Maurice Flanagan: shot in the right lung in Cathedral Street.

Ignatius Flynn: severely wounded in the Imperial Hotel and had his big toe amputated in Dublin Castle hospital; he never recovered from his wound and died of meningitis in the Mater Hospital in 1922, while being treated for gangrene of the foot.

Patrick Flynn: received a slight head wound from the accidental discharge of a shotgun in North Earl Street.

Michael Heffernan: injured as a result of an accident at barricade and taken to Jervis Street hospital and then to Dublin Castle hospital.

Richard Gibson: wounded in Moore Street with The O'Rahilly.

Michael Giffney: wounded in the knee in Henry Place.

Tom Harris: wounded evacuating the GPO and spent three months in Dublin Castle hospital.

Fred Higgins: wounded in the back in the GPO yard.

Patrick Hughes: wounded in the throat in O'Neill's outpost in Liffey Street.

John Hynes: wounded in the leg, crossing Sackville Street to the GPO.

Luke Kennedy: wounded three times in Sackville Street.

Jack Kenny: wounded twice in Moore Street when accompanying The O'Rahilly.

James Kenny: slightly wounded by the accidental discharge of a shotgun by Antti Makapalis, the Finnish sailor, in the GPO.

John King: severely wounded in the hip, evacuating the GPO.

Michael Knightley: taken to Jervis Street hospital from GPO with a carbuncle on his throat.

Hugh Lee: wounded in the leg on the roof of the GPO.

Joe Lee: severely wounded on the roof of the GPO.

Noel Lemass: wounded in the ankle, crossing Sackville Street.

Paddy Mahon: badly injured in Cathedral Street.

Harry Manning: shot in the instep of his left foot in Waterford Street.

Pat McCrea: slightly wounded in hand in Jervis Street on Tuesday and wounded again in Marlborough Street on the next day.

Joseph McDonagh: wounded in the right hand in the Cathedral Street area.

John McEntagart: seriously wounded in the left thigh in Moore Lane on morning of the surrender.

Liam McGinley: received shrapnel injuries in Sackville Street, when fired on by Volunteers in the Imperial Hotel.

Michael McGrath: injured during the evacuation of the GPO.

Paddy McGrath, Junior: shot in the chest and head on the roof of the GPO; he lost an eye and lived with a bullet lodged in his skull, which caused epilepsy.

Dominic Mulvey: wounded by machinegun fire at Hopkins & Hopkins.

Steenie Mulvey: slightly wounded by machinegun fire, crossing Sackville Street.

William Mulvey: wounded by shrapnel on the roof of the GPO on Friday.

Michael Murphy: wounded in the foot, crossing Henry Place and Moore Lane.

Patrick J. Murray: shot in the right knee in Moore Street with The O'Rahilly.

Ernie Nunan: received a superficial wound on the ground floor of the GPO.

William O'Brien: slight wound over his right eye, evacuating the GPO.

Kevin O'Carroll: wounded in the abdomen in Moore Street with The O'Rahilly.

James O'Connor: wounded in Moore Street, near Coles Lane, with The O'Rahilly.

Ted O'Kelly: wounded in the heel in the GPO.

Patrick O'Moore: wounded in the hand at a Henry Street outpost.

Michael Ó Murchú: wounded in the foot in Moore Lane, from machinegun fire.

James O'Neill (ICA): wounded in the ankle, evacuating the GPO.

William O'Toole: wounded in the leg in Moore Lane.

Matt Parnell: received head injury when he fell twenty feet from a window, evacuating the Imperial Hotel; his early death in 1918 was attributed to his head injury.

Leo Ring: wounded in the arm in Moore Lane and was taken to Dublin Castle hospital.

Liam Roche: wounded by an accidental shotgun discharge in the GPO.

Dan Ryan: wounded in the GPO.

Charles Saurin: wounded in Henry Place, evacuating the GPO.

Frank Scullin: wounded in the back at Reis Chambers.

Peter Slattery: slightly wounded by accident, entering the GPO on Easter Monday.

Charlie Smith: received a sledgehammer blow to the knee, while boring through the walls of a building adjacent to the Imperial Hotel; his injuries never healed and his leg was amputated in 1933.

Jack Stafford: slightly wounded in the hand, in the Hibernian Bank, when his rifle butt was shattered by a sniper's bullet.

Padraig Supple: wounded in GPO on Friday.

James Tallon: wounded in the leg, during the retreat from Cabra Bridge to the GPO.

Frank Thornton: wounded twice in the GPO.

Paddy Thornton: slightly wounded at Fairview.

Cormac Turner: wounded evacuating Noblett's, at the corner of North Earl Street, on Thursday evening.

Frank Turner: wounded in the GPO on Friday.

Joseph Turner, Junior: wounded at the Metropole Hotel on Thursday.

Joseph Turner, Senior: received an injury to his back in the *Freeman's Journal* office on Friday.

Tim Tyrrell: was wounded by shrapnel while in Parliament Street on Tuesday.

Laurence Whelan: wounded in the arm, entering the Hibernian Bank.

Appendix 3: Known addresses of members of GPO Garrison

Dublin City

Amiens St, No. 82.

Arbour Hill, Mountpelier Hill, No.(?).

Artane: Kilmore Cottage.

Aungier St., No.77 (*2*).

Ballsbridge : Ailesbury Rd, No.22; Northumberland Rd, No.54; Stanley Cottages, No. 3.

Ballybough : Ballybough Lane, No.3; Ballybough Rd, No.24; Ballybough Rd, No.31; Ballybough Rd, No.61; Ballybough Rd, No.89; Clonliffe Ave, No.15; Clonliffe Ave, No.27; Clonliffe Ave, No.30; Clonliffe Rd, No.69 (*2*); Clonliffe Rd, St James's Ave, No.(?); Clonliffe Rd, St James's Ave, No.35; Clonmore Rd, No.1; Clonmore Rd, No.16 (*2*); Clonmore Terrace, No.17; Sackville Ave, No.13; Sackville Gardens, No.4 (*2*); Sackville Gardens, No.5; Sackville Gardens, No.6; St Mary's Terrace, No.41.

Beresford Place, No.10.

Blackpitts, St Michael's Terrace, No.23.

Blessington St: Blessington Place, No.8; Blessington St, No.36.

Bride St: Bride St No.73; Bride St, Iveagh House, No.(?); Bride St, Upper, No.10, (*2*).

Buckingham St: Buckingham Buildings, No.9a; Buckingham St, No.22; Buckingham St, Lower, No.14; Buckingham St, Upper, No.36; Buckingham St, Upper, No.49.

Burgh Quay, No.12.

Camden St: Camden Place, No.2; Camden St, No.21; Camden St, Lower, No.51.

Capel St: Capel St, No.2 (*2*); Capel St, No.94 (*2*); Capel St, No.98.

City Quay, No.33.

Clontarf: "Cluny", Clontarf Rd (*3*); St Lawrence Rd, No.106; Seafield Rd, No.3; Strand Rd, Strandville, No.6; Vernon Ave, Joseph's Square, No.16; Vernon Ave, The Cottage.

Coombe: Hanbury Lane, Chatworth Terrace, No.1; Newmarket, No.17.

Dollymount, Byrne's Lane, No.12.

Dominic St: Dominic St, Lower, No.1; Dominic St, Lower, No.2; Dominic St, Lower, No.8, (*2*); Dominic St, Lower, No.65.

Dorset St: Dorset St, Lower, No.35; Dorset St, Upper, No.138; St Joseph's Parade, No.14; St Joseph's Parade, No.32; St Joseph's Place, No.32.

Drumcondra: Botanic Ave, Florence Villas, No.2; Botanic Ave, Victoria Lane, No.93; Carlingford Terrace, No.14; Clements Rd, No.13; Clements Rd, No.14; College View Terrace, No.4; Drumcondra Park, No.18; Drumcondra Rd, No.23, (*3*); Drumcondra Rd, No.108, (*2*); Fitzroy Ave, No.(?); Fitzroy Ave, No.79, (*2*); Millbourne Ave, No.4; Richmond Ave West, No.7; Richmond Rd, No.251; Richmond Rd, No.257; St Brigid's Rd, No.8; St Colomba's St Lower, No.16 (*2*); St Ignatius Rd, No.24; St Joseph's Ave, No.18; Susanville Rd, No.38; one other Drumcondra address, street unknown.

East Arran St, No.(?).

East Wall: Merchants Rd, No.1; Wharf Rd, Rose Terrace, No.1 (*2*).

Erne St: Erne St, Lower, No.31; Erne St, Lower, No.33.

Fairview: Fairview Strand, No.25; Fairview Strand, No.76; Marino House, Gate Lodge; Philipsburgh Ave, Sallypark Cottages, No.2; Philipsburgh Ave, St Joseph's Parade, No.4; Philipsburgh Ave, St Joseph's Terrace, No.3; Richmond Ave, No.31; Richmond Rd, No.(?); Windsor Villas, No.5.

Findlater's Place, No.(?).

Fitzwilliam Lane, No.16.

Fleet St, No.15.

Foley St: Foley St, No.43; Foley St, No.110, (*2*).

Fownes St, Upper, No.4.

Francis St, Garden Lane, No.17.

Gardiner St: Gardiner Place, No.3; Gardiner Place, No.16; Gardiner Place, Grenville Lane, No.(?); Gardiner St, Lower, No.47; Gardiner St, Lower, No.92; Gardiner St, Lower, No.99; Gardiner St, Lower, No.192; Gardiner St, Lower, Moore's Cottages, No.7 (*2*).

Geraldine St, No.43.

Glasnevin: De Courcy Square, No.30; Lindsay Rd, No.102; St Ignatius Rd, No.25.

Gloucester St: Gloucester Place, Upper, No.11; Gloucester St, No.24; Gloucester St, Lower, No.57; Gloucester St, Upper, No.18.

Grantham St, No.17.

Great Brunswick St, No.27 (*2*).

Haddington Rd, No.96.

Harcourt St: Harcourt St, No.58; Harcourt St, No.(?).

Hardwicke St: Hardwicke St, No.13; Hardwicke St, No.46; Hardwicke St, No.(?).

High St, No.48.

Inchicore: Inchicore Rd, No.(?); Emmet Rd, Myra Lodge, No.(?).

Kevin St: Kevin St, Lower, No.27; Kevin St, Church Lane, No.8.

Kilmainham: street address unknown.

Leeson St: Leeson St, No.102; Leeson St, Wilton Terrace, No.3.

Liberties, Dean Swift Square, No.1.

Liffey St: Liffey St, Upper, 14; Liffey St, Upper, 30.

Little Denmark St: Little Denmark St, No.8; Little Denmark St, No.30.

Lombard St: Lombard St, No.(?); Lombard St East, No.(?); Lombard St West, No.4.

Luke St, No.21.

Marino: Grace Park Terrace, Upton Cottages, No.(?); Marino Ave, No.3; Marino Ave, No.5.

Marlborough St: Marlborough St, Lower, No.6; Marlborough St, Pro-Cathedral.

Mespil Rd, No.(?).

Milltown: Old Bridge House (*3*).

Moore St: Horseman's Row, No.9; Sampson's Lane, No.25.

Mountjoy Square: Mounjoy Square, No.11; Mountjoy Square, Grenville St, No.1; Mountjoy Square, Grenville St, No.12.

Nelson St: Nelson St, No.17; Nelson St, No.(?).

Nicholas St: Nicholas St, No.19 (*2*); Nicholas St, No.23.

North Circular Rd: Arranmore Ave, No.23; Arranmore Terrace, No.50; Belvedere Ave, No.13; Belvedere Place, No.16, (*2*); Belvedere Place, No.(?); Belvedere Rd, No.40; Fitzgibbon St, No.2, (*2*); Jones's Rd, No.55; Kenmare Parade, No.17; Killarney Parade, No.6; Killarney Parade, No.14; Killarney Parade, No.15; Mountjoy St, No.44; Mountjoy St, No.51; North Circular Rd, No.181, (*6*); North Circular Rd, No.487; North Circular Rd, No.508; North Circular Rd, No.559; North Circular Rd, No.582; North Great Charles St, No.24; North Great Charles St, No.58; North Richmond St, No.17, (*5*); North Richmond St, Branvilla, No.2, (*3*); North Summer St, No.10; North Summer St, No.15; Richmond Cottages, No.3; Richmond Cottages, No.20; Richmond Cottages, No.25; Richmond Parade, Richmond Parade, No.14; Richmond Place, No.34; Russell St, No.4; Russell St, No.16; St Joseph's Terrace, No.5, (*2*); Sherrard St, No.11.

North Frederick St: North Frederick St, No.18; North Frederick St, No.28, (*10*).

North Great Georges St: North Great Georges St, No.7; North Great Georges St, No.23; North Great George's St, No.(?).

North King St: North King St, No.4, (*2*); North King St, No.64.

North Strand: Annesley Square, No.9; Bayview Ave, No.24; Bessborough Ave, No.23; Charleville Ave, No.8; Charleville Ave, No.24; Leinster Ave, No.32; Northbrook Ave, No.21; Northbrook Ave Upper, No.3, (*2*); North Clarence St, No.(?); North Strand Rd, No.68; North Strand Rd, No.149; North Strand Rd, No.155; Portland Row, No.44; St Brigid's Ave, No.6; St Brigid's Ave, No.7; Seville Place, No.(?); Seville Place Cottages, No.10, (*2*); Seville Place, Oriel Place, No.2; Strandville Ave, No.15; Strandville Ave, No.30; * *and one other North Strand address, street unknown.*

North Wall : Guild St, No.31; Mayor St, Lower, No.42; Mayor St, Lower, No.44;

Newfoundland St, No.9; Newfoundland St, Heuston Cottages, No.2; Old Church St, No.34; St Laurence St, No.12; Sheriff St, Commons St, No.38.

Parnell St: Parnell Square, No.16; Parnell St, No.36; Parnell St, No.93; Parnell St, No.163; Parnell St, No.184; Parnell St, No.196.

Phibsboro: Cabra Rd, No.19 (2); Cabra Rd, No.24; Dalymount Terrace, No.(?), (3); Phibsboro Rd, No.88; Broadstone, Royal Canal Bank.

Ranelagh: Elmesgrove, No.25, (2); Mountpleasant Ave, Walker's Cottages, No.2; Ranelagh Rd, No.3; Ranelagh Rd, No.19; Sandford Rd, No.42.

Rathmines : Bessborough Parade, No.7; Castlewood Ave, No.28.

Rialto: 11 Herberton St.

South Circular Rd: Curzon St, No.9 (2); Lennox St, No.33; Lombard St West, No.70; Synge St, No.18; Wharton Terrace, No.2.

South Great George's St, No.49.

South Dock, Eden Gardens, No.6.

Stoneybatter: Stoneybatter, No.23; Murtagh Rd, No.63.

St James's St, Grand Canal Harbour, No.12.

Summerhill : Rutland Place, No.14; Rutland St, Lower, No.8; Rutland St, Lower, Rutland Cottages, No.20; Rutland St, Moore's Cottages, No.8; Rutland St, Upper, No.(?); North William St, No.13; North William St, No.23, (2); Summerhill, No.8; Summerhill, No.10, (3); Summerhill, No.22; Summerhill, No.27; Summerhill, No.49; Summerhill, No.71, (2); Summerhill, No.74; Summerhill, Lower, No.24; Summerhill Parade, No.12; Willet Place, No.4.

Talbot St: Talbot St, No.62; Talbot St, No.63a; Talbot St, No.82.

Temple St: Temple St, No.6; Temple St, No.31.

Usher's Quay: Usher's Quay, No.31; Usher's Lane, No.4.

Waterford St, No.12.

Westland Row: Hamilton Row, No.9; Hamilton Row, No.(?).

York St, No. (?).

Dublin County

Baldoyle: Burrowfield Cottages; Station Rd, No.18.

Castleknock: Dunsink Cottages, No. (?); River Rd Cottage;

Chapelizod: The Brass Castle, No. (?).

Dalkey: Bullock, Harbour View, No.8.

Dundrum: street address unknown.

Dun Laoghaire: street address unknown, (2).

Harold's Cross: Harold's Cross Rd, No.58, (2); Mountainview Ave, No.16; Tivoli Ave, No.2.

Howth: *street address unknown.*

Lucan: St Catherine's.

Lusk: Chapel Green, No. (?); Collinstown; Lusk, street address unknown (2).

Mulhuddart: street *address unknown.*

Oldtown: street address unknown.

Rathfarnham: Ballyboden; Butterfield Ave, No.1 (*2*); Castleview, No.5; Edmondstown; Fonthill Abbey, No.(?) (*2*); Grange Ave, No.(?); Grange Rd, Washington Lodge; Grove Cottages, No.(?); Lower Rathfarnham; Main St, No.10; Main St, No.(?) (*2*): Newbrook; Rathfarnham Castle; St Patrick's Cottages, No.29 (*2*); St Patrick's Cottages, No.38; Strand Cottages, No.4; Vicarstown House; Whitechurch Cottages, No.(?); Willsbrook Terrace, No.10; three other Rathfarnham street addresses are unknown.

Stillorgan: street address unknown.

Sutton: street address unknown.

Swords: Commons West; Rathbeale; Saucerstown.

Counties outside Dublin

County Antrim: Belfast.

County Carlow: Hackettstown, Clonmore; Tullow (*2*).

County Cavan: Cavan Town (*2*); Kingscourt; Virginia.

County Clare: Tulla; one other address unknown.

County Cork: Bandon (*3*); Bantry; Cork City (*2*); Glandore; Skibberreen; Tracton; Tullylease.

County Derry: Coleraine; Magilligan.

County Donegal : Burtonport; Letterkenny.

County Down: Bangor; Downpatrick; Newry.

County Fermanagh: Aughanagh, Letterbreen.

County Galway: Carraroe; Dunmore; Inisheer, Aran Islands.

County Kerry: Ballybunion; Ballylongford; Caherciveen (*3*); Milltown; Rathmore (*2*); Tralee (*4*).

County Kildare: Carbury (*2*); Cloncurry (*2*); Salmon Leap, Leixlip; Maynooth (*10*); Prosperous.

County Kilkenny: Kilkenny City: Thomastown, one other address unknown.

County Leitrim: Kiltyclogher.

County Limerick: Glin; Killoghteen; Limerick City (*3*); Monegea; Newcastle West.

County Longford: Ballymahon; Keenagh; Lenamore; Longford Town.

County Louth: Donore; Drogheda (*5*); Dundalk; Blackrock; Omeath.

County Mayo: Ballina (*2*); Newport.

County Meath: Dunsany; Gormanstown; Kells; Kilskyre.

County Monaghan: Carrickaboy; Carrickmacross (*2*); MonaghanTown.

County Offaly: Birr; Edenderry; Tullamore (*2*).

County Roscommon: Ballaghaderreen.

County Sligo: Curry; Dromard; Drumcliffe; Sligo Town.

County Tipperary: Emly; Nenagh; Templemore; Thurles, Rossmore; Tipperary Town.

County Tyrone: Omagh.

County Waterford: Cappoquin; Ring (*2*).

County Westmeath: Athlone.

County Wexford: Blackwater; Enniscorthy (*2*); Ferns; New Ross; Taghmon; Wexford Town (*3*).

County Wicklow: Avoca; Bray (*3*); Carnew; Collentra; Newcastle.

Locations outside Ireland

Argentina: Buenos Aires.

Australia: Sydney.

England: Colchester; Isle of Wight; Liverpool (*16*); London (*9*); Manchester (*2*); Newport, Cumberland; Norwich.

Finland: Helsinki.

France: Nice.

Scotland: Edinburgh; Glasgow (*4*).

Sweden: unknown but noted in witness statements and other sources.

United States: New York; Philadelphia.

Appendix 4: Known occupations of members of GPO Garrison

Accountant: Michael P. Murphy, J.K. O'Reilly & John R. Reynolds

Actor: Arthur Shields

Agricultural Worker: Dan Brophy, Pat Colgan & John Hynes

Auctioneer's Assistant: John Fitzharris

Author: Brian O'Higgins (Brían na Banban)

Baker: Patrick Bird, James Byrne, Thomas Kilcoyne, Michael Murphy, Patrick Swanzy & Michael White

Bank Official: Michael Cowley & Patrick F. English

Blacksmith: Patrick Devereux, Larry Mackey, Michael Mackey & Seán Price

Bricklayer: Dave Begley, Peadar Doyle, Paddy Garland, Paddy Mitchell & Patrick Tuohy

Brush Maker: William Egan

Builder's Providers Worker: Liam Breen

Building Contractor: John O'Neill & James O'Neill

Carpenter / Cabinet Maker: Andrew Carmichael, Wally Carpenter, William Darcy, Robert Eustace, Ignatius Flynn, Richard Hickey, James Hunter, Jack Kenny, Tom Mangan, Christopher Ring, Joe Ring, Leo Ring, Patrick Ring, Seán Russell, Pat Weafer, Laurence Whelan & William Whelan

Carter: Michael Boland, Dick Corbally, Joe Lee, John Lynch, Andy Mulligan & Ned Walsh

Cattle Dealer: Patrick Gallagher & Jack Maguire

Chauffeur: James Minahan & Matthew Reilly

Chemist's Assistant: Joe Cripps & Frank Keogh

Cinema Operator: James McEvoy & Frank Murtagh

Civil Engineer: Rory O'Connor & Peter Slattery

Civil Servants: Joseph Bracken, Michael Cremen, Joe Derham, Matt Flanagan, Gerald Griffin, Seán Hayes, James McElligott, Patrick Moore, Michael Mulvihill & Colm Ó Murchadha

Clerk: James Cassells, Michael Collins, Harry Colley, Seán Conway, Patrick Corless, Denis Daly, John J. Doyle, Maurice Flanagan, James Heery, Seán Hegarty, Martin Hore, Seamus

Kavanagh, Hugh Kearns, Diarmuid Lynch, Garret McAuliffe, Seán McGrath, John McQuaid, William Mulvey, William J. O'Brien, Páidí Ó'Caoimh, Patrick O'Connor, Patrick O'Moore, Joe O'Reilly, Thomas Rath, Liam Ring, Charles Saurin, Jack Stafford, Charles Steinmeyer & Thomas Weafer

Coach Builder: Andrew Bermingham, Seán Bermingham, Austin Kennan & Patrick Nugent

Commercial Traveller: Joe Murray

Cooper: Patrick O'Connor

Concreter: Joseph Turner (Junior)

Delft Merchant: Gerald Crofts

Dock Worker: Peter Carpenter, John Doyle, John Geoghegan, Tom Leahy, Thomas Meehan, John Moore, Tom O'Brien (Bryan), Joseph O'Reilly, Michael O'Shea, William O'Toole & James Sexton

Domestic Servant: Elizabeth McGinty (nee Burke)

Draper: James Cassidy & Peter Paul Galligan

Draper's Assistant: Charles Purcell

Dressmaker / Tailoress: Julia Grenan & May McLoughlin

Dublin Corporation Worker: Thomas Dunne, Patrick Hughes & Vincent Poole

Electrical Engineer: Liam Daly & Sean McEntee

Electrician: Andy Fitzpatrick, Joe Good, Fred Higgins, Thomas Hughes, John Madden, Seán McGarry, Johnny (Blimey) O'Connor & Thomas O'Reilly

Farmer: Patrick Caddell, Tom Harris, Edward Lawless & John McNally

Fitter: Seamus Daly, Frank MacPartland, Liam Roche & Joe Toomey

Garage Manager: Liam Cullen

Garage Worker: Joseph Kelly

Gardener: Paddy Donnelly, Paddy English & Micheál MacRuaidhrí

Grocer Assistant /Barman: John Bolger, Dan Canny, Andy Conway, Charlie Donnelly, John Dunne, Michael Foley, James Gavan, Jack Graves, Richard Healy, James Kenny, Patrick Lynch, Thomas McEvoy, Henry Moughan, Patrick Murray, Patrick O'Donoghue, Andy Redmond, John Redmond, Dan Ryan & Hugh Thornton

Groundsman (Golf Club): Batt Burke

Groundsman (Racecourse): James McCormack

Hairdresser: Christopher Byrne, Patrick Flynn, Francis Macken, Jimmy O'Byrne & Harry Ridgeway

Hotel Proprietor: John O'Mahony

Hotel Worker: Martha 'Birdie' Walsh

Insurance Superintendent: Michael W. O'Reilly

Insurance Agent: James Flanagan; George King

Journalist: William Brennan-Whitmore, Patricia Hoey, Michael Knightly, Micháel Ó'Murchú & John J. Scollan

Labourer: Nicholas Burke, James Byrnes, Peadar Carroll, John Cooper, Thomas Corbally, Dan Courtney, Edward Doyle, Peter Higgins, Jack Kelly, Tom Kerr, Bob Killeen, Michael Largin, Patrick McDermott, Joseph McDonagh, Seamus McGowan, Dan McMahon, Seán McMahon, Joe Murray, John O'Brien & James Wardick

Laundry Worker: Brigid Doran (nee Lambert), Ellen Hartnett, Martha Murphy (nee Kelly) & Ellen Stynes (nee Lambert)

Library Assistant: James O'Byrne

Lock Keeper: Joe Ledwith

Machinist: Frank Turner

Mattress Maker: Seán McLoughlin

Medical Doctor: Dr. John J. Tuohy

Medical Officer: John J. Doyle

Medical Student: Eamon Dore, Dan McLoughlin, Ted O'Kelly & James Ryan

Mechanical Engineer: Luke Kennedy

Messenger Boy: Art Hannon

Milliner: Maeve McDowell (nee Cavanagh)

Motor Driver: John Bolger, Joseph Callan, Tom Crimmins, Joseph Dunne & Pat McCrea

Motor Mechanic: Davy Golden, James Minihan & William O'Reilly

Monumental Sculptor: Willie Pearse

Night Watchman: Christopher Tallon

Nurse: Molly Adrien, Eva Burke, Linda Kearns & Catherine Treston (nee Ryan)

Painter & Decorator: James Conroy, Frank Devine, Joe Gahan, Harry Gannon, Jack Kealy, Henry Kenny, William McCleane, Patrick Meagher, Michael O'Brien, Charlie Rossiter, Frank Sheridan & James Sheridan

Plasterer: Peter McPartlin

Plumber: Bernard Friel, Tom Kearney, Peter O'Connor, Liam Parr & Joseph Trimble

Porter: John Boylan, Michael Croke, Thomas Croke, John Halpin, Paddy Halpin, Edward Kelly & John Reid, Thomas Roche

Post & Telegraph Worker: Andy Fitzpatrick, Sam King, John Twamley & Henry Willis

Priest: Fr. John Flanagan

Printer: James Behan, Michael Behan, Frank Dunne, Albert Dyas, Joseph Gleeson, Frank Henderson, Joe Hutchinson, Henry Kenny, John McDonnell, Paddy McGrath (Senior), Paddy McGrath (Junior), Paddy Mahon, Peadar Murphy, Tom Murray, Kevin O'Carroll, Billy O'Neill, John O'Reilly, James O'Sullivan, Thomas Ryan, Joe Stanley, Oscar Traynor & Charlie Walker

Purveyor: John McEntagart

Railway Worker: Tom Ennis, Mick Fox (coach painter), Richard Gibson, Michael Heffernan, Harry Manning, Michael McGrath (clerk), Thomas Mooney & Patrick Sealy

Rope Maker: Edward Cosgrave

Salesman: Gerald Keogh

Scholar: Roddy Connolly, Jimmy Fleming, Richard Gogan, Seán Lemass, Charlie McMahon & Tony Swan

School Teacher: Leslie Bean de Barra (nee Price), Eamon Bulfin, Frank Burke, Bridie Connolly, Louise Gavan Duffy, Veronica Gleeson (nee Ní Riain), Brian Joyce, Thomas McDonagh, Mary Josephine Mulcahy (nee Ryan), Máire ní hAinle, Annie O'Higgins, Brian O'Higgins, Kathleen Patton (nee Murphy), Bridie Richards, Joseph Tallon & Seamus Tallon

Seaman / Sailor: Thomas Jones, Seán Kerr, Neil Kerr (Junior), Antil Makapaltis, Swedish Seaman (name unknown), Paddy Weafer & Jack (Blanco) White

Sewing Machine Agent: Dominic Mulvey

Shoemaker: Arthur Agnew

Shopkeeper: Michael Brady, Tom Clarke, Paddy Kilmartin, Paddy Mahon, Seán Milroy, Dómhnall Ó'Buachalla, Peter Reynolds, J. J. Walsh & Thomas Weafer

Shop Assistant: Jack Graves, Con Keating, May Kelly (nee Chadwick), Mike Keough, Patrick Kirwan, Liam McNieve, Patrick Murray, John Newman, James Norton, Liam O'Raogain & Catherine Rooney (nee Byrne)

Slater: Harry Coyle

Springsmith: James Quinn

Stationer's Assistant: Paddy Stephenson

Steelworks Worker: Patrick Mahon

Steeplejack: Paddy Morrin

Stockbroker's Assistant: Liam Clarke

Stonemason: Peadar Bracken, Patrick Connaughton, Michael Murphy & Thomas O'Connor

Student: John Kilgallon, Conor McGinley, Eunan McGinley, Máire Nic Ainle, Fintan Murphy, Fergus O'Kelly, Phyllis O'Kelly (nee Ryan), George Plunkett, Jack Plunkett, Desmond Ryan & Joseph Sweeney

Tailor: Harry Boland, Charles Carrigan, Thomas Fogarty, John Griffin, Liam McGinley, Patrick McGinley & William Ross

Timber Sawyer: Michael Dwyer

Trade Union Official: Winnie Carney & John O'Neill

Tram Conductor: Pat McCrea

Typist: Brigid Foley

Upholsterer: Joseph Billings, Seamus Hayes & James O'Neill

Van Driver: Matt Caffrey, Jimmy Carrigan, Herbert Conroy & Tom McGrath

Waiter: Oliver Ryan & Arthur Wicks

Watchmaker: Kevin McCabe & George Oman

Wireless Operator: Liam Daly

Victualler: James Heron

Appendix 5: Members of GPO Garrison who were related to other combatants in 1916

(**Note:** Those listed are siblings, unless otherwise stated)

Begley: Dave & Dan (*Four Courts*), first cousins

Behan: James & Michael

Bermingham: Andrew & Sean

Boland: Harry, Ned & Gerry (*Jacobs*)

Brooks: Christine (nee Stafford) & Fred (*Mendicity Institute*), husband & wife

Burke: Elizabeth (nee McGinty) & Tom (*Jacob's*), husband & wife

Burke: Eva & Frank

Byrne: Alice (Coogan), Catherine (Rooney), Jack, Patrick & Peter

Byrne: Tom & Lucy (nee Smyth), husband & wife

Carpenter: Peter & Wally

Colley: Gertie (Murphy) & Harry

Connolly: James, Ina, Nora & Roddy, father, daughters & son

Corbally: Dick & Larry, father & son

Coyle: Harry & Thomas (*City Hall*)

Croke: Michael & Thomas

Daly: Seumas, Frank (*Cabra Bridge* & *Ashbourne*) & Paddy (*Four Courts*)

Daly: Laura (O'Sullivan) & Nora (Dore)

Devereux: Patrick & Mary (*St Stephen's Green*)

Dore: Eamon & Nora (nee Daly), husband & wife

Dowling: Michael & Andrew & John (*both Four Courts*)

Duffy: Edward & Christopher (*Four Courts*), son & father

Dunne: Joseph & Thomas

Fagan: Margaret (MacSherry) & Brian (*South Dublin Union*)

Flanagan: James & Matt, first cousins

Flanagan: James & Marie (nee Perolz), husband & wife

Fleming: Jimmy & Michael (*Four Courts*)

Fogarty: Tom & Patrick (*Four Courts*)

Foley: Brigid (Martin), Kate, Nora, Vera & Michael (*Four Courts*)

Gahan: Joe, May (O'Carroll) & Matt (*Four Courts*)

Gleeson: Joseph & Martin

Griffin: Gerald & Florence (nee Meade, *Four Courts*), husband & wife

Grimley: Lucy (nee Gibney) & Michael (Four Courts), husband & wife

Hannon: Art & James (*Jacob's*)

Henderson: Frank & Leo

Holahan: Hugh & Patrick (*Ashbourne*) & first cousins of Garry & Michael Holohan (*Four Courts*)

Kavanagh: Michael & Seamus; Patrick & Peter (*both Boland's*) & Seán (*Marrowbone Lane*)

Kearns: Hugh; Frank, John, Joseph & Tom (*all Jacob's*)

Kelly: Joseph & Thomas (*Boland's*)

Kenny: Jack & Michael

Keogh: Frank & Gerald; Cyril (*St Stephen's Green*)

Kerr: Niall, Seán & Thomas

Kilmartin: Patrick & Mary (*Four Courts*)

King: Sam; Arthur & George (*City Hall*), Martin (*St Stephen's Green*)

King: George, John & Patrick

Lambert: Brigid, Ellen (Noone), Ellen (Stynes) & Thomas (*City Hall*), father, daughters & aunt

Lawless: Edward & Mary, & Frank & James (*both Ashbourne*)
Lemass: Noel & Sean
Mahon: Paddy & Tommy
McDowell: Maeve (nee Cavanagh) & Cathal (*Boland's*), husband & wife
McEvoy: James & Patrick (*Jacob's*)
McGallogly: James & John
McGinley: Conor & Eunan
McGinley: Liam & Patrick
McGrath: Michael & Sean
McGrath: Paddy (Senior) & Paddy (Junior), father & son
McLoughlin: May & Sean
Mackey: Larry & Michael
Maguire: Jack & Matt
Mulvihill: Michael (*killed in action*) & Austin Kennan, brothers-in-law
Mulvey: Dominic & William
Murphy: Michael & Martha (nee Kelly), husband & wife
Murphy: Robert & Hubert (*Four Courts*)
Murray: Mae & Patrick
Ní Riain: Áine & Éilis (*Four Courts*)
Norgrove: Fred; George, Annie, Emily (*all City Hall*) & Maria (*St Stephen's Green*), father, mother, daughters & son
Nunan: Ernie & Sean
O'Brien: Eoghan & Peadar (*Marrowbone Lane*)
O'Hanrahan: Mary & Edward & Joseph (*both Jacob's*)
O'Connor: Thomas & Peter, father & son
O'Donoghue: Patrick & Tomás
O'Leary: Diarmuid & David (*St Stephen's Green*)
O'Mahony: Eamon & Matt
Oman: George & Bob (*Four Courts*) & William (*City Hall*)
O'Moore: Esther (nee Wisely) & Seán (Four Courts), husband & wife
Ó'Mórdha: Donagh & Patrick
O'Reilly: J.K., Desmond, Donal, Sam & Thomas; & Kevin (*Four Courts*), father & sons
O'Reilly: Thomas (*killed in action*), John (*Four Courts*) & Patrick (*St Stephen's Green*)
O'Sullivan: Seamus & Laura (nee Daly), husband & wife
Pearse: Pádraig & Willie
Plunkett: George, John & Joseph
Poole: Vincent, Christy (*St Stephen's Green*), Jack (*City Hall*)
Price: Leslie (Bean de Barr) & Seán & Eamon (*Jacob's*)
Redmond: Anne & Patrick (*Jacob's*), husband & wife
Redmond: Andy & John
Reynolds: John & Molly, father & daughter
Ring: Christopher, Joe, Leo, Liam & Patrick

Ryan: James, Mary Josephine & Phyllis
Scullin: Frank & Paddy
Simpson: Tilly & Jerry (*Jacob's*)
Slater: Martha (nee Walsh) & Tom (*Jacob's*), husband & wife
Stafford: Matt, Christine (Brookes) & Jack, father, daughter & son
Staines: Michael & Liam (*Mendicity Institute*)
Stephenson: Paddy & Mary (nee Kilmartin, *Four Courts*), husband & wife
Swan: Tony & Patrick (*Four Courts*)
Sweeney: James & Patrick
Tallon: Christopher, James & Joseph
Tannam: Liam & Michael (*Boland's*)
Thornton: Frank, Hugh, Nora & Paddy
Toomey: Joe & Stasia (Byrne); Jack (*Jacob's*)
Turner: Frank, Henry, Joseph (Junior) & Joseph (Senior), father & sons
Walker: Charlie; Mary (Máire Nic Shiubhlaigh, *Abbey Actress*), John & Michael (*all Jacob's*)
Walpole: Harry & Leo (*Boland's*)
Walsh: Christy & Edward
Walsh: Margaret (Jenkinson), Mark, Martha (Slater) & Mary Jo (Rafferty)
Weafer: Paddy & Tom; John & Patrick (*both fought in Enniscorthy*), father & sons
Whelan: Laurence & William

Appendix 6: Members of GPO Garrison who served in armies outside Ireland

British Army
Michael Boland: British Army and served in the Boer War, South Africa
W.J. Brennan-Whitmore: Royal Irish Regiment and served in India
James Connolly: King's Liverpool Regiment
Tom Craven: British Army and served in the Boer War, South Africa
Thomas Croke: discharged from the Royal Irish Guards, in 1903
Patrick Dalton: British Army, 1916-1922
John J. Doyle (C. Coy): British Medical Auxiliary Medical Service, 1914-1915 and served with the British Naval Auxiliaries in WW1
Fergus Kelly: British Army Signals Corps and was a wireless operator
Vincent Poole: British Army and served in the Boer War, South Africa
Joe Turner, Senior: served in a militia unit of the British Army prior to the Rising

B. Armies outside Britain
Tom Byrne: Irish Brigade and served in the Boer War; he was later decorated by the South African Government for services rendered

Appendix 7: Sporting organisations to which members of the GPO Garrison belonged

Members of GPO Garrison who were members of the GAA (club/county in brackets)

Dave Begley: St Laurence O'Toole's

Ned Boland: O'Donovan Rossa's; Parnell's

Harry Boland: O'Donovan Rossa's; Rathmines HC; Faugh's & Dublin

Michael Brady: St Laurence O'Toole's

Dan Brophy: Lusk HC

Eamon Bulfin: Collegians (UCD)

Frank Burke: Collegians (UCD) & Dublin

Patrick Caddell: Lusk HC

Matt Caffrey: Michael Dwyer's GFC

Tom Clarke: St Laurence O'Toole's

Pat Colgan: Kildare County Board Secretary

Thomas Corbally: Michael Dwyer's GFC

Harry Coyle: Davis HC

Michael Cremen: Davis HC

Tom Crimmins: St Laurence O'Toole's

Michael Croke: St Laurence O'Toole's (founder member)

Thomas Croke: St Laurence O'Toole's (founder member)

Denis Daly: London Irish; Kerry G.A.A. County Board Chairman

Pat Dennany: Croke's GAC & Donore (Secretary & Treasurer)

Joe Derham: Skerries Harps

Charlie Donnelly: Geraldine's & Michael Dwyer's

Paddy English: St Margaret's; Erin's Isle

Tom Ennis: St Laurence O'Toole's & Dublin

John Fitzharris: St Laurence O'Toole's

Matt Flanagan: Davis HC

Pat Gallagher: Ballyboden Wanders

Paul Galligan: Kickham's

John Halpin: St Laurence O'Toole's

Frank Henderson: Árd Craobh Hurling Club; St Laurence O'Toole's

James Hunter: Celtic HC, (founder member)

Brian Joyce: Collegians (UCD) & Dublin

Tom Kearney: Ballyboden Wanderers

Con Keating: Keating's GFC

Seán Kerr: St Laurence O'Toole's

Tom Leahy: St Laurence O'Toole's

Larry Mackey: St Laurence O'Toole's

Michael Mackey: St Laurence O'Toole's

Jack Maguire: Maynooth & Kildare

Matt Maguire: Maynooth & Kildare
Seán McDermott: Saint Laurence O'Toole's
Conor McGinley: Collegians (UCD)
Eunan McGinley: Collegians (UCD)
Tom Mangan: Maynooth & Kildare
Charlie McMahon: St Kevin's, Young Ireland's, St Laurence O'Toole's & Dublin
Pat Mitchell: St Laurence O'Toole's
Stephen (Steenie Mulvey): Bray Emmets & Dublin
John Newman: Marino Gaels
Thomas O'Donoghue: involved in the G.A.A. in London
Mary O'Hanrahan: Oliver Bond HC
Brian O'Higgins: Saint Finian's HC
Seán T. O'Kelly: Confederate HC
Thomas O'Reilly: Emeralds
James Quinn: Hibernian Knights
John R. Reynolds: John O'Mahony HC
Seamus Robinson: Oscars HC, Belfast
Thomas Roche: St Laurence O'Toole's
Dan Ryan: Faugh's
Frank Sheridan: Michael Dwyer's GFC
Tilly Simpson: Dublin, (camogie)
Joe Stanley: Geraldine's
Patrick Swanzy: Emeralds
James Sweeney: Michael Dwyer's GFC
Patrick Sweeney: Michael Dwyer's GFC
Frank Thornton: St Laurence O'Toole's
Joe Toomey: Fianna HC
Tim Tyrrell: Maynooth & Kildare (captain)
Domhnall Ua Buachalla: Maynooth & Kildare, (captain)
Paddy Weafer: Emeralds & St Laurence O'Toole's
Tom Wheatley: St Laurence O'Toole's

Summary of Club affiliations

Árd Croabh HC, (1); Ballyboden Wanderers, (2); Bray Emmets, (1); Celtic HC, (1); Collegians (UCD), (5); Confederate HC, (1); Crokes GAC, (1); Davis HC, (3); Donore GAC, (1); Emeralds GFC, (3); Erin's Isle, (1); Faughs HC, (2); Fianna HC, (1); Geraldines GFC, (2); Hibernian Knights GFC, (1); John O'Mahony HC, (1); Keatings GFC, (1); Kickham's GAC, (1) London Irish, (1); Lusk HC, (2); Maynooth GAC, (5); Marino Gaels GFC, (1); Michael Dwyers GFC, (6); New Ireland HC, (1); O'Donovan Rossa GAC, (2); Oliver Bond HC, (1); Oscars HC, Belfast, (1); Parnells GAC, (1); Rathmines HC, (1); St Finians HC, (1); St Kevin's HC, (1); St Laurence O'Toole GAC, (21); St Margaret's GAC, (1); Skerries Harps GFC, (1).

Numbers of GPO garrison who played inter-county
Dublin (7); Kildare (5).

Other sports:
Paddy Donnelly: Tug-o-war team trainer
Paddy Kilmartin: Amateur boxing
Pat Mitchell: Amateur boxing referee & delegate
Eamonn O'Mahoney: Lifelong association with Bohemians FC
Joe Ring: Richmond Utd, as a player & Drumcondra FC, as a trainer
James Sexton: Lifelong association with Stella Maris FC
Liam Tannam: Lifelong association with Clonliffe Harriers Athletics Club
Oscar Traynor: Belfast Celtic FC, as a player & FAI president

Appendix 8: The GPO Garrison in the Civil War

Members of GPO Garrison who remained neutral in the Civil War (Total: 180)
Arthur Agnew; David Begley; James Behan; Michael Behan; Seán Bermingham; Patrick Bird; Joseph Bracken; Liam Breen; Tom Brien; Seamus Brennan; Eamon Bulfin; Frank Burke; Nicholas Burke; James Byrne; Patrick Caddell; Peadar Carroll; Patrick Clinch; Patrick Connaughton; Seán Conway; John Cooper; Tom Craven; Tom Crimmins; Liam Cullen; Mark Cummins; Dan Davitt; Tom Devine; John J. Doyle (E. Coy); Joe Duffy; Frank Dunne; Joseph Dunne; Thomas Dunne; Albert Dyas; Paddy English; Patrick Francis English; Michael Finnegan; Mabel Fitzgerald; John Fitzharris; Maurice Fitzsimons; Thomas Fogarty; Michael Foley; Joe Gahan; Pat Gallagher; Paul Galligan; Harry Gannon; Louise Gavan Duffy; Richard Gibson; Julia Grenan; Gerald Griffin; Art Hannon; Seamus Hayes; Dick Healy; James Heery; James Heron; Richard Hickey; Peter Higgins; Hugh Holahan; Patrick Hughes; Thomas Hughes; James Hunter; Joe Hutchinson; John Hynes; Margaret Jenkinson; Con Keating; Chris Keeling; Jack Kelly; Luke Kennedy; Niall Kerr, Junior; Tom Kerr; Bob Killeen; Patrick Kilmartin; John King; Joe Lee; Patrick Lawler; Diarmuid Lynch; John Lynch; Larry Mackey; Jack Maguiure; Matt Maguire; Patrick Maguire; Frank MacPartland; Michael MacRuardhaí; Tommy Mahon; Jerry Malone (Joseph Coughlan); Harry Manning; Thomas Mason; Kevin McCabe; William McCleane; Patrick McDermott; John McDonnell; James McElligott; John McEntagert; Michael McGarvey; Conor McGinley; Eunan McGinley; Liam McGinley; Christy McGrane; Dan McMahon; Patrick McManus; Brian McMullen; John McNally; Liam McNeive: Peter McPartlin; James Minihan; Jim Mooney; Patrick Mooney; John (Edward) Moore; Andy "Dazzler" Mulligan; Dominic Mulvey; Martin Murphy; Michael P. Murphy; Peadar Murphy; Patrick Murray; Tom Murray; Francis Murtagh; Michael Nugent; Eoghan O'Brien; John O'Brien; Michael O'Brien; Tom O'Brien; William O'Brien; James O'Connor; Patrick O'Connor; Eamon O'Mahony; Matt O'Mahony; Michael Ó Murchú; George Oman; James O'Neill (ICA); John O'Neill (ICA, East Arran St); John O'Neill (ICA, Ballybough Rd); Billy O'Neill;

Joseph O'Reilly; Liam O'Raogain; Sam O'Reilly; Kathleen Patton (nee Murphy); James Quinn; Thomas Rath; Matthew Reilly; Peter Reynolds; Bridie Richards; Christopher Ring; Joe Ring; Leo Ring; Liam Ring; Patrick Ring; William Ross; Charlie Rossiter; Dan Ryan; Desmond Ryan; Oliver Ryan; Thomas Ryan; John J. Scollan; James Seville; Arthur Shields; Charlie Smith; Joe Stanley; Padraig Supple; James Sweeney; Patrick Sweeney; Christopher Tallon; James Tallon; Joseph Tallon; Joe Toomey; Joseph Trimble; Henry Turner; Joseph Turner, Jr; Joseph Turner Sr; Joe Twamley; Peggy Viant (nee Downey); Helena Walsh; Mark Walsh; James Wardock; Paddy Weafer; Tom Wheatley; Joseph Whelan; John White; Michael White; Henry Willis; Esther Wisely; James Wren; Nancy Wyse Power.

Members of GPO Garrison who supported the Treaty and took the Free State side in the Civil War (Total: 105)

John Bolger; W.J. Brennan-Whitmore; Dan Brophy; Batt Burke; Christopher Byrne; Eddie Byrne (killed in the Civil War); Patrick Byrne; Peter Byrne; Tom Byrne; Matt Caffrey; Patrick Caldwell; Joseph Callan; Jimmy Carrigan; James Cassells; Patrick Colgan; Michael Collins; Herbert Conroy; James P. Conroy; Patrick Dalton; James Daly; William Daly; Charlie Donnelly; John Doyle (C. Coy);Paddy Drury; Michael Dwyer; William Egan; Tom Ennis; Desmond Fitzgerald; James Flanagan; Jimmy Fleming; Mick Fox; Andy Furlong; Joseph Gleeson; Martin Gleeson; Davy Golden; Joe Good; Seán Hayes; John J. Horan; Martin Hore; Thomas Kearney; Hugh Kearns; Edward Kelly; Henry Kenny; Jack Kenny; Michael Kenny; Bernard Keogh; Patrick King; John Lafferty; Michael Largin; Joe Ledwith; Hugh Lee; Rory MacDermott; John Madden; Louis Marie; Pat McCrea; James McEvoy; Seán McGarry; Patrick McGinley; Con McGinn; Michael McGrath; Paddy McGrath, Jr; Paddy McGrath, Sr; Charlie McMahon; Seán Milroy; Paddy Mitchell; Charles Molphy; Henry Moughan; Robert Murphy; Joseph Murtagh; John Newman; Patrick Nugent; James O'Byrne (A.Coy); James O'Byrne (F.Coy); Padraig O'Caoimh; Patrick O'Donoghue; William O'Donoghue; Colm O'Murchadha; J.K. O'Reilly; Joe O'Reilly (Lon. Coy); John O'Reilly; William O'Reilly; Gearoid O'Sullivan; Jim O'Sullivan; Charles Purcell; John Redmond; Thomas Roche; William Roche; Larry Ryan; Charles Saurin; Peter Slattery; Jack Stafford; Michael Staines; Charles Steinmeyer; Tony Swan; Patrick Swanzy; Joseph Sweeney; Frank Thornton; Hugh Thorton; Cormac Turner; Frank Turner; Jack Twoomey; Harry Walpole; Christy Walsh; J.J. Walsh; William Whelan.

Members of the GPO Garrison who opposed the Treaty and took the Republican side in the Civil War (Total: 156)

Mary Adrien; Leslie Bean de Barra; Andrew Bermingham; Joseph Billings; Ned Boland; Harry Boland; Michael Boland; David Bourke; Michael Brady; Peadar Bracken; Christine Brooks (nee Stafford); Eva Burke; Louis Byrne (Junior); James Byrnes; John Caffrey; Matt Caffrey; Dan Canny; Winnie Carney; Peter Carpenter; Walter Carpenter; Patrick Carroll; May Chadwick; Liam Clarke; Seán Cole; Harry Colley; Bridie Connolly; Roddy Connolly; Ina Connolly-Heron; Nora Connolly-O'Brien; Thomas Corbally; Patrick Corless; Dan Courtney; Michael Cremen; Joseph Cripps; Denis Daly; Frank Devine; Paddy Donnelly;

Michael Dowling; John J. Doyle (C. Coy); Peadar Doyle; Edward Duffy; Jack Early; Marie English; Patrick Flynn; Paddy Garland; John Geoghegan; Lucy Gethings; May Gibney; Richard Gogan; Jack Graves; Tom Harris; Michael Heffernan; Frank Henderson; Leo Henderson; Seán Hegarty; Fred Higgins; Linda Kearns; Frank Kelly; Joseph Kelly; May Kelly; James Kenny; Mike Keough; George King, (killed in Civil War); Patrick Kirwan; Brigid Lambert; Ellen Lambert; Tom Leahy; Noel Lemass; Seán Lemass; Patrick Lynch; Michael Mackey; Margaret MacSherry; Patrick Mahon (C.Coy); Tom Mangan; Garrett McAuliffe; Joseph McDonagh; Seán MacEntee; Thomas McEvoy; Seamus McGowan; Seán McGrath; Tom McGrath; May McLoughlin; Seán McLoughlin; Patrick Meagher; Steenie Mulvey; William Mulvey; Gertie Murphy; Martha Murphy; Michael Murphy; Michael P. Murphy; Stephen Murphy; Joseph Murray; Mae Murray; Ellen Noone; Fred Norgrove; James Norton; Ernie Nunan; Seán Nunan; Matt O'Brien; Dómhnall Ó'Buachalla; Kevin O'Carroll; May O'Carroll (nee Gahan); Johnny "Blimey" O'Connor; Peter O'Connor; Rory O'Connor; Tomás Ó'Donnachada (Thomas O'Donoghue); Mary O'Hanrahan; Brian O'Higgins; Fergus O'Kelly; Seán T. O'Kelly; Dr.Ted O'Kelly; John O'Mahony; James O'Neill (A.Coy, 3rd Batt); Desmond O'Reilly; Donal O'Reilly; Molly O'Reilly; Tommy O'Reilly; Donough O'Mordha; Patrick O'Mordha; Joe O'Rorke; Michael O'Shea; Liam Pedlar; George Plunkett; Jack Plunkett; Vincent Poole; Seán Price; Annie Redmond; John Reid; Áine ní Riain; Seamus Robinson; William Ross; Seán Russell; Dr. James Ryan; Frank Scullin; Patrick Scullin; Patrick Seely; James Seville; James Sexton; James Sheridan; Tilly Simpson; Martha "Birdie" Slater; Matt Stafford; Paddy Stephenson; Jim Stritch; Ellen Stynes; Aoife Taaffe; Liam Tannam; Annie Tobin; Oscar Traynor; Joseph Trimble; Patrick Tuohy; George Tully; Tim Tyrrell; Michael Wade; Laurence Whelan; Esther Wisely.

Appendix 9: Political Involvement of members of GPO Garrison post-1916

Winnie Carney: member of the Labour Party.

Harry Colley: founder member of Fianna Fáil; TD for Dublin North East, 1944-1957; member of the Seanad, 1957-1961.

Michael Collins: Minister of Home Affairs and later Minister of Finance in the Sinn Féin Provisional Government, 1919-1922; President of the IRB in 1921; member of the Irish Delegations at the Anglo–Irish Treaty Negotiations in 1921; Chairman of the Provisional Government and Commander-in-chief of the Free State Army, until his death in 1922.

Roddy Connolly: joined the Socialist Party of Ireland in 1917; founder member of the Communist Party of Ireland in October 1921; joined the Labour Party in 1928; a member of Bray Trade Council in 1931; elected Labour TD for Louth, 1943-1944 & 1948-1951; member of the Seanad, 1975-1977; chairperson of the Labour Party, 1971-1978.

Nora Connolly-O'Brien: member of the Seanad for fifteen years, nominated by both Éamon de Valera & Seán Lemass.

Denis Daly: member of Fianna Fáil; TD for the Kerry Constituency, 1933-1937.

Desmond Fitzgerald: Sinn Féin MP for the Dublin Pembroke Constituency in 1918; Director of Publicity of the 1st Dáil in 1919; TD for Dublin County, 1922-1932 & Minister for External Affairs, 1922-1927; TD for Carlow County,1932-1937 & Minister for Defence, 1927-1932; member of the Seanad, 1938-1943.

Andy Fitzpatrick: Sinn Féin Councillor for the Usher's Quay Ward in 1918.

Paul Galligan: Sinn Féin MP for West Cavan in 1918; TD in the 1st Dáil in 1919.

Richard Gogan: founder member of Fianna Fáil; TD for Dublin North West, 1954-1977.

Tom Harris: elected Kildare County Councillor in 1920; founder member of Fianna Fáil; TD for Kildare, 1927-1937 & TD for Carlow / Kildare, 1937-1948.

Seán Hayes: Sinn Féin MP, 1918-1922; Military Governor for Newbridge Internment Camp during the Civil War.

Seán Hegarty: founder member of Fianna Fáil.

Linda Kearns: founder member of Fianna Fáil & a member of the Seanad.

Seán Lemass: Sinn Féin MP for Dublin South in 1924; Secretary of Fianna Fáil at its foundation; Minister for Industry & Commerce, 1932-1948 & 1951-1959, (also Minister for Supplies, during the emergency years); Tánaiste,1945-1959; Taoiseach, 1959-1966; retired as a TD in 1969.

Diarmuid Lynch: Sinn Féin MP for Cork South in 1918.

Sean MacEntee: Sinn Féin MP for Monaghan South in 1918; founder member of Fianna Fáil; TD for Dublin County in 1927; Minister for Finance, 1932-1939; Minister for Industry & Commerce, 1939-1941; Minister for Local Government & Public Health, 1941-1948; Minister for Finance, 1951-1954; Minister for Health, 1957-1959; Tánaiste, 1959-1965; retired as T.D. in 1969; he was the last surviving member of the First Dáil at his death in 1984.

Seán McGarry: Sinn Féin MP for Mid Dublin in 1921; Cumann na nGaedheal TD, 1923-1924; founder member of the National Party.

Seamus McGowan: member of the Labour Party.

Seán McLoughlin: founder member of the Communist Party of Ireland in October 1921.

Seán Milroy: Cumann na nGaedheal TD for Cork, 1923-1924; member of the Seanad, 1928-1936.

Páidí Ó'Caoimh: Secretary of Sinn Féin and responsible for organising the campaign for the 1918 General Election; Sinn Féin MP for Cork North, 1918-1921.

Tomás Ó'Donnachada (Thomas O'Donoghue): Sinn Féin MP for Kerry North & Limerick West, 1921-1922; founder member of Fianna Fáil in 1926.

Brian O'Higgins: Sinn Féin MP for Clare West in 1918.

Seán T. O'Kelly: Sinn Féin MP for the College Green Division, Dublin in 1918; Ceann Comhairle of the First Dáil in 1919; Irish Envoy to the Paris Peace Conference in 1919; founder member of Fianna Fáil in 1926; Vice-President of the Fianna Fáil Executive Council, 1932-1937; Minister for Local Government, 1932-1939; Minister for Finance, 1941-1945; Tánaiste, 1937-1945; President of Ireland, 1945-1959.

John O'Mahony: Sinn Féin MP for Fermanagh & Tyrone in 1918; member of the Sinn Féin Executive.

John O'Neill: Labour candidate in the Municipal Elections of 1915.

Gearóid O'Sullivan: Cumann na nGaedheal TD for Carlow / Kilkenny, 1921-1923 & for Dublin County, 1927-1937; Judge Advocate General, 1927-1932.

Liam Pedlar: General Secretary of Fianna Fáil until 1931.

Annie Redmond: founder member of Fianna Fáil in 1926.

Seamus Robinson: Sinn Féin MP for East Tipperary in 1921; founder member of Fianna Fáil in 1926.

Dr. James Ryan: founder member of Fianna Fáil; TD for Wexford, 1927-1965; Minister for Agriculture, 1932-1947; Minister for Health & Social Welfare, 1947-1948; Minister for Finance, 1951-1954 & 1957-1965; on retiring as a TD, he served in the Seanad until 1967.

Matt Stafford: founder member of Fianna Fáil & a member of its National Executive, 1926-1947; served in Seanad, 1937-1948.

Michael Staines: served in the Seanad, 1930-1936.

Paddy Stephenson: founder member of the Communist Party of Ireland in October 1921.

Oscar Traynor: joined Fianna Fáil in 1927; Minister for Posts & Telegraph, 1936-1939; Minister for Defence, 1939-1948 & 1951-1954; Minister for Justice, 1957-1961.

Domhnall Ua Buachalla: Sinn Féin MP for Kildare North in 1918; founder member of Fianna Fáil in 1926; TD for Kildare, 1927-1932; served as nominal Governor General from 1932 to 1937 when the office was abolished.

J.J. Walsh: Sinn Féin MP for Cork City in 1918; Cumann na nGaedheal TD for Cork Borough, 1923-1927; Postmaster General, 1922-1924; Minister Posts & Telegraphs, 1924-1927.

Appendix 10: Members of GPO Garrison who were subsequently employed in the Public Sector

Health

Molly Adrien: Chairperson of the Balrothery Board of Guardians & Secretary of the Balrothery Old Age Pensions Committee

Leslie Bean deBarra (nee Price): a member of the Irish Red Cross Society from 1939 and its Chairperson, 1950-1973; Chairperson of the Irish National Committee for Refugees, 1955-1960 & National President of Gorta, 1960-1965

Eva Burke: nurse

Julia Grenan: employed in the Irish Hospital's Trust

Frank Henderson: Secretary of Dublin Board of Assistance

Linda Kearns: National Council of Nurses

Garrett MacAuliffe: Limerick Health Board

Doctor Dan McLoughlin: South Dublin Union Hospital & GP in Rathmines and Cabra

Seamus Ó Braonán: National Health Inspector in the 1930's & President of the Polio Fellowship of Ireland

Elizabeth O'Farrell: midwife in the National Maternity Hospital, Holles Street

Doctor Ted O'Kelly: had a medical practice in London

Seamus O'Sullivan: member of the Hospital's Trust in Dublin and later in Limerick

Matt Stafford: member of the Central Midwives Board & a member of the Grangegorman Mental Hospital Committee

Joe Sweeney: member of the Irish Red Cross Society 1950-1962, including General Secretary, 1956-1962

Doctor John J. Tuohy: the oldest medical practitioner in Dublin at his death in 1936

Catherine Treston: nurse

Dublin Corporation

Eva Burke: nurse

Tom Byrne: clerk

Patrick Caldwell: clerk

Jimmy Carrigan: lorry driver

Harry Colley: rate collector

Patrick Connaughton

Thomas Dunne: employed in the Waterworks Dept

Paddy Garland: bricklayer in the Sewers Dept

Frank Henderson: Dublin Corporation Councillor in 1934

Patrick Hughes: caretaker in the Housing Dept

Tom Kearney: employed in the Architect Dept

Tommy Mahon: inspector in the Waterworks Dept

Conor McGinley: Assistant Dublin City Architect, 1924-1936 & Dublin City Architect, 1936-1959

Christy McGrane: painter

James Norton: employed in the Waterworks Dept

James O'Byrne: library assistant in Kevin Street Public Library until 1947

Rory O'Connor: civil engineer in the Engineering Dept

Seán T. O'Kelly: Dublin Corporation Councillor

Diarmuid O'Leary: Dublin Corporation Councillor

Vincent Poole: employed in the Sewers Dept

James Sexton: inspector in the Paving Dept

Matt Stafford: Dublin Corporation Councillor

Michael Staines: Dublin City Alderman until 1925

Paddy Stephenson: Dublin City Librarian

Jim Stritch: inspector in the Paving Dept

Liam Tannam: employed in the Rates Dept

James Wren: rent collector.

County Councils
Steenie Mulvey: employed in the Bray Urban Council
Charlie Donnelly: rate collector in Dublin County Council
Jack Kelly: employed in Dublin County Council
Jack Stafford: employed in the Dublin County Council Health Authority
Eamon Bulfin: Chairman of Offaly County Council.

Board of Works / Office of Public Works
Louis Byrne, Junior
Larry Corbally
Thomas Corbally
Joe Derham: accountant to the Commissioner of Public Works
John Horan
Thomas Hughes: head electrician in Government Buildings, Leinster House
Mike Keough: employed in the Botanical Gardens for over thirty years
Christopher Ring: carpenter
Joe Ring: carpenter.

Semi-State Bodies
Donagh Ó Mórdha: CIE, Clerical Dept
Mick Fox: CIE, Inchicore Works
Patrick Corless: ESB
Johnny (Blimey) O'Connor: ESB
William O'Donoghue: ESB
William O'Reilly: ESB
Jack Plunkett: electrical engineer in the ESB
Frank Scullin: ESB
Leo (Paddy) Scullin: ESB
Fred Higgins: engineer in the Dublin Port & Docks Board
Peadar Doyle: employed in the Dublin Gas Company
Frank Murtagh: employed in the Dublin Gas Company.

Schoolteachers
Leslie Bean deBarra (nee Price)
Frank Burke: headmaster in St Enda's, until his retirement in 1935
Bridie Connolly: schoolteacher at Clonsaugh National School
Louise Gavan Duffy: schoolteacher and founder of Scoil Bhríde, Dublin's first all-girls school
Veronica Gleeson (nee Ní Riain)
Tomás Ó'Donnachada: schoolteacher in Limerick VEC until he lost his job for refusing to take the Oath of Allegiance
Annie O'Higgins: teacher in the School of Music, Dublin
Brian O'Higgins: Secretary of O'Curry College, Carrigaholt, County Clare

Bridie Richards: schoolteacher at Gardiner Street Convent School
James Tallon: vocational schoolteacher until his retirement in 1959, founder of Coiste na
bPáiste & President of the Gaelic League
Joseph Tallon: schoolteacher in Dungarvan, Omagh, Dundalk & O'Connell Schools, Dublin

An Garda Síochána/Prison Service
Patrick Byrne: until his retirement in 1961
Peter Clinch: until his retirement in 1944
Herbert Conroy: detective sergeant until his death in 1926
John Doyle (C.Coy): until his retirement in 1949
Jack Graves: from 1933 until his retirement in 1954
Martin Hore: detective officer
James Kenny: detective in the Special Branch
Martin Lynch: Chief Superintendent of An Garda Síochána for Wexford
John O'Reilly (F.Coy): from 1924 until his death in 1946
Michael Staines: the first Commissioner of An Garda Síochána
Patrick Dalton: Prison Officer

Civil Service
Arthur Agnew: civil servant until his retirement in 1967
David Bourke: employed in the Irish Land Commission
Joseph Bracken: employed in the Congested District Board, prior to the Rising & clerk in
the Dept of Defence until his retirement in 1951
Peadar Bracken: clerk in Tullamore District Court
Eamon Bulfin: Consul to Argentina, in 1919 & tax collector for the Revenue Commissioners
Batt Burke: employed in the Stationery Office
Nicholas Burke: civilian employee in Army Corps of Engineers
Peter Byrne: civil servant
Tom Byrne: Captain of the Guard in Leinster House
Patrick Caldwell: clerical officer in Customs & Excise
Patrick Carroll: employed in the Dept of Social Welfare
James Cassells: civil servant
Michael Cremen: Private Secretary to various Ministers of State; Secretary to the Military
Services Pensions Board
Thomas Croke: employed in the Dept of Local Government until his retirement with a
disability in 1935
Seamus Devoy: member of the High Commisioner's Staff in London from 1941 to 1967
Jack Early: civil servant, based at Gardiner St Labour Exchange for over thirty years
Andy Fitzpatrick: inspector, Post & Telegraphs, Engineering Dept
Martin Gleeson: clerical officer in the Revenue Commissioner's Office
Seán Hayes: executive officer in the GPO, Stores Branch
James Heery: clerical officer, Post & Telegraphs, Engineering Dept

Seamus Kavanagh: employed in the Dept of Local Government until his retirement in 1945

Frank Kelly: principal officer in the Dept of Local Government

Joseph Kelly: porter in the Dept of Posts & Telegraphs, GPO

Jack Kenny: usher in Government Buildings, Leinster House

Michael Kenny: civilian employee in the Dept of Transport, Power & Aviation from 1940

Bob Killeen: postman, Dept of Posts & Telegraphs

Michael Knightly: editor of the Dáil Debates in Dáil Éireann, in 1922; official censor of newpapers during the emergency years

Paddy Mahon: employed in the Dept of Education

Harry Manning: civilian employee in the Dept of Defence

James McElligott: Financial Advisor to the Government, in 1923; Secretary of the Dept of Defence and Head of the Civil Service in 1925; Secretary of the Dept of Finance until 1953; Governor of the Central Bank from 1953 to 1960

John McGallogly: employed in the Dept of Post & Telegraphs, the Dept of Industry & Commerce and the Dept of Social Welfare

Eunan McGinley: a Local Government Dept auditor until his death in a motor accident in 1923

Patrick McGinley: employed in the Dept of Customs & Excise and was the Customs & Excise Office for Howth for 30 years

Con McGinn: employed in the Dept of Customs & Excise and was a Customs & Excise Officer at Dublin Airport

Michael McGrath: civil servant, based at the Employment Exchange in Tralee from 1925

Patrick McManus: employed in the Dept of Posts & Telegraphs, Engineering Dept

Patrick Mooney: civilian employee in the Army Air Corps, Baldonnel Aerodrome

Henry Moughan: civilian employee in the Army Corps of Engineers, Collins Barracks

Michael Murphy: employed in the Irish Placenames Commission

Ernie Nunan: employed in the Irish Marine Service in 1939

Seán Nunan: Private Secretary to Éamon de Valera on his visit to the United States in 1919; Diplomatic Service in London, New York & Washington; Assistant Secretary & then Secretary of the Dept of External Affairs until his retirement in 1955

Eoghan O'Brien: employed in the Dept of Education

Matt O'Brien: employed in the Dept of Social Welfare

Páidí Ó'Caoimh: Assistant Clerk in the Seanad, from 1938 until his retirement in 1947

James O'Connor: civilian employee in the Army Corps of Engineers

Tomás Ó'Donnachada: civil servant in 1932

Diarmuid O'Leary: Industrial Inspector, Dept of Industry & Commerce in 1927

Colm Ó'Murchadha: Assistant Secretary in the First Dáil & First Clerk of Dáil Éireann; OireachtasTranslation Dept

Billy O'Neill: employed in the Stamp Dept, Dublin Castle

J.K. O'Reilly: Head of the Financial Dept in the First Dáil

Joseph O'Reilly (ICA): civilian employee in the Army Corps of Engineers

Joe O'Reilly (Lon, Coy): Aide-de-Camp to Michael Collins; Aide-de-Camp to W.T. Cosgrave; Director of Purchases of the Commissioners of Public Works

Charles Purcell: employed in the Public Record Office, Four Courts

Patrick Rankin: civilian employee in the Army Corps of Engineers

Liam Ring: senior translator and later Chief Translator in Dáil Éireann

Séamus Robinson: Advisory Committee of the Military Service Board in 1935, Bureau of Military History in 1949 & Military Registrations Board in 1953

Thomas Roche: employed in the Stationery Office, Beggar's Bush

Charlie Rossiter: employed in the Dept of Social Welfare

Padraig Supple: employed in the Dept of Supplies

Joe Twamley: employed in the Dept of Posts & Telegraphs, Engineering Dept

Charlie Walker: printer in the Dept of Defence

Christy Walsh: usher in Government Buildings, Leinster House

Thomas Wheatley: employed in the Dept of Finance

Henry Willis: employed in the Dept of Posts & Telegraphs, Engineering Dept.

Appendix 11: Members of GPO Garrison who were subsequently Trade Union Officials

Winnie Carney: worked for the I.T.G.W.U. after the Rising and joined the Labour Party in 1924

Peter Carpenter: I.T.G.W.U.

Wally Carpenter: founder member of the Communist Party of Ireland, in 1921 and a former President of the Irish Trade Union Congress

Maeve McDowall (nee Cavanagh): I.T.G.W.U.

Roddy Connolly: member of Bray Trade Council

Andy Conway: full-time official with the I.T.G.W.U.

Gerald Griffin: General Secretary of the Clerical Worker's Union

Leo Henderson: Secretary of the Irish Local Government Officials' Union

William McCleane: Amalgamated Society of Painters

Seán McLoughlin: Branch Secretary in the W.U.I., in 1924

Brian McMullan: organiser in W.U.I.

Patrick Meagher: Executive Member of the Irish House & Shop Painter's Union

John Moore: W.U.I.

Michael Murphy: organiser in W.U.I.

Robert Murphy: Secretary of the Union Stationary Engine Driver's Trade Union

Tom Murray: Founder member of the Irish Bookbinder's Union in 1920

Michael Nolan: Branch Secretary, W.U.I.

Diarmuid O'Leary: assisted in reorganising the I.T.G.W.U. after the Rising and was employed in the head office from 1919 to 1927

James O'Neill (A. Coy, 3rd Batt): Secretary of the Amalgamated Union of Upholsterers from 1923 to 1936

John O'Neill: Branch Secretary in the I.T.G.W.U. in 1911

Donal O'Reilly: Executive Committee Member of the Plasterer's Union; Delegate to the Dublin Trades Council and the Irish Congress of Trade Unions

James O'Sullivan: Dublin Typographical Providence Society, (Printer's Union)

Christopher Ring: Branch Secretary, Amalgamated Woodworkers' Union

Laurence Whelan: Assistant Secretary & Treasurer of the Irish Society of Woodcutting Machinists.

Appendix 12: Members of GPO Garrison who emigrated after the Rising

Dave Begley: originally from Liverpool, he returned to England in 1921; his last known address was 68 Brondesbury Villas, High St, Kilburn, London, in 1939.

John Bolger: to United States; he married in Chicago in 1927 and died in Barrington, Illinois in 1974.

Alice Byrne: to Glasgow in 1919 where he died in 1972.

Christopher Byrne: to England and he died in Birkenhead in 1981.

James Byrne: to England after his release from Frongoch and lived in Islington, London.

Peadar Carroll: to Birmingham, where he died in 1992.

James Conroy: to the United States in 1923; he died in Stanton, Orange County, California in 1981.

John Conway: to Scotland in 1919; he died at his residence at 75 Ashby Crescent, Knightswood, Glasgow in 1959.

Tom Craven: to the United States; he died in Akron, Ohio in 1955.

Tom Crimmins: to the United States in 1920 and returned to Ireland on his retirement in 1964; he periodically returned to America, before finally settling in Ireland in 1985 where he died in 1988.

Joe Cripps: to the United States after the Civil War and resided there for over forty years; he returned to Ireland on his retirement and died in 1975.

Mark Cummins: to the United States in 1920; he died in the U.S. Marine Hospital, San Francisco in 1943.

Patrick Dalton: to London after the Rising and returned to Ireland in 1923; he lived intermittently in England over the years, before settling in Dublin where he died in 1989.

Seamus Devoy: lived for many years in England & the United States, before returning to Dublin where he died in 1982.

Brigid Doran (nee Lambert): to England; she died in Watford in 1961.

Joe Duffy: originally from Liverpool, returned to England seeking employment in 1918; he later returned to Dublin where he died in 1972.

William Egan: to the United States in the late 1920s; he died in New York in 1985.

Davy Golden: to the United States in 1926; he died in Chicago in 1967.

Paddy Halpin: to the United States and resided at Long Beach, California.

Art Hannon: to the United States in 1917; he died in San Diego in 1973.

Hugh Holahan: to the United States in December 1920; he died in New York, in the- 1960s.

Frank Keogh: to Liverpool sometime after the Rising.

Seán Kerr: to the United States in the 1920s; he returned to Ireland in 1930.

Thomas Kilcoyne: to England; he died in Cheltenham, Gloucestershire in 1971.

John Lafferty: to the United States; he died in Chicago in 1958.

Tom Leahy: to Glasgow in 1924: he died there in 1958.

Michael McGarvey: returned to Liverpool after his release from Frongoch and emigrated to the United States in 1917; he died in New York, in 1949.

Seán McLoughlin: to Hartlepool in 1924; he died in Sheffield in 1960.

John McQuaid: to New Zealand after serving in the British Army on his release from Frongoch.

James Minihan: to England and returned to Dublin, after twenty years in 1948.

Jim Mooney: to Manchester in 1919 and then to the United States in 1920; he died in New York in 1961.

Martin Murphy: to Chicago in 1920; he returned to Sligo in 1950.

Robert Murphy: to the United States in 1924; he returned to Dublin in 1932.

Tom Murray: to England in 1917; he returned to Dublin in 1920.

Joseph Murtagh (John O'Connor): to the United States in 1929; he returned to Dublin in 1939; when his health broke down, he went to live with daughter and died at her residence in London in 1964.

John Newman: to Boston in 1929; he died in Houston in 1969.

Patrick Nugent: to England in 1926; he returned to Dublin, in 1932; he emigrated to the United States in 1951 and died in New Jersey in 1967.

William O'Brien: to the United States in 1920: he died in Gulfport, Mississippi in 1972.

May O'Carroll (nee Gahan): to Australia; she died in Sydney in 1988.

James O'Connor: to England after the War of Independence; he returned to Dublin some time later.

Patrick O'Donoghue: to England in 1929; he lived there for over forty years, before he returned to Galway.

Ted O'Kelly: to London where he had a medical practice at 30 Oakley Square; he died in the London Blitz in April 1941.

Patrick O'Moore: to Australia in 1926; he died in Brisbane in 1958.

James O'Neill (ICA): to South Africa in 1947; he died in Pietermaritzburg, Natal in 1952.

Sam O'Reilly: to the United States in 1922; he died in New York in 1988.

Joe O'Rorke: to South Africa in 1925; he returned to Dublin in 1932.

Peter Reynolds: to England in 1926; he died in Hemel Hempstead in 1979.

Dan Ryan: to Australia in 1928; he died in Brisbane in 1958.

Thomas Ryan: to England; his last known location was in Birmingham in 1936.

Arthur Shields: to the United States in 1936; he died in Santa Barbara in 1970.

Joseph Turner (Junior): to England; he died there.

Mark Walsh: to England; he died in Peckham, London in 1972.

William Whelan: to Canada; he died in Toronto in 1969.

Jack (Blanco) White: to Liverpool after the Rising; he died at Hampstead Way, London in the late 1930s.

Appendix 13: People whose obituaries state they were in the GPO Garrison but do not appear in official sources

Walter Bell: 265 Blackhorse Avenue; he died 10th December, 1943, *Irish Independent;* F. Company, 1st Battalion.

Christopher Caffrey: 28 Oak Road, Donnycarney; he died 29th September, 1943; *Irish Press;* C. Company, 1st Battalion.

Mrs. Ann Carolan nee Dixon: 44 Shandon Gardens; she died 7th February, 1961; *Irish Press;* Cumann na mBan.

Elizabeth Coakley: Matron, Crooksling Sanitarium; she died 22nd April, 1933; *Irish Press.*

Francis Dowling: Ballyhackett, Co. Carlow; she died 21st March, 1967; *Irish Independent.*

Sean Fitzpatrick: 27 Donelan Avenue; he died 10th March, 1963; Sunday Press; 3rd Battalion; General Secretary, National Graves Association.

Senator John McKean: 30 Claireville Road,, North Circular Road; he died 21st September, 1936; *Irish Press.*

Edward Mallon: 11 Saint Fintan's Road, Cabra; he died 24th March, 1959; *Irish Independent;* Irish Citizen Army.

Michael O'Brien: 158 Iveragh Road; he died 9th October,, 1952; *Irish Press.*

Diarmuid O'Sullivan: 30 Seafield Road, Clontarf; he died 26th July, 1952; *Irish Independent.*

Patrick Ryan: 281 North Circular Road; died 13th May, 1940; *Irish Independent.*

Francis Timony: 13 Shandon Drive; died 17th March, 1961; *Irish Press.*

It is stated in a number of other obituaries that the deceased had taken part in the 1916 Rising but no garrisons or locations are given.

Appendix 14: Members of GPO Garrison whose biographies are in the Dictionary of Irish Biography

Thomas (Tom) Clarke, vol.2, pp 559-62, by James Quinn

Harry Colley, vol. 2, p.670, by Pauric Dempsey

Michael Collins, vol. 2, pp 678-82, by M.A. Hopkins

James Connolly, vol. 2, pp 756-61, by Fergus A. D'Arcy

Roderick (Roddy) Connolly, vol. 2, pp 765-7, by Lawrence William White

Louise Gavan Duffy, vol. 3, pp 514-5, by Mary Kotsonouris

 (Thomas Joseph) Desmond Fitzgerald, vol. 3, pp 820-4, by William Murphy

Frank Henderson, vol. 4, pp 598-9, by Pauric J. Dempsey and Sharon Boylan

Michael Knightly, vol. 5, p.240, by Pauric J. Dempsey

Noel Lemass, vol.5, pp 431-2, by Anne Dolan

Seán Lemass, vol. 5, pp 433-44, by Ronan Fanning

Diarmuid Lynch, vol.5, pp 618-9, by Marie Coleman

Seán Mac Diarmada (Mac Dermott), vol. 5, pp 911-14, by Lawrence William White

Seán (John Francis) MacEntee, vol. 5, pp 995-8, by Deirdre McMahon

Seán McGarry, vol. 5, pp 1014-15, by Lawrence William White
Linda Kearns McWhinney, vol. 6, pp 208-9, by Seán Kearns
Seán Milroy, vol. 6, pp 517-8, by Marie Coleman
Seán Nunan, vol. 6, pp 991-2, by Michael Kennedy
Nora Connolly-O'Brien, vol. 7, pp 69-71, by Lawrence William White
Roderick (Rory) O'Connor, vol. 7, pp 271-4, by Lawrence William White
Elizabeth O'Farrell, vol. 7, p. 453, by Frances Clarke,
Brian O'Higgins, vol. 7, pp 561-2, by Patrick Maume
Seán T. O'Kelly, vol. 7, pp 615-9, by Patrick Maume
Michael J. O'Rahilly (The O'Rahilly), vol. 7, pp 828-30, by Patrick Maume
Joseph F. O'Reilly, vol. 7, p. 861 by Marie Coleman
Gearóid O'Sullivan, vol. 7, pp 967-9, by Patrick Long
Pádraig Pearse, vol. 8, pp 19-27, by J.J. Lee
William (Willie) Pearse, vol. 8, pp 27-8, by William Murphy
George Oliver Michael Plunkett, vol. 8, pp 179-80, by Lawrence William White
Joseph Mary Plunkett, vol. 8, pp 183-7, by Lawrence William White
Séamus Robinson, vol. 8, p.549, by Marie Coleman
Seán Russell, vol.8, pp 660-1, by Brian Hanley
Desmond Ryan, vol. 8, pp 683-5, by Lawrence William White
James Ryan, vol. 8, pp 692-4, by Patrick Maume
Philomena Frances Ryan, vol. 8, pp 702-3, by Cathy Hayes
Arthur Shields, vol. 8, pp 923-4, by Tom Feeney
Michael Joseph Staines, vol. 9, pp 1-2, by Tom Feeney and William Murphy
Joseph Aloysium Sweeney, vol. 9, pp 178-9, by Tom Feeney
Frank Thornton, vol. 9, pp 358-9, by Seán Collins
Oscar Traynor, vol. 9, pp 456-7, by Marie Coleman
Domhnall Ua Buachalla (Daniel Buckley), vol. 7, p. 108, by Marie Coleman
James Joseph Walsh, vol. 9, pp 737-9, by Patrick Maume
Frances Brennan-Whitmore, vol. 9, pp 911-12, by Patrick Long

Index of Biographies

Thomas Ryan 319
William (Dan) Ryan 320
Charles Saurin 320
John J. Scollan 321
Francis (Frank) Scullin 322
Leo (Paddy) Scullin 323
Patrick J. Seely (Sealy) 323
James Seville 324
James Sexton 324
Francis (Frank) Sheridan 325
James Sheridan 326
Arthur Shields 326
Patrick Shortis 327
Matilda (Tilly) Simpson 328
Doctor Peter Slattery 328
Charles (Charlie) Smith 329
Lucy Smyth (Mrs Lucy Byrne) 330
Christine Stafford Brooks 330
John (Jack) Stafford 331
Matthew (Matt) Stafford 332
Michael Staines 333
Joseph (Joe) Stanley 334
Mary Jane Stapleton (Mrs. Mary Slevin) 335
Charles Steinmayer 335
Patrick J. Stephenson 336
James (Jim) Stritch 337
Padraig Supple 338
Anthony (Tony) Swan 339
Patrick Swanzy 339
Swedish Seaman (Name Unknown) 340
James Sweeney 340
Joseph (Joe) Sweeney 341
Patrick Sweeney 342
Aoife Taaffe 342
Christopher Tallon 343
James Tallon (Seamus Ó Tallamháin) 343
Joseph Tallon (Seosamh Ó Tallamháin) 344
Liam Tannam 345
Francis (Frank) Thornton (alias Frank Drennan) 346
Hugh Thornton 347
Nora Thornton 347
Patrick (Paddy) Thornton 348
Annie Tobin (Mrs. Annie Soalfield) 348
Maurice Tobin 349
Joseph (Joe) Toomey 349
Stasia Toomey (Mrs. Stasia Byrne) 350
Oscar Traynor 350
Joseph Trimble 352
George Tully 352

Doctor John J. Tuohy 353
Patrick C. Tuohy 354
Cormac Turner 354
Francis (Frank) Turner 355
Henry Turner 356
Joseph Turner (Junior) 356
Joseph Turner (Senior) 357
John J. (Joe) Twamley 357
Timothy (Tim) Tyrrell 358
Domhnall Ua Buachalla (Daniel Buckley) 359
Michael Wade 360
Charles (Charlie) Walker 360
Robert Henry (Harry) Walpole 361
Christopher (Christy) Walsh 362
Edward J. (Ned) Walsh 362
Helena (Eileen) Walsh 363
James J. Walsh 363
Margaret Walsh (Mrs. Margaret Jenkinson) 364
Mark W. Walsh 365
Martha (Birdie) Walsh (Mrs Martha Slater) 365
Mary Josephine (Mary Jo) Walsh (Mrs Mary Jo Rafferty) 366
James Wardock 367
Patrick (Paddy) Weafer: (1896 - 1946) 367
Patrick (Pat) Weafer: (1890 -   ) 368
Thomas Weafer 368
Thomas (Tom) Wheatley 369
Joseph Whelan 370
Laurence Whelan 370
William Whelan 371
Jack (Blanco) White 372
John J. White 372
Michael White 372
W.J. Brennan-Whitmore 373
Arthur Wicks, (alias John Neal) 374
Henry Willis 375
Esther Wisley (Mrs. Esther O'Moore) 376
James Wren 376
Nancy de Paor (Wyse Power) 377